The Afrikaner Bond

THE
AFRIKANER BOND

The History of a South African
Political Party, 1880–1911

BY

T. R. H. DAVENPORT

Reader in History at
Rhodes University
Grahamstown

Cape Town
OXFORD UNIVERSITY PRESS
London New York
1966

Oxford University Press, Ely House, London W. 1

GLASGOW NEW YORK TORONTO MELBOURNE WELLINGTON
CAPE TOWN SALISBURY IBADAN NAIROBI LUSAKA ADDIS ABABA
BOMBAY CALCUTTA MADRAS KARACHI LAHORE DACCA
KUALA LUMPUR HONG KONG TOKYO

Oxford University Press, Thibault House, Cape Town

PRINTED IN SOUTH AFRICA BY THE RUSTICA
PRESS (PTY.) LTD., COURT ROAD, WYNBERG, CAPE

Contents

List of illustrations and maps   *page* vii

Preface   ix

Publisher's Note   xi

PART ONE: THE AFRIKANER BOND IN ORIGIN

1 The Pressure of British Rule   1

2 Farmers in Politics   10
   I. The Z.A. Boeren Beschermings Vereeniging   14
   II. The Eastern Vereenigingen   19
   III. The Measure of Hofmeyr's Achievement   25

3 Nationalist Foundations: from the Genootskap to the
   Afrikaner Bond   28
   I. The Genootskappers of Paarl   29
   II. The Birth of the Bond   34
   III. A Rhapsody in Blue   40
   IV. The Spread of a Popular Movement   42
   V. Ignis Fatuus   49

4 Amalgamation   54
   I. The Graaff-Reinet Congress   54
   II. The Cradock Congress   57
   III. Hofmeyr joins the Bond   60
   IV. The Richmond Congress   67

PART TWO: THE AFRIKANER BOND IN ACTION

5 Assault on the Imperial Factor   71
   I. The Wreck of Sprigg's South African Policy   72
   II. Hofmeyr and Scanlen: an Experiment in Co-operation   75
   III. Upington, the Bond and Bechuanaland   89

6 The Failure of Pan-South Africanism   95
   I. The Effects of Depression   95
   II. A House Divided   99
   III. Links of Iron and a Golden Chain   101
   IV. The Collapse of the Republican 'Provinces'   107

7 The Consolidation of a Cape Colonial Party   111
   I. An Approach to English Farmers   111
   II. Obstacle Race   113
   III. The Problem of the Franchise   118
   IV. Canons of Faith and Order   123

8   The Hofmeyr–Rhodes Alliance   127
       I. Fair Play   127
      II. The Partnership Under Fire   134
     III. The Harvest of Goodwill   139
      IV. General Post and General Election, 1892–4   145
       V. Glen Grey and Scab   152
      VI. The Raid Crisis   159

9   Recessional   166
       I. 'Lest We Forget'   166
      II. Wild Tongues   176
     III. The Tumult and the Shouting   183

10 Diplomatic Breakdown   189

11 War   210
       I. The Breaking of the Moderates   210
      II. Martial Law and Disfranchisement   222
     III. Polarized Loyalties   226

12 Recovery   236
       I. The Suspension Movement   237
      II. Chamberlain's Visit   241
     III. Afrikaner Bond and South African Party   243
      IV. The Nadir of Afrikaner Fortunes   251
       V. Conciliation   253
      VI. The Afrikaner Revival   264

13 Union   270
       I. Divided Interests   271
      II. The Unification of South Africa   280
     III. The Unification of Leadership   290
      IV. The Unification of Parties   297

       PART THREE: THE AFRIKANER BOND IN RETROSPECT

14 The Afrikaner Bond as a Political Party   305

15 The Afrikaner Bond and Nationalism   320

Notes   333

Appendix: Office-bearers of the Afrikaner Bond in the
           Cape Colony   397

Bibliography   399

Index   409

List of Illustrations and Maps

I   J. H. HOFMEYR, 1883, *by W. H. Schröder*   *facing page* 58

II LEADERS OF THE BOEREN VEREENIGINGEN: 59
D. P. van den Heever
H. P. du Preez, *by W. H. Schröder*
Jotham Joubert, *by W. H. Schröder*
J. S. Marais, *by W. H. Schröder*

III FOUNDERS OF THE AFRIKANER BOND: 72
Ds. S. J. du Toit
D. F. du Toit
Carl Borckenhagen
General P. J. Joubert

IV THE CHAIRMEN OF THE AFRIKANER BOND,   73
CAPE COLONY:
J. J. Janse van Rensburg, *by W. H. Schröder*
R. P. Botha, *by W. H. Schröder*
P. J. du Toit
T. P. Theron
H. C. van Heerden, *by E. Roworth*

V   PROMINENT CAPE BOND LEADERS: 248
N. F. de Waal
Dr. T. N. G. te Water
Dr. J. M. Hoffman
F. S. Malan, *by E. Roworth*

VI PROMINENT ASSOCIATES OF THE AFRIKANER BOND: 249
J. Tengo Jabavu
C. J. Rhodes, *by Sir William Nicholson*
W. P. Schreiner, *by John St. Helier Lander*
John X. Merriman, *by E. Roworth*

VII T. P. THERON, *by D. C. Boonzaier*   264

VIII J. H. HOFMEYR, 1908, *by 'Mac'*   265

MAP 1 Distribution of political and farmers' organizations
in South Africa on the eve of the Richmond
Congress, May 1883   *following page* xi

MAP 2 District Besturen, 1898, in relation to electoral
divisions in the Cape Colony   *following page* 396

vii

TO BETTY,
HER PARENTS AND MINE,
FOR THEIR OWN SPECIAL CONTRIBUTIONS
TO THE WRITING OF THIS BOOK

Preface

THIS book is concerned with the first real political party to emerge in South Africa. The *Afrikaner Bond*[1] was conceived in the mind of the Reverend S. J. du Toit in June 1879, its earliest branches were established during 1880, and it took the decision to dissolve itself on 7 December 1911. It was primarily a Cape Colonial party, though for a brief period during the 1880's it attempted to operate across the internal frontiers of South Africa, with affiliated branches in the Orange Free State and the South African Republic. After the unification of South Africa it joined up with its opposite numbers in the Transvaal (*Het Volk*), in the Orange Free State (the *Orangia Unie*) and in Natal (the *Volksvereniging*), and with a number of individual South Africans who had no previous party attachment, to form the South African National Party (better known as the South African Party), over which General Louis Botha was elected to preside, and from which General J. B. M. Hertzog's Nationalists would in due course break away. The Afrikaner Bond was thus the chief lineal ancestor of both the government party and the major opposition party of mid-twentieth century South Africa. It had an important formative influence on both of them.

Although it was a factor of major importance in the determination of political trends in the three decades before Union, the Afrikaner Bond has attracted relatively little attention from historians. Mentioned briefly in many published works, it has received detailed treatment only in the biographies of the elder Jan Hofmeyr and S. J. du Toit,[2] its co-founders, and in a small handful of published and unpublished monographs on related topics. English historians, unfamiliar with the records of the Bond, or with the language in which they were written, have too often accepted the stereotype presented by hostile contemporaries like Worsfold, Thomas and Slater. Afrikaner historians, for their part, have tended to interest

---

[1] Official party documents referred usually to the 'Afrikaander Bond'. The variants 'Afrikander Bond' and 'Africander Bond' were commonly used by contemporaries, the latter only by English speakers. 'Afrikanerbond' is the normal rendering in modern Afrikaans. The form used here, which comes most easily to mid-twentieth century readers, is that consistently used by S. J. du Toit in his newspaper, *Die Afrikaanse Patriot*, though he sometimes hyphenated the name.

[2] For the full titles of works referred to in the notes, see sections V and VI of the bibliography at pp. 404–8, below.

ix

themselves in Republican rather than in Colonial political developments in the period after the Great Trek. The Bond has—with
notable exceptions—been ignored by the *nasionaalgesind*, perhaps
because Pretoria never became its Mecca, nor Paul Kruger its
prophet.

In the following pages, therefore, I have attempted to encompass
the broad story of the Afrikaner Bond. In the first part of the book,
which covers the origin of the Bond and its fusion with the *boeren
vereenigingen* (farmers' associations) of the Cape, I have followed a
path somewhere between the accounts in the biographies of 'Onze
Jan' Hofmeyr and S. J. du Toit, and deviated to some extent from
the conclusions of J. Albert Coetzee, whose *Politieke Groepering in
die Wording van die Afrikanernasie* is the fullest documented account
to date of Afrikaner political movements. In the second part, which
deals with the impact of the Afrikaner Bond on the development of
South Africa, and of external events on the Bond, an approach to
the main stream of history through the Bond records has suggested
some new perspectives and confirmed some existing ones. The third
part contains an analysis of the Afrikaner Bond under two main
headings, its organization and its aims, which is based on the
factual material handled in Parts I and II.

*   *   *   *

It gives me great pleasure to acknowledge a substantial debt to
those scholars who have given advice at various stages of the work.
These include Professor L. M. Thompson, then of the University of
Cape Town, under whose helpful supervision a portion of the work
first saw light as an academic thesis, and Professors J. S. Marais,
W. A. Maxwell, Sir Keith Hancock and G. H. L. le May, Dr. R. F.
Currey, Mrs. P. Lewsen, Mr. N. G. Garson and Mr. Leo Marquard,
who gave comments and criticism of great value. My debt to colleagues in the University of Cape Town, where the whole of this
work was written, is immense.

The late Hon. Charles te Water, Mr. B. D. Malan, Mr. J. G.
Sprigg and the Trustees of the Smuts Archive kindly gave me access
to private papers listed in the bibliography. I am also deeply indebted
to the librarians and staff of the South African Public Library, the
Library of the University of Cape Town, the Library of Parliament,
Cape Town, the Library of Rhodes House, Oxford, and the Library
of the Royal Commonwealth Society, London, and the staff of the

Cape Archives and of the Public Record Office, London, for their helpful assistance.

The maps were drawn by Mrs. D. Sprigg from information supplied by the author.

For permission to reproduce the photographs of Carl Borcken-hagen, General P. J. Joubert and P. J. du Toit, I am indebted to the Archives in Bloemfontein and Cape Town, and of Tengo Jabavu to the Library of Rhodes University. The portraits of H. C. van Heerden, F. S. Malan, W. P. Schreiner, C. J. Rhodes and J. X. Merriman, and the cartoon of T. P. Theron, are in the Sibbett Collection, University of Cape Town. The portrait of W. P. Schreiner is reproduced with the kind permission of P. R. S. Scott and the J. W. Jagger Library.

T. R. H. DAVENPORT

PUBLISHER'S NOTE

IN this book the reference mark * directs the reader to the Notes (mainly sources) beginning at page 333, where the relevant note may be found according to the word immediately preceding the reference mark in the text. Notes that have a closer bearing on the text are numbered and placed at the foot of the page to which they refer.

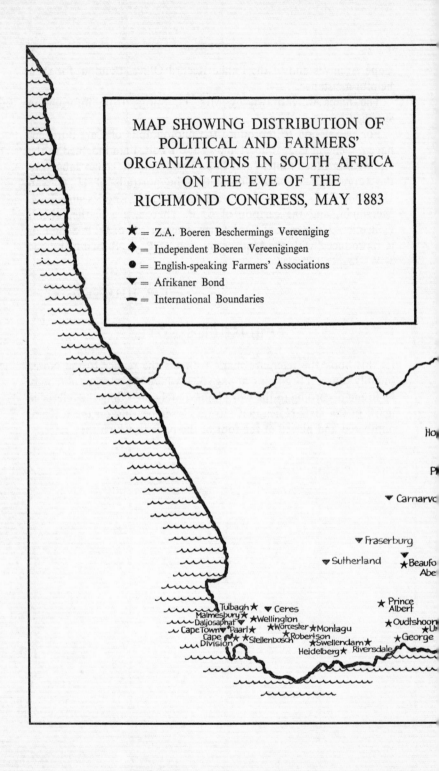

MAP SHOWING DISTRIBUTION OF
POLITICAL AND FARMERS'
ORGANIZATIONS IN SOUTH AFRICA
ON THE EVE OF THE
RICHMOND CONGRESS, MAY 1883

★ = Z.A. Boeren Beschermings Vereeniging
♦ = Independent Boeren Vereenigingen
● = English-speaking Farmers' Associations
▼ = Afrikaner Bond
━ = International Boundaries

Ho

P

▼ Carnarvo

▼ Fraserburg

▼ Sutherland ▼ Beaufo
★ Abe

★ Prince
Albert

Tulbagh ★ ▼ Ceres ★ Oudtshoon
Malmesbury ★ ★ Wellington ★ Un
Daljosaphat ▼ ★ Worcester ★ Montagu ★ George
Cape Town ▼ Paarl ★ ★ Robertson
Cape ★ ★ Stellenbosch ★ Swellendam ★
Division Heidelberg ★ Riversdale

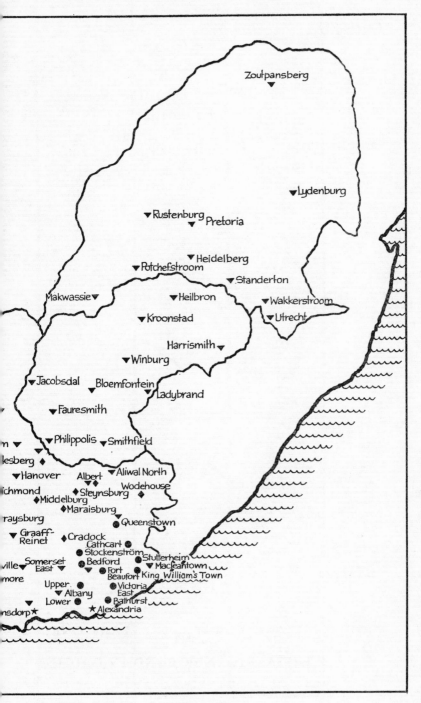

MAP 1

PART ONE:

THE AFRIKANER BOND IN ORIGIN

1

The Pressure of British Rule

THE Voortrekkers left the Cape Colony partly because they would not accept the changes in law and social practice which had followed the establishment of British rule; but they represented only a small fraction of the Afrikaner people.[1] A much larger number of Afrikaners—farmers and townsmen—stayed behind. A decision not to emigrate did not, however, imply an acceptance of the changes which had been introduced, and very little happened between 1840 and 1870 to change the outlook of the rural Afrikaner, the austere, religious, unbookish, fully acclimatized individualist who formed the backbone of Colonial society. For example, ideas expressed about the proper relations between master and servant in Piet Retief's manifesto, the classic formulation of Voortrekker grievances, can be shown still to have commanded general assent in the rural areas of the Colony at the latter date. From about 1870, major economic changes followed the discovery of diamonds and a further wave of immigration from Europe. These developments helped to precipitate the growth of Afrikaner political activity, and new political organizations emerged which became powerful in the land almost as they saw the light of day. Their emphasis, however, was for the most part conservative. They stressed the need to protect Afrikaner society from the destructive impact of the new influences —influences which seemed dangerous to the Afrikaner community because it possessed neither the political power which would have enabled it to control developments nor the linguistic and cultural ascendancy which it had once been able to take for granted, and

[1] Throughout this book, I use the term *Afrikaner* and its variants in the normal mid-twentieth century sense of a white Afrikaans-speaking South African. For the extent to which it acquired a wider meaning, see below, p. 326.

1

which would have enabled it to participate more effectively. It was of great significance for the history of the Colonial Boer that he embarked on a political revolution before he had really begun to show much interest in new forms of economic activity, like digging for minerals or even running retail shops; and that, once stimulated to political action, he was torn between an urge to condemn these new practices as alien incursions on his way of life, and a desire to take over the practices for the material advantages which they brought, or for the sake of breaking free from the aliens who ran them.

To what extent did the British dominate the life of town and country, and the politics of local and central government? It is the purpose of this chapter to show what avenues were available, and what avenues were not, for the Afrikaner who wished to make his way in public life in the 1870's. This will help in turn to show what kinds of frustration and disability underlay the Afrikaner's decision to launch his own political movement.

After the permanence of the British occupation had been secured by treaty in 1815, it became the policy of the Imperial Government to endow its new colony with institutions of a British type, sometimes by replacing those which already existed. The policy was neither ruthless nor in the end sustained, but it touched the Dutch Colonial on what he would come to regard as a tender spot. For the policy meant subjection to a form of cultural conquest through the introduction of British governmental institutions and some facets of British law (though the Roman-Dutch legal system was left largely intact); through the substitution of English for Dutch as the official language of the legislature, the civil service and the courts, as the medium of instruction in at least the secondary schools, and, in practice, as the language of business transactions; through the introduction of English and Scottish teachers and ministers of religion; and through the aided immigration of British settlers, who, in addition to buttressing an insecure frontier, would add to the sum of loyalty and propagate their way of life among the inhabitants. It is beside the point to labour the rights and wrongs of this policy, but some estimate needs to be made of the extent of its success, and here it is helpful to draw a distinction between what happened in the Cape Peninsula and what happened in the country districts.

The Cape Peninsula and immediate neighbourhood was the home of a Dutch-speaking aristocracy before the British arrived.

It retained this character, though in a progressively diluted form, throughout the nineteenth century. The Dutch language survived in common speech, and was kept alive in the worship of the Dutch Reformed Church and through educational institutions like *Tot Nut van 't Algemeen*, founded in 1805, and a Dutch language press which the capital was never without after 1826. The foundation of cultural associations like the *Aurora Rederijkerskamer*, a dramatic and debating society, gave the Cape Dutch focal points for their community life over and above that provided by their church, which for the greater part of the century enabled them to tolerate the spread of English institutions with equanimity. Thus fortified, the Cape Dutchman was prepared to adapt himself to the new exigencies of British rule, by learning English in order to qualify for a post in the civil service, for example, or by opening his church for the holding of services in English. He usually accepted the British Crown and British political institutions as part of his own heritage. This easy-going tolerance characterized the relationship between Dutch and English until the late sixties, and it was only then that the leaders of Dutch opinion came to realize that their own cultural tradition was being forced into the background, and that much which they treasured had been taken too much for granted or signed away. *Tot Nut van 't Algemeen* closed its doors in 1870, at a time when the use of the Dutch medium in secondary education had all but disappeared. Services in the English language had become so much a part of the life of the Groote Kerk that the church authorities were becoming concerned at the number of Cape Dutchmen who were attending these rather than the services in their own language. More serious (since this was undoubtedly at the root of the problem), the use of English had come to be regarded by many as a hallmark of breeding, a necessity in polite society.* Thus the strength of the Dutch cultural tradition had become its weakness. It would take all the efforts of the devotees of this tradition to evoke a sufficient response to such an insidious challenge; but when that response came, it stood every chance of being moderated by a conviction that much of what had evolved in the common white society of the Cape Peninsula was intrinsically good and worth preserving.

The problem in the rural areas was different. Here the spoken language was generally an immature form of Afrikaans, unsupported, except in the long-established homes of the west, by any significant amount of cultural activity; and unsupported by a literature, for the language of worship and of the Bible, which was often the only book in the household, was High Dutch. The spoken language was not catered for in the schools, nor was Dutch encouraged as a subject of study in its own right. Anglicization of the educational system had gone furthest in regions where it was practically impossible to build up an indigenous educational tradition to compete with it. But in spite of this fact, the Afrikaner way of life on the platteland was much safer from English influences than that in the capital. Schooling was not compulsory. For the sons of farmers who were short of labour and far from towns, it was often impracticable. As the editor of the *Cape Argus* pointed out in 1882, 'no system which could be devised would enable children to be at work on a farm and learning their lessons at the same time'.* Two of the commonest Boer objections to the administration of local government in the Colony were that resident magistrates could not speak the language of the people, and that the farmers could not understand the proceedings in the courts of law because they were conducted in English. These objections did not apply only during the first few decades after 1827, when the exclusive use of English was first made compulsory in the courts; for Jan Hofmeyr, the father of Cape Afrikaner political movements, stated at a dinner in Bloemfontein in May 1883 that the Colonial Boer took little interest in Colonial politics because he could not read the published reports, and that he was at sea in the courts because he could not understand the proceedings.* Yet it must follow that, to the extent to which the language of the administration was not understood by the Boer, the policy of anglicization had been a failure. Official policy, indeed, took cognizance of this fact. It was both permissible and common practice for field-cornets, for example, to submit their reports in Dutch,* and although the *Government Gazettes* contained many more notices in English than in Dutch, they usually contained a few pages of Dutch language notices where the application was local rather than general. Government could not have been carried on in the rural areas unless such practices had been permitted.

The platteland Boer was protected from the direct influences of anglicization by the isolated conditions under which he lived; and one must, of course, take into account the factor of opposition to cultural conquest. But the Boer of the seventies was not as isolated as his forebears of the thirties had been, chiefly because of the quickening of commercial activity in the interior, where English and other immigrant settlers were beginning to gain control of the towns. The building of towns was not, of course, an exclusively British contribution to the growth of South Africa. Quite apart from centres like Graaff-Reinet, which was an important town long before the British occupation, the siting and founding of most towns of the interior was the result of Boer enterprise.* Only after the towns had been sited and established did the nation of shopkeepers step in. The middle years of the nineteenth century witnessed the still largely uncharted spread of English settlers, accompanied by immigrant Jews, Germans and others, fanning out from the coastal towns, especially those of the Eastern Province. Sometimes they farmed, but more often they set up trading establishments and offices in the villages already established by the Dutch. If one reads local newspapers of the seventies and eighties, one is forced to conclude that by this time the cultural life of the majority of centres was conducted for the most part on English lines. To start with, these newspapers were nearly always owned and edited by British settlers, whether they appeared in English or Dutch or both. As for the society described in the newspapers, it was a world where debating societies and horse-racing, and cricket matches between 'Home born' and 'Colonial born', or shooting matches referred to as 'Wimbledons', were among the leading recreational pastimes. Local chambers of commerce began to appear in a number of these centres from the sixties onwards, and these were chiefly English-speaking bodies.* The surnames of the original committee of the Burghersdorp Chamber, founded in 1877, whose activities were soon to awaken Afrikaner political activity in the Albert district, were Sichel, Tennant, Mosenthal, Stuart and O'Brien.* None of the leading tradesmen in the town who advertised their businesses in the local newspaper had Afrikaner names. What was true of Burghersdorp by this standard was generally true of other towns in the eastern and north-eastern Cape. In the west, the position was not quite the same. Thus at Worcester, where, according to Scholtz, it was advisable for the English trader to learn Dutch, the list of retail licences issued by the Sub-distributor of Stamps in January 1883 contained thirty-nine names, which included a Bosman, a Meiring, a Joubert, a Hoffman, two De Villiers's and two Du Toits: the exotic element was dominant, but not in complete control.

The argument that the farther east one went, the slenderer grew the Afrikaner's control over urban life applies to a slightly lesser extent with regard to the municipal boards. In the western Cape—apart from the capital itself, where the participation of Afrikaners in city government was by no means negligible—town councils often contained a majority with Afrikaner names. This was so in Worcester after the municipal elections of 1883.* Members of the Beaufort West town council at the beginning of 1882 included four Afrikaners of whom one, C. J. M. van der Spuy, was chairman of the local farmers' union, or *Boeren Vereeniging*.* When Richmond elected a new municipal board in 1883, Hofmeyr's paper noted that the new body was thoroughly 'Hollandsch-Afrikaansch', and rejoiced accordingly because this was something new.* But the municipal commissioners in Burghersdorp and Dordrecht were still mainly English-speaking.

Although the Afrikaner carried little weight in many of the Colonial towns, especially in the east, this does not mean that he was excluded from local government even in the east. Field-cornets, who were men of his own flesh and blood, no longer exercised the powers they had once held; but a great deal of the work of local administration still fell on their shoulders, and on those of the divisional councils. The constitution of these councils had been consolidated in 1865.* With the exception of the Cape division, each fiscal division of the Colony was divided into six wards. Each ward returned one representative to the council except the town ward—in which the civil commissioner's office was situated— which returned three. A divisional council of eight members, presided over by the civil commissioner who had no casting vote, might thus be expected to contain a majority of farmers over townsmen of five against three, though as the residential qualification for membership applied to the division as a whole and not to the individual ward, it sometimes happened that the urban representation was somewhat larger. A high fixed-property qualification for membership, however, tended to encourage the better-off farmers to stand for election. The reward for their public spirit was the power to supervise the local school committees; and to see that the divisional roads were maintained in good repair, for which purpose they were empowered to levy a road rate, raise and spend revenue from tolls, appoint road inspectors and determine their salaries. The reports of divisional council meetings given in the press indicate that these afforded valuable experience for men who hoped for political careers. An examination of the names of divisional councillors elected throughout the Colony in 1882 has shown that approximately one quarter of the successful candidates were, at that time or within a year or so, committee members of the local branches of the Afrikaner Bond or of the various *boeren vereenigingen*. The names of councillors elected in 1867—the first election after the consolidation of the councils— included not a few who were to become prominent leaders of the Afrikaner Bond, among them J. J. Janse van Rensburg, later M.L.A. for Cradock and chairman of the Bond's Cradock congress in September 1882. More than one witness testified to the superb way in which Van Rensburg handled the Cradock congress, and it is hardly fanciful to suggest that it was a short term in Parliament, preceded by long experience of divisional council work, which had equipped him for his task.*

Whereas it was not difficult for the Dutch-speaking Boer to find his niche in politics at the local level, it was quite another matter for him to find his way into Parliament. Despite the numerical preponderance of Dutch-speaking people in the Colony, members with English names normally outnumbered those with Dutch names by about two to one in Parliament. The main reason for this was undoubtedly the embargo on the use of Dutch in either House, which had been challenged several times in the fifties without result.* Failure to secure the right to speak Dutch in the early days of representative government had given rise, in turn, to two further complementary developments. The one was that the Boer came to look with growing indifference on an institution which for practical reasons largely excluded his own representatives; the other was the emergence of carpet-bagging on a fairly extensive scale, by semi-professional politicians with English names who came mainly from the three urban centres of Cape Town, Grahamstown and Port Elizabeth. 'Grahamstown had most say in everything, and the country was almost entirely ruled by that town', Janse van Rensburg told the Cradock *Boeren Vereeniging* in 1882, commenting on the situation in 1858 as he remembered it. The leading Afrikaner newspapers deplored the extent of Boer indifference and tended to jibe at the carpet-baggers.* Carpet-bagging was not in itself a social evil, as the members of the Afrikaner Bond would have been bound in honesty to admit, for they practised it extensively enough in later years. People deplored it because the language restrictions had helped to produce it, and because it was prevalent before any political parties had come into being in the Colony, at a time when the constituencies might therefore have been expected to return local men.

No law expressly debarred the Afrikaner from entry into any field of public life, and he was legally entitled to hold any position of authority in the public service from the field-cornetcy to the Bench; but the practical difficulties in the way of his promotion in the public service, or of his entry into professional life, were very real for the Boer from the country districts, as distinct from his urban counterpart. 'The misfortune of the young Afrikander', wrote F. J. Dormer, 'is that he is either so untrained altogether that nothing but a life of unscientific and comparatively profitless farming is before him, or, by the self-sacrifice of his parents, he has been brought up to one of a few professions which already show indications of being overstocked.'* Dormer was not lacking in charity for the Boer, and his point was a valid one. Afrikanerdom was by no means devoid of professional men, above all clergymen, lawyers and doctors; but there were few careers open to men without a knowledge of English. The language barrier injured the Boer's dignity, once he cared to think about it, and blocked his way to advancement in public life. The Afrikaner of the platteland was affected by this restriction in a different way from the Afrikaner of the large town. Preferment was indeed harder for him, but he missed it less. His contact with the alien culture was direct, but it was only occasional. He might have sat for irregular periods at the feet of a Scottish schoolmaster, and perhaps even struck up a friendship with him, while at the same time noting the irrelevance to his own situation of some of the things he was required to learn. He would do regular business with the shopkeepers in the nearest town, and perhaps suspect that he was being overcharged, without being in a position to withdraw his custom. From time to time he would appear at the magistrate's court to discharge the burdensome obligation of unpaid jury service, or alternatively to appear as plaintiff or defendant in a case, as likely as not between himself and his own servant. He would thus make direct contact with the extended arm of an alien legal system which was, from his point of view, remarkable not so much for its impartiality as for the enormous inconvenience which it caused him, its unfamiliar procedure, its unprofitable judgments, and—insult of insults—its 'kaffir' interpreter to help make good his own deficiencies in the English tongue.[1] But the backvelder lived his own life, so far as he

[1] The attitude of the Boer to the Colonial legal system is discussed more fully in ch. 7. For the 'kaffir' interpreter as a figure, see below, p. 117.

was able. He would not take the lead in disturbing these arrangements, and it might not even have occurred to him that they ought to be disturbed, for they had already been in operation for several decades. But as soon as a prophet arose among his own people—he tended to think in biblical terms—he would be more than willing to follow the man raised up to lead him, and work for the emancipation of the *Volk*.

Such leadership, however, could only be expected to come from the western Cape, where the inroads into the Afrikaner way of life had been most marked, and where alone the resources in educated manpower and organizing ability were sufficiently concentrated.

2

Farmers in Politics

AT the end of the 1860's, the leaders of Cape Dutch opinion were gradually able to turn their energies to secular politics as their preoccupation with ecclesiastical politics declined. A conflict between the orthodox and the modernist sections of the Nederduits Gereformeerde Kerk—which had turned on questions of theology and church government, and reached a climax with the trial for heresy of three clergymen in 1864, had resulted in an initial victory for the liberal Erastian minority despite their paucity in numbers.* By 1870, however, the conservative majority in the synod was well on the way to regaining control, and the interest of the general public began to turn away from ecclesiastical controversy towards events in the field of secular politics. Jan Hendrik Hofmeyr, who had handled much of the orthodox propaganda as editor of the *Volks- vriend*, amalgamated this paper with the struggling *Zuid Afrikaan* in 1871, and likewise began to pay more attention to secular affairs.

Recent political events which had helped to bring about this change included the British annexation of Basutoland in 1868 and of the Diamond Fields in 1871, under circumstances which had aroused the anger of the Government of the Orange Free State. Though the motives behind British imperial expansion were manifold and not always what the Boer leaders thought they were, it was clear that the doctrine of British paramountcy in southern Africa, which had gone into almost total eclipse in the 1850's, was now being vigorously reasserted. This could be seen in the development of British efforts to confederate South Africa, of which the grant of responsible government to the Cape Colony in 1872 was one aspect, and Shepstone's annexation of the Transvaal in 1877 another. From the Boer Republican point of view, any assertion of British supremacy

north of the Orange River was a breach of the conventions of 1852
and 1854, and therefore unacceptable. Furthermore, the period saw
the outbreak of a succession of serious frontier wars between white
men and black men in different parts of South Africa, in two of
which—on the Cape eastern border and in Zululand—the imperial
authorities were directly involved. This meant that questions of
native policy were also drawn to the forefront of political debate,
and old antagonisms revived.

Colonial Dutch opinion could not fail to be excited by these
developments. Disputes between the Imperial Government and the
Boer Republics divided Cape Afrikaners' loyalties and made them
conscious of their blood ties with the emigrant trekkers, thus leading
many of them to look upon the Great Trek for the first time in the
light of a national saga. Modern Afrikaner writers have suggested
that the awakening of an historical sense among the Afrikaner
people—it might be described as a sense of manifest destiny—
occurred suddenly and quite dramatically during the storms of the
late 1860's and early 1870's.*

In Paarl, some thirty miles across the Cape Flats from the capital,
this new mood would show itself in a dedicated effort to revive the
indigenous Afrikaner culture in all its aspects. This will be discussed
in the following chapter.

In Cape Town, as already indicated, the consolidation of Afrikaner
opinion was more difficult to achieve, and the continuing lack of
unity, even in the face of the political developments mentioned above,
is well illustrated by the inability of the two leading Dutch papers,
the *Volksblad* and Hofmeyr's *Zuid Afrikaan*, to form a common
front. The habit of disagreement had been fostered by the church
quarrel, in which they had taken opposite sides; but it extended
to such political issues as the Imperial Government's policy of
confederation, which the *Volksblad* continued to support, in defiance
of political realities, even after Shepstone's annexation of the
Transvaal. B. J. van de Sandt de Villiers, editor of the *Volksblad*, was
a liberal, inclined at times to be doctrinaire. His rival, Hofmeyr, was
essentially a pragmatist, and inclined to be cautious in his political
judgements. Neither provided the sort of literary fodder which could
be expected to awaken the national feelings of Afrikaners, but
Hofmeyr knew better than De Villiers how to exploit the situation.

There was nothing about the background of Jan Hendrik Hofmeyr
('Onze Jan') that singled him out in advance as a likely leader of an

2

Afrikaner nationalist movement. The son of a wine farmer, he was born in Cape Town in 1845 and spent the greater part of his life in the capital, being educated at *Tot Nut van 't Algemeen* and afterwards at the South African College before he took up journalism. The cultural environment in which he moved was largely English, and it has been suggested that he found difficulty in speaking Dutch, though he never had much difficulty in writing it.* His biographer has noted a reference made by him to the 'National Party' during the early months of the Molteno ministry,* but Hofmeyr saw no special virtue in the formation of an Afrikaner party on an ethnic basis, either then or at any other time. He was indeed concerned to awaken Afrikaner self-respect outside the political field, and acknowledged that the Afrikaans language, support for which was already gaining currency in Paarl as a substitute for Dutch, was valuable as a vehicle of 'sound national feeling'. But as an educational medium he preferred Hollands to Afrikaans because it possessed a literature. Through it, he considered, Afrikaner children could also read and appropriate the epics of Dutch history, so that later generations of South Africans 'should boast of the exploits of De Ruijter, as well as those of Blake'.*

As the seventies advanced, his political outlook tended to harden, and after Shepstone's annexation of the Transvaal his natural moderation gave place to a disciplined anger. In June 1878 he refuted in strong terms the suggestion that the annexation was popular among the burghers. The following February he endorsed the advice of the Paarl paper, *Die Afrikaanse Patriot*, that the Transvalers should offer passive resistance rather than armed defiance, and held to this line until fighting broke out between the British and the Boers in December 1880. The advantage of passive resistance, he wrote, was that it kept the British on the alert in case violence should break out, and also involved them in heavy military expenditure.* Time and the workings of the British parliamentary system might be expected to bring a cure. But the restoration of the Transvaal's independence had to come, and to that end Hofmeyr sponsored a petition to the Queen and maintained a barrage of criticism directed against the agents of Imperial policy, more especially against the High Commissioner, Sir Bartle Frere, whom he described as a thorough-going representative of British land-hunger.*

It was over the crisis in the Transvaal and the related question of confederation that Hofmeyr scored his first major success at the expense of the *Volksblad*. He used the Transvaal situation to demonstrate that he had the Afrikaner cause at heart, whereas the *Volksblad* missed the opportunity. Soon afterwards, the imposition of an excise duty on Colonial brandy by the Sprigg Government gave Hofmeyr an opportunity to fight a battle on behalf of the Western Province farmer—a chance which he grasped with both hands and which the *Volksblad* again missed. It proved to be a significant move and led directly to the establishment of Dutch-speaking farmers' associations, known as *boeren vereenigingen*, all over the Cape Colony. These would gradually assume responsibility for the protection, in the broadest sense, of the interests of the Afrikaner Boer. At first, Hofmeyr managed to keep the farmers' difficulties and those of the Afrikaner in separate compartments; but eventually the pressure of circumstances forced him to jumble the two together. It is not clear that he ever really expected to be able to keep them apart.

The *boeren vereenigingen*, which should not be confused with English-speaking farmers' associations, of which some already existed, fell broadly into two categories: first, the group situated in the western Cape, known collectively as the *Zuid Afrikaansche Boeren Beschermings Vereeniging*, for the establishment of which Hofmeyr was mainly responsible; and secondly, individual *boeren vereenigingen* set up in various parts of the eastern Cape and the Cape midlands, which had no constitutional link with Hofmeyr's group, but which would make an important contribution to the development of the Afrikaner farmers' movements and assist their eventual unification when all the *boeren vereenigingen* and the Afrikaner Bond amalgamated in May 1883. Hofmeyr's Vereeniging was the earliest political organization set up by Cape Afrikaners, and it became Jan Hofmeyr's means of effective entry into political life, giving him the status and authority he would need. Of the independent *vereenigingen*, that established in the Albert district of the north-eastern Cape is of special interest because it shows clearly in its own history the kind of local tensions which could bring a farmers' association into being. As a farmers' association representing a politically subordinate Afrikaner community, it gradually enlarged its platform to include cultural demands: it wanted rights for Dutch-speakers as well as a tax on imported mules. As it happened, the Albert Vereeniging would also fulfil an important mediatory role between the followers of Hofmeyr and of Du Toit, having drawn on the ideas of both.

I. THE Z.A. BOEREN BESCHERMINGS VEREENIGING

When Sprigg decided to tax the Cape brandy producers in June 1878, his object was to find extra revenue with which to pay the interest on a substantial loan needed to cover the cost of new railways and the Gaika–Gcaleka war. The need for the money was pressing and, as the *Volksblad* repeatedly pointed out, there was much to be said in favour of the particular tax proposed. There was no machinery for taxing incomes; a uniform poll tax, which the farmers tended to favour, would have spread the burden inequitably between rich and poor. If the tax appeared to victimize a particular interest, its defenders could reply that other sectors of the economy, notably the importers of merchandise, already carried a heavy share of the tax burden. Further, once the Excise Bill had become law, it did not turn out to be so great a burden as the farmers had anticipated.

But Sprigg miscalculated the political effects of his decision; for the Bill, and the manner in which it was introduced, contained all the ingredients for a good agitation. It hit a struggling industry just at a time when it was attempting to apply to itself the good Victorian virtue of self-help; for the wine farmers, who had run into heavy weather since the loss of their privileged position on the British market during the middle years of the century, had formed their first co-operative society, the *Wijnbouwers Vereeniging*, as recently as October 1877. Hofmeyr, whose *Zuid Afrikaan* had played a leading part in the establishment of the Wijnbouwers Vereeniging, was quick to point out the Bill's defects. It would encourage the producers to adulterate their product, he argued, if they wished to maintain their profit levels. He deplored the provisions for inspection, the inevitable increase of paper work, and the penalties for infringement laid down in the Bill. He complained with overt special pleading that it was not the 'brandy-distilling West' but the 'brandy-drinking East' which ought to pay the tax—the Sprigg ministry was composed of easterners—and invoked the support of Adam Smith and J. S. Mill to prove that the tax ought not to be imposed at all.* The Bill was pushed through with indecent haste. The Opposition's request that it be referred to a select committee was turned down, and even the *Volksblad* agreed that the practical interests of the wine farmers had not been sufficiently considered.

The agitation which followed the introduction of the measure was not wholly due to the *Zuid Afrikaan*, for Hofmeyr could not have created a grievance where none existed. Public meetings held before the end of June at Paarl, Stellenbosch, Montagu, Cape Town, Wellington and Worcester, the first of which reminded J. S. Marais, a local member of Parliament, of the anti-convict agitation of 1849, displayed considerable spontaneity. But Hofmeyr made use of the agitation to exploit what, on analysis, appeared to be a hopeful situation. The Bill duly became law; but he summarily rejected the idea put forward by the *Patriot* that the farmers should retaliate by refusing to produce.* His own answer recalled, either consciously or unconsciously, a suggestion first made by the *Patriot* over a year earlier that the farmers of the Western Province should organize themselves as a political force.* He had in mind not simply an organization to fight the brandy excise, but an all-embracing farmers' association for farmers of all kinds, with regularly established branches and a head office in Cape Town, whose function would be to bring pressure to bear in Parliament on any matter affecting farmers' interests. As an association, it would show an interest in the registration of voters and the choice of suitable candidates for Parliament, somewhat after the manner of Cobden's Anti-Corn Law League, to which Hofmeyr referred in editorials at the time.* Once the excise law had been gazetted, the only action Hofmeyr would recommend was parliamentary action. Several directors of the Wijnbouwers Vereeniging visited his office on the day the law came into force, accepted his arguments, and entrusted to Hofmeyr and a Cape Town attorney, H. P. du Preez, the task of drawing up rules for an association of the sort Hofmeyr had in mind.

The draft regulations proposed by Hofmeyr and Du Preez were considered by a meeting of farmers in the Stellenbosch town hall on 12 August, and accepted after discussion.* Hofmeyr then rose to commend the formation of what he now referred to as a *boeren beschermings vereeniging* (farmers' protection association). He hoped it would create among the farmers of the west a political sense comparable with that of their eastern counterparts, whose farmers' associations had already been in existence for years. If the westerners came to realize that their interests could be furthered by their own efforts, he said, it would matter little if the excise law remained on the statute book. His enthusiasm carried a sympathetic meeting. A provisional committee was elected, and a decision taken to canvass for members in the districts of Stellenbosch and Paarl. Other meetings quickly followed, and a formal act of association was made at a meeting of delegates in Cape Town on 31 October.

The most complete description of the aims, methods and organization of the Vereeniging is to be found in the constitution which this second general meeting adopted.* According to this document, it sought to protect Colonial farmers of all kinds, stock-raisers as well as crop-raisers. (There was no suggestion that it should operate outside the borders.) It planned to secure the election to Parliament of men who would oppose measures considered oppressive to the farming population; who would work for the repeal or at least the reduction of the brandy excise; who would support the special interests of the farmers in legislation dealing with masters and servants; and who would back judicious schemes for the subsidization of farming projects out of public revenue. The Vereeniging would attempt, secondly, to secure the registration as voters of all who had an interest in farming, and guard against the abuse of the franchise. In the third place, it would provide suitable means of keeping farmers informed about projected legislation thought likely to affect their interests. The head office was to be in Cape Town, with local associations—spread throughout the Colony—of which full members were to be entitled to attend and vote at general meetings called by a head committee, or *hoofdbestuur*. The *hoofdbestuur* was to call a general meeting each year for the purpose of making a report and holding fresh elections. It was to control the purse, receiving all the money raised through subscriptions, and it was to be responsible for the selection of candidates for parliamentary seats.* Local *vereenigingen*, whose committees had to include representatives from each field-cornetcy in the division, were empowered to draw up their own regulations subject to the terms of the general constitution. Life members, who had paid a lump sum of £10 0s. 0d., and general members, who paid an annual subscription of £1 1s. 0d., could vote at general meetings of the Vereeniging; and provision was made for a further grade, that of the local member paying 10s. 6d. yearly, who could participate only in the proceedings of his branch.

At the time of the formal inauguration of the Vereeniging on 31 October 1878, a few branches already existed in the western Cape, and the number grew in the next few months. Procedure for the formation of branches quickly became standardized. A public meeting would be called, at which either Hofmeyr or Du Preez was usually present. The constitution would be read and explained, and resolutions adopted, often without dissent, accepting the rules and agreeing to form a branch. Thereupon a provisional committee would be elected, care being taken to see that each ward in the district was represented by two people who would be instructed to canvass for members. Subscription lists would then be opened, and in some cases generous donations were made on the spot. Finally, a date would be fixed for a subsequent meeting at which the Vereeniging was to be formally constituted and a proper committee elected. Thus a meeting was held at Paarl on 18 August, the preparatory work done, and the local Vereeniging constituted on 18 September. At Wellington it took rather longer, because the local members required an assurance, which they only received on 31 October, that their branch would be independent of Paarl. The Stellenbosch branch was established early in September. Tulbagh held its first public meeting on 2 October, and formed its branch on the 23rd. Du Preez used the opportunity of the western circuit to set the movement on foot in the south-western districts, but in spite of the optimism of the report which he made on his return,* it soon became apparent that there was far less enthusiasm beyond the mountains of the Western Province. At Prince Albert, Riversdale, Heidelberg and Swellendam, his first efforts to form branches failed, though all eventually joined. Montagu and Caledon both formed branches, but the former branch succumbed in 1879, while the latter did so in 1880 and was never resurrected. The branch at Worcester, founded by Hofmeyr in September 1878, remained in being but was very inactive.* It did not contribute to central funds until 1882. Apart from the fickle Caledon, only one branch was formed in a predominantly grain-producing district during the initial drive. This was at Malmesbury. Here torrential rains did not prevent a good attendance, when Hofmeyr, forgetting for the moment the debt which he owed to the Anti-Corn Law League, frightened his audience by saying that there was a move on foot in parliamentary circles to abolish the duty on imported grain. Malmesbury's interest in the Vereeniging was thereupon immediate and lasting.

The first efforts to establish the Boeren Beschermings Vereeniging in the rural districts barely carried it outside the four electoral divisions of the Cape, Stellenbosch, Paarl and Malmesbury. This was in spite of the stimulus of Upper and Lower House elections in

1878–9, in which the successes of the Vereeniging were considerable, if one takes into account the fact that it was not given proper time to organize its campaign.[1] However, once the excitement of the elections was over, the *hoofdbestuur* had the utmost difficulty in encouraging even the well-established branches in the western circle to do very much. At the first annual meeting in 1879, the members talked at great length about the brandy excise but neglected to discuss any other matters of interest to farmers. The report of the *hoofdbestuur* a year later made sorry reading. It had itself been active, more especially in the fields of viticulture and parliamentary registration; but its report grieved over 'the increasingly obvious lack of tangible interest in the Vereeniging', illustrated by the fact that not a single branch had paid its subscriptions as required by the constitution.*

A change came over the Vereeniging in 1881, mainly as a result of the Transvaal war of independence and the emergence of the Afrikaner Bond as an open rival for the Afrikaner's political allegiance. In that year Hofmeyr, who had entered Scanlen's Cabinet without portfolio, undertook two branch-forming tours in the southern coastal districts of the Colony, with the result that the number of branches had more than doubled by the end of 1882.*[2] But his efforts to persuade the members of the Vereeniging to lend their support to cultural objectives in addition to agricultural reform met with only moderate success, and when the Vereeniging associated itself with the current campaign for the extension of Dutch language rights at a special meeting in March 1882, it was handling this subject officially for the first time.*[3]

[1] These elections are discussed below, p. 72.

[2] The spread of the *Z.A. Boeren Beschermings Vereeniging*, as shown in the references to branches in the minutes of the annual general meetings, was as follows (see map 1):

Oct. 1879   Branches existed at Paarl, Stellenbosch, Cape Division, Tulbagh, Malmesbury, Wellington, Worcester and Caledon.

Nov. 1880   Caledon had ceased. A new branch existed at Prince Albert.

Sept. 1881   New branches existed at Beaufort West, Oudtshoorn, George and Uniondale.

Aug. 1882   New branches existed at Robertson, Swellendam, Montagu, Heidelberg Riversdale and Humansdorp.

May 1883   New branches existed at Willowmore and Alexandria.

[3] For Hofmeyr's efforts to enlarge the aims of the Vereeniging in 1881–2, see below, pp. 45–6, where they are considered in relation to the challenge of the Afrikaner Bond.

II. THE EASTERN VEREENIGINGEN

There existed in the eastern Cape, by the early eighties, a handful of Dutch-speaking *boeren vereenigingen* which were independent both of their English-speaking counterparts and of Hofmeyr's Vereeniging in the west. From the start, Hofmeyr tended to look upon these *vereenigingen* as necessary adjuncts to his own movement, and their existence as a valid reason why his own efforts should be confined mainly to the west. Thus, early in October 1878, after he had heard that plans were afoot to set up a body of this kind in Graaff-Reinet, he took the opportunity of suggesting that the Graaff-Reinet body might take over the western Vereeniging's constitution, set itself up as a local *hoofdbestuur*, form more branches in the east, and send delegates to the meetings of his own Vereeniging in Cape Town.* But Hofmeyr apparently lost interest in this new body, and he did not find another occasion to discuss developments in the east until the Albert *Boeren Beschermings Vereeniging* was founded in the middle of 1879.

The beginnings of the Albert Vereeniging are difficult to ascertain because the two near-contemporary accounts which exist are mutually contradictory and both unreliable. The one, published by a foundation member of the Vereeniging in *De Tolk* over three years after the event, almost certainly explained the origin of the Vereeniging in terms of a movement of public opinion which developed only after that body had been formed, and used phrases to describe its organization which did not become current until after the formation of the Afrikaner Bond.* The other—written after the same interval of time by the editor of the local newspaper, who possessed no esoteric knowledge—cannot be reconciled with the contemporary reports in the same newspaper, and dates the foundation of the Vereeniging a full year too early.* The fact that St. P. O'S. O'Brien, the editor of the *Burghersdorp Gazette*, did not enjoy the confidence of the founders of the Vereeniging lies near the root of the difficulty, for this meant that much of its activity was not reported at all.

The division of Albert had been politically awake for some years before its *boeren vereeniging* was formed, and had taken a lead in the efforts to secure the use of Dutch in Parliament in the fifties. A Burghersdorp Chamber of Commerce and Association for General Purposes, founded in January 1877, was active in the election campaigns of 1878–9. All three candidates who were returned in these elections—J. A. Vermaak for the Council, and George Sichel and Andries Stockenstrom for the Assembly—received requisitions signed by prominent men in town and country, of both language groups, while the election of Vermaak was strongly approved by the *Zuid Afrikaan*.* But there was one notable absentee from the list: F. H. Hopley, a farmer who had represented the constituency in Parliament almost continuously since 1864. Hopley had aroused the anger of an important section of the electorate by failing to support the Prime Minister, Sir John Molteno, when Sir Bartle Frere dismissed him from office in 1878, and the *Gazette* gave him no mercy.* He was still nursing his grievance at a meeting in October the following year, when, according to the *Gazette*, he ascribed his failure in the 1879 election 'mainly . . . to town influence'.* It was to the Albert Boeren Beschermings Vereeniging, which had in the meantime come into existence, that Hopley made his complaint.

The first meeting of the Vereeniging to be reported in the press took place on 26 May 1879.* The occasion was a joint meeting of representatives of the Vereeniging with the committee of the Chamber of Commerce, to interview George Sichel, the new member of Parliament, and 'make known to him the opinions of the said Committee'. They presented him with a document containing nineteen points, all of them to do with the real or imagined interests of a farming community, a precise mandate for their member to follow. A foundation member of the Vereeniging, Jotham Joubert, later referred in a letter to the *Gazette* to 'the nineteen points brought forward by the chairman, *at the first meeting of the Society* (the Board of Commerce being present, at the request of the Society to co-operate . . .) and handed to Mr. Sichel'.* This must refer to the same occasion, and makes it reasonably certain that the Albert Vereeniging did not exist before May 1879.

The nineteen propositions given to Sichel contained no suggestion whatever that the Vereeniging was interested in the political or cultural claims of the Afrikaner. But the *Patriot* was read in Burghersdorp, O'Brien having already indulged from time to time in an attack on its views. Between this first meeting of the Albert Vereeniging and its second, held at Vinkelfontein on 2 July, S. J. du Toit had published his appeal for the formation of an Afrikaner Bond,[1] and the chairman of the Vereeniging had evidently read it. This was D. P. (Oom Daantje) van den Heever, a farmer from Ventersburg, whose rock-like personality stands out among the

[1] *Patriot*, 20, 27 June 1879. See below, pp. 35–6.

Afrikaner politicians of the late nineteenth century. His rhetorical gifts could sway an audience, as the Bond would discover to its cost during the dispute over scab in 1895, and to its advantage during the elections of 1898, when Oom Daantje would be called upon to bolster the position of several hard-pressed candidates. At Vinkelfontein, he gave a demonstration of his powers, calling on his audience to 'wake up and dig out our rights from under the rubbish heap of indifference'. He gave the meeting five objectives to work for: the right to speak Dutch in Parliament (if that is what he meant by 'onze moedertaal'), the redemption of the Colonial debt, the raising of the franchise, the punishment of corrupt practices in elections, and finally, 'Not only the Farmers' Protection Committee [*Boerenbeschermings Comité*] but an Afrikaner Bond, a compact bound together by loyalty and interest [*een Afrikaanderbond, een aaneengeschakelde overeenkomst van getrouwheid en belangstelling*], in which every Afrikaner may feel at home. Then South Africa will become what it must be, and then the alien tongue [*uitlandsche taal*] will no longer dominate South Africa.'* What the meeting thought of this speech is not recorded; but it seems that something of the group exclusiveness breathed by the *Patriot* had found its way into the Albert Vereeniging on the morrow of an electoral feud which threatened to drive a wedge between town and country.

The situation was given no chance to quieten down, for in September Stockenstrom resigned from the Assembly to take up an appointment on the Bench, while Sichel, on his return from Cape Town the same month, felt called upon to 'regret exceedingly, that the Community should be divided on matters of the utmost importance'.* The Vereeniging, however, was not to be soothed by gentle words. It held a meeting on 17 October and chose Jotham Joubert as its parliamentary candidate to succeed Stockenstrom, the Chamber of Commerce having already met on the 6th and chosen F. R. Tennant. The former was a farmer, the latter a merchant who dealt *inter alia* in agricultural implements; and both were local men. Hopley was the moving spirit in the choice of Joubert, and it was he and Van den Heever who put his name forward on nomination day, Tennant having meanwhile withdrawn his candidature in the interest of local peace.* The Albert Boeren Beschermings Vereeniging had thus won its first political victory and, as O'Brien saw the position, Hopley had had his revenge. And now, for the first time, the Vereeniging began to attract the attention of the Afrikaner leaders in the western Cape.

The Albert Vereeniging had already begun to express support for the efforts of Ds. W. P. de Villiers to secure the recognition of Dutch in Parliament, which led S. J. du Toit to describe it in October as the 'most wide awake and fiery' of the three Afrikaner political associations.* Hofmeyr went further. He looked upon the Albert address to De Villiers 'as one more proof that a feeling of nationality really is beginning to sprout among our Afrikaners. . . . Such associations as that in Albert will be able to accomplish an incalculable amount towards the joining together of East and West and towards the nurturing of a true Afrikaner spirit.'* When the *Volksblad* asserted that the western Vereeniging was bent on incorporating the eastern in itself, Hofmeyr vigorously denied the charge. All he wanted, he said, was an informal alliance between the two bodies on a basis of complete administrative independence and mutual consultation.* He expressed these ideas again with some urgency the following March when he learnt of the establishment of a *boeren vereeniging* at Maraisburg.* When he heard, at about the same time, that the Albert Vereeniging planned to hold a large meeting on 19 March, to which representatives from other *vereenigingen* would be invited, he took the opportunity of making fresh proposals for the organization of the eastern *vereenigingen*. These were that each electoral province should have its own *hoofdbestuur*, which could meet in the various towns of the province in rotation. Each *bestuur* could then look after its own parliamentary elections.*

The western Vereeniging was not represented at the meeting in Burghersdorp on 19 March, but it set up a special committee to attend to its relations with the easterners and plied the men of Albert with its own literature, which was gratefully acknowledged. The Albert Vereeniging reciprocated with an address to Hofmeyr which amounted in effect to an acceptance of his political leadership: 'We ask you to proceed with the defence of our people and our language, and we will follow you wherever necessity requires.' Hofmeyr replied with thanks, and an exhortation to further action: 'The organization started in Albert needs to be spread into all eastern districts where there are Dutch Afrikaners (*Hollandsche Afrikaanders*), to make them realize what great political power they possess if only they will learn to use it.'*

Contact had been made between the *boeren vereenigingen* of east and west, and in December 1880, the month in which the Transvalers threw down the gauntlet before the Imperial power, the Albert committee decided to develop the link still further. They sent Oom Daantje van den Heever on a progress to Cape Town in January, armed with credentials and a sheaf of formal introductions to merchants, lawyers and the '*Boerenbeschermings-comité van de Westelijke Provincie*'. There were letters to various parliamentarians and to the Prime Minister in person, and Oom Daantje took a private secretary with him to assist in what promised to be a very full programme. He travelled through Beaufort West and set up a *vereeniging* there which later joined Hofmeyr's body; on his arrival in Paarl he had talks with members of the local *boeren vereeniging*, including its parliamentary team, and also appeared on the same platform as S. J. du Toit at a public meeting to discuss the Transvaal crisis.* He then moved on to Cape Town, met the Prime Minister and the *hoofdbestuur* of the western Vereeniging, and after a visit to the branch at Malmesbury returned to the capital for an audience with the Governor. This took place on 16 February, after which Oom Daantje returned home fully satisfied with the success of his mission.* He had cemented the good relationship between the *vereenigingen* of east and west, and (though this did not become apparent until after he had returned home) he had also laid the foundations for an alliance between the Albert Vereeniging and the Afrikaner Bond, which would have considerable importance in the future.

In the month that D. P. van den Heever went to Cape Town, an open-air meeting in Middelburg was addressed by Janse van Rensburg, Hofmeyr's parliamentary ally from the Cradock division, who, in the opinion of the editor of the *Middelburg Gazette*, 'spoke as disloyally as the warmest supporter of the Opposition could desire'.* This was an important meeting for the people of Middelburg, who had come together under the auspices of their local *boeren vereeniging* to discuss the important political issues of the day. It was the first time that the Middelburg Vereeniging had shown any lively interest in matters outside farming, and it was now prepared to argue in favour of Dutch in Parliament, express itself on conscription and the troubles in Basutoland, listen to a fiery tirade by Van Rensburg on the successful resistance of the Transvalers against British arms, and demand a place on the political map for the district, which for the moment was split between the electoral divisions of Cradock, Albert, Colesberg and Graaff-Reinet.

Middelburg, like Albert but unlike Aliwal North and Dordrecht,[1] possessed a local newspaper whose editor looked upon Boer political activity with profound mistrust. O'Brien of the *Burghersdorp Gazette* would eventually turn cat in pan and join the Afrikaner Bond. Heathcote, his Middelburg contemporary, could never have gone so far; but his mistrust of the local *vereeniging* soon landed his paper in difficulties, and at the same time provided an entry into Colonial politics for a talented Hollander who quickly built up in the midlands a strong personal influence which he always used to support the policies of Jan Hofmeyr.

Nicolaas Frederic de Waal, the son of a banker, was born in Rotterdam in 1853, received a commercial education in Brussels, studied law privately, and had travelled in Europe and America before a chest complaint brought him to South Africa in 1880.* He met Hofmeyr soon after his arrival, and a friendship developed before De Waal moved to the midlands—first to Graaff-Reinet where he was employed by a firm of general agents and auctioneers, and subsequently to Middelburg where he opened a new agency at the beginning of November 1881. He immediately set about the propagation of his political ideas through the only available medium, namely Heathcote's newspaper, to which he contributed the first of a number of articles on 15 November. On 20 December he took over the paper, under contract with Heathcote, for a period of three years, renamed it *De Middelburg Getuige*, and changed its editorial policy, greatly increasing the amount of space devoted to Dutch news and comment. Like many Hollanders of his day, De Waal was able to identify himself quite easily with the aspirations of the Colonial Afrikaner, though his nationalism was not extreme. It was not long before he was active in the local *boeren vereeniging*—he was elected secretary and treasurer in March 1882—and he used his influence to keep the Vereeniging on the moderate Hofmeyr path. In this he succeeded, though attempts were made to affiliate with the Afrikaner Bond; and it does not seem that his newness to South Africa was held against him.

Boeren vereenigingen were set up at Maraisburg and Cradock in January and June 1880, and the reports in the *Cradock Register* suggest that both of them were moderate in their politics.* With the

---

[1] Francis Hamilton of the Aliwal *Northern Post*, and O'Brien's namesake of the Dordrecht *Frontier Guardian*, both looked on the emergence of *boeren vereenigingen* as legitimate and desirable developments.

formation of further *vereenigingen* of the same type at Petrusville, Colesberg, Murraysburg, Wodehouse, Aliwal North, Steynsburg and Somerset East (but apparently nowhere else), all before the end of 1881, the network of such associations was complete. They stretched from the Cape Peninsula to Aliwal North.[1] West and south of Beaufort West they were affiliated to Hofmeyr's *hoofdbestuur* in Cape Town. From Murraysburg eastwards they were independent units with no co-ordinating machinery, though all used the Dutch language —the only sure distinguishing mark between them and the English farmers' associations—and none felt obliged to limit the range of its interests to purely agricultural matters. The pull of the Afrikaner Bond came to be felt more strongly by some than by others. The Murraysburg Boeren Vereeniging, for example, called itself a branch of the Bond from about May 1881, but in April the following year it reverted to its original name.* The Aliwal North Vereeniging went over to the Bond in April 1882, following a move from its Lady Grey members the previous July.* The Colesberg Vereeniging fought a war on two fronts; against the English in the dorp on the one hand, and on the other against Bond branches in the neighbourhood which refused to allow it to affiliate with them unless it dropped the name *'Boeren Beschermings Vereeniging'* from its official title.[2] But whatever reasons these associations had for choosing to retain this nomenclature, it may be regarded as certain that most of them were apprehensive about the direction which the Afrikaner Bond was taking. The idea of fusion with the Bond had its attractions, but the eastern *boeren vereenigingen* were no more ready than the western to sell their souls in order to get it.

III. THE MEASURE OF HOFMEYR'S ACHIEVEMENT

The first *boeren vereenigingen* to come into existence were created with the sole publicized object of looking after the farming interests of their members, and their concern for the cultural interests of the Afrikaner was a subsequent development. In the case of the Albert Vereeniging, whose earliest documents contained not a trace of Afrikaner nationalism, the transition was almost immediate; but it meant little in practice until after Van den Heever's visit to Cape

---

[1] See map 1.

[2] This storm in a teacup raged for approximately two and a half years, and was only resolved with the fusion of the Bond and the *boeren vereenigingen* in May 1883.

Town in January 1881. The cultural interests of the Afrikaner did not feature strongly in the politics of the western Vereeniging either, until the same year. But by that time, against the background of the Transvaal war, the campaign for Dutch language rights in the Colonial Parliament, and the early successes of S. J. du Toit's openly nationalist Afrikaner Bond, the several *vereenigingen* were coming to concentrate more and more on cultural issues while still retaining their primary interest in farming matters.

Hofmeyr not only permitted this change of emphasis, but actually encouraged it to develop. His correspondence with the Albert Vereeniging, together with his campaign for Dutch in Parliament, indicates that he was at least as interested in the cause of the '*Hollandsche Afrikaander*' as in that of the farmer. Did he therefore vest his energies in the farmers' movement as a way of concealing his real intentions? Was the bluff 'Sir John Falstaff' of South African College days, as Sir John Kotzé remembered him, already on the way to becoming Merriman's 'Mole'?

When the *Volksblad* noted on 9 July 1878 that 'there appears to prevail, in some quarters, an opinion that the opponents of the Excise Bill are, in reality, fighting the battle of Dutch *versus* English', Hofmeyr was angry. It seems clear, in fact, that he shared the *Volksblad's* abhorrence of naked racialism; but he considered that the absence of a strong Afrikaner group feeling could no longer be taken for granted. According to his diagnosis it already existed, and the problem for the statesman was to ensure that it developed in a healthy manner and remained under control. He called for a resurgence of Afrikaner self-esteem, not from a hatred of things English, though he hated some current manifestations of Imperial policy, but from a feeling that unless the Englishman could be persuaded to look upon the Afrikaner as his equal and grant him full equality of opportunity, the existing ascendancy of the one group over the other would continue and perhaps grow worse. That, he felt, would be to the enduring disadvantage of a Colony where harmony between the two white groups was essential if self-government was to work, or if the ultimate withdrawal of Imperial authority was to be a sensible and desirable step.

Hofmeyr's interpretation of the position was probably correct. It can be argued, however, that by using a farmers' movement as a vehicle for the development of Afrikaner solidarity, he helped to smother at birth a possible Colony-wide Anglo-Dutch farmers' party.

The widespread agricultural depression of the early eighties, together with the opposition of many farmers to a number of laws affecting their social and economic position, and the fact that the farming interests were, if anything, under-represented in Parliament, provided a considerable stimulus for the formation of such a party.* Before it could come into existence or draw support from farmers of both language groups, racial politics would have had to be excluded from the *boeren vereenigingen* and the farmers' associations. But racial politics were not excluded from the former, with the result that when the situation was peculiarly ripe for the Dutch and English farmers to sink their differences, in the period between 1886 and 1895, an inner tension prevented the leaders on both sides from effectively spanning the gulf of suspicion which kept them apart. Too much passion was generated in the years 1881 to 1884. For this, the Afrikaner Bond was in large measure responsible, though the fires of mistrust were also fed by the anti-republican feeling which developed among English-speaking colonials during the Transvaal crisis. Hofmeyr, who can hardly be blamed for not seeing how events would develop, found himself in the awkward position of having to keep in check a nationalist movement which he had himself done something to promote, and at the same time to spur his own *vereeniging* on to a more forthright adoption of cultural objectives, for fear that the Afrikaner Bond should steal all his thunder.

3

3

Nationalist Foundations:
From the Genootskap to the
Afrikaner Bond

THE *boeren vereenigingen* had come into being in the first instance for the same reason as the English-speaking farmers' associations which preceded them: to protect the material interests of the farmer. But the *Genootskap van Regte Afrikaners* (Fellowship of True Afrikaners), which was launched at Paarl on 14 August 1875 by a small group of dedicated men, proclaimed the intention '*om te staan ver ons Taal, ons Nasie en ons Land*' (to stand for our Language, our Nation and our Country). Its members fastened on to the concept of the Afrikaner people as a culturally distinct element within the population of South Africa: a blending of Hollander, German and Huguenot for the most part, knit together by two centuries of common history into a national group fully identified with the South African soil and speaking a common language, Afrikaans. To propagate such an idea was to impart a new intensity to the nationalist feelings which were beginning to stir within Afrikanerdom, and it will be the purpose of the present chapter, after an initial survey of the *Genootskap* itself, to trace the extension of the *Genootskap's* activities into avowedly political channels, where it would take shape as S. J. du Toit's project of an 'Afrikaner Bond'.

An organization with forthright aims of this kind might be expected to appeal strongly to Afrikaners who were apprehensive about their chances of cultural survival as a group. But at first this did not happen. The evidence seems to suggest that this was largely because S. J. du Toit antagonized the leaders of opinion in the Church of which he was a minister and to which nearly all Cape Afrikaners belonged. At all events, the Afrikaner Bond made no headway worth mentioning until after the Transvaal war of independence, when it did take root in the Cape, Orange Free State and South African Republic. But in the course of the next two years it rejected the leadership of the men from Paarl who had brought it into being, and turned to Jan Hofmeyr, though he had in the first instance dissociated himself from its aims and methods. A nationalist movement which had suddenly acquired momentum after early setbacks as suddenly checked itself in mid-course, abandoned nationalist polemics, and began to conciliate those whom it had first set out to antagonize. This further development seems to have taken place because the leaders of the Afrikaner Bond inferred too much from their initial success. The rank and file Bondsmen would not participate in controversial trade boycotts as they were asked to do, nor subscribe to statements of principle which they did not understand. They came to prefer Hofmeyr's more tolerant, less doctrinaire approach to the problem of relations between groups.

I. THE GENOOTSKAPPERS OF PAARL

Stephanus Jacobus du Toit and his brother Daniel François were the thirteenth and twelfth children respectively of a wine farmer in Daljosaphat, near Paarl.* Daniel François was a schoolmaster. Stephanus Jacobus had entered the Paarl Gymnasium in 1867 at the age of 19, and had proceeded from there to the Stellenbosch seminary to receive the theological training which would eventually qualify him for the ministry of the Nederduits Gereformeerde Kerk. At the former establishment he had come under the influence of two notable exponents of Dutch culture. One was Ds. G. W. A. van der Lingen, who had battled successfully to maintain the independence of the school and keep Hollands as the medium of instruction. The other was a talented linguist, Arnoldus Pannevis. At the seminary, his chief mentor was Professor N. J. Hofmeyr, an uncle of Jan Hendrik and a very strict Calvinist. He was also strongly influenced by the Dutch theologian, Dr. Abraham Kuyper. Both these influences, the cultural and the theological, left a lasting impression on him, and were developed by his busy brain into a coherent philosophy which sought to combine the cultural and political ambitions of Afrikanerdom and fix them in a theocratic mould. An early visit to the Transvaal filled him with admiration for the burghers of that state. After being called for short periods to various congregations in the western Cape, he accepted a call to Noorder Paarl in July 1875. This was a new congregation, created as a result of a split in the

Paarl community on the question of religious education in schools,*
and Du Toit accepted the call as an advocate of Christian National
Education—a philosophy which he would soon develop in print and
subsequently apply in practice as Superintendent General of
Education in Kruger's Transvaal.

The arrival of S. J. du Toit in Paarl was followed almost immediately by the foundation of the Genootskap van Regte Afrikaners.
The background to this dedicated and to some extent clandestine
organization must be briefly told.* For many years there had been
attempts by individuals to encourage the literary use of Afrikaans,
and in the view of Pannevis and C. P. Hoogenhout this had become a
necessity. The former, with his sensitive feel for language, regarded
Dutch as too far removed from the experience of South African
youth to serve as a satisfactory educational medium. The latter, a
well-known educator, began a campaign in April 1873, which grew
in intensity over the next few years, for the recognition of Afrikaans.
It was in order to provide the necessary organization for
such a campaign that the Genootskap van Regte Afrikaners was
formed.

The foundation of the society was partly the outcome of a meeting
between S. J. du Toit and a representative of the British and Foreign
Bible Society named Morgan. They met to discuss the translation
of the Bible into Afrikaans.* Religious enthusiasm, indeed, provided
much of the drive behind the society's activities. Members had to be
professing Christians; they looked upon the Afrikaans language
essentially as something God-given, and they were not deterred,
though they seem to have been driven into anonymity, by the *odium
theologicum* which resulted from their efforts to change the language
of divine worship.*

The *Genootskappers* began under difficulties which arose not only
from the conservative opposition of the clergy, but also from the
emergence of a rival campaign for the recognition of Hollands in
public life; from a desperate initial shortage of money; and from the
fact that they embarked upon an ambitious programme of public
education without possessing a printing press. The campaign for
Dutch got under way in 1878, inspired largely by Jan Hofmeyr in
the columns of the *Zuid Afrikaan*. Attempts to amalgamate the two
campaigns proved unsuccessful, with the result that Hofmeyr
decided to publish a new *Zuid-Afrikaansche Tijdschrift* as a venture
entirely independent of the Paarl society.* But good sense prevailed

on both sides, and a disagreement over which language should be developed as the *volkstaal*, which could have destroyed the effectiveness of both campaigns, was not allowed to develop. The Afrikaans *Genootskappers*, while continuing to publish material in Afrikaans, gave their support to the campaign for the recognition of Dutch, and in fact published a great deal in both languages.* The money shortage was met by the self-sacrifice of the *Genootskappers* themselves, notably that of S. J. du Toit in person, who financed the movement largely out of his own pocket and claimed to have sold books out of his own library to defray the printing costs.* The initial lack of a printing press was met by the good offices of Jan Hofmeyr in Cape Town. In addition to receiving and forwarding applications for membership, which had to be addressed to 'Oom Lokomotief',[1] he undertook the publication of their monthly newspaper, *Die Afrikaanse Patriot*, and in 1877 published the first edition of their much-read essay in historical interpretation, *Die Geskiedenis van ons Land in die Taal van ons Volk*. By the beginning of 1877, the Genootskap had acquired its own printing press and took over responsibility for the *Patriot*. The firm of D. F. du Toit and Company, printers and bookbinders, first advertised itself in 1878.

To limit a discussion of the Genootskap van Regte Afrikaners to its efforts to propagate the Afrikaans language would be to ignore its more fundamental significance. The recognition of Afrikaans was, of course, an end in itself. But the Afrikaans language was also the vehicle of a bigger idea, as yet only vaguely formulated, which involved the self-conscious cultivation of a distinctive Afrikaner outlook rooted in the religion and the history of the people, to be attained by an all-embracing programme of popular education. Here the starting point of the *Genootskappers* was the concept of Christian National Education, which had first appeared in the Netherlands with the establishment of the *Vereeniging van Christelijk-Nationaal Onderwijs* in 1860, and had begun to take root in South Africa under the influence of Ds. G. W. A. van der Lingen of the Paarl Gymnasium. S. J. du Toit, who wrote his *De Christelijke School in hare verhouding tot Kerk en Staat* in 1876, aimed in particular to do two things: to restore the Church's influence over the minds of the young by securing the principle of confessional religious instruction in the schools, and to protect those same minds from the

[1] Initially this was the sobriquet of the anonymous editor, but it attached itself in the course of time to D. F. du Toit in person.

cultural domination of things English. The first of these aims represented a protest against the secularist trend of the education ordinances of 1839 and 1865, but it did not enjoy the support of the clergy as a whole. At a time when they felt capable of keeping theological liberalism in check, the clergy placed their confidence in Christian teachers rather than in an overhaul of the school system, and to that end secured the establishment of their own normal college in Cape Town in 1878.

Fewer obstacles attended the efforts of the Genootskap to turn the minds of Afrikaners inwards towards their own 'national' traditions and way of life, and there is no better example of its aims and methods in this respect than the *Geskiedenis van ons Land in die Taal van ons Volk*. This was a joint effort, but the greater part was the work of S. J. du Toit.* In a modest preface the authors deplored the lack of adequate source material in the Dutch language, but claimed to have set inquiries in motion to make good the deficiency. The book was directed at the Afrikaner public, and was intended to enthuse as well as to teach. The authors' method was boldly eclectic, and those aspects of South African history which did not lend themselves readily to the case they were expounding—for example, the story of the constitutional development of the Cape Colony— were compressed into a narrow compass. It was romantic history of an exaggerated kind, in which the hero was the Afrikaner Boer. He was pictured, first of all, trying to build a colony, caught between the upper and nether millstones of the Dutch East India Company and the 'wild nations'; and was seen to prevail over both because the Lord was on his side. The Huguenots were discussed at considerable length, and their fusion with the Cape Dutch was likewise brought within the scope of the Providential plan. The writers' emphasis moved to the Republics from the time of the Great Trek onwards, with the implication that from that time the spiritual home of the Afrikaner lay beyond the Orange River. The authors, partly to offset distortions in the English textbooks then in circulation, played down the contribution of English-speaking people to the development of South Africa, and they sought to arouse the group patriotism of the Afrikaner by a skilful use of melodrama, best seen in their account of the Slagters Nek executions in 1815. When a second edition was published in 1895, a new section was added covering the period from 1877 to 1895, from which anti-British sentiment, which was then out of fashion, was excluded; but it was

not suppressed in the rest of the book. The *Geskiedenis* provided a
good foundation for a nationalist mythology, even if that mythology
was not as complete as it was later to become.[1] Only five hundred
copies of the first edition were printed, and the demand so far
exceeded the supply that the *Patriot* repeatedly advertised for unsold
copies to be returned. So it was evidently much read. But, great
though its impact on the unlettered mind of the average Boer must
have been, it is likely to have been small by comparison with that of
the *Patriot* itself.

Die Afrikaanse Patriot first appeared, as a monthly, in January
1876. It became a weekly in January 1877 and the editorial burden
fell mainly on the two Du Toit brothers until Stephanus Jacobus
accepted a government post in the Transvaal in 1882. Daniel
François then took on full responsibility. From the start the paper
cultivated a friendly, informal relationship with its readers, and was
not afraid to talk down to them. 'Oom Lokomotief' was a topical
enough nickname for the editors to choose at the beginning of the
South African railway age. It was funny, familiar, and above all
avuncular. 'Oom' encouraged his readers to write to him, and the
correspondence columns were usually full, sometimes to overflowing,
with letters—nearly always in Afrikaans—from all over the Colony
and the republics. At first the paper's news service was exceedingly
poor, though this improved rapidly as it acquired more and more
correspondents throughout South Africa. It does not seem to have
had its own parliamentary correspondent for the first few years of
its existence, and relied on the *Zuid Afrikaan* and the *Volksblad* for
much of its political news. It did not report the parliamentary session
of 1877 until it was over, and then dismissed its lengthy deliberations
with the terse comment, 'as usual, more *talk* than *action*'.* The
following year it carried brief parliamentary reports, with the
explanation that 'what we give here is what every Afrikaner *ought*
to read'—and no more. Its editorial coverage was narrow, the policy
being to pick on fruitful themes and 'plug' them. Thus six of the
seven issues between 24 December 1880 and 4 February 1881
contained leading articles supporting the establishment of a
Huguenot memorial, which in fact received better editorial coverage

[1] It is of some interest that the authors could make a strong attack on the
missionary societies (other than the Moravians) without so much as mentioning
the name of Dr. John Philip, and that they could write a narrative history of the
Great Trek without any reference to the covenant before Blood River.

than the Transvaal war of independence then taking place. Four consecutive issues in March and April 1882 were devoted to an attack on the Standard Bank, and many other instances of this repetitive technique are to be found. The paper's arguments were usually couched in the simple, monosyllabic form to which the Afrikaans language so easily lends itself.* Its aim was to instruct rather than to inform, and it tended to do this somewhat in the manner of a schoolmaster preparing pupils for an examination, setting out its arguments in simple language, numbering its points, sometimes reprinting editorial sequences in pamphlet form where they related to a common subject. Meanwhile its subscribers grew from fifty, who took the first issue in 1876, to about 3,700 at the end of 1881, by which time the paper's agencies in the Colony were nearly as numerous as those of the *Zuid Afrikaan*, and in the Transvaal considerably more so. The circulation of the *Patriot* in the Transvaal would eventually have great importance for the Paarl movement, though not until 1881.

Within a year or two of its inception, the leaders of the Genootskap van Regte Afrikaners had achieved much in focusing the attention of Afrikanerdom on the unsatisfactory features of its position in society. Their enthusiasm was infectious, and their methods were well suited to stirring up the elemental fervour of an intense, conservative and unsophisticated people. But they were not methods which appealed to the taste of all Afrikaners, namely those whose relationship with their English-speaking fellow Colonials was reasonably cordial; those who regarded the retention of the Dutch language as necessary for the growth of their own civilization, and scorned the patois offered as an alternative; and the theological moderates, the middle-of-the-road Calvinists who would no more accept Christian National Education than the theories of Charles Darwin. The Genootskap's approach was strong because it captured the spirit of the platteland. It was weak because it alienated most of the men who would have been qualified to provide a national movement with wise or moderate leadership. The fervour of its crusade was marred by the crude aggressiveness of some of its propaganda—but this in itself made it a force to be reckoned with.

II. THE BIRTH OF THE BOND

The Genootskap van Regte Afrikaners paid next to no attention to the question of political organization during the first three years of its existence, but its nature was such that it could, without incongruity, step into the political arena at any time. As soon as the supporters of either *volkstaal*[1] began to show that they were really serious, the language question was bound to become a political issue, and the connexion between language and politics in the outlook of the *Genootskappers* was emphasized by members of the society both at the time and afterwards.* It was in fact during the course of a discussion in the press on the language question that S. J. du Toit first developed his political programme.

During June 1879, all three leading Dutch papers focused attention on the need for the extension of Dutch language rights, and all recognized that the time was ripe for the institution of an organized campaign for this purpose.* The *Zuid Afrikaan* looked for a parliamentary leader who would give his life to the cause, backed by 'an alive organization spread through the land'. The *Patriot* considered that the editor of the *Zuid Afrikaan*, who had himself recently entered Parliament as member for Stellenbosch, measured up to the qualifications which that paper looked for, and it saw in the attitude of its contemporaries an example of rare unanimity in the Dutch-Afrikaans press, a sign of a general awakening of national feeling which ought to be seized upon. On the 20th, therefore, S. J. du Toit launched a proposal for the formation of:

AN AFRIKANER BOND, in which any Afrikaner can feel at home and work together for the good of a United South Africa;

AN AFRIKANER BOND, in which no nationality divides us from each other, but in which everyone who recognizes Africa as his Fatherland can live together and work as brothers of a single house, be they of English, Dutch, French or German origin, with the exclusion only of those who talk of England as their 'home' or of Holland and Germany as their 'Fatherland', and only want to fill their pockets with African wealth in order to go and spend it in Europe;

AN AFRIKANER BOND, which therefore furthers the true interests of our land and of all parties, and prevents the sacrifice of Africa's interests to England, or those of the Farmer to the Merchant;

[1] i.e. Hollands and Afrikaans. This and *landstaal* were the smokescreen terms usually employed to mask disagreement on the language issue.

AN AFRIKANER BOND, which keeps its eye on politics, to keep traitors out of the council chamber, and see that the true friends of the Fatherland take their places there;

AN AFRIKANER BOND, which sees to the development of the *whole* population, and does not spend millions of pounds on the education of one section of the population, while another and larger part is totally neglected; and which must therefore naturally ensure that in education the language of all sections of the population must have equal recognition in School and Office, Law-court and Council chamber;

AN AFRIKANER BOND, which develops Trade and Industry for the benefit of the land and not to fill the pockets of speculators; which above all does not permit our money market to be dominated by English banks; which will develop factories as soon as opportunity comes;

AN AFRIKANER BOND, which includes Free State and Transvaal; with separate branches over all South Africa to look after particular interests, and a Bond Council or Central *Bestuur* to safeguard general interests;

We need such a Bond; each day the sense of need for such a Bond grows; such a Bond will be applauded by thousands and tens of thousands, and the future of Africa cannot do without it.

Hofmeyr paid tribute to the idealism of these proposals, but was not attracted by them. He had been able to reach an understanding with Du Toit on the language question after a certain amount of give and take on both sides; but these new proposals made only incidental mention of language, and drew into the discussion a wide range of potentially explosive issues which he did not really care to see raised. His published reply dealt mainly with points of detail. He asked how it would be possible to cast a wide enough net to contain both farming and mercantile interests. There were patriotic Afrikaners, he wrote, who thought that the money market ought to be free, and who were therefore unwilling to obstruct the activities of English companies. Difficulties could arise within an organization which embraced both the Colony and the Republics, especially on tariff questions. There was consequently a real danger that a clash of interests would drive many true Afrikaners out of such a Bond, focus attention on their disagreements rather than their group cohesion, and thus weaken the position of their parliamentary party when issues affecting language came before the House.*

Du Toit was not convinced by Hofmeyr's arguments, which he rebutted seriatim on the 27th. On 4 July he published a draft constitution for his Afrikaner Bond,* which reaffirmed the main points made in the editorial of 20 June, and which he would use as the basis for a further series of articles at the end of the year.

The surprising feature of Du Toit's proposals, for all Hofmeyr's unwillingness to accept them, was their moderation. This is very apparent if they are compared with the tone of *De Christelijke School* and the *Geskiedenis van Ons Land*, written three and two years earlier, or the *Programme of Principles* and the commentaries upon it which Du Toit wrote between two and four years afterwards as a statement of political faith for the Afrikaner Bond.[1] These other documents were the outpourings of a convinced Afrikaner nationalist, unafraid to speak his mind however unpalatable his words might be to Afrikaners who did not belong to his own school of thought. But the proposals of June and July 1879, for all their implied criticism of the English immigrant, were loaded with liberal platitudes. They contained no colour bar, no discrimination against Anglo-Saxons as such, and no Christian National Education. These omissions suggest that on this occasion Du Toit had a different purpose. The Afrikaner cause, as he saw it, was being cared for by several separate groups of devotees: his own Genootskap, Hofmeyr's Boeren Vereeniging, the promoters of the *Zuid Afrikaansche Tijdschrift*, the Transvaal *Volks Comité* around whom the resistance to British rule was growing, and (as he made a special point of noting in October 1879) the Albert Boeren Vereeniging. Co-ordination between their activities was poor; none was organized on a sufficiently comprehensive basis to absorb the others in itself; yet unity was essential if the Afrikaner cause was to triumph. A formula for unity was what he hoped to supply. Considered in this light, his proposals of June and July 1879 make good sense, and they seem to have been directed mainly at Hofmeyr. Though he had been a keen supporter of the Boeren Beschermings Vereeniging since its foundation, and backed it whole-heartedly in the elections of 1878–9, Du Toit did not consider that it provided a rich enough fare to sustain a real national movement. Yet its success in the elections[2] made it the

[1] On the first two works, see above, pp. 31–3, and on the Programme of Principles, see below, pp. 51–3.

[2] See below, p. 72.

natural spearhead for a political offensive, while Hofmeyr's status among the Afrikaner people by virtue of that success and of his editorial activities could not be left out of account.

Hofmeyr turned down Du Toit's proposals and chose not to refer to them again, thus defeating the latter's immediate object. Du Toit, however, made a second attempt in November and December, when he wrote a series of editorials attempting to rouse the feelings of Afrikaners against political carpet-baggers, urging them to register as voters, and telling them to look for suitable parliamentary candidates—not necessarily good speakers, but faithful mouthpieces (*'manne wat mar reg stem'*). He told his readers in simple terms how branches of the Bond could be formed:

'Any locality or ward can make a start. Where two or three think the cause good they can call a little meeting, read out the Rules. Make a resolution in which they approve it. Choose a local Committee to make their own rules and begin to work. And let this then work further in the district. Tell the *Patriot* about it, and others then will surely follow.'*

Nothing could have been easier, yet nothing happened for a good six months.

There is good reason for thinking that Du Toit's lack of success in his efforts to form an Afrikaner Bond in the period preceding the Transvaal war of independence can be largely attributed to his unpopularity in ecclesiastical circles. His austere Neo-Calvinism, based on the doctrines of Dr. Abraham Kuyper in the Netherlands,*[1] together with his support for Afrikaans as the language of worship and his periodic criticism in the *Patriot* of the teachings of individual clergy, drew upon him the wrath of moderate Calvinists in the Cape Church who considered their orthodoxy to have been vindicated by their successful stand against modernist trends. Matters came to a head in October 1880, shortly after the *Patriot* had incited the Transvalers to open rebellion against British rule, when the Cape synod decided 'to investigate, whether and to what extent they shall

---

[1] Neo-Calvinism, the form of theology associated with Kuyper and Groen van Prinsterer, stressed the literal acceptance of the Heidelberg Catechism and the canons of the Synod of Dort, demanding *inter alia* a more resolute preaching of predestination, and proclaiming as a rule of church government the autonomy of the individual congregation (*kerkgenootschap*) against the over-riding authority of the central synod.

pronounce judgement over the spirit and the trend, in religion as well as in politics, of the weekly named *Die Afrikaanse ,Patriot'*. The discussion was allowed to continue for long enough to leave no doubt that hostility towards the *Patriot* was shared by many of those present.*

But if Du Toit's poor standing in the Cape Church adversely affected the success of his political activities, the converse was also true: namely, that wherever he found support for his theological views, he was likely to find supporters for the idea of an Afrikaner Bond. There was an obvious connexion in his mind between the idea of decentralized church government and the principle of extreme decentralization on which he desired to base his Bond. His concept of the autonomy of the local community, whether in a political or an ecclesiastical sense, had its reverse side in his criticism of the top-heavy organization of the Boeren Beschermings Vereeniging, and his resistance to the authority of the Colonial synod.

Two of the three branches of the Afrikaner Bond formed during 1880 appear to have arisen out of the ashes of a local ecclesiastical dispute. The first was formed at Hopetown, where a fierce dispute broke out in the local congregation after a spectacularly successful temperance mission, conducted by Ettie Schreiner shortly before the middle of the year. The minister became a convert, and nine of the church council members resigned in protest. Abstinence from liquor (*afschaffing*) was one of the 'methodist' tendencies which Du Toit wished to see eradicated from the Dutch Reformed social teachings. Within a week or so, on 16 June, a branch of the Afrikaner Bond was set up at Hopetown, and at least two of the men who helped to establish it, P. J. du Toit and B. J. Badenhorst, were interested enough in the ecclesiastical dispute to write letters to the *Patriot* about it.* During the debate on the *Patriot* at the synod in October, one of the delegates affirmed that 'on a few evenings he had met some of the church council members of Hopetown, who were strong supporters of the *Patriot*'.* At Petrusville, six months later, a comparable situation arose. Men of undoubtedly fundamentalist convictions, who seem to have had only vague ideas of the political significance of what they were doing, met on 9 December and 5 January to form a branch of the Bond.* What seems to have given urgency to their deliberations was the fact that the Colesberg Ring of the Church had denied the Petrusvillers the right to become a

separate congregation, and though the latter, according to
Oberholster, put behind them all thought of secession, they did
write to Oom Lokomotief asking him 'if he can recommend a *Patriot*
clergyman (*predikantjie*) for them'.* Within a year the people of
Petrusville had obtained their ecclesiastical independence, and four
of the six office-bearers in their new church were almost certainly
men who had taken an active part in the establishment of the Bond
branch.*

The Petrusville branch of the Bond was only the third to be
established, and it must have seemed to S. J. du Toit at the end of
1880 that his efforts had been largely in vain. His plans for the
propagation of Afrikaans had been eclipsed by the movement in
favour of Dutch. The ideas which he had expressed in the field of
theology and religious education had aroused the opposition of the
moderates and done much to undermine his influence. His first
attempt to launch a political movement had aroused hardly any
response at all. But his harvest was brought very much nearer by the
success of the Transvaal revolt at the beginning of 1881.

III. A RHAPSODY IN BLUE

On 1 April 1881 the editors of the *Patriot* celebrated the conclusion
of the Transvaal armistice by printing their newspaper in blue ink.
They had cause to rejoice, for it was their attitude to the British
annexation of the Transvaal, more than any other single factor,
which earned them the support of the Colonial Dutch. On 2 February
1877, eleven days after Shepstone's arrival in Pretoria, the *Patriot*
had crisply warned the Transvalers to look to their independence,
and advised them to choose Paul Kruger rather than T. F. Burgers
at the forthcoming presidential election. All through the period of
the British occupation, the editors kept their fingers on the pulse of
the Transvaal burghers, advising, criticizing, restraining, and finally
helping to unleash their energies, in a manner which gave no doubt
of their fellow-feeling and with a buoyancy resting on the conviction
that sooner or later the republicans would regain their independence.
At a time when the Transvaal papers, including the *Volksstem*, gave
the opponents of the annexation little lead, the republican leaders
often looked to the *Patriot* for guidance.* The Du Toit brothers built
their hopes round Kruger, though they momentarily lost faith in him
when he returned empty-handed from London in 1878. Why had the
deputation produced no report of their visit when they addressed a

meeting at Mooi River on their return?—they could still write one
'for the historical record'. Had the delegates received money from
Carnarvon—then let Kruger say so openly and have it publicly sent
back.* Passive resistance was the *Patriot's* counsel for the time being,
as it was that of the *Zuid Afrikaan*, and so it remained until the
second half of 1880. In April and May that year the Transvaal
leaders—Kruger, Jorissen and Joubert—visited the Western Province
to build up opposition to the Sprigg policy of confederation, and
they received a warm welcome in Paarl. The *Patriot* then intensified
its campaign, and as soon as it became clear that Gladstone was not
prepared to fulfil the hopes aroused in the Transvalers by his
Midlothian speeches, it parted company with the other Dutch papers
and issued a call to real though unspecified active resistance:

'Up to now we have always said *passive* resistance. But now no
longer. Passive resistance is now futile resistance [*Lydelik verset word
nou ydelik verset*]. From the latest handling of Transvaal affairs in
the imperial parliament it is clear to see that there is no chance or
hope of getting independence, unless something happens to cause a
change in the political situation in the Transvaal and South Africa.
But to sit still any more and wait for it is disadvantageous only for the
Boers, since they cannot work with heart and soul for the betterment
of agriculture and the progress of the land; while the English gain
all the more influence through the arrival of more Settlers and a
section of the Afrikaners is indifferent.'

The *Patriot* therefore rejected the advice proffered by the *Zuid
Afrikaan* and the *Volksblad* to send another deputation to London
to seek a qualified independence, and continued:

'With weapons let them demand their land back. We have indeed
always discouraged war, cannot, may not and will not now encourage
it; because we foresee that the Transvaal will become unoccupiable,
even if the evil day is again postponed with a deputation.

'Now this is just a summing up to make everyone reflect. Later we
hope to return to the matter. In the meantime let us wait on the Lord.
His hand can yet provide a solution before the Meeting of burghers
called for 8 January, which we pray, hope and wish for. Only this we
say now: Things cannot remain longer as they are. It must now come
to a head. *Lydelik verset word nou ydelik verset*.'*

No wonder that the Colonial Secretary's office in Cape Town
filed the *Patriot* from October 1880 onwards!

The *Patriot* did not organize the outbreak of the Transvaal war of independence. That erupted in its own way, at a moment determined by events in the Transvaal, though the Boer leaders were certainly encouraged by editorials from Paarl. But whereas the other Dutch papers in the Colony and the Transvaal had been restrained by a sense of propriety from advocating extreme courses, the *Patriot* had not. It could point to its record during the whole period of the British occupation, from before the annexation to the moment when the British forces were defeated by Boer arms, and claim in retrospect to have been unerringly right. The blue issue of 1 April really celebrated a double victory, and gave the *Patriot* a standing in the Republics and the Colony alike, which would hold much significance for the political developments within Afrikanerdom during the next few years.

IV. THE SPREAD OF A POPULAR MOVEMENT

Before the war of independence, the progress of the Afrikaner Bond had been negligible. Afterwards it was rapid, not only in the Cape Colony but also in the Orange Free State and the Transvaal.[1]

Let us first consider the developments in the Colony. By the end of 1881, Bond branches stretched from the Orange River southwards, mainly to the east of a broad arc drawn through Hopetown, Aberdeen and Albany. The spread must be attributed largely to the enthusiasm of local branches, which carried their propaganda into the surrounding districts and began at an early stage to build up district organizations. The outstanding example of this was in the Colesberg electoral division, from which there survive reports of combined meetings of delegates from widely scattered centres. Thus on 3 August a meeting was held at Philipstown, attended by delegates from Bond branches in the wards of Onder Zeekoe Rivier, Petrusville and Rietfontein (Hanover) as well as the local branch, and a decision was taken to set up a district *bestuur*.[2] Hopetown and Britstown were drawn into the orbit of this group, but its influence was unable to penetrate far to the south owing to opposition or

[1] See map 1.

[2] I retain the Dutch term *bestuur* wherever it is used to describe the organization of the Afrikaner Bond, owing to the absence of a precise English equivalent. 'Executive', 'directorate', 'board', 'committee', and even 'congress' could be understood by this word. There was no provision for district *besturen* in S. J. du Toit's draft constitution. The phrase emanated from the Orange Free State, to which Bond branches tended to look for their organizational pattern.

indifference to the Bond in the districts of Richmond, Middelburg, Murraysburg, Maraisburg and Cradock, in the last four of which *boeren vereenigingen* were established.

The spread of the Bond into regions where the eastern *vereenigingen* already existed engendered some political friction, as already noted in the case of Murraysburg and Colesberg.[1] But the strength of the Bond's appeal is shown by the fact that some of the *vereenigingen* went over to it, notably those of Albert, Steynsburg and Aliwal North. The decision of the Albert Vereeniging proved in the long run to be the most consequential. There is no sign in the reports of D. P. van den Heever's visit to the Western Province in January 1881 that he went to explore the possibility of affiliation with the Bond. But at the meeting held in Burghersdorp on 12 March, at which he reported on his visit, a resolution was taken to unite the Vereeniging with the '*Afrikaanschen Bond*', and to draw up a new constitution accordingly.* This decision did not however involve any weakening of the Albert Vereeniging's link with Hofmeyr's movement.

Bond branches were also set up in the regions of English settlement farther south, where the farmers' associations were strong. There is some evidence that the English farmers viewed this infiltration with distaste, and showed little desire to co-operate with a movement for cultural emancipation which was external to themselves. Many of them, according to the *East London Dispatch*, found some views expressed at Bond meetings 'so radically opposed to enlightened principles that they can have nothing to do with them'.* The Cathcart Farmers' Association contemplated amalgamation with the local Bond branch, but decided against it. In the Queenstown district there was undoubted friction, though the situation was mellowed by a certain amount of give and take.*

Greater tension accompanied the developments in the Bedford district, where the local situation has a peculiar interest because of the destructive influence of the Bedford Bondsmen, during the subsequent movement for amalgamation between the Bond and the *vereenigingen*. Bedford was an 1820 Settler district. Its Dutch-speaking community was small and did not yet possess its own church. It succeeded however in setting up Bond branches in two of the wards in July and August 1881, and it was only when it tried to form one in a third that opponents attended in sufficient numbers to defeat its purpose and form a farmers' association instead.* The

[1] See above, p. 25.

4

Bondsmen took umbrage.[1] When they found that none of the three Bedford weeklies took kindly to their cause,* they started a fourth, the *Opregte Afrikaner*, which was edited by the secretary of the Bedford branch, N. P. van der Meulen, a very convinced Afrikaner nationalist of the *Patriot* school. In the more harmonious political climate of 1882, when attempts to fuse Bond and *vereenigingen* made considerable progress, the Bedford Farmers' Association adopted a more tolerant attitude towards the Bond; but the Bondsmen remained intolerant, and were by no means appeased after the wholesale defeat of Bond by Association candidates in the local divisional council elections at the end of the year.*

Most of the opposition to the formation of Bond branches occurred, however, in the western half of the Colony, the region which Hofmeyr rather tended to look upon as his own political preserve. *Patriot* and *Zuid Afrikaan*, which had differed over Transvaal policy since October 1880, continued to disagree over the terms of the proposed settlement, and Du Toit, confident that he possessed the psychological initiative, determined to outbid Hofmeyr in a competition for Afrikaner support everywhere. On 18 March he threw down the gauntlet with an editorial which castigated the Boeren Beschermings Vereeniging. Its name, he said, was too long; Afrikaners could not pronounce it, let alone spell it. It had no all-embracing object. As a farmers' body its membership was too limited, and it took no account of the need to awaken national feeling. Its organization was top-heavy, and it lacked drive (*werkkrag*) because the few leaders on whom the work devolved already had their hands full with other matters. These criticisms were exaggerated, but there was enough truth in them to hurt, once it became clear that Du Toit was trying to set up Bond branches in the west.

It is unlikely that any sort of agreement existed between Hofmeyr and Du Toit, under which the former concentrated on the west and the latter on the east, and friction occurred between the Bond and the Vereeniging as soon as Du Toit's movement began to gain momentum. The first head-on collision occurred at Oudtshoorn in July 1881. A by-election had taken place in the early part of the year, resulting in the victory of Herman van der Spuy, who had been adopted by the Vereeniging as its candidate and had also received

---

[1] A correspondent in the *Patriot*, 16 Sept. 1881, was angered by the English opposition, but found solace in aloofness: 'Oom, . . . ek is bly dat ek nie rooinekagtig is nie.'

the support of the *Patriot*.* Neither the Vereeniging nor the Bond had a branch in the Oudtshoorn district at the time, but the stimulus of the election campaign prompted the sponsors of both bodies to take action. The Vereeniging acted first, and gave timely notice of a public meeting to be held on 6 August. The Bond's supporters then tried to present their rivals with a *fait accompli* by convening a meeting at Hazenjagt, outside the town, before the end of July. They failed, however, in their plan to turn the August meeting to their own purposes. It was well attended, with Van der Spuy and Jan Hofmeyr both present (the latter on a branch-forming tour through the southern districts following the end of the parliamentary session), and a decision to establish a local *boeren vereeniging* was carried without resistance. The Bondsmen met again at Hazenjagt on the 12th and established their branch; but it apparently failed to take root, for it seems that C. Behr, the man chosen as their local chairman, was a member of the local *boeren vereeniging* at that body's next meeting on 10 September.* But if the Bond failed at Oudtshoorn, it had more success elsewhere. On 2 August, Hofmeyr had visited Prince Albert and restored the local *vereeniging* to life. On the 27th, a meeting was held there to establish a branch of the Bond.* On 10 September, a branch of the Bond was set up in Du Toit's home district of Daljosaphat, north of Paarl.*

Du Toit, meanwhile, continued to goad the Boeren Beschermings Vereeniging in his editorials, urging on 4 November that it had failed to take root among the people, and was kept going by the touring activities of influential orators who wound the engine up, only for it to run down again after their departure; all this in contrast with the Afrikaner Bond, which 'grows up . . . slowly but healthily, under misunderstanding and opposition, without recourse to extraordinary methods, out from the heart of a willing people'. Hofmeyr was very conscious of the Vereeniging's weaknesses, and he tried hard to immunize it against the scurrilous attacks to which it was being subjected. Thus at the annual meeting on 21 September 1881 he proposed an amendment to its constitution which would bring the 'national' as well as the material interests of the Boer within the Vereeniging's official cognizance.[1]* This was appropriate

---

[1] Hofmeyr proposed to add the italicized words to the objects clause, as follows: 'The object of this Association is *while maintaining every respect for established authority*, to watch over the *national as well as* over the *material, the indirect as well as the direct* interests of our Farming population [*Boerenbevolking*] and to protect them' [Dutch original].

enough to the changing outlook of the Vereeniging—which was beginning to lose its earlier unanimity over the excise*—for several of its branches had already begun to press for the permissive use of Dutch in public life, in support of a campaign which Hofmeyr had begun to carry into the parliamentary arena.[1] But the meeting failed to adopt Hofmeyr's proposal. Early in 1882 he tried again, repeating his proposal in editorials on 18 and 25 February, and adding two further suggestions for making the constitution of the Vereeniging more democratic: the removal of the rule that the *hoofdbestuur* must be situated in Cape Town, and a new procedure for the election of that body by a special meeting of accredited delegates from the branches, on a basis of one vote for every £5 contributed by the branch to central funds during the preceding year. But when a special meeting of the Vereeniging was called on 10 March to enable members to debate current issues before the opening of Parliament, Hofmeyr's proposals were not even discussed.* The Bond had actually established few branches in the western Cape, and it had antagonized the western Boeren Beschermings Vereeni- ging; but it had drawn Hofmeyr to a position closer to its own than the Vereeniging as a whole was prepared to accept.

The Bond began to spread into the Orange Free State from the moment that Carl Borckenhagen, the German editor of the Bloemfontein *Express*, began to take an interest in it; but Borcken- hagen's interest awoke slowly, and at first the exclusive Afrikaner spirit which animated the men of Paarl seems to have eluded him. When the *Patriot* issued its appeal for action in the Transvaal in October 1880, he ignored it, and it was not until January 1881 that he committed himself to supporting an 'African' political movement, with the object of building up opposition to the 'organised anti- African party' responsible for the troubles in the Transvaal and Basutoland.* He appealed to South Africans to organize themselves 'throughout the whole country' to achieve control of their own affairs by constitutional means: 'Disregardful of nationality and creed, independent of position and place, free from private motives, let all those who have the future of South Africa at heart unite.' There was no racialism in this sincere but vague appeal.

Borckenhagen's main contribution to the growth of the Bond was to set out an extremely tidy proposal for a constitution, which appeared without indication of its authorship in the issue of 7 April.*

[1] See below, pp. 76, 79.

This *Express* constitution set out the aims of the Bond in the broadest terms, without any reference to the fact that the Afrikaner had special interests to protect. Its chief importance lay in its provision of an integrated pattern of committees, from that of the ward at the base of the pyramid, rising through those of the district and the province to a central *bestuur* at the apex. Borckenhagen followed Du Toit in assuming the existence of a South African nationality which transcended the existing political barriers, and planned accordingly. His 'provinces' coincided with the existing colonies and republics. His Central *Bestuur* was a small committee, representative of each province, required to meet in each territorial capital in rotation, and empowered to direct the main lines of policy for the Bond as a whole. Only in December 1882, when the *Express* constitution came up for review at a meeting in Bloemfontein, were the powers of this supra-territorial committee significantly whittled down.

Though some Bond activity had taken place in the Free State before the publication of the *Express* constitution, the events which really set the movement going took place at Bloemfontein in May. A branch was formed in the capital on the 11th, and five days later a meeting took place at Grey College to inaugurate the movement in the Free State as a whole.* Those involved in the proceedings included the acting moderator of the N.G. Kerk in the Republic, and the entire Free State Bench. Chief Justice F. W. Reitz was elected chairman of the Bloemfontein branch and presided over the meeting at Grey College. He was not apparently concerned about the propriety of his actions, which he would soon crown in more spectacular ways.

Reitz's bravado and Borckenhagen's constitution gave the Free State Bond a flying start, but at the price of arousing the antagonism of President Brand. While on circuit at the end of May, Reitz tried unsuccessfully to establish a branch of the Bond at Smithfield. The opposition was considerable, but by the end of June a branch was in existence,* and it gave the President an address of welcome when he visited the town on 19 October. The tone of the address was respectful enough, but it drew from Brand a stinging rebuke. He claimed, like them, to be a patriotic Free Stater, so that Bond membership was no necessary badge of patriotism. On the contrary, its organization seemed to presage the establishment of a state within the state, and to threaten the authority of the established government.* Borckenhagen's editorial reply was specious, but seems to have satisfied public opinion.*[1] The Smithfield Bondsmen were unrepentant and the *Patriot* was scornful, while even Oom Daantje van den Heever tried after an interval of a few months to provoke the Free State President into repeating his charge.*

The fact that Brand's remarks came to be linked in the public mind with a similar utterance by John X. Merriman to the Bondsmen of Graaff-Reinet a few days later,[2] did much to undermine their effect, and the Free State Bond probably spread faster because he had made them. By the end of September 1882 there were one or more branches in the magisterial districts of Bloemfontein, Smithfield, Philippolis, Fauresmith, Jacobsdal, Winburg, Kroonstad, Heilbron, Harrismith and Ladybrand—a total of twenty ward *besturen* out of a possible fifty-one.* The Free State provincial *bestuur* had been constituted by the end of 1882, a good six months before the Bond in the Cape Colony was able to bring such a body into existence, and its president, the indomitable Reitz, actually played a major role in the establishment of the Cape *bestuur*.* But events would show that the Free State Bond could not maintain the influence which it had acquired with such remarkable ease, and the conclusion is inescapable that one of the reasons for this was the sustained opposition of President Brand.*

The Transvaal lagged slightly behind the Orange Free State in the establishment of Bond branches, though General Piet Joubert publicly supported the Bond cause in a meeting at Heidelberg as early as April 1881.* A gathering at Potchefstroom on 30 July led to the establishment of a branch at Rustenburg in August.* The Bond's supporters then decided to take advantage of the Volksraad session to call a meeting in Pretoria on 17 October, the initiative coming from Joubert and the editor of the *Volksstem*, J. F. Celliers. The initial response was good, and members undertook to work for the establishment of branches in their constituencies, though when the meeting was resumed on the 22nd the attendance was noticeably poorer—on account of bad publicity, said Joubert from the chair. He offered them an account of Bond objectives as vague as Borcken-

---

[1] Borckenhagen wrote: 'The Afrikaner Bond must either be looked upon . . . as a national or a party move[ment]. In the case of the former, it seems anomalous that any statesman or leading politician should adopt a hostile position towards it; in case of the latter it is indeed without precedence [*sic*] that the Head of a State should violate "The Majesty of his exalted position" to join in or oppose a party movement.'

[2] See below, pp. 76–7.

hagen's and calculated perhaps to reassure the strangers in the gate;*¹ but little was done to set the movement on its feet until the middle of 1882.

The call for the setting up of a provincial *bestuur* was made by 'old Jacob Middel', secretary of the Komatie branch, and it was through his initiative that members came together in Pretoria on 16 May 1882 to discuss a draft constitution, which Middel and S. J. du Toit had in the meantime drawn up. It was probably the best-attended meeting that the Transvaal Bondsmen ever had, with over a hundred people present and nine centres represented. But although the constitution was approved, no provincial *bestuur* was formed— perhaps, as Coetzee suggests, because many of those who attended did not represent Bond branches.*² The heads of the Transvaal state seem at first to have smiled on the venture, while the appointment of S. J. du Toit as Superintendent-General of Education at the start of 1882 endowed the Bond with vigorous leadership in the Transvaal. But internal troubles within the state, notably tribal unrest, delayed the first meeting of the provincial *bestuur* until 12 January 1884, when it was attended by delegates from only Lydenburg, Standerton, Pretoria, Middelburg and Potchefstroom.* Like its Free State counterpart, the Transvaal Bond failed to maintain the impetus with which it had started, and before long its fortunes would recede with those of its leaders, Joubert and Du Toit. Kruger, like Brand, would come to find it an embarrassment, and his opposition would prove as hard to overcome.

V. IGNUS FATUUS

A year after the Transvaal had liberated itself from British rule, the Du Toit brothers could look with some satisfaction at the way in which their political movement had progressed. In proportion as the Bond grew, so they were encouraged to broaden their appeal by offering the Afrikaner a wider range of objectives, some of which

---

¹ Joubert said: 'Hij die de belangen van Zuid-Afrika ter harte neemt, afgezien van welke nationaliteit hij is, is welkom bij ons, en is lidmaat van den Afrikaner Bond' ['He who takes the interests of South Africa to heart, whatever his nationality, is welcome among us and a member of the Afrikaner Bond'].

² The centres represented were Zoutpansberg, Rustenburg, Heidelberg, Pretoria, Wakkerstroom, Standerton, Makwassie, Potchefstroom, Lydenburg and Utrecht.

had been foreshadowed in the aims of the Genootskap van Regte Afrikaners but for tactical reasons had not been emphasized between 1879 and 1881. Our consideration of the early growth of the Bond may conveniently be drawn to a close with an account of the more important of these projects: the attempt to encourage the Boer to become economically independent by establishing his own trading co-operatives and banks, and the attempt to saddle the Bond with a Neo-Calvinist programme of principles.

Opposition to the Imperial banks was by no means new in South Africa in the eighties. They had long been looked upon by some as leviathans with large appetites and a special taste for small banks and Colonial money. It was not difficult to present the large dividends paid by the Standard Bank as evidence that good money was being drawn out of the Colony.* The *Patriot* did so in March and April 1882, and drew the conclusion that a national bank should be formed. This bank, it urged, should be formed from the amalgamation of a large number of local banks set up through local initiative, rather like Bond branches, and should eventually replace the Standard Bank as the government bank of the Colony, just as the National Bank of the Orange Free State had achieved that position with the aid of the diamond fields compensation money and the legislative eviction of its rivals. These bold suggestions were accompanied by a direct attack on the Standard Bank, both as an agent of imperialism, and on the ground that its operation under conditions of limited liability constituted a threat to the security of Colonial depositors.* The detailed proposals contained in the *Patriot's* scheme were not very practicable in 1882, when money was tight, and the *Zuid Afrikaan* criticized them roundly in October; but at the same time it admitted that if there was any issue over which Afrikanerdom was united, it was the desirability of founding a national bank.*

Du Toit had found a talking point around which the indignation of hard-pressed farmers could be rallied. This was perhaps, from his point of view, all that really mattered. But, having struck the right chord, he encouraged the volume of protest to develop by urging the establishment of *boerewinkels* (farmers' co-operative stores) in every dorp. These could break the stranglehold of an alien commercial class—foreign exploiters who squeezed the Boer and corrupted him at the same time:

'And therefore we say outright: it is now the duty of every true Afrikaner not to spend a copper at an Englishman's if he can avoid it. It is our bounden duty to help no Englishman and no supporters of Englishmen. Buy nothing at an Englishman's, or at an English-minded Afrikaner's; or even from anyone who advertises in an English paper.'*

Rather let the Boers form their own little trading companies and thus secure their economic independence, he urged. Even Hofmeyr looked sympathetically on this suggestion, provided the accent lay on the achievement of independence and not on the boycott.*

The *Patriot's* agitation produced some results, but no more than the economic realities of the day might have been expected to allow. The prospectus for an abortive Hopetown Bank, with a nominal capital of £30,000, half of which was to be called up in stages, appeared in the paper on 1 September 1882. The Stellenbosch District Bank, formed in December 1882 with a share capital of £15,000, of which one-third was paid up, was more successful though it would have to close down temporarily in 1889. The idea does not seem to have been taken up anywhere else in the Colony. There is evidence of attempts to establish *boerewinkels* at a few places.[1] But it proved practically impossible, even if they acquired sufficient working capital, to make them independent of the merchant impor-ters at the coast. Even in the Transvaal, where the *boerewinkels* enjoyed considerable support from the Zuid Afrikaansche Handels-Maatschappij of Amsterdam, such bodies fought a losing battle against real trading difficulties.*

S. J. du Toit's last act, when he left the Colony to take up his appointment in the Transvaal in February 1882, was to make available for Bondsmen a draft Programme of Principles (*Program van Beginsels*) in the hope that they would adopt it.* He described it as 'the Programme of the anti-revolutionary or Christian historical party in the Netherlands . . . changed according to our circumstances'. This was the party led by Dr. Abraham Kuyper, whose theological views Du Toit closely shared and to whom Du Toit acknowledged his debt on all major points of principle.* Du Toit's document of twenty articles and the commentary which he published on it, give a comprehensive picture of his political philosophy.* They disclose a theocratic view of the relations between Church and State, and a doctrine of divine sovereignty which left no room for a sovereign legislature or even a sovereign people and regarded existing political

[1] In the Albert district, at Petrusville, Middelburg, Sutherland, and perhaps elsewhere.

authorities as divinely ordained. But to acknowledge the divine origin of the *status quo* did not preclude for Du Toit the possibility or desirability of change. Departing from the monarchist Kuyper when it came to matters of local detail, he expressed a preference for a republican form of government on historical, cultural, theological and practical grounds, and looked forward to the establishment of a united South Africa under its own flag. This aim, he wrote, should be proclaimed boldly, and should be worked for in a constitutional manner, without resort to violence. A petition should be addressed to the Queen by her Colonial subjects, affirming their present loyalty but urging the confederation of the South African states and colonies, especially for the sake of a common native policy, and pointing out that the British flag was the sole obstacle in the way of such a step. The Queen was therefore to be asked to take her flag away—without entirely relinquishing responsibility for South Africa, for Du Toit desired the continued protection of the British fleet. The function of the Bond was to educate public opinion along these lines, and see that the right steps were taken at the right time.

Du Toit's *Program van Beginsels* revealed a narrower political philosophy than his draft constitution of July 1879 and contained important points of similarity to his earlier *Geskiedenis van ons Land*. At the same time it revealed marked differences from the political outlook of Jan Hofmeyr. In the first place, he used the term 'Afrikaner' in a restricted sense as applying pre-eminently to people of Dutch or Huguenot descent, a limitation which Hofmeyr annotated on his own copy of the draft Programme. In the second place, he showed a marked distaste for liberal institutions of the British type, which may in part have been a projection of his abhorrence of theological liberalism into the political sphere. We have already noted that the *Geskiedenis van ons Land* practically ignored the story of the growth of self-government in the Cape Colony, and that the *Patriot* manifested a singular lack of interest in the activities of the Colonial Parliament, which it treated as exotic and inconsequential at least until the end of 1877. If Du Toit thought it was important that Afrikaners should organize themselves for the purpose of fighting elections, this is to say no more than that he was prepared to play according to the rules of the political game as he found them, and he certainly did not commit himself to an acceptance of the principle of a sovereign legislature. On such questions he differed radically from Hofmeyr, who had ceased to blow hot or cold on theological issues, was himself the product of a liberal education, and held the British parliamentary system in great respect. Furthermore, whereas Hofmeyr limited his political movement to the Cape Colony, Du Toit took cognizance of Afrikanerdom beyond the Colonial frontiers. It was in keeping with the rest of his outlook that he should do so, for his plans did not stop short with the formation of a political movement. Political independence for the Afrikaner people was indeed part of his goal, but he was even more concerned that the Afrikaner *volk* should find itself in relation to his own idea of its culture, its religious past, and its linguistic present, as well as its political future.

But events would show that Du Toit had been lured away by a will-o'-the-wisp, for the mass of Colonial Afrikaners were either sceptical of his flights of fancy, or—as was the case with the *Program van Beginsels*—failed to comprehend them.

4

Amalgamation

I. THE GRAAFF-REINET CONGRESS

THE unfriendly rivalry between Hofmeyr and S. J. du Toit during most of 1881 did not provide an auspicious background for a movement towards closer union between their respective organizations, yet signs were not lacking that even in this year of conflict each would have welcomed amalgamation (*samesmelting*) on his own terms. Du Toit suggested a merger from time to time, though never in such a way as to indicate that he would sacrifice the more controversial elements in his own policy for the sake of such a result.* Hofmeyr, though he disagreed with the Bond leadership, was prepared to speak in defence of a Bond branch when he felt that it had been slighted by one of his Cabinet colleagues, John X. Merriman, in October.[1] But it is to the Albert Boeren Vereeniging that we have to look for the only attempt made in 1881 to bring the various Afrikaner organizations together.

The Albert Vereeniging had established an informal relationship with the western Vereeniging in January, and joined up with the Afrikaner Bond in April. On 14 May Van den Heever wrote to the *Patriot*, urging people to write to him about the holding of a congress of the various 'B.B. Vereenigingen' in the Colony and requesting that suggestions should reach him by 1 August.* He subsequently enlarged his appeal to include other interested bodies in the Cape, Free State, Transvaal and Natal, and this the *Patriot* supported to the full if time were given to establish the Bond in the Transvaal before the congress took place.* The implementation of Van den Heever's proposals did not, however, follow the lines which he had planned. On 16 July, representatives of several north-eastern *boeren vereeni-*

[1] On Merriman's Graaff-Reinet speech, see below, pp. 76–7.

gingen met at Ventersburg to welcome Jotham Joubert on his return from Parliament, and the opportunity was taken to discuss the idea of a congress.[1] The press reports do not agree on all particulars as to what happened; but according to the *Patriot* the meeting agreed to fix a venue for a gathering of representatives of the *vereenigingen* and the Afrikaner Bond, and to appoint a committee for this purpose.* Van den Heever, according to the correspondent of the *Zuid Afrikaan*, was empowered to nominate this committee and he selected names from the Bond and the *vereenigingen*;*[2] but there is no evidence that this well-scattered committee ever met.

At all events, over seven months elapsed between the Ventersburg meeting and the calling of a congress at Graaff-Reinet for 1 March 1882. They were months in which the Bond and the western Vereeniging hardly moved closer to one another, and whatever negotiations took place during this time have apparently gone unrecorded. All that may be said with certainty is that on 17 February 1882 an advertisement appeared in the *Patriot*, unsigned, but dated from Graaff-Reinet on the 8th, inviting delegates from Bond and Vereeniging to a congress which was intended to be a combined meeting of both.[3]

This congress was not, as Hofmeyr's biographer implies, the first step taken by Onze Jan to infiltrate into the Afrikaner Bond and guide its policy from within.* He was not present himself, nor was his newspaper represented, nor, with the exception of the Albert and Steynsburg delegates, whose organizations were already amalgamated with the Bond, was there any Vereeniging man present.*[4] Yet

---

[1] Delegates attended from Albert, Aliwal North, Colesberg, Maraisburg, Philipstown and Steynsburg. The Philipstown delegates were almost certainly Bondsmen.

[2] Van den Heever nominated Jan Hofmeyr, 'Lokomotief' du Toit, Daniel de Waal of Stellenbosch, M. J. Herholdt (chairman of the Murraysburg Bond), J. J. Janse van Rensburg (chairman of the Cradock Vereeniging), Gerrit Bekker of the Maraisburg Vereeniging, and himself.

[3] The notice ran: 'Hiermede wordt vriendelyk ieder dorp of distrikt waar de Afrikaner Bond of de Boerenbeschermingsvereeniging opgerigt is vriendelyk [sic] uitgenoodigd hun afgevaardigden te zenden naar Graaff-Reinet op den eersten dag van Maart 1882 op welke vergadering verschillende belangryke zaken tot welvaart van land en volk besproken zullen worden; derhalwe worden alle afgevaardigden dringend uitgenoodigd tegenwordig te zyn.'

[4] The districts represented were: Graaff-Reinet, Sneeuwberg, Camdeboo, Albert, Steynsburg, Bedford, Somerset East, Pearston, Aberdeen, Britstown, Murraysburg and Bethesda. They are all in the eastern and central Cape. There

although Hofmeyr had nothing to do with this congress, its outlook and its decisions conformed very closely to his views. It lavished compliments upon him, stood to carry a unanimous resolution of confidence in him as the 'leader of the Afrikaner party in the Cape Colony', urged him not to accept nomination for the Transvaal presidency (for which his name had been canvassed), and looked to him to place its resolutions before Parliament. The delegates talked rather vaguely about setting up a 'central *bestuur*', which in terms of the existing Bond constitutions was beyond their powers; but for the rest they aired matters which could have been discussed at a meeting of any *boeren vereeniging* without incongruity—among them the Dutch language, Basuto policy, the raising of the franchise, the masters and servants law, and education. The debates were severely practical, and the reluctance of the delegates to become involved in idealogical discussions can best be seen in their handling of S. J. du Toit's *Program van Beginsels*. They acknowledged receipt of this embarrassing document, gave shortage of time as their reason for not discussing it, and referred it to the branches. More significant for the continuity of Afrikaner political development, they resolved, on a motion from the chair by R. P. Botha of Graaff-Reinet, to convene a congress of Vereeniging men and Bondsmen at Cradock on 12 September. Jan Hofmeyr, D. F. du Toit, D. de Waal (probably Daniel, of Stellenbosch) and H. P. du Preez were to be sent special invitations, while arrangements were left in the hands of the committee appointed to consider forming a 'central *bestuur*'.[1]

The Graaff-Reinet proceedings pleased Hofmeyr, who had previously been dubious about fusion. He expressed the hope that the Bond would soon establish its own provincial *bestuur* which could then negotiate with the *vereenigingen*, and advised the eastern *vereenigingen* to set up a *hoofdbestuur* of their own for the same purpose.* But if the *Zuid Afrikaan* was in a conciliatory mood, the

are slight discrepancies as to the total number of delegates. The *Patriot* listed twenty-five. Hofmeyr's biographer gives eighteen. At all events it was not a large congress attributable perhaps to its having been convened at short notice.

[1] The projected congress was described as an 'Algemeene Vergadering van afgevaardigden' called 'om te trachten de Z.A.B.B. Vereeniging en den Afrikaner Bond te vereenigen'. The members of the continuation committee were: R. P. Botha, M. J. Herholdt, D. P. van den Heever, J. J. Bouwer of Bedford, Thomas Theron of Britstown, and J. J. Janse van Rensburg of Cradock. Van Rensburg was not a Bondsman.

Patriot, now in the hands of D. F. du Toit, began to fight shy. Its editor sensed that something had gone wrong at Graaff-Reinet, and he asked some unsettling questions: what had the congress meant by its talk of a central *bestuur*? why had the Free State and the Transvaal been excluded? why was it necessary to pass a motion of confidence in Hofmeyr? why had the congress not resolved in favour of the voluntary principle in schools? He hoped that the branches would see that these deficiencies were put right.*[1]

II. THE CRADOCK CONGRESS

It was therefore against a background of some uncertainty that the Cradock congress met on 12 September. In accordance with the resolution taken at Graaff-Reinet, invitations were extended to all branches of the Bond and the *boeren vereenigingen* to what was termed in the press announcement an '*Afrikaansch Nationaal Congres*'.[2] The Bond delegates outnumbered those of the eastern and western *boeren vereenigingen* together, so that the Bond malcontents who subsequently complained that they had been swamped by *vereeniging* men at Cradock had no substantial case.[3] They were in fact strong enough to carry any proposal they wished, provided they acted together. The *vereenigingen*, though their delegates were in a numerical minority, were strong in parliamen-

[1] The term 'voluntary principle', which had been applied originally to Saul Solomon's campaign for the disendowment of the churches, was taken over by the advocates of Christian National Education to signify the disendowment of public education, so that schools giving confessional instruction would be able to compete on equal terms with the public schools, which were not allowed to do so.

[2] The correctness of this procedure has been disputed by Coetzee on the ground that the Graaff-Reinet congress had intended a *Bond* congress to meet at Cradock. It would indeed have facilitated fusion between Bond and Vereeniging if the Bondsmen had first come together to form their own provincial *bestuur*, as the procedure subsequently adopted at Richmond in May 1883 showed clearly. But when it is borne in mind that the Graaff-Reinet congress had technically been a meeting of both organizations, and that it had instructed its continuation committee to summon an *algemeene vergadering* to Cradock (see above, p. 55 n. 3), it is clear that this committee would have exceeded its instructions had it limited attendance at Cradock to Bondsmen.

[3] An analysis of the delegates, allowing for inconsistencies in the published lists, has shown that there were between 9 and 13 representatives of the western Vereeniging present, and between 20 and 23 representatives of other *vereenigingen*, giving all *boeren vereenigingen* a total representation of between 29 and 36 delegates. Against these, there were between 60 and 67 Bondsmen.

tarians (who by virtue of their status were given seats of honour on the platform, and by virtue of their debating skill were denied the right to vote). But it is not true, as has sometimes been implied, that the *vereeniging* representatives went to Cradock to force amalgamation through. They had no mandate to do that. The annual meeting of the western Vereeniging, which had taken place at Stellenbosch a short while before, had only carried a guarded resolution on the subject—blessing co-operation between the two bodies but reserving judgement on the matter of fusion until its own branches and the Cradock congress had declared themselves. Of the branches, it seems that by that time only Worcester and Oudtshoorn had approved of fusion in principle.*

At least half a dozen newspapers sent their correspondents to cover the Cradock debates—an indication that contemporaries viewed the congress as a significant event.* The editor of the *Uitenhage Times* described how the opening of the congress was 'announced to the public at an early hour by a black boy bearing the usual "bell and board". Some time before that hour, however, ninety-six delegates . . . had taken their seats at long tables covered with green baize, each delegate being accommodated with a sheet of cream-laid foolscap and a black lead pencil ready sharpened.' The English-speaking journalists evidently expected worse than they got, and gave high praise to the orderliness of the meetings, the 'remarkable absence of what might be called "twaddle"', and above all the impartiality, patience and good humour of the chairman, J. J. Janse van Rensburg.

The conference was opened with a prayer, which was already becoming normal practice at Bond meetings. The agenda was very long, but the delegates dealt first with the controversial issues, of which the question of amalgamation was the most important. They discussed this in terms of two contradictory motions, both of which focused attention not on the desirability of fusion or otherwise, but on the name which the combined organization should bear. One, sent in by four branches of the Bond, insisted that there should be no amalgamation 'unless the Afrikaner Bond keep its name and constitution'. The other, contributed by the Murraysburg Boeren Vereeniging, referred to 'the desirability of the fusion of the two Associations (*Vereenigingen*) . . . under another name'. This concern about the name, as something of seemingly greater import than the substance of unification, seems to have represented the heart of the

1.   J. H. HOFMEYR ('ONZE JAN')
1883

II. LEADERS OF THE BOEREN VEREENIGINGEN

D. P. VAN DEN HEEVER
Co-founder of the Albert Boeren
Vereeniging

H. P. DU PREEZ
Co-founder of the Z.A. Boeren
Beschermings Vereeniging

JOTHAM JOUBERT
Co-founder of the Albert Boeren
Vereeniging

J. S. MARAIS
Co-founder of the Z.A. Boeren
Beschermings Vereeniging

problem to many present. The name 'Afrikaner Bond' had already acquired a pseudo-mystical significance for devoted readers of the *Patriot* and *De Tolk*, and it is difficult to read the reports of local Bond meetings, especially in the period between the Cradock and Richmond congresses, without receiving the impression that loyalty to the name 'Afrikaner Bond' was not only widespread, but inspired by sentiments of a semi-religious kind.* From the point of view of the non-Bondsmen, of course, the opposite was the case. Some feared that, by giving in over the name, the *boeren vereenigingen* might lose more than their identity. Others considered that to retain the name 'Afrikaner Bond' would be to stigmatize the new united body in the eyes of English-speaking people, and thus reduce the chance of building any sort of bridge between the two white groups.*

The Cradock congress did not remove this rock of offence; it circumvented it. Several speakers, Hofmeyr among them, suggested that as a temporary solution the two names should be strung together, until they grew tired of them and thought of something better.[1] Hofmeyr helped to set the tone of the debate in a well-conceived speech which, without treading on the toes of the Bondsmen, emphasized the need to build up a right relationship between the two white language groups. He could find nothing to object to in the constitution of the Bond. It had been accused of incitement to rebellion, he said, but that was far from the truth—on the contrary, the Bond made Afrikaners loyal because it made them satisfied. There was no question of the Bond's trying to drive the English out of the land: the national feeling of English- and Dutch-speaking people had to be developed and welded together. Their English friends, however, had to learn to respect the Afrikaner and above all his language. If the Bond caused ill feeling between Afrikaners and Englishmen, it would be a curse not a blessing; and there could be no question of abandoning the English flag for at least fifty or a hundred years, though they could not always remain attached to England's apron strings.* He received warm support from Oom Daantje van den Heever, whose speech glowed with cosmopolitan goodwill and showed from the applause which it received that the day was carried.* The final outcome of a long debate, which had taken much of the afternoon and evening of the 12th, was the decision of congress to appoint a commission to draft a constitution

---

[1] They never did, so 'Afrikaner Bond en Boeren Vereeniging' remained the official designation of the Cape body until its dissolution in 1911.

for a united Bond and Vereeniging, and a standing executive committee to convene a further congress as soon as the constitutional commission had done its work.* The commission was to consist of Hofmeyr, D. F. du Toit and J. M. Hoffman, a doctor from Paarl, while the members of the executive committee were D. P. van den Heever, Jeremias van Heerden* and T. P. Theron.

No sooner had the constitutional commission been appointed than Theron rose to move the abandonment of the other controversial item on the agenda. This was S. J. du Toit's *Program van Beginsels*. He urged that the constitutional commission was the proper body to look into this, and there is no suggestion in any of the reports that this proposal called forth audible opposition. But the *Patriot*'s unhappy correspondent later expressed his personal disappointment in somewhat bitter terms.[1]

III. HOFMEYR JOINS THE BOND

The reactions of Bond and Vereeniging branches to the Cradock proposals for amalgamation were generally very favourable; but one outcome of the congress was the early emergence of an opposition group, scattered geographically yet united in the main points of their argument, who exerted a great deal of pressure in the succeeding months. The lead came from D. F. du Toit in the *Patriot*. He criticized the Cradock constitutional proposals immediately after the congress, apprehending a marriage between the two organizations 'like that concluded between *Zuid Afrikaan* and *Volksvriend*, wherein the former indeed kept its name. but was in fact dissolved in the latter'.* By November, Oom Lokomotief was still more positive in his denunciation:

'To be brief, the Bond suffered total defeat at the Congress, and the Vereeniging obtained a great victory. Bondsmen present there yielded up everything. . . . We repeat that we do not see the necessity for amalgamation; expect no good from it, and have already suffered disadvantage from the resolution.'*

These doubts about the decisions taken at Cradock came forcefully from one who had expressed misgivings before the congress began, and whose absence from the congress excused him from any responsibility for them.

---

[1] 'Eers is dit uitgestel tot di aand sitting en toen is dit weer in di doofpot gedaan.'

The first serious friction occurred at Ceres. Hofmeyr went there on 29 September, according to his biographer, with the object of founding a branch of the Boeren Vereeniging; but 'immediately after his departure one finds other counsels prevailing and a Bond branch established instead'.* Two reports in the *Patriot*, however, make it clear that on this occasion Hofmeyr was defied to his face.* These indicate that after Hofmeyr had finished speaking, a local man rose and moved the formation of a Bond branch, and carried his proposal against Hofmeyr's counter-suggestion of a joint organization. Hofmeyr expressed his disappointment. A branch of the Bond was duly established, and at a meeting on 16 October it decided to oppose the plan for amalgamation accepted at Cradock.*

On 12 October, N. P. van der Meulen reported on the Cradock congress to a gathering of about sixty Bedford Bondsmen.* The editor of the *Opregte Afrikaner* told his audience—quite correctly—that he had previously attended the Graaff-Reinet meeting, and—quite incorrectly—that he had seen at that meeting 'just as many members of B.B. Vereenigingen as Bondsmen', though he had supposed it to be an exclusively Bond meeting. He had regretted at the time that no provincial *bestuur* had been set up at Graaff-Reinet, and been amazed when the suggestion had come up that the Bond should merge with the *boeren vereenigingen* and change its name. His audience no doubt appreciated the force of this remark in the light of their own local situation. However, Van der Meulen continued, he had relied on the congress at Cradock to put matters right, only to find at Cradock 'a far from friendly attitude towards the Bond' even among those who said they were its supporters—even indeed among some who had joined it as members. The appointment of a constitutional commission at Cradock had prevented him from taking the resolute stand he would have liked to have done. He therefore urged his audience to work together 'without any external (*vreemde*) influence' and make the Bond a vehicle of prosperity for land and *volk*, which was its proper destiny; and he made a proposal to the following effect: that a further congress of the Bond in the Colony should be held not later than 27 November, at either Hanover or Richmond, for the purpose of setting up a Bond provincial *bestuur*; and that this new *bestuur* should then send two delegates to the forthcoming festival at Paardekraal in the South African Republic, which was due to be held on 16 December, with the object of bringing into being a central *bestuur* for the whole Bond in South Africa.* Van der Meulen's proposal was greeted with applause, and he set about its implementation, assuming the role of convener of the proposed congress, and on 14 November announced in the press that it would meet at Richmond on the 28th.

It was about this time, apparently, that Hofmeyr determined, in the words of his biographer, 'to effect from within the Bond what it seemed impossible to accomplish from without'.* After taking a few moderate Englishmen into his confidence to safeguard himself against any possible misconception of his motives, he formed a Bond branch in Cape Town on 28 October. Among those who joined was F. J. Dormer, editor of the *Cape Argus*, and Victor Sampson has related how 'Dormer explained privately that their intention was to get hold of the organization and control it'.* Hofmeyr was elected chairman on 2 November, and the new branch immediately adopted the broad aims and objects set out in the Free State Bond constitution.* It was a clever move, and seems to have been made with the immediate object of enabling Hofmeyr to attend Van der Meulen's congress as a delegate, and thus put a stop to the 'wild work' of which Sampson said he disapproved.

Van der Meulen's plan got a mixed reception. Some Bond branches considered it to be in conflict with the Cradock resolution;* some, with the agreement of the *Patriot*, were alarmed at Van der Meulen's haste;* while the Richmond Bondsmen, who had been asked to act as hosts, complained of the burden during the harvesting season, and gave only reluctant assent.* Hofmeyr's main concern was lest the ground gained at Cradock might be lost, especially if an unrepresentative minority of the Bondsmen took control at Richmond and constituted themselves as a provincial *bestuur*. Under such circumstances the Bond itself might easily split.* Thus, although his prompt action in founding a Cape Town branch of the Bond has been represented by both friendly and hostile writers as a clever move designed to extend his personal influence, it also needs to be said that his intervention may well have saved the Bond from itself. This construction is fully borne out by his conduct at Richmond.

The congress was nearly a sorry fiasco. It was poorly attended,[1]

[1] Two district *besturen* (Bedford and Carnarvon) and fifteen branches (Sterkstroom, Rietfontein, Hanover, Philipstown, Oost Uitvlugt and Zuid Winterveld [Richmond], Richmond dorp, Hamelfontein [Colesberg], Cape Town and the six wards of Graaff-Reinet) were represented. The *Notulen* were published in the *Zuid Afrikaan*, 7 Dec. 1882.

partly owing to inadequate notice, and a good proportion of the delegates doubted either Van der Meulen's right to call it or the right of the meeting to take any decisions which conflicted with those taken at Cradock. J. S. O. Brink of Richmond ruled from the chair that the congress was lawful because it consisted of accredited delegates, but that it was bound by the Cradock decisions—a ruling which was contested by several speakers on both sides. It was only after the debate had reached something like stalemate that Hofmeyr intervened with a lengthy motion which broke away from the unprofitable discussion of the meeting's legality and contained the following substantive proposal: that the three office-bearers of the congress, Brink (chairman), Paul J. van der Merwe (vice-chairman) and Daniel F. Berrangé (secretary) should smooth out the difficulties in consultation with the standing executive committee appointed at Cradock and arrange to convene a provincial, and ultimately a central, *bestuur*.[1] This proposal was accepted by fifteen votes to five, the minority consisting of Van der Meulen and his supporters, who had taken their stand on the necessity of constituting a provincial *bestuur* there and then; and the acceptance of Hofmeyr's proposal brought the formal business of the congress to an end.

Hofmeyr had made no attempt to thwart Van der Meulen's main purpose, which was to establish a Bond provincial *bestuur*.* He had prevented an unrepresentative congress of the Bond from asserting an authority which it obviously did not possess; but he had also called for the summoning of a properly constituted Bond congress after a suitable interval, which would establish a provincial *bestuur*, and even—a point which he had never accepted on principle before—appoint delegates to a central *bestuur* whose authority would cover the Bond in all South Africa. This was a major concession, and brought Hofmeyr into line with the brazen spirits in Paarl and Bloemfontein who planned to turn the Bond into an inter-territorial movement. His purpose in bringing the office-bearers of the

---

[1] Deze vergadering thans uiteen gaat, maar het opdraagt aan haren voorzitter, den assistent-voorzitter en den secretaris, zamen met de heeren Thomas P. Theron, [Jeremias van Heerden] en D. P. van den Heever, om in den loop der maand Maart e.k., op zoodanige plaats als zij zullen goedvinden, eene Provinciale Vergadering te beleggen van een lid van elk Distriktsbestuur, ten einde daarop eene Constitutie aan te nemen, en leden te kiezen van het Centraal Bestuur.'

Hofmeyr omitted Jeremias van Heerden on the supposition that he was not a Bondsman, but on being assured to the contrary agreed to include his name.

Richmond congress into contact with the Cradock executive was to prevent the two committees from working at cross purposes, and he could hardly have foreseen the objections, rooted in misunderstanding, which the Cradock committee subsequently raised.

T. P. Theron thought that the Richmond congress had arbitrarily increased the size of the Cradock committee, and at first refused to accept Hofmeyr's explanation that the three men appointed at Richmond were a separate committee whose task was to convene a meeting of the Bond, and whose relationship with the Cradock committee was to be purely consultative.* He therefore retaliated by summoning a Bond congress to meet as soon as the formation of ten district *besturen* had been reported to him, naming February as the target date.* Hofmeyr answered back. How, he asked, could the differences in the Bond be resolved if two authoritative committees issued contrary instructions? At Richmond it had been agreed that each district *bestuur* should send one representative to a provincial congress in March; but now the order had gone out for each to send two representatives to a rival congress in February. This, he urged, was a slap in the face for the Cradock congress, which had not authorized the executive committee to summon any congress from which the *boeren vereenigingen* were excluded; and to make matters worse, the report of the Cradock constitutional commission had not yet been made public.* Theron continued to deny that the Richmond committee had any standing;* but his committee met at Hanover on 7 February to reconsider their proposals. The outcome of their deliberations was a fresh circular which urged the rapid grouping of Bond branches into district *besturen*, so that when a sufficient number had come into being, an equal number of Bondsmen and representatives of the western Boeren Vereeniging could meet under an impartial chairman to consider the draft constitution soon to be published. All reports of the formation of district *besturen* were to reach Theron by 15 March for this purpose.* Hofmeyr was still not entirely satisfied, but he was prepared to accept the Hanover circular as a working basis, and made the further suggestion that the eastern *vereenigingen* should seek representation through the secretary of the western *hoofdbestuur*.*

Even this, however, was not the end of the story. The congress which was originally planned for March did not open until 22 May owing to administrative difficulties, and by that time the principle of equal representation for the Bond and the *vereenigingen*, as laid down in the Hanover circular, had been abandoned in favour of a more sensible proposal that each party should send as many delegates as it thought fit, but that all decisions on the matter of fusion should only have binding effect if carried by a majority vote within each delegation. The idea of holding a separate Bond congress before the combined meeting still held, and both were arranged to meet at Richmond—the Bond on 22 May, and the combined meeting on the 24th. The *hoofdbestuur* of the western Vereeniging had in the meantime arranged to hold its annual general meeting much earlier than usual, on 29 May at Beaufort West. It would thus be able, if the Richmond congress went according to plan, to dissolve itself as a separate organization.

The success of that congress was bound to depend a great deal on the skill and harmony of the constitutional commission appointed at Cradock, to whose activities we must now turn. Its report was completed by 20 January and made public on 3 February.*[1] It drew on all the foundation documents of the Bond and the Boeren Beschermings Vereeniging, and put out two draft instruments: a general constitution for the united organization and a provincial constitution for its Cape branch. The main points at issue concerned the organization and the aims of the united body, and the drafts are therefore most suitably considered under these heads.

The commission looked to the various Bond constitutions, with their correlation of ward, district, provincial and central *besturen*, to provide the organizational pattern, in preference to the less adaptable structure of the western Boeren Beschermings Vereeniging. They paid some attention to local idiosyncrasy by allowing each province to have its own constitution, and recommended that the Cape should be allowed to retain 'Boeren Vereeniging' in its official title; but their proposal that the central *bestuur* should have power to amend the general constitution 'with the agreement of a majority of the provincial *besturen*' was essentially unitary in character, and gave that *bestuur* a residual authority which would in the long run prove unacceptable to the Cape provincial congress, despite attempts to tone it down.[2] The commission decided to set out the aims and

[1] The members, it will be recalled, were J. M. Hoffman (chairman), J. H. Hofmeyr and D. F. du Toit.

[2] 'With the agreement of a majority of the Provincial *Besturen*' became, at the Richmond congress, 'with due account taken of the feeling of the lower *besturen*' ['met inachtneming van het gevoelen der lagere besturen']—a vaguer formulation which left the power of the central *bestuur* essentially undisturbed.

objects of the combined Bond and Vereeniging in words taken almost verbatim from the *Express* constitution:

'The Bond knows no nationality of any kind save that of the Afrikaners, and considers as belonging to it everybody, of whatever origin, who aims at the welfare of South Africa.

'The object of the Afrikaner Bond is: the formation of a South African nationality, through the nurturing of true patriotism.

'The Bond will strive towards this objective, by encouraging the Afrikaners to assert themselves as a nation both on political and on social grounds.'[1]

It would have been difficult even for opponents of the Bond to take exception to these aims; but they seemed insufficiently robust to D. F. du Toit, who preferred the equivalent clauses in the constitution of the Bond in the Transvaal:

'The Bond establishes itself among the white population of all South Africa. It admits to membership all who recognize South Africa as their fatherland, and adopt the Principles of the Bond, whether they were born in South Africa or have come here from abroad.

'The immediate objective of the Bond is the formation of a South African Nationality; by joining together and co-operating, as preparation for the achievement of the final goal: *a United South Africa under its own flag.*'[2]

This was much more controversial, with its bold assertion of a demand for South African autonomy (which would seem to have been the purpose in agitating for a distinctive flag), its oblique

[1] 'De Bond kent geene nationaliteit hoegenaamd, dan alleen die der Afrikaanders, en beschouwt als daartoe te behooren, een ieder, van welke afkomst ook, die de welvaart van Zuid-Afrika beoogt.

'Het doel van den Afrikaander Bond is: het vormen van eene Zuid-Afrikaansche nationaliteit, door de aankweeking van ware vaderlandsliefde.

'Naar dit doel zal de Bond streven, door de Afrikaanders aan te moedigen zich zoowel op staatkundig als op maatschappelijk gebied te doen gelden als een natie.'

[2] 'De Bond vestigt zich onder de blanke bevolking van geheel Zuid Afrika. Hy neemt in zich op allen, die Zuid Afrika als hun vaderland erkennen, en de Beginselen van den Bond aannemen, hetzy zy in Zuid-Afrika geboren zyn of van buitenlands derwaarts gekomen.'

'Het naaste doel van den Bond is de vorming eener Zuid Afrikaansche Nationaliteit; door aaneensluiting en zamenwerking, als voorbereiding tot bereiking van het einddoel: *een Vereenigd Zuid Afrika onder eigen vlag.*'

acceptance of S. J. du Toit's *Program van Beginsels*, and its firm affirmation of a colour bar. The only other important point of controversy, on which D. F. du Toit was outvoted on the commission, was his desire to specify 'Christian' education as the only kind to which the Bond would lend its support.[1]

All three members of the commission appended their signatures to the final report, but D. F. du Toit felt at liberty, through the columns of the *Patriot*, to campaign for the adoption of points on which he had been outvoted.* He had some following; but although the volume of opposition was now greater than it had been at the time of the Cradock congress, there is no room for doubt that the opponents of the commission's proposals made up only a small fraction of the total Bond membership, and that these proposals received the full support of the *boeren vereenigingen*.* Prospects for fusion at Richmond were therefore extremely favourable, and even D. F. du Toit reluctantly considered that it would be 'driven through'.

IV. THE RICHMOND CONGRESS

The Bondsmen were the first to arrive at Richmond, thirty-nine of them representing twenty-three district *besturen*, and including in their number D. F. du Toit, Oom Daantje van den Heever, and Jan Hofmeyr. The Free State Bond was represented by its imperturbable Chief Justice and one other; but there was no representation from the Transvaal, though S. J. du Toit sent a message of good will, hoping that 'a way towards union or co-operation' between Bond and Vereeniging would be found, and exhorting the Cape men to choose their representatives on the Central *Bestuur*.*

At their first meeting on 22 May, the Bondsmen constituted themselves as a provincial *bestuur*, and elected office-bearers. Two days later the *vereeniging* delegates arrived, and after some difficulty had been experienced in finding a suitable place of meeting, they assembled with the Bondsmen in the public school building. The Bondsmen, who now numbered forty, sat to the right of the chair, Hofmeyr among them; twenty-four delegates, representing nine western and four independent *boeren vereenigingen*, sat to the left. The chair itself was occupied by J. J. Janse van Rensburg, whose success at Cradock had resulted in his being put there again by an all but unanimous vote. D. F. du Toit was elected as his deputy, and

[1] The term 'Christian' did not feature in the educational sections of any of the original Bond constitutions.

Thomas P. Theron of Britstown was given the secretaryship, which he would continue to hold for many years to come.

After a few preliminaries the meeting devoted attention to the draft constitutions, taking the general one first. Each was discussed clause by clause, and an amended version of both received the approbation of both groups of delegates; but it is necessary to ask how easily this was achieved in view of the differences which had built up over the preceding months. Du Toit's party did not move the total rejection of the commission's proposals—they had not in any case prepared themselves by submitting an alternative document —but they tried, on controversial points, to secure the adoption of the Transvaal formulae. They expected a stormy debate over the proposed name for the united body in the Cape, and they complained that the closure was applied too soon, though it is clear from the *Zuid Afrikaan* that A. S. le Roex of Fraserburg was allowed to move an amendment for the deletion of 'Boeren Vereeniging' from the proposed title. They also failed, after extensive argument when minds were still fresh, to secure the incorporation of a colour bar — and failed by the impressive margin of forty-nine votes to six; but the discussion centred on political tactics rather than political principle, and defeat did not mean that membership would be thrown open to non-white people.[1]

Du Toit's supporters did not, however, go away empty-handed. They obtained their 'Christian' education, and went a long way towards securing the Transvaal formula covering aims and objects. This last was really the most controversial topic of all. The article in question, as set out in the draft general constitution, read: 'The object of the Afrikaner Bond is: the formation of a South African nationality, through the nurturing of true patriotism.' To this, Chief Justice Reitz proposed to add: 'as preparation for the achievement of the final goal (*einddoel*), a united South Africa', while D. F. du Toit proposed to complete this quotation from the Transvaal Bond constitution by adding the words 'under its own flag'. J. S. Marais, of the western Vereeniging, and D. P. van den Heever both rose to object to these amendments. The debate became acrimonious and personal after Van den Heever had accused Reitz of indelicacy 'in coming to make such a proposal on English territory', as the report in *De Tolk* put it. Reitz retorted that he was not afraid to speak his

[1] The question of non-white membership of the Bond is discussed below, pp. 118–19.

mind anywhere, even in the presence of the Queen herself. As at the earlier Richmond congress, Hofmeyr waited for the right moment and then entered the debate on wings of peace: let Reitz substitute the words 'final destiny' (*eindbestemming*) for 'final goal', he suggested, and thus meet his own supporters half-way. Reitz agreed. *Eindbestemming* was a less provocative word to use, and it satisfied those who, like Marais, had opposed Reitz's amendment for tactical reasons. When the matter was eventually put to the vote, Du Toit's amendment was rejected by an overwhelming majority,* and that of Reitz, incorporating Hofmeyr's verbal change, agreed to by each delegation.

Procedure for the amalgamation of the Bond and the *vereenigingen* was clarified at Richmond, and rather clumsily incorporated in the provincial Bond constitution, from which it would later have to be removed when that amalgamation had taken place. The Bondsmen ratified the agreement under their own chairman, and on a proposal by D. F. du Toit admitted the *vereeniging* delegates to membership. A fresh election of office-bearers for the enlarged provincial *bestuur* took place the next day, and resulted in the choice by a large majority of Janse van Rensburg as chairman. D. F. du Toit was elected vice-chairman, narrowly defeating Hofmeyr, who was elected treasurer, while Theron retained the secretaryship. Hofmeyr and Du Toit were then chosen as members of the Central *Bestuur*, with Van Rensburg and Theron as their respective alternates. After these formalities had been concluded, there was little time left for discussion of a long and varied agenda.

The Boeren Beschermings Vereeniging went through the motions of dissolving itself, without any fuss, at Beaufort West on 29 May, when the *hoofdbestuur* met and reconstituted itself as a public meeting.*

The reports of Bond branch meetings in *De Tolk* between June and December 1883 reveal overwhelming support for the Richmond decisions. A few branches dissented, as was to be expected.[1] But in view of the general support which the Richmond decisions received, there was no course open to these branches save silence or secession. Prince Albert apparently did secede, for the Bond statistical records make no further mention of a branch there until 1892; but the action of this branch did not precipitate a general movement. For every

[1] e.g. Bedford, Prince Albert, Klein Drakenstein, Fraserburg and Gouph No. 5, Beaufort West.

report which indicated some sort of dissent there were ten or more which showed either that the combined name had been accepted without dispute, or that the Richmond decisions were acclaimed.

At Richmond the delegates accepted a proposal by Chief Justice Reitz that the Colonial members of the Central *Bestuur* should consult with their Free State and Transvaal counterparts, with a view to holding a meeting at Bloemfontein on 15 October. It was chiefly the unpreparedness of the Transvaal which prevented this proposal being followed up, and the Central *Bestuur* was farther away in 1883 than Bondsmen at the time imagined. By the time of the next Colonial congress, at Graaff-Reinet in March 1884, the Transvalers had put their house in order and elected their central members, Piet Joubert and P. J. Naude.* S. J. du Toit was not available as he was still absent in Europe, after helping to negotiate the London Convention with the Colonial Office. On the suggestion of T. P. Theron,* the first meeting of the Central *Bestuur* was therefore deferred until the father of the Bond was in a position to take part, and it did not occur until February 1886. This meeting took place at a time when the prospect of co-operation between the colonies and republics of South Africa was brighter than it had ever been since the birth of the Bond, or was to be again until after the Anglo-Boer war. It represented the high-water mark of the Bond's influence as an interterritorial political movement; but, for reasons which will appear later, the Bond failed to make use of the opportunity which it was then given to build up that spirit of South African unity to which it was dedicated on principle.

5

Assault on the Imperial Factor

THE *boeren vereenigingen* and the Afrikaner Bond did not wait to iron out their internal disagreements before plunging into public affairs. Hofmeyr's Boeren Beschermings Vereeniging first scored considerable successes in the general election of 1878–9. The amalgamated Bond and Boeren Vereeniging then improved on these in the election of 1883–4, and came near to winning a controlling influence in the Cape legislature, in which it was at first the only organized political party. How would it use the influence thus rapidly and easily acquired?

During J. G. Sprigg's ministry of 1878–81, Hofmeyr and his followers usually voted on the opposition side, and in due course helped to overthrow the Government. They then joined forces with the new ministry under T. C. Scanlen, and for a brief period Hofmeyr held a seat in the Cabinet, only to find that membership of a non-Afrikaner government undermined his position among the members of the Bond. Thus warned, he resigned from the ministry and never took office again, preferring rather to act the part of king-maker by throwing the weight of his party behind a sympathetic outside candidate, thereby allowing such a person to attain the premiership and hold it with the help of Bond votes for as long as Afrikaner interests were served. This method, first followed during the Scanlen ministry of 1881–4, worked well. It enabled Hofmeyr and his parliamentary followers to gain their objective with regard both to the repeal of the excise and to the extension of Dutch language rights, the two questions which had led to their entry into politics.

But in one major field the Bond politicians failed. A basic uncertainty of approach in the face of difficult decisions, coupled with an anxiety not to disturb the inter-territorial structure which the Bond had built up, led them into serious errors of judgement in their eagerness to keep the Imperial factor out of Basutoland and Bechuanaland. They failed in both areas, and, as will be shown in the following pages went far towards destroying the Bond's inter-territorial structure in the process.

I. THE WRECK OF SPRIGG'S SOUTH AFRICAN POLICY

The Z.A. Boeren Beschermings Vereeniging was barely in existence before it found itself involved in elections for both Houses of Parliament. The Council election of 1878 was the first to be fought under the Seven Circles Act of 1874,* which had amended the system of representation in the Upper House by dividing the Colony into seven electoral provinces, each returning three members, in place of the two large existing constituencies (the western and the eastern provinces), returning eleven and ten members respectively. Because the new law had been drafted in order to 'remove the preponderance of the towns',* it is arguable that the farming interest would have increased its numerical strength even without the influence of Hofmeyr's Vereeniging; but the Vereeniging undoubtedly had great influence on the rural voters, whipping up opposition among them to the excise, and securing eight of the twelve seats in the three western and the midland circles. It finished with control of nine seats in a House of twenty-one, and with better organization in the western and south-western circles might have secured a bare majority*—a goal which still eluded it, however, in subsequent by-elections.

The Assembly elections of 1879 did not give the Vereeniging and its allies a corresponding position of strength in the Lower House, but even here they acquired nearly one-third of the seats. The successful candidates included twelve members of the Vereeniging, among them Jan Hofmeyr, who was returned for Stellenbosch. Six others who won seats, though probably not members of the Vereeniging, were sponsored by it. Thus was Hofmeyr's Vereeniging spared the ordeal of a period in the political wilderness before winning a position of influence in Colonial politics. Few political movements can have enjoyed a more auspicious beginning.

J. G. Sprigg, who had acceded to the premiership under the cloud of Molteno's dismissal in 1878, following the latter's dispute with Sir Bartle Frere over the conduct of the frontier war, was the chief butt of the Vereeniging's criticisms in these elections. Devoted to the causes

III. FOUNDERS OF THE AFRIKANER BOND

REV. S. J. DU TOIT
Founder of the Afrikaner Bond

D. F. DU TOIT
('Oom Lokomotief')

CARL BORCKENHAGEN
Founder of the Orange Free State
'province' of the Afrikaner Bond

GENERAL P. J. JOUBERT
Chairman of the Afrikaner Bond in
the South African Republic

IV. THE CHAIRMEN OF THE AFRIKANER BOND
IN THE CAPE COLONY

J. J. JANSE VAN RENSBURG
M.L.A. (Cradock), Chairman
1883–6

R. P. BOTHA
M.L.C. (Midland circle),
Chairman 1886–92

P. J. DU TOIT
M.L.A. (Richmond)

Chairman
1892–8

T. P. THERON
M.L.A. (Richmond), Chairman
1898–1908

H. C. VAN HEERDEN
M.L.A. (Cradock), Chairman
1909–11

of confederation and the extension of the railways, as well as to the energetic pursuit of rebellious African tribes, his ministry enjoyed the confidence of the Governor, Sir Bartle Frere, for all its collective mediocrity. But Hofmeyr's Vereeniging hated Sprigg's brandy excise. They had no objection on principle to his native policy, but they disliked the Peace Preservation Act of 1878—which gave the Government power to relieve African tribes of their recently acquired fire-arms—chiefly because they did not think the Act could be enforced without creating major disturbances among tribesmen. They also disliked his confederation policy because they felt strongly that confederation was unacceptable before the independence of the Transvaal was restored.

Confederation appeared to offer a way of escape to the Imperial Government: a means whereby it could extricate itself from its difficulties in the Transvaal without either reversing the annexation or admitting its error. But Hofmeyr and his followers were adamant in their opposition. In response to an appeal from the Transvaal leaders in April 1879, the *Zuid Afrikaan*, *Volksblad* and *Patriot* circulated a memorial urging retrocession, and obtained over seven thousand signatures.* It did not reach the Colonial Office until July, however, by which time Sir Michael Hicks Beach, successor to Lord Carnarvon, had already intimated his adherence to the policy of confederation and expressed the hope that the Cape Parliament would come forward with concrete proposals for its introduction.* Hofmeyr and a strong deputation called on Frere in November and offered terms: they would co-operate with the confederation policy provided Frere allowed the Transvalers, in a freely elected convention, to declare their attitude to the annexation.* Frere rejected these overtures, though he knew the state of feeling among the Transvaal and Colonial Dutch,* and the deputation went away empty-handed. The following March, however, under the inspiration of Gladstone's Midlothian campaigns, the Dutch papers, together with the *Cape Argus*, decided to appeal directly to Gladstone.* Furthermore, in April and May, Kruger, Jorissen and Joubert visited the Cape, held a series of successful meetings, made contact with the Afrikaner leaders in Paarl and Cape Town, and soon showed that they had cut the ground from under Sprigg's feet when he moved in the Assembly on 22 June for the calling of a conference to discuss confederation. Sprigg's motion was defeated without a division. The defeat put confederation out of court, for it was unthinkable without Cape

6

support, and the recall of Frere followed in September. The impracticability of confederation would soon be underlined by the successful revolt of the Transvaal.

The central importance of the Transvaal revolt of 1880–1 for the growth of Afrikaner nationalism has already been noted.[1] Only a small minority of Colonial Afrikaners expected this revolt to succeed, and most of the public meetings called in the Colony after the outbreak of fighting urged an early ending to hostilities and an impartial examination of burgher grievances by a royal commission.* The success of Transvaal arms consequently filled the Colonial Afrikaner with immense pride of race and stirred up in him a profound contempt for the arrogant and unimaginative diplomacy of the Imperial authorities. The second of these factors was as important as the first, for in spite of Gladstone's decision to agree to a truce after Majuba, which most Boers warmly applauded, one legacy of the Transvaal crisis was the emergence among Afrikaners of a deep suspicion of Imperial motives in the period until 1886. They were years in which a much chastened Imperial Government continued to play a role, albeit a subdued one, in a succession of South African crises, beginning with the revolt in Basutoland which had already broken out.

The unwisdom of Sprigg's attempt to disarm the Basuto has been generally recognized. It would have been better, as De Kiewiet has stated, 'to take away their grievances and leave them their guns than to take away their guns and leave them their grievances', for the Basuto were, with good reason, in a state of chronic disaffection.* Disarmament was not applied in Basutoland until July 1880, but stiff resistance speedily followed. Sprigg, aware of the poor cooperation between Imperial and Colonial forces during the Gaika–Gcaleka war of 1877–8, had resolved, and would probably have been obliged, to master the Basuto with Colonial forces alone, and he had already reorganized them to meet such a contingency.* But the Basuto resistance necessitated at an early stage the call-up of conscript burghers, though these were intended only as a last line of defence. Their performance was poor, their resentment great, and it was not until February 1881 that the Basuto showed an interest in peace terms. After refusing an offer by Sprigg, they accepted the mediation of the High Commissioner at the Cape, Sir Hercules Robinson, who published an award on 29 April requiring the Basuto, in return for a

[1] See above, pp. 40–2.

complete amnesty, to pay a fine of 5,000 cattle, to compensate white traders for damage incurred, and to surrender their guns, which they could receive back again on payment of an annual licensing fee of one pound.* Before having to face the ordeal of enforcing the Robinson award, however, the Sprigg Government went out of office.

The grant of parliamentary representation to the newly incorporated province of Griqualand West had strengthened the precarious position of the Ministry at the beginning of 1881, and enabled it to survive a motion of censure on 27 April. But respite for Sprigg was brief. The new members, Francis Orpen and Cecil Rhodes, turned on him, rejected his disarmament policy—had not the Basuto bought their guns with honest labour at the diamond fields?—and criticized his failure to give them a railway.* Sprigg, aware that he was lost, resigned early in May. Persistent pressure by Hofmeyr's followers had helped to bring this about, but they could not have achieved it without the support of the still-diminutive diamond lobby.

II. HOFMEYR AND SCANLEN:
AN EXPERIMENT IN CO-OPERATION

Thomas Scanlen, the senior member for Cradock and Leader of the Opposition since 1879, agreed to form an administration in May 1881.* His team was stronger then Sprigg's, and Scanlen was careful to ensure Hofmeyr's support by offering him a position in his Cabinet, which Hofmeyr, to his almost immediate embarrassment, was persuaded to accept. The Vereeniging members therefore trooped across to the government benches, and began their first experiment in co-operation with a ministry the bulk of whose members stood outside their own political movement.

Hofmeyr considered it 'imperative that at least one sound Africander should go in', and accepted membership of the Government after he had failed to persuade J. S. Marais of Paarl to do so;* but he was careful to remind the readers of his newspaper that he had accepted neither salary nor portfolio, and still reserved full freedom of action.* Aware of the growing antagonism towards the Vereeniging in *Patriot* circles, and anxious to press for the extension of Dutch language rights, Hofmeyr was keen to avoid the collaborator's stigma; nor did he wish to find his hands tied. He quickly discovered that membership of the Cabinet exposed him to both these dangers.

His attempt to obtain the recognition of Dutch in Parliament during the 1881 session failed, partly because he moved too late in the session, but mainly because he was unable to get Cabinet agreement to the measure, and had to leave it in the hands of a private member.[1] Meanwhile the *Patriot* began a sustained attack on his person, his newspaper, his policy, and his new position. On 20 May it inferred that the *Zuid Afrikaan* was encouraging the renewal of the Basuto war, at a time when Hofmeyr was trying hard to dissuade the Cabinet from making a definite statement on this very issue. On the 27th, at a moment when Hofmeyr was embarrassed by lack of Cabinet support for his language motion, the *Patriot* claimed to be the only newspaper 'which *works* for Hollands'. In an editorial on 3 June which approved the new Government's radical pruning of Sprigg's railway plans—a pruning for which Hofmeyr himself was largely responsible—the *Patriot* discounted the support given by the *Zuid Afrikaan* with the explanation that 'that paper is no longer a *popular organ*, but a *government organ*, now the editor himself sits in the Ministry'. The following week it asserted that Hofmeyr and President Brand had been working in the interest of the British in their efforts to procure a truce in the Transvaal, and thus unleashed a controversy which Hofmeyr dealt with, under the circumstances, with remarkable restraint.* If it be recalled that the middle months of 1881 were those in which the Boeren Beschermings Vereeniging and the Afrikaner Bond began their open struggle for the conquest of Afrikaner opinion, Hofmeyr's sensitivity to the *Patriot's* shafts needs no explanation. The cares of office were indeed heavy, even without portfolio or pay.

Nor did Onze Jan's troubles end there. His plans for Dutch in Parliament temporarily defeated and his reputation blackened, he devoted his attention during the recess to restoring the weakened position of the Boeren Vereeniging in the country districts. Merriman, his Cabinet colleague, who was also on tour in October, was presented on the 26th with an address of welcome by the Graaff-Reinet branch of the Afrikaner Bond, which stressed two things: the need for Dutch in Parliament, and the Bond's lack of revolutionary intent.* Merriman saw red. He did not want Dutch in Parliament, and he was not interested in the means which the Bond intended to use, so long as he disapproved of their ends; and he had probably not taken the trouble to distinguish between the mild Graaff-Reinet

[1] Ds. W. P. de Villiers, member for Beaufort West.

Bondsmen, led by Hofmeyr's friend Dolf Botha, and the fire-eaters
in Paarl. He unbosomed himself of a written reply, which, considered
out of context, reads like a sane warning against the dangers of
racialism; but in the context of Brand's remarks at Smithfield a few
days earlier, and of the Graaff-Reinetters' apparent courtesy, it
appeared both impetuous and provocative. Though Merriman and
Hofmeyr travelled back by sea together from Mossel Bay, a rift
developed between them. The *Zuid Afrikaan* of 1 November showed
that Hofmeyr took Merriman's attack personally, intimating that
the Graaff-Reinet Bond's address was 'precisely the kind to which
the Z.A. Boeren Beschermings Vereeniging could have subscribed',
though it did not miss the opportunity of lashing out at the Paarl
leadership of the Bond for having put such mistaken ideas into
Merriman's head. The next day an article appeared in the *Argus*—
inspired, so Hofmeyr thought, by Merriman—which, though not
disapproving of Hofmeyr's efforts to build up the Boeren
Beschermings Vereeniging, charged him with a breach of constitutional etiquette in 'conducting a political campaign which aims at
altering the law, while he was a Minister of the Crown . . . without
first assuring himself that he has the concurrence of his colleagues'.
The writer can only have had Hofmeyr's advocacy of Dutch in
Parliament in mind, though he did not explicitly say so. The *Zuid
Afrikaan* answered the charge on the 3rd, suggesting that membership
of the Cabinet had brought Hofmeyr no advantage to offset the
weakening of his support among Afrikaners.

Scanlen returned to Cape Town from the Eastern Province
towards the end of the month, earlier than expected. By the 28th
Hofmeyr had decided to resign, and drew up a confidential memorandum for the Cabinet, explaining his reasons, which his biographer
has published in full.* This should be compared with the reasons
given in the *Zuid Afrikaan* on 3 December. They differ, though they
are not mutually contradictory. In the press article he denied that
either the Dutch language question or Merriman's Graaff-Reinet
utterance was at issue, and he went out of his way to state that he
would continue to support the Scanlen Government. The '*Afrikaander
partij*', he reminded his readers, was not strong enough to form a
government of its own, and there were more well-disposed Englishmen on the government than on the opposition benches. The
Cabinet memorandum made two main points. On the one hand
Hofmeyr turned the charge of improper conduct against Merriman,

by asserting that his communication to the editor of a newspaper of 'intelligence, which is calculated to brand me as unworthy of a seat in the Cabinet' was a violation of Cabinet secrecy. On the other hand, he argued that since 'it is impossible for both of us to remain in the Cabinet', the onus was on himself to resign, because Merriman 'endorsed the Premier's utterance in the House of Assembly, which I did not'.* It was a matter of collective responsibility, and the issue at stake was policy in Basutoland. Hofmeyr knew that any further association with the policy to which the Government was now committed in Basutoland would lose him the leadership of the Afrikaner movement in the Colony; but he could not say so in public for two reasons. One was the necessity of not embarrassing Scanlen if the campaign for Dutch in Parliament was to succeed. The other stemmed from the fact that neither Hofmeyr nor his supporters either inside or outside Parliament had any constructive Basuto policy to offer. All they were sure about was that a continuation of Sprigg's methods was wrong.

Hofmeyr's refusal to embarrass Scanlen paid two important dividends, for the Government let him have his way with regard both to the excise and to the Dutch language. At the end of March 1882, still adhering to the fiscal arguments which had brought the Boeren Beschermings Vereeniging into existence, Hofmeyr moved the total repeal of the excise, even though the producers no longer unanimously condemned the tax. Myburgh, his fellow member for Stellenbosch, moved an amendment whereby the duty would be doubled on brandy distilled with imported materials, and would remain unaltered if home-grown materials were used; but eventually he and Hofmeyr compromised with a proposal that the former grade should pay a shilling duty and the latter go duty free. The Government, reluctant to lose an important source of revenue, attempted to delay the issue by referring it to a commission, but when this proposal was defeated they accepted the appointment of a select committee, to include Hofmeyr, with instructions to draft a bill to give effect to the Hofmeyr–Myburgh proposal. This bill became law in the same session. The Government manfully resigned itself to a reduction in tax receipts and never dared to touch the question again, though the following ministry would be compelled for a short while to raise the excise to an unprecedented level.*

Victory for the Dutch language followed. The eighty-ninth section of the Constitution Ordinance, which laid down that 'all debates and discussions . . . journals, entries, minutes and proceedings' should be in English, had been assailed by spasmodic petitions since the fifties, but all had been turned down. No petitions had been presented during the session of 1880, but in that year the synod of the N.G. Kerk had sponsored the cause, and when Hofmeyr and De Villiers raised the matter during the 1881 session a flood of petitions poured into both houses as part of an organized campaign. No longer tied by membership of the Cabinet, Onze Jan returned to the attack in 1882, with a masterly speech delivered on 20 March.* His motion that the use of Dutch be permitted in Parliament was carried with few remonstrances and without a division, and a bill to give effect to it was law by 9 June.

The importance of this decision for the subsequent development of the Afrikaner political movement was immense. Henceforth rural electors would no longer be influenced in their choice of parliamentary candidates by a consideration which ought, in fairness, to have been irrelevant. The ability of candidates to speak English had not always been a decisive criterion in the past, and several members of Parliament were in fact unmuzzled by the new law—the first step in a long development which would lead eventually, after some real setbacks, to the establishment of approximate parity in the use of Dutch and English in public life. Once Dutch was permitted in Parliament, it could not logically be debarred in other fields—in the courts, in the public service, in the secondary schools, where Dutch-speakers were at a great disadvantage. The efforts of J. S. Marais during the 1882 session secured an amendment to the public school regulations, to allow governing bodies of first and second class schools to determine the language of instruction. This was in accordance with the advice of the De Villiers Commission of 1880, though it would be some time before the change came to mean anything in practice.* A commission appointed in 1881, of which Hofmeyr was a member, considered the question of Dutch in the public service, and when its report was tabled in 1883 the Government agreed to make a knowledge of Dutch (or in the case of the Native Affairs Department, 'Sesuto or Kaffir') obligatory for third class clerks in the higher division—a concession from which subsequent extensions of compulsory Dutch in the public service sprang.* The use of Dutch was made permissive in the higher courts, at the discretion of the presiding judge, and fully optional in the lower, by an Act of 1884.* It became a compulsory subject for civil service candidates in 1887.*

Most of the legislative changes necessary for placing the Dutch language on an equal footing with English were made before 1890. Little parliamentary friction accompanied them, for no government which valued the support of Afrikaners was prepared to alienate them on such issues. The language movement thus strengthened the position of Afrikaners in Parliament, and in its early stages directly affected the relationship between Hofmeyr's Vereeniging and the Scanlen ministry. Once Scanlen had taken the first important step, Hofmeyr's dependence on his good offices was immediately diminished, and if Scanlen's policy failed to measure up to the Boers' needs in other respects, it would be easier now for Hofmeyr to abandon him.

Basutoland provided an acid test. Scanlen, faced with the problem of carrying out the High Commissioner's award, which the people had shown little inclination to accept, announced during the session of 1881 that he intended to enforce it with the continued use of Colonial troops, even though Hofmeyr, who knew a great deal about the unpopularity of the war in the Colony, had warned him against an early declaration of policy for political reasons. Desertions from the burgher forces reflected the malaise, which debates at Boer congresses explained.* Boers complained that the burden of conscription was too unevenly distributed; they resented the use of burgher forces on campaigns beyond the Orange River; they wanted the Coloured levies placed under their own commandants, not under special officers; they were critical of the general strategy; while generations of commando warfare lay behind their suggestion that instead of cash payment the burghers should receive two-thirds of the land confiscated from the beaten tribes, with double shares for the commandants. They had made bad soldiers, they urged in effect, because they had been denied their traditional organization and their traditional incentives for fighting.

Lack of success against the Basuto made them ask whether Colonial forces ought to be in Basutoland at all. The feeling prevalent in the sixties—that Basuto affairs were the concern not of the Cape, but of the Orange Free State—easily revived, and gave rise to the slogan that the Colonial frontier ought to be the Orange River 'from the Drakensberg to the sea', which found expression at many a Bond meeting. This ingenious argument for evading responsibility in Basutoland, and incidentally for surrendering control of Griqualand West, did not preclude the settlement by Cape farmers of the fertile southern slopes of the Drakensberg, which many coveted; but it made no allowance for the Free State's reluctance to be burdened either with West Griqualand or with the Basuto problem, and may therefore be consigned to the realm of fantasy. When it came to suggesting a practical solution for the Basuto difficulty, the Afrikaner political organizations had in fact no policy to offer. The western Boeren Vereeniging's special congress in March 1882 admitted defeat and left the problem to 'Parliament and the Government'.* The congress of Bondsmen at Graaff-Reinet the same month indulged in the Orange frontier dream,* while the Cradock congress voted hesitantly in favour of disannexation.* A wide range of alternative policies had received support in the branches of both organizations, and all that can usefully be said in general terms about their attitude is that those who favoured a Colonial withdrawal were probably more numerous than those who were prepared to accept a continuation of the war; but withdrawal seemed likely to lead to a reintroduction of Imperial control, and this engendered queasy second thoughts.

Such indecision did not make the position easy, either for Scanlen or for Hofmeyr. From December 1881, however, Scanlen trimmed his sails and began to talk of the withdrawal of Colonial authority from the territory.* The Basuto ignored an ultimatum of 15 February, to accept the Governor's award within a month on pain of its withdrawal. Realizing that the war was unpopular, Scanlen decided on 27 March to withdraw both the award and the disarmament proclamation and leave a skeleton force in Basutoland to keep order while tempers had a chance to cool; and he announced that he would appoint a commission to examine the claims of the loyal Basuto and traders and would seek the support of the Free State.* Hofmeyr and the *Vereeniging* parliamentarians trailed behind him, voting against an Opposition motion on 4 April which required the Government to enforce the disarmament proclamation, while most of them voted against a Basutoland Annexation Repeal Bill on the 14th. But unfortunately for Scanlen and the Vereeniging, the new policy did not work. Nothing came of the proposed collusion with the Free State, whose Government considered itself well clear of the problem.* The inclination of the paramount chief, Letsie, to submit to Scanlen's easy terms was not shared by his subordinates, while further troubles broke out at the end of the year in the Leribe district between two contestants for tribal succession rights. To deal with these new difficulties, Scanlen summoned a special session of Parliament in January 1883.

He now proposed that the Colony should recall its magistrates from Basutoland, thus abandoning the internal administration of the territory, but should retain a resident there to supervise its external relations—more particularly to keep order on the Free State frontier, which the Colony was bound to do in terms of its inherited obligations under the Aliwal Convention of 1869. He no doubt expected the support of political Afrikanerdom for this policy; but Hofmeyr thought otherwise, arguing that the abandonment of Basutoland should not even be considered for fear of readmitting the Imperial factor. The ministry, Hofmeyr now considered, should 'go to the British Government and claim the right to regulate the native question according to our own pleasure, and for that purpose, if necessary, to enter into alliances with other States and races in South Africa.* At the beginning of May, Hofmeyr went to Bloemfontein and tried to secure the co-operation of the Free State in a policy of joint action.* He failed, but the Richmond congress that month was undeterred by his failure.*

Meanwhile Scanlen had reached the conclusion that disannexation was the only way out, having toured Basutoland and consulted Brand in March. The Government therefore informed the Colonial Office on 30 April that the existing regime would no longer be continued, and suggested that if the Imperial Government intended to fill the void left by the Colonial withdrawal they would be advised to act quickly.* Merriman went to London to raise a much needed loan and to apply pressure at close quarters, while Brand reminded the Colonial Office of its obligations under the Aliwal Convention. Lord Derby, the new Secretary of State, then outlined the conditions on which British control of Basutoland might be resumed: an undertaking by the Free State to police its side of the border, willingness of the Basuto to co-operate, and consent from the Cape to make over to the High Commissioner an annual sum equal to the customs duties levied on goods destined for Basutoland.*

Scanlen introduced a Disannexation Bill on the strength of Derby's dispatch, in terms of which the Colony was to make good any shortfall in the revenue of the territory up to an annual maximum of £20,000.* Hofmeyr dissented, and moved an amendment on 13 July which called for an appeal to the constituencies before such a momentous decision was taken; but this attempt to scotch the Government's plan by delaying tactics failed. The amendment was thrown out by forty-two votes to twenty-one, and the 'Noes' included five members of the Boeren Beschermings Vereeniging. Hofmeyr therefore fell back on his second line of defence by supporting a further amendment moved by Upington that 'no Legislative Measure for the Disannexation of Basutoland should be accepted which contains any provision other than one for the Repeal of the Basutoland Annexation Act'. This time the margin was narrowed to ten votes, but none of the Vereeniging's rebels returned to the fold. On the contrary, they allowed the Disannexation Bill to pass through all its stages, and when Upington failed by the margin of one vote to introduce a clause into the Bill during the committee stage, to terminate all Colonial liabilities in Basutoland, the opposition of these rebels saved the Government's plan.* The measure was eventually confirmed, in a form acceptable to the Imperial Government, by an Order in Council of 2 February 1884.*

The Afrikaner politicians had paid the penalty for their inconsistency, for, as Janse van Rensburg said at Graaff-Reinet in March 1884 (though he was the only speaker to admit this), Scanlen's Government had been obliged to renounce responsibility for Basutoland because of the Cradock congress vote in favour of disannexation.

Having decided to abandon Basutoland, the Scanlen Government was prepared to go further and hand over to the Imperial authorities the administration of the greater part of the Transkei.* This plan appeared to provide a solution to an intractable problem which the Sprigg regime had handed down, at a time when affairs in Basutoland were going badly and the Colony's financial resources were desperately low. It would also help to rationalize a situation under which Tembuland and adjoining territories, though administered by Colonial magistrates remained under tribal law, and, were neither part of the Colony proper nor represented in the Colonial Parliament, but were governed by the High Commissioner under a separate commission from the Queen.*[1] But the policy commended itself neither to the Imperial Government, which did not desire to increase its responsibilities, nor to the Boers of the north-east frontier, who looked upon parts of Tembuland and Emigrant Tembuland as desirable regions for white settlement.

---

[1] The Transkeian Annexation Act of 1877 had brought Fingoland and Griqualand East under Cape control, but Tembuland remained outside its provisions.

During the Basuto rising of 1880, a section of the Tembu who had taken up arms against the white men in the frontier war of 1877–8, decided to open hostilities again.* They were subdued by burghers of the adjoining districts of Barkly East and Dordrecht, who took advantage of their victory to move into the northern part of Tembuland and settle there. The Scanlen Government was prepared to issue grazing permits to those who applied, but soon found itself faced with a situation in which homes had been built and land brought under the plough, by men who gave themselves a sort of prescriptive right to the conquered land and obviously had no intention of leaving.* These squatters received the warm support of Hofmeyr, in whose imagination there grew the idea of a broad belt of white settlement from Queenstown to Kokstad, separating the Basuto in the north from the Tembu and the Pondo in the south, as a means of bringing order to the tribal areas and extending the opportunities for the white farmer.*

The tact of Scanlen and of the civil and military administration persuaded the squatters not to take the law into their own hands but to await the findings of a commission, which the Premier undertook to appoint with a view to regularizing the *de facto* position by putting the land up for sale.* A commission was duly appointed, and when the Cradock congress represented to Scanlen that it contained no representatives of the squatters' point of view, he immediately set their minds at rest by inviting their chairman, Janse van Rensburg, and Jotham Joubert of Albert to join it.* The commission in due course recommended that the squatters' lands should be put up for sale to whites and annexed to the Colony;* but a storm of protest soon greeted the Government from squatters who thought they should have been given first option on the land at cheaper prices, and resented the presence of armed police in their midst. They appealed to the Richmond congress in May 1883, and the congress resolved to help them by sending a deputation to Parliament and by organizing petitions, over twenty of which reached the House of Assembly. Parliament was prevented from taking a decision on the Tembuland Commission's report by a Speaker's ruling that the only course open was to petition the Queen, since the territory lay outside Colonial jurisdiction.* But although a private member moved accordingly, and Irvine's motion appeared repeatedly on the order paper, it was never taken to a vote. The Government had decided to leave the territory in the nominal hands of the Imperial Government, husband its meagre resources by arranging for the recall of its magistrates, and stand on this decision at the forthcoming general election, even at the risk of covering its head with coals of fire.

The Bond congress of March 1884 was very angry indeed. No speaker defended the Government. A letter was read from the Tembuland trekkers' committee which complained of their power-lessness 'under Kaffirs' magistrates and Kaffirs' laws', and demanded the incorporation of Tembuland and Griqualand East in the Colony and the enfranchisement of the settlers. Nobody denied that Tembu-land was legally Imperial territory; but the delegates preferred to take their stand on *de facto* occupation by Colonial settlers, and they thought, with Dolf Botha, that there was no danger of Imperial intervention if they made up their minds to stay there.* Scanlen and the Bondsmen had clashed head on, despite Scanlen's earlier attempt to treat his allies fairly, over an issue that was wreathed in legal ambiguity and aroused the elemental instincts of the Colonial frontiersman.

A Colonial party energetically backing the claims of its fellow-countrymen to settle in a region outside the borders of the Colony was not likely to stand in the way of blood relations in a neighbouring state who were trying to do the same thing. This basic similarity between the situations in the Transkei and in Bechuanaland deserves some emphasis, for it helps to explain the attitude of the Bond when the latter region became a scene of crisis during 1884. In practice, the events connected with the establishment and disestablishment of Stellaland and Goshen were of greater significance in the developing maelstrom of South African politics, because they threatened to cause a revival of hostility between the Imperial and Transvaal governments, and took place in a region of great strategic and commercial importance.

The problem of the western border of the Transvaal, which had not been solved by the Keate Award of 1871, was clarified when Colonel Moysey made his report on it in December 1880. He dis-covered that no proper survey had been carried out; that overlapping grants had been made from Pretoria; that enterprising settlers were laying claim to extensive tracts of territory on the basis of legally-suspect agreements with the chiefs of the region; and that the area of paper claims had far outrun the zones of effective white settlement. Confronted with this situation, Moysey had proceeded on the eve of the war of independence to draw a western border for the Transvaal which ignored paper titles however impressive, but recognized effective European occupation even where the original native inhabitants had been dispossessed. His aim had been to fix the frontier and prevent further penetration by whites, and his report, despite its unpopularity among the Transvaal Boers, became the basis of the frontier settlement under the Pretoria Convention.* Trouble broke out in these western areas, however, before that Convention was signed. The pattern which soon emerged was that of a conflict between two rival pairs of chiefs, of whom Moshete and David Massouw looked to the Transvaal for protection, and Montsioa and Mankoroane to the Imperial Government. Each of these chiefs had his retinue of European concessionaires, variously described as 'volunteers' or 'freebooters' according to the point of view, some of whom came from the Transvaal, others from the diamond fields, and yet others from as far away as the western Cape.

During 1882, plans were set in motion by the Transvaal 'volunteers' to set up independent states to the west of the Moysey line. They drove Mankoroane, despairing of help from his Imperial patrons, to appeal to the Transvaal for protection in June. Paul Kruger, after testing the British Resident in Pretoria, declined to take him under his wing, but also, in company with President Brand and the Cape Government, rejected the British High Commissioner's suggestion of a four-power police force to control the area, unless the frontier provisions of the Pretoria Convention were first amended to the Transvaal's advantage. Meanwhile Montsioa capitulated to a commandant of the South African Republic in October. Before the year was out, the Republic of Stellaland, based on Vryburg, and the Republic of Goshen, based on the farm Rooigrond near the Transvaal border, were in being, and the Government of the South African Republic was ready to absorb them both as soon as conditions were favourable for it to do so.*

The Imperial Government had not provided itself, under the Pretoria Convention, with a ready method of employing sanctions against the Transvaal, and when Lord Derby took over the Colonial Office in January 1883 he soon showed an inclination to take the line of least resistance. Once his proposal for a joint police force had been turned down, he suggested that Mankoroane and Montsioa might be provided with alternative homes in the Cape; but pressure from the Colony, and from the missionary and commercial interests which desired to keep the road to the north open, soon drove this suggestion out of court. At the end of the year, when a Transvaal delegation visited London to negotiate for the amendment of the Pretoria Convention, he was sufficiently under the influence of these pressure groups to reject the delegation's proposal that the Transvaal should annex the two mushroom republics and in return neutralize the northern road. He proposed to give the Transvaal 'as much of this territory as can be given without including the road', and made acceptance of this offer a condition for the reopening of other disputed questions. What Derby would have liked best of all, however, was the annexation of the disputed territory by the Cape.*

The Cape Government had viewed the mounting crisis from the sidelines, divided as to the course which it ought to pursue. Rhodes, the new member for Barkly West, campaigned energetically for annexation. He was already thinking in terms of opening up the interior, for which the maintenance of the northern road was vital. He therefore secured his own appointment to a commission which investigated the northern frontier question in May 1883, and soon determined on a policy of 'dividing the free-booters, bribing those of the south with the promise of their lands to acquiesce in the expulsion of their northern neighbours'.* He urged Scanlen to prevent Derby from allowing the Transvaal to expand, and to 'have the courage' to take Bechuanaland for the Colony, and he made his celebrated 'Suez Canal' speech in the Assembly in August; but he failed to persuade Scanlen to grasp 'the neck of the bottle'. At the end of the year the Colonial Office tried to persuade Scanlen to annex, or at least to participate in a joint protectorate with the Imperial Government; but Scanlen would not act without the acquiescence of the Transvaal Government, even after the Transvaal delegation had accepted a modified frontier under the London Convention in February 1884.* When the Imperial Government appointed the missionary John Mackenzie as Resident Commissioner in Bechuanaland, the Scanlen Government looked on the appointment with disfavour.

It was, by general agreement, primarily pressure from the Afrikaner Bond which tied Scanlen's hands. Hofmeyr's attitude was less conspiratorial than Agar-Hamilton has suggested;[1] but Onze

---

[1] In his chapter entitled 'The Mole, the Bug, the Warming-Pan and the White House', Agar-Hamilton has understood Hofmeyr's biographer to state that 'as soon as the London Convention was *signed*' [i.e. in February 1884] Onze Jan

Jan firmly believed that Bechuanaland lay within the Transvaal's sphere of influence, and he held this view at least until August 1884. He saw no advantage in the restoration of Imperial authority on the western border of the Transvaal, either in its sole majesty or in conjunction with the authority of the Cape Government. He was not personally concerned, as Rhodes was, with the security of the northern road, but urged that this road stood a better chance of remaining open if it ran through the South African Republic, than if it passed through unstable satellite states dependent on transit dues for their revenue—an argument with which Rhodes had no quarrel, though he was less concerned than Hofmeyr over the Transvalers' fear of Imperial encirclement. The weakness of Hofmeyr's argument lay in the fact that the Transvaal had already begun to raise a tariff wall against imported Cape goods,* which meant that the free use of the northern road could not be taken for granted if it fell under Transvaal control. Logically he might have been expected to favour annexation of the disputed territory by the Cape, which would have untied Scanlen's hands without damaging Cape Afrikaner interests and would, incidentally, have obviated the crisis of 1884. But Hofmeyr held strong views because he was involved in a problem of loyalty, not so much to the Transvaal, as to the Afrikaner Bond, whose internal developments were peculiarly bound up with the Bechuanaland crisis.

The Cape Bond congress in March 1884 favoured abstention by the Cape Government from the affairs of Bechuanaland,* mainly, it seems, because the Transvaal Bondsmen were deeply committed to an expansionist policy on their western border. Piet Joubert had invested his reputation in the project, and had taken it upon himself to supply the Republican 'volunteers' with the sinews of war.* He encouraged these 'volunteers' to join the Bond, according to a letter which he wrote to N. C. Gey van Pittius, president of Goshen. The Goshen branch of the Bond was in existence at the beginning of October 1883, centred at Rooigrond, according to an undated report in *De Tolk*, and there was a branch in December at Rietvallei in the Molopo district, of which Gey van Pittius himself was chairman.* The Transvaal Bondsmen were playing for

'abandoned the idea of annexing Bechuanaland to the Transvaal in favour of control by the Cape'. But Hofmeyr's biographer actually states that Onze Jan continued to support annexation by the Transvaal until that convention was *ratified* in August 1884.

high stakes, and it would have been difficult for Hofmeyr and the Colonial Bondsmen to take the sort of action in Parliament which would have split their organization on territorial lines in the first flush of their new-found unity.

The further development of the Bechuanaland crisis belongs to the period of Upington's ministry. Like the question of Tembuland, it was unsolved when, to general surprise, Scanlen elected to go out of office 'on a bug'. His relaxation of quarantine measures against phylloxera was hardly in itself an issue of confidence, important though it was to the wine farmers, and the event was a pretext rather than the cause of his decision to relinquish power. Scanlen had performed useful services for the Afrikaner party, and, aware of the need of their support if he was to hold his own against Sprigg's opposition group, he had been prepared to pay for it. Hence his willingness to grant their request over the language question, his anxiety not to lose their support over the excise, and his willingness to allow them to call the tune, to begin with, over Basutoland, Tembuland and Bechuanaland. But questions involving the Imperial factor broke the alliance. To call Scanlen an imperialist, as the Bondsmen began to do, was to misrepresent the main springs of his policy. He was the victim of hard times, and of Sprigg's legacy of intractable problems, and his appeal to the Imperial Government over Basutoland and the Transkei was in both cases an admission of defeat rather than a declaration of principle. But from the Bond's point of view, Scanlen had proved too willing to abandon his difficulties to London. It was not that the Bond had more viable policies to offer, or that the imperialism of Gladstone's second ministry was of a particularly rampant kind; but the Bondsmen were in buoyant mood, with strong branches in the Cape and the two Republics, and they were encouraged to press all the harder for a united and independent South Africa by their success in the Colonial elections of 1884.

III. UPINGTON, THE BOND AND BECHUANALAND

The general election of 1883–4 was the first which the Bond and Boeren Vereeniging fought as a united body, and it had good reason to be satisfied with the results. The Council elections, completed in December 1883, gave it a nominal majority of twelve against ten, while in the new Assembly Hofmeyr's followers numbered nearly half the House.

On Scanlen's resignation, Hofmeyr declined the offer to form a ministry 'because if I formed a Ministry, my opponents would raise the racial issue, and I hate racial issues'.* He was quite right. Within six months, affairs in Bechuanaland would cause a resurgence of emotional jingoism among English-speaking Colonials, directed against Hofmeyr, which would assuredly have been more vigorous had he been in office. Ill health was a contributory cause of Hofmeyr's refusal, but it is unlikely to have been the main one, especially as Hofmeyr found a willing ally against Scanlen's policy in Thomas Upington, a Cape Town lawyer of Irish origin who represented Caledon.

Upington assumed office in May, and brought the Irishman's mistrust of Downing Street to the defence of Colonial authority in South African affairs. Basutoland, on which Upington and Hofmeyr had first drawn together, was irretrievably lost; but Upington considered that the Transkei could be saved, and was prepared to leave Bechuanaland in the Transvaal's sphere of influence. In his first session as Premier, he secured the annexation of the Umzimvubu region, including Port St. John's, and extended the legal authority of the Cape Government over the whole of Tembuland in 1885. He also made a determined but ultimately disastrous attempt to follow the Bond's policy on the northern border, refusing to agree to take over Stellaland, until developments in that region had reached such a pass that a reluctant Imperial Government decided to take charge of its own interests without relying on Colonial support.

Lord Derby had made the tactical mistake of placing John Mackenzie, the Resident Commissioner in Bechuanaland, under the authority of the High Commissioner at the Cape; for whereas Mackenzie favoured the extension of British authority in Bechuanaland, Sir Hercules Robinson preferred the extension of that of the Cape Colony. Mackenzie, going beyond the terms of the London Convention, which made no mention of a British protectorate over Bechuanaland, ran up the Union Jack at the request of one group of Vryburg settlers, but aroused the hostility of others on a multitude of grounds, and soon found that he had not the means of maintaining law and order.* Robinson accordingly recalled him and sent up Rhodes in his place. But Rhodes, whose chief aim was to get the Transvalers out of the disputed territory, clashed with Piet Joubert, who was equally determined that they should remain; and it was Joubert, with force at his back, who got the better of the encounter.*

However unscrupulous Joubert's expansionist aims may have

been, and they are well authenticated, it seems clear that the break-down of law and order in Bechuanaland in the middle of 1884 required speedier and more decisive action than the Imperial Government was at first willing to take, even under pressure from Pretoria. When Montsioa asked Joubert for the Transvaal's protection on 30 August, shortly after the Volksraad had ratified the London Convention (which left the bulk of his lands outside the Transvaal), the Executive Council was divided in its views. Chief Justice Kotzé warned the President that even a qualified annexation of his territory amounted to a breach of the Convention, while Kruger and S. J. du Toit disagreed, advancing the claims of humanity.* These claims would have looked more convincing had Transvalers played a smaller part in fermenting the Bechuanaland disorders, but they gave a plausible pretext for the 'provisional' annexation of the satellite republics on 16 September, which was gazetted in Pretoria on the 18th. The annexation was to be subject to the Queen's consent, and S. J. du Toit was sent off immediately to put it into force. The political predikant would try to succeed where, from the other side, the political missionary had failed.

The beginning of Du Toit's commission marked the ending of Joubert's,* but signified no change of policy except so far as the annexation was concerned. Du Toit arrived at Rooigrond on 22 September, concluded a treaty with Montsioa on the 25th, taking him over in the name of the South African Republic, and on 3 October ran up the Vierkleur at Rooigrond to the accompaniment of what Agar-Hamilton has not unfairly called 'a passionate oration beside which the most flamboyant utterance of contemporary jingoism seems pale and flaccid'.* Kruger, however, ordered him to pull the flag down on the 6th, recalled him on the 10th, and issued a further proclamation on the 13th which cancelled that of 16 September, on the ground that the Government's 'object of establishing peace on the western border had been attained, and . . . the way was now open . . . for the establishment of a permanent peace, [which] the said provisional proclamation . . . may retard'.*

The reputation of S. J. du Toit suffered as a result of his Goshen adventure, the gravamen of the charge against him being that his hoisting of the flag was a contravention of his instructions.* His biographer has denied this, and it can hardly be maintained that the raising of such a symbol was necessarily incongruous with the order to annex provisionally, though Du Toit ruined a plausible case in his old age by even denying that annexation had been intended, if his biographer is to be believed.* What seems to have happened is that the Kruger Government lined itself up behind the policy of annexation, but in such a way as to deny credit for it to Joubert, and to give itself a safe line of escape (the 'provisional' nature of the annexation) in case the Imperial Government were to react vigorously, as it subsequently did. Du Toit, who had accepted the commission partly on account of a current feud which he had with Joubert, had not the wit to see that the flag demonstration, which was not detailed in his instructions, would enable his enemies in Pretoria to turn him into a scapegoat for a policy which had failed; and he was powerless to prevent their doing so.* His private feud with Joubert, whatever its cause, was soon over; but the fact that both he and Joubert had quarrelled with the real rulers of the Transvaal damaged both their reputations, and incidentally had a calamitous effect on the growth of the Afrikaner Bond in the Republic.

The Transvaal Volksraad had ratified the London Convention in August, and the Executive Council, after trying in a guarded manner to defy it in September, reverted to a policy of honest adherence on 13 October. The Republican leaders were now prepared to accept the annexation of the lands of Montsioa and Mankoroane by the Cape, if only as a *pis aller*.* Hofmeyr's hands were freed, and he too began to press for the annexation of Bechuanaland by the Colony. The German proclamation of a protectorate over Namaqua–Damaraland on 7 August helped to confirm his change of view, just as the attitude of the Transvaal Government was being transformed by the evident intention of Whitehall to insist on observance of the Convention by commissioning General Warren to lead an army into Bechuanaland and make a show of military force. If the Cape took over the road, as Hofmeyr now saw the position, the Germans would be unable to cut it from the west, and the Warren expedition would not be necessary. Lack of Imperial zeal in one quarter, and a superabundance of it in another, could be made up for at a single stroke, and all Afrikanerdom could breathe more freely.

The policy which Upington followed in attempting to avert the Warren expedition accorded therefore with Bond plans. It was, under the circumstances, a difficult policy to pursue, because of the stirring of British Colonial sentiment which followed the news that Warren was on his way, and the evident antipathy between the Ministry and the Governor. On 17 October the Cape ministers told

Robinson that the expulsion of the Goshen 'volunteers' by force would make the subsequent annexation of Bechuanaland by the Colony difficult, and they proposed that the Premier and one of his colleagues should go to Rooigrond and negotiate a settlement with Gey van Pittius's men. Robinson gave his reluctant approval, cautioning the ministers that they should on no account sacrifice the lands of Montsioa, who had come under severe pressure from the Goshenites. The Imperial Government agreed to hold up military operations, but not preparations, for six weeks, pending the outcome of their visit, and on 4 November Upington and Sprigg set out for Goshen. The terms which they made with the Goshenites were, however, unacceptable to Robinson, and the year ended to the tune of rising party cries as Warren duly set foot on Cape soil to carry out his assigned task.

An Imperial League had been founded in the capital on 23 October, in opposition to the conciliatory policy of the Government. It was an ephemeral thing, confined almost entirely to the western Cape,* and its bubble would be pricked by the actions of Warren himself before many months were out. But the excited temper of public opinion can be gauged from the fact that Hofmeyr received threatening letters through the post, purporting to emanate from the League, while Sprigg of all people suffered arraignment at the hands of his East London constituents on a charge of disloyalty. The Cape Town Bondsmen, meeting on 28 October (that is, five days after the formation of the League and a week before Upington and Sprigg set out for the north), worked hard to counter the League's influence by carrying resolutions urging the Government to negotiate with all interested parties, and affirming their own loyalty to the Empire;* but no efforts on their part could prevent the Warren expedition from setting out.

Warren's armada encountered no resistance. Kruger restrained the Goshen 'volunteers' and gave way to Warren's show of force when the two met at Fourteen Streams in January 1885.* But Warren's conduct of affairs in Bechuanaland soon alienated the parties which had been interested in sending him there, as well as those who had objected to his going. He preserved the tribesmen in the remnant of their land, and brought them peace. But he crossed swords with Rhodes, with Sir Hercules Robinson, and with Downing Street, where the scale of his unofficial empire-building was viewed with impotent alarm. He had not only annexed the territory south of the Molopo River as the Colony of British Bechuanaland, but declared a Protectorate over a vast region to the north of it. The Transvalers abhorred the establishment of Imperial rule along their western border. Upington's Cabinet, piqued by the rejection of its negotiated settlement in December 1884, declined to relieve the Imperial Government of its new commitments when subsequently asked to do so. The Bondsmen, who at Beaufort West in 1885 expressed regret at the rejection of Upington's settlement, as well as anger at Warren's activities, did not even discuss the subject at Grahamstown in 1886.* In Bechuanaland as in Basutoland, their concern for the territorial interests of their republican neighbours, combined with their fear of the consequences of any extension of Imperial authority, had produced a vacillating policy which led in both cases to the extension of British rule and therefore to the defeat of their primary objective.

6

The Failure of Pan-South Africanism

I. THE EFFECTS OF DEPRESSION

AT the beginning of 1886 a turning point was reached in the history of the Afrikaner Bond. With provincial *besturen* now functioning in the Cape, Orange Free State and Transvaal, it was poised to become a truly inter-territorial party once the Central *Bestuur*, which was due to meet in February, had promulgated a general constitution. Yet the moment could hardly have been less propitious for such a crowning ceremony. The manifest failure of the Bond to control and turn to its advantage the recent border crises, especially that in Bechuanaland, was a bad omen for any future attempt to give expression to the pan-Afrikaner ideal. The Warren expedition had gone far to dispel the clouds of glory which had hung for five years round the summit of Majuba, and the Imperial factor, re-established in Basutoland and on the Transvaal's western border, seemed to be in full command once more. Equally significantly, the sustained economic depression which had hit South Africa during the early eighties made further inroads into the pan-Afrikaner movement in two main directions: it drew attention to the conflict of economic interests between the several South African states, both before and after the discovery of gold on the Witwatersrand, thus driving a wedge between the Bond's various 'provinces'; and at the same time it drew the Dutch and English farmers of the Cape Colony together in a common attempt to deal with their agricultural problems, dousing the bright flame of national feeling with the cold water of economic need.

The six Bondsmen who met at Bloemfontein on 17 February as

the first representative Central *Bestuur*[*1] seem hardly to have been aware that it was no longer possible to take the inter-territorial structure of the Bond for granted. They used the powers given to them under the general constitution approved at Richmond not only to ratify that constitution but to amend it, bringing back the contentious word *einddoel* ('final goal') to define the Bond's attitude to South African union, and even toying with the expression *onder eigen vlag*.[2] After reviewing current political developments in South Africa, they issued a pastoral letter (*Bondsbrief*) for circulation to all branches, in which they referred to the desirability of a South African customs union in terms which criticized the tariff policies of the Cape.

No wonder the *Zuid Afrikaan*, in a very critical editorial, raised the question whether so small a *bestuur* ought to have so much uncontrolled authority.* The Murraysburg Bondsmen took to the Grahamstown congress, which assembled in March, a proposal that the Central *Bestuur* should be abolished and replaced by liaison committees in the various 'provinces'. The proposal was defeated, but it received much support, and Congress resolved firmly that the united South Africa to which it looked forward was to be 'under British protection'.* The Central *Bestuur* thus survived, but as shadow rather than substance, as the events of the following year would demonstrate.

To appreciate the Cape Bondsmen's lack of ideological fervour in 1886, it is helpful to note the extent to which they were caught in the toils of depression. The statistics are striking. Wool exports, which had exceeded £3,000,000 in value in the early seventies, had fallen from £2,400,000 in 1880 to £1,400,000 in 1885: the wool farmers had been afflicted by drought and had failed to combat the ravages of burr-weed (*Xanthium spinosum*) and scab.* Ostrich feather exports, which had reached a record value of £1,000,000 in 1882, had fallen to barely half that figure in 1886: over-production was one cause of distress, as is suggested by the dramatic increase of insolvencies in the Oudtshoorn district in the boom year 1882.* Wheat

---

[1] They were S. J. du Toit and P. J. Joubert, representing the Transvaal; J. G. Grabe and C. J. Visser, representing the Orange Free State; and D. F. du Toit and T. P. Theron representing the Cape Colony. S. J. du Toit was elected to the chair.

[2] See above, pp. 66–9.

imports, which varied inversely with the Colonial crop, rose to the unusually large quantity of over 40,000,000 lb. in the years 1882–4, and reached a record figure of 52,000,000 lb. in 1885: the wheat farmers were victims of a succession of bad seasons, during which the crops gathered were sometimes hardly equal to the quantity of seed sown.* The importation of agricultural implements and machinery, which had reached a peak in 1880, had almost stopped by 1884.

One consequence of the depression was the sudden imposition of a credit squeeze by the banks, whose discounts were reduced in 1881–4 by nearly 50 per cent, leading to a threefold increase in the Colonial insolvency rate.[1] Though the traditional picture of the platteland farmer as one reared on a subsistence economy is largely correct, it should not be imagined that he was untouched by the system of easy credit which had grown up during the seventies. The newspapers of those years carried large pictorial advertisements (in both languages) of expensive agricultural machinery, and when Oom Daantje van den Heever visited Cape Town in January 1881 he was given special instructions to call on the sellers of such machinery. Moreover, farmers were as often the victims of other people's speculations as their own, as the *Argus* indicated in January 1882:

'We have been accustomed to say that commercial disturbance was purely local, and strictly confined to the circle of those affected by speculation in diamond scrip; but we are sorry to see disproof of that position in the very large proportion of farmers to be found amongst the insolvents. The immediate causes of these agricultural insolvencies are twofold—pressure from the storekeepers, who in their turn have been pressed by the town merchants, and unexpected pressure from the banks who had hitherto made advances freely upon what may be called ostrich scrip.'*

Of the 250 insolvents whose occupations were published by the *Zuid Afrikaan* during the first quarter of 1883, 113 were farmers; and it seems unlikely that the Dutch farmers fared any better than their English-speaking fellows, if the insolvency rate in some of the

[1] On 31 Dec. 1881, the total discounts on issue by the banks amounted to £1,050,000. This figure was steadily reduced to £310,000 by 31 Dec. 1886. Insolvencies, which had always totalled less than 400 in the years 1876–81, rose to 1,000 in 1883.

worst hit and predominantly Dutch farming districts is taken into account.*

To add to the difficulties of the farmers, the pressure on the land was also becoming more acute. The impoverishment of farmers consequent upon repeated subdivisions of the original farms had caused some alarm in the early seventies. The first reference to the poor-white problem at a Bond congress was made in 1884, at a time when the farmers knew that, bar unexpected windfalls, the frontiers of settlement were now closed.

The farmers recovered rather more slowly from the depression than did the commercial firms, and continued to preach retrenchment as late as 1887, at a time when other interests were being quickened by the gold discoveries on the Rand. Their doctrine of retrenchment did not stand alone, but was accompanied by a persistent demand that the farming interest ought, like a poor relation, to be the recipient of special favours: of government loans on first mortgages, drawn on the security of their farms and repaid on sinking-fund principles—as urged at the Bond congresses of 1886 and 1887, and in Parliament by M. M. Venter;* of state-aided irrigation schemes; and—a hardy annual—of railway branch lines.

The protective policy to which the Cape farmers adhered was inspired in large measure by the tariff policy of the Transvaal, which raised walls against imported produce of many kinds, and linked these with an internal system of monopolies—for example the brandy monopoly sold to A. H. Nellmapius—which directly affected the markets of Cape producers.* Transvaal brandy, distilled from non-grape products and excise-free, was not only protected on its home ground but threatened to impinge on Colonial markets, at a time when the Colonial producers of the genuine article were having to face competition from the local producers of *dop*. No wonder that the item of imported liquor received special attention at the Bond congress of 1884.* There was some opposition among the Bondsmen to a tax on essential foods, and the principle of a sliding scale found support among them; but, as will be shown below, the corn producers were so concerned over the importation of grain from the inland states that when the last opportunity arose for the Cape to enter a South African customs union (before the discovery of gold on the Rand made it virtually impossible to do so advantageously), the wheat farmers caused the chance to be thrown away.

II. A HOUSE DIVIDED

Before the discovery of gold on the Rand, the desire for economic federation was never sufficiently universal among the states of South Africa for its achievement to appear probable. Natal and the Cape each tried to bring the Free State within its own sphere of influence, to the exclusion or at least the embarrassment of the other. The Free State, meanwhile, obliged like the Transvaal to pay duty as well as freight charges on its own imports without benefit to its treasury, was only interested in a system of internal free trade which neither coastal colony would have. President Brand's call for a customs conference in 1884 therefore met with no response from the colonial governments, at a time when Kruger was busy negotiating for a railway of his own from Lourenço Marques. However, there was some doubt in the middle of 1885 whether Kruger's Delagoa Bay project would materialize, and in July Kruger sent the financier Sammy Marks to sound the Cape Government about the possibility of a customs agreement, following this with an offer to remove the duty from Colonial brandy and wagons if the Cape would reciprocate by giving free entry to Transvaal tobacco.* Upington's reply was extremely cautious; but in January 1886 he was subjected to pressure from both the Free State and the Transvaal. Brand wrote to Sir Hercules Robinson on the 8th, suggesting a conference for the discussion of a *Zollverein*, on the basis of an equitable distribution of customs dues between the coastal and inland governments, while Kruger sent his Chief Justice to Cape Town to discuss mutual free trade and the extension of the Kimberley railway to Pretoria.* The Central *Bestuur* of the Afrikaner Bond, at its Bloemfontein meeting in February, supported the idea of a customs union on the broadest possible basis.*

Had the Cape wished for a customs union, therefore, it seems to have been there for the taking. But Upington, under the influence of Robinson and Sprigg, fought shy, and no strong free trade movement developed in the Colony to force his hand. The Afrikaner Bond was conspicuously backward in coming forward. Though we are told that in 1884 Hofmeyr favoured an agreement with the Free State which could later be extended to the other states, and that early in 1887 he 'came prominently forward' in favour of a general union,* there is nothing to suggest that he was at all prominent during the first half of 1886, which was, from the Cape's point of view, the crucial period. Nor did the Cape Bondsmen even discuss the Central

Bestuur's resolution of 17 February when they met in Grahamstown on 22 March.

Most of the opposition to a customs union came from the Cape farming interests, especially the wheat growers. Thomas Louw, a Bond member for Malmesbury, asked the Prime Minister on 4 May whether he was aware that grain from across the border—which Upington interpreted as meaning from the Free State and Basuto-land—was flooding the market at the diamond fields. Upington replied that he was, tabled papers which had passed between the Colonial and republican governments on the subject of tariff policy,* and undertook to make certain proposals when members had had a chance to study the papers. The outcome was his motion of 20 May, for which he took good care to obtain Bond acquiescence by asking Theron to act as his seconder:

'That the Government be empowered to appoint a person or persons who shall be authorised to act with persons appointed by the neighbouring States and Colonies in any inquiry which may be held into the question of Border Customs and Duties: Provided that such person or persons so appointed by the Government shall not have authority to bind this Colony, but shall report to Parliament, for its decision thereon, the result of such inquiry.'

In his supporting speech, Upington ruled out discussion of the customs duties at the ports and defended their exclusion from the motion on the ground that the Cape had never admitted the principle that the inland states had any claim on these, thus rejecting out of hand the main argument on which the Free State's case rested.* All he was prepared to empower Colonial representatives to recommend was the adjustment, removal, or possibly even the increase of border dues, affecting only that part of the trade between the South African states which concerned locally produced goods—Transvaal and Free State tobacco for example, brandy, and, most important, wheat. It was unfortunate for the economic growth and the political harmony of South Africa that at this particularly favourable moment for the establishment of a customs union, a counter-agitation should have been set in motion for the protection of Colonial grain, fostered by the Prime Minister of the Cape, who himself represented an important grain-producing district.* During the ensuing debate some speakers, notably Scanlen and Rhodes, criticized Upington's speech for its excessive caution; but Rhodes's attitude was very inconsistent,* no opposition member was sufficiently convinced of the need for a customs union to call for a division, and no Bondsman spoke at all. The *Zuid Afrikaan's* editorials of 22 and 26 May, with which Hofmeyr was presumably in agreement, had no constructive proposals to offer. The writer recognized Delagoa Bay as being the 'natural harbour' of the South African Republic, and ruled out the extension of the railway from Kimberley as lying outside the scope of practical politics. He approved Upington's motion, provided that the Cape sent to the suggested customs conference a representative who appreciated the point of view of the Transvaal. He warned that there were certain aspects of the Cape's existing policy from which no departure could be made—one is left to infer that the protection of certain producer interests was intended; and finally, after acknowledging Rhodes's point that increased ties of sentiment would contribute to South African union, and after rejecting his further point that something constructive should be done to tie the commerce of the Cape and the Transvaal together, he diverted his argument to a discussion of native policy: if only, he wrote, the Cape would shed a tradition associated with the names of Wilberforce and Burke, it would be able (after losing the commercial leadership) to assume the moral leadership of South Africa in the one big question which concerned all states, namely 'who will be *baas*, Colonists or Natives'. No wonder the Bond had nothing to offer, when its most responsible newspaper evaded the issue like this.

After the end of the parliamentary session, the Government set about implementing the resolution of 20 May by requesting the High Commissioner to communicate with the heads of the Free State, Natal and Transvaal governments and to seek their co-operation over the holding of a customs conference. These overtures failed. The Free State was vaguely interested, Natal not at all, while the Transvaal, in a position to bargain as never before because gold was now known to exist in large quantities on the Witwatersrand, treated the Cape to a blunt refusal.*

III. LINKS OF IRON AND A GOLDEN CHAIN

The Transvaal Bond leaders, even after the discovery of gold, pressed Kruger to accept a rail link with the Cape and opposed his plan to establish a line from Delagoa bay, which had been entrusted to a Dutch firm, the Netherlands South African Railway Company. Their motive was not entirely above suspicion, for both S. J. du Toit and Piet Joubert had an interest in the firm of Lewis and Marks, which was trying to obtain the contract for a Kimberley extension.* Their criticism of the Kruger regime, which had stemmed from the Stellaland episode of October 1884, now included a growing antagonism to the concession policy,* and a growing resentment at the influence of a 'Hollanderkliek' in the affairs of state. But it is ironical that in the middle months of 1886, when it was clearly to the Cape's advantage to press for closer economic ties with the Transvaal, the Transvaal members of the Bond should have looked after the long-term Cape interests better than the Cape members did themselves. The Zuid Afrikaan persisted in the view that it was in Kruger's interest to work with the Netherlands Company and not with Lewis and Marks, and rebuked the Patriot as late as October 1886 for suggesting that the Kruger regime was tottering to its fall.*

The gold discoveries, however, worked a change in the outlook of Colonial Bondsmen, for not much time was to elapse before several of their more prominent members began to speculate on the Rand. S. J. du Toit related how, at the tail end of the rush, a Paarl syndicate was able to buy part of the farm Langlaagte for £8,000 cash down, on the basis of which transaction the Paarl-Pretoria Company and the Langlaagte Estate Mines were established.* Further light is shed on the speculative activities of Cape Afrikaners in the memoirs of Charles Kohler, who collaborated with D. F. du Toit to form a syndicate with a capital of £6,000. Both men went to the Transvaal; but after they had quarrelled Du Toit was obliged to return, while Kohler remained to collect unto himself the managership not only of their syndicate, now called the National Gold Mining Company, but of the Aurora and the Paarl-Pretoria as well.* Daniel Malan, father of F. S. Malan who became a leading Bondsman in the nineties, went from Paarl to the Rand in 1887 to study the prospects.* Thomas te Water, a leading Bondsman from Graaff-Reinet, bought shares in Paarl-Pretoria, for which he paid the last instalment in April 1888.* The first evidence that comes to light regarding Hofmeyr's interests is from the end of 1888, when he already possessed a number of well-spread investments on the Rand and a knowledge of the share market which suggests that he was not new to the game. He was investing through a broker in Kimberley, and in collaboration with Rhodes.*

It would have been surprising if, in the light of the new opportunities, the Cape Bondsmen had not changed their political tune. The

first clear indication of a change came when the Cape Town branch
approached the Government in January 1887, and asked it to press
for immediate negotiations with the Transvaal Government for the
extension of the Kimberley railway and the laying of plans for an
eventual customs union.* Sprigg, who had taken over the leadership
of the Government, needed no convincing, and decided to send a
deputation to Pretoria. Colonel Schermbrucker, the Commissioner,
was chosen to negotiate and David de Waal, who no doubt had a
watching brief over the interests of the Colonial farmers, was
appointed as his interpreter.

The change of heart which had occurred within the Cape Town
Bond was matched by a more constant enthusiasm in the Central
Bestuur, which issued a second *Bondsbrief* on 17 February over the
signatures of S. J. du Toit and T. P. Theron, interpreting the signs
of the times to its no doubt confused provincial bodies with an air of
unmitigated optimism.* It had held no meeting 'on account of
various hindrances', but it was moved to state that the gold discoveries would not threaten the Bond's 'youthful, highly promising
nationalism', or divert it from its goal of a united South Africa. They
had striven hard towards such a goal in the past without much
apparent success, ran the message; 'but now there comes a Higher
Hand, which governs the destiny of Peoples and States, and wills to
bind us to each other with a *golden chain*'.[1] Their objective should be
a customs union, governing at least the internal trade of South
Africa, and—if certain practical difficulties could be overcome—its
overseas trade as well. Meanwhile the Bond should press for the
building of a single line of railway 'from the Cape to Delagoa Bay',
passing through the Orange Free State, to which other junction lines
could be added in due course. The Cape provincial *bestuur*, meeting
in March, did not exhibit the same keenness for a railway; but it
considered the formation of a customs union, to include even an
agreement for the more equitable distribution of port revenues, 'not
only desirable but necessary'.* In April the Transvaal provincial
bestuur followed suit.*

For all their increased interest in economic federation and the
Rand, however, the Colonial Bondsmen had played their cards too
late, as can be plainly seen from the pages of Schermbrucker's
report, made on his return from Pretoria and Bloemfontein in April.*

---

[1] 'Nu komt een Hooger Hand, die het lot van Volken en Staten regelt, en wil
ons met een *gouden keten* aan elkander verbinden.'

Kruger and he had found little difficulty in reaching a basis for negotiation on tariff questions; but Kruger had refused either to enter into any sort of customs union or to countenance the extension of any Cape railway into his country, because the Delagoa line seemed likely to move ahead again under the stimulus of the gold discoveries. The Colonial envoys had met the usual courtesy and the usual hard bargaining from President Brand, who had insisted on complete free trade across the border, and would only meet the Cape's desire to build a railway through his state if he were given an equal share in the port customs on goods destined for his country. The Cape had lost the initiative, but the situation was not entirely hopeless, for there was still substantial agreement within the Bond over the desirability of a customs union.

The Cape Town Bondsmen, trading on this, approached Kruger and the Bond in Pretoria in August, with a memorial in support of free trade between the Colony and the Transvaal. They intimated that, while not wishing to stand in the way of the Delagoa Bay railway, they desired also to construct a line through the Free State to the Transvaal.* But Kruger not only turned down their overtures in his reply of 21 September, but withstood the attempts of the Transvaal Bond leaders to make him change his mind. When Joubert and Du Toit decided to appeal to the party members and convened an extraordinary Bond congress at Potchefstroom in November 1887, they obtained the necessary support for a customs union, but found to their dismay that the rank and file favoured Kruger's railway policy—a policy for which he had as good as won Brand's support by persuading him, on a visit to Bloemfontein in October, not to allow the extension of any railway northwards from Bloemfontein for ten years.* Kruger, having turned the Transvaal Bondsmen against their leaders, was therefore in a strong position to turn down an invitation from Sprigg to send representatives to a customs and railway conference in Cape Town in January 1888.

This Cape Town conference, which was called to clear the ground for a proper customs and railway agreement, was, however, attended by delegates from the Free State and Natal. The Natal Legislative Council subsequently withdrew its support on the ground that the tariff rates proposed were too high. But the conference did reach tentative agreement on tariff rates, at least so far as the Cape and the Free State were concerned, and on the desirability of railways entering the Free State from the Cape and Natal sides. In May the

Cape Bondsmen supported these recommendations,* but in the knowledge that the Free State Bondsmen, who had met in congress at Kroonstad in January, were now as opposed to having a Cape railway in their territory as the Transvaal Bondsmen were to having one in theirs.* Had they possessed slightly greater strength in the Volksraad, the Free State Bondsmen would have been able to destroy the provisional railway proposals accepted at Cape Town. As it was, though a motion for a customs union was carried by a fair majority, another to authorize a railway survey was passed only with the chairman's casting vote.* This movement of Free State opinion towards the idea of closer economic union with the Transvaal was an understandable consequence of the gold discoveries, and it gave the Cape little reason for satisfaction, especially when Brand, whose sympathies lay towards the Cape, died in office in July 1888.

When Sprigg faced the Cape Parliament in the same month, he had no difficulty in winning support for a Bill to authorize a customs union with the Free State; but the railway problem raised difficult tactical issues. Extension from the railhead at Colesberg to the Orange River offered no certain prospects of a line into the Free State while the anti-railway forces there were so strong. But it might be coupled with extension from Kimberley to the Vaal, which implied a threat to circumvent the Free State should Kruger ever decide to admit a Cape line to his own territory; and if Kruger refused, the Kimberley line could be extended along the western border of the Transvaal northwards in the direction of Matabeleland, where prospectors were already busy. Sprigg proposed that both the Colesberg and the Kimberley extensions should be undertaken. Hofmeyr, with the backing of most of the Bondsmen, was more anxious to establish free trade with the Transvaal than to risk the loss of it by provocative railway building. He made very careful soundings of responsible opinion in both Republics, and reached the conclusion that the risks involved in Sprigg's policy were too great.* S. J. du Toit, however, identified himself with Sprigg's policy of forcing Kruger's hand, and he threatened that he and his brother would work through the *Patriot* against any efforts that might be made to oppose it:

'You really must believe me,' he wrote, 'we are not doing this out of a desire to be awkward. But until the neck of Kruger's policy is broken all your beautiful plans are so many soap bubbles. Sprigg's policy will undermine Kruger's; but the policy now followed among our people gives Kruger and his Hollanders a dictatorship not only over the Transvaal but over the whole of South Africa.'*

But Onze Jan was unmoved. On 18 July, during the debate in committee, he had attempted to insert a proviso into the Railway Bill whereby, should the Transvaal Government obtain authority to introduce free trade with the Colony by 1 October, the Kimberley extension would be held up pending further consideration by Parliament. This he subsequently withdrew in favour of an alternative proviso by Theron, designed to apply pressure not only to the Transvaal in respect of free trade, but also to the Free State in respect of its own railway undertakings, and giving both Republics until 31 December to make up their minds. Rhodes, in cautious mood, also supported the Theron proviso, banking on the chance that the Delagoa Bay railway would not after all materialize;* but the proviso was rejected in committee and again at the third reading by a margin of twenty-four and sixteen votes respectively.* Sprigg and the majority had decided that Kruger's hand could be forced by a firm decision.

S. J. du Toit was right in his view that Kruger would not welcome a strong policy in the Cape. The thought of a railway outside his control, running along the western border of the Transvaal and tapping its trade, did not please him, especially during the year in which Colonial concession hunters, Rhodes among them, were beginning to show an active interest in 'the North'. He therefore appealed to the Cape Government not to begin operations on this line until he had been given a chance to persuade the Free State Volksraad, which was due to meet in January 1889, to authorize the extension of the Colesberg line at least to Bloemfontein.* Kruger was as good as his word. The anti-railway forces which attended the special Volksraad meeting in Bloemfontein, convened primarily to install F.W. Reitz as President, were well organized and might well have carried the day; but the initiative was taken from them by a well-timed telegram from Kruger urging the Free Staters to allow the construction of a line as far as their capital—a telegram inspired in the first instance by Hofmeyr, who with the help of Ewald Esselen in Pretoria had persuaded Kruger to take this step.* Reitz in fact went further, and when Sprigg visited Bloemfontein in the same month he was able to persuade the new President to convene a customs conference there, to be held in March.

Ironically, Sprigg abandoned his strong railway policy before the fruits of it began to fall into his lap, for the idea of a railway through Bechuanaland released a flood of humanitarian objections in Britain,* and this, combined with the disapproval of the Bondsmen, had the effect of pushing him into less adventurous paths. This however helped him little, because the doughty Transvaal President, encouraged by the information that the Portuguese Government was about to clean up the incompetent railway company responsible for the Moçambique end of the Delagoa Bay–Pretoria line, had decided to put on a bold front again. Freed from the danger of a line along his western border, he now resumed his efforts to block the approach of a line through the Free State. He met Reitz at Potchefstroom on 4 March and concluded a defensive alliance and commercial treaty with the Free State, together with a railway agreement under which both states undertook to act in consultation with each other, and not to permit any other rail links through their territories save the Delagoa, Harrismith and Colesberg lines, while Kruger made it clear that he did not want the Colesberg extension to proceed beyond Bloemfontein until the Delagoa line was sufficiently well advanced to reach Pretoria first.* Only then would he agree to have a Cape line, or to allow Cape products into the Transvaal duty free. Reitz could not persuade him to send a delegation to the Bloemfontein customs conference due to be held at the end of the month.

The Colonial Bondsmen, meeting at Middelburg from the 4th to the 8th, still wanted a customs union and the extension of the Colesberg railway 'without delay towards the Transvaal'.* They stood four-square behind Sprigg's modified policy, and gave the Cape delegation a strong hand when it met those from the Free State and Natal in Bloemfontein on the 20th. Although the Natalians once again refused to enter a customs union because the Cape and the Free State insisted on too high a transit tariff, and on too large a share of that tariff for the inland republic, the Cape and the Free State decided to ignore this objection, and reached an agreement between themselves on the basis of the Cape Town resolutions of the previous year.

IV. THE COLLAPSE OF THE REPUBLICAN 'PROVINCES'

The customs convention of 1889 affords a convenient resting-point. At long last the negotiations for the economic federation of South Africa had produced one small fruit, though few could pretend that this achievement offered very bright prospects for the future. Natal had elected to go its own way. The South African Republic had not yet deviated from its policy of isolation, though its attempts to bring the Free State over into some sort of partnership vis-à-vis the coastal colonies had achieved only partial success. Though satisfied that one of its railways would now enter the Free State, the Cape had little assurance that this line would one day reach the Rand, and it had been obliged to forgo the extension of its other line in the direction of Bechuanaland and the Zambezi—a region already marked out for exploitation. For these reasons, it would soon become clear that the convention of 1889 was no more than an episode in the railway and customs struggle, a struggle which would soon be further complicated by the intrusion of extraneous issues. But it is important at this stage to reach some conclusion over the use which the Bond had made of this opportunity to give its pan-South African idealism practical expression.

The outstanding fact here is that it had achieved very little, and the incidental reasons for this have been noted in the course of the foregoing narrative. Before the discovery of the Witwatersrand's gold, Republican Bondsmen had been interested in a customs union and Colonial Bondsmen had not. After this discovery, the Colonial Bondsmen became unity-minded, the Free State Bondsmen found an affinity with the Transvaal and turned their backs on the Cape, and too many of the Transvaal Bondsmen found peace of mind in the isolationist policy of their President to support the cause of South African unity to which they were in theory committed.

Lack of statesmanship among the Bond leaders is a fair verdict, provided the Bondsmen are not made to share more of the blame than is their due; other corporate interests had been similarly unforthcoming and even Rhodes had equivocated. So far as the Free State was concerned, local interest and the essential requirements for a pan-South African railway and tariff agreement went hand in hand, and this fact was a real asset to the diplomacy of Brand and Reitz. But even under these favourable circumstances the showing of the Free State Bondsmen was not impressive. They threw up no real leaders during these crucial years, and their hostility to Brand suggests that their antipathy towards him following the Smithfield episode of October 1881 had not been allowed to die down.[1] They sought to throw in their lot with the Transvaal during 1887–8, at a

[1] See above, pp. 47–8.

time when Brand and his successor were trying to reach an agreement which satisfied wider interests, and nearly succeeded in blocking the presidential policy.

In the Transvaal the situation was of unusual interest because there the Bond leadership maintained a consistent opposition to the fiscal, concession and railway policies of the Kruger regime, but failed in the long run to retain the support of the rank and file, as became evident at the Potchefstroom congress of November 1887. This was fatal to S. J. du Toit's position in the councils of the state. Two months afterwards, the Volksraad resolved to deny offices of profit to company directors, and Du Toit, as the chairman of ten, was squeezed out. Kruger reinstated him in his post as Superintendent of Education on the eve of his departure for Europe in 1889; but while Du Toit was in Holland, attending mainly to his business interests, he seems to have tried to ingratiate himself with the Dutch directors of Transvaal enterprises instead of having it out with them, and lost a good deal of face. Kruger continued to treat him with moderation, perhaps because he realized that his bubble was pricked, and allowed him to resume his post on his return in 1890. But in November, by which time his activities in Europe had given rise to a smear campaign against him in the Transvaal, he deemed it wise to return to the Cape, not only discredited but also penniless. The volatile Du Toit was no rival for the ox-like Kruger, who matched him in religiosity and more than matched him in constancy.* Nor was Joubert a rival, after his overwhelming defeat at Kruger's hands in the presidential election of 1888.

The Cape Bondsmen, like the mass of their fellow-Colonials, had missed a favourable opportunity for a railway and customs agreement in 1886, and nothing which they tried to do subsequently could make up for this initial error, though they tried responsibly enough to bring pressure to bear on the Republics once the gold discoveries had provided the incentive. Apart from a certain tardiness to recognize the isolationist possibilities of Kruger's Delagoa Bay scheme, and a reluctance to risk too forthright a railway policy lest this should jeopardize a customs agreement, their support for the Government was consistent but, for the reasons mentioned, not very effective.

The Bond was thus unable to direct the negotiations along lines which harmonized with its own principles because the interests of the 'provinces' were too diverse. But the events made a lasting impression on the Bond itself. By demonstrating how insubstantial the desire for economic integration was, even among Bondsmen, they helped to transform the Bond into a Cape political party, because the effectiveness of the provincial organizations in the Republics was destroyed and the Central *Bestuur* was liquidated. The Free State Bond went into a gradual decline, though it experienced a partial recovery after 1896 during the presidency of M. T. Steyn.* The Transvaal Bond had all but ceased to exist by 1890, and never recovered.* The Central *Bestuur* never met again in its original form, though the Cape continued faithfully to elect its central members in 1888, 1890, and finally in 1896, when the matter was raised for the last time. When the term 'central *bestuur*' was resurrected after the South African war, it applied not to the original body, but to the congress of the Cape Colonial party.*

7

The Consolidation of a Cape Colonial Party

I. AN APPROACH TO ENGLISH FARMERS

THE Bond congress at Beaufort West in March 1885 instructed its secretary, Thomas Theron, to write to the chairman of the congress of English-speaking farmers' associations, Arthur Douglass of Grahamstown, inviting their general co-operation.* Douglass duly placed Theron's letter before the farmers' congress at Port Elizabeth in March 1886, whereupon the secretary of the congress gave an account of the earlier negotiations between the Dutch- and English-speaking bodies. He had first approached Hofmeyr in 1883, he said, and Hofmeyr had then agreed to co-operate but not to amalgamate 'as he stated that would be impossible on account of the differences of language'. Onze Jan had, however, promised to 'draw up a document' as a basis for joint action, but owing to the untimely death of his wife this had never been done.* Subsequent speakers betrayed considerable anxiety over the close relationship existing between the Colonial Bond and its branches in the Republics, and over its attitude to the flag, and for these reasons the Port Elizabeth congress decided to return a guarded answer to Theron, suggesting that the respective presidents should arrange 'the preliminaries . . . for a conference of a deputation from each', without either body being committed to anything.

The Bondsmen accepted the proposal at their congress in Grahamstown the same month,* and a small conference was arranged between five Bondsmen and three representatives of the farmers' associations in Grahamstown at the beginning of April.* The atmosphere was rather stiff. The representatives of each group agreed that the other should be represented at its congresses, with the right to speak but not to vote. They also discussed the question

111

of amalgamation, but they had not been authorized to take positive steps and therefore could not do so, though the Bondsmen went out of their way to assure the associations' representatives that they did not intend to get rid of the Union Jack, and Theron went so far as to say that 'the Bond was now no longer a political union properly so called, but one for the maintenance of farming interests'.[1] The establishment of a white farmers' party appeared to be on the horizon.

The farmers had been drawn together by a common anxiety over tariff policy, and by the depression and its effects. Rural crime, more especially stock-thieving, was on the increase, and prosecutions under the master and servant and pass laws had reached abnormally high levels in the early eighties.* The amalgamation of the Bond and the farmers' associations would have been a logical step for the farming community to take if they intended to remedy their difficulties by parliamentary action. Yet, although no English-speaking political movements which were inspired by any appreciable degree of ethnic fervour came into existence between the collapse of the Imperial League in 1885 and the formation of the first Progressive Party in 1893,* and although fraternization regularly took place between the Bond and the farmers' congress in the years 1886 to 1891, no amalgamation took place. The embers of the mutual suspicion which had been aroused by the events of the preceding decade between people of Dutch and English speech had not really been allowed to die down. By 1886 there is reason to believe that the Boer's fear of British imperialism and the English-speaking Colonial's fear of exclusive Afrikaner nationalism were on the wane; but they continued to keep each other at arm's length because of the influence of other less tangible differences which stemmed from the roots of their different cultures. Neither the Bond nor the farmers' congress followed up the Grahamstown overtures by encouraging the free use of both official languages at its own meetings, though in this respect the Bond went further than the English farmers.* Bond representatives were sometimes made to feel unwanted at farmers' congress meetings—notably in 1889, when a delegate from the Zwartruggens Association queried the right of Dolf Botha and Thomas Theron to speak and vote. When the same person later wrote to Te Water to invite him to join the Zwartruggens Association, the latter declined

---

[1] 'De Bond was thans niet eenmaal een eigenlijke politieke vereeniging meer, maar een tot handhaving van boerenbelangen.'

for fear of introducing a 'discordant element'.*

Boer and Settler each set much store by his group loyalties, and each, in his own way, betrayed a feeling of insecurity by doing so. The Boer, aware of his comparative lack of sophistication, and mistrustful of his ability to hold his own in debate with the self-confident Englishman, found safety of a sort in group isolation behind the protective shield of his own resurgent culture, which focused on the campaign for the extension of Dutch-language rights. The English-speaker, on his part, feared numerical swamping, and this fear resulted in a tendency to belittle the Boer as a narrow, unenlightened person who could not be trusted to govern the country in a responsible manner. Furthermore, the play of colour attitudes upon this sensitive lens of white group relationships exposed those relationships to too fierce a glare, and exaggerated the contrasts in attitude in an unfortunate way. The very existence of Afrikaner nationalism often forced the English Colonial, for reasons of self-defence, into the position of the *kafferboetie* ('black man's pal'), and invited him to enjoy the advantages of a liberalism which in many cases was probably no more than a pose. To speak the language of the enlightened without assimilating the philosophy was to play Tartufe, as the Boer did not hesitate to remind such people. But the Bondsman who assumed as a matter of course that the man of colour was his political adversary, and refused to question those social attitudes which had led to this result, had no real cause for complaint.

II. OBSTACLE RACE

It would be invidious and probably impossible to draw a rigid distinction between the attitudes of English- and Dutch-speaking Cape Colonials on social questions connected with race relations during the late nineteenth century; but if we are to have a clear understanding of the environment in which the Cape Bond developed its distinctive political programme on racial matters, we must at least allow the evidence to speak for itself. On such matters as pass legislation, stock thieving, squatting, and other questions of pressing importance to the farmer, a complete range of views could and did find expression at congresses of the Bond and of the farmers' associations, varying from the humane to the brutal in both cases. An analysis which takes these into account for other than purely illustrative reasons would therefore lead nowhere; but where congresses took decisions on particular questions, these at least had some claim to be representative, and may be treated—with reservation—as indicative of the attitude of the group as a whole. When this criterion is employed, certain differences between the viewpoint of the Afrikaner Bond and that of the farmers' congress do emerge.

The question of the administration of justice in country districts is a case in point. Bondsmen frequently harked back to the tradition, killed with good reason in the 1820's, under which powers of petty criminal jurisdiction had been entrusted to untrained white field-cornets. This was a matter to which the Colonial legislators had given considerable attention. Because of the sheer inaccessibility of justice in the remoter parts, a situation had resulted where, in the words of a select committee appointed in 1880, 'much crime goes unpunished . . . and there is a strong temptation to farmers . . . to take the law into their own hands, or to compromise with accused'.* To meet this difficulty, Parliament had authorized the appointment of special justices of the peace in 1876, and entrusted these officers with petty master and servant jurisdiction in 1882;* but it would go no further, though Bondsmen urged the restoration of the judicial authority of field-cornets at nearly every congress between 1884 and 1889, and attempted to introduce legislation in Parliament with this probable object.* No such demand emanated from the farmers' associations, which looked rather to improvements in the field-cornet's conditions of service and to an enhancing of the dignity of the office by the appointment of 'proper persons' to it.*

The Bondsmen seem, on the whole, to have been less sympathetic than the English farmers to the divisional police system which operated in the Colony. They liked to take justice into their own hands, thought that they could apprehend criminals more effectively than the professional police, resented the cost of local forces, and often advanced the view that the local forces should either be abolished or brought under the control of the divisional councils.* The farmers' congress, on the other hand, periodically asked for an increase in the local police establishment, together with improved methods of detecting crime and the grant of wider powers of search.*

There was wide agreement among the farmers of both language groups that when an accused servant had been found guilty in the magistrate's court he should be given corporal punishment rather than the statutory sentence of a fine or imprisonment. They claimed, with a good deal of justification, that the existing penalties were liable to hurt the farmer without having an obviously corrective value for the miscreant; but they sometimes ruined a good case by arguing that the lash was suitable for the black man but unsuitable for the white, or by contending on insufficient grounds that the courts administered the law to the disadvantage of the white man.* Frustrated Bondsmen and English farmers might suggest savage punishments for stock thefts, but both bodies in congress rejected the proposals of these angry individuals.* Yet when P. J. du Toit, a Bondsman, introduced his notorious 'Strop Bill' in the session of 1890, no English-speaking farmer voted in favour of it, whereas nearly all the Bond members did.[1]

An affinity of language and a long association bound the Boer and the Coloured man together, and militated to some extent against the rigidly hierarchical social order which had developed over the years in western-Cape society. Such a relationship lay largely outside the experience of the English-speaking farmer, who had more contact with the native African of the frontier districts. But Dutch-speaking farmers also had widespread contact with Africans, with whom, as was the case with the Settlers, they had no intimate cultural bonds—they had only a memory, and that a very recent one, of conflict over land and stock, which merged into an actual fear of further hostilities in the future. Both groups, therefore, adjusted themselves to the blacks under what might be described as equal conditions. But the English-speaking community made closer contact with Africans than did the Boers, and generally acquired a better understanding of tribal ways. This is not altogether surprising. The English missionaries were active among them, whereas all Dutch Reformed missionary activity within South Africa was directed towards the Coloured people. Political factors, as will be noted later, had a moderating influence on the English-speaker's attitude towards the African.[1] The Boers, for their part, tended to look upon the African less as a challenge to their civilizing mission than as a standing threat to their security, and consequently developed no native policy which deserved the name of coherent, because they were unable to disentangle the problems involved from considerations of their own group interests. It is possible to suggest this broad distinction between Boer and Settler views because on certain key issues the reactions of the Afrikaner Bond and of the farmers' associations

[1] Rhodes supported the 'Strop Bill'. Hofmeyr abstained.
[2] See below, pp. 118–20.

were significantly different.

Both bodies, it should be emphasized, desired to preserve and tighten the pass laws. The system of passes for Africans, which had first been instituted to protect the Colonial Fingo from 'being mistaken for Kaffirs[1] and thereby aggrieved', had developed into an instrument 'for the better protection of property',* and farmers of both language groups were very anxious to maintain it for this purpose. They wanted a sure means of knowing whether an African seen driving cattle was on bona fide business or absconding with somebody else's stock.*

But Bondsmen and congress men differed in their attitude to African squatting in white farming areas. In 1884 the Bond congress carried a resolution to permit squatting only in cases where the landowner could show his squatters' means of livelihood, and where he accepted liability for stock losses in the neighbourhood.* An Act of Parliament the same year made it unlawful to establish new locations without the agreement of the divisional council and the permission of the Governor.* But the Bond congresses wished, further, to penalize individuals who maintained squatters on their land, and to place all locations under the supervision of the divisional police.* To a considerable extent their demands were met by a further law in 1892, which made the revocation of location licences possible, limited the number of adult males in any one location to forty, and compelled the owners to keep up-to-date registers of the huts, the occupants and their stock.* Thus encouraged, the Bondsmen became more forthright in their demands, and in 1893 they accepted a motion from Albany and Albert which urged the Government to abolish locations which already existed.* The Government referred the matter to a select committee of the Assembly, which reported unfavourably.* In seeking to remove this sort of 'nuisance' by legislative action, the Bondsmen exhibited a naïve misapprehension of the real nature of the problem, as was shown in the evidence led before the select committee by P. J. du Toit, the chairman of the provincial *bestuur*, when he was examined on the subject of the congress debate:

'Was any suggestion made as to what is to be done with natives turned off farms?—No. That did not come before the Congress.

'Does it not occur to you that there would be some difficulty in

---

[1] i.e. immigrants from across the frontier.

providing for such a large number of natives as would be likely to be turned off?—No. There was nothing brought forward with reference to that.'*

A good many of the Bondsmen hoped that the abolition of the locations would force more Africans on to the labour market by making them dependent on the mercy of some farmer for a place of abode; but this was no way to approach the problem of the farm-labour shortage, as a select committee appointed in 1892 firmly emphasized.* The farmers' associations might urge, as they did in 1886, that squatters should be compelled to take out individual titles or depart, or they might call for the registration of location stock, as they did in 1889; but when a motion came up in 1889 to prohibit squatting they threw it out.*

Bond congresses consistently and fervently demanded a reduction in the amount of public money expended on native education.* Their attitude was governed by the argument that, as the education budget was limited, a greater proportion of the funds available ought to be devoted to the third-class rural and district boarding schools, upon which many sons of Boers were dependent for such education as they were able to receive. Unfortunately, from their point of view, the cost of these schools per pupil was very much greater than that of the public, mission and aborigines' schools which served the mass of the population, and although the education of white children accounted for the greater part of the government expenditure, rural white children certainly received less than was desirable from every point of view.* The farmers' congress took up this issue, sometimes positively by recommending an increase in the grant to rural white schools,* and on one occasion by adopting the Bond's negative approach and urging a reduction in the mission school vote, which the African journalist, Tengo Jabavu, was quick to notice;* but they do not seem to have approached the question with the same intensity of feeling as the Bondsmen. Underlying the Bond attitude—and this was a feeling shared by English-speaking farmers, but not to the same extent—was a repugnance towards the educated African, especially if such a person held a position of authority in relation to the white man and thus disturbed the accepted 'white supremacy' myth. The type of educated African who caused the greatest irritation was the court official who stood between the white citizen and the magistrate, either as clerk or as interpreter*—but only the Boer was likely to need an interpreter.

Both Bondsmen and English farmers expressed the view from time to time that the African child at school represented a direct loss to the farmer's labour supply, and it seems impossible to differentiate between them in this respect.*

Fear for the security of their group, rather than a studied attempt to arrest the development of the African, explains the Bondsmen's attitude over native education. They looked upon the African as a minor and were in no hurry to elevate him to adult status, though it is unlikely that they deliberately calculated to keep African society permanently at the primitive tribal level. They wanted to break up the tribes for military reasons. They wanted African labour. They were offended by certain aspects of tribal custom which seemed to them immoral, such as polygamy and the *lobola* system (*vrouenhandel*, as they termed it), and desired to see them removed. Education in school might not, for a totally different set of reasons, be the proper way to get rid of these practices; but congress after congress believed that they could be removed by some sort of legislative action.* In the late eighties the feeling grew among Bondsmen that the African with more than one wife ought to be denied the vote. In the same crab-like manner, the 1887 congress carried a resolution to deny legal recognition of communal land titles, not with the object of encouraging individual tenure, which they did not wish to force upon the African, but in order to limit the number of Africans possessing the property qualification for the franchise.* Without the same fear of the African vote, the farmers' associations were inclined to encourage individual tenure by Africans, sometimes with the object of forcing them either to accept it or to vacate their holdings to the advantage of potential white buyers, but on at least one occasion for more responsible reasons.*

III.   THE PROBLEM OF THE FRANCHISE

When Bondsmen discussed native policy, their minds were too often preoccupied with the relationship between native policy and political power to view the question objectively. Their tension was unavoidable, given the traditional social values and rigid colour distinctions of Boer society on the one hand, and the egalitarian political system on the other. For the farmers' associations there was no comparable tension, for two main reasons: first, they were not faced with the decision of admitting non-whites to or excluding them from membership, because they were not, strictly speaking, political organizations, and only set out to cater for the needs of farmers as farmers;* in the second place, they did not object to the enfranchisement of non-whites because they knew that a black vote usually meant a vote for the 'English' candidate, and they needed black votes to give them control of several marginal constituencies.

Unencumbered by non-racial franchise laws, the Transvaal and Free State Bond branches wrote a colour bar into their constitutions.* The Cape Bond, after extensive soul-searching and careful calculation, did not. But this decision is to be explained, not in terms of a difference in its basic attitude, but in terms of the necessity for winning non-white support. When the Richmond congress decided in 1883 to leave membership theoretically open to all races, it covered the Bond against the likelihood of its ever becoming a multi-racial party by the very safe step of leaving the right of admission to membership in the hands of the ward *besturen*.* These local committees seldom had to exercise discretion in cases of non-white applications, and when a Coloured man tried to join the Geelhout-boom branch in the Humansdorp district in 1883, the branch's ostentatious refusal to admit him was treated as an object lesson and given prominence by the editors of *De Tolk*.* The Coloured applicant, who seems to have tried to turn his application into a test case, was ceremoniously reprimanded by the chairman, and expelled in company with his white proposer. The branch no more considered that Coloured people ought to be admitted, than the Bond as a whole considered that membership should be extended to women.*

It was to be expected that a party which excluded non-white people from membership would try to reduce the political power of non-white people; but this was difficult to achieve without making the sort of public attack on the existing franchise which would invite non-whites to vote against Bond candidates in elections, and almost certainly deprive the Bond of any chance of winning a parliamentary majority. The balance of power between the Bondsmen and their opponents was always delicate, and the Bondsmen knew that a direct attack on the non-white franchise would fail; but other circumstances, notably the dependence of the Bond on poor-white votes, sealed off the obvious alternative approach—that of standing for higher non-racial qualifications.*

Before we consider the manner in which Bondsmen dealt with the franchise question, it must be emphasized that they tended to assume as a matter of course that the African vote would normally be cast against their candidates, and that they would have to count on the opposition of a high proportion of Coloured voters too. Hofmeyr, who claimed to draw support from Coloured voters in his own constituency, noted in November 1882 that in recent by-elections the Coloured people had been reluctant to support Dutch candidates, and attributed this to a failure of Afrikaner politicians to take sufficient account of the political power of the Coloured people—a shallow diagnosis, but social taboos prevented a frank appraisal.* Immediately after the general election of 1888, a *Patriot* editorial expressed the view that 'in the Western Province the coloured . . . often vote against the boers', though it added with somewhat forced cheerfulness that the Coloured people were not possessed by 'the hatred of boers which inspires the kaffirs'.* The Afrikaner Bond made no serious attempt to win African supporters until the Assembly elections of 1898, and even then its achievements were not impressive.[1] What was worse from their point of view, some Bondsmen suspected their English-speaking opponents of deliberately turning the receptive minds of the Africans against the Colonial Dutch. In December 1881, at a time when feelings ran high, the *Port Elizabeth Telegraph* did exactly this. After arguing against the legalization of the Dutch language on practical grounds, and defending the right of the African to enjoy the franchise because it would give him 'an opportunity of cultivating an intelligent interest in public affairs', the paper went on to state:

'We have continually expressed our conviction that if the Africander Bond is to be well beaten it will have to be done by the assistance of the black vote. Look at the question as we may, we always come back to the fact that the Dutch in the colony are to the English as two to one, and that if they combine they can outvote us, and inflict upon us all the absurdities of their national and economic prejudices. We earnestly hope that the attempt may not be made . . . but we shall not be forced into retrogression without using every legitimate opposition.'*

The *Zuid Afrikaan* reacted sharply to this frank statement of aims.* Yet Hofmeyr and his followers knew that the Bond's policies were not likely to attract the support of the Africans—a truth of which they would in due course be constantly reminded by the editorial activities of Tengo Jabavu, whose King William's Town newspaper,

[1] See below, pp. 184–6.

Imvo Zabantsundu, consistently attacked the Bond, and told its readers on one occasion:

'History shows unmistakably that the votes of the natives have been used discreetly in the best interests of the country and of civilization, and that they have steadily and consistently been employed to strengthen the English or the party of right and justice in the House.'*

The Bondsmen's complaint that African voters could normally be expected to support their opponents was considered by contemporaries of all shades of opinion to reflect the actual situation. The African voters held the balance in several of the eastern constituencies. Thus in the 1888 general election the liberal farmer W. J. Warren headed the poll in King William's Town on the strength of their support, according to the testimony of *Imvo*; Mackay won at Uitenhage for the same reason, on the testimony of the *Uitenhage Times*; and Orpen won in Wodehouse with the aid of a solid African vote, on the testimony of the *Zuid Afrikaan*.* Under these circumstances, it was natural that Bondsmen should try to eliminate African voters from the roll, and equally natural that the Bond's opponents should try to place as many as possible on it. There is plenty of evidence in the records of both kinds of activity,* as also of attempts by both Bondsmen and their opponents to buy the votes of the supposedly more corrupt non-white electorate.*

But the franchise was the key, and Bond congresses devoted a great deal of attention to the problem of raising the qualifications for electors in such a way as to exclude Africans from the vote in practice without appearing to do so in theory. The Cradock congress of 1882 proposed the ownership of land in the Colony as a necessary condition for African enfranchisement but not for white. All kinds of fancy franchises were proposed at Graaff-Reinet in 1884, but no conclusion was reached.* The Bond, it seems, would have had a very slender chance of success but for Upington's incorporation of the Transkei in the Colony in 1885, which placed the whole question in a different perspective by creating the possibility of a vast increase in the number of enfranchised Africans.*

Before Parliament assembled in 1886, the Bondsmen had met in Grahamstown and the farmers' congress in Port Elizabeth. The farmers' congress decided that the question of franchise reform was outside their competence.* The Bondsmen, however, approved higher qualifications and a literacy test, and accepted in substance a proposal, made by Upington during the preceding session but withdrawn after the second reading, for an elective Native Council in the Transkeian territories; but they added the rider that only Transkeian Africans of considerable substance should have a parliamentary vote.* They also urged that communal tenure should cease to be regarded as a qualification for the franchise. Strengthened by this expression of opinion, Upington proposed in 1886 that the Transkei should be represented by two members: one elected by whites possessing the ordinary qualifications and by Africans holding land worth £500 in individual tenure, the other chosen indirectly by a Native Elective Council, itself elected by all male Africans who paid the hut tax. The Bondsmen were satisfied, though Hofmeyr was troubled by the introduction of racial discrimination and supported it only as a temporary measure.* The Opposition, however, rose up in arms, and several representatives of rural as well as urban constituencies gave expression to the pure milk of liberal doctrine. They mustered a narrow majority for a significant amendment before the third reading, and Upington, in disgust, decided to discard the amended Bill.*

When Sprigg, who had in the meantime resumed the premiership, returned to the attack in 1887, he had prepared his ground more carefully. He first asked Parliament to accept a new Registration Bill, which cut some of the ground from under the liberals' feet by re-interpreting the Constitution Ordinance without altering the text, so as to exclude communal tenure from the electoral qualifications, both in the Colony proper and in the Transkei.* Having with difficulty obtained parliamentary support for this, and secured its enactment, he then introduced a Transkeian Representation Bill to give Griqualand East and Tembuland one member each, which became law on 5 August. Sprigg claimed that he had laid his plans without consultation with the Bond; but the Bond's Uitenhage congress had already given its blessing in advance.*

The franchise reforms of 1887 were in essence a compromise. The Bond obtained a safeguard against the likelihood that the voters' roll would be swamped in the foreseeable future by 'blanket' voters; but, as the elections of 1888 indicated, they did not thereby gain any immediate increase of strength in the constituencies. The liberals had failed to prevent a potentially serious limitation in African voting strength, but they had at least frightened the

Government away from the course of naked racial discrimination. The members of the government party who were not Bondsmen, of whom Sprigg was representative, had forced the measure through from a calculation that the distant threat of African political power was a greater danger to their society than the alternative possibility of a Bond majority. Jabavu saw the point when he urged, with a mixture of exaggeration and prophetic insight, that Sprigg's proposals had been put forward 'to weaken and silence the English party in the Legislature by disfranchising its devoted allies, the Natives, and . . . to seal the supremacy of the Bond in the land'.*

IV. CANONS OF FAITH AND ORDER

'I feel more strongly every day that what this poor Colony wants is a strong government', Dormer told Rhodes in September 1888, 'that shall be able to travel along one road or the other—I do not very much care which—without having to ask itself at every turn and corner, not what the verdict of the country will be, but what will be the thought of some irresponsible member of Parliament whose shadow is always interposed between the country and itself. . . . I regard it as treason to the Colony . . . for a man in Hofmeyr's position to endeavour to keep our Executive weak, never knowing whether it stands or falls, when the Executive in the republics is so strong.'*

J. W. Sauer also regretted a situation in which 'office and power are separated'.* Both men disapproved of Hofmeyr's refusal to form a Bond ministry, and both looked to Rhodes to bring office and power together in his own magisterial hands. They did not count their blessings; for the delicate balance of forces in the House of Assembly was the main guarantee against serious discriminatory legislation at the expense of any section of the community during the late nineteenth century. Despite the complaints of Dormer and Sauer, full credit for this state of affairs should not be given to Hofmeyr. Sprigg himself, by shifting his balance alternately between the Bond on the one hand and two mushroom political organizations —the Frontier Party and the Tariff and Excise League*—on the other, was encouraging the instability which these men deplored. Hofmeyr, for his part, told Rhodes that Dormer's account of their conversation was 'not quite correct'.

'*I would be delighted to have a majority*', he added, 'but I never have had a majority in the House and I do not expect to have one next session. There is too much narrow localism and personal feeling in the Afrikander ranks being exhibited in the course of the present elections for that. . . . I now only advise my friends to vote for men with good sound Africander views and independence of feeling who will not pin their faith to either opposition or ministry, but judge for themselves. . . . I see that you will not take office because you would be subject to an "irresponsible majority". Well, that is very much my position. However, do your best and I'll do mine.'*

The general election of 1888 bore out Hofmeyr's gloomy prognosis, but this very fact provided the impetus for a significant change. It was an election like other elections, in that it provided the Bond with substantial strength but no independent majority. The Bond, as the chairman told the Middelburg congress, had shown 'power in numbers and influence, but weakness in discernment and team-work'. He invited the congress to consider how this could be put right.* The details in fact made sorry reading. In the Uitenhage constituency the Bondsmen had been thoroughly outwitted by their opponents.* The two Bond candidates in Graaff-Reinet had struggled home, but only after the outbreak of near-anarchy within their organization,* and much the same had happened in the Richmond constituency. In Cradock, the inefficiency of the chairman and the secretary had led to the election of only one candidate. In another case, Bondsmen had cast their votes against the officially nominated candidate, and there was nothing in the constitution to prevent them from doing so.* A committee of congress recommended a number of constitutional changes designed to obviate a repetition of such occurrences, the most important of which was the appointment of a disciplinary committee, to be known as the *Commissie van Toezicht op Elekties*, which would assume the overall direction of electoral campaigns. These proposals were accepted.*

The *Commissie van Toezicht* was to consist of three Bondsmen. It was to see that nomination meetings were properly called, to call them itself if the local chairman failed in his duty, and to take the initiative in the summoning of circle meetings to nominate candidates for the Upper House. In two further respects it was to be endowed with important discretionary powers: first, all disputes concerning elections could be referred to it by either party in any constituency, and its judgement was to be final. Secondly, if there was no chance of returning a Bondsman to Parliament and there was no properly chosen Bond candidate in the field, the *Commissie* was to have authority, on request by any branch, to direct members to vote for particular non-Bondsmen. The former power would give the *Commissie* complete control over the settlement of nomination disputes, especially when, as often happened in later years, it demanded a written declaration of submission to its authority by both parties before it would agree to arbitrate in any dispute. The second of these powers would give the *Commissie* some initiative in the choice of outside candidates for marginal constituencies, though not as much as Hofmeyr would find he needed in the general election of 1893–4. The first three members of the *Commissie van Toezicht* were J. H. Hofmeyr, R. P. Botha and N. F. de Waal, nominated by the chairman with the assent of the delegates.

Congress dealt with questions of order only after it had disposed of questions of faith. To appreciate the extent of its achievement in this other respect, it is necessary to relate it to a long history of discord within the party ever since S. J. du Toit's original *Program van Beginsels* had been referred by the Graaff-Reinet congress to the branches, and by the Cradock congress to a constitutional commission.[1] Ineffective efforts by the Richmond, second Graaff-Reinet and Beaufort West congresses had led to the appointment of a commission of three (Hofmeyr, D. F. du Toit and J. M. Hoffman), but they reported failure to agree at the Grahamstown congress in 1886.* D. F. du Toit stuck to a bowdlerized version of his brother's earlier draft, while Hofmeyr and Hoffman produced a new concept, less narrowly nationalist in tone and stripped of Neo-Calvinist terminology. In other respects the two drafts had much in common. The Bond was declared in both to be an independent political party, prepared to co-operate with outsiders in so far as this could be done without compromising its principles. These principles included the assumption that South African nationality was Christian and European. They proclaimed the obligation of governments not to impede the spread of the Gospel, and, in more detail, to permit freedom of worship, to compel Sunday observance, to control public morals and public health without trespassing on legitimate privacy, to administer impartial justice, levy impartial taxes, and protect the economic and cultural interests of the people. In addition to these general principles, both documents referred to the goal of a united South Africa, to the need for reform of the electoral system, the

[1] See above, pp. 56, 60.

reform of the master and servant law, and the achievement of complete local South African control over native policy. Both went some way towards meeting the new conciliatory spirit which prevailed between the two white language groups, Hofmeyr's further than Du Toit's.* But the Grahamstown, Uitenhage and Paarl congresses were unable to decide between them, and in 1888 the original commission of three was invited to try again, with simplicity and clarity as their watchwords. The result was the Bond's acceptance, with only minor amendments, of the Hofmeyr–Hoffman draft.* The Cape Bondsmen, without the aid of their Transvaal and Free State brethren, had come down, after seven years of indecision, on the side of a moderate statement of principles. Hofmeyr had won through with an appeal for a broadly tolerant white South African patriotism, which would serve the Bond well during the exhilarating period of its alliance with Cecil Rhodes.

The changes effected at Middelburg could not transform the Bond overnight from a rather aimless and undisciplined association into a political party with a sense of purpose; but they created a foundation on which Hofmeyr would be able to build. As chairman of the *Commissie van Toezicht*, he had been given the sort of power that he wanted. He could begin to develop the Bond on the lines enunciated in his own Programme of Principles, and he could now face the outside world confident in the knowledge that the Bond had confidence in him. In particular, he would cease to address Rhodes with the air of one buffeted by uncontrollable circumstances, and would begin to drive hard bargains with Bond votes for counters, while the other man drove mercenary ones on the basis of his Chartered shares. It would take a few months, however, before either would be able to profit from the respective positions of strength which each was in the process of gaining. Rhodes applied for his charter in April 1889, but he did not get it until 29 October, the same date on which he finally achieved an agreement with the Cape Government for the building of the Bechuanaland railway. Hofmeyr, meanwhile, had to shepherd a parliamentary flock no stronger than that of the previous year, if the observations of members of his parliamentary team are to be trusted.* He and Sprigg were both marking time, each in his own way dissatisfied with the other, and ready to break their alliance as soon as the way became clear.

8

The Hofmeyr–Rhodes Alliance

I. FAIR PLAY

THE partnership of Rhodes and Hofmeyr was a gradual growth, a coming together of dissimilar personalities who each, to his surprise, discovered in the other a respect for the traditions and interests of his own people which went beyond mere lip-service. Rhodes was the prime mover, and success may be said to have attended his overtures from the moment that he was able to win Hofmeyr's support for his policy in the North.

At the time of the 1888 general election, Hofmeyr had had strong reservations about the expansion of Colonial influence into Bechuanaland and Zambesia, a point which his biographer has stressed convincingly.* He jibbed at the thought of an advance by the Colony at the expense of the Transvaal into an area which in his view required development by the co-operative efforts of the two governments. Had Hofmeyr refused to move from this position, a political alliance with Rhodes would have had no *raison d'être* from the latter's point of view. But Hofmeyr altered course. His conversion had several facets, and the point to which he drew most attention himself was that the Transvaal Government had let him down: 'Had Kruger fulfilled my expectations, and fallen in with my advice, then Rhodes and I might have agreed to differ.'* These remarks referred to the failure of his efforts, after the customs convention with the Free State had been agreed upon in March 1889, to persuade Kruger to allow free trade between the Transvaal and the Cape. Between April and July, Hofmeyr put steady pressure on Kruger, both directly and through President Reitz, to induce him to bring the Transvaal into the customs union. He tried to impress on Kruger that, while continuing to build the Delagoa Bay line 'with the greatest energy', he ought to look after his own interests by encouraging the Free State to build a line as rapidly as possible to the Vaal River, where it should divide into two arms, one to Johannesburg and Pretoria, the other through Potchefstroom and Klerksdorp to the western Transvaal. The Johannesburg line, he suggested, might subsequently be extended northwards to the Limpopo. Such action, Hofmeyr urged, 'would reap the support of every true Africander', 'completely take the wind out of the sails of the Bechuanaland Syndicate', help to build up co-operation between the Cape and the Transvaal, 'give an enormous push to the development of Republican industries and agriculture', and 'lead the whole traffic with Central Africa through your State'.* These were persuasive words. The Transvaal Government pondered them and replied cryptically but not unfavourably.* But ten days later, on 29 July, the Volksraad turned down by twenty-six votes to six a motion put forward by the Executive Council in favour of a limited customs agreement with the Cape. In spite of Kruger's eloquent advocacy of such an agreement, the Raad decided not to commit itself until the following session—a decision which, as Hofmeyr's biographer rightly observes, 'practically determined what was to be the position of the Republic in the development of the North'.* Rebuffed by the Transvaal, Hofmeyr walked into the arms of Rhodes just at the moment when the latter was most anxious to receive him.

Rhodes left England in August 1889, confident that he would get his charter, and determined that the extension of the railway from Kimberley into Bechuanaland should proceed. He went almost immediately to Kimberley, where Hofmeyr paid him a visit, and the nature of their discussions is clear from a letter which Hofmeyr received from Rhodes after returning to Cape Town.* The British South Africa Company, in anticipation of its charter, had secured an option on the land through which the northern railway would have to pass; but it would still have been possible to prevent the building of the railway by a special Act of Parliament, and Rhodes needed Hofmeyr's support to make sure that this would not happen. Hofmeyr objected that the rail extension would call forth a great deal of opposition. Rhodes attempted to allay his fears by disclosing his intention of placing the affairs of the Company under the control of a local South African board, and the two men agreed—on whose suggestion it is not clear—to consult James Sivewright, himself a Bondsman and an expert on communications, over the desirability of proceeding with the railway plan. Rhodes's letter to Hofmeyr intimated that he had found Sivewright 'heart and soul' behind the idea, and 'enthusiastic' over the suggestion of a local board; but he proposed to 'do nothing until the atmosphere clears as to [the] railway, and I know Reitz's views'. Hofmeyr replied, advising him *in his own interest*, to suspend [the] Kimberley extension' until the arrival of Sir Francis de Winton, who had been commissioned by the Imperial Government to negotiate with the Transvaal over Swaziland, and would be able to sound Reitz; and in the meantime to take no steps without consulting Sprigg. On 29 October an agreement between the Cape Government and the Chartered Company was signed at Sivewright's home in Somerset West, under which the Cape undertook to raise enough money to take the railway to Vryburg without extra cost to the Company, and the Company agreed to complete the next section as far as Mafeking if the Colonial Government had purchased the first section by August 1891. These terms were not to Hofmeyr's satisfaction; but by January 1890, when the Imperial Government agreed to make over a strip of land in Bechuanaland to the Company for railway purposes, Hofmeyr had come round to full support of the northern extension, to the great satisfaction of the Colonial Office.*

Hofmeyr's performance in the Swaziland negotiations of 1890 is intelligible only on the assumption that his conversion was now complete. This was not a subject of particular concern to Cape Bondsmen, who never discussed it formally at their congresses; but it had a direct bearing on Rhodes's northern policy and assisted the development of the Rhodes–Hofmeyr alliance, both positively by depriving Transvalers of the right to cross the Limpopo, and negatively by undermining Hofmeyr's standing with the Government of the South African Republic.*

Settlers from the Transvaal, together with seasonal trekkers and concession-hunters, had by this time penetrated into Swaziland beyond the borders laid down by the London Convention, and the Swazi tribal authority had already been substantially undermined. The Transvaal Government desired to intervene for the dual purpose of restoring order and of establishing its own access to the sea in the region of Kosi Bay, as yet unappropriated by European Powers. Pressure of public opinion in Britain, however, prevented the Imperial Government from following its inclination to allow the Transvaal a free hand. Sir Francis de Winton, who was accordingly appointed at the end of 1889 as special commissioner to examine the Transvaal's claims on the spot, recommended that the Transvaal claims should be accepted provided that the Republic abandoned all interest north of the Limpopo, granted free trade in Colonial products, and admitted railways from the coastal colonies into the Transvaal. After the establishment of a joint temporary administration, Sir Henry Loch, the High Commissioner, met Kruger at Blignaut's Pont on the Vaal on 12 March 1890 to discuss this question, together with problems arising from a proposed trek into Mashonaland by a group of Transvalers—the abortive Bowler trek. As a party interested in Mashonaland, Rhodes was also present. Loch presented Kruger with a draft convention under which Kosi Bay was to go to the Transvaal together with a connecting strip, in return for the Transvaal's entry into the customs union, while a joint administration of Swaziland was to continue. Kruger, who agreed to submit these terms to his executive, was given until 18 July to add his signature, under the threat of the replacement of a joint administration by the authority of a British commissioner. Kruger subsequently claimed, against Loch's insistence, that he had entered into no obligations at Blignaut's Pont. He failed, as might have been expected, to secure the ratification of the terms offered there, and Loch, who was unwilling to force a crisis at this stage, asked Hofmeyr to go to Pretoria and negotiate on his behalf.

Hofmeyr accepted and reached Pretoria on 5 July, with instructions not to give way on the main points of the 'agreement entered into . . . at Blignaut's Pont'.* By 2 August he had successfully negotiated a settlement, though it is clear that it was really a threat from Loch to use armed force which caused Kruger to yield.* Hofmeyr was not a welcome guest, as was apparent when Kruger called him a traitor in public;* but he served his new political allies faithfully, above all when it came to steering the Transvalers away from an interest in the North. Piet Joubert had been one of the leading Transvaal advocates of northward expansion, and while Hofmeyr was in Pretoria Joubert was in Cape Town on his way to England, on a mission of which the purpose was not publicly known. In fact he had not been sent to undermine Hofmeyr's diplomacy,* but Hofmeyr's insistence that Joubert should not obtain a hearing betrayed real anxiety on his part.* Rhodes's Pioneer Column had already set out and it was vital to his plans that Transvaal activity north of the Limpopo should be prevented. E. A.

Lippert, who was angling for a concession from Lobengula covering land rights not yet secured by Rhodes's company, wrote to Hofmeyr in Pretoria asking him to help two of Lobengula's indunas to secure an interview with Sir Henry Loch, with a view to having the claims of his own syndicate 'impartially and calmly examined into' and the dispute 'fairly adjusted'. Hofmeyr forwarded the letter, as requested, to the Imperial Secretary in Cape Town, but with the further request that it be shown to Rhodes, in whose possession it finally rested.* Furthermore, the terms which Hofmeyr obtained from Kruger differed from those offered by Loch at Blignaut's Pont in that any concessions made to Kruger in relation to territories east of the Transvaal were made conditional on his absolute renunciation of interest in the North, and this now became irrevocable.* It is clear, therefore, that a working agreement between Rhodes and Hofmeyr was in existence before the fall of Sprigg's Government in July 1890.

For some months the net had been closing round Sprigg. Tudhope, his Colonial Secretary, had migrated to the Rand in September 1889, and both Hofmeyr and Sivewright had declined the vacant portfolio. Sprigg, aware that Bond support for his Government was dwindling, tried to buy it back during the session of 1890 with extravagant proposals for new railway branch lines.* Strenuous agitation for a local line had come to be regarded almost as the acid test of a member's competence during the sessions of 1888 and 1889, when few private proposals had earned more than a third of the votes. By 1890 the enthusiasm had diminished but by no means disappeared. The Bond congress rejected a proposal to build a line from Klipplaat to Beaufort West, but it did approve by small majorities the construction of lines from Middelburg Road[1] to Molteno and Graaff-Reinet. When Sprigg announced his proposals, several of Thomas te Water's Bond correspondents expressed their qualified approval, one even averring that 'had Sir Gordon been able to do without the Klipplaats–King Williamstown line, he would I think have had the unanimous support of the Midlands and West'.* But it was an unwise gamble, especially as Sprigg seems to have intended to start all the new lines simultaneously.* The proposals brought Rhodes back to Cape Town in unpremeditated haste, to take part in the winding up of a Government which was losing not only its hold on the House but also its sense of responsibility.

The Railway Bill defeated, Sprigg resigned on 10 July. Sauer, the

[1] Now Rosmead junction.

Leader of the Opposition, considered that the premiership should be entrusted to 'one who might be able to combine in his government a wider representation of the several parties in the country', and recommended Rhodes.* Rhodes preferred to serve under Hofmeyr, who was still in Pretoria. But Hofmeyr, acting his usual part as a 'sort of Colonial Warwick',* declined either to form a government or to serve in one formed by Rhodes. Rhodes, who was by this time confident of Hofmeyr's support, swallowed his disappointment, accepted the offer of the premiership, and set about the appointment of a ministry with the broadest possible basis, containing both liberals and Bondsmen—the two groups which potentially formed the most vocal opposition to his policies.

No Cape premier had ever consolidated his position with such care, both inside and outside Parliament. James Rose Innes, as spokesman for the liberal section, agreed that Rhodes should make terms with the Bond caucus.* Rhodes then secured Theron's support for the Charter, and on 16 July met the Bond parliamentarians to receive the assurance of 'fair play' for which he asked.* Finally, on 6 September, he defended his actions to his business associates at a banquet in Kimberley, explaining that in his view it was necessary to take the Bondsmen into fuller confidence for the sake of removing internal tensions in the Colony, the better to pursue its proper interests beyond its borders.* His plan to set up a local board of directors for the South Africa Company fell through because he was unable to lure Chief Justice De Villiers or Jan Hofmeyr into a public relationship with Mammon; but it was Rhodes himself rather than the London directors who came to occupy the power void. Nor did he find it difficult to create a vested interest in the Charter in other ways, notably by offering potential supporters or critics Chartered shares on favourable terms, or alternatively a farming interest in the North.

Many writers have alluded to the distribution of Charter shares by Rhodes as a means of winning political support, but few details have been published of these transactions. It is known however that Rhodes received a substantial number of £1 shares for distribution in the Cape Colony, and that when he distributed them in 1890 at par, Charter shares were not being offered on the open market. There is no agreement among authorities as to the number distributed,* though it is certain that Bondsmen were among the recipients.* The distribution seems to have taken place both before and after Rhodes's assumption of the premiership in July 1890, while all the evidence of purchases by Bondsmen dates from the end of that year. There has been much discussion of these and other deals, which were turned into political ammunition against the Bond on two subsequent occasions: in 1896, when Rhodes used them to blackmail Hofmeyr into silence during the Colonial investigation into the Jameson Raid; and during the 1898 general election, when Dr. T. W. Smartt, an ex-Bondsman who stood as the Progressive candidate for the Wodehouse constituency, tried to discredit Hofmeyr by alleging that he had cleared £30,000 profit from Charters—an insinuation which Hofmeyr was almost certainly justified in denying.* Hofmeyr's only big transaction of which the evidence survives, and which may have been the real foundation for both attempts at blackmail, was a large deal in De Beers shares which he made in August 1895, of which Rhodes kept the evidence.* Rhodes never carried out his threat to publicize it, however, and contemporaries were left to suppose that it was a deal in Charters. The awakening of Colonial interest, including that of Bondsmen, in the farming possibilities of the North belongs mainly to the year 1891, the year in which Rhodes brought his struggle with rival concessionaires to a successful conclusion; but when he visited Mashonaland with the High Commissioner in October 1890, he took D. C. de Waal and another Bondsman, M. M. Venter of Philipstown, with him,* and Dolf Botha, who was chairman of the Cape provincial *bestuur* at the time, visited the North in December and wrote enthusiastically to Te Water about the farming prospects.*

The ground was therefore well prepared for Rhodes's appearance at the Bond congress in March 1891. This congress, by a happy decision taken a full year earlier, was due to meet in Kimberley. Dolf Botha, in his opening address, referred to the 'great personal sacrifice' which Rhodes had made in accepting the premiership, and anticipated that he would follow a 'true national policy'. Rhodes travelled to Kimberley by train with Hofmeyr, arriving on the last day of the congress, and in the evening attended a love feast (*vriendschaps maaltijd*) at which he took the opportunity of explaining his policy in terms which made sense to Bondsmen.* He sought to enlist the support of the Colony in the development of the North, and assured his audience that his aim was to work for the unification of southern Africa on terms most favourable to the Cape, without trespassing on the independence of the Republics or destroying the link with Great Britain. He urged the Colony not to throw away any of the cards in its hand, and appealed to the Bond for co-operation, in conformity with its own professed intention to work for South African union. The speech was received with the bonhomie usually accorded to after-dinner orations, and Rhodes was no doubt satisfied that a good proportion of the Bondsmen present were already converts to his expansionist policy. But he still needed to make sure of the rank and file, some of whom had tried only that morning to drag the name of De Beers through the dirt,[1] and there were other Bondsmen who would soon show that they were very determined opponents of his northern schemes, not least among them Oom Lokomotief du Toit.

II. THE PARTNERSHIP UNDER FIRE

1891 was a year of testing for the alliance between Rhodes and the Afrikaner Bond, but by the end of the Stellenbosch congress in April 1892 it had safely survived the test. Two bids were made in this year to wreck it: the first, an attempt to enlist Afrikaner opinion behind a rival agency for the colonization of land north of the Limpopo, generally known as the Adendorff (or Banyailand) trek; the second, an effort by Bondsmen in Barkly West to secure a denunciation by congress of the De Beers monopoly.

In the course of 1890 two Transvaal burghers, L. D. Adendorff and Barend Vorster, organized a trek into the south-eastern part of Lobengula's territory, known as Banyailand, which the British South Africa Company claimed lay within its own sphere.* On his return from the North at the end of 1890, therefore, Rhodes broke his journey at Pietersburg to interview Adendorff and Vorster, who appear to have been more interested in selling their concession to Rhodes than in using it as a title for effective occupation.* Rhodes repudiated their claim and proceeded to Pretoria, where he was courteously received by the President.* Early in 1891, however, Adendorff threw caution to the winds. On 24 March, a few days before Rhodes won his diplomatic triumph at the Bond's Kimberley congress, he addressed a letter to the press inviting others to join his trek which was about to get under way.* He issued a direct challenge to the Company, and announced that further information could be obtained from D. J. Malan, Lokomotief du Toit, and J. P. Toerien (another Bondsman from Paarl), who had set themselves up as a

[1] To be considered in the following section.

secretariat in Pretoria.

At first the campaign waged by Rhodes and the Bond leaders to defeat the trek went entirely according to plan. Kruger frowned on the trek in public, and the Transvaal Volksraad decided in April to apply penal sanctions against any who took part in it. Furthermore, Rhodes received energetic support from S. J. du Toit, who had returned to the Colony from Pretoria at the end of 1890. A letter from Du Toit to Hofmeyr on 14 March 1891 indicates that he was then contemplating an approach to Rhodes.* Whether or not it was Hofmeyr's influence that finally persuaded him, it is clear that he was a strong supporter of Rhodes at the Kimberley congress,[1] and after resuming the editorship of the *Patriot* he brought its policy round full circle to support of Rhodes in April.* He was also in communication with Rhodes by this time on the question of handling the Banyailand trekkers, and the idea on which Rhodes subsequently acted of sending a party of Colonial farmers to Charterland to examine the farming prospects there, emanated from him.* By the middle of April the organization of such a party was in the hands of a committee on which Du Toit, Hofmeyr and David de Waal all served, while the *Patriot* increased its efforts to discredit Adendorff.* Rhodes made a major speech at Paarl on 23 April, addressing himself to the farming interest in general, and working up to a peak of indignation with an attack on the Banyailand trekkers.* It was obviously intended as a *tour de force*. Rhodes was anxious because of the weakness of his own title to surface rights in Charterland, and Innes has recorded how, when questioned by a Stellenbosch student in May as to the right of the British Government to dispose of land in the area, 'by way of reply Rhodes made another speech'.* But events appeared to play into Rhodes's hands in spite of his insecure title. The Colonial farmers set off on their mission as intended, and when a few of Adendorff's more determined followers arrived at the Limpopo on 24 June with the intention of crossing, they were turned back by the tact of Dr. Jameson and the appearance of a force of Bechuanaland Police.

Adendorff's friends, however, were strong and well spread. Carl Borckenhagen was disturbed over the support Rhodes was winning in Bond circles, though it was not long before he too began to make overtures to Croesus.* The trek leaders, undeterred by the reverse of 24 June, put their case into the hands of a committee of three Free

[1] See below, p. 138.

Staters, headed by Johannes van Soelen of Ladybrand, and this committee worked in association with D. J. Malan and J. S. Joubert, into whose hands the concession had now passed. D. F. du Toit continued to associate himself with their cause, and his influence caused Rhodes's supporters much concern.* The *Graaff-Reinetter*, the most influential Bond paper in the Cape midlands, went over to the trekkers' side, adding the weight of its propaganda to that of Borckenhagen's *Express*. Ds. W. P. de Villiers felt strongly that defeat for the Adendorff trekkers would spell 'Ichabod' for Afrikaner nationalism in all its facets.* As late as October 1891 S. J. du Toit was expressing concern at the growing success of the opposition: 'In the Free State the Trekkers are gaining ground. At Aberdeen our best men are *for* them. At Pearston . . . the Bond has passed a resolution *against* us.'* The ever-industrious Du Toit had been to the Transvaal in August in an attempt to smell out the trekkers' plans, and he informed Rhodes that they intended to renew their attempt to trek in 1892.* After his return, the Bond leaders in the western Cape were able to arrange an interview between Rhodes and one of the concession-holders, D. J. Malan. Du Toit worked hard on Malan, confiding the details of his discussions to Hofmeyr,* and Rhodes was able to persuade Malan to accept a proposal for arbitration by the Chief Justices of the Cape and the Orange Free State over the trekkers' claims. No sooner had Malan departed, however, than a telegram arrived from a fellow-concessionaire in Pretoria, which Du Toit said he had received authority to open, ordering Malan to stop all dealings with Rhodes forthwith, and another from the trekkers' committee in Bloemfontein, declaring that Malan had negotiated without authority. Settlement of the dispute by negotiation therefore seemed out of the question, and Du Toit told Hofmeyr that they should be prepared for a 'minor bataille'.*

It soon transpired, however, that the trekkers had shot their bolt. The Colonial farmers returned from Charterland in October, suitably impressed by the prospects, and held successful meetings at Hopetown and Paarl, where, on the latter occasion, Hofmeyr spoke strongly in favour of Rhodes's northern policy.* On a second trip to the North in November, Rhodes made a special point of visiting the Banyai chief to try to get Adendorff's claim refuted at its source, and appears to have succeeded in his object.* Even before this, though, the trekkers' committee had begun to see the virtue of

compromise, and—perhaps through the mediation of Borckenhagen*
—agreed to meet in conference with Rhodes's supporters at
Burghersdorp on 4 November.

The Burghersdorp conference was a meeting of Bondsmen, though
outsiders were allowed to attend without voting rights.* Its discussions were not limited to the trek question, but the trek was the
central issue. Hofmeyr and S. J. du Toit arrived to put the case for
the Rhodes party, while Lokomotief du Toit and Van Soelen put
that of the trekkers. The rivals agreed on a formula whereby the
High Commissioner should be asked to approach the Imperial
Government with a view to the institution of an inquiry under
articles 2 and 9 of the B.S.A. Company's Charter, so that the
question could be permanently settled.[1] This seemed to be the end
of the matter but was not; for the trekkers' committee refused to
accept the assumption of the Imperial authorities that Banyailand
was British territory subject to British law as the condition for
further arbitration.* Understandably, the trekkers' committee felt
they had been tricked, but then fell back on the weak argument that
the Burghersdorp conference had been rigged, and that the voting
on the resolution had been out of order.* It was not the first time
that D. F. du Toit had fought this sort of rearguard action in
Colonial politics, but it was the last, for after his defeat he pulled up
his roots from the Colony and emigrated to the Free State.* Whatever justice there was in his case—and it was presented too late to
look really convincing—there is little doubt that the Rhodes party
had gone to some trouble to arrange the Burghersdorp meeting
under conditions favourable to themselves. A large number of
applications for farms in Charterland had already come from that
district;* the leaders of the Bond in the Albert division were known
to be supporters of the Company, and one of them (Jotham Joubert)
was in the chair;* and meetings had been arranged to take place in
other parts of the Colony—notably at De Aar, Kimberley, and
Rietfontein near Hanover—to endorse the Burghersdorp decisions
as soon as these were known to be favourable to Rhodes's policy.
When Rhodes bought the Lippert concession in December 1891,

[1] Art. 2 of the Charter declared concessions invalid if they infringed earlier
concessions granted by the chiefs concerned. Art. 9 empowered the Secretary of
State to prevent the Company from exercising authority in any part of its
territories 'on the ground of there being an adverse claim to or in respect of that
part'.

10

thus securing the surface rights in Charterland which had so far
eluded him, and when in the following April the Imperial Government stood firm on the ground that Banyailand was British territory
and could not be considered in any other light, the resistance of the
trekkers wilted.* Of all the factors which had led to their defeat,
perhaps the most important was the widespread feeling among
farmers throughout southern Africa that the securest titles to land
north of the Limpopo were those which had the Company's
guarantee. Floods of applications reached Rhodes, especially from
Bondsmen in the Cape Colony,* and—irony of ironies—even Piet
Joubert found it necessary to warn his Transvaal compatriots that
it was unpatriotic to trek away from the Republic's soil.*

Among the services rendered to Rhodes by S. J. du Toit during
the formative months of the Rhodes–Bond alliance must be included
his claim to have prevented the passage of a resolution criticizing
the De Beers monopoly on the very day that Rhodes arrived in
Kimberley as the guest of the 1891 Bond congress.* Du Toit secured
the appointment of a committee, consisting of himself, D. C. de
Waal and P. J. Marais, to look into the question and report to the
next congress. He pictured himself as a kind of arbiter between De
Waal the Rhodes-ite and Marais his opponent. His action, however,
achieved no more than delay, for it proved impossible to call the
committee together, and Marais, who described himself as a specu-
lator and owner of farm property, and had been responsible for the
original attack on De Beers, was ready by the following congress
with a report standing in his own name and that of H. D. Stiglingh,
the other Kimberley delegate, which passed severe strictures on the
Company.* The Griqualand West mines, this report declared, were
capable of supporting four times the population of the Colony,
provided they were not collared by a European company. By closing
down Du Toit's Pan and Bultfontein, both well-paying mines, De
Beers was said to have dispensed with the services of thousands
and to have cut down the local demand for Colonial produce.
Local commerce had been severely compromised by the introduction
of the compound system and truck payments. The value of fixed
property had fallen by over 75 per cent.

Many people on the diamond fields were undoubtedly experiencing
hardships as a result of the extension of De Beers' control. This is
apparent from the report of a parliamentary select committee
appointed during the session of 1891, which drew attention to the

fact that between 1888 and 1891 the population of Kimberley had halved, the total valuation of fixed property in Beaconsfield had fallen by approximately one-third, while the market dues paid to the Kimberley council had fallen from over £4,000 in 1886 to under £1,600 in 1890.* Upington and Sprigg, in a minority report, considered that the distress was widespread, that the closing of certain mines had caused real harm to local business interests, and that intervention by the Government was called for;* but the majority rejected these arguments, attributing the fall-off in trade and employment in Kimberley to the 'feverish state of prosperity consequent on the amalgamation of the local companies in 1887–8', and declaring that 'the entire weight of evidence is in favour of the [compound] system', even if it had not been 'of equal advantage to the small retailers'. They recognized that the closing down of Du Toit's Pan had been 'detrimental to Beaconsfield', but doubted whether the total number of persons engaged in the production of diamonds had grown less, and refused to commit themselves on the principle of the monopoly.*

The Bond congress at Stellenbosch therefore had the evidence of two parliamentary reports and another by two of its own members to consider. Had there been a disposition among the Bondsmen to dissociate themselves from Rhodes's commercial practices, the evidence was available to support their case. But instead, congress contented itself with a neutral resolution which left its political relationship with Rhodes entirely unimpaired.* Disgruntled Bondsmen from Kimberley had failed to tarnish the image of Rhodes, and although they succeeded in securing the passage of two motions at the 1893 congress which implied a criticism of De Beers on the lines of the Marais report, these issues were not pressed after 1894.* There was no talk during the Rhodes period, as there had been in 1887–8, of clamping a tax on diamond exports, though the anti-Rhodes element in the Kimberley Bond survived to give the alliance considerable trouble during the general election of 1894.

III. THE HARVEST OF GOODWILL

Rhodes therefore began to feel confident in his Bond support, and he profited immensely from it. By the middle of 1892 he was secure in Charterland, his railway had reached Vryburg, and the strong political majority which he commanded in the Colony was united by a common vested interest in the North. But it would be misleading to suggest that the Bond, in electing to follow his lead, had made a simple sacrifice of its political principles before the lure of material gain. The history of the partnership over its five-year course refutes this over-simple judgement, which takes no account of the fact that the early years of Rhodes's premiership witnessed a recovery by the Bondsmen of much of the political initiative which they had lost under the distracting influences of the late eighties. A new spirit overtook Bond thinking, a spirit which echoed the enthusiasm of the early eighties—less intense perhaps, decidedly more tolerant in outlook, and guided by a real sense of purpose.

Its manifestations were varied. On his return from the Transvaal, S. J. du Toit busied himself once again with a campaign to establish a national bank. Arndt's comment, that Du Toit had little under-standing of banking but had in mind the formation of a truly national institution, makes the essential point.* In October 1890 the Taalbond was inaugurated, to propagate the Dutch language and culture in the schools.* The devotees of Afrikaans had so far made little progress against the advocates of Dutch; but the latter had much influence, and Rhodes, like his predecessors, found it desirable to yield to their pressure by appointing an educational commission in 1891 to look into the teaching of Dutch in schools, and by abandoning his plan for a teaching university in the English-dominated Cape Peninsula.* The removal of legal disabilities in the way of Dutch-speakers was so much a part of public policy that the campaign had begun to move out of the parliamentary arena.

The Bond profited from its rejuvenation, for the early Rhodes period was marked by a more rapid growth in its membership than at any other time in its history.* This may have been due in part to an influx of English-speaking members; but Englishmen had begun to trickle into the Bond before 1890, and the increase was too well spread geographically for that to be the whole explanation.

The growth in membership was accompanied by real success in the Council elections of 1891, which was the first occasion on which the *Commissie van Toezicht* was given a chance to prove itself. The Bondsmen and their allies won sixteen of the twenty-two seats. Disappointments in the eastern and north-eastern circles, where the Bondsmen had hoped to do better than they did, were matched by triumphs in the midlands, where the *Commissie* worked hard to secure the return of all three Bond candidates against stiff opposition, and in the south-eastern circle, largely Settler country, where the

Bondsmen concentrated their efforts on one candidate and secured his return at the head of the poll.*

But the most outstanding achievement of the Bond in the early Rhodes period concerned the press. Not without reason, S. J. du Toit denounced his brother, Carl Borckenhagen and J. E. McCusker as the three leading trouble-makers in the Adendorff affair, for a difference of opinion between the Bond leadership and the editors of the *Patriot, Express* and *Graaff-Reinetter* had been a major cause of party division. Even before the Adendorff crisis the need had been felt for a Bond paper in the Dutch language to circulate in the Eastern Province, while in the early part of 1891 a demand grew for another to feed the region of Victoria West and Carnarvon. In some areas, the Bondsmen complained of literary under-nourishment; in others, if McCusker's critics are to be believed, they were suffering under a diet of editorial champagne. The Bond could still count on a bevy of local newspapers which served a useful if limited function. Thus N. F. de Waal, who had been obliged to return the *Middelburg Getuige* to its owner, Heathcote, on the expiry of his three-year contract, had succeeded in driving Heathcote out of business when he started the *Nieuwe Middelburger* in 1885.*[1] But local papers could not make up for deficiencies in the larger journals, and in the early nineties it was these which caused the Bond leadership the greatest concern. *De Tolk*, that stodgy concentrate of branch news, lightened by a very thin layer of editorial butter, had ceased in 1885 without loss to the cause. But the defection of the *Graaff-Reinetter* was a serious blow, while the *Patriot*, which had been brought back into line with the orthodoxy of the moment when S. J. du Toit resumed the editorship, soon ran into severe financial difficulties.* In the course of the same year the *Zuid Afrikaan*, which was then edited by Dr. J. W. G. van Oordt, incurred the opprobrium of the Bond leadership because it had not adjusted itself sufficiently to the requirements of the new policies. Its shortcomings are not easy to discern, for in 1891 it gave strong support to the alliance with Rhodes on most contentious matters; but Van Oordt stood out against any watering down of the Afrikaner cause, and he may have resisted pressure to translate his editorials into English.*

By April 1892, however, the position had entirely changed, and the Stellenbosch congress saw reason for gratitude in the foundation since the last meeting of *Ons Land, De Paarl, Onze Courant*, the

[1] See above, p. 24.

Philipstownsche Weekblad and *Het Oosten*, 'which alone have declared themselves to be based on our Programme of Principles'.* *Ons Land* had appeared in Cape Town with the avowed object of driving the *Zuid Afrikaan* out of business—an objective achieved in exactly two years.* Not only was the *Patriot* still going, but the Paarl Drukkerij were turning out *De Paarl* in Dutch for the benefit of Boland readers. *Het Oosten*, published in Somerset East, was edited by a devoted Bondsman, J. A. Vosloo, and C. H. O. Marais ran *Onze Courant* in Graaff-Reinet—a first-rate production in both the technical and the editorial sense.*

Hofmeyr understood the importance to the Bond of an efficient press. 'It is a matter of dire necessity', he wrote to Te Water, 'for our party to be possessed of trustworthy and resolute organs'.* For S. J. du Toit, 'The press is the greatest power and strongest factor in politics. And we have the chance to get the press of the Colony in our hands to such an extent that we can dominate [*beheerschen*] public opinion.'* His imagination, assisted no doubt by the straitness of his financial circumstances, took in the concept of a vast press union, which would provide some form of centralized direction for a chain of newspapers feeding all the important districts of the Colony; and he communicated this idea to Rhodes, on the suggestion of David de Waal, as early as April 1891, with the caution that 'having lost everything in the late crisis I am not in a position to provide the funds'.* It was clearly to the advantage of Rhodes that the Bond press should be a force in Colonial politics, and to the advantage of both parties that any financial assistance provided by Rhodes should be given *sub rosa*. Consequently, though the sudden appearance of five new Bond newspapers in the course of a year is difficult to explain without allowing for the accretion of new funds from some external source, it is difficult if not impossible to link these developments positively with Rhodes. Both the *Zuid Afrikaan* and the *Patriot* denied having received aid from Rhodes shortly after Du Toit had drawn Rhodes's attention to his shortage of money.* When *Onze Courant* first appeared, the *Graaff-Reinetter* alleged that it was backed by Rhodes's money, and Te Water asked Hofmeyr's advice as to whether this gave sufficient grounds for a libel action. Hofmeyr thought not. He had advised the foundation of *Onze Courant* as a private company, with a high proportion of the shares held in Cape Town in order to provide a ballast against the ups and downs of local politics. 'Please ask Botha not to talk of loans from Rhodes or any other Cape T[ow]n man', he had written. 'Cape Town men will take *shares* to the tune of five hundred pounds, if necessary'.* But the identity of the 'Cape Town friends' who undertook to rescue the *Patriot* and set *Onze Courant* on its feet has not been positively revealed.*

The economic policy of Rhodes's first ministry was geared to the interests of the Bond, with its emphasis on the need for developing the natural resources of the Colony above and below ground. For the farmers this involved special emphasis on four points: the encouragement of potentially valuable export products by a tariff policy adapted to their interests; the development of the internal and external railway system so as to increase the flow of goods at the smallest possible capital cost; the application of scientific knowledge to specialized branches of farming, especially those which were handicapped by disease; and the solution of the labour problem.

Tariff and railway questions both had a direct bearing on the relations between the Cape and the Transvaal, and Rhodes was able to attract Bond support by his energetic defence of Colonial interests. He was helped initially by the gold crisis of 1890–1, which made the Transvaal Government look abroad for the funds necessary for the completion of the Delagoa Bay railway.* With the keen support of Merriman, Rhodes sent Sivewright, his Commissioner, to negotiate a deal, offering to advance Kruger the necessary funds on condition that he agreed to construct a railway from Johannesburg to the Vaal which would link up with the Cape–Free State line. Unable to help himself, Kruger accepted the condition and allowed the Cape to win the railway race. From September 1892, therefore, the Cape enjoyed a near monopoly of the Rand traffic, and prospered accordingly. The boom was at best temporary, and could not be expected to last beyond the anticipated opening of the Delagoa Bay line in 1894; but Cape merchants were surprised and annoyed when the Kruger Government, after reducing the general *ad valorem* duty on imports to 5 per cent in 1891 in response to agitation from the Rand, decided to push it up to 7·5 per cent in 1892, having, not unnaturally, decided to make what it could out of the sudden increase in the Cape trade. The Transvaal Government was moving away from a policy of South African free trade without much respect for the feelings of potential allies beyond its borders, and when the issue came up in the Cape Parliament on 24 August, Rhodes had to turn to his Bond supporters and urge them to moderate their language for the sake of restoring good relations with the northern Republic.* But in spite of the friendly representations which he immediately made to Kruger, Rhodes received no satisfaction. At Queenstown in March 1893 the Bond congress manifested extreme annoyance:

'That . . . with regard to the tariff now in force between the Colony and the South African Republic, our farming population is severely handicapped by the prohibitive import duties of the Republic whereby trade in farm produce from the Colony is utterly obstructed, and thinks that our Parliament ought to devise plans to move the Transvaal Government to change this tariff and allow us free trade with our countrymen and fellow-Afrikaners across the Vaal.'*

They were particularly annoyed because Free State produce could enter the Transvaal duty free. But their representations came to nothing, and the chairman's report to congress the following year indicated that the situation had gone from bad to worse.* Rhodes had lost the customs battle with the Transvaal; but he had lost it in the Bondsmen's cause, and his failure was offset to a considerable extent not only by the opening of the railway to the Rand, but also by the sensible construction of new lines within the territories under his own control. The Bechuanaland railway reached Mafeking in 1893, and with the construction of branch lines between Stormberg and Middelburg Road, and between Burghersdorp and Springfontein via the Bethulie bridge, Rhodes brought the three main Colonial ports into rail communication with each other and with the Rand, in a manner calculated also to facilitate the transport of Colonial produce to the centres of population at the coast—all at a tenth of the cost envisaged for Sprigg's expensive proposals in 1890.*

Rhodes looked upon agriculture as an industry of enormous potential profit to the Colony, and sought to develop it primarily from that point of view. Though unable to help the wine export trade by obtaining a more favourable tariff on the British market, he took the trouble to have the problem of phylloxera investigated by appointing a commission under the chairmanship of Hofmeyr, and acted on its advice to import American root stocks.* His motive was not entirely disinterested, for he appreciated the value of placating the liquor lobby, to which several of his more intimate political friends, notably D. C. de Waal and S. J. du Toit, were closely bound. But he also helped to save the citrus industry and practically created the deciduous-fruit industry. He took pains to improve the breed of all manner of livestock, and his interest in this field is well illustrated by a decision of the Bond congress in 1895 to refer a resolution in favour of improving the '*donkeys ras*' to the Minister of Agriculture. This official was himself a product of Rhodes's effort to cultivate the farmers' support, after the Bondsmen had prodded him for three years to make the portfolio change involved.*

Not all aspects of Rhodes's agricultural policy found favour in Bond circles, however. As already noted, they got no significant master and servant legislation from him (though he did personally support their Strop Bill), and little satisfaction over the problem of rural squatting.[1] When rural conservatism pointed one way and economic realities another, Rhodes was hard pressed to keep his Boer supporters in line, as would become abundantly clear during the scab crisis of 1894–5.[2] He might go a long way to meet them in other directions, for example by agreeing to oppose the running of Sunday trains, but he would not yield on points which materially affected his major aims.

IV. GENERAL POST AND GENERAL ELECTION, 1892–4

To describe the government of the Cape Colony during the Rhodes period as a straight partnership between Rhodes and the Afrikaner Bond would be to over-simplify the reality and to misinterpret Rhodes's own intentions. Rhodes was not a lover of the parliamentary system, and might well have been happy in a one-party state. His overriding concern was that the government over which he presided, whoever happened to belong to it, should be loyal to its leader, strong in talents, secure in the votes it could count upon, and untroubled by clever men on the opposition benches. An arch-pragmatist infused with a sincere if superficial idealism, he tried not to take sides in the quarrels which divided his Cabinet colleagues, and saved his energies for the work of reconciliation, or, if this proved impossible, for that of changing his ministers.

His first Cabinet had a liberal and a conservative wing, and was not an harmonious body. Friction developed, above all between Innes and Merriman on the one hand, whose standards of public conduct were strict, and Sivewright, the Commissioner, whose standards were not. Sivewright's handling of his Johannesburg

[1] See above, pp. 115–17.
[2] See below, pp. 155–8.

waterworks concession,* of the Bamberger affair,*¹ and finally of the Logan railway refreshment contract*² earned him the disrespect of the liberal section, and the fact that he was a Bondsman made the situation awkward for Rhodes.* Rhodes hoped at first that by cancelling the Logan contract he had sufficiently allayed public criticism, just as he had previously assuaged Innes by reversing the Cabinet's decision to reinstate Bamberger. But he was more prepared for a Cabinet change than was commonly supposed. In the month in which the contract was offered to Logan (September 1892) Rhodes on his own initiative held private talks with Sprigg, the Leader of the Opposition, with a view to giving him a place in the Cabinet in lieu of Merriman.* The negotiations fell through because Sprigg would not serve in the same Cabinet as Sauer, whom Rhodes was not yet prepared to do without; but they reveal the workings of Rhodes's mind at a particularly fluid moment in Cape political history when it was apparent to many that the personal antipathies dividing the ministry were bound soon to cause it to split open.* Rhodes did not want to drive out the entire liberal wing, though their united resistance to Sivewright's continued membership of the Cabinet led him to this view early in 1893. But he did want to decapitate the Opposition, and it was not long before he had developed his plans for keeping the 'three musketeers' who were about to lose their portfolios away from the Opposition benches: Merriman to have the agent-generalship in London in succession to Sir Charles Mills, Innes to follow Upington on to the Bench, and Sauer to go into temporary and voluntary retirement. But Merriman turned the offer down, and Innes would have done so had Rhodes actually made one to him.* The removal of Sauer was probably inspired by a request from Sprigg, who on 1 May informed Rhodes that he was willing to bury the hatchet and serve under him. This offer removed Rhodes's predicament, for it enabled him to form a new government himself instead of serving in one under Chief Justice De Villiers, who had already indicated his willingness to enter politics when approached by Rhodes, but was not interested in the premiership if Rhodes and Hofmeyr insisted on nominating his

¹ Bamberger was a magistrate whom Upington had transferred to other duties on account of misconduct. During Innes's absence abroad in 1891, the Rhodes Cabinet decided to reinstate him and news of the decision leaked to the *Zuid Afrikaan*, presumably through Sivewright's indiscretion.

² The contract had been awarded to James D. Logan, a friend of Sivewrights', without being advertised for public tender.

Cabinet for him.*

If there was any issue which might have been expected to send Bondsmen and liberals into different lobbies, a proposal to amend the franchise was such an issue—a consideration which must add importance to the in any case significant Franchise and Ballot Bill of 1892. The franchise legislation of 1887,[1] which had removed the political threats to white electoral supremacy that might have resulted from the enfranchisement of the Transkei, did not lift franchise questions above debate because it had not increased the political influence of the Afrikaner Bond in those eastern constituencies where the African vote could determine election results, and had not therefore killed Bond resentment of African voting rights. The Bond, however, still refused to come out in favour of a racially discriminatory franchise, and at its 1891 congress adopted a motion by S. J. du Toit in favour of a multiple-voting system, with extra votes for men with property worth £200 or a matriculation certificate.* The proposal went from congress to the Bond caucus, and from caucus via Hofmeyr to Rhodes and the Cabinet, as a prelude to a motion proposed by Hofmeyr on 4 August, that the Government be asked to consider reform of the franchise 'in order to secure due weight in the future for the material and educational interests of the country, with a view to legislation during the next session of Parliament'.* The motion seemed to presume that reform was necessary, which would have been too big a concession for the liberals to make; but, on the understanding that no major point of principle was involved, Hofmeyr accepted an amendment by Sauer asking the Government to consider 'whether any legislation is required', which was easily carried.* In fact, the liberal members of the Cabinet were not in favour of the Bond's proposed multiple vote, which the Bondsmen themselves abandoned, and took their stand on the argument that the demand made by nearly all white Colonials for a raising of the qualifications could not be resisted, and ought therefore to be accepted in principle with a view to minimizing its effects in detail. The changes made in the franchise law during the 1892 session—an increase of the occupational qualification from £25 to £75, and the introduction of a very simple educational test*—did result in a fall-off in Coloured and African registration, but they did not improve the political position of the Bond one iota if the results of the 1893–4 election in the marginal

[1] See above, pp. 122–3.

eastern constituencies are compared with those of the 1888 election.[1]
It is in fact difficult to see what the Bondsmen expected to gain by
the change. Racial discrimination would have suited their interests
far better, yet they did not press for it, though in their 1892 congress
they had asked for some sort of civilization test;* and while propa-
gating their plural-vote proposals, Hofmeyr had even paraded the
argument that these would increase the voting strength of town
against country—which could well have been true. On the whole,
the Bondsmen showed much less interest in franchise reform than
they did in the redistribution of seats, though they never succeeded
in working out a convincing argument why the rural areas should
have more members than they already had.* It was a pity for the
reputation of the Afrikaner Bond that the remarkable moderation
of its attitude during the 1892 deliberations should not have extended
into 1893, when, to a man, they voted for the abolition of plumping
in the Cape Town constituency in order to destroy the possibility
that Ahmed Effendi, the leader of the Cape Malay community,
might win a seat in the House.*

The franchise debates and the Cabinet crisis did nothing to clarify
political alignments in the Assembly, which remained very confused.
One English-speaking group, led by T. E. Fuller, made a deal with
Hofmeyr for the sake of securing the easy passage of the Franchise
Bill and thus restricting the non-white vote.* Others, however, over
whom Fuller also claimed to preside, felt more concerned to check
the Bondward tendencies in Cecil Rhodes, if possible by offering
him an alternative basis of power.* But this section, after casting
round in vain during the 1893 session for a leader and a programme,
were still far from realizing the expectation of Victor Sampson that
after the dismissal of the Innes group from the ministry a new
liberal, anti-Bond political party would emerge.* They were too
heterogeneous. With some, like Colonel Brabant, dislike of the Bond
was strong,* whereas Arthur Douglass could talk of giving 'independent support' to the Government,* and J. Frost, another of its
members, could actually accept the portfolio of Native Affairs in
Rhodes's second ministry. Although it was by the last quarter of

[1] The constituencies in question are Aliwal North, Fort Beaufort, Griqualand
East, King William's Town, Queenstown, Tembuland, Victoria East and
Wodehouse. In the 1893–4 general election the Bond gained one seat in Aliwal
North, where the non-white vote, as in most constituencies, had decreased, and
lost one seat in Queenstown, where the non-white vote had increased.

1893 already the fashion, despite the confusing nomenclature of Fuller's rival lobby, to refer to this group as the Progressive Party, they were by no means united at the time of the general election at the end of the year.

Brabant issued a nine-point manifesto at Bedford in September, Innes a different programme at Woodstock in October, and a new organization, the Queenstown Political Association, came out with yet another in November.* Brabant, by expressing an interest in the rehabilitation of poor-whites; by insisting that if the excise were reintroduced it should fall on the consumer; by not pressing for a redistribution of seats (which could only have been made, in fairness, to the advantage of the urban areas); and by standing for a native policy of 'firmness coupled with justice', bade fair to attract marginal Bond voters. At the same time, he supported Rhodes's plan to allow individual title to Africans; to introduce a general Scab Act; and to work for the unification of South Africa. The emphasis of the Innes and Queenstown programmes, which had much in common with each other, was more radical. They were unequivocal in their opposition to the Bond, Innes accusing it of irresponsibility in refusing to form a government and thus undermining the proper working of a two-party system. The two programmes attacked the social policy of the Bond—the Queenstown document demanding 'an uncompromising rejection of Strop Bills, Compulsory Labour Bills, and all such kindred attempts at obnoxious class legislation, as being ineffectual in their application and brutalising in their tendency'. They also pressed for redistribution, which did not find favour with the eastern farmers' associations and was indicative of the rift within the English-speaking community between urban and rural interests.

The Afrikaner Bond, which already had leadership and a policy, had problems of a different order as it prepared for the general election. Hofmeyr knew that, however hard his followers worked, they stood little chance of increasing their representation by very much. His concern was therefore over the quality of the Bond candidates. *Ons Land* posed the problem on 1 February 1894, when it urged that what the Bond needed was greater debating strength ('*mannen van groote zeggingskracht*') in Parliament, above all lawyers.* But how could such men be chosen if, as was likely to be the case, they had to be found outside the Bonds' ranks? The party constitution, which left the choice of candidates to the branch representatives at a special meeting in each constituency, and prevented the *Commissie van Toezicht* from intervening except in the case of disputed nominations, and even then from taking the initiative in selecting a suitable candidate, contained no remedy.[1] The *Commissie* (on which S. J. du Toit had now replaced Dolf Botha) were, however, equal to the occasion. They proceeded, after a careful selection of constituencies and by a calculated violation of the Bond constitution, to secure the nomination of several candidates of their choice, and once the shouting was over they had good reason to congratulate themselves on their achievement.*

Places were found for three medical men of calibre: Thomas te Water and Arthur Vanes, who were returned as members for their home constituencies, Graaff-Reinet and Uitenhage respectively; and Thomas Smartt of Britstown, for whom the *Commissie* secured the Wodehouse nomination after a great deal of angry correspondence.* Something also had to be done for poor Sivewright, the sitting member for Griqualand East, whose reputation within the Bond was clouded because of the Logan affair. The Bondsmen in his constituency had decided to reject him in favour of L. S. Zietsman, a non-Bondsman of somewhat ambivalent views, though not unfavourably disposed towards the Bond. The Griqualand East Bondsmen were within their rights to nominate Zietsman, which they did. The *Commissie van Toezicht*, however, cancelled the nomination and ordered another meeting, which confirmed the previous decision. Thereupon the *Commissie* released the Bondsmen from their constitutional obligation to vote for the properly nominated candidate or abstain. Sivewright won the election.

Then there was W. P. Schreiner—not himself a Bondsman, but a desirable candidate because he was a lawyer and had for a short while been Attorney-General in Rhodes's Cabinet.* The *Commissie*

[1] The *Commissie's* power in this respect was defined as follows: 'De Commissie zal het recht hebben, op aanzoek van eenigen tak, om goed te keuren, dat eenig kandidaat, geen Bondskandidaat zijnde, ondersteund worde door den Bond, mits er geen kans schijnt om een Bondskandidaat in te krijgen en mits er geen Bondskandidaat volgens constitutie benoemd is, die daardoor zou schade lijden en *alleen* in zulke gevallen waar het noodzakelijk is in het belang van den Bond'. ['The *Commissie* shall have the right, on application by any branch, to approve that any candidate, not being a Bond candidate, shall have the support of the Bond, provided there appears to be no chance of getting a Bond candidate elected and provided there is no constitutionally nominated Bond candidate, who would thus suffer deprivation and *only* in such cases where it is necessary in the interest of the Bond'].

decided to put him up to run with Rhodes in Barkly West, after the local Bond branches had already chosen P. J. Marais, the critic of De Beers. Marais was willing to stand down; but his alternate, H. D. Stiglingh, who had also criticized De Beers, was not. There was bound to be local opposition to this move, so the *Commissie* decided to take Barkly West by stealth rather than by storm. They invalidated the previous nomination, and S. J. du Toit, who was already in the running for the Bond nominations in Victoria West and Paarl, went to Barkly West and secured the nomination at a second meeting. Stiglingh still stood up for his rights as the original secundus; but Du Toit called a special meeting in the constituency, at Campbell, and persuaded the meeting to choose Schreiner in preference to Stiglingh. This it did after deliberations behind closed doors, 'with the full confidence that the Primarius will go forward as candidate'. But before the end of January 1894 Du Toit, who presumably intended this manoeuvre all along, stood down in favour of Schreiner, and became a candidate for Paarl, where he was, perhaps deservedly, defeated. Hofmeyr rode the storm of abuse from deceived Barkly West Bondsmen, and parried their blows with arguments about party discipline, telling the electors shortly before polling day that if Schreiner lost the party would not have a single barrister in the House. Rhodes and Schreiner both scraped home.*

The *Commissie* had strained the Bond constitution to its limits, even violated it, in what they regarded as the party's wider interest. But Hofmeyr, though exhausted almost to the point of throwing up the sponge by the disputes and their aftermath, was able to prevent the party from falling apart. He persuaded S. J. du Toit not to take his opponent, J. S. Marais, to court after the latter had beaten him by a narrow margin in Paarl. He also persuaded the Barkly West Bondsmen not to expel Stiglingh from the party, with the result that Stiglingh did not take his case to the provincial *bestuur*, as he had threatened. But a sordid dispute arose and dragged on in Hofmeyr's own constituency of Stellenbosch, where Pieter de Waal, brother of David, had narrowly defeated the other sitting member, W. A. Krige, by six votes. Hofmeyr had easily headed the poll, and preferred De Waal as his fellow-member; but Krige decided to lay a charge against certain of De Waal's supporters, alleging bribery, and De Waal brought a counter-charge against Krige personally on the same ground. Both cases were still pending when, towards the end of May, Hofmeyr left for Ottawa to attend the Colonial Conference.

He was already weary of the struggle;* and, exasperated by this further development, he drafted letters to the Speaker of the Assembly, Sir David Tennant, resigning his seat, and to his Stellenbosch constituents, informing them that if the election petitions went against De Waal he would have to consider his next step.* Both plaintiffs succeeded, De Waal losing his seat and Krige his political rights for five years. Hofmeyr's resignation was not, under the circumstances, sent in, though Gideon Krige, stepping into his brother's shoes, defeated De Waal at a by-election later in the year; but Hofmeyr would give up the unequal task before another year had passed.

For the Bond as a whole, the election results were moderately satisfactory. Its alliance with Rhodes had held fast, and the ministerialists were returned with a comfortable majority over the Progressives and associated groups. Of thirty-eight candidates who had stood with the blessing of the *Commissie*, twenty-seven had been returned, and these, with the addition of a further twenty who supported Rhodes, gave the alliance not far short of two-thirds of the seats in the Assembly.

For Rhodes, the position was very satisfactory. Without a major transference of weight, he could now lean either on the Bond or on the Progressives—even, as events transpired, on the liberal elements in the Opposition—in order to secure the legislation he desired; for neither the re-formation of the ministry after the Logan crisis nor the general election of 1893–4 had really disturbed the subtle balance of forces in the House. Rhodes would need the liberals' support to deal effectively with the problem of Glen Grey, and the support if the Progressives if he was to face up to the Bond over scab.

V. GLEN GREY AND SCAB

Glen Grey lies to the west of Emigrant Tembuland, the northern part of which had been occupied by white settlers after the frontier war of 1877–8. Attempts had been made periodically from 1864 to persuade the Tembu, who had been allowed to settle in Glen Grey in 1852, to move to alternative lands across the Indwe River; but although there had been small migrations in 1865 and again in 1885, the inhabitants had never left *en masse*, and the Government had not resorted to compulsory eviction. During the Basuto war of 1880, a number of Glen Grey Tembu rebelled, and left their lands. They could have been prevented from returning but were not, and by the early nineties, when the arrival of squatters from other tribes had made over-population a serious problem, it was no longer easy either to identify ex-rebels or to find an equitable reason for evicting anybody. The district comprised 250,000 morgen of high mountains and fertile valleys, supporting a population of 40,000 and an excess of stock, and providing a *pied-à-terre* for an indeterminate number of migrant labourers on short-term employment in the Colony.

Rhodes appointed a commission to examine the Glen Grey problem in 1892, partly on the insistence of the Bond.* Its report* recommended the grant of individual tenure to Africans in the district, on a basis of 55 morgen per family; those who received no title to be obliged to seek work in the Colony, as seemed fitting. It accepted the plea of most would-be title-holders that their lands should not be executable for debt for three or four years, except with government consent; and in view of the prevalence of burr-weed and the neglected state of the roads, it recommended that the district should be proclaimed a fiscal division of the Colony. Its recommendations had the support of a clear majority of the African residents, on the understanding that they would have to pay for the survey, and on the assurance that they would not lose commonage rights or pay more in quitrent than they already paid in hut tax.

The liberals in Parliament recognized the value of individual title as a civilizing force, and wanted to see it granted without its beneficiaries being obliged to surrender their existing rights, including the right to vote. They also wanted to prevent the purchase of Glen Grey lands by white men, and it was mainly for this reason that Innes, 'after consultation with Sauer, Merriman, [Richard] Solomon and others', stressed the need to 'regulate the disposal during life and the devolution after death' of these lands, when he moved an amendment to Frost's motion for the adoption of the report in 1893.*

For many Bondsmen, on the other hand, Glen Grey was a coveted region. In 1886 congress had congratulated the Government for the steps it had taken to remove some Glen Grey Africans to the Qumbu district, and expressed the hope that it would either remove more from the region or compel those who remained to pay taxes on the same basis as white settlers.* The Glen Grey commission in due course repudiated the argument that there was land available for white settlement in the district, and went out of its way to quote the evidence of Bondsmen to that effect,* but congress explicitly resolved

11

in 1893 that if individual tenure were introduced in Glen Grey, there should be no restrictions on the owners' right of sale.*

The Bond's attitude to the Glen Grey problem seems to have been materially influenced by Victor Sampson, who corresponded freely with Hofmeyr and Te Water on the question, and told Hofmeyr in November 1893 of the pleasure which it gave him 'to know that any ideas of mine had a share in determining you to oppose Frost's motion'.* Sampson, who was the Bond-sponsored candidate for Tembuland in the 1893–4 election, had thought in terms of individual tenure for Africans at least as early as June 1891, but had then confessed that he could not see how individual title could ever be granted on a large scale 'without some limitation to their right to vote'.* By 1893 he was rejecting the 'silly notions' of Merriman and Innes of 'making the Transkei a native preserve', and felt that white people should be settled there in order to prevent over-population.* Titles, he now urged, should be limited to existing huts and gardens; there should be a grouping of settlements into villages; land not built upon or cultivated should be strictly treated as commonage, with the important qualification:

'I think I should be inclined to help the poor whites to some of the land so saved. At any rate, considering how we . . . have given land to other natives, at Matatiele, at Qumbu and at Tsomo, I do not think we should be blamed for giving our own kith and kin and colour a few of the crumbs that fall from the natives' table! Do you ?'*

A further letter to Hofmeyr objected to the Glen Grey Commission's proposal to give 55 morgen to each family, on the ground that this would not stop squatting. Sampson then put forward the suggestion of primogeniture, and coupled it with that of a ban on the subdivision of properties, so that younger sons would 'have to go to the Colony in search of labour'.*

The legislation which resulted from these conflicting pressures carried the marks of both.* Individual tenure, accepted in most quarters, formed the basis of the new land system; but the 4–morgen holding agreed upon was far closer in size to Sampson's hut-and-garden allotment than the 55 morgen recommended by the Commission. The law met part of the liberals' case for safeguards on the alienation of land, but the land nevertheless remained executable for debt. Primogeniture, as proposed by Sampson, became the basis of succession. The occupational qualification for the franchise—

property worth £75 held in individual tenure—was abolished with respect to Glen Grey but not with respect to any other district. This the liberals abhorred, though the establishment of a district council with limited local governmental powers was some compensation to them, since it was not introduced as a substitute for representation at the parliamentary level. Had the labour tax to force the landless to seek work outside the district been collected, which it never was, the Bondsmen, being employers of labour, would no doubt have appreciated it. Innes considered it a 'blot on the measure', though this part of the 'Bill for Africa' has since had rather stiffer parallels in other parts of the continent. The Glen Grey Act has the appearance of a truce between two groups of contenders for control over the native policy of the Rhodes Government. That policy had its seamy side, as was shown by the Matabele war of 1893, and by the series of developments in Pondoland which began with a machine-gun demonstration as a prelude to annexation and finished with the Sigcau affair of 1895. When Innes described the Glen Grey Act as Rhodes's greatest legislative achievement, he implied that it differed in quality and intention from these other actions, which contained no suggestion that Rhodes's patriarchal views on native policy were inspired by a conscious desire to civilize his wards. On the other hand, the Rhodes-Bond alliance was not endangered by the Act, for if the Bondsmen had failed to gain their point over the alienability of the lands, they had at least obtained a limitation of the freehold African vote.

In the case of the Scab Act, however, the alliance with Rhodes proved harder for the Bond to maintain and came within an ace of foundering. The ravages of the scab insect caused losses to Colonial farmers of perhaps £500,000 a year, by reducing the quantity and quality of the wool and mohair clip and by causing the death of thousands of sheep in times of drought. Though the disease had been endemic in the Colony since the seventeenth century, it was not until the late nineteenth century that research proved the possibility of controlling it by dipping and quarantine methods. Legislation accordingly followed in 1886 and subsequent years. Inspectors were appointed, with power to prosecute for infringements, and an indication of the growing zeal with which they performed their task may be gleaned from the increase in the number of prosecutions from 47 in 1887 to 1,568 in 1893.* The Scab Disease Commission appointed by Rhodes in 1892 was satisfied that the control methods

were effective but noted great diversity of outlook among the
farmers on many aspects of the problem. Some farmers exhibited
'a sentimental feeling that legislation referring to their flocks inter-
fered with what they considered their sacred liberty'—a notion which
was sometimes accompanied by an astonishing degree of ignorance.*
The Act of 1886 had worked well in the south-eastern Cape and had
the general support of the farmers' associations and Bond branches
in that region; but in the north-west, where the incidence of drought
was most severe and the ignorance most profound, there was strong
resistance to scab legislation even in the face of high stock fatalities,
which farmers often attributed to the arduous journey to the dipping-
tanks rather than to the disease. The commissioners decided,
nevertheless, to recommend a general compulsory Scab Act, with
limited provision for its suspension in particular areas under very
special circumstances.

Bond congresses normally trod cautiously when they discussed
scab, because of deep differences of opinion among members. But
the Paarl congress of 1888, which set the tone of Bond policy in
subsequent years, voted for a modification of the 1886 law in favour
of less compulsion and the granting of more discretion to the
divisional councils.* When the Government introduced a general
compulsory Scab Bill in 1894 to implement the Commission's
report, the Bond caucus therefore opposed it.* Rhodes agreed to
defer the second reading to give the Bondsmen time to work out
their amendments, which were numerous, and he agreed to accept
them in return for a guarantee of sufficient support to ensure the
passage of the measure. The amendments were designed to ease the
position of farmers who objected to the legislation; but the Bill
remained in substance general and compulsory, and the Bond
parliamentarians soon became aware that they had signed away
more than their followers would accept.

Towards the end of the year, opposition mounted. The Brandvlei
Bondsmen from the Calvinia district began to call for petitions in
September, while in December close on a hundred representatives
from thirty-two farming centres met at Victoria West to organize a
campaign for the abrogation of compulsory scab legislation. The
malcontents found a leader and spokesman in the fluent Oom
Daantje van den Heever, and bade fair to challenge the parliamentary
leadership of the Party at the forthcoming congress, perhaps even
to split the Bond in twain.*

S. J. du Toit, ever one to declare his thoughts on paper, set about 'feeling the pulse of the Bond' and told Hofmeyr that he feared the opponents of the Act would have a majority at the following congress.* At his suggestion he went with Hofmeyr to see Rhodes, who agreed that they should try to persuade congress to accept the legislation for a trial period of three years. But in the meantime Du Toit calculated that the opposition would be even stronger than he had previously thought, and felt obliged to change his tactics. He therefore suggested to Te Water that the Act should be made compulsory east of a line drawn from Warrenton to Mossel Bay, and voluntary west of it, and that committees under local magistrates should be set up to arbitrate between farmers and scab inspectors.*

The possibility of a dividing line had been envisaged in the Scab Commission's report,* and the Bondsmen were certain to welcome any proposal which really placed the relationship between the farmer and the inspector on a more equal basis;* but the opposition were firm in their resolve to obtain a permissive Act and conscious of their superior strength. They therefore pressed home their advantage by forcing through a motion at the Port Elizabeth congress demanding a permissive Act in unambiguous terms, against which thirty-eight delegates recorded their names in the minority.* But, having delivered this severe reproof to the parliamentary leadership, congress then proceeded to close its ranks by expressing 'complete disapproval' of the popular agitation set off by Van den Heever. It then assented to a motion by N. F. de Waal to the effect that the Bond was the only channel through which Bondsmen made their grievances known and had them redressed.*

A split was thus avoided in the provincial *bestuur*, but not in all the branches.* Opposition to the Act spread through the platteland during 1895. A large deputation of farmers went in accordance with the congress resolution to interview the Government. Hofmeyr acted as go-between—with perhaps rather more reluctance than his biographer suggests.* At first the Government was inclined to brave the opposition, and Sprigg, with a bravado he would live to regret, referred to the agitators as victims of the 'Demon of ignorance and prejudice'. A Bondsman, D. J. A. van Zyl, introduced a Bill to make the Act permissive. Frost, now Minister of Agriculture, moved its rejection. The government caucus reconsidered the matter, and decided that no further steps should be taken during the session but that during the recess an inquiry should be conducted into the working of the 1894 Act, with the prospect of further legislation in 1896 if it were found necessary.* Innes, who was in a minority of twelve in the division, observed that Rhodes did not carry out his undertaking to visit the disaffected districts at the end of the year, since when the time came he was 'less lawfully engaged'; but his memory played him false when he asserted that Rhodes had changed his front.* The Act remained general and compulsory, and if its administration was softened, which seems to be a legitimate inference from the greatly reduced activity of the courts, it continued to bring forth protests from the hard-hit country areas. A severe drought afflicted the north midlands in 1895, and Ds. W. P. de Villiers appealed to Rhodes from Carnarvon in September: 'If it does not rain, I am sure you will have reason enough to suspend the Act. The drought is getting worse every day, and to crown all the misery, myriads (literally not figuratively) of springboks are coming in from all quarters of the compass'; and again in December: 'Some people have had to trek for want of water. And yet the act is not suspended.'*

Opposition did not 'die away', as Hofmeyr's biographer supposed, without causing the Bond and the next Government a great deal more trouble; but its later developments belong to the period after the Jameson Raid, when the forces of unity within the Bond were stronger then those of division. By 1896, moreover, though a further attempt was made to make the Act permissive, the policy of systematic dipping and quarantine began to justify itself by a reduction in the number of infected sheep and an increase in the value of wool exports.

'It must be remembered', wrote Victor Sampson, 'that the scab law was one of the burning questions of the day, and that Hofmeyr, as I happen to know, retired from Parliament because he feared to weaken his prestige with, at any rate, one section of his followers, by his attitude in the House on any question connected with this subject.'* The Port Elizabeth congress carried its motion in favour of a permissive Scab Act on 18 March 1895, and Onze Jan submitted his resignation from the Stellenbosch seat on the 30th. A connexion is therefore probable, though it is certain that this is not the only explanation. Somewhat obscurely, J. T. Molteno traced his decision to resign back to his 'false step' in supporting Sivewright in the Logan affair.* His illness in Canada in 1894 featured prominently in the telegrams of commiseration which Onze Jan received when his resignation had been made public.* But Stellenbosch was prominent among the causes. 'He is bitterly sick of Stellenbosch', wrote David de Waal to a Bond M.P. on 1 November 1894, at a time when Onze Jan was clearly considering resignation.* The family vendetta was still going on, and to make matters worse the Stellenbosch branch of the Bond had collapsed.

Although the Port Elizabeth scab resolution provided the occasion for Hofmeyr's resignation, the causes are likely therefore to have been more general. If he interpreted the congress resolution as a vote of no confidence in himself, his logical action would have been to resign from his position as chairman of the *Commissie van Toezicht*, which he did not do. Had he remained in Parliament, his inability to hold the caucus together would have been bound to reflect adversely on his authority in the *Commissie*, and would perhaps have weakened his leadership still further. His work for the Bond and his work as leader of the Bond parliamentary group seem to have been separate activities in his mind, and he seems to have abandoned the latter so as to be able more effectively to carry out the former. There is no proof that Rhodes in any way 'willed' him out of Parliament, despite Innes's observation that Rhodes's speech in the House when he heard of the Bond leader's decision was not tinged with any expression of personal loss.* Hofmeyr's fiftieth birthday celebration, at which both men made ostentatious display of their friendship, was held on 4 July, while his big share transaction with De Beers took place in August.[1] If Hofmeyr's absence from the House facilitated the development of Rhodes's secret plans for the North at the end of the year, the argument that Rhodes in any way contrived to bring it about must rest on pure conjecture.

VI. THE RAID CRISIS

Hofmeyr's resignation from Parliament coincided almost exactly with the return of Sir Hercules Robinson for a second term of office as Governor and High Commissioner at the Cape. Bondsmen had regretted his departure in 1889, having come to look on him as a renegade imperialist and a convert to the Colonial point of view. His successor, Sir Henry Loch, had done much, however, to alleviate their disappointment, for he had successfully hidden most of his militant imperialism from their gaze and struck up a friendly

[1] See above, p. 133.

relationship with Hofmeyr, especially during the difficult Swaziland negotiations in 1890. Loch had also been able to work with Rhodes, up to a point. Somewhat reluctantly, he had agreed to accompany Rhodes to the North in 1890. Together they had beaten the Adendorff agitation. They were at one in their effort to end the uncooperative behaviour of the South African Republic over railway, customs and—a later development—uitlander problems. But whereas Rhodes worked in the interest of the Company, Loch sought similar ends in the name of the Imperial Government, and distrusted companies. When Loch decided to resign while on leave in 1894, Rhodes was therefore pleased to be rid of a High Commissioner who had been of use to him in the past but was likely to be an obstacle in the future. By investigating the possibility of a revolt in Johannesburg and by placing Bechuanaland police on the Transvaal's western border, Loch had provided Rhodes with the rudiments of the plan he and Jameson were to develop later; but its proper execution required a High Commissioner 'relegated to an assistant role'.* Sir Hercules, an old man now, a shareholder in the Chartered Company, an ex-director of De Beers and the Standard Bank, was far less likely to stand in Rhodes's way, and might—as some feared at the time—even assist him. But it was the liberals, not the Bondsmen, who were apprehensive; and the latter went out of their way to welcome their former friend on the same evening that the Cape Town liberals, led by Innes and Sauer, made a public protest.*

The Sivewright railway agreement with the South African Republic lapsed by effluxion of time at the end of 1894. Kruger had allowed a line from Natal to enter the Transvaal in February that year, and the Delagoa Bay railway would be ready for traffic by June 1895.* Knowing therefore that Kruger was free to regulate tariffs and allocate traffic as he chose, Rhodes sent his Commissioner, Laing, to meet Middelberg, the head of the Netherlands South Africa Railway Company, in Pretoria in August 1894. But Laing, ignoring Sivewright's warning against provoking the Transvaal, demanded half the Republic's heavy traffic and threatened to undercut the other lines when Middelberg offered him only one-third. By way of retaliation, Middelberg persuaded Kruger to increase the rates between the Vaal and Johannesburg, and subsequent Cape pressure failed to make him change his mind. The Cape merchants therefore organized the conveyance of their goods from the Vaal to the Rand by ox-wagon, an expedient which was not likely to be effective for long against the competition of other railways, but which had the merit of keeping the controversy open. Meanwhile the Bond congress at Port Elizabeth expressed its perennial indignation at Transvaal tariff policy, and the Cape Government sought to escape from the tangle by convening a conference in Cape Town in April—a conference which ended in deadlock because the Natal and Transvaal delegates would not meet the Cape's minimum demand, which had now decreased to two-fifths of the Rand traffic.*

Rhodes's Government had lost face, and it had lost it at a bad time, for it was now known almost for certain that the Portuguese would not surrender control over Delagoa Bay to any outside power,* and it was also known that a geological survey of Charterland by the American, John Hays Hammond, had not disclosed the anticipated mineral deposits. Mineral discoveries were needed to recoup shareholders for the expenses of the 1893 Matabele war, and when Rhodes met them in London in January 1895 he was unable to promise dividends.* Anxious also on the ground of his own health, Rhodes became increasingly hungry for 'federation within the year'.

He hoped to achieve this by the application of force to the Transvaal from the inside and from the outside: internally, by a rising on the Rand, and externally by an invasion of the Republic by armed forces whose affiliations would not compromise the Imperial or Cape governments. His plan was first to secure the transfer of British Bechuanaland to the Colony, so that the Bechuanaland Border Police could be released by the Imperial Government for Company service, and the transfer of the Protectorate to the Company to provide a base from which the invasion itself could start. Rhodes carried a motion with this double purpose through the Cape House in early June.* In the same month Joseph Chamberlain succeeded Lord Ripon in the Colonial Office; but it was not until after the conflict with the South African Republic over tariffs had ended in November that he gave his partial consent to the double request, allowing the Cape to take over the Crown Colony and granting to the Company a strip of territory along the Protectorate–Transvaal border.

The Bond was not an accessory before the fact, but Bondsmen did earnestly desire the incorporation of British Bechuanaland. There were Bond branches in the territory which, though technically outside the Colony, had been sending representatives to Cape congresses since 1891. The Vryburg district *bestuur* grew from 84 members in March 1895 to 453 at the time of the 1896 congress, such was the stimulus it received from the prospect of incorporation. Indeed, without waiting for the Imperial Government's consent to annexation, the Bond began to prepare for an election contest in the territory and S. J. du Toit, who remembered the local support which he had received during his unfortunate escapade in 1884, took what seems to have been an unusually keen interest in securing the nomination—which, however, he failed to get.*

The tariff crisis meanwhile developed to Rhodes's advantage. Had Kruger ignored the Cape's boycott of the Vaal–Rand line, the other lines would soon have driven the drifts traffickers out of business; but instead he proclaimed on 20 August that the drifts were to be closed from the beginning of October. The closure was enforced; the Cape protested that it was a violation of the London Convention—a point raised quietly on Rhodes's behalf by Schreiner, who ascertained that this was also Chamberlain's view, and obtained from the Imperial Government an undertaking to back an ultimatum with an expeditionary force, provided the Cape would contribute substantially in men and material aid if violence proved necessary.* With the assent of Schreiner and Laing, who were on their way to Pretoria on the Transvaal Government's invitation to discuss the railway deadlock, Rhodes advised Chamberlain to send his threat. It arrived in Pretoria on 4 November, the day before the railway conference was due to begin, and although the conference itself broke down, Kruger bowed as usual to the threat of superior force and opened the drifts. His earlier impetuosity had done nothing to solve the tariff question; but it had established accord between Rhodes and Chamberlain, it had kept alive the unrest in Johannesburg so essential to Rhodes's plans for a rising there, and it had helped Rhodes to retain the support of the Cape Bondsmen who, without knowing his real intentions, shared in the general indignation against the Transvaal.* Kruger's reopening of the drifts, on the other hand, in no way deflected Rhodes from the action he had planned.

When Jameson crossed the Transvaal border on 29 December 1895 (though the plans for a simultaneous Rand rising had fallen through), he did so without the prior knowledge of any member of the Cape ministry except Rhodes. When Schreiner saw Pieter Faure on the 30th, the latter expressed astonishment that Rhodes had allowed such a thing to happen without consulting his Cabinet.* Schreiner saw Rhodes the same evening and, after obtaining confirmation of the essential accuracy of the telegraphic reports, made his own position plain: he was in no doubt that Rhodes ought to resign, and would in any case do so himself as soon as blood was known to have been shed.

Hofmeyr, who learned the news only on the following day, experienced a *bouleversement* more shattering than Schreiner's. The Raid showed up—or so it must appear to the mass of his supporters —a gigantic error of judgement on his part. Not only were his dreams of co-operation destroyed, but his authority would be undermined among his own people unless he took prompt and unequivocal action to dissociate himself from the events which were taking place, and if possible unearthed the guilty party. He wasted no time, therefore, before sending a message of encouragement to President Kruger.* He then called on the High Commissioner, whose private knowledge of the invasion plans he did not suspect, and persuaded him to issue a proclamation, as Robinson put it in an apologetic message to Chamberlain, 'publicly repudiating Jameson's action on behalf of Her Majesty's Government and calling on all British subjects to refrain from aiding or abetting him in armed violation of territory of friendly State'.* Hofmeyr passed on the substance of this decision to the Transvaal President;* but the order to oppose Jameson was toned down at Graham Bower's suggestion, and further softened by Edmund Garrett, editor of the *Cape Times*, whom Robinson allowed to inspect the draft proclamation after Hofmeyr's departure. This necessitated delay in its dispatch while Hofmeyr was sought to approve the alteration, and Hofmeyr in consequence began to suspect a move in the High Commissioner's office to make the proclamation nugatory, wrongly attributing the evil genius to Bower.

Having obtained an official British repudiation of the Raid, Hofmeyr met Rhodes the same afternoon in Bower's office, and emerged from the interview convinced that Rhodes himself was implicated in the events, both because of his failure to warn the Transvaal and because of his silence in the presence of his own ministers.* When Rhodes refused the challenge of publicly repudiating Jameson and instituting criminal proceedings against him, Hofmeyr considered his guilt to be beyond doubt. He still trusted the High Commissioner, however, and recommended to Kruger that he should invite him to Pretoria to help with the maintenance of peace and order.* The Republican Government, understandably keen to show that the invasion had been put down by their unaided resources, at first demurred, but ultimately accepted his advice on 1 January.* Hofmeyr declined Robinson's invitation to accompany him, pleading ill health and explaining that he wished to withhold his diplomatic services until the moment of 'supreme necessity . . . which is not yet'.* It is probable that he desired to remain in Cape Town to probe the conspiracy still further, and to discuss the situation with the Bond leaders. He was in communication with S. J. du Toit, who was already trying to arrange a meeting between Rhodes and the Afrikaner leaders, so that Rhodes could explain his actions to them; but Hofmeyr was opposed to this idea.*

The news of Jameson's defeat reached the Cape on 2 January, and Hofmeyr sent off a congratulatory telegram to Kruger the same day, urging him at the same time to be generous.* On the 4th, he entered into correspondence with Chamberlain on the latter's invitation, which apparently stemmed from Robinson's report of their interview of 31 December. Hofmeyr seems to have been pressing his investigations too hard for the Colonial Secretary's liking, and Chamberlain sought to reassure him of the Imperial Government's bona fides:

'Inform Hofmeyr', he told Robinson, 'that Her Majesty's Government repudiates Jameson's action, and are doing all in their power to counteract the mischief he has done. I have no doubt that the influence of Hofmeyr will be used in the same direction.'

Onze Jan's reply contained a pointed reference to 'men of high reputation in British financial and military circles, as well as in Her Majesty's Service' who had taken an active part in the events leading to the Raid, and he asked for a radical change in the government of the Company's territories and a 'searching inquiry . . . through impartial and energetic men' into the origins of the Raid. 'There shall be full inquiry', Chamberlain replied on the 7th, and he asked Hofmeyr to 'telegraph this to High Commissioner to save time and publish'.*

The following day, on the intercession of Adriaan Hofmeyr, he met Rhodes again at Groote Schuur. Rhodes was apparently indifferent about the interview: 'A chat will do the country no harm, but I leave it to you', he replied to Hofmeyr's message of acceptance. However the chat apparently did some good, for they met again next day at the home of Thomas Louw, and Hofmeyr kept a record of the discussion.* He advised Rhodes to resign or stay away from

Parliament during the following session, and to 'issue a manifesto in interest of reconciliation and peace', which he was willing to write for him. Rhodes 'proved very nervous about his charter', though Hofmeyr reassured him: 'If I could give any information to promote thoroughness of enquiry I would do so; but for the present my chief object was not anti-Charter agitation but to throw light on Bower's doings.' David de Waal, who acted as a go-between, told Hofmeyr the next day that Rhodes intended to go to Bulawayo, but could not because he feared that Hofmeyr was going to attack the Charter. Hofmeyr repeated his assurance of the previous day. The memorandum, however, complains that Rhodes failed to accept Hofmeyr's assurance and spurned his advice:

'Rhodes never gave me any further information re manifesto or seat in P[arliamen]t.—He left for Kimberley within a few h[ou]rs instead of next day—instead of promoting peace and reconciliation he made bluffing speech at Kimberley—sent irritating wire to America, sneaked off to England, allowed *Times* to be filled with invidious fictions.'

Eventually, when Rhodes accused Hofmeyr of actually attacking the Charter, the latter lost patience and sent Rhodes a message via de Waal that 'if Johannesburg fictions in *Times* continue' he would 'cable exposure signed by himself and other prominent men'.

It is impossible to page through the sheaf of letters, memoranda and telegrams in the Hofmeyr Papers which deal with the Jameson Raid, without gaining an impression of the sincerity, moderation and integrity of Onze Jan as he set about the unravelling of the mystery—counselling the victors to clemency and the Imperial authorities to honesty, and telling the rumour-mongers to hold their peace. By the time of his final communication with Rhodes, he had contributed a great deal towards the solution of the crisis. He had succeeded to some extent in softening the indignation of the Government and people of the Transvaal; he had tested Rhodes's sincerity and found it lacking; and he had forced the Imperial Government and its local representative into the position of having to declare not only their opposition to the Raid but also their intention of holding a public investigation into the causes of it. Here, at least, was some achievement to offset his bitter personal disappointment.

9

Recessional

I. 'LEST WE FORGET'

RHODES's resignation followed on 7 January, as expected, but it was not easy to find a new premier who could replace a man so firmly entrenched in power. Chief Justice De Villiers and Hofmeyr both declined the offer,* and it was at best doubtful whether the devotees of 'ignorance and prejudice' would find themselves able to rally behind the ever-available Sprigg. But Sprigg was game to try, and desperately sought an indication of more than sufferance from the Bond, telling Hofmeyr that he wanted Pieter Faure and Thomas te Water in his Cabinet, and asking him to bring pressure to bear on the latter.* Te Water's anxieties were reflected in a telegraphic conversation which he must have had with Hofmeyr shortly after the dispatch of Sprigg's note.* He did not want to take 'any step which our party might not cordially approve'. Onze Jan intimated that a government under Sprigg was perhaps the best that could be had under the circumstances, at a time when it was 'all bosh to stand out for a complete programme of Principles', and when the country needed 'an administrative ministry that will see us through far greater questions than the details of Scab and the weight of the penny loaf'. 'Decide for yourself', he concluded. 'I see you are pretty well determined not to give me the advice I require', Te Water complained. Had Schreiner been prepared to follow Sprigg, Te Water would have found the decision easier; but Schreiner did not think Sprigg could win the confidence of the Republics.* But by 13 January, after further pressure from Sprigg, Te Water had accepted the Colonial Secretaryship and Faure had accepted Agriculture.* The Bond was committed, therefore, at least to leaving Sprigg alone. But this would not be an easy position to hold if the

Bondsmen were to atone for their error in trusting the Colossus, for demands would soon come from the Transvaal for their support for the effective punishment of Rhodes and the Chartered Company,* simple acceptance of which would have made their continued association with Sprigg impossible.

The Raid gave birth to a new form of self-conscious Afrikaner nationalism, at once self-critical and self-congratulatory, which laid stress on the exclusiveness of the wronged group and its need to close its ranks. Some, like F. S. Malan, the new editor of *Ons Land*, saw the best hope for Afrikanerdom in a spiritual rebirth, and urged Afrikaners to keep their heads and their hearts pure and uncontaminated by the 'spirit of materialism which flows in on us from Europe'.* The same ideas were reflected in a series of articles contributed to *Ons Land* by Ds. P. J. G. de Vos of Stellenbosch, published under the title *Nationale Vraagstukken* (National Questions) during the course of this troubled year. According to De Vos, the Raid had resulted from the Englishman's fundamental disrespect for the Afrikaner. Anglicized Afrikaners therefore came in for his special reprobation, above all those who still looked on Rhodes as a benefactor. These he compared to small birds which had escaped from a trap and remembered the gift of grain offered as bait, but not the intention to kill. So he told Afrikaners to recover their self-respect, prize their language as never before, and return to their Bible.

In a negative sense, these feelings found expression in a renewed suspicion of the alien, of whatever origin. S. J. du Toit urged in his first note to Hofmeyr after the Raid that firmness was necessary 'or we shall give the Hollander party a case against ourselves'.* There were many Cape Afrikaners who blamed the Dutch railway company for the Transvaal's high tariffs, and others who resented the treatment they had received when they offered their services as teachers in Mansvelt's Transvaal Education Department. Dutch firms in the Transvaal had begun to sense even before the Raid that their presence was not popular among the burghers, and began therefore to make exaggerated professions of loyalty to the Republic.* But the new Afrikaner patriotism was something in which outsiders could not share, and even the correspondence of the moderate Chief Justice Kotzé reflected this exclusive spirit, as he wrote to Hofmeyr asking him to use the Cape press and the Bond to break the influence of the 'little foreign gentlemen' (*buitenlandsche heertjes*) on Kruger.*

The indications are that Hofmeyr took these remarks seriously, as did Kruger in due course, when he came to see the practical wisdom of removing Hollanders from his leading offices of state.

There was, however, a small but influential group of Cape Afrikaners who were not only unwilling to lend their support to a narrow nationalist revival, but reluctant even to sever their ties with Rhodes. David de Waal, Hofmeyr's brother-in-law, was one of these.* So was Tom Louw, in whose house Rhodes and Hofmeyr had held their final meeting.* Rhodes's 'My Dutch', some of whom would soon find it impossible to remain within the Bond, were initially part of a larger fellowship, held together by a sense of obligation to Rhodes, or by disapproval of precipitate action, or by the feeling that the South African Republic was not, after all, entirely free from blame. Hofmeyr himself was alive to the weaknesses of Kruger's state, and although he turned down Chamberlain's proposals for the establishment of local autonomy on the Rand, which Sir Hercules Robinson submitted to him for comment in February, he agreed in May, on Robinson's instance, to submit a private memorandum which contained far-reaching ideas for the reform of the Transvaal.*[1] S. J. du Toit wanted Rhodes to be given a chance to explain himself, refused to consider the abrogation of the Charter, and considered that if separate they must, then Rhodes and the Bond should do so in a friendly manner.* When Rhodes's departure for Kimberley made Du Toit's idea of an interview impossible, he still desired to suspend judgment though he admitted to Hofmeyr that he believed Rhodes to be guilty.* There was as yet no real rift between Du Toit and Onze Jan.

Du Toit's breach with the Bond majority did not take place at the Burghersdorp congress in March 1896. F. S. Malan and Du Toit gave notice of contradictory motions on this occasion, the former blaming Rhodes for the Raid, the latter placing the onus on Jameson. Malan spoke eloquently to a motion which congratulated the Transvaal on its defeat of the raiders, thanked Hofmeyr for his stand and assured him of the Bond's support, held the Imperial Government to its promise of a full inquiry, urged Sprigg to call an early meeting of Parliament with a view to instituting a local investigation of the

[1] Hofmeyr proposed the grant of municipal government to Johannesburg, the elimination of the procedure of legislation by simple resolution [besluit]; considerable relaxation of the Transvaal franchise law in favour of uitlanders; the abolition of the Second Volksraad and the enlargement of the First.

plot, and censured Rhodes for his actions both before and after the Raid, with the clear implication that unless he gave a satisfactory explanation of them it would be impossible for the Bond to co-operate with him in the future. Du Toit rose immediately to second the motion, explaining his decision not to move the one which stood in his name. He spoke of Rhodes with greater reverence than Malan thought the occasion warranted, though he referred to his federal ideas as 'the amalgamation of the snake which swallows up the little mouse', and praised Hofmeyr's stand. When he sat down, unanimity reigned, though Malan's biographer may be right in representing the episode as a trial of strength between her father and Du Toit, in which the former won a brilliant victory.[1]

In Parliament on 12 May the Bond maintained a front as unbroken as at the Burghersdorp congress when Merriman, furious at the recent manifestations of the capitalism which he loathed, moved the revocation or alteration of the B.S.A. Company's Charter. Congress had not asked for this, and the Bond members therefore supported an amendment by Schreiner which called for the appoint-ment of a select committee of inquiry, and asked the Imperial Government to alter the governance of Rhodesia so as to prevent the possibility of a repetition of the Raid. It is possible, as Walker has suggested, that Schreiner dissuaded Hofmeyr and his colleagues from supporting Merriman's proposal, but it is more probable that he and they together decided on a form of words which corresponded with the Burghersdorp congress resolution, as Schreiner's motion did.*[2] The Bond members were bound to follow the lead of congress on a point of this kind. The amendment was duly carried and a

---

[1] The 'David and Goliath' quality of the account in Cloete (p. 128) is not reflected in Malan's version (*Ons Land*, 17, 21 Mar. 1896), or in Du Toit's (*Patriot*, 19 Mar. 1896, and the unofficial minutes reprinted from *De Paarl*), or in the version taken over from the *Express* in Hofmeyr, N. J., pp. 398–416, or in the official *Notulen*, pp. 9–10. None of these versions suggest that an open clash took place on the floor of congress, followed by an adjournment for the purpose of lobbying, followed by an unexpected decision on Du Toit's part to admit defeat before seconding Malan's motion. They indicate rather that the whole question was disposed of, from beginning to end, on the morning of Saturday 14 Mar., apparently without undue friction. There may, of course, have been a clash behind the scenes.

[2] The Burghersdorp resolution had not asked for the revocation of the Charter, but merely expressed the wish 'that sweeping changes [*ingrijpende veranderingen*] in the administration of Rhodesia shall be brought about in order to prevent such attacks as that of Dr. Jameson in the future'.

12

select committee was appointed under Upington. Its report, attributing responsibility for the Raid to Rhodes, was adopted without opposition on 24 July.*

It is not known beyond all doubt why S. J. du Toit should have persisted, even after the adoption of the select committee report, in his refusal to admit in public that Rhodes was guilty. The suggestion that he was bought by Rhodes is, however, difficult to resist. Nine days before the Assembly's adoption of the Raid report, a new Dutch-language newspaper, *Het Dagblad*, appeared in Paarl under the editorship of S. J. du Toit. The paper was to replace *De Paarl*, though the *Patriot* would still appear as its week-end supplement. *Het Dagblad* claimed to be a Bond organ, affirmed Bond principles, and professed to aim at the reconciliation of the Dutch and English sections of the population. It is often confidently asserted that Rhodes subsidized the new journal but the argument rests mainly on reasonable conjecture, although Du Toit's biographer does not directly deny the charge.*

Having left the Colony in January 1896, Rhodes did not return until after his dramatic ending of the Matabele rebellion in October. He then made a triumphal progress through Natal and the Cape Colony before sailing for England from Cape Town in January 1897, to attend the Imperial Commission of Inquiry into the Raid. *Het Dagblad*, despite the wave of jingo feeling which Rhodes's return inspired, contained little to which the faithful Bondsmen could legitimately take exception before Rhodes's departure for England. It deprecated the idea that Rhodes should be given a public reception when he arrived in Cape Town in January, and still placed the onus on him to prove his innocence in respect of the Raid.* But this was the position Du Toit had held a year earlier, whereas the Bondsmen in general were now openly condemning Rhodes's actions and waiting to see him punished.

The Malmesbury congress was the turning point. A delegate from Colesberg moved the repudiation of the editorial policy of *Het Dagblad*, and the rejection of its claim to be a Bond organ. The fact that the paper had not yet committed a major indiscretion was borne out by the lack of unanimity in congress.* S. J. du Toit put up a spirited defence, but the meeting carried by 35 to 25 an amendment by J. M. Hoffman of Paarl to the effect that recognition should be withheld on the ground that it had never been granted. Congress then clarified its position on other related issues and, taking the findings of the Cape select committee as sufficient justification for a final breach with Rhodes, roundly declared that 'all considerations of national self-respect, political honour and good faith command the National Afrikaner Party not to lend Mr. Rhodes any more political support at all, whether at public meetings, in the press, at the ballot-box, in Parliament, or anywhere else'.* It disowned two Rhodes men, Thomas Louw and M. M. Venter, who had been summoned to the London inquiry to present the 'Dutch point of view', and spent £10 on a cable to London declaring that they were unrepresentative.* It also decided to warn all branches against the danger of weakening the 'good cause of Afrikanerism' by compromising with other parties whose principles were repugnant to those of the Bond. With congress in this mood, Du Toit must have realized that the parting of the ways had come; but he still chose to remain in the Bond in the vain hope that he might be able to check its new trend from the inside.

His hope was vain because it was not possible, in the hardening political climate of 1897, to build up by such methods a moderate centre party which was capable of holding its own against the twin pressures of the Afrikaner Bond and its emergent imperialist rival, the South African League. The League, which had come into being since the Jameson Raid,* was rapidly gaining in strength, and had a membership in the Colony of 4,500 by July 1896,[1] distributed through branches which increased from twenty-four in May 1896 to seventy-four in October 1900. Its structure was federal; it had associated branches in the Transvaal and Natal, and an affiliated ally, the South African Association, in England. The League fought for British supremacy in South Africa, appealing to English ultra-loyalists, urban free-traders and progressive sheep-farmers alike. It charged the Afrikaner Bond, somewhat gratuitously, with racism, and presented the novel spectacle in Colonial politics of a political organization which seriously set itself the task of forcing the Bondsmen on to the Opposition benches.

Standing in the same sort of relationship to the League as Du Toit's splinter group stood to the Bond, though it claimed no integral connection with the League, was the South African Political Association founded by Innes in May 1895, with a platform of cheap bread, dear brandy, and a humane native policy.

The emergence of a centre party thus depended on the ability of

[1] The official Bond membership in Mar. 1896 was 8,511.

Innes's and Du Toit's groups to reach across the cultural gap and find each other. The political climate in mid-1897 was not entirely unfavourable to such a development. Sir Alfred Milner, the new Governor and High Commissioner, had only recently arrived and was still taking stock of the situation in an unprovocative manner. Rhodes, who was back in Rhodesia, had not yet announced his intention of returning to Colonial politics. The ministry, for all its tensions, and for all the pressure being put on Te Water to induce him to resign,[1] showed no signs of breaking up. In these circumstances, Innes might have come forward with an appeal to moderate Bondsmen. He did not, partly because he did not believe that his own position was a strong one,* and partly because he did not receive sufficient encouragement from the other side. *Het Dagblad* considered and rejected the idea that Innes might lead a centre party.* This was a role which Du Toit assigned, with strange insensitivity, to the Bond, in a series of articles in August and September, entitled 'Our Political Earthquake' (*Onze Politieke Aardbewing*). On 29 October *Het Dagblad* said:

'We have been advocating for more than a year . . . that a strong moderate party should be formed in Parliament, by which means the progressive Africanders and the moderate Englishmen can join each other and can co-operate in a broad, healthy South African policy. . . . The reason why the Bond on the one hand and the League on the other so often go over to extremes cannot be ascribed to their principles as laid down in their programmes, but to the sentiments of their individual members.'

But, he added, 'the door of the Bond is open still', and he urged moderates of both language groups to join the Bond and turn it from its mistaken ways.

Du Toit would have done better to make a clean break with the Bond and with Rhodes, both for the sake of his own public image and to assure Innes and other moderates of his good faith. But he was perhaps the wrong person to make the gesture, for it was the weakness of all the Bond renegades, the 'Nicodemuses who visit me by night' as Innes remembered Rhodes describing them, that they were unable to convince the public mind of the disinterestedness of

<hr>

[1] Between May and September 1897, Te Water received letters urging him to resign from C.H.O. Marais, Ds. W. P. de Villiers, D. P. van den Heever and several others (Te Water Papers).

their motives. Furthermore, Du Toit's influence in the Bond had been destroyed at the Malmesbury congress just at a time when, as at the start of his political career, he found himself cut off from his fellow clergy on account of his attempts to launch another schismatic movement, the *Gereformeerde Kerke Onder die Kruis* (Reformed Churches under the Cross), in the Cape Church.[*1] The moment when Rhodes was making up his mind to resume his political career, as he did in January 1898 at the head of a new Progressive Party, was not one at which the leadership of the moderates should have been in ineffectual hands, for he and the Bond were in the mood to crush independents.[2] The manner of the crushing may be seen in the Western Province Legislative Council election of 1898.

At the end of August 1897, on the evidence of interviews conducted by a group of Bondsmen, the Paarl district *bestuur* decided to back the candidature of J. A. Faure, a Paarl wine farmer, in preference to M. L. Neethling, a Legislative Councillor of longer standing, in the knowledge that there was no chance of more than one Bondsman winning a seat.[*] Innes was also interested in Faure's candidature.[*] But before the end of the year Faure had begun to show signs of having come under the influence of Rhodes.[*] The South African Political Association and the Cape Town Bondsmen therefore decided to drop him, and a section of the Paarl Bondsmen led by Dr. J. M. Hoffman set out to have his nomination cancelled. The *Commissie van Toezicht* then ruled that in the event of the official nomination day's occurring after the expiry in December of the term of office of existing Bond *besturen*, which it did, all Bond nominations for Council seats were to be regarded as invalid, and fresh ones were to be made by the new *besturen*.[*] Because of the Paarl situation, as David de Waal told Rhodes, Hofmeyr 'upset the whole election in the Colony'.[*] But the Paarl district *bestuur*, which represented three-quarters of the Bondsmen in the circle and in which the influence of S. J. du Toit was still dominant, saw red. They turned down, on a technicality, Hoffman's application to set up a new branch of Zuider Paarl, which would have supported Neethling, and instead founded Noorder Paarl, which backed

[1] Meetings of the faithful had been held in Paarl in Jan. 1896 and Jan. 1897, but had failed to make much impression on the mass of the church people.

[2] Michell records that Rhodes said at Port Elizabeth on 17th Sept., 'I can respect your Bondsmen, and I can fight your Bondsmen. . . . But these Independents! I cannot stand them.'

Faure.* Meanwhile the Cape Town Bondsmen nominated Neethling and invited the delegates from the Paarl district *bestuur* to attend a meeting in Cape Town on 29 December to elect the candidate for the circle. But when Du Toit and Van Eyk arrived on the appointed day, the Cape Town delegate, Tielman Hofmeyr, was not present— by design, as it subsequently transpired, in order not to be involved in a meeting which would certainly have chosen the Paarl candidate.*

The Paarl district *bestuur*, meeting on 12 January, therefore asked the *Commissie van Toezicht* to declare Faure the lawful candidate. Onze Jan found an excuse for not doing so: he had only received the request on 24 January, which did not give him time to investigate the question before official nomination day on 5 February; he was therefore unable to do more than judge according to the bare facts of the case, which were that a quorum had not been present at the *cirkelvergadering*; but he would willingly refer the case to his alternate (J. P. du Plessis, member for Cradock, who was on his deathbed). N. F. de Waal concurred. Du Toit, the third member of the *Commissie*, correctly referred the matter to his alternate, T. P. Theron; but Theron endorsed Hofmeyr's view.* The *Commissie* had acted dictatorially to bring a branch to heel, because in its view the branch majority was out of step with congress. Understandably, *Het Dagblad* protested over the 'Bond dictatorship [which] has definitely been established at the *Ons Land* office'. Faure and Neethling were both in due course returned to the Legislative Council.

There was a contested election for the *Commissie van Toezicht* at the Worcester congress, where seventeen candidates were proposed to fill the three positions.* After three ballots, only Hofmeyr was left of the original *Commissie*—S. J. du Toit being rejected in favour of his Paarl opponent, J. M. Hoffman, and N. F. de Waal losing by a narrow margin to T. P. Theron. Du Toit's influence was thereby excluded, and the majority proceeded to dig themselves in by adopting two changes in the constitution as proposed in the outgoing *Commissie's* majority report:* one empowered the provincial *bestuur* to dissolve and reconstitute any ward or district *bestuur* in the event of its coming under any influence 'which is disadvantageous for or hostile towards the organization';* the other gave the *Commissie* the sort of discretion it had already used in the case of the Western circle election, namely, the right to refuse recognition as a Bond candidate to any person so chosen, should it consider that the interests of the Bond would be furthered by such refusal.* Theron was very uncomfortable over the congress decision and feared a major upheaval in the party. He suggested to Frederic de Waal that an open letter to all Bondsmen should appear in the press, urging them to petition for a delay in the reprinting of the constitution until the next congress had had a chance to consider the Worcester amendments. De Waal passed the letter on to Hofmeyr with adverse comments, which Onze Jan endorsed.*[1] The amended constitution was therefore published and the seal set upon the schism.

Meanwhile the Progressives won the Council elections—a victory which Du Toit interpreted as a vindication of the attitude which he had gone down defending in congress:

'One thing is perfectly clear: the future belongs to the Progressives. There is only one remedy for the Bond party; namely, to pursue a moderately progressive policy, to leave the retrogressive course they have lately been following, and not to run candidates with such extreme views. If this is declined, the result of the Legislative Assembly election will be a more crushing defeat to them than was the case at the Council election.'*

These remarks, a curious compound of moderation and defeatism, illustrate his frame of mind when, on 23 April, he and his Paarl supporters established a new political party, the Colonial Union (*Koloniale Unie*), to witness to the errors into which the Afrikaner Bond had fallen.

The nucleus round which Du Toit built his new party was those members of the Paarl district *bestuur* who had backed the candidature of J. A. Faure. They had two main objectives: to remove hatred between the two European nationalities, and to operate at all levels of the party machine on the strict majority principle.* Could one join the new party while remaining in the Bond? Du Toit turned this awkward question aside at the inaugural meeting, for it exposed the pathos of his own position: his severance in practice, though not by any formal act of resignation or expulsion, from the party of his own creation.* But it was evident that the Colonial Union men would have to oppose the Bond in the forthcoming Assembly elections, and the only question was whether they would fight as an independent

[1] Hofmeyr noted: 'To follow Tom's advice could be interpreted as incitement of branches to defiance of Provincial Bestuur. . . . I have no liberty to advise anything else than to adhere to your instructions.'

middle party or join forces with Rhodes and his Progressives. In fact they did the latter,[1] and thereby destroyed what slender chance they had of drawing moderate men away from the Bond. Though they met in congress in 1899,[2] the party never gathered momentum. In the meantime, in September 1898, Du Toit had had to admit that the publication of a Dutch-language daily 'does not serve the purpose we had expected to attain'.* *Het Dagblad* ceased forthwith, though *De Kolonist* continued with lesser frequency. Du Toit, after fighting and failing to win Richmond in the 1898 election, quietly withdrew from politics, the better to serve his religious and linguistic interests.

The departure of S. J. du Toit into the wilderness marked the end of a political career which was full of contradictions and in which only two constant features stand out: his devotion to neo-Calvinist doctrine and his desire to secure the acceptance of the Afrikaans language in public life and public worship. Beside these aims, both of which preceded and outlasted his venture into politics, all else was fickle. A prolific writer, with a firm grasp of academic principles within a narrow field, he seems to have lacked the originality of the real scholar. Impetuous to a fault, given in some degree to casuistry, he was the sort of person who probably did not know when he was bluffing himself. To one writer he has appeared as a 'lonely Ishmael',* to another as the victim of a disappointed idealism.* He possessed a rare gift for getting out of step with his closest political allies, and was a bad politician largely because he had the courage of his own unstable convictions. There is a suggestion of classic tragedy in a career which began with the brash uncouthness of a political revivalism largely of his own making (though it grew out of a real need), and ended in tempestuous days with a mellow but sadly ineffectual plea for political peace.

II. WILD TONGUES

Sprigg was ever on the look-out for parliamentary allies who might replace the Bondsmen on the Government benches. His association with the Bond brought constant problems owing to the uncertainty of Te Water's position and the Bondsmen's deep division over scab, to which was added further friction in 1897 over the way to handle

[1] See below pp. 186–7.

[2] The branches then represented, at Paarl, Barkly West, Prieska, Britstown and Cape Town (see Coetzee, p. 188), were chiefly in areas where the *Kruiskerk* movement had attracted some following.

a serious rinderpest epidemic.* In April 1897 the majority of the Bond members had voted against the Government in a 'no confidence' division, and the Government owed its survival to the backing of the official Opposition, the casting vote of the Speaker, and the timely return of Rhodes from his ordeal in London. But Sprigg was not one to forsake one group of political supporters without making sure that their opponents would serve him better. He therefore continued to cultivate Bond support by voting for P. J. du Toit's peace motion in April 1897—a very wordy appeal for the reciprocal observance of obligations and treaties, which the House carried against Innes's motion for the redress of 'legitimate uitlander grievances'. He ended the Langeberg rebellion in Bechuanaland by the traditional method of confiscating tribal land for white occupation, to the consternation of Milner and the glee of the Bond.* He went out of his way to resist the growing agitation in the towns for the removal of agricultural protection, and the Bondsmen appreciated his efforts.* Despite this show of co-operation, however, the partnership wore thinner by the day. Sprigg left Cape Town in the middle of June to attend Queen Victoria's diamond jubilee celebrations and the colonial conference in London. He responded to the spirit of the occasion, and took liberties with the benevolence of the Cape Parliament, by offering a warship to the Imperial navy on his own initiative. 'That battleship' became a live political issue at the Cape from the moment Sprigg laid her imaginary keel until the Schreiner Government settled the question with an annual grant of £30,000 to the Imperial navy and the handing over of the Simonstown dockyard. The Bondsmen, who charged Sprigg with irresponsibility, at the same time offered to pay for a deep-sea west coast cable,* though the South African League, with some assistance from Milner,* sought to use the Bond's attitude over 'H.M.S. *Africander*' as a pretext for imputing disloyalty to them.

Such imputations of disloyalty, the first ranging shots in the League's electoral campaign, were perhaps to be expected at such a heady time; but their damaging effect on South African public relations deserves emphasis. Given a reasonable show of confidence from the Imperial authorities, the Bond could well have been a potent force for peace in the tense year of 1899. But League propaganda effectively cast doubts on the Bond's bona fides, sowing suspicion not only in the mind of Milner (where it found receptive soil) but also in the Colonial Office in London, whose historians have stressed the *assumption* of the responsible British statesmen of the day that the Bondsmen's hearts were in Kruger's camp.* This was a tragedy for South Africa, for the additional reason that the case made against the Bond was a very bad one.[1] The Bondsmen admittedly spent little time in congress discussing how to strengthen the Imperial tie, and their contribution to Imperial development was largely wrapped up in the not inconsiderable efforts of Jan Hofmeyr at the colonial conferences of 1887 and 1894, which congress never troubled to endorse;* but they had consistently shown at least

[1] If the attitude of the Afrikaner Bond during the crisis of 1898–9 is to be seen in proper perspective, the extent to which this attitude was misrepresented in contemporary and subsequent literature must be taken into account. It was a common device in writings hostile to the Bond at the time of the South African war, of which Josiah Slater's *The Birth of the Bond* and Scoble and Abercrombie's *The Rise and Fall of Krugerism* were typical examples, to base the charge of Bond disloyalty during the late 1890's on the evidence of the more extreme Bond propaganda during the excitements of the early 1880's. This was unhistorical and it was dishonest; and the book in which the most unscrupulous use of this technique was made, C. H. Thomas's *The Origin of the Anglo-Boer War Revealed* (*c.* 1900), has mesmerized later writers to a remarkable degree.

Thomas, who claimed to have been an Orange Free State burgher, knew so little about the Afrikaner Bond that he thought it had originated in and that it derived its direction from Holland. He charged this 'Dutch' body with responsibility for the South African War. He thought that Paul Kruger was a member. He almost ignored the Bond in the Cape, save for giving at pp. 64–9 what he described as 'Memoranda of Bond Programme, Emanating from Holland (Translation from Gleanings)' which appear to owe something to *Patriot* editorials during its early anti-British phase, but do not read like authentic quotations. W. B. Worsfold, in his *Lord Milner's work in South Africa*, took over this passage from Thomas and gave it a more authentic look (pp. 48–57). In A. P. Newton's *Select Documents relating to the Unification of South Africa*, (i, 86), the same extract has become a 'document' tentatively dated 1881, but one to be regarded as 'not authoritative' and 'reprinted . . . as illustrating a particular point of view'. Headlam, however, relying on one or other of these sources, used the same material without reservations of any kind (i, 44–7). From Headlam, the legend has passed to J. E. Wrench, *Alfred, Lord Milner: The Man of No Illusions*, p. 175, and it even has the dignity of a footnote in E. A. Walker's *History of Southern Africa*, p. 389.

Not all contemporary works in English maligned the Afrikaner Bond, however. Of those which did not, F. J. Dormer's *Vengeance as a Policy in Afrikanderland* and J. A. Hobson's *The War in South Africa* were perhaps the most dispassionate. Dormer, whose South African experience had brought him in close touch with Saul Solomon, Jan Hofmeyr, and the newspaper world in Cape Town and Johannesburg, was particularly well qualified to assess the situation. Hobson saw the situation as an outsider and a critic of imperialism.

formal respect for the throne, they had never given encouragement
to any other imperial power to set foot in southern Africa, and they
had always taken British naval protection for granted as their first
line of defence.* They therefore resented the allegations made, and
angrily rejected them at Worcester in February 1898, in a resolution
which Hofmeyr was instructed to present to the Governor.*

Milner, on arrival in South Africa in May 1897, had expressed a
desire to establish cordial relations with the Afrikaner people. He
learned the Dutch language, he soon claimed that he was keeping
abreast with comment in the Dutch-language newspapers, and he
took the earliest opportunity after his arrival to go on an extended
tour of the country districts in order to meet the people. 'We are
getting on capitally with the Dutch', he told Chamberlain in July.
'Feeling all round much better than when I came, but'—and then
followed the illuminating but ominous comment—'improvement
began with and depends on [their] conviction [of the] determination
[of] Great Britain not to be ousted'.* His attitude seems to have been
determined less by an empirical effort to understand the views and
ideals of Colonial Afrikaners, than by a notion that such views as
they held, and which he claimed to understand, could not in the
nature of the case be reconciled with the aims of Imperial policy as
he thought these ought to be. A letter to Sir Clinton Dawkins in
Egypt, which contained the question 'Would the French Canadians
be loyal, if the United States were a *French* Republic?'; and another
to Sir Edward Grey almost two years later, in which he described
the Afrikaner party as consisting of an extremist element of
republican rebels and a less extreme section who would sing 'God
save the Queen' if allowed to govern themselves, but would not
support a wholesale clean-up of the Transvaal administration
for fear that this would endanger Afrikaner ascendancy in the
Republic*—these are indications of the depth of Milner's mistrust
of Afrikanerdom, which an episode in March 1898 would
underline.

In that month Milner went to Graaff-Reinet to open a new railway
line. The local Bondsmen had been considering for some weeks, in
a political atmosphere which seems to have grown heated, how best
to use the occasion to demonstrate their loyalty. C. H. O. Marais
indicated to Te Water how difficult it was to choose the right form
of words for an address, and asked the minister to prepare a draft
—in Dutch if Milner could understand it—with a view to a private

presentation when Milner reached the town.*[1] How or if Te Water
replied may never be known; but he accompanied Milner to
Graaff-Reinet, and it is at least likely that he had something to
do with the address which Marais read to Milner in Dutch on
his arrival at the station. It was a carefully worded address,
in which the Bondsmen welcomed Milner as their Queen's
representative, deplored the allegations of disloyalty which had been
made against themselves, and asked Milner to clear them of the
stigma. They professed the intention of making their own section of
the population better subjects, and a desire 'to assure to our blood
relations in South Africa the rights which Her Majesty our Respected
Queen has graciously vouchsafed in the past'.* The Governor
reserved his reply (which he composed during brief interludes in a
crowded day) until the official banquet held that evening. He was
not the first person to be placed in an embarrassing situation by the
formal and possibly unexpected attentions of Bondsmen. Their
address did not contain affirmations of loyalty only; there was also
a phrase which might be construed as a criticism of Imperial policy
towards the Transvaal. It was presented just at a time when Milner
was beginning to feel that the screw on the Transvaal should be
tightened; and it came from an organization whose congress a
fortnight earlier had warmly congratulated President Kruger on his
successful re-election.* Furthermore, the Colonial Council elections
were in full swing, and there was some reason for construing the
address as an attempt by midland Bondsmen to obtain a certificate
of political decency for electoral purposes. Milner said he was glad
to be assured of their loyalty, but he would have preferred to be able
to take it for granted. Then, after extolling the advantages of life
in the Colony under British rule, he said he felt conscience-bound
to mention certain 'unpleasant facts'. He went on to assert that when

    [1] After beginning in Dutch, Marais continued in English as follows: 'Is it not
possible for you to draft me a copy in pencil so that we can have the right thing—
of course everything will be kept private. Please try to assist me in this matter
and please let me know if the address must be in Dutch or English. I prefer
Dutch if the Gov[ernor] can understand it. [Then follows an account of how
Marais had opposed an attempt by members of the reception committee to have
Rhodes invited to the opening of the railway.] . . . My intention is not to give the
address to the Governor on his arrival but we want you so to arrange it that a
deputation of the Africander party meet him at his house to give him an address
as the address which is drawn up by the comite [sic] is for the whole town and
district—please let me know also what you think of it and also let me know by
whom the address is to [be] signed.'

disputes arose between the Imperial Government and the South
African Republic, 'a number of people in the Colony at once
vehemently, and without even the semblance of impartiality,
espouse the side of the Republic'.* He declared that it was 'improper
for a Governor, especially at a time of electioneering, to concern
himself with rebutting charges brought by one party against another'.
But, so far from rebutting the charges, he had underlined them. The
local *Advertiser* interpreted Milner's address in this way. But Marais
rode the blow with apparent composure:

'The "Advertiser" appears to look on the Bondsmen as children
in political matters, or it would have realized that by asking a direct
question the Bond wanted to evoke [*uitlokken*] a direct answer. . . .
We have evoked criticism in our address, and therefore expected
criticism, and, thanks be to God, Bondsmen can take criticism.'*

Deliberate provocation, therefore? But the original intention
seems to have been to present the address in private.

Barely had Milner uttered, than Rhodes took up the refrain in
an interview with the *Cape Times* on 8 March, making his first open
attack on the 'little gang in Camp Street' (the street in Cape
Town where Hofmeyr lived) to mark the occasion of his
return to Colonial political life.* The return of their unrepentant
prodigal, together with victory in the Council elections, had put the
Progressives in buoyant mood and done much to weaken the link
between the Bond and Sprigg. But the Bondsmen gained too, by
attracting anti-capitalists of all hues, with some big names among
them such as John X. Merriman. He had little enough sympathy
for sectional nationalism, but nurtured a growing dislike for Rhodes
and the Chartered Company, and a conviction that the Imperial
factor worked only harm.* With Merriman, almost as a matter of
course, went Sauer. W. P. Schreiner followed after rather more
hesitation. His political association with Hofmeyr dated back to
1894, when Hofmeyr had arranged for Schreiner to stand as a Bond
candidate for Barkly West. He was still in the pre-liberal phase of
his development, having given his backing to the Langeberg confisca-
tions and fathered a Transkeian Territories Act which armed the
Governor with extensive powers of arbitrary arrest and detention
in the tribal areas.* Strong family pressure, notably from his sister
Olive, at first kept him at a distance from the Bondsmen, as did his
friendship with Rhodes, which was shaken by the Raid but not

broken until they met on the way to the London inquiry in January 1897. Even then he would not become a Bondsman, though he began to see the Bond, for all its lack of sophistication, in the light of a sober counterpoise to the dangers of Rhodes's unprincipled bid for power. When Parliament met, he would soon be brought into a close relationship with the Bond through the very fact of becoming *de facto* Leader of the Opposition.*

It was redistribution that finally killed the alliance between Sprigg and the Bond. Given the fact of very unequal constituencies and the absence of any system of regular redelimitation,[1] it was to be expected that at this moment of political crisis the Progressives would agitate for more equal representation, for this held out to them the prospect of clear political advantage. The Bondsmen, though they tried to work up arguments for a redistribution in favour of the rural constituencies,* were really more concerned to ensure that the subtle balance of forces in the legislature should not be disturbed to the advantage of a party of which their *bête noire*, Rhodes, was emerging as the real leader. Yet the case in favour of redistribution was so strong, considered mathematically, that even the Bond members of Sprigg's redistribution commission in 1897 agreed that some was desirable*[2]—and legislation was therefore bound to follow in 1898. When he learned that Sprigg intended to go ahead with his redistribution plans, Te Water resigned from the Cabinet, to the relief of many of his Bond supporters.*[3] His resignation removed all necessity for the Cabinet to continue to hold a middle course, as Milner fully realized,* and assisted the polarization of political forces in the Colony which it was perhaps already too late to prevent.

Sprigg based his Redistribution Bill on the more extreme minority report of the previous year and, with the help of the Opposition and

[1] The greatest disparity was between Victoria East, which in 1897 had 782 voters, and Port Elizabeth which had 6,560. Each returned two members. The details of the representation had been laid down in the Constitution Ordinance of 1853, subsequent changes being made by statute.

[2] Sprigg was chairman; T. P. Theron, I. J. van der Walt and A. S. du Plessis represented the Bond, the other members being Innes, Fuller and Douglass. All agreed to the creation of 15 new seats, while the minority, consisting of the last three, wanted 18.

[3] Ds. W. P. de Villiers, for example. Pieter Faure and Sivewright, the other Bond members of the Cabinet, had changed their loyalty and would fight against the Bond in the following elections for Namaqualand and Stellenbosch respectively.

most of the Innes group, he carried the second reading by 42 votes
to 35. Schreiner, realizing with Hofmeyr that if Sprigg were not
immediately defeated the Progressives might well entrench themselves in power, moved a vote of no confidence on 31 May. With the
help of some of the moderates, who wanted redistribution but did
not want Rhodes, he achieved the defeat of Sprigg.* Milner dissolved
the Assembly at Sprigg's request at the end of June, and the parties
began to prepare for the fiercest general election in the Colony's
history.

III. THE TUMULT AND THE SHOUTING

The 1898 Assembly election was fierce because the stakes were high
and the result was expected to be very close. It was the first Cape
election in which two recognizable parties were ranged against each
other, and each feared that the other's victory would be followed by
an attempt to change the constitution with a view to the permanent
exclusion of its opponents from power. Under these circumstances
the bitterness and the dishonesty of much of the electioneering was
understandable, though there was a great deal more of it than usual
—most of it on the side of the Bond's opponents.

On the whole the Progressives' allegations of Bond corruption
did not stick. There were several charges made: that Hofmeyr had
been venal, though the charge was made in such a way that Onze
Jan could truthfully deny it;[1] that secret agents from the Transvaal
played a prominent part in developing the Bond's election campaign;*
and that the Bond was assisted by contributions from the Transvaal
secret service fund.* The inherent probability that there were
Transvaal agents in the Colony gives some colour to the second of
these charges, though if agents there were—a fact which even
Kruger seems to have admitted*—it would be difficult to show that
they were doing more than the work of an ordinary intelligence
service. So far as the financial allegation is concerned, the evidence
is conflicting, inconclusive, and partly suspect for the reason that
the Progressives admitted the receipt of substantial funds from
Rhodes and clearly desired to show that the Bond was similarly
endowed from outside.* The records of the *Commissie van Toezicht*,
which handled all the regular disbursements connected with the
election, not only contain no evidence of outside help (apart from a
sum of £4,500 attributed by Hofmeyr to his ever-anonymous 'Cape

[1] See above, p. 133.

Town friends'), but suggest strongly that the Bond fought the election on a shoestring.[1] The theory that Transvaal money was paid, not through the normal channels but privately through J. W. Sauer, looks convincing on the surface because Sauer nearly lost his seat on a petition which alleged bribery; but Sauer was not unseated, for all Chief Justice De Villiers's qualms over his injudicious distribution of free blankets.*[2]

It is less difficult to establish corruption on the part of the Progressives because the worst charges against them were proved in the subsequent election petitions, and this resulted in the unseating of three of their candidates.[3] Whether, as was suggested in Bond quarters, Rhodes's money was instrumental in turning Coloured voters against the Bond, would be difficult to prove even though the disbursement of money to Coloured people was demonstrated in the Stellenbosch constituency.* But since the Progressives lost the campaign, it cannot be held that their corrupt practices were decisive.

The Bond's marginal victory on a substantial minority of votes was due in no small measure to luck*—the smile of fortune, perhaps, on the relatively cleaner campaign, but also on Hofmeyr's shrewd electoral tactics. On 28 March he spoke at Cape Town and, with his mind on the non-white electorate, proclaimed that he had not voted for the Strop Bill, had 'never tried to deprive a single Native of the vote which he had already acquired', and 'never joined in the insensate cry of "Equal rights for all white men south of the Zambesi" '.* The claims were modest enough, and the Bond papers

[1] There are no consolidated election accounts in the Bond archives and, contrary to normal practice—whatever the reasons—the financial statement at the 1898 congress was tabled but not minuted. The treasurer's report to the 1899 congress showed a payment to the *Commissie van Toezicht* of just over £300, presumably for electoral purposes, while the Bond's main capital asset, a fixed deposit in the Standard Bank which had stood at £450 in 1897, had now fallen to £300. Although precise figures for disbursements by the *Commissie* do not exist, an undated balance sheet indicates that it spent only £113 16s. 6d. on the Council elections, of which it was able to recoup £56 12s. 0d. from branch and private contributions. Grants made to candidates for Assembly seats out of provincial *bestuur* funds by the *Commissie* were usually for amounts of £25 or £50, and it is impossible from the records to account for more than about £250 distributed in this way.

[2] H. D. Stiglingh, Rhodes's opponent in Barkly West, took Rhodes to court for alleging that he had used Transvaal funds, and won his case.

[3] Sivewright in Stellenbosch, Haarhoff and Fincham in Vryburg.

reporting the speech did not choose to dwell on its 'negrophilist' aspects; but this was the first purposeful attempt by a Bondsman in authority to look for the votes of non-white people, and Tengo Jabavu, faced with the problem of loyalty to men such as Merriman and Sauer who were now allied to the Bond, decided to take his words at face value, even though *Imvo* had been counselling Africans to vote against Bond candidates as late as 10 March. He described Hofmeyr's speech as an 'epoch-making address in the politics of the country', paid tribute to him as a tactician, and continued:

'He has discerned the Progressive wave, evidenced by the Legislative Council elections, which has deprived him of an absolute Bond majority in the Upper House; and, like a wise man, he counts the cost of entering into a fight with those commanding larger forces than himself, and makes terms of peace. . . . The decadence of the Bond offers him a surcease from his labours, and he reverts to type, unfurling as liberal and progressive a programme on the Native question that [*sic*] any political leader could lay before the country. . . . It would not be right not to give Mr. Sauer credit for this magnanimous utterance of Mr. Hofmeyr's. . . . So that when it was said that Mr. Sauer had gone over to Mr. Hofmeyr, we clung to the belief that it was Mr. Hofmeyr who had returned to Mr. Sauer, by whom he fought side by side in 1879–81 in the great Disarmament struggle.'*

Jabavu would have preferred Innes to Schreiner, the likely candidate for the premiership; but he too was a tactician and offered Hofmeyr an electoral alliance in the constituencies fought by his liberal friends who had broken away from Rhodes.* The victory of Merriman and the Bondsman P. J. de Wet in Wodehouse, and of Sauer and the Bondsman J. N. P. Botha in Aliwal North, brought the alliance two important electoral gains—not, it would appear, as a result of increased African votes for Bondsmen, because the Bond had won a seat in each of these constituencies in 1894, but because Merriman and Sauer, with Bond support, were able to beat the Progressive vote. This being so, it mattered little that the Bond failed for the most part to attract the African vote elsewhere—in Queenstown, where Jabavu promised neutrality;* in King William's Town, where Richard Solomon, Jabavu's preferred candidate, declined to stand;* in Fort Beaufort, where their position was so hopeless that no Bond candidates entered the lists. To look after the

Coloured and African vote in the key constituency of Barkly West, Hofmeyr could count on the support of Cronwright-Schreiner and his still abler wife, Olive, who at least set about exploding Rhodes's 'negrophilism' with imagination. They accepted Hofmeyr's suggestion that an article should be written on 'Mr. Rhodes's Oppressive Native Policy', accompanied by a photograph from *Peter Halket*,[1] provided Olive was spared the publicity. 'Say simply', Cronwright suggested, 'that this is a photograph taken at Bulawayo, showing how natives are treated in Rhodesia. And *don't mention the Transvaal*.'* But Rhodes, in the course of an election campaign which his biographers usually choose to dwell on, was more than a match even for opposition of this kind.* With the help of Colonial Union supporters who split the local Bond branches, he secured not only his own return but that of a little-known colleague as well. The Bond programme contained no new deal for the black or coloured man, nor could its agents compete with the lucrative attractions which Rhodes's men had to offer, and by and large they failed to attract their votes.

The influence of Hofmeyr's 'negrophilists' was largely offset by that of Rhodes's 'My Dutch'. One of these, Gert Olivier, secured an Oudtshoorn seat after the Speaker, Sir Henry Juta, whom the Bondsmen would have supported as an independent, ruined his chances by going over to the Progressives.* Danie Haarhoff, another of Rhodes's Dutchmen, secured a Vryburg seat. This was a constituency which the Bondsmen ought to have carried; but one of their candidates was killed in a railway accident after nomination day, and another factor was that the League had taken the precaution in the previous year of placing on the voters' roll many volunteers who had participated in the suppression of the Langeberg rising, and of making arrangements for them to return and record their votes.*[2] It was Piketberg, however, which presented Hofmeyr with his

[1] The first edition of Olive Schreiner's *Trooper Peter Halket* (1897) carried a frontispiece showing five African corpses hanging from a tree, with white men standing nonchalantly below.

[2] The Progressives were later unseated on petition, and though their supporters organized a mass immigration into the constituency for the subsequent by-election, the Cape Bondsmen arranged for the presence at Vryburg of two Stellenbosch students 'thoroughly at home in the working of cameras' and warned their candidates to have 'a good strong contingent of detectives at polling station'. These precautions proved sufficient to ensure a Bond electoral victory.

biggest poser. David de Waal was too strong locally to be dislodged, chiefly on account of his past stewardship on behalf of the grain farmers and his fight to secure a local railway. Though still a Bondsman, he had remained close to Rhodes and followed an independent line in Parliament. After first demurring, the *Commissie van Toezicht* decided to support him.* In the next Parliament, De Waal would find himself on the point of balance between the parties, able to throw his weight whichever way he chose.

The contribution of the Colonial Union men to the Progressive electoral successes was slight but not entirely negligible. The Richmond Bond candidates complained to Hofmeyr of the activities of the Colonial Union in that constituency, where the members of the Colonial Union and the *Kruiskerkers* were usually the same people, and where S. J. du Toit was able to poll 646 votes. Strydenburg, near Hope Town, where the first *Kruiskerk* had been founded in 1897, was reported to be full of Colonial Union supporters, while there were allusions in the Bond correspondence to '*Kruiskerkers in de spoorweg* [railway]'.* A. S. le Roex, an old stalwart from Fraserburg, who had a long-standing affinity with S. J. du Toit, stood against the official Bond candidates in the Victoria West constituency. He had the support of one branch in Victoria West, two in Fraserburg, and one in Williston, and only just failed to get the nomination for a constituency which he had already represented for fifteen years. He stood as a Progressive but failed to win a seat.* The most stubborn loyalty to Du Toit still seems to have come from those regions where the Bond had most easily taken root in the early eighties, a fact which would emerge even more clearly during the by-elections which followed redistribution in 1899. In the 1898 general election, however, the clearest evidence of the activities of the Colonial Union comes from the *Commissie van Toezicht's* files relating to Barkly West. These show how the local Bond branches were riven with discord on the vital question of the attitude to be adopted towards Rhodes, and suggest that the divisions were chiefly due to the activities of Colonial Union men.*

Once the tumult and the shouting was over, and the unfair practices had been set right by the courts, the *Commissie van Toezicht* expressed its delight at the election result, describing it as 'not only encouraging but extremely surprising'.* The swing towards the Progressives which the Council elections appeared to indicate had been checked, and the Opposition had won, despite the influence of

Rhodes's Dutchmen, by the narrowest of possible majorities. When the results were known, both Sprigg and Rhodes hoped that the Government would be able to remain in office, its position strengthened by favourable judgments on the electoral petitions which they proposed to bring forward. Milner (to his credit, for he was personally strongly in sympathy with the Government party) deprecated such a course on constitutional as well as tactical grounds, and refused to listen to Sprigg's plea that the opening of the new Parliament should be deferred until such time as the Progressives were able to consolidate their position in the manner they proposed.* The new Parliament therefore met on 7 October; a Progressive, Dr. Bisset Berry, was elected Speaker on the strength of Opposition votes; and on the 10th Schreiner proposed his second 'no confidence' motion of the year, carrying it by 39 votes to 37. In a division in which the marginal votes were crucial, Innes had refused to vote with a party led by Rhodes, and David de Waal had remained faithful to the Bond.* Sprigg resigned on the 12th, and Schreiner immediately agreed to form an administration.

10

Diplomatic Breakdown

THE main task of Sprigg's Government had been to keep the administration of the Colony going during the period of disillusionment after the Raid. The main task of Schreiner's was to maintain the status of the Cape as a self-governing colony in the months immediately before and immediately after the outbreak of the South African war, and to use its influence on the side of peace. When Schreiner assumed office in October 1898, opinion in the Colony was hardening in two directions and the moderates were being forced to the wall. The Colonial Office had recovered some of its lost initiative, and was beginning to reassert its claim to paramountcy in southern Africa, though it had so far refrained from reviving awkward issues with the South African Republic. The new Government would fail to prevent the South African war, and it would fail to keep together for more than a few months once the war had started. But the dice were loaded heavily against it, and the wonder is rather that under the circumstances it was able to achieve anything at all.

Onze Courant of 20 October 1898 described Schreiner's Cabinet as the 'first Bond ministry properly so called', though only two of its members, A. J. Herholdt (Minister of Agriculture) and Thomas te Water (Minister without portfolio),* were members of the Bond. Schreiner who was already referring to his parliamentary followers as the 'South African Party'—a name which would stick—realized that he would have to look beyond the Bond for support if he was to stay in power, and therefore made Richard Solomon his Attorney-General and brought in Merriman and Sauer as Treasurer and Commissioner respectively. He took the Colonial Secretaryship himself.* There is no indication that he had any difficulty in forming his Cabinet, though there is some doubt as to whether he considered including David de Waal.* The inclusion of Richard Solomon caused some consternation in the Bond press, for he was liberally inclined over racial issues and had as yet no seat in the legislature. Merriman, for his part, was not entirely happy serving under a much younger man. But Schreiner's initial troubles would arise not from discord within the ministry, though this would come in the end, but from the fact that he had no majority in the Upper House and an extremely slender one in the Lower.

The extent to which Schreiner was not his own master can be seen in his inability to resist Opposition pressure over the introduction of a Redistribution Bill during his first month in office. To placate his opponents, who were in any case hardly satisfied, he introduced a measure based on the more conservative majority report of the 1897 Commission; but even after this gesture, his plan was waylaid by David de Waal's motion of 4 November, calling for an inter-party conference with a view to working out an agreed measure, which was seconded by Rhodes and carried with the Speaker's vote. Schreiner, conscious of the fact that the Speaker had already come to the rescue of his Government two days earlier, and afraid for the Supply Bill in the event of his refusal to call such a conference, had no choice but to succumb.* De Waal does not seem to have intended to stab the Bond in the back, and it is doubtful if he expected quite such high praise as he received from Rhodes, or quite such sharp hostility as the Bond meted out to him.* But, seen in perspective, his action did not damage the Bond in the way his contemporaries feared—or hoped—because success in their electoral petitions just covered Bond losses in the by-elections which followed redistribution, enabling the Government to keep its head above water.[1]

To Schreiner's difficulties arising out of his slender majority must be added those which sprang from the Governor's unwillingness to allow him a free hand. It was not that Milner objected to the new Cabinet on substantial grounds. 'They were all absolutely unobjectionable', he informed Chamberlain in a confidential dispatch on 19 October, and he went on to stress the weight of their collective experience, the 'high average capacity' of the individual members, and the policy of 'compromise and conciliation, or, perhaps it would

---

[1] The Progressives won 9, the Government 7, of the new seats created; but the Government had gained 3 seats from the Progressives as a result of election petitions.

be more correct to say, of comprehension' which the new Prime Minister was expected to follow.* At the same time, however, he betrayed a desire that they would soon be superseded by a Progressive government rid of the 'flabbiness on questions of Imperial interest' which had condemned Sprigg's regime in Milner's eyes. 'We have got a Bond Ministry', he told Chamberlain, 'but so far'— one can sense his feeling of relief—'we have not got a Bond policy.' The new administration, as he saw it, was fit to run the Colony until the Progressives recharged themselves with imperial fervour; but it was not to be encouraged to throw its weight around.

Soon after the new Government came to power, however, Milner returned to England on leave, having left his military deputy, General Sir William Butler, in control. Butler began his short term of civil office between November 1898 and February 1899 under the firm impression that the chief inflammatory agents in South Africa were not the Republicans and the Bondsmen, as Milner supposed, but Rhodes, the League and the jingo press. He later claimed to have detected 'an acerbity in political and journalistic life, a seeking for causes of offence, a girding and goading at the Dutch in and beyond the Cape Colony' which needed to be checked.* Like Milner, Butler may have been too set in his opinions, and he admitted that his impression of Rhodes was not based on personal acquaintance.* But if he lacked Milner's intellect, he outweighed him in South African experience, having been a member of Sir Garnet Wolseley's team in Natal in the 1870's, and he was prepared to take the Cape ministers into his confidence in a way that Milner was not. When the Edgar incident, involving the death of an uitlander at the hands of a Republican policeman,* took place in Johannesburg in December 1898, causing bad blood between the uitlander community and the authorities, the former petitioned the Queen for intervention; but Butler, partly on the advice of his Cape ministers, refused to send the petition forward. His action, based on the information that the avenues of judicial redress had not yet been properly explored, and that the petition had been prematurely published, was correct.

But far from merely trying to undermine uitlander influence in the Transvaal, the Cape ministers practised a policy of positive conciliation. Merriman, acting on his own initiative, approached Kruger at the end of the year with the suggestion that concessions to Cape trade by the Transvaal might help Bond candidates in the 1899 by-elections. He asked Steyn whether he was prepared to 'play the part of honest broker', and on receiving a favourable response set off for Pretoria in mid-January with Steyn's chief adviser, Abraham Fischer, to lay the basis for a South African conference. He hoped that agreement on relatively innocuous subjects such as the establishment of a joint health board, mint and university might induce the right frame of mind in South African statesmen for the profitable discussion of more controversial issues. The evident willingness of Lippert, the dynamite concessionaire, and the leaders of the Transvaal Government to reach an accommodation with the Rand capitalists over the dynamite monopoly seemed to suggest moreover that Merriman's effort was well timed.*

In the event, however, neither Merriman's conference plans nor the capitalist negotiations reached fruition. The gold magnates, led by Sir Percy Fitzpatrick, broke off the dynamite negotiations, which they do not seem to have entered into with any spirit of genuine compromise,* while Merriman's conference plan was successfully 'boshed' by the failure of Milner and the Free State leaders to agree on the role to be played by the High Commissioner. Both developments may be construed as manifestations of the tougher line which Chamberlain and Milner had agreed upon during the latter's leave in London. The capitalist negotiations brought Chamberlain and the mining magnates together, and enabled Milner and Greene, the British Agent in Pretoria, to 'reconstitute the reform movement of pre-raid days on the Rand'.* They lifted what Milner at first described as a 'capitalist question pure and simple' into an issue between governments. To assist this development, Milner bombarded the Colonial Office during March and April with a sequence of strongly-worded dispatches while the Johannesburg uitlanders collected signatures for a second petition of grievances,* which was in Milner's hands before the end of March. So far as the proposed South African conference was concerned, Milner told Merriman that he had no objection to it provided it was purely deliberative, that it did not stray beyond the topics which Merriman had listed, that the German and Portuguese colonies were excluded, and that he himself should be present as High Commissioner.* This, in view of the attitude taken by the Republics when Steyn had tried to convene a conference on immigration in 1897, was tantamount to a refusal, though Merriman remained optimistic. Milner would have no conference from which the Imperial representative was excluded, for this reflected on Britain's paramount status; but the Republics would not risk the creation of a precedent for any new kind of Imperial intervention in their affairs.*

The Colonial Government, unaware that Milner was getting ready to resume the diplomatic offensive in his own way,[1] devoted their energies during April to preparing the ground for the sort of conference which Milner could not avoid for reasons of protocol: a meeting between the Republican presidents and himself. Schreiner persuaded Chief Justice De Villiers to go to Pretoria and meet the Transvaal leaders, and paved his way by making overtures to J. C. Smuts, the State Attorney. De Villiers, who reached Pretoria on the 26th, avoided Kruger but gave Smuts, Reitz and Schalk Burger the impression that it would be discreet to make early offers of reform despite their rebuff at the hands of the mining magnates. They agreed to work for franchise reforms and an inquiry into the dynamite monopoly on condition that the Imperial Government made a complete and final presentation of its demands, and they admitted that some hope might lie in a conference between the High Commissioner and the two presidents.* De Villiers telegraphed this information to the Cape Government, and within two days of the receipt of his message Hofmeyr was able to pass on encouraging advice from Sivewright, who had retired from Cape Politics and was living in London, and had seen Chamberlain on 4 May. Sivewright urged that Kruger should invite Milner to Pretoria to discuss the dynamite question, and intimated that he had 'best grounds for believing such invitation would be accepted'—that is, presumably, by the Colonial Office on Milner's behalf.* Sivewright, wittingly or otherwise, had misinformed Hofmeyr, but in such a way as to make it difficult for the Imperial authorities to refuse the overtures without losing face. Plans for the conference therefore went ahead. Subsequent discussions between Hofmeyr, Schreiner and Sauer led these men to see the advantages of Bloemfontein over Pretoria as a venue for the proposed meeting, and they separated with two tasks to perform: to persuade Steyn to act as host and convener, and to impress upon the Transvaal Government a sense of the seriousness of the situation, with a view to securing a real offer of reform and the presence of Kruger at the conference table. Steyn was willing to play his part. There were signs of irritability, perhaps of excessive confidence, in the reactions of Reitz and Smuts, both of whom Hofmeyr thought it desirable to caution;* but by 17 May both

[1] For his 'helot' dispatch of 4 May, see below p. 196.

Kruger and Milner, the latter with Chamberlain's approval, had accepted Steyn's invitation to go to Bloemfontein.*

The conference proposal had thrown out the timing of Milner's diplomatic offensive, and he described it to Greene as 'a very clever move [which] has already produced one effect, viz. that of mollifying the British Press a bit and relaxing for the moment, unfortunately as I think, the screw upon the enemy'.* In the interest of his own plans, he had either to use the conference to force concessions out of the Transvaal, or to cause the negotiations to break down. To this end, he ensured that the form and procedure of the conference followed his own lines, not those urged on him by the Cape Government. The Cape ministers wanted active participation by Steyn and Schreiner; but Milner refused to allow Steyn the role of a go-between, and decided 'not to tell [Schreiner] to come', as he put it to Chamberlain, even though Chamberlain thought Schreiner's presence might be advantageous.* Procedurally, Hofmeyr had hoped for 'an informal friendly talk . . . free of formalities', followed by the publication of a joint communiqué. But Milner insisted on a verbatim report of the discussions—a decision no doubt reassuring to the uitlanders, whose petition still lay unanswered, but one which had the inevitable effect of turning the Bloemfontein conference into a verbal fencing match from which each side would seek to derive propaganda value.*

The conference, which opened on 30 May, failed because the maximum concessions which Kruger was prepared to make with regard to the uitlander franchise (on which Milner required agreement before moving on to other topics) amounted to less than the minimum demands on which Milner had decided to insist.*[1] The Bond leaders and editors greeted the news with regret, but soon came to the conclusion that Kruger had been accommodating and Milner unreasonable.* The ministers composed a minute of protest, but, unaware of the importance that Chamberlain attached at that moment to their point of view, decided not to present it formally, even though Schreiner came away from an interview with the High Commissioner extremely dissatisfied with the latter's unbending

---

[1] Milner insisted on the vote for uitlanders after five years' residence, with retrospective effect—a proposal calculated to enfranchise a considerable number of them immediately. Kruger's offer would admit none to the vote, except under the existing law, for two years, and laid down a minimum period for future immigrants of seven years.

attitude.* Hofmeyr thought that Kruger 'displayed an unexpectedly liberal spirit at Bl[oemfontein], and I am sure he w[oul]d have done a great deal more if he had been encouraged by the other side'.* Like the members of the Government, he believed that Kruger's proposals, even if not adequate as the basis for a settlement, might have been made so after fuller discussion. He proposed therefore to try to pull the fat out of the fire. On 9 June Te Water told Steyn that Onze Jan was about to call a meeting of the Cape Town Bond, at which he proposed to 'damn those who still talk of war', thank the parties to the Bloemfontein conference for the trouble they had taken, express regret that Kruger's proposals were not more fully discussed 'as they contain germs of satisfactory settlement', urge Kruger to carry out dynamite and franchise reforms and make provision for uitlanders on the Rand of seven years' standing to receive the vote within a year, allow uitlanders changing their allegiance to retain their old citizenship until they became full burghers of the South African Republic, and urge the Transvaal to withhold the presidential vote from residents of less than ten years' standing.* Fischer, who had accused the Cape Bondsmen of indifference in a letter to Hofmeyr on the 8th, reacted unfavourably to Hofmeyr's proposed amendments to Kruger's plan on the ground that they would create new divisions, while Smuts (who had not yet seen Hofmeyr's proposals) continued to urge Afrikaner unity behind the President's stand.* The Transvalers insisted on the submission of outstanding disputes to a three-man tribunal under a foreign president as the price of further franchise concessions, and when Milner told Schreiner on 11 June that their proposed franchise legislation was unacceptable, the Cape friends became very uneasy. Te Water explained Hofmeyr's predicament to Fischer:

'Jan sounded men of authority and considered question from all aspects; thinks that if Bond should now adopt another course than more or less in direction indicated in my former telegram it would do harm rather than good here. He feels, now that nothing but President's proposals are insisted on, so very strongly on subject, sees so many difficulties, and is with all of us so firmly convinced that there is no ground for the hope that the President's proposals as formulated will be accepted by the other party, that he has decided to hold no meeting tomorrow but to wait until he obtains more light from Sec[retary of] State for Colonies' despatch as well as from Pretoria and Bloemfontein.'

After stressing the need for keeping the franchise and arbitration questions distinct, and Hofmeyr's readiness to speak in favour of the latter, the message ended with a request that Fischer should visit Cape Town for consultations.* Fischer agreed to make the journey, in a telegram full of regrets that Hofmeyr's meeting had not been held.*

Meanwhile telegraphic summaries of Chamberlain's reply to the uitlander petition and of Milner's dispatch of 4 May reached Cape Town, and created much consternation in Bond circles. For though he had been mainly concerned with the Transvaal, Milner had stated:

' . . . a certain section of the press, and not in the Transvaal only, preaches openly and constantly the doctrine of a Republic embracing all South Africa, and supports it by menacing references to the armaments of the Transvaal, in alliance with the Orange Free State, and the active sympathy which in case of war it would receive from a section of Her Majesty's subjects. I regret to say that this doctrine, supported as it is by a ceaseless stream of malignant lies about the intentions of the British Government, is producing a great effect upon a large number of our Dutch fellow-colonists. Language is frequently used which seems to imply that the Dutch have some superior right even in this colony to their fellow-citizens of British birth. Thousands of men peaceably disposed, and, if left alone, perfectly satisfied with their position as British subjects, are being drawn into disaffection, and there is a corresponding exasperation on the side of the British.'*

After initial expressions of incredulity, the Bond editors reserved their judgments until the arrival of the 'blue book' in July, when the *South African News* considered that Milner's remarks would create a 'profound and painful impression in this country', and *Onze Courant* mockingly suggested that the *Patriot* must have been in Milner's mind, since that was the only Colonial paper which had ever stood for a South Africa under its own flag.*

Here was the disloyalty charge again, boldly asserted. Was it justified? There are indeed fragments of evidence which may be held to give substance to Milner's accusations.* But if the tone of Colonial Dutch journalism is considered as a whole during the months immediately prior to the 'helot' dispatch, the charge must be dismissed as ludicrous. Neither *Ons Land*, nor *Onze Courant*, nor *Het Oosten*, the three most influential Bond papers in the Colony, either stimulated disaffection or indulged in republican propaganda of the kind suggested by Milner. They devoted extraordinarily little editorial space to the Transvaal;[1] and when they mentioned the crisis the Bond editors tended to press for a peaceful settlement rather than encourage Republican resistance. In so far as they made appeals for Afrikaner unity, these were normally in the context of the current election campaigns. They were in fact working under conditions of self-imposed restraint. Until the middle of July they took the line, which had apparently been agreed upon but not minuted at the March congress, that the handling of the crisis was a matter for their leaders, whose work was most likely to prosper with the minimum of publicity. Bondsmen were counselled not to hold public meetings on the crisis for fear of provoking League counter-demonstrations.* They would not depart from this rule of conduct until they received a cue from the Prime Minister himself, and this did not come until the middle of July.*

Bond committees responded to their leaders' request for restraint, and maintained their discipline well, with one important exception a month *after* the 'helot' dispatch had been sent. The Albert Bondsmen lost patience and decided to hold a public meeting on the crisis to coincide with the Bloemfontein conference. Hofmeyr tried to stop them in telegrams to Professor Cachet of the Burghersdorp seminary and 'Oom Daantje' van den Heever,* but his advice was ignored. About 150 people attended the meeting and heard Professor Cachet deplore the congress decision not to discuss the Transvaal or hold public meetings. *Ons Land*, which reported the meeting as discreetly as could be desired,[2] described Cachet's performance as 'an excellent patriotic address which made all hearts vibrate with sympathy for the Transvaal'. A local English trader and erstwhile opponent of the Albert Boeren Vereeniging rose to support Cachet. An old Boer twitted Jotham Joubert with feigned but effective naïveté about the rights of the Transvaal. Another clergyman, who thought that the Bloemfontein conference was a mistake, dismissed the idea that Britain was a military danger to the Republics, basing his logistics on the writings of General Butler. A member of the Free State Volksraad added his contribution to what evidently became

---

[1] Of the thirty issues of *Onze Courant* between the beginning of 1899 and the writing of Milner's 'helot' dispatch, only two discussed the Transvaal in editorials.

[2] By contrast with the anti-Bond *Patriot*, which gave prominence to a report culled from the Burghersdorp *Bondsman*.

an extremely lively meeting. But as a meeting it was exceptional. Milner may have deplored the sympathies of Bondsmen, but he had little ground for criticizing their conduct.

The knowledge that Milner and Chamberlain had been getting ready for a showdown with the Transvaal while the ground was being prepared for the Bloemfontein conference did not ease the atmosphere at the time of Fischer's visit to the Cape; but there were other grounds for hope. A letter from Smuts showed Hofmeyr that the fire-breathing State Attorney was coming to appreciate the difficulties of Cape Afrikaners, and to see that open support for the Transvaal could destroy their influence in the Colony. Smuts urged them to support the Republican Government's franchise reform proposals in principle, while suggesting amendments in detail; to give discreet support to the idea of arbitration; and to carry a motion in favour of peace, so that 'it cannot be said by the other side that the Bond is a wing of the republican party'.* Meanwhile Milner and Chamberlain, lacking the military reinforcements which the unwarlike tone of British public opinion and the influence of General Butler on the War Office had so far denied them, found that they did not have the means with which to build up pressure against the Transvaal. Fischer's visit therefore caught Milner in a moment of doubt, and Milner gave at least his *nihil obstat* to Fischer's going to Pretoria with a set of proposals, drawn up in collaboration with Hofmeyr and the Cape ministers, which asked for less than the 'minimum demands' put forward by Milner at Bloemfontein.*

Fischer, who was in Pretoria from 25 to 28 June, found Kruger prepared to go some distance to meet his arguments, but he was unable to persuade the Republican leaders to agree to submit their reform proposals to a representative of the Imperial Government for scrutiny before laying them before the Volksraad.* This appeared to savour of undesirable intervention, to which the Republican authorities were naturally, but perhaps excessively, sensitive, for nothing would have reduced the tension quite so much as an agreed measure. For a start, it would have made nonsense of the warlike speech made by Chamberlain at Birmingham on the 26th, which so effectively undermined Fischer's influence as a conciliator.*

Fischer's negotiations were therefore inconclusive, though not entirely fruitless; but in view of the delicacy of the situation the Cape ministers prevailed on Hofmeyr, accompanied by Herholdt as representative of the Cabinet, to visit Pretoria and complete the work which Fischer had begun. The two Cape Afrikaners immediately set off for Bloemfontein at the beginning of July, and there met Smuts and Grobler, the Transvaal Under-Secretary for External Affairs, to whom they delivered a memorandum setting out suggested improvements to the reforms proposed by the Republican Government.* The Transvaal emissaries agreed that their proposals did not increase the danger to the Republic's independence; but Kruger and his advisers were at first reluctant to invite them to Pretoria lest their mission should fail and their usefulness to the Transvaal thereby cease. They were allowed to proceed, however, and evidently found the Republican authorities very attentive to their advice. The Volksraad, with astonishing lack of political sense, had on the eve of their arrival narrowly resolved to swamp any increase in the representation of the Rand by adding fifteen seats to the old burgher districts.* The Cape delegates, however, secured the withdrawal of this proposal in the course of meetings with the Executive Council and with the combined Volksraads in secret session. Using arguments on which the records throw no certain light, they persuaded the assembled legislators to accept the substance of the proposals which they had brought with them.* These proposals did not include Milner's five-year retrospective franchise, or even the seven-year maximum which Hofmeyr had himself put forward, and thus failed to ensure the immediate enfranchisement of the large number of uitlanders who, according to Milner's calculations, had entered the Transvaal in 1890–5.* But Hofmeyr had obtained nearly all the major points which Fischer had asked for, and Fischer's proposals had had at least the tacit assent of Milner.*

It was because Hofmeyr had obtained what Fischer had set out to get that Schreiner, who had been cabling sombre thoughts about the 'darkest hour' on the morning of 6 July, was able to inform Herholdt the same afternoon that the Cabinet had considered his coded report of the Volksraad proceedings and regarded them as a substantial basis for peace.* They were 'adequate, satisfactory and such as should secure a peaceful settlement', he informed the press, after badgering the emissaries for permission to break silence and send London 'something simple and definite from Pretoria'. Smuts also thanked Hofmeyr for what mattered most to him: the restoration of Afrikaner unity.* This the mission had certainly achieved.

A meeting of Bondsmen took place in Cape Town on the evening of the 12th, the day after Hofmeyr's return.* Onze Jan asked from the Chair whether the time had not now come for the Bondsmen to break silence. 'It had been thought best', he told his audience, 'not to hold any big meetings, nor to get up an immense demonstration throughout the country, but to work in silence as they had done. . . . Before the Bloemfontein Conference they had been in uncertainty. Now, however, this period of doubt had passed away.'

Motions were then carried unanimously: in favour of the maintenance of peace and the settlement of the Transvaal franchise dispute, moved by F. S. Malan; in favour of the arbitration of disputes under the London Convention, in the light of the attitude taken by British delegates at the recent Hague Convention, moved by Hofmeyr; and of thanks to the Cabinet for their Transvaal policy. A fourth, condemning the reference to Colonial Boer disloyalty in the 'helot' dispatch, was ruled out of order by Hofmeyr. The Bond editors responded favourably, echoing their leaders' belief that the cause of peace and unity was about to triumph, and that the time had come to break silence, hold mass meetings, and openly declare their approval of the terms which Hofmeyr had secured.* The meetings, and the appropriate resolutions, most of them in identical terms to those carried at the Cape Town rally, duly followed.* Their mood, however, was rather that of doing battle in a cause than of a victory celebration, for the Imperial authorities still needed to be convinced.

Milner and Chamberlain wanted the Republican Government to hold its legislation back until they had been given a chance to examine, approve, and guarantee its contents, for they were mindful of the Republic's record over franchise legislation and would not recommend a new law to the uitlanders without being satisfied that it really safeguarded their interests and could not subsequently be invalidated.* Their suspicion was indeed well grounded; but so was that of the Republican leaders, who objected that any attempt by the Imperial Government to control the form of their franchise legislation would be an infringement of their autonomy in this field.* They would offer concessions over the franchise only as part of a general settlement in which provision was made for the arbitration of disputes—an issue which Milner had insisted on treating separately. The Transvaal's legal right to resist interference was beyond question; but the wisdom of doing so at that moment was more debatable, on the argument that if Milner had been prepared to allow Fischer and Hofmeyr to act as go-betweens, and

Chamberlain had shown an interest in the Republic's own proposals for reform, it was a time not for balking the negotiations on a point of principle, but for keeping the discussions open. The Colonial Bond leaders urged the Transvaal to accept the Imperial Government's request for delay and consultation.* So did Steyn.* But the Transvaal leaders stuck to their guns, making it possible for Milner not only to deplore their uncooperativeness, but to cast doubts on the efficacy of their proposed reforms.

The peace which Hofmeyr hoped he had achieved was therefore no peace, and the predicament of Colonial Afrikanerdom and the Cape ministers deepened. Talk of Afrikaner *volkseenheid* (unity), that dangerously imprecise expression which took no account of frontiers, began to grow more frequent in the correspondence of Boer leaders in the Colony and the Republics, stimulated by the outpourings of devotion to Milner by uitlander and Leaguesman, with the result that suspicions continued to deepen on both sides of the political fence. The refusal of the Transvaal Government to admit any British influence in the drafting of their new franchise Bill was rooted partly in the belief that, thanks to Hofmeyr, the formula for *volkseenheid* had been found. They could now count on the moral support of the Colonial Afrikaners. But Hofmeyr had left Pretoria with nothing more than a promise, and that of doubtful acceptability to the Colonial Office. He and the Cape ministers therefore bombarded the Transvaal Government, either directly through Smuts or indirectly through the Free State, with detailed suggestions for and criticisms of the proposed Bill. The Executive Council could accept from them ideas which it had become politically impossible to entertain if they came from the British, and on the whole they showed a disposition to listen to advice. 'It will be dealt with in accordance with your work and Hofmeyr's. . . . We are doing our best with the improvements and I shall do my best to have your suggestions of yesterday carried out. . . . Have in past few days worked with all strength to get art[icle] 4 fixed at seven years. There is no chance of success. Therefore send immediately a very stiff telegram to strengthen my hands.' These extracts from telegrams sent by Smuts to Te Water and Hofmeyr between 12 and 17 July illustrate the concern on Smuts's part to work out an acceptable measure.* Consequently the Cape friends were able to secure improvements on Hofmeyr's earlier terms, including the offer of a seven-year retrospective franchise.*

14

Milner's doubts persisted, however, with regard both to the meaning of the new law, which was very complicated even with the annexure of an explanatory memorandum, and to its probable effects. The Colonial Office, ever anxious to retain the initiative and still led by Milner, therefore began to press at the end of July for a joint Anglo-Transvaal inquiry into its provisions.* In view of the Transvaal Government's earlier rejection of approaches of this kind, this was a stiff demand, savouring as much of intervention as the earlier requests, though it was now moderated by an offer to discuss 'arbitration without introduction of foreign element' once the franchise question had been disposed of. The Cape ministers and Hofmeyr urged the Transvaal once again to accept the Imperial condition, believing, as Milner hoped they would, that not to accept it meant to risk war.* The Bond parliamentarians corroborated this advice:

'We, the undersigned Africander members of Parliament, thoroughly sympathising with our Transvaal relatives in their troubles and appreciating the concessions already made by them in the interest of peace, yet beg to urge the expediency of their still doing their very utmost short of sacrificing their independence, to avert the horrors of war. While agreeing that the Commission of Enquiry proposed by Mr. Chamberlain can not be asked for as a matter of right, we believe that such a commission might provide a way out of existing difficulties, which are fast approaching a crisis, with results which might prove fatal to the best interests not only of our Transvaal and Free State brethren, but also of the Africander party in the Cape Colony. In the presence of an immediate danger and of the momentous issues awaiting the decision of your Honour's Executive and Volksraad, even the risk of being misunderstood or misrepresented is of minor importance. We beg that your Honour will lay these words which are only dictated by a keen sense of our common interests and risks privately before your Executive and Volksraad, and remain, your Honour's obedient servants.'*

Fischer, to whom this message was sent for transmission to Kruger, protested that acceptance of a joint commission would be 'tantamount to surrender of independence'. 'Any other course', Te Water replied on Hofmeyr's behalf, 'would be fatal to them, to you and to us.'* Fischer therefore addressed himself to Pretoria, if not to persuade the Transvaal to accept the joint commission, then at least to help it find a satisfactory alternative.

The Transvaal leaders saw the mirage of Afrikaner *volkseenheid* dissolving before their eyes, and began to argue among themselves. 'Had yesterday telegraphic communication with President and Smuts', Steyn cabled to Hofmeyr on 14 August. 'President does not seem to agree with Smuts. Will speak [to] them again today.'* The same message contained the following communication from Smuts:

'Have just had private conversation with Greene who informed me that object of joint commission was to bring Johannesburg into the matter and then to go further than at Bloemfontein. Uitlanders have gathered all facts which will then be brought before Commission to bring opinion of world over to their side. The only way open for this Government was to accept Bloemfontein proposals as alternative to prevent investigation and greater demands. The honour of High Commissioner and Ministry were bound to [?regard] Bloemfontein proposals as minimum. Kindly inform Hofmeyr of this. Perhaps he may persuade High Commissioner to bring his proposal to settlement basis. Can Fischer not go to Cape Town immediately?'*

Smuts had met Greene on Saturday, 11 August, and with the authority of his Government had offered important concessions to the uitlanders: Milner's five-year retrospective franchise, with immediate effect, for both Volksraad and presidential elections; eight new first Volksraad seats for the Rand, bringing its representation up to a quarter of the House, with a guarantee that it would not fall below that ratio; and the right of the British Agent to participate in discussions over the franchise law and any other points in dispute. In return he assumed that the British Government would not look upon this offer as a precedent for intervention, would allow the Queen's claim to suzerainty* over the Republic, based on the Pretoria Convention of 1881 quietly to drop, and, as soon as the new franchise scheme had become law, concede the principle of arbitration from which the foreign element was now to be excluded. The Transvaal leaders were now prepared to pay more than Milner's original price to avoid a joint inquiry. Smuts's message to Steyn suggests that fear of the effects of such an inquiry was one reason for this; but the offer was also intended to bring Britain's purposes out into the open. If the uitlanders were her real concern she would accept Smuts's terms; but if the assertion of paramountcy was her aim, she would of necessity reject them. 'If the British Government now decides to reject our proposals,' Reitz told Hofmeyr, 'then there would be but a slender chance for peace—but if she does so then our conscience is clear.'* Smuts meanwhile derived courage from this assurance. If Britain declined the offer, he wrote, she would put herself in the wrong in the eyes of the world, and if it came to a showdown, 'I believe that the two republics will be able to look after themselves. We have about 50,000 men, whose equals as marksmen and intrepid fighters are unknown to the world.' Like Butler, he still believed Britain would need three times their number to get level with the republican forces; but he advised Hofmeyr not to run the Bond ministry into too much danger lest Milner should dismiss it and replace it with another under Sprigg or Rhodes.*

Smuts's objective, however, was only partially attained. He was able to manoeuvre Chamberlain and Milner into declaring their intention to establish British paramountcy,* and they turned down Smuts's offer to Greene after assuming, on very slender grounds, that there was ambiguity in the Republic's terms.* In a position to accept the Republican offer without dishonour, they chose instead to 'move in to the kill',* and they succeeded in their manoeuvre without bringing into being that solidarity within Afrikanerdom for which Smuts had been prepared to sacrifice so much.

The Schreiner Government, which had found itself in trouble with the Opposition, with the Free State Government, and with Milner himself over the related questions of Imperial troop movements in the Colony and the passage of arms and ammunition to the Free State,* was not kept informed over the detailed plans of the Imperial Government,* and felt increasingly powerless to avert the impending clash. Hofmeyr, while appreciating the genuineness of the Smuts proposals, criticized them before he knew what the British reaction would be: '*You gave too much*', he told Smuts, 'and at the same time *asked too much*, spoiling the first by the second, and thereby playing into the hand of the enemy.' The Transvalers, he said, had played their cards badly: 'By refusing to restore the "Conference spirit", all your concessions have acquired the appearance of being forced. By giving them by fits and starts,[1] you have made no impression on the general public in foreign countries.' He thought there was still time for them to accept the joint inquiry, and pressed them to do so 'although it is rather late, and the terms will

[1] 'Dribbling out reforms like water from a squeezed sponge' was Chamberlain's way of putting it.

become harder. Think of the Sibylline Books.'*

On 2 September the Transvaal Government answered Chamberlain's objections to their offer of 19–21 August, but at the same time withdrew that offer, while remaining non-committal towards Chamberlain's further suggestion of another conference between the heads of states in Cape Town.* Hofmeyr protested that this reply was totally inadequate. 'We consider a dilatory policy as most dangerous', he told Fischer, who was again in Pretoria;* and it was partly owing to the pressure which he exerted through Fischer that on the 8th the South African Republic decided to accept Chamberlain's demand for a joint inquiry—only for its offer to be outdated by Chamberlain's demand on the same day for the unconditional acceptance by the Transvaal of its own offer of 19 August, minus the conditions which had then been attached to it.* It was the Smuts offer, not the July franchise law, that Chamberlain now wanted a commission to examine.

The position of the Cape friends now became impossible. Hofmeyr tried once more to keep negotiations open by counselling the Transvaal, through Fischer, to return a conciliatory reply to Chamberlain's latest demand, to the effect that they 'renew their offer in paragraphs 1, 2 and 3 in note of 19th August and accept invitation to joint enquiry and conference, of course without detriment to their independence and existing rights'.* Fischer's reply indicated that at last the Free State and the Cape friends had parted company, for neither he nor Steyn felt that they could conscientiously advise the Transvaal to accept the latest demand.* Hofmeyr's rejoinder, that Brand had yielded over the Diamond Fields and saved his State, 'and today there is none to censure Brand', had no effect.* Kruger's message of the 16th registered the parting of the ways:

'Although we fully acknowledge and appreciate your good intentions, we however regret that it is no longer possible for us to further accede to extravagant and impudent demands of British Government. It was in co-operation with you and on your advice that we lowered the franchise and accepted joint Commission of Enquiry, acting under same conviction which you probably shared. All this was of no avail. . . . We are determined not to go any further than we have latterly done, and we are convinced that we cannot accept Secretary [of] State [for] Colonies' proposals regarding franchise after 5 years residence, now that all assurance for our

independence embodied in our proposals has been taken away. . . .
We are fully impressed with the very serious position in which we
are placed, but with God before our eyes we cannot go further
without endangering, if not totally destroying, our independence.
The Government, Parliament and people are unanimous on this
point.'*

On the 18th, Hofmeyr abandoned his attempt to influence the
Republics, wishing Kruger 'wisdom to select the right way and
strength to pursue it'.*

Two days later the Bond parliamentarians met and found nothing
constructive to say. They noted with satisfaction that the South
African Republic had accepted the joint inquiry, and trusted that
this would prevent the outbreak of hostilities; but as war seemed
probable they raised the question of a subscription list for the
Republican wounded, widows and orphans for discussion at a later
date.* On the 21st, the Cape ministers petitioned the British Government to approach the Transvaal leaders in a 'spirit of magnanimous
compromise', which elicited from Chamberlain a formal and
unyielding reply.* A further attempt by them to frame a peace
motion which might win the unanimous support of Parliament
failed owing to ministerial disagreement over the contents of
Schreiner's draft.* On the 28th, the ministers and their parliamentary
supporters petitioned the Queen, laying stress on their 'ties of blood
relationship, inter-marriage and friendship, with residents in the
South African Republic', the preparedness of the Republican
Government to institute adequate reforms, and the desirability of
holding a joint inquiry. It received a somewhat chill response, and
its effect was largely offset by a counter-petition signed by Sprigg
and nearly as many members of Parliament, deprecating 'the
attempts which have been made to encourage the Government of
South African Republic to continue their resistance to the just
demands of Her Majesty's Government', and underlining their
support for Milner's policy.* Thus, to the sound of hollow formalities, South Africa drifted slowly towards war.

An assessment of the role of the Afrikaner Bond in the crisis of
1899 must take cognizance of a wide range of viewpoints, the more
especially since the interpretations of contemporaries have tended
to enjoy a long half-life. At one end of the scale stands the assumption of imperialist writers that the Bond was an 'unmixed curse' to
South Africa because it had taught the Dutch Boers to 'identify

themselves with the Republics rather than with their own country and Queen'.* Even Dormer, whose *Vengeance as a Policy* was oddly classified by the collector Mendelssohn as pro-Boer, considered that 'the loyal Afrikanders . . . sent their remonstrances to the wrong address', because 'it was their part to admonish Mr. Kruger that he would get no aid or countenance from them if he should be so headstrong as to push things to the last dread arbitrament'.* On an earlier occasion, though the analogy is applicable to 1899, the Bloemfontein *Express* had seen the Bond as a tame elephant used by a hunter (the Imperial Government) to trap its wild Republican blood-brother beyond the Colonial borders.* A rather different simile chosen by L. S. Amery stressed the Bond's ineffectiveness in the crisis. He saw the Cape Afrikaners as 'resembling nothing so much as some chorus of ineffective old men in Greek tragedy . . . now in secret lamenting their hero's madness, and counselling prudence in rhythmic platitudes, now in public defending the justice of his cause and denouncing the conduct of his adversaries'.*

It is impossible, in the light of the foregoing narrative, to take the the charge of insidious republicanism seriously. The negotiations of 1899 revealed only too clearly what a fragile plant Afrikaner *volkseenheid* was, and the Transvalers, who banked on its vitality, discovered at the time of the Smuts–Greene negotiations how grievously they had been mistaken. The concept of Afrikaner unity, which came to mean a great deal in Steyn's Free State, meant little more to the Colonial Bond leaders than a compulsion to give moral support to their Republican kinsmen. But this was qualified in their minds by the conviction that the Republican leaders could have played their cards better.

Equally difficult to sustain is the argument that the Bondsmen set out to undermine the resistance of the Transvaal. Concern that the Republican leaders should not sacrifice their independence, whatever else they yielded, was as constant a theme of Hofmeyr's and Schreiner's advice as their insistence that the Transvaal should improve its case in the eyes of the world by removing the causes of genuine uitlander grievance. But did the Bond have a corrosive influence on the Republican resistance? It might be urged that Milner used the Fischer and Hofmeyr missions as a means of penetrating the Transvaal's moral defences; but the force of this argument disappears once it is appreciated that Milner looked upon these missions as unwanted interruptions of his own diplomatic offensive. On the other hand, the fact that the South African Republic withdrew by stages from the position which Kruger had taken up at Bloemfontein, and thereby exposed itself—rightly or wrongly—to the charge of equivocation, did follow as a result of pressure applied by Hofmeyr and the Cape Government. But a distinction must be drawn here between the steps which the Transvaal authorities took and those which Schreiner and Hofmeyr advised them to take.* Had their counsel been followed at an early stage, and a generous and simple extension of the vote to the uitlanders been given—with stiffer qualifications, perhaps, for the presidential vote, for which the Republicans put up no real defence—the negotiations could hardly have been shipwrecked on the sharp rock of misunderstanding, the Imperial Government would probably have been forced to show its hand sooner, and the issue for the Colonial Afrikaner would have been clearer cut. Briefly, questions related to the uitlander demands would have been separated from the more fundamental issue of British paramountcy, with the connected issues of the Queen's suzerainty and arbitration. Hofmeyr believed that the uitlanders had something of a case—how much it is difficult to say, but he at least saw that the Republic's refusal to extend political privileges to them damaged its own case in the eyes of the world. On the broader issues, however, he supported the Transvaal, indicating his readiness to speak in favour of arbitration, and showing constant concern lest the Republic should abdicate sovereignty unnecessarily. It was one of the essential weaknesses of the Transvaal Government's handling of the crisis, that by allowing negotiations to become bogged down on the question of uitlander rights, over which the moral arguments were not more than half in their favour, they failed to give Colonial Afrikanerdom a satisfactory basis on which to pledge its support, and at the same time gave the Imperial Government excellent cover under which to develop its doctrine of paramountcy.

If no tame elephant, then, was the Bond a Greek chorus? Some urged, as did Cachet at Burghersdorp, that if the Colonial Bondsmen had given open and vociferous support to the Transvaal from the beginning of the year, the Imperial Government would not have dared to press its case. This argument, however, presupposes a very questionable estimate of Milner. Alternatively, they might have sided strongly with the Transvaal after the latter had indicated its readiness to accept the joint inquiry in September. This was the moment at which the Government of the Orange Free State clearly saw their path of duty, feeling, as Fischer did, that the latest British demand was 'palpably dishonest and insulting and makes it only too clear that Transvaal was deliberately trapped'.* The Free Staters had made up their minds that the Colonial Office intended to take from the Transvaal all that was needed for the effective assertion of British paramountcy. The Cape leaders, on the other hand, continued to advise the Transvaal to give ground until the latter would hear no more of it, on the assumption that Britain might still be persuaded to ask for something less. The evidence of the correspondence between Milner and Chamberlain indicates that the Free Staters were right. But the position of the Boers in the Free State and in the Colony was not the same. The Free State was master of its own destiny, seeking, with troops at its disposal, to honour a treaty with a threatened ally. The Cape friends, had they followed the Free State lead, would have run the risk of unleashing civil war, with all the additional hazards incumbent on those who commit high treason. They would have enlarged the area of conflict at a time when it was too late to divert the Imperial Government from its main purpose, or—so far as might reasonably be expected—to affect the end result.

11

War

I. THE BREAKING OF THE MODERATES

THE outbreak of the Anglo-Boer war on 11 October 1899 caused Schreiner and his colleagues to consider but also to reject the idea of resignation.* It was constitutionally impossible for them to remain neutral, and they were unable to assure Steyn that the Colony would not become a base of operations against the Republics.* Schreiner knew, furthermore, that Milner would not hesitate, if sufficiently provoked, to follow Frere's precedent and replace the ministry by one of a stronger loyalist persuasion.* He did the best he could for Colonial Afrikaners, therefore, by obtaining from Milner the guarded undertaking that Colonial troops would not be required to serve against the Republics ('except in the last resort') save for purposes of defence.* He then turned his energies, with the support of the Bond executive, to the task of preventing a popular rising in the country districts. While he directed circulars to the magistrates and approached the moderator of the Nederduits Gereformeerde Kerk,* the Bond executive issued advice to party members through the press, urging them to 'keep quiet, and . . . hold no meetings with reference to the existing situation, neither of Ward nor of District Councils [*Besturen*], nor any meetings of the public, in order that our voices may be heard at the highest meeting of our organization, where resolutions can be discussed and considered by our Delegates [*wettige afgevaardigden*]'. To this end, they proposed to call a special congress in November.*

Perhaps if Imperial forces had been strong enough at the beginning of the war to prevent the invasion of the Colony by Republican commandos, the Cape Government's efforts to prevent rebellion would have achieved universal success. Their efforts were, however, thwarted in the districts along the Orange River by early Boer victories. Free State commandos crossed into the Colony and annexed the frontier districts of Colesberg, Albert, Aliwal North, Barkly East and Dordrecht during November, while the Transvalers, who had taken Vryburg on 21 October, advanced through Prieska, Kenhardt and Gordonia during February and March 1900. Wherever Republican forces moved into the Colony, local supporters flocked to their banners in substantial numbers—'half the registered voters . . . and about two-thirds of the males not on the voting list', according to the magistrate of Albert; 502 of 884 voters in the Vryburg constituency; all but two of the Dutch-speaking adult males at Taung.*

There is no reason to suppose that members of the Afrikaner Bond acted with greater restraint than other Afrikaners in these frontier districts. Least of all was this true in Barkly East, where leading Bondsmen almost certainly invited a Republican commando to cross the border and take over the district.* The magistrate, D. A. Campbell, who lacked the necessary sang-froid for handling such an invasion threat, had a sufficiently alert intelligence service to enable him to predict the pattern of the subsequent rising with fair accuracy. The double game of Bondsmen like Carl van Pletzen and others, who assured Merriman of the innocence of their intentions on the one hand, and plotted to overthrow the Cape Government's authority on the other, did the Bond much harm in the long run by giving its opponents tangible evidence on which to base their disloyalty charges.* One of the Barkly rebels was W. J. Sauer, brother of Schreiner's Commissioner of Crown Lands. This may have been Schreiner's reason for sending J. W. Sauer to pacify Merriman's constituency in November. He reached Dordrecht towards the end of the month, by which time Barkly East was already in rebel hands, and although he secured overwhelming support at a public meeting in favour of standing firm, he could not prevent the district from falling into Free State hands, with at least a measure of local encouragement.* A year later the Colonial Office was more than pleased to receive evidence that of the thirty-three Bond office-bearers in the Wodehouse constituency, no less than twenty-four had been found guilty of aiding the Republics.*[1]

[1] Special sheets were prepared with a view to proving the complicity of the Afrikaner Bond in the rebellion, bearing the printed heading: 'List of the Officials of the Afrikaner Bond for the District of . . . in the Cape Colony, extracted from

Furthermore, three Bond parliamentarians, Jotham Joubert of Albert, I. J. van der Walt of Colesberg and Ds. C. W. H. Schröder of Prieska, associated themselves with the Republican invaders and thus forfeited their seats in the legislature.*¹ In most areas the invaders commandeered local Afrikaners, using sufficient pressure to guarantee a considerable following, at the same time requiring English sympathizers to declare their neutrality or depart, leaving behind their firearms.* Had the Republican commandos penetrated deeper into the Colony, as they might well have done during the early weeks of the war, there is no reason to suppose that the rebellion would have stopped where it did. Strydom's comment, that the Cape Afrikaner would not have rebelled without outside help, but that whenever his district was occupied by fellow-Boers, and the Vierkleur run up, he would 'saddle his best mount, take leave of wife and child, and ride off with the Boer commando', reflects this mood with sufficient accuracy.* But whatever the activities of local Bond committees, the suggestion that in its higher echelons the Bond encouraged rebellion is (the actions of a few members of Parliament excepted) wide of the mark. Some assisted the Boers in a non-belligerent manner, like the Cape Town working committee which organized a widows and orphans fund for the Republics,* or Dr. Hoffman, who formed an ambulance unit on the Boer side, ruined his health in the process, and spent the first half of 1900 convalescing in Pretoria. Others worked actively to prevent the spread of violence. Thus Theron, in his capacity as president, personally assisted Kitchener in persuading the Prieska rebels to lay down their arms in March 1900. During the martial law debate in August, Schreiner described how P. J. du Toit, member for Richmond and ex-chairman of the provincial *bestuur*, 'went through Griqualand West urging and striving to keep the people true to their fealty'. He also referred to F. J. van der Merwe, member for Clanwilliam, 'to whose efforts it was largely due that the north-western districts of the Colony remained quiet'. He had a report from the acting magistrate of

the Seventeenth Provincial Meeting, opened at Victoria West on 9th March 1899, with particulars affecting certain of the individuals mentioned in the list.' But although Hely-Hutchinson intimated that lists from other districts would be sent, only those from Wodehouse appear to have been dispatched. The methods used to confirm identity between Bond officials and rebels of the same name do not appear from these sheets, whose veracity is nevertheless probable.

¹ Joubert and Van der Walt left the Colony. Schröder surrendered and suffered a period of imprisonment. All three forfeited their seats in the Assembly.

Kenhardt on the latter's performance.*

The Bond executive, having agreed to hold a congress in November 1899 with the apparent object of imposing discipline on their members, decided on 30 October to postpone it indefinitely, for the surprising yet obviously sincere reason that they then considered the danger of widespread rebellion to be over.* The regular committee elections were, however, allowed to proceed as usual, and Theron urged Bondsmen to demonstrate their sense of responsibility (*verstand*) when they met.* Congress, then fixed for March, was postponed again by executive decision on 24 February at the request of Milner and Schreiner, and deferred to the eve of the parliamentary session, whenever that might be.*

While the Boers were in the ascendant the Bond leaders held their members in check, and Milner himself referred to the existence of a 'truce of God' in Cape politics. But this did not long survive the change in the fortunes of war, when it first began to look as if the Republics themselves were in danger of being overrun.

A leading cause of the change in the Bond's attitude was the conciliation movement, which had been started in Britain by Frederick Mackarness and other prominent men.* Conciliation committees were formed in the Cape Colony from March 1900 onwards, and Schreiner received a typed leaflet setting out the aims of the movement on the 20th.* Albert Cartwright, editor of the *South African News*, played a prominent role in Cape Town, but the moving spirit behind the campaign was Ernest T. Hargrove, an Englishman who was on a visit to South Africa at the end of 1899.[1] In November of that year he was in Dordrecht with Sauer, and was chosen as a 'guest' of the deputation elected at Sauer's meeting there to exhort the Free State commandant Olivier not to invade the district.* He subsequently went to Pretoria via Delagoa Bay, met Kruger in January, received £1,000 from the Netherlands South Africa Railway Company on the recommendation of F. W. Reitz, to further his peace campaign, and after meeting Steyn returned to the Colony, where in mid-March he began a speech-making tour which culminated in a mass meeting at Graaff-Reinet on 31 May.* His object and that of the conciliation committees was to preserve

[1] Hargrove was described by the *S.A. News* on 19 Mar. 1900 as 'an English gentleman of means and leisure, a Public School man, a former member of the Middle Temple and an author of some note'. He was said to be well travelled, with an American wife and homes in both London and New York.

the independence of the Republics in the face of Britain's determination to annex them, and to bring about peace on these terms. The movement was not directly associated with the Afrikaner Bond, whose congress in June laid emphasis on its spontaneous and independent origin;* but in most places where committees were set up the local Bondsmen had prominent roles.*

For Milner, the conciliation movement was an 'agitation got up by the most extreme section of the Bond party in the Colony to advocate the continued independence of the Republic[s] and to threaten Great Britain with the permanent disaffection of the Dutch of South Africa, if she does not adopt that policy'.* He would not allow that it was spontaneous, or that it had a wide following, or indeed that it aimed at conciliation. This however was going too far. Hargrove may have been a tactless meddler, and the movement may have provided the setting for a spate of anti-Imperial speeches, but the meetings were not seditious, and the *Cape Times* reporter at the Graaff-Reinet gathering, who was a hostile witness, could not resist noting its orderliness. Its purpose was well enough indicated in the resolutions carried at this unusually large gathering,* which claimed, not unreasonably, to represent majority (white) opinion in the Colony. It censured the Imperial Government for causing the war by intervening in the affairs of the South African Republic. It protested at the lack of opportunity for the Colonial ministers to exert proper influence during the pre-war crisis, at the charges of disloyalty levelled against Colonial Boers in the jingo press, and at the obstacles in the way of presenting the Cape view to the British public. The delegates voted against the annexation of the Republics by Britain, and in favour of their continued independence, with provision for the settlement of disputes by arbitration. They wanted a voice in the selection of their own governor. They agreed to establish a fund to cover the cost of a deputation to England, and possibly to other parts of the Empire, bearing a popular petition; and they resolved to publicize their resolutions widely.* Had Milner considered, side by side, the silence of Colonial Afrikanerdom during the months of Boer victory and the disciplined protests which they made during the months of Boer defeat, he might have been more restrained in his criticism of the conciliation movement. It was subversive only on the assumption, which Milner made, that anything short of unconditional surrender by the two Republics would involve the undermining of Imperial interests. Milner was correct in protesting that it was the conciliators, rather than their rivals, who broke his 'truce of God', for it was they who opened their mouths first. But within a short while pro-Imperial vigilance committees, together with various English-speaking church groups and municipal authorities, were conducting an equally vigorous propaganda in favour of the annexation of the Republics.*

On his visit to the South African Republic in January, Hargrove had given Kruger some reason for informing Steyn that he had 'come here . . . from Sauer and Merriman, who are ready to range themselves openly on our side, to make propaganda in the Cape Colony provided an official declaration is given that the Republics only desire to secure complete independence'.* This telegram was found in Steyn's correspondence when the British forces captured Bloemfontein in mid-March. Milner handled the information with scrupulous correctness, declaring that he refused to believe 'that any Minister of the Crown in this Colony would send a private communication to the head of a State with which Her Majesty was at war without the knowledge of the Governor, much less a message of the character alleged', and he handed the matter over to Schreiner for action. Merriman and Sauer both emphatically denied having sent messages to Kruger, and the former extracted from Hargrove a written explanation of Kruger's 'misconception', in which he affirmed that as Merriman and Sauer had been unaware of his intention to visit Kruger, he could not possibly have been the bearer of a message from them. He had merely told Kruger, he wrote, of a conversation with Sauer in which the latter, speaking in his personal capacity, had supported in principle the guaranteeing of independence to the Republics in return for the withdrawal of Republican forces from Colonial soil.* Hargrove's explanation did not satisfy Milner, who recommended the publication of the full correspondence and perhaps desired to embarrass the ministers concerned. They, on the other hand, were more interested in burying the past, on the argument that publication would inflame popular feelings and that Kruger's original telegram was not public property; but Schreiner, who looked on Hargrove's explanation as 'laboured, lame and unsatisfactory' and meriting exposure, supported Milner's recommendation.* Not surprisingly, the Schreiner ministry never associated itself with Hargrove's agitation. Some weeks before the embarrassing revelations Richard Solomon had advised Schreiner to have nothing to do with it—a view which Schreiner shared.

Hofmeyr, who was not unsympathetic, also kept aloof.* But such restraint would not be of much avail, for by April 1900 the Cabinet crisis which would lead after two months to their downfall was already in being.

The question of how to handle the Colonial rebels had been discussed personally and in letters between Richard Solomon and Kitchener in January, when the Cabinet showed signs of being divided, and Chamberlain raised it again in a secret dispatch to Milner on 10 March.* Milner informed Chamberlain that 'the answer to this question will in all probability split the Ministry. Even if it does not', he continued, 'there are other questions which would be likely to lead to the same result, notably the annexation of the Republics'.* He had for some time been drawing the attention of the Colonial Office to the difficulties likely to ensue from the existing ministry's continuing in power; for, as he explained to Chamberlain on 17 January:

'If, when our troops have withdrawn, the Government remains in the old hands, the Colony will be part of the British Empire only in name. On the other hand, if a loyal Government can be secured for only a few years, the position will, I believe, be saved for ever. The Bond unsupported from the outside would die a natural death in the Colony, unless it could artificially strengthen itself by the possession of power and patronage. It is only the Imperial Parliament which can deal with the situation. No local Parliament elected by the present constituencies including rebels would support a loyal Ministry.'*

Chamberlain rejected the conclusion which Milner drew from this observation, namely that the rebel districts should be disfranchised; but the letter, and others like it, make it clear that Milner did not intend to lighten the load of the Schreiner Government now that the military situation appeared to be under control, and the end of the war in sight.

The first problem was to decide whether the rebels should be tried by normal jury procedure or by special courts, or indeed whether they should be tried at all. Milner and Richard Solomon, who in late March together toured the frontier districts recently evacuated by the enemy, agreed that under the exceptional circumstances jury trials were likely to defeat the ends of justice.* Te Water, however, argued vehemently that this was not the case, and treated the suggestion as a slur on the integrity of the Colonial Afrikaner.* By 27 April this issue had been settled within the Cabinet, with the adoption of a ministerial minute favouring the establishment of a special court. This should be composed, the ministers argued, not in the manner suggested first by Chamberlain and subsequently by Milner, of three ordinary lawyers of whom only one would be required to have a reputation for lack of bias, but two judges of the Supreme Court assisted by a barrister of ten years' standing. They were to be competent to try treason cases, and, when assisted by a jury, ordinary criminal cases as well.* The question of the court's constitution, however, raised further problems. Chamberlain had not discussed the issue in his secret dispatch to Milner. Milner tried to persuade the Colonial Government to institute the new procedure itself.* Solomon, on whose shoulders as Attorney-General the problem largely fell, preferred to sacrifice some constitutional independence by leaving the matter in the hands of the Imperial authorities, rather than assume responsibility for setting up a special court without the assurance that the Colonial Parliament would either support such an institution or carry the necessary Act of Indemnity.* But the sacrifice of constitutional rights, as might be expected, did not commend itself to Merriman, who would not give way to Solomon on this point and protested that only a court established on the authority of the Colonial Parliament would satisfy him.*

More serious than the procedural and constitutional difficulties, however, was the question of how convicted rebels ought to be punished, for on this the ministry split wide open. Reacting to Solomon's original suggestion of a special court, Merriman advised Schreiner to work for 'the very widest and broadest measure of amnesty' for all rebels save those indictable for common law offences. His views found expression in a ministerial minute on 28 April, in which the Cabinet proposed that although the ringleaders should stand trial and receive exemplary sentences, the Queen should be asked, as an act of grace, to grant a general amnesty to the rest. The Ministers sought to prove that the precedent of generous treatment accorded to the Canadian rebels in 1837 was applicable in the Cape Colonial situation.* But on 4 May Chamberlain rejected the arguments based on the Canadian analogy and urged that disfranchisement should be applied even in the case of rebels who could 'satisfactorily prove that they acted under compulsion', with the infliction of severer penalties on the ringleaders, the perpetrators of outrages, the looters, those who had acted 'contrary to the usages of civilized warfare', and those who had gone into rebellion of their own free will.*

The ministers' proposals for a general amnesty therefore found no favour with Chamberlain; but he had not quite closed the door. Solomon therefore made an attempt to meet him, accepting the substance of Chamberlain's proposals for all categories of rebels save those who had acted under compulsion. As these had been unable to help themselves, Solomon urged, they should not be punished. For other classes of offenders, as Chamberlain had left the period of disfranchisement unspecified, he suggested a maximum of five years. 'It appears to me,' he wrote, 'after a careful perusal of Mr. Chamberlain's message, that if this Government would, in the main, adopt the views which I have expressed, there ought to be no difficulty in the two Governments agreeing on a policy.'* But Solomon had banked on Chamberlain's not insisting on life-disfranchisement, and Chamberlain soon made it clear that he would not consider a shorter term.* 'Disfranchisement for life', he wrote, 'does not seem to Her Majesty's Government to be a very serious punishment for rebellion.' To be sure it was not, considered as a penalty for individual rebels; but, as Schreiner's Bond supporters now urged with all the force at their command, disfranchisement would penalize the Afrikaans-speaking community as a whole, by upsetting the parliamentary balance of power, and would perhaps create—neither Hofmeyr nor Merriman could resist the analogy—a class of Dutch helots in the Colony.*

The South African Party caucus met on 8 June, in a last attempt to resolve the Cabinet deadlock before the opening of Parliament on the 22nd. The issue before the meeting was not to choose between Chamberlain's ideas on disfranchisement and Solomon's, for Chamberlain's were not yet public knowledge, but to decide whether any kind of disfranchisement should be imposed. Three members of the caucus, Frederic de Waal, David de Waal and Merriman, have left accounts of the proceedings, of which Frederic de Waal's, given to the Bond congress a week later, is the fullest.* He spoke of the policy dispute in the Cabinet and of Schreiner's desire 'to know definitely what the members of the Africander Party [sic] thought of the matter', and then turned to the motion which Schreiner had put to the caucus as a test of their confidence in himself:

'That this meeting of members of the Legislative Council and House of Assembly will support the Government in reasonable legislative measures—

(1) For the provision of an indemnity for the Acts properly done under the proclamations of Martial Law;

(2) For the establishment of a special tribunal for the trial of those who are prosecuted as ringleaders or principal offenders against the law of High Treason;

(3) For the enactment of a measure protecting from criminal prosecution those offenders not to be so prosecuted, but providing for their disenfranchisement for a period of five (5) years unless they shall prove that they have acted under compulsion.'

Strong argument ensued, some members urging that, having sanctioned martial law, the Government could not refuse the responsibility for dealing with misdemeanours committed under it. The majority, however, rejected this view, Frederic de Waal among them. It might have been possible, he continued, to accept the first two points in Schreiner's motion; but 'Point 3 . . . had admitted of no compromise, for it was one upon which the party could not join hands with the Ministry. Every member said it was a measure of which the party could not approve. They felt that they could not go to Parliament and bring in a Bill providing for the disfranchisement of those men who had taken up arms against Her Majesty's troops, well knowing . . . that these men had been forced into rebellion; well knowing that they would never have taken up arms if they could have helped it; well knowing, too, that the Opposition would dearly like to take away or curtail the electoral privileges of as many of the Africander party as possible.'

Rather than take a hasty decision, the caucus met again on the 9th, this time without the ministers. But after discussion they confirmed their attitude over point 3. Schreiner, on being informed of this, asked what decision had been reached over his first two points, and received the answer 'that if it was made a condition of his remaining in office that they should agree to these points they were prepared to do so, reserving however the right to amend or alter any measure in committee as they thought fit. At the same time the meeting expressed its opinion that this was not a fit time for the Ministry to resign.' For the sake of keeping the Government in office, therefore, the caucus was prepared to accept in principle an

Act of Indemnity and a special tribunal; but if disfranchisement was the price of the partnership's continuance, an overwhelming majority considered it too heavy. Schreiner, realizing that he no longer had majority support either in the party or in the Assembly, resigned on 13 June.*

Although disagreement over disfranchisement had been the main cause of the ministerial split, and of the break between Schreiner and the parliamentary party, it was not the only issue. There was, as Milner had anticipated, disagreement in the Cabinet over the future of the Republics. When Schreiner drew up a memorandum in favour of their continued independence under British paramountcy, for discussion at a Cabinet meeting on 30 March, he subsequently endorsed it 'unanimity impossible'.* Solomon decided after the same Cabinet meeting that he had 'no wish to go through such a painful experience again', accused Merriman and Sauer of suppressing their objections to his handling of the Justice Department, and referred to Te Water in contemptuous language as Hofmeyr's Cabinet informer.* 'It is inconvenient, to say the least of it,' Schreiner commented at the foot of one of Te Water's minutes on 24 April, 'to note strong protests from a Minister who rarely, if ever, takes part in the councils of his colleagues.'* Schreiner had also begun to fall out with Hofmeyr, whose advice was nevertheless in constant demand,* while Merriman was regularly irritated by Schreiner's overbearing manner.* Thus the weaknesses and the personal antipathies within the ministry, and between some of the ministers and their Bond allies, had come to the surface some weeks before the final break. But for all the pent-up feelings, it was not a break like that of 1896. The South African Party had not turned on Schreiner and all that he stood for: rather, they had refused to associate themselves with proposals for the punishment of rebels which threatened to undermine the basis of their power.

The mood of the Bond as a whole was bound to be important under the circumstances, and that mood, when it was at last able to express itself in congress at Paarl on 15 June, was truculent and bitter but not uncontrolled. There had been many irritants: not only had the date and venue of congress been repeatedly changed, but when it eventually met most of the frontier district *besturen* were of necessity unrepresented; *Ons Land* and other Dutch papers had been banned in certain districts, which made the dissemination of party information difficult, and annoyed Bondsmen because similar restrictions were not imposed on the *Cape Times*;* white people had been disarmed in some districts, and non-whites armed in others, to the great chagrin of party members;* Boer cattle had been impounded by Imperial troops; people had been arrested and kept waiting for trial. Congress therefore appointed a strong commission to draw up a comprehensive statement on the war, and unanimously accepted its findings in a motion introduced by F. S. Malan.* The motion expressed strong disapproval of the policy of the Imperial Government, which had led to 'the bloody and unjust war', for showing little consideration for the feelings of a majority of the Cape Colonials, for going back on the promise of a joint inquiry, and for refusing arbitration to the Transvaal even though England had supported it at the Hague conference. It went on to ask for the speedy restoration of peace under conditions which allowed the Republics to keep their independence 'unimpaired', and for the establishment of a parliamentary grievances commission to investigate the infringement of private property, personal liberty and constitutional privileges during the war. Malan, who was acquiring the reputation of a mischief-maker on account of his allegedly provocative articles in *Ons Land*, spoke to the motion with a lengthy indictment of the Imperial record since the Jameson Raid—an indictment marked by firmness, incisiveness, and (it is perhaps desirable to add) restraint.

'Like Peter, we are on the stormy waves of the sea,' he said, 'and if we look only to the hurricane which roars around us, we will in all probability be lost men. And the man who wishes to be our leader in these times must come forward in a firm and decided manner; he must know his own mind; and further, he must have the courage to extend a helping hand to us. Given such a leader, and a firm resolve on the part of our people to follow him, I regard the future with confidence; then I already see the dawn of salvation of our people and our country.'

Malan's words were optimistic—too optimistic, perhaps, for a speech made a mere ten days after the British occupation of Pretoria. More in keeping with the needs of the moment were the concluding sentences of Thomas Theron's opening address:

'And now, friends, what are we going to do? Are we going to take revenge? Beware of that. It is one of the worst means that we can have recourse to. To express our feelings in certain resolutions and to discuss and pass such resolutions? That is permissible, but let us even in our speech act as men whose heads are above their hearts, and let us never forget that even if we are Afrikanders we are yet British subjects, and let us, even in criticising matters, however sharp our criticism may be, never allow ourselves to lose sight of the sound rules of criticism, and let us never make ourselves guilty of descending to personalities under the name of criticism. May God give each member of this meeting His Grace and the guidance of His Spirit.'*

Theron's quiet example would continue to be a source of strength and unity for the Bondsmen; and, should he fail, there was N. F. de Waal, whom Merriman had spotted during the Cabinet crisis as one who had 'displayed tact and great ability, and evidently leads his party'.* New leadership would in any case be necessary, for Hofmeyr was about to depart for Europe, where he would spend the remainder of the war years living the life of an invalid.

II. MARTIAL LAW AND DISFRANCHISEMENT

The Paarl congress emphatically endorsed the action of the South African Party caucus in withdrawing its support from Schreiner.* But although the break was clean on the issue of disfranchisement, congress was careful to 'reciprocate in full' the hope expressed by Schreiner, in his letter of explanation to Frederic de Waal, that he would be able to co-operate with the Bond frequently in the future. 'They mourn over him in affectionate sorrow', Milner told Chamberlain, 'but are wise enough not to attack him'.* It seems that when Parliament opened on 22 July Schreiner still considered himself to be a member of the party caucus, but that, without wishing to cause him any offence, the caucus itself had assumed the contrary.* In the last resort, his actions and those of his fellow 'Adullamites' during the session would settle the issue. They sat on the cross-benches, and Sprigg, who had succeeded in forming his fourth ministry on 18 June, was aware that their votes would be necessary to keep him in office.

The delicacy of the parliamentary situation was well reflected in a letter written by Louis Abrahamson to Rhodes, urging him to return to Parliament in order to make Sprigg's tenure secure:

'If the four rebel members[1] (two of whom are in jail and two are supposed to have left the country) don't turn up and if Schreiner,

---

[1] P. J. de Wet (Wodehouse), Jotham Joubert (Albert), I. J. van der Walt (Colesberg) and Ds. C. W. H. Schröder (Prieska). De Wet voted twice during the session, Van der Walt once, the other two not at all.

Solomon and D. de Waal support the Ministry the parties will just balance. If therefore Sonnenberg, Wessels[1] and Wienand vote with us we will have a majority of four or six. That is if none of the rebel members should be released on bail meanwhile, as Botha[2] another member has already been released. . . .'*

Most of Schreiner's faithful band are mentioned here, though the names of Charles Searle, member for George, and A. J. Herholdt need to be added. H. J. Raubenheimer, who also represented George, had supported Schreiner in the caucus meeting in June.* Not much, apart from a different view of what was practical politics, divided these men from the Bond majority.

The return of Jameson and the threatened return of Rhodes to active political life were of doubtful value to Sprigg in this delicate situation, for it was essential that the Government should strike a moderate pose. But Innes's acceptance of the Law Department was of inestimable value to the new Government, more especially since it was the Attorney-General who had to handle the two most controversial debates of what proved to be a very stormy session: on Merriman's motion calling for an end to martial law, and on the Government's Indemnity and Special Tribunals Bill.

Merriman moved the immediate repeal of all martial law proclamations on 24 July, giving as his grounds the termination of armed resistance in the Colony, the reopening of civil courts in the districts recently relinquished by the enemy, and the obnoxious character of martial law itself—'a law of force, the abjection of all law'.* For one Bond speaker after another, martial law spelt frustration and hardship, often injustice. Several were indignant at the activities of General Brabant's Horse in the north-eastern districts, though this force had its energetic defenders in C. P. Crewe and Brabant himself. Some, like T. P. Theron and A. S. du Plessis, objected to the arrest of individuals for treason 'on the evidence of . . . Kafirs'. On the whole, however, the debate did not go well for the Bondsmen. It was easy for Innes to point out that it was the previous Government which had introduced martial law, and that within five weeks of attaining office their successors had already ended martial law in several districts where the local magistrate had advised the step. Sensing as the debate developed that the categorical tone of Merriman's motion was out of harmony with the realities

[1] The S.A. Party members for Vryburg. Wessels was a Bondsman.
[2] J. N. P. Botha (Aliwal North).

of the military situation, the Bondsmen, through Theron, moved as
an amendment:

'. . . that this House, without disapproving of the proclamation of
martial law in the proclaimed districts, is of opinion that the continuance of martial law, and the punishment and prosecution of
persons under the forms of martial law in districts in which armed
resistance to Her Majesty's forces has ceased, and in which it is not
indispensable for the success of the operations of Her Majesty's
forces in the field, is contrary to the inherent rights of British
subjects, and that in such districts it is therefore expedient that the
proclamation declaring martial law should now be repealed.'*

The amendment was blunted by excess of verbiage, yet it was lost
by only 41 votes to 45. With the exception of Raubenheimer,
however, none of the Adullamites voted with the Bond.

The debate had given rise to a good deal of unsavoury sniping
across the floor of the House; but the heat generated was as nothing
when compared with the debate on the Indemnity and Special
Tribunals Bill. In its main provisions this measure echoed the
proposals first made by Richard Solomon, who in any case helped
to draft it.* A blanket indemnity was proposed for offences committed in good faith under the compulsion of martial law. There
was to be a special court for the trial of ringleaders, consisting of
two judges of the Supreme Court plus a practising advocate of at
least ten years' standing. Except in the case of persons who had
surrendered under specific proclamations, who could not be executed
or imprisoned, the court had discretion in the imposition of sentences,
and within certain broad limits the definition of a ringleader was
left to the Attorney-General. Special commissions of three men, of
whom one at least had to be a practising advocate of seven years'
standing, were to examine the cases of the rank and file rebels, who,
if found guilty, were to lose their civil rights for five years—the old
Roman loss of status, explained Innes when introducing the Bill:
'a mild and most fair punishment'.

There was a general, if sometimes reluctant, disposition on the
part of Bond speakers to agree that rebel ringleaders had to receive
punishment, though every kind of argument was advanced in
extenuation: that they had acted under compulsion, that prior
responsibility lay with the Imperial authorities for not making sure
that the frontiers were adequately defended against invasion, that

the rebels were dupes of Republican propaganda, and so on. But the real emphasis of the debate lay neither here nor on the indemnity, which many Opposition speakers found far too sweeping, but on the proposed treatment of the rank and file.

Bondsmen argued, first, that the Schreiner Government had allowed the case for a general amnesty for the rank and file rebels to go by default. Had they resisted Chamberlain's demand, these speakers contended, Britain would not have presumed to press her case for punishment. The ministerial defence, which Schreiner endorsed, rested on the twin arguments that the British Government had pressed the point in a manner not to be resisted, and that as the prerogative of mercy had not been extended to the Colonial Parliament, it could not be used except by the Queen as an act of grace, and on the advice of her ministers in London. When Bond speakers, notably Dr. Beck of Worcester, asked whether in this kind of case the Queen should seek the advice of 'ministers who, for the time being, were at the head of affairs in a particular colony, or [of] ministers six thousand miles away in England', Innes's answer was to distinguish between internal and Imperial questions and to claim that the treatment of Colonial rebels fell in the latter category. The weight of tradition lay behind the reply, which Lord Durham himself might have given; but in an area governed by convention rather than strict law, the Opposition case was at least arguable. This was the kind of issue on which the authority of tradition was bound to be challenged, and had been—eloquently so—by Albert Cartwright at Graaff-Reinet and F. S. Malan at the Paarl congress, who both contended that because the Colony paid £5,000 annually to the Governor and £3,000 to the High Commissioner, the Queen's representative was bound to listen to his Cape ministers' advice in both capacities.*

The other main claim put forward repeatedly by Bond speakers was that disfranchisement, so far from being the mild punishment which Government supporters alleged, was hardly a punishment for a serious crime, was no punishment at all for the rebel who was not yet on the voter's roll, and yet was a punishment for all political opponents of the Government, most of whom had remained loyal, because disfranchisement on the scale envisaged could deprive the Afrikaner Bond of the reasonable prospect of power. Merriman complained that the Government was planning 'to shift the balance of political power, not by fair political fight'. 'For every man they disfranchise', he said in the debate on the third reading, '. . . they are turning him into a republican. This was a Bill for the manufacture of republicans in South Africa.' There were, of course, arguments on the other side. The Colonial law, as amended in 1892, laid down the life disfranchisement of convicted traitors—a far worse penalty than that proposed by the Government, since this was only the minimum sentence, as Chamberlain had reminded the previous ministry. Sonnenberg and Wessels, the two members for Vryburg, both of whom had been Bond candidates in the previous election, had visited their constituency since the withdrawal of the Republican forces, and both claimed to have received from the rebels in their constituency a mandate to support the disfranchisement proposals, if rank and file rebels might thereby avoid a prison sentence or loss of property.* The Adullamites found the proposals satisfactory, and gave the Government a majority of nine votes at the second and third readings.

Schreiner and his supporters kept Sprigg in office through the session, though the Government survived a division by only two votes on 24 September. Thereafter they would find the wilderness increasingly lonely, as is evident from the correspondence which ensued between Schreiner, who scrupulously held a private referendum in his own constituency and resigned his seat on the strength of it, and Herholdt and Charles Searle, who both suffered local hostility but decided to retain their seats.* Solomon resigned from Parliament and went for a while to London. As a group, if they ever were one in any formal sense, the Adullamites faded out; but as Parliament did not meet between October 1900 and August 1902, this had at best a delayed significance.

III. POLARIZED LOYALTIES

Between the British occupation of Pretoria on 5 June 1900 and the crossing of the Cape frontier by commandos under Kritzinger, Scheepers and Hertzog in mid-December—a period of growing exasperation for the Imperial military command, though not one of encouragement for the Colonial pro-Boer—there was a marked deterioration in the public mood at the Cape. The events of the session had contributed to this, with the constant stream of Progressive complaints at rebel treachery and Bond disloyalty, and antiphonal protests by South African Party leaders—by Theron, against the activities of Rimington's Scouts in the Britstown area, where Smartt also complained of property losses at the hands of local rebels; by Hoffman, who still waited to learn why the British had seized his ambulance; by Merriman, on the ground that a letter which he had written to restrain P. J. de Wet, his fellow member for Wodehouse, from rebelling had not only been seized before it reached the addressee, but had been published by Chamberlain in an Imperial command paper 'for a paltry political advantage', without any permission having been obtained from the writer, who was an Executive Councillor of the Colony at the time.* During these months the Colonial Afrikaners had also to witness the failure of the peace delegation which had been sent to Britain on the decision of the Graaff-Reinet mass meeting in May. The delegation returned in October having found 'time and sentiment against them', and the British people 'bitten by the mad dog of Jingoism'.*

Then the British command, incensed by the extent of collaboration between civilian Boers and the commandos in the field, began to destroy farm properties and to concentrate the occupants in camps under military supervision. The practice preceded by several weeks the general order issued by Kitchener on 21 December, and it gave rise to a sharp and bitter reaction among Afrikaners, in the Colony no less than elsewhere. In the first place, it led to demonstrations by Boer women. Many gathered at Somerset East in October to hear, at second hand, the impassioned lament of Olive Schreiner: 'Now, England is dead to me.'* Two thousand women met at a farm outside Paarl in November, where, under 'tall, pollarded oaks in full foliage', they listened to a denunciation of the farm burnings in a message from Marie Koopmans de Wet, who still pressed for the ending of the war on terms of independence for the Republics.*

The fury of the women produced, and was partly produced by, the fury of the journalists, who accepted, without the sort of verification which would have been desirable, stories of gross brutality alleged to have been committed by British troops, even by British generals, in the enforcement of the farm-burning policy.* Not without provocation, Milner wrote to Chamberlain that the 'unbridled licence of press and pulpit, and . . . the unchecked extravagance of the rebel party in the Assembly' had 'altered the whole tone of the country population'.* He was quite clearly afraid that the Colonial Afrikaners would rise in arms.

So was Merriman, who wrote to the secretary of the Afrikaner Bond on 23 November and told him that 'this women and children

business seems to me to be the last straw, and I frankly tell you I
dread the result'.* Malan and others had begun to organize a mass
protest meeting to take place in Worcester, on the lines of that held
at Graaff-Reinet, in order to show the Imperial authorities the full
depth of their abhorrence of the new military policy, and Merriman
feared that it was being 'engineered by political agitators' and might
well get out of hand. N. F. de Waal, though he later claimed to have
disapproved of the Worcester gathering,* recorded at the time that
he thought Merriman was being unduly apprehensive, for although
he feared that the proposed resolutions were not likely to achieve
much practical good, 'yet at the present time any opportunity for
people to relieve their pent-up feelings in a legitimate manner should
be looked upon as a sort of safety valve'. But Theron looked upon
the meeting with 'fear and trembling' and thought its convening the
height of unwisdom.*

The Worcester mass meeting of 6 December, like its Graaff-Reinet
predecessor, was not a meeting of the Afrikaner Bond, whose
executive had decided not to become officially involved.* Two
Bondsmen, Jacob de Villiers and F. S. Malan, filled the positions of
chairman and secretary respectively, and there were a dozen Bond
members of Parliament present, as well as many ordinary members
of the party. But the appeal had gone out for a 'People's Congress',
and of the large number present—estimated at between seven and
twelve thousand by the *South African News*—many were not
Bondsmen. It was, in fact, the non-Bondsmen on the platform who
made the excited speeches. Cronwright-Schreiner, who during a
recent visit to Britain had been attacked by an angry crowd at Leeds,
blamed capitalism for atrocities committed by the British army, and
went on to demand the recall of Milner on the unusual ground that
he was intellectually incompetent. The frankest praise for the Boer
commandos came from the Rev. Dr. Kolbe:

'If we all hung on to De Wet's coat tails we could not keep him
from fighting. It is not we who encourage them: it is they who
encourage us. If they were to give in now and surrender, we shall say:
"You have done all that honour suggests." But if they go on fighting
we shall say: "You are even greater heroes than we took you for"'.

Kolbe moved to censure the Governor himself, and asked the
gathering to claim 'the full recognition of the right of the people of
this Colony under its constitution to settle and manage their own

affairs'—a national petition of right, he called it. Bond contributions to the discussion were more modest, though they included a motion by Dr. Reinecke, chairman of a Ceres branch, who would soon himself be the victim of controversial detention, urging the 'termination of the war now raging with its untold misery and horrors, such as the burning of houses, the desolation of the country, the extermination of a white nationality, and the treatment to which women and children are subjected'. He also got the meeting to support a demand for the retention of independence by the Republics. Two other Bondsmen, H. J. H. Claassens and Dirk Viljoen, then persuaded the meeting to agree to act only in a constitutional manner, and to send a deputation to the Governor to request the transmission of their resolutions to the British Government.

Though he had looked upon the authorization of the Worcester meeting as 'perfectly monstrous', Milner agreed to meet its deputation and to forward the resolutions as requested; but he made it abundantly clear that he disagreed with them, and held out no hope that the policy of annexation would be reversed.* Chamberlain in due course confirmed that the resolutions would not affect British policy.*

Kolbe had proposed a 'petition of right'. Merriman, in his anxiety to avert the dangers which he feared would follow from the Worcester meeting, had conceived the idea of a 'grand remonstrance', to be delivered by an accredited delegation of the South African Party at the bar of the House of Commons, embodying an authoritative statement of their point of view. His proposal, which De Waal accepted, that the Party should meet at Beaufort West or Cradock to draw up such a remonstrance, was not therefore designed to supplement the Worcester meeting, but was conceived originally as an alternative to it and was intended to ensure that the party made its voice heard in the most effective way possible, while at the same time remaining under discipline.* A meeting of South African Party members of Parliament accordingly took place, not at Beaufort West as has been commonly supposed, but in Cape Town on 7 January, at which the members resolved to send Merriman, Sauer, and—if they could get him—Hofmeyr, on a deputation to England.*

Hofmeyr, however, was not prepared to make the journey from Munich to London for a cause which he considered hopeless. When Merriman suggested to him that the British Government might consider 'autonomy under their own flag for the Republics, coupled with a general confederation of S. Africa under the Br[itish] flag', he replied that any proposal for a genuine grant of autonomy to the Boers was bound to be turned down. He preferred direct government from Downing Street, where there would not always be a Chamberlain in power, than that the Republics should be 'hood-winked and sucked dry by a Brummagem President and Volksraad'.* Despite this friendly rebuff, Merriman and Sauer went through with their mission, based their petition on the assumption that the British Government would not go back on its declared policy of annexing the Republics, and asked simply to be allowed to appear at the bar of the Commons to testify against the inappropriateness of crown colony rule for colonies which had known self-government, and to 'offer suggestions as to other alternatives which would hold out a more secure promise of a peaceful settlement'.* The British Government refused the request, however, as Hofmeyr, James Bryce and others prophesied they would, and the Cape delegates had to content themselves with a few opportunities to address public meetings—some hostile, some friendly—and a couple of not very profitable interviews with Chamberlain.* They had tried and failed to find a middle term between annexation and independence as a basis for negotiations on which to end the war. Their effort coincided in point of time with the Middelburg negotiations between Kitchener and Botha, and broke against the same obstacles.[1] 'I do not, as things are, see any way out of the *impasse*', wrote Hofmeyr, 'except a complete victory on either the one side or the other. The more's the pity, but so it is.'*

The changed military situation gave good ground for Hofmeyr's pessimism, for the second Boer invasion of the Cape presented new and difficult military problems. The annexation of territory no longer mattered. It was now a war of movement in which regular troops fought against large mobile commandos under skilled guerrilla leaders, who relied on the Cape population not so much for overt acts of rebellion as for moral support, military information, new mounts and fresh supplies of food. The success of the Boer commandos in disrupting communications, in breaking up small concentrations of British troops (many of them raw recruits, in

---

[1] Botha rejected Kitchener's Middelburg terms on 16 March. The British Government refused Merriman and Sauer a hearing in the Commons on the 28th.

mid-1901), in eluding Kitchener's increasingly elaborate network of blockhouses, and in maintaining their resistance on captured arms and ammunition, food and clothing, together with the retaliatory steps taken by the military command, tried the patience and the courage of the Colonial supporters of both sides.

Boer successes, above all the brilliant elusiveness of De Wet, did much to restore the hopes of the Colonial pro-Boers, and left the leaders of the Bond with a difficult problem: to avoid giving the impression that, while their representatives were seeking peace in Britain, they in South Africa were dedicated to a continuation of the war. The South African Party newspapers continued to criticize Imperial policy and to protest vigorously against British military methods. While holding that it would be wrong for Colonials to rebel and join the invaders, they also asserted that, as it was a British war, it was the responsibility of the British to drive the invaders out. In April the Government put four of the editors on trial: Malan of *Ons Land*, J. E. de Jong of the *Worcester Advertiser*, and Vosloo of *Het Oosten*, for publishing an article which accused General French of inhumanity towards women and children, and Albert Cartwright of the *South African News* for taking over from an English newspaper a report which alleged that Kitchener had given an order not to take prisoners.* Malan, who was refused permission to call witnesses from concentration camps in Natal because he could not show what particular line of defence would be helped by their presence, was found guilty of maliciously trying to injure French's reputation, and sentenced to a year's imprisonment. Vosloo and De Jong, on the same charge, were sent to prison for six months. Cartwright's plea that he had published his article with a view to obtaining Kitchener's denial, which he had also published, was dismissed by the court, and he received the same sentence as Malan. The effect of these trials on the Opposition press was considerable. *Ons Land* went out of circulation in early January, while the preparatory examination of its editor was in progress, and did not reappear until July 1902. The *Advertentieblad*, which took its place, steered clear of all controversial reporting. The *South African News* continued to appear until October and it continued to oppose Imperial policy; but its circulation was restricted to Cape Town and it was in severe financial straits. As the other Bond journals on which the executive relied to disseminate instructions to the branches were not permitted to circulate in martial law districts, a situation had arisen in which it was almost impossible for the party leaders to communicate with the rank and file.*[1]

It was under these conditions that Theron received a direct approach from the Boer Central Peace Committee, a body formed by surrendered burghers of the Orange Free State with the approval of the British military authorities. They asked the 'Afrikaner Party' to support their appeal to the commandos still in the field to lay down their arms, by sending a deputation to inform the commandos that they did not propose to give them any military assistance.* Theron, who, as Dr. Beck observed, had been 'all the time in a martial law district [and] entirely ignorant of what was going on',* made the journey to Cape Town to interview the delegation. They met him before he got there, at Wellington, and put their argument to him. According to their story, Theron 'agreed with us on all points, but he saw some difficulty in giving effect to them', and therefore sent telegrams to N. F. de Waal, [P. J. ?] du Toit and [D. J. A. ?] van Zyl, asking them to meet him at Worcester. 'In essentials', ran the Peace Committee's fuller memorandum, 'he was entirely at one with us.'* But then, 'on the 20th, five days after our meeting, Mr. Theron suddenly breaks off all further communication with us, and disappears from Cape Town without even replying to our letter in reply to his'. Theron's letter to them stated:

'As it is impossible for me, after enquiry, to recognise the status of your deputation, and further since it is beyond my power, in accordance with the programme of principles of the Afrikaner Bond, to enter into any official negotiations with anybody, if thereby our principles would be prejudiced, I shall not and cannot, meet you in this matter, or negotiate with you. [But] having been always anxious to promote the restoration of peace in South Africa on terms honourable to both parties, I am still prepared to use all the efforts in my power and in accordance with those principles, and the resolutions of our party, and for that purpose I would gladly tender my services to the constituted authorities.'*

[1] According to Varley, the *S.A. News* was suspended between 15 Oct. 1901 and 19 Aug. 1902. *Onze Courant*, the date of whose suppression is not clear, only appeared 81 times between 4 Mar. 1901 and 2 July 1903. *Het Oosten* seems to have gone out of circulation after 28 Mar. 1901, the date on which it carried an official notice banning it, along with *Ons Land*, the *S.A. News*, *Onze Courant*, *Ons Weekblad*, the *Nieuwe Middelburger*, and various imported journals, from distribution in the Somerset East district.

Much was made of this incident during the Assembly debate on the Afrikaner Bond in 1902, by Progressive members anxious to show that the Bondsmen had behaved in a disloyal manner; and the story was put abroad that Theron had been prepared to accept the proposals of the Peace Committee until he came under disloyal influences in Cape Town which led him to change his mind.* We have, unfortunately, only partisan accounts of the episode; but in Theron's favour must be cited his claim during the parliamentary debate to have gone 'straight to the Prime Minister and explained the whole thing', in the presence of Dr. Smartt (who was one of his leading critics) as soon as the interview was over, and there to have offered to take any terms the Government cared to offer to the enemy, even if he could not agree with them.* Smartt did not refute Theron's statement. As to the propriety of the Bond leader's conduct in refusing to co-operate with the '*hensoppers*', it seems clear that he acted on advice, and that it would have been politically impossible for him, as it was for the Cape *Kerk* leaders on the same occasion, to follow any other course. He and De Waal later claimed to have drawn up and signed, at the request of General French, an appeal to all rebels to lay down their arms in July 1901, and to have transmitted it to French, who, for reasons unknown, had not sent it out.* Together they made out an impressive case for their own sense of responsibility and that of their party. When the war ended in May 1902, the elected leaders of the Afrikaner Bond could honestly claim to have acted consistently in a discreet and honourable manner.

How many Bond rebels had there been? The answer to this question must be considered in the light of the fact that the second Boer invasion, and therefore the rebellion, were by no means confined to the frontier districts. When the Royal Commission under Baron Alverstone arrived to review sentences passed under martial law after the end of the war, it found ringleaders still serving sentences from nearly every magisterial district in the Colony—100 from the Cradock district, 26 from Aberdeen, 42 from Somerset East, 18 from Willowmore, 25 from Calvinia, 8 from Malmesbury, 4 from Paarl, to name at random some of the districts away from the borders.* There is almost no correlation between the names of the 721 Cape ringleaders mentioned in the Commission's report and the names in the only complete list of Bond members ever published; but as this was drawn up in 1893, and most of the rebels were by common repute very young men, this is not surprising.* When in September

1902 N. F. de Waal asked for a select committee to examine the charges levelled against the Bond during the war he carefully limited his motion to include only Bond parliamentarians.* The select committee, which consisted of an equal number of supporters and opponents of the Bond under the chairmanship of H. T. Tamplin, member for Victoria East, disagreed over its ability to make a proper inquiry. Since only the Bond's supporters really wanted one, the majority secured the committee's discharge after examining only two witnesses.* Its report revealed nothing beyond what was contained in a letter from the secretary of the Law Department stating that, though seven members of the House of Assembly whose names figured on a list supplied by De Waal had been under consideration for criminal charges, only one of them, F. S. Malan, had been found guilty.*[1] Had the Progressives succeeded in their attempt to broaden the inquiry to include other members of the Bond, they would undoubtedly have been provided with a stronger case against their opponents; but without being able to count on the Adullamites they were not strong enough to insist on a broader inquiry in 1902,* though Smartt could make bold assertions during the debate on De Waal's motion, so far as treasonable activity by Bond office-bearers was concerned:

'Under the heading of Barkly West was the name of the chairman of the district bestuur and delegate to congress [H. M. van der Rijst]; Griquatown or Hay, the secretary of the district bestuur and delegate to congress [J. C. Maritz, secretary; J. J. Heyns, delegate to congress]; Gordonia, the chairman of the district bestuur and delegate to congress [no Gordonia branch existed in 1899: Upington was admitted that year]; and Prieska, Mr. Smeer, the erstwhile

[1] Charges against J. N. P. Botha (Aliwal North) and C. J. Lötter (Jansenville) had been withdrawn after preliminary examinations. P. J. de Wet (Wodehouse) had been tried for high treason and acquitted. The case of J. H. Schoeman was treated as common knowledge. (He had been sentenced to hard labour and a fine, but was subsequently exonerated by a parliamentary select committee in 1903 and awarded compensation.) Proceedings against A. S. du Plessis (Albert) by the military authorities had been quashed following his appeal to the Attorney-General. There was still one case under consideration (almost certainly that of T. N. G. te Water who, according to evidence in his own papers dating from July and August, was considering returning from Europe, where he had gone into voluntary exile, in spite of information that he might be arrested on his return). De Waal's list did not include the names of Jotham Joubert, I. J. van der Walt and Ds. C. W. H. Schröder, whose earlier association with the enemy had led to the forfeiture of their seats.

"landdrost" of the town. Under the heading of Colesberg he placed the name of . . . A. G. van Rensburg, secretary of the district bestuur and delegate to congress [N. A. J. van Rensburg].'*

What the Progressives could not get from Parliament, however, the Governor got from the Law Department. On 4 December 1902 the Governor's private secretary asked for details of the number of Bond officers who had been convicted for high treason, which the Attorney-General's office sought to answer by sending parallel lists of convicted rebels and Bond office bearers to the resident magistrates for identification purposes. A partial answer was ready by 21 January 1903:

'Of the 587 men mentioned upon this list [of Bond office-bearers], it is found that 21 have been convicted of High Treason. Of these, one was convicted by the Special Court established by Act 6 of 1900; ten by the Special Commission appointed under the provisions of that Act; one by the Supreme Court; one by Military Court, and eight by Courts of Resident Magistrates. One other person mentioned upon the list is at present a refugee in German territory. Should he return to the Colony a charge of High Treason will be prosecuted against him.'*

The inquiry was not exhaustive—none of the districts from which Smartt had drawn his illustrations, for example, were investigated; but it would seem that it was the comparative fruitlessness of the initial sample that led to the abandonment of the search.[1]

[1] The magistrates of the following districts only were interrogated: Aliwal North, Aberdeen, Barkly East, Bedford, Calvinia, Carnarvon, Ceres, Cradock, Elliot, Fraserburg, Graaff-Reinet, Herbert, Jansenville, Malmesbury, Middelburg, Molteno, Murraysburg, Namaqualand, Philipstown, Piquetberg, Richmond, Somerset East, Steynsburg, Sutherland, Tarkastad, Uniondale, Van Rhynsdorp, Victoria West and Willowmore.

12

Recovery

WHATEVER the actual performance of the Afrikaner Bond during the war, the failure of the select committee of 1902 to convict the Bond parliamentarians of disloyal acts was no reassurance to those of their opponents who did not want to be reassured. One fruit of their mistrust, though it was prompted mainly by Milner's desire to ensure British control over the whole of South Africa in the reconstruction era, was a movement for the suspension of the Cape constitution. After a good deal of acrimonious debate, following which Joseph Chamberlain visited South Africa, this movement failed. But out of its ashes emerged the first experiment in conciliation between Boer and Briton, when leaders of the Afrikaner Bond succeeded in establishing a personal *rapport* with Chamberlain. From the time of his visit in early 1903, the political tensions in post-war South Africa gradually relaxed. The Bond and the South African Party, though weakened by disfranchisement, returned with remarkable ease to their peacetime activities. If Milner's policy in the Transvaal and the Orange River Colony (as the O.F.S. was now called) remained firm and uncompromising, it did not obstruct—indeed, in a negative way it even stimulated—the resurgence of political activity among Afrikaners in those territories. They established their own political parties, they agitated for and soon won self-government from their British overlords, and they went on to win the first elections after self-government had been granted. They revived their language agitation of pre-war days, with political demands for the restoration of rights lost through the war, and a renewal of the debate over the relative merits of Dutch and Afrikaans. And all this happened under the banner of conciliation, which, on pragmatic as well as ideological grounds, became the password for most aspirant leaders of Afrikaner opinion during the years until 1910.

I. THE SUSPENSION MOVEMENT

The suspension of the constitution of the Cape Colony had some forceful advocates in the closing stages of the war, but the balance of public opinion was against it even though it had not been possible to summon Parliament during 1901 or to hold the statutory registration of voters during that year, and a *de facto* suspension seemed already to have taken place. Milner had advocated suspension since the first month of the war, and continued to repeat the advice to Chamberlain at intervals,* though Chamberlain always disagreed and warned him that the British Parliament was unlikely to support such a plan.* By the middle of 1901 support for suspension had begun to spread. A majority of the Graaff-Reinet Vigilance Committee petitioned Hely-Hutchinson for it in May, urging that an election in the near future would 'contain all the elements of dangerous discord and would tend to keep alive the racial animosity which exists, and which your petitioners are so anxious should be allowed to die out'.* An identical petition from over a hundred inhabitants of Colesberg was forwarded by Hely-Hutchinson to Chamberlain on 17 June, together with similar documents from the Albert district. Significantly, however, the executive of the South African Vigilance Committee in Cape Town, whose comments Hutchinson also forwarded, still felt that 'no good reason exists for the demand'.*

Support for suspension was still lukewarm among the backers of the Government in mid-1901 because, like Chamberlain, they were aware of the seriousness of such a step, which had no precedent in the history of the second British Empire and would require legislation by the British Parliament. There were some, too, who still thought that their problems could be solved by a Cabinet reshuffle, with the replacement of Sprigg by Rhodes in the premiership, and of Frost and Sir Pieter Faure by men such as Jameson and Victor Sampson. The *Diamond Fields Advertiser* and the *Eastern Province Herald* used arguments such as these to counter the suspensionist views of the *Graaff-Reinet Advertiser* and the *Cape Times*.* The cure they proposed throws light on the nature of the malady. It apparently stemmed mainly from the fear of some Progressive politicians that their artificial hold on the Cape legislature, which was itself a result of wartime circumstances, would end with the restoration of peace. They mistrusted Sprigg for having given the Bond treason legislation which they regarded as disgracefully lenient, expected that he would be driven into closer association with the Bond, and feared that unless they entrusted the leadership of their party to a more forceful personality, the party itself would not only lose the initiative but run the risk of disintegration.

The discomfiture of the Progressives was, it might be thought, a signal for Bond complacency. But the Bondsmen were every whit as perplexed over the right course to follow. Some Bond leaders, among them David Graaff, also considered the possibility of approaching Rhodes. Graaff put the idea to Hofmeyr as one of several possible courses, urging that 'we will be able to get more out of Mr. Rhodes than even out of a Bond Ministry', and explaining that this was 'the opinion of people who care to think on the matter'.* 'Oh!' Hofmeyr commented distastefully in the margin. 'Humiliation —can't.' He replied that he thought further collaboration would be worthless.* He much preferred Graaff's final proposition: that the Bond parliamentarians should go quietly about their business of looking after their constituents, should guard against administrative corruption, and refrain from unnecessary attacks on Imperial interests. This was a 'policy which need not fear the judgment of the future historian, nor of our own posterity'. But, to confuse the picture further, Hofmeyr was not perturbed over the dangers inherent in constitutional suspension:

'As for the "abolition of the Constitution", do not worry yourself about threats under that head. If our Jingo friends wish to turn South Africa into a worse than Ireland, let them. We live inter-mingled with one another. If *we* have to suffer under autocratic Government, so will *they*. And if such Government has to come over us I for one would rather see it exercised by a Governor from England (who will not always be a Milnerite) sent over by the Imperial Government (who will not always be Chamberlainites) rather than, under the specious forms and fictions of Constitutional Government, by a bitterly anti-Dutch Colonial Jingo party. . . .'

He evidently assumed that the suspensionists would be content with a simple moratorium on party politics, and that they did not intend to use a reversion to Crown Colony status as an opportunity to press for a revised constitution with a more favourable distribution of political power.

On 15 May, however, Sprigg firmly indicated that he had no intention either of changing his Cabinet to suit the *Diamond Fields Advertiser*, or of supporting the suspensionist movement.* This set a term to the speculations of both sides. Repeated prorogations of Parliament then removed the need for immediate realignments, and it was not until after the New Year that the campaign for suspension was revived. This time, however, it had far more support. To begin with, the suspensionists made a successful effort to enlist Rhodes himself in their cause. Milner approached him on 30 January, and again in March. S. J. du Toit, writing as chairman of the Paarl Vigilance Association, told him on 4 February that local loyalists considered that a vigorous policy was necessary to eradicate sedition, 'which could be carried out only by suspension of the Constitution or by a strong hand at the helm here'.* Rhodes's signature duly appeared on a petition to suspend the constitution which was presented to the Governor on 10 May, six weeks after his death.

The petition in question, signed by forty-one members of the Cape Parliament, and by another five who subsequently changed their minds, asked for a temporary suspension of the constitution provided that the Colonial Office made it clear what kind of regime it would propose to substitute.* The signatories expressed a vague preference for 'an interim Government appointed by the Crown, assisted by a nominated Council with legislative powers'. They declined to endorse, but nevertheless enclosed, an annexure by Sir Henry Juta supporting parliamentary redistribution, and they asked for guarantees that suspension would not result in any subordination of the Cape point of view to that of Natal, or take place at all in the event of a change of government in Britain. Milner was asked to add his support and did so unofficially, to Chamberlain's great embarrassment, in a letter which was published in the press.* But contrary pressure was exerted from many quarters: by Sir Henry de Villiers, by Speaker Berry, by Sprigg and the other Colonial Premiers when they visited London for the diamond jubilee celebrations, by J. T. Molteno, who was also in England at the time, and by several members of the British Cabinet. Chamberlain, who was himself not in favour of suspension, and felt sure it would not be possible to win acceptance for it in his own party, rejected the petition in a telegraphic dispatch which was a model of discreet reasoning.*

The suspension issue drove Chamberlain and Milner apart, for in spite of Chamberlain's rebuke for his open support of the Cape petition, Milner still held that the strategy of suspension was correct. He raked over the coals of the dispute for several months after the main issue had been settled, referring in September to a 'failure to prevent the Cape relapsing into the hands of the Bond' as the price which had been paid for not listening to his advice.* He even talked of resigning, and might have done so but for Chamberlain's visit to South Africa at the end of the year, during which the two men were able to reach an understanding. Meanwhile Chamberlain was strongly influenced, not only by the objections raised in England to Milner's suggested policy, but by a fear, which Hely-Hutchinson shared, that if he were to pick a quarrel with Sprigg it might not be possible to find an alternative prime minister for the Colony.*

Hofmeyr, in exile, was carefully pondering over the same problems.* In June he had been prepared to state that Sprigg and his supporters were using their opposition to suspension as a way of working for a new deal in parliamentary seats, and that it was really Smartt and his fellow suspensionists who were the 'more honest'. The problem, as he saw it, was whether to accept indemnity legislation and redistribution as a probable price for the Sprigg alliance, or to oppose both and force suspension by using blocking tactics in the House. But he soon reached the position that indemnity legislation, even without a promise of amnesty for the rebels, could be supported provided the Progressives did not ask for redistribution, though it might be necessary for the South African Party to demonstrate its dislike of an Indemnity Bill by abstaining from voting at the second reading. Finally, in a letter dated 22 July, came the advice on which the Party was to act during the 1902 session: it was the suspensionists who were not to be trusted, Hofmeyr now concluded, for they had themselves begun to reveal their insincerity by talking of blocking tactics; therefore the Party would have to make terms with Sprigg, offering their support for the indemnity legislation if Sprigg was willing to refrain from asking for a fresh delimitation. The way to beat Milner, he might have added, was to give Chamberlain a chance of proving that Sprigg was right in his claim that parliamentary government at the Cape could still go on.

It hurt, but when Parliament met in August the Bond members did it. They spoke in injured tones of the Government's refusal to give them a grievances commission, but they allowed the indemnity legislation through without insisting on one.* Sprigg, in return, voted with them against a majority on the Government benches in most of the divisions of the session, with the result that motions standing in the name of ultra-loyalist members were usually defeated by comfortable margins—Smartt's for a stronger treason law, for example, which went down by 34 votes to 13. Hofmeyr's counsel of moderation was not, however, uniformly observed. Merriman, with the strong support of his party, spoke up for the principle of self-government. In a fiery speech he covered the suspensionists with obloquy, though several of them had acknowledged the error of their ways. But his motion, though successful, may well have had the effect of building up the anger and the cohesion of the ultra-loyalists in preparation for the general election of 1904.* Whether a decision to let bygones be bygones would have helped the Bond in the subsequent election is, of course, an open question; but as the penalties imposed on the rank and file rebels had been altered neither by the terms of the treaty of Vereeniging nor by legislation during the session of 1902, it was a safe assumption that in the forthcoming elections a substantial body of Bond supporters was likely to remain without a vote.

II. CHAMBERLAIN'S VISIT

Chamberlain decided in November 1902 to visit South Africa, and landed at Durban at the end of the following month.* Though the problems of the new colonies absorbed much of his attention after his arrival, he and Milner were agreed that the establishment of a politically reliable government in the Cape Colony was essential if Britain's long-term hold over the ex-Republics was to endure. But neither believed that the working agreement between Sprigg and the Bond gave the kind of security required. Milner privately asserted that 'to have any "truck" with the fundamentally and incurably disloyal organization which has caused all the mischief, and is as full of devilry as it ever was, would be an even greater blunder than the suspension mess', while Chamberlain told an audience at Port Elizabeth that he saw a certain humour in the continuance in power of a government which rested on the votes of ten thousand disfranchised electors.* But in spite of Milner's apprehension lest Chamberlain should be hoodwinked by the Bond, the Secretary of State's visit contributed substantially to peace because he was able and prepared to learn from what he saw. When a South African Party deputation met him in Cape Town at the end of his visit, they told him that if he had visited South Africa three years earlier 'our history would have taken an entirely different course'.*

Frederic de Waal seems to have administered the first shock, when he accompanied Chamberlain from Graaff-Reinet to Middelburg and there made a speech of welcome in his capacity as mayor:

'It had been noticed [De Waal said] that Chamberlain asked assurances from the Dutch-speaking population that they should abandon the idea of a Dutch Republican South Africa and should in the future bear true allegiance to British authority. Well, this assurance was extremely easy to give, *and just because the Dutch population of the Cape Colony never desired a Republican form of Government. All that was wished for was that the late Republics might have retained their independence. As for ourselves, we had sufficient liberty under the British flag and would under no circumstances exchange it for any other.* He [Mr. De Waal] spoke for himself and those who worked with him politically when he said that in the future, equally as in the past, there was not the slightest desire to sever themselves from the British connection. *We propose to prove our loyalty by our acts. We propose to assist in the great future scheme that you [Mr. Chamberlain] have laid down. We wish to show by our lives that we wish to live in amity with our fellow men.* We have now in South Africa one country, one ruler, one flag. Why should it not be possible to become one people? . . .'[1]

De Waal's effort was effective because, although he announced no new policy, rather claiming that the objectives which Chamberlain set for the Colonial Dutch had been Bond policy all the time, he nevertheless proved amenable to Chamberlain's suggestions, agreeing for example that the Cape should make an increased naval contribution; and he sent Chamberlain on to Cape Town with his mind attuned to receive further conciliatory gestures from Hofmeyr and the other leaders of the party, who had already decided to compliment his action over suspension as being true to the liberal

[1] My italics. This is a composite quotation from Garvin and Amery, iv, 367 (quoting the *Cape Times*, 18 Feb. 1903), and the *Midland News*, 17 Feb. 1903, which gives the text as supplied by De Waal. The second italicized passage was omitted by De Waal—deliberately, suggests Amery, 'perhaps because he thought he had gone too far'. The first italicized passage, essential to an understanding of the tone of the speech, was omitted by Amery.

traditions of Fox and Gladstone, 'with something about magnanimity and conciliation added'.*

On the day of his arrival in Cape Town (18 February) Chamberlain was given a civic reception in the morning and conferred with Onze Jan in the afternoon.* On the 19th he interviewed Theron and Malan, and on the 21st he received a large South African Party deputation at Government House. Hofmeyr was more cautious on the subject of a naval contribution than De Waal, and apparently caused Chamberlain to drop it as a talking point by proposing that a generous gift might buy a general amnesty for the imprisoned rebels. Nor, according to Chamberlain's biographer, would he listen to the Secretary of State's proposal for a 'realignment of parties' so that ethnic factors should cease to matter in the determination of political loyalties—perhaps because in the post-war political climate the gains made for the Dutch language before the war were in danger of disappearing. But by assuring Chamberlain that he abhorred the boycotting of loyal Dutch Colonials by fellow-Afrikaners, and by appealing publicly for a cessation of this sort of activity, he was able to persuade Chamberlain of his own good faith, which led Chamberlain in turn to agree to press for the release of the political prisoners in Tokai jail.

The Chamberlain–Hofmeyr encounter was an undoubted success at the personal level. They exchanged photographs and cordial letters after Chamberlain's departure.* On the level of public policy its effects are much less easy to estimate. Chamberlain did not leave the Colony with his confidence in the Colonial Dutch fully restored, or he would not have felt obliged to warn Sprigg against the danger of an early re-enfranchisement of the rebels—this at a time when the commission appointed under the Special Tribunals Act of 1900 was still busy purging the voters' rolls. His letters to Hofmeyr do not reflect a mind fully alive to the grievances of the Colonial Afrikaner— hence Hofmeyr's concern to show him that there was a sense of injury on both sides of the ethnic fence by quoting examples of the victimization of Dutchmen;* but they do betray a warm sense of the value of conciliation, of the pricelessness in a torn society of the generous gesture which compels a generous response.

III. AFRIKANER BOND AND SOUTH AFRICAN PARTY

It was not easy for the Afrikaner Bond, after the serious dislocations which it had experienced during the war, to resume normal political activities after the restoration of peace. The party had been disorganized from top to bottom. Contributions—or rather *the* contribution—from the branches to the provincial treasury in 1901 and 1902 amounted to less than £5, which meant that the party could not have afforded to hold a congress in those years, even supposing that the martial law regulations had made this possible. There had been no election of office-bearers in 1902 as required under the constitution, and the *Commissie van Toezicht* had had to improvise a method for nominating party candidates for the by-elections of that year, because it was impossible to summon the regular nomination meetings. Furthermore the weight of the disloyalty propaganda had been enough for some—among them even Hofmeyr—to consider seriously whether it was wise policy to revive the Bond organization at all.*

Under these circumstances it was remarkable that the Bond's return to normalcy should have been so rapid and so complete. Very few district *besturen* were not represented at the first post-war congress, held at Somerset East at the end of April 1903.[1] The official party-membership figure released at the congress was 11,469, only eighteen lower than that for 1899, without taking the absentee branches into account. The branches went far towards making up their debts to the central treasury by contributing £450, which was approximately double their annual pre-war contributions. An indemnity resolution condoned the liberties taken by the executive to keep the party in working order, and members turned their attention to its constitution, so as to bring the Bond into line with the realities of the post-war situation.

The revision of the constitution was a matter to which Hofmeyr had given thought during his wartime exile, and at the end of the 1902 session he conferred about the subject with a group of South African Party members from both Houses.* The recommendations made by this group were then considered and further amended by the Cape Town branch in December, the outcome of their deliberations being circulated to the branches over the signatures of Hofmeyr and F. S. Malan. Delegates to the Somerset East congress were therefore well prepared to receive the changes proposed, and adopted them without amendment.* The changes included a decision to marry the Afrikaner Bond to the South African Party, an extra-parliamentary movement to a parliamentary group, with a common

[1] The only important ones were Aliwal North and Vryburg.

set of political principles as their symbol of union. The original programme of principles of 1889 had been ascribed to the 'South African National Party'. Now the adjective 'National' was dropped, and the relationship was clarified in a new First Article of the Bond constitution, which declared that the Bond itself was based on the programme of principles of the South African Party.

The principles themselves were amended in important particulars. In place of the original aim ('the formation of a pure Nationality, and the preparation of our people [*volk*] for the establishment of "a United South Africa" '), for example, congress now declared itself dedicated, under Providence, to 'the development of a feeling of unity among the different nationalities of British South Africa, and the unification of the British South African colonies in a Federal Union, with consideration for the mutual interests of the colonies and of the superior authority of the British Crown'.* The next section of the programme of principles, which referred to the firm linking-together (*hechte aaneensluiting*) of the different European nationalities, was now taken—somewhat vaguely—to mean a relationship similar to that existing between the English and French nationalities in Canada, while the Canadian and Australian examples were quoted to illustrate the party's objective of South African autonomy (*zelfstandigheid*).* The general constitution of the Afrikaner Bond was technically beyond the reach of the provincial *bestuur* because only the defunct Central *Bestuur* was entitled to change it, after 'taking into account the feelings of the lower besturen'. With punctilious regard for form, therefore, congress went through the motions of electing two representatives, J. M. Hoffman and F. S. Malan, to the Central *Bestuur*, and these two, in the absence of other representatives from the defunct Transvaal and Free State provinces, formally sanctioned the constitutional amendments proposed to them by the Cape congress. The effective assumption of full constitutional powers by the Cape Bondsmen was obviously desirable in itself. Congress, therefore, with the endorsement of the two central representatives, proceeded to amalgamate the provincial and the general constitutions into a single instrument, and now gave *itself* the name of 'Central *Bestuur*, with power to enter into friendly relations with any kindred political movements which might arise in the other colonies. The Cape Bond had thus become, for the first time in a strict constitutional sense, a fully autonomous body, linked by a common set of political principles to the South African (parliamentary) Party.

A desire to broaden the basis of Bond and South African Party support stands out clearly in the constitutional reforms of 1903, and Malan specifically alluded to this when he introduced the proposals in congress.* This was sensible enough, especially under the circumstances of 1902–3, when association with Sprigg and the cross-benchers seemed to be the only formula for political influence. It had worked in 1902, to the satisfaction of *Ons Land*.* But for all the care taken not to disturb the anti-suspensionist alliance, and in spite of the disadvantages to both sides if it were to disintegrate, Sprigg and the Bondsmen moved farther apart during the session of 1903, and parted company at the end of it.

The occasion for the split was Sprigg's refusal, despite an unqualified undertaking given to Merriman during the session of 1902, to appoint a commission to look into martial law grievances.* The more serious martial law sentences—those involving the death penalty and long-term imprisonment—had been examined by the Alverstone commission, which had substantially reduced the penalty in most cases.* But there were many instances where individuals had undergone periods of detention without trial,* or had not received adequate compensation for losses suffered during the war, which the Opposition expected Sprigg to put right because he and Graham, the Attorney-General, had said that they would do so. The South African Party waited for them to make a move, and their impatience increased with the months. Why had Sprigg not acted before the prorogation of Parliament? Merriman challenged him directly, and received an equivocal answer.* Why, when he made a major policy speech in March 1903, did Sprigg say nothing on the matter?* In public speeches and in congress, the Bondsmen left no room for doubt as to their strong feelings; but Sprigg made no move during the 1903 session. On the anniversary of his written promise to Merriman he spoke and voted against the motion when Henry Burton, on whose shoulders had fallen the task of defending many of the accused, asked for a one-man judicial commission to review all martial law and war compensation claims.* Then, for the first time, he defended his inaction. He claimed that his promise to appoint a commission went back three years, and had been invalidated by the second invasion. He asked, with better reason, how a single judge could possibly review the 60,000 cases which the war losses commission had so far investigated, or the 25,000 which it had still to look into. If the motion went through, he continued, the House could expect to have to double the sum of £1,800,000 which had already been voted for compensation—which was a good reason, as he should have seen, not for refusing a commission but for appointing one.*

On 25 August the Government went down in defeat on Burton's motion by 32 votes to 22, 32 members having paired. From the South African Party's point of view, Sprigg had made a promise on a subject very dear to them and, after securing the passage of his indemnity legislation, had gone back on his word. This was a matter of principle which weighed more than immediate political advantage.* As some Progressives saw it, the South African Party, after holding the Prime Minister at their mercy for two sessions, had gambled on being able to bend his will, and had unexpectedly had their bluff called when Sprigg, in a final gesture of defiance, announced his intention to go to the country and to drop the legislative programme still to be carried through—particularly the Railway Bills on which the Bondsmen had set their hearts—in the hope of securing personal reinstatement in the Progressive ranks.* If this was true, it was a major error in tactics on the part of the South African Party leaders to press Burton's motion to a division. It is certain that Merriman and his supporters were in fact taken by surprise. As Colvin writes, they 'lost their balance' and pleaded with Sprigg to withdraw his decision to regard the defeat as a matter of confidence, as soon as they realized the boomerang effect of their stand.* But the Progressives' pressure on Sprigg was as relentless as their own, and the Prime Minister, whatever his real reasons for obstinacy, was not to be turned.

The dissolution of Parliament in September, following the Bond's retaliatory refusal to pass the Appropriation Bill, therefore occurred at a moment of sudden clarification in the political atmosphere. The voters were given a clear choice between the South African Party and the Progressives, with only a handful of independent candidates to complicate their choice. The Prime Minister, not having returned to the Progressives, was among these.

The Progressives, now led by Jameson, were better organized and disciplined than ever before, their candidates being obliged to take a pledge of loyalty to the party.* Helped by the disfranchisement of rebels, they were in confident mood and expressed their determination to fight the South African Party rather than outbid it, by putting out a programme which emphasized the differences between the two. They made much of the Imperial connection, above all in economic questions, whereas the Bondsmen had no enthusiasm for Imperial preference and argued for an autonomous, federal South Africa rather than for the further strengthening of Imperial ties. The Progressives aimed at a redistribution of parliamentary seats on the principle of more equal constituencies, as opposed to the balance of urban and rural interests which was the Bond argument for retaining the *status quo*.* The South African Party laid most stress on the righting of wartime wrongs—amnesty for rebels, compensation for those wrongfully injured through the war (not 'loyalists' only), the restoration of the farmer's right to keep firearms, and the reaffirmation of Dutch language rights in education and the public service, where these rights had suffered eclipse during the war.

The Council elections took place in November, and the outcome was the same as in 1898: the South African Party won the same eleven seats and the Progressives the same twelve as they had each won on the previous occasion. The poll was appreciably higher in 1903, especially in the western circle but even in the midland, though there was no contest in Griqualand West, British Bechuanaland and the north-eastern circle. The combination of a cumulative voting system and three-member constituencies had imposed a pattern on the voting tactics of the parties with which they were now familiar. The South African Party in the western, eastern and south-eastern circles, and the Progressives in the south-western, north-western and midland, concentrated on securing the return of a single candidate, while their opponents distributed their votes in the certainty of obtaining at least two seats and possibly a clean sweep.[1] In every case the minority party succeeded in its purpose, the undistributed vote in three instances securing the return of the party's candidate at the head of the poll. In the north-eastern circle, where Bond disfranchisement had been particularly severe, the

[1] The tactics can be illustrated from the Bond records. Thus Hofmeyr instructed that the 'whole strength of [the eastern] circle must be used to support one candidate only'. In the midland circle, Bondsmen were advised as follows: to give one vote each to Claassens, Du Toit and Maasdorp in Graaff-Reinet, one to Claassens and two to Du Toit in Beaufort West and Richmond, and two to Claassens and one to Du Toit in Victoria West and Prieska. In the south-western circle, by contrast, the Bond electoral conference at Mossel Bay on 17 September 1903 resolved to recommend strongly that no plumping be done at all (Hofmeyr Papers).

V. SOME LEADERS OF THE AFRIKANER BOND

N. F. DE WAAL
(LATER SIR FREDERIC)
Secretary-Treasurer of the Afrikaner Bond, 1898–1908, and member of the Commissie van Toezicht, 1889–92, 1910–11. M.L.A. (Colesberg)

DR. T. N. G. TE WATER
Colonial Secretary, 1896–8, Minister without Portfolio 1898–1900. M.L.A. (Graaff-Reinet)

DR. J. M. HOFFMAN
Member of the Commissie van Toezicht, 1898–1905. M.L.A. (Paarl)

F. S. MALAN
Editor of *Ons Land*, 1895–1908, Member of the Commissie van Toezicht, 1905–11. M.L.A. (Malmesbury)

VI. PROMINENT ASSOCIATES OF THE AFRIKANER BOND

J. TENGO JABAVU
Editor of *Imvo Zabantsundu*

C. J. RHODES
Prime Minister of the Cape Colony
1890–6

W. P. SCHREINER
Prime Minister of the Cape Colony
1898–1900

JOHN X. MERRIMAN
Prime Minister of the Cape Colony
1908–10

South African Party reached an agreement with the Progressives not to nominate more than two candidates if the latter nominated only one, and they thus avoided a contest. But it was the western circle which provided the South African Party's thorniest tactical problem, that of finding a candidate capable of attracting a sufficient proportion of the greatly increased urban electorate.* Dr. A. H. Petersen, a member of the Cape Town ward *bestuur*, was their eventual choice. Hofmeyr would not accept him as an official Bond candidate, apparently because he was not confident of Petersen's party loyalty, but agreed to back him as an independent.* This was a valuable nomination because Petersen subsequently acquired the backing of the newly founded Political Labour League, which controlled most of the organized labour votes, together with that of Dr. A. Abdurahman's African Political Organization and Isaac Purcell's Working Men's Union in District Six.* Petersen, thus supported, headed the poll, and thereby emphasized the value for the South African Party of a link with urban labour, which it would assiduously cultivate over the next few years.

The Progressives, after securing a bare majority in the Upper House, proceeded early in 1904 to win the Assembly elections as well, with a majority of approximately six seats. Now, as in 1898, the victims of the election were the mugwumps: Sprigg in East London, beaten by Smartt; Douglass in Grahamstown, beaten by Jameson; Schreiner, beaten at Caledon by two Bondsmen anxious to show that his 'non-S.A. policy of 1900' did not pay. But the voting did not show a swing towards the Progressives. Over the Colony as a whole, if the effects of disfranchisement are taken into account, the 1904 results are best explained by the assumption that, among the still-enfranchised voters, support for the South African Party had actually increased. The example of Wodehouse bears this out. Here Merriman, who had headed the poll with 1082 votes in 1898, polled only 587 in 1904 and failed to retain his seat. His failure led to considerable soul-searching among his supporters, many of whom do not seem to have expected it. Merriman, whose letters to his wife betrayed little patience with uneducated African voters, thought that it was they who had let him down—a view Tengo Jabavu was only half inclined to accept.* H. M. Neville, his campaign partner, thought that the Dutch voters had deserted them, which might have been true in his own case but could hardly have been so in Merriman's.* But, if the disfranchise-

17

ment figures are taken into account, Merriman should have fared
worse than he did; for his poll dropped by only 495 votes on the
1898 figure, whereas the number of Wodehouse voters disfranchised,
all of whom could be presumed to be South African Party supporters,
was certainly well over 800.* If, as may have been the case,
Merriman's black supporters proved amenable to Progressive
methods of persuasion,* he could only have obtained the votes he
did as a result of a favourable swing in white public opinion. Sauer,
similarly, polled 247 fewer votes in Aliwal North than he had
received in 1898; but at least 400 potential South African Party
voters had been removed from the roll, and the electorate had
diminished by 307.

There were forty-six constituencies in the Colony in 1904, in
thirteen of which there was no contest. Of the remaining thirty-three,
a comparison of voting trends in the elections of 1898 and 1904 is
possible in seventeen, where straight fights between South African
Party and Progressive candidates took place in each year. Of these,
the percentage of the electorate voting for the most successful
South African Party candidate increased in twelve and diminished
in five by comparison with the 1898 figure, whereas the fortunes of
the Progressives in the same constituencies showed an improvement
in seven and a deterioration in ten. Using the same constituencies
as a yardstick, the percentage of the electorate voting for South
African Party candidates remained stable, whereas the percentage
voting for Progressive candidates showed a significant decline.[1]
The constituencies chosen do not include the three main urban
concentrations in the Colony, where the Progressives could expect
to have the greatest advantage; but in each of these centres the
absence of serious South African Party competition, combined with
the expansion of the electoral roll, resulted in a relatively much
lower Progressive poll.

[1] In 1898 and 1904 respectively, the S.A. Party percentages were 40·50 and
40·96, and the Progressive Party percentages 39·00 and 32·29. The South African
Party vote went up in relation to the number of registered voters in Beaufort
West, Caledon, George, Namaqualand, Oudtshoorn, Paarl, Queenstown,
Richmond, Somerset East, Stellenbosch, Tembuland and Victoria East. It went
down in Aliwal North, Colesberg, Swellendam, Uitenhage and Wodehouse. For
the Progressives, the improvement occurred in Aliwal North, Caledon, George
Somerset East, Tembuland, Uitenhage and Wodehouse; and the deterioration
in Beaufort West, Colesberg, Namaqualand, Oudtshoorn, Paarl, Queenstown,
Richmond, Stellenbosch, Swellendam and Victoria East.

There were reasons, therefore, for optimism in the South African Party, and Smuts would soon be assuring Merriman that the current Jingo fever was no more than 'a moral and political distemper which must work its way'.* But from the standpoint of 1904 this was a truth apprehended by faith rather than by sight.

IV. THE NADIR OF AFRIKANER FORTUNES

Afrikanerdom had first to look into the pit, for with the Progressive victory in the Cape Assembly elections the nadir in its political fortunes had been reached. Milner's fear that the last outpost of Afrikaner strength might not succumb to the Empire's pressure had proved unfounded. A new uniformity had been created in the political conditions of South Africa, because in every colony there were now governments dedicated to the maintenance of British supremacy, and three of them owed their position directly or indirectly to the victory of British arms. Afrikaners throughout South Africa therefore had good reasons for fearing fresh inroads into their way of life, and in every colony a sense of common destiny developed among the defeated communities, inspired by the realization that, whether beaten on the battlefield or at the polls, their interests overlapped as never before.

The human problems arising directly out of the war occupied much of their attention. Between one and two hundred thousand people had to be returned from the prison camps or from protective custody and rehabilitated,* and although Milner's administration as good as completed its repatriation programme in the first year of peace, at a cost far in excess of that anticipated in the peace treaty, the resettlement of the Boers was seriously handicapped by drought and embittered by disputes over the allocation of the money set aside for relief work under article 10 of the treaty. There were recriminations between Transvalers, on whose behalf the Free Staters had entered the war, and those Free Staters who were still prepared to go on fighting when the Transvalers declared in favour of surrender. Resentment of the Republicans existed, too, among the Cape rebels, when it was found that their interests were not looked after under the treaty of Vereeniging, but left to the discretion of the Cape and Natal regimes. But the hardest gulfs of all to bridge were those between the *bittereinder* and the *hensopper*, and—worse still—between the former and the 'national scout' who had actually worked for the British. This rift affected even the religious life of the people, when the ostracism of collaborators led to the foundation of the 'Scouts' *Kerk'*. The Afrikaner people were not only broken materially, but also riven with discord among themselves.*

They also faced the vision of a destiny controlled by that nightmare figure of their pre-war past, the capitalist mine magnate, the Hoggenheimer of Boonzaier's cartoons, who was not only thought to have landed the Transvaal with a massive war debt, but was also known to have demanded the importation of 20,000 indentured Chinese labourers to the Rand as a means of speeding up output and paying off that debt. The magnates, it seemed to many a Boer, were threatening to bring about racial pollution of a land which his forefathers had won and set aside for the white man, and they were doing it without a proper investigation of labour needs in general, or those of the displaced Afrikaner in particular.* The Cape Progressives actually professed opposition to Chinese immigration during the 1904 elections; but they were not taken seriously by their Bond opponents, who accused them of opportunism, and saw them as instruments of capitalism led by none other than the original Raider. Cronwright-Schreiner told Merriman in April 1904 that if the South African Party leaders would not recognize capitalism as their main enemy they would be 'stormed by the back benches', who did.*

Milner had made it clear, in his much-quoted letter of December 1900 to Major Hanbury Williams,* that he intended to use the victory over the Republics as an opportunity to extend English cultural influences and restrict Dutch. So English was made the only official language of the new colonies. It was also to be the medium of instruction in the schools, and the number of hours devoted to Dutch, the teaching of which had been guaranteed under the terms of peace, was kept within narrow limits.*[1] The image thus arose in Boer minds of female British teachers entering South Africa in droves to complete in the schoolroom the task of conquest begun by their menfolk on the battlefield.* Meanwhile the Dutch language had lost status in the Cape Colony too. Regulations of 1901 had waived the obligatory knowledge of Dutch as a qualification for entry into the civil service,* and the level of Dutch teaching had by general admission deteriorated—and neither of these was a consequence of either military defeat or normal legislative action.

Faced with these difficulties, the Boer leaders were constantly

[1] Three hours per week, with a maximum of five if the two hours set aside for confessional instruction were also used.

reminded of their political impotence and driven to think hard around the problem of power. Military administration soon gave way to civil government in terms of the peace treaty and Milner's 'kindergarten' took control of the two administrative systems and of the new Inter-Colonial Council. But there were in 1904 as yet no signs of the 'representative institutions, leading up to self-government' which had been promised; nor was there much reason for hoping that self-government would be granted before Milner had settled an English-speaking political majority on the soil of the new colonies. Botha, Smuts and De la Rey were offered seats on the nominated Transvaal Legislative Council, colloquially referred to by the Boers as Milner's *debatsvereeniging* (debating society); but they knew well that to accept such an offer would be politically suicidal, and they declined.* In the Cape, meanwhile, it took the Jameson ministry less than two months after assuming office to drive an Additional Representation Bill through the Assembly, providing for three new Upper House seats, all of which it later won, and twelve new Lower House seats, seven of which it won.* Even though there were strong statistical arguments for such redistribution, the South African Party could hardly be blamed for regarding it, in context, as a bid to entrench the Progressives in power, especially when the Government declared that it had more radical changes in mind.

V. CONCILIATION

It is customary to label Afrikaners, according to their reaction to the post-war situation after 1902, as either 'conciliators' or 'isolationists'.[1] By the term 'conciliator' is meant a person who aimed to bring three kinds of adversary together—the *bittereinder* and the national scout, the Dutch-speaker and the English-speaker, the South African colonial and the Englishman—with a view to the building of a united (white) South African nation within the British Commonwealth. The 'isolationist', on the other hand, preferred to retire into ethnic seclusion in order to preserve the values of his group so that these should remain intact against the ultimate restoration of republican autonomy on some happier future occasion. But these are crude labels when it comes to the measurement of actual individual attitudes. As the years until 1914 would reveal, there were

---

[1] 'Two-streamers', in the sense later used by General Hertzog to describe those who wished to keep Afrikaner and English groups apart, conveys more accurately the sense intended, but this expression was not used before Union.

conciliators (like General J. B. M. Hertzog) whose very enthusiasm for conciliation produced in the long run an isolationist result; and there were others (like some of the leaders of the 1914 rebellion) who remained within the conciliationist camp yet may have intended all along to fight for the restoration of republican independence when Britain was sufficiently preoccupied elsewhere. Even for Botha and Smuts, whom some mistakenly placed in this category, conciliation was probably not in the first instance the fruit of any irrational desire to bury the hatchet, but above all a practical expedient dictated by urgent political necessity—the only available course, perhaps, to men deprived of effective bargaining power. Few Boers in 1903 would have followed a leader who lauded the British Empire for any reason, though many looked hopefully towards His Majesty's Opposition for some sort of counterpoise to Tory imperialism. Only after the Liberal electoral victory in 1906, and the grant of responsible government to both ex-Republics which followed it, did appreciation of their membership of the British Empire begin to colour the political outlook of ex-Republican Afrikaners.

Where Cape Afrikaners were concerned, of course, this generalization did not apply, for it was part of the Bondsman's normal thinking to regard himself as a British subject. Not surprisingly, therefore, it was in the Cape that the policy of conciliation was first applied towards the Imperial authorities. The Afrikaner Bond successfully pioneered the new diplomacy in its handling of Chamberlain in February 1903, at a time when Botha and Smuts, and after them Hertzog, were still dealing with him according to the old formula of sullen, even defiant, antagonism.*[1]

By September 1904, F. S. Malan had sufficiently mastered his personal feelings to address a Cape Town audience (the South African Liberal Association) on 'The True Ideal of South African Politics' in similar conciliatory strains.* He began by parading various false ideals before his audience: the money ideal, which he found to be dominant in the Progressive Party; the Downing Street ideal, which led the Progressives to look towards their 'bigger brother' across the water whenever things went badly for them in South Africa; and, along with these, the 'independence ideal' of the ex-Republics, which was not a sound principle, said Malan, because it divided 'the permanent population of South Africa . . . largely on racial lines', enabling the 'real enemy at the gate', which

[1] See above, pp. 240-3.

was the capitalist power, to 'threaten the very life of our civilisation' by introducing Chinese labour. Did the war have to continue in their hearts, he asked, while such dangers existed? Malan thought that there was an alternative, and to the accompaniment of some rather banal rhetoric he proclaimed 'a free united South Africa under the Union Jack' as the proper ideal to cherish. There was a note of reservation in his voice, prompted no doubt by an awareness of the difficulty which he would have in convincing many Afrikaners of the soundness of his proposition; but his reply to those who doubted was: 'Let them try it.' Concluding, he invited English-speakers to show tolerance towards the Dutch language, urged that the voters' rolls should be made 'clean and accurate'—in the expectation that this would return to Parliament 'men whom they could trust to work for the attainment of the ideal they had in mind'—and suggested to the townsmen that they might well make common cause with the farmers behind a general protective tariff policy. Malan's biographer has imaginatively described the agonies of mind which her father went through before delivering this speech, which made a sensation at the time. But if the gesture was hard to make, the advice at least carried its own justification. Malan had delivered a very clever party political speech, in which he had stressed the virtue of reconciliation within the 'permanent population of South Africa' as the best way of combating the influence of capitalists and Progressives, and of courting the authorities in Britain, in whose hands the prospect of further advance largely rested.

Cape Afrikaners might put out probes of this kind; but before their kinsmen in the new colonies could follow suit they had first to test the strength of their position vis-à-vis the occupying Power. This the Transvalers began to do in the months immediately following Chamberlain's visit. Botha told Milner, after receiving letters from 'all parts of the land', that he proposed to call a public meeting at Heidelberg on 2 July 1903. Milner ordered the South African Constabulary to attend in force, but he did not forbid the meeting, and the Transvaal Boers made good use of their now acknowledged right of political assembly.* Encouraged by an address of welcome from the veteran officers of the Heidelberg commando, Botha gave expression to the chief Boer grievances against the Milner regime. He described what the Dutch Reformed Churches were doing to resist the Government's educational policy. He attacked with feeling the proposal to import Chinese labour, and criticized Chamberlain for settling a large war debt on the Transvaal. The passing of appropriate resolutions on all three points gave the leaders public backing for the protests which they then took to the authorities, and when these protests were in turn rejected, both by the authorities on the spot and by the Colonial Office in London, the minds of the Boers turned easily in the direction of political action.*[1] But the power of physical resistance, which had been the final arbiter a generation earlier, was lacking in 1904.

They began therefore to organize under the cover of farmers' associations, such as that of the Zoutpansberg described by G. G. Munnik, who was one of the moving spirits.* 'I am going up tomorrow to Krugersdorp to attend the conference of the "Agricultural? Society" ', wrote one of Merriman's correspondents revealingly in March. This was a meeting at which farmers Botha, De la Rey, J. Kemp and C. H. Muller[2] sat on the platform, and the chairman affirmed that 'the Association could not debar politics from its discussions any longer'.* It already had eight branches. By the end of May the Transvaal Boers were sufficiently well organized, and sufficiently full of purpose, to meet in congress in Pretoria and take the decision to form a political organization. The committee appointed to draft a constitution had completed its labours by January 1905, and at a series of meetings, beginning in Pretoria on the 28th, they set about the systematic establishment of branches of the 'Organization of the People (Het Volk)'.[3]

The Rand Daily Mail alleged that the renewed political activity of the Boer leaders followed on secret negotiations which they had conducted with the Afrikaner Bond and a recently formed Transvaal group, the National Democratic Federation, whose members professed a strong aversion to Chinese labour. The leaders of the N.D.F. energetically denied any association with the Bond, and

[1] Though the Boer petition was signed by fourteen well-known men, of whom three had been pre-war Executive Councillors and ten had participated at Vereeniging, the Secretary of State declined to accept their signatures as representative. In view of the Boer leaders' refusal to serve on the Legislative Council, this was strictly correct; but the rebuff angered Boer public opinion.

[2] All were ex-Boer generals.

[3] The Transvaal Leader of 28 Jan. 1905 reports Het Volk's inaugural meeting in Pretoria, while issues of the same paper in February give details of the branch-forming tours of the Transvaal by Het Volk leaders, who usually worked in pairs: Botha and Esselen, Beyers and Wolmarans, Smuts and De la Rey.

they probably had none.* About a month later Merriman answered a request for advice by a Transvaal correspondent, Ernest Sheppard (who was connected with the Boer revival and would attend the formation of Het Volk's Krugersdorp branch in January 1905), as to whether he thought it desirable for the leaders of the Transvaal movement to associate with the Bond. Merriman thought such association would be unwise, and suggested rather 'the formation in your colonies of a South African Association upon broad liberal lines', which would work to 'secure the development of our liberties on the lines of the Australian and Canadian Commonwealths', while maintaining allegiance to the British connection, and which would aim at the government of South Africa by those willing to make the country their home, would look after the educational needs of the people, decentralize public authority where possible, and maintain an efficient control over the spending of public money.*

The seed sown by Merriman in fact germinated first in the Cape, not the Transvaal, with the foundation in June of the South African Liberal Association. Merriman was the only speaker at its inaugural meeting, which adopted (with minor additions) the programme he had first sent to the Transvaal.* The purpose in setting up the Liberal Association seems to have been, firstly, to create a political movement with pan-South African possibilities—hence the very general nature of its principles, and of Merriman's speech in support of them;* secondly, to create a movement which did not look like the Afrikaner Bond in sheep's clothing, as the South African Party did, so as to attract English-speaking artisans and immigrants and keep them out of the Progressive camp;* and thirdly, to establish liaison with the British Liberal Party, which seems to have been achieved when Herbert Easton, the Association's first secretary, spent much of 1905 in Britain canvassing the Liberal leaders. He did his best to see that South African issues were placed constantly before the public, on the eve of what proved to be a very important general election in which the Liberals were swept back to power.*

But if the Liberal Association took root in the Cape, at least the ideas behind it interested Smuts. He had previously heard—perhaps not through Sheppard—of Merriman's idea of 'substituting for the Bond a broader organization which would not have to contend with the same rooted prejudices', and asked Merriman to supply a programme of principles for 'an organisation on broad national lines' in which 'every fair-minded Englishman can take his place . . .

beside the Boer'.* It was the Liberal Association's principles that Merriman sent him in return, and the impact which they had on Smuts can be traced in the draft programme which he drew up for Het Volk in 1906, in which some of Merriman's ideas reappeared.* The formula eventually adopted by Het Volk in December 1906 differed considerably from Smuts's draft, however, though, like Merriman's original proposal, it could not be described as an instrument for the protection of exclusive Afrikaner interests.*

This characteristic of the Het Volk programme reveals the essential moderation of the approach by Botha and Smuts to the political tasks of post-war South Africa. It was dictated largely by the assumption of Het Volk's leaders that the acquisition of power would depend on their ability to come to terms with at least a section of the English-speaking community in the Transvaal. An electoral alliance concluded between Het Volk and the Transvaal Responsible Government Association in April 1905 was their answer to this problem; and when the 'Responsibles' merged with other groups to form the National Association in September 1907, the alliance was kept up.[1] The Boer leaders were not interested in constitutional half-measures of the kind embodied in the abortive Lyttleton constitution of April 1905, which offered only representative government as a substitute for Milner's rule. But to obtain substantive self-rule they had to convince the British Government of their bona fides as well, and if necessary at a price. Smuts saw the point very clearly, as is shown by his reply to Merriman's criticism of the way in which Het Volk bargained with the West Ridgeway constitutional committee in 1906:

'You *cannot* expect any British Government to put in the wrong their own compatriots in the Transvaal, even in the year 1906; and when these compatriots are such as you and I know them to be, the position of a poor devil of a "Dutchman" becomes very difficult indeed. No wonder that you sometimes surprise us in a little supper with the devil, but we do our best to use long spoons. Let us never

[1] Spoelstra, gives the terms of the alliance as published by A. G. Pakeman, secretary of the Transvaal Responsible Government Association, in the *Volksstem* of 26 Apr. 1905 (pp. 373–4). Members of the National Association soon came to be called *Nationalists*, and as such should not be confused with the associated Afrikaner parties (South African Party, Het Volk, Orangia Unie and Natal Volksvereniging) which were collectively referred to as *Nationalists* in the election campaign of 1910.

be in too great a hurry, knowing that "the good can well afford to wait" and will yet assuredly arrive. Our English friends have to be conciliated and their suspicions have to make way for whole-hearted confidence and loyalty of spirit before we shall succeed.'*

Thus considerations of practical politics, coupled with the infectious warmth of Botha's exhortation to 'put back the past so far that it no longer has any power to keep us apart',* determined the course which Het Volk would follow on the unexpectedly short road back to power. The policy had its opponents among the Afrikaners of the Transvaal; but the most eloquent, like General C. F. Beyers, protested from within the fold and could therefore be contained.*

Even in the Orange River Colony, where some of the bitterest post-war resentments lurked, the mood of conciliation came to prevail, as in the Transvaal, after an initial outburst of anger. The equivalent of Botha's Heidelberg meeting took place at Brandfort in December 1904, when the whole of the first day was devoted to the airing of grievances over the administration of compensation funds.* Strong resolutions on language rights and other subjects followed, and all were sent to the Lieutenant-Governor with the request that he would place them before the King. The Imperial Government's reply, for which the Boers had to wait seven months, admitted none of the complaints and was greeted with anger when the congress resumed its deliberations at Bloemfontein in July 1905.* According to Hertzog, who had by this time emerged as the leading spokesman of the O.R.C. Boers, it was 'much better for us to go to the grave with our grievances than to His Majesty's Government any longer'. The meeting decided to follow the example of the Transvalers and launch a political movement, which eventually announced itself as the *Orangia Unie* in May 1906 and was committed to the achievement of self-government. By the time of this first party congress, however, Hertzog's viewpoint had undergone a considerable change. There were by this time good prospects for the early establishment of self-government in the new colonies, and this led him to speak hopefully about the future:

'We come together to start a new life. Broken friendships are restored, and we must now conduct ourselves as men who have been purged in the fires and are determined to give a true account of ourselves, and so to labour that the people of this land shall be cemented together to build up a great and worthy country. Our constitution must be broad and all-embracing, to receive into its fold all men of whatever nationality, who have come to South Africa to make this country their home.'*

If humane idealism prompted these remarks, it was coupled with a sense of the politically expedient which had led Hertzog to argue in Bloemfontein a week earlier that, since the English-speakers were bent on forming a 'racial party', the 'best tactic now was to plead for co-operation and equal rights', and to forgive even *hensoppers*, 'whose vote was necessary'.*

The principles of the Orangia Unie paid more attention to Afrikaner interests than did those of Het Volk, affirming, for example, the party's support for a monument to the Boer women who had fallen during the war. But the Orangia Unie had no cause to fear the power of the O.R.C. Constitutionalists, led by Sir J. G. Fraser, as Het Volk had to fear that of the Transvaal Progressives, and its outlook reflected this position of greater strength. If responsible government were restored to Orangia, the Unie would undoubtedly obtain power.

Even in Natal, where the Afrikaners had no prospect of power, they began to organize themselves with renewed vigour. A *boerenvereeniging* with several branches and its own newspaper, the *Natal Afrikaner*, had existed there since the 1880's but had all but perished during the war. It was revived as the *Boerekongres* at a meeting in the Blood River district in March 1906, the Afrikaner community having gained strength from the incorporation of the erstwhile Transvaal border districts of Utrecht and Vryheid. The Boerekongres continued to hold regular meetings and, like its counterparts in the other colonies, sought to conciliate the English-speakers.*

The main recommendation for the policy advocated by Malan, Botha and Hertzog was that it worked. Between 1903 and 1908 Afrikanerdom not only shook itself free from the chains of defeat, but went far towards the eradication of the internal divisions caused by the war.

In the first place, conciliation brought the restoration of self-government to the ex-Republics. Milner, before handing over his authority to Lord Selborne in April 1905, had accepted the principle of representative government for the Transvaal at an early date. But the Boer leaders objected to the Lyttleton constitution, which Selborne was sent to introduce, because it did not go far enough, and they secured its abandonment by the Liberals after their victory

in the British election of January 1906. When Smuts visited London
in February he persuaded Campbell-Bannerman, the new Premier,
to investigate the governmental problem in the Transvaal.* This the
West Ridgeway Committee duly did between April and June, and
the Imperial Government followed its recommendations by granting
responsible government to the Transvaal in December. The Committee's recommendations were similar with regard to the Orange
River Colony but, because the English-speaking population was so
small, the British Government did not agree to home rule until the
middle of 1907.

The grant of responsible government was followed in each
colony by a general election, which the pro-Boer parties proceeded
to win. Het Volk and its English-speaking allies, who called themselves Nationalists, took forty-three seats of sixty-nine in the
Transvaal Lower House,[1] while the Orangia Unie won thirty-one of
thirty-eight in the O.R.C. Assembly. Then, to complete the triumph,
the South African Party followed with landslide victories—the first
in Cape Colonial history—in the Council and Assembly elections of
January and March 1908.

The elections in both the northern colonies revealed a continuing
cleavage between the outlooks of rural and urban voters, which no
party could effectively bridge. In Orangia, Sir John Fraser's Constitutionalists pictured themselves as the 'party of progress and
development', and expressed alarm at the power of the 'remschoen'
(reactionary, literally 'brake-shoe') element in the Unie to saddle
their party with a 'Dopper' educational policy.* But they conceded
that the Unie's politics had a practical as well as an ideological side:

'If the enquiring stranger will turn his ear veldwards he will hear
a different and more practical type of oratory. Federation and the
usual political tags have their place . . . at the end of a speech. . . .
[But] what really interests the audiences is Scab Law and Locust
Destruction, Railway rates for farming material and sheep dip, grain
rates and stock disease, irrigation problems and wool prices.'*

The Unie, meanwhile, making good use of its English-speaking
as well as its Dutch-speaking leaders, sought to present a broad

[1] Het Volk 37, Nationalists 6, Progressives 21, Labour 3, Independents 2.
This generally accepted breakdown is correct. 'Knop', p. 51, gives Het Volk 35,
Nationalists 7, Progressives 23, Labour 3 and Independents 1, making a total of
only 68. I am indebted to Mr. Noel Garson for information that H. C. Hull,
usually thought to have been a Nationalist, was in fact a member of Het Volk.

front to the electorate, and vigorously denied that it was a 'purely Dutch organization'. It contested all the seats but one, whereas the Constitutionalists left nearly all the rural seats to independent candidates, who fared extremely badly.[1] The Transvaal Progressives were no more venturesome in this respect, and their independent rural candidates were no more successful. But north of the Vaal the fight was often triangular, with the urban vote split between Progressive and Labour candidates and Het Volk's Nationalist allies. Although Smuts jokingly derided the Nationalists in borrowed phrases as showing 'flabbiness in [their] political texture . . . and an inherent tendency to . . . wobble',* they won seven closely fought contests and gave Het Volk a margin of safety in the new legislature which it might not otherwise have had. Het Volk's uneasiness towards them sprang essentially from their earlier equivocation on the subject of Chinese labourers, whom their leaders had not been anxious to repatriate immediately; but the Nationalists withdrew their objections on this issue. Their reward was two seats in the Cabinet formed by Louis Botha in March 1907.[2] Abraham Fischer's Orangia ministry, by contrast, was composed entirely of Unie members; but, like Botha's, it was drawn from both European language groups.[3]

A pronounced swing in Cape public opinion was apparent from the moment that results of the January Council elections began to come in—the first being the unexpected return of two S.A.P. candidates, David Graaff and A. H. Petersen, at the head of the poll in the western circle. The South African Party had criticized Jameson's creation of extra seats for the western, eastern and south-eastern circles, partly on the ground that it was a partisan measure, yet in 1908 the South African Party won two of the four seats in each

[1] 17 independents contested seats in Orangia, 15 of them in straight fights with Unie candidates (all losing), while 2 were returned unopposed. In the Transvaal there were 33 independent candidates, of whom only 2 won seats.

[2] Botha's Cabinet was composed as follows: Louis Botha (Prime Minister and Minister of Agriculture); J. C. Smuts (Colonial Secretary); J. de Villiers (Attorney-General and Minister of Mines); J. Rissik (Minister of Lands and Native Affairs); H. C. Hull (Colonial Treasurer) and E. P. Solomon (Minister of Public Works). Solomon was a Nationalist.

[3] Fischer's Cabinet was composed as follows: A. Fischer (Prime Minister and Colonial Secretary); J. B. M. Hertzog (Attorney-General and Minister of Education); A. E. W. Ramsbottom (Colonial Treasurer); C. H. Wessels (Minister of Public Works, Lands and Mines); C. R. de Wet (Minister of Agriculture).

of these circles. Their cause was undoubtedly helped, too, by the re-enfranchisement of the war-time rebels, for in most of the electoral provinces a substantial number of citizens had regained voting rights.[1] Public dissatisfaction with the Jameson Government, above all on account of its financial policy—for which hard times were at least as responsible as ministerial failings, also contributed to the result; but it was a matter for some surprise that the swing should have been so decisive after Jameson had apparently succeeded in living down a good deal of the odium which he and his ministers had to face in their first few months of office. Sir James Molteno, who wrote of the Jameson Government's policy in 1904 as being 'war to the knife against the Dutch inhabitants of South Africa', went on to describe him during the later part of his ministry as a 'friend of Afrikanerdom'.* Jameson, who had been forced to dissolve by the defeat of a supply Bill, took the Council election result as a vote of no confidence and resigned, leaving to Merriman as leader of the South African Party the task of forming a new administration.* Merriman's Cabinet, which included four Bondsmen,[2] took office on 3 February and entered the House of Assembly election contest with the assurance that the issue was already decided. With a Prime Minister and Treasurer well known for his financial ability, and a ministerial team anxious to achieve South African unification without sacrificing cherished Cape rights, the South African Party secured an unprecedented strength of sixty-nine seats to the thirty-three held by the Unionists[3] and five by Independents.

The victories of Het Volk, the Orangia Unie and the South African Party put the star of Afrikanerdom well in the ascendant, though six years had not yet passed since the humiliation of Vereeniging.

[1] According to a memorandum prepared for Hofmeyr by A. B. du Toit, the following numbers of voters had been re-enfranchised:

Western province	..	.. none	Eastern province	..	.. 2,468
S.W. province	..	.. 34	S.E. province	..	.. 102
N.W. province	..	.. 1,008	N.E. province	..	.. 1,736
Midland province	..	.. 1,889	British Bechuanaland		no figures
			Griqualand West	..	no figures
					(Hofmeyr Papers).

[2] Merriman's Cabinet was composed as follows: J. X. Merriman (Prime Minister, Treasurer and Minister of Native Affairs); J. W. Sauer (Commissioner); H. L. Currey and D. P. de V. Graaff (Ministers without Portfolio); N. F. de Waal (Colonial Secretary); F. S. Malan (Secretary for Agriculture); H. Burton (Attorney-General). The last four were Bondsmen.

[3] The new name adopted by the Cape Progressives.

VI. THE AFRIKANER REVIVAL

The defence of the cultural interests of the Afrikaner formed no part of the declared objectives of the parties under discussion, as their published principles clearly indicated;[1] but the existence of these parties afforded a good protective shield behind which the broken institutions of Afrikanerdom could be rebuilt. Thus there is no incongruity in the fact that the age of conciliation between Boer and Briton was also an age of Afrikaner cultural reassertion.

As a first step in this direction, Hofmeyr and a group of Cape Afrikaners, some of them scholars from Stellenbosch, had revived the Taalbond in the early part of 1903.* They drew up a new constitution in which the original aims of the movement were reaffirmed: the development of popular knowledge of the *volkstaal* and the creation of 'sound national feeling', to be realized through the holding of yearly examinations in the Dutch language and in South African history, the publication of school books in Dutch, and the award of prizes for works of literary merit.

The leaders of the second language movement, which this revival heralded, were plagued by the same problem that had bothered the leaders of the first: which language to encourage, simplified Dutch or Afrikaans? Hofmeyr and the Taalbonders continued to defend the Dutch language with a simplified form of spelling, and issued *De Goede Hoop* (under the editorship of J. H. H. de Waal, a son of David de Waal), to popularize their cause.* Their arguments centred on the richness of the Dutch literary tradition and the absence of significant literature in the language of common speech, and on the place that Dutch already had in the religion of the people and in the educational system. But the devotees of Afrikaans—northerners in the first instance, like Gustav Preller, editor of the *Volksstem*, and Eugène Marais, editor of *Land en Volk*—argued their case with passionate conviction: that Afrikaans was the language of the people; that, if not allowed to express himself on paper in the language which he spoke in everyday life, the Afrikaner would inevitably fall back on English; that even the clergy unwittingly spoke Afrikaans in the pulpit and at synod (Preller produced examples taken down in shorthand); that the Dutch and Afrikaans languages ought to be kept distinct from each other; and that if Afrikaans had no literature it was up to the people to put this right. When Hofmeyr made a plea at Stellenbosch in March 1905 that

[1] See below, pp. 271 ff.

VII. T. P. THERON

VIII. J. H. HOFMEYR ('ONZE JAN')
1908

Afrikaners should take Dutch seriously, Preller answered him in a sequence of editorials arguing the case for Afrikaans,* in which he tactfully refrained from challenging vested interests, and provided a formula for a transitional period: 'Until Afrikaans becomes the generally written language we are taking it as our rule of action: to write and speak Afrikaans, to learn Dutch, and to read both.' He formed an *Afrikaanse Taalgenootskap* (Afrikaans Language Association) in Pretoria in December 1905,* to the great consternation of the Cape Taalbonders, especially F. S. Malan, who still spoke for the conservative interests as editor of *Ons Land*. But De Waal's editorial experience was leading him, too, to the conclusion that Afrikaans was the natural vehicle for Afrikaner self-expression, and in November 1906, assisted by a group of men of whom some had belonged to the original Genootskap van Regte Afrikaners, he established an *Afrikaanse Taalvereniging* (Afrikaans Language Union) in Cape Town.* The Cape front was now split, and the success of De Waal's organization in establishing branches all through South Africa could well have brought bitterness in its wake and have destroyed the effectiveness of the language movement as a whole. The Afrikaner Bond, doubtless influenced by the views of Hofmeyr, F. S. Malan and N. F. de Waal, himself a Hollander, made regular contributions to the Taalbond at each congress from 1907 to 1911, and never sent any money to the Taalvereniging.* But ill will was not permitted to develop. Malan gave the Taalvereniging space in *Ons Land*. Taalbonders and members of the Taalvereniging (which soon eclipsed Preller's Taalgenootskap in importance) conferred at Paarl at the end of 1907 and agreed to work for the establishment of a central organization to preserve and promote the 'Dutch-Afrikaans' language, while in August 1908 the chairman of the Taalvereniging, Dr. D. F. Malan, urged reconciliation as a matter of urgency in the Afrikaner national interest, and added:

'Give the young Afrikaner a written language which comes easily and naturally to him, and in that way you will have set up a bulwark against the anglicization of our people. . . . Raise the Afrikaans language to a written language, make it the vehicle of our culture, of our history, of our national ideals, and you thereby also raise up the people who speak it. But keep the *volkstaal* at the level of a half-civilized provincial dialect, and in that way you keep the people too at the level of a half-civilized, illiterate class of yokels [*volksklasse*].'*

18

Taalbond and Taalgenootskap, he said, were really working towards each other, not in opposite directions, and it was his hearers' duty to assist this process. The foundation at a conference in Cape Town in January 1909 of the *Akademie voor Taal, Letteren en Kunst* (Academy for Language, Literature and Art)* resolved the basic problem for the time being by providing a method for accommodating two irreconcilable points of view until the time was ripe to choose between them—as it eventually was in 1925.

An important aspect of the language question was the external struggle of the Afrikaner to maintain the status of his language in public life. Although the official language in the ex-Republics after the conquest was changed from Dutch to English, the letters patent which granted self-government eventually restored Dutch to a position of near equality in both colonies, though Het Volk and the Orangia Unie continued to press for a fully bilingual public service.* In the Cape the Bondsmen made a similar stand.* During the parliamentary session of 1905, F. S. Malan attempted to establish the principle of strict equality of English and Dutch in the civil service, and the subject received considerable airing in a long debate.* The Jameson ministry, after winning its initial battle over redistribution by the application of *force majeure*, was not disposed to irritate the Opposition on this kind of point, and though Government members were far from conceding that the Dutch-speaker could demand language equality as of right, the debate was notable for its lack of acrimony. Malan's motion was defeated on a party vote, however, and referred back to the Civil Service Commission.* The Bond congress of 1906 asked for, and was in due course given, a select committee to examine the language question in all its aspects. This committee failed to agree, the majority continuing to insist that success in Dutch should not be a condition of entry into the civil service; but eventually, in 1907, the Government agreed to make Dutch obligatory for civil servants within two years of their appointment.*

The safety of Dutch language rights was closely bound up with educational policy, and the new parties were bound to take notice of any attempt by the various regimes to use education as a means of advancing English culture at the expense of Dutch. In the northern colonies, where British policy aimed to do this, the Dutch Reformed Churches had revived the Christian National Education movement directed towards the education of the Dutch-speaking children in their own privately financed schools which were controlled by elected school committees. Shortage of funds caused the movement in the Orange River Colony to founder, but not before the C.N.E. leaders had met the Lieutenant-Governor in March 1905 and had extracted from him the right to have a bare majority of elective members on the public-school committees, which had the power to select teachers from lists supplied by the Education Department.* This made the amalgamation of the public and private school systems possible without loss of face to either side. In the Transvaal, negotiations in 1903 between Milner and the clergy broke down on the twin points of language instruction and parental control,* and the C.N.E. schools remained in existence in many cases until after the grant of responsible government. When Lord Selborne succeeded Milner in 1905, however, the Administration began to experiment with mainly elective school committees, as in the O.R.C., and cautiously relaxed the rules governing the language medium without departing from its aim of promoting English at the expense of Dutch. Teachers were to use either English or Dutch as a medium of instruction 'so long as they make themselves understood to the children', provided English were used 'as soon as the children are able to follow the teacher's instruction in that language'.*

After the achievement of responsible government, the position of Dutch was made safe in the schools under the Smuts and Hertzog Acts. The Smuts Act left Dutch in a subordinate position in the Transvaal, laying down mother tongue instruction up to standard three, but requiring that English should be the medium thereafter in all subjects save two, and making the study of English obligatory and of Dutch optional. There were reasons for Smuts's decision not to insist on equality of rights—his friendly understanding with Dr. J. E. Adamson, who had been Director of Education under the crown colony regime and remained at his post under Smuts;* the electoral pact which Het Volk had struck up with the 'Responsibles' under which the Afrikaner party had agreed to allow the English language a certain priority;* and —it seems safe to add—Smuts's view that a concession on this sort of point was worth while if it helped to allay the mistrust of the English-speakers, which was one of the major tactical problems of the Het Volk Government after its rise to power.

Hertzog's approach, by contrast, depended on logic rather than finesse. In August 1908 he carried through the O.R.C. legislature a law which made the English and Dutch languages strictly equal in education.* All children were to be educated in their home language through the first four standards, while being introduced gradually to the other language until they were able in due course to receive instruction through the medium of both. He was less willing than Smuts to allow discretion to the parent on this point save under special circumstances, arguing that a bicultural state had the right to impose standards of bilingualism on its future citizens. Even Smuts allowed no option when it came to the learning of English, but in this respect he merely continued an existing compulsion whereas Hertzog sought to create a new one. Both laws came in for a great deal of criticism. Smuts's was attacked at the Het Volk congress of 1909, for not going far enough; Hertzog's angered many English-speakers, whose case was strengthened by the administrative difficulties which followed its introduction, and the unfortunate friction which developed between Hertzog and some members of his own department. Yet both laws, for all their differences of emphasis, gave the Dutch language as a taught subject and as an educational medium a far greater security than it had enjoyed during the years of direct British control.

That Cape Afrikaners feared for the future of Dutch in education can be seen from some of their comments. Thus Dr. Meiring Beck, member for Worcester, wrote that 'of course Jameson will attack the education citadel next, of course he will attempt to crush the Dutch Church, and to invest Muir [the Superintendent-General of Education] with autocratic power', while Ds. G. A. Maeder of Victoria West suspected a careful plan 'to crush the Dutch Ref[ormed] Church and fight the Dutch people *scholastically* as well as politically and underhandedly'.* The Bondsmen feared the worst, but in practice their expectations were not fulfilled. Under the School Board Bill of 1905 the Government planned to introduce a system of district school boards, less democratically chosen than the existing school committees, as agencies for the enforcement of compulsory school attendance by white children. The Bondsmen had no objection to the Progressives' plan of discriminating between the children of 'European parentage or extraction' and others, and they attached much importance to the Government's plan to subsidize the schooling of children of indigent parents; but they feared that the boards would deprive the individual school committees of their traditional control over language medium and the appointment of teachers, and they looked on compulsory education with misgiving but not disapproval, failing to see how it could be enforced.* The Government, however, arranged an inter-party conference, agreed to soften the introduction of compulsory education by making its adoption permissive by districts, and accepted stronger local representation on the school boards. In this way the Afrikaner community was largely reassured, with the result that in the Cape the movement for Christian National Education barely took root. It was only after the achievement of power by a South African Party government in 1908 that the Bond began seriously to agitate for the amendment of the legislation of 1905 and the provision of government support for schools ministering to the 'Protestant, religious character of our people'.*

13

Union

IF 1904 was the nadir of Boer fortunes, 1908 may be described as their zenith, in the context of the present narrative. By the middle of the latter year the shattered political structures of Afrikanerdom had been rebuilt and Afrikaners held effective power in three of the four self-governing colonies. In the Cape, the Afrikaner Bond had established a regular liaison at the parliamentary level with the governing South African Party, sharing a common political programme and an overlapping membership, while in the Liberal Association it had acquired an agency for recruiting the support of town dwellers and working men of all races. In the Transvaal, Het Volk was in firm control of the rural areas, and it had begun to exert pressure on the urban voter through its alliance with the anti-capitalist organizations on the Rand, and had even established branches and won seats on the Rand itself.[*1] The Orangia Unie was undisputed master of the O.R.C. In Natal too there were signs of Afrikaner political revival.

This resurgence of Afrikaner political activity had much to do with the timing of the movement for the unification of South Africa which was completed in 1910, just as the immediate past experience of the Afrikaners had much to do with the shape of the Union as it emerged from the deliberations of the National Convention. Union was, without doubt, a remarkable achievement. The extent of the achievement is best measured against the magnitude of the obstacles that had to be overcome, as recent work on the unification of South Africa has amply demonstrated. Though we are concerned here only with the part played by political Afrikanerdom in the movement

---

[1] At Randfontein in 1907 the Het Volk candidate had beaten a Progressive by 793 votes to 226, and at Vrededorp by 865 to 198.

towards Union, it is noteworthy that the associated Afrikaner parties,[1] did constitute the strongest of all the pressure groups which directed the course of events. Their situation was not unlike that of the various Bond 'provinces' in the mid-1880's, bound together as they were by strong emotional ties, yet representing conflicting geographical and occupational interests. After failing to make common cause in the 1880's, could they succeed under the new conditions of the twentieth century? As we shall see, their task before Union was considerable; but Union was as much the beginning as the end of their problems. The parties needed another eighteen months before they found a way to resolve the problem of their combined leadership and amalgamate as a single body.

I. DIVIDED INTERESTS

After the first Anglo–Boer war, the politically-minded Afrikaners had built up a pan-South African organization and had then found that they could not operate its inter-territorial machinery. After the second Anglo–Boer war they remembered this lesson. N. F. de Waal even told the Liberal Association in December 1906 that 'it was a matter of extreme regret that it was ever contemplated that the Afrikander Bond should exist in the late Republics as well as in this Colony'.* They therefore took care to see that each territorial political organization had complete local autonomy and no constitutional links with its opposite numbers in the other colonies. But the four parties which ran parallel courses from 1906 onwards did not operate in complete isolation from each other. Despite major differences in terminology, their constitutional structures bore clear similarities and signs of interdependence. They made a special point of keeping in touch with each other, the Bond taking a lead in this respect;* and they found themselves occupied with the solution of similar problems.

A synoptic view of the programmes of Het Volk, the Orangia Unie and the lesser Liberal Association reveals not merely a substantial community of outlook between these organizations, but also some important new emphases in the public interests of political Afrikaner-dom.* All three, drawn up before the return of their respective organizations to power, stressed that the government of South

---

[1] The expression 'associated parties' was not used by contemporaries, but has been used in the present narrative to denote the Bond, Het Volk, the Orangia Unie and the Natal Boerekongres collectively.

Africa should be managed by South Africans, the Boer parties relating this point specifically to native affairs. There was a new emphasis in the manifesto of each organization on the need to improve and regulate the relationship between capital and labour, with the explicit rider that labour stood in the greater need of protection. The fact that the Boer parties paid so much attention to industrial problems before the Afrikaner had really begun to move into industry testifies not so much to their leaders' ability to estimate future trends—the Rand strike of 1907 would hasten the emergence of an Afrikaner proletariat—as to their awareness of the need to seek allies among the urban workers. This was the real motivation behind Het Volk's defence of collective bargaining, or the Orangia Unie's insistence on an eight-hour day for white workers, or the Liberal Association's demand for minimum-wage legislation.

It was an axiom of the new Afrikaner movements that a community of interests existed between the farmer and the urban proletarian, their assumption being that it was to the advantage of both to join forces against the capitalists. This was reflected in their taxation proposals—in the Bond's revival of its demand for a tax on diamond exports, which it had not made since it had entered into alliance with Rhodes and in the advocacy of a graded profits tax by the Liberal Association and Het Volk. Yet such a philosophy had no real place for the capitalist farmer, nor for the urban worker who wanted cheap food even if it had to be imported. Nor did it suggest a solution to the disagreement between the coastal townsman and the farmer over the best forms of indirect taxation, on which the Cape depended for most of its revenue:* the townsmen generally looked to low import duties and high railway tariffs, whereas the farmers who used the railways for the transportation of goods in bulk preferred the imposition of high duties on imported goods, to ensure that the burden of indirect taxation was fairly borne by the towns, and that their own produce could vie with imported goods at competitive prices.

But if it was hard to convince town and country that they had interests in common, it was even harder to convince the citizens of different colonies of the same point. At first it indeed seemed that the bringing of all South Africa under British control had provided a solution to the baffling customs and railway deadlocks of pre-war years. Customs and railway conferences convened at Bloemfontein in March 1903 brought agreements between the colonies on both major issues, settling the vexed question of railway rates, laying down a detailed schedule of duties, and introducing a preferential rate for British and other Empire produce.* But even without an independent Transvaal to block an agreement, and with the O.R.C. and Transvaal railways under joint control, the colonies would only allow the new arrangements a trial period of two years. The differences between them were indeed vast. The Cape and Natal were dependent on high duties and high transit tariffs for revenue purposes, though Natal was prepared to lower tariffs for the sake of attracting trade. The O.R.C. relied appreciably less on indirect taxes of this kind, while the Transvaal's main concern was to pay as little as possible under either head, which meant in practice using the Delagoa Bay route as fully as possible at the expense of the Natal and Cape lines. The preference given to Delagoa Bay under the *modus vivendi** which Milner had arranged with the Portuguese in December 1901 had the additional advantage that it guaranteed a labour supply for the Rand mines. At the Bloemfontein conference the Transvaal delegates insisted that the *modus vivendi* should be accepted as a basis for negotiation.

Short of bringing all the rival railroad systems under joint control, which was difficult to envisage without some form of political amalgamation of the South African colonies, there appeared to be no answer to the deadlock reached at Johannesburg in February 1905 and again at Pietermaritzburg in March 1906, when further conferences tried unsuccessfully to unravel the difficulties. The most serious consequence of the dispute was the imbalance—fostered by the customs and railway agreements—between the economy of the Transvaal, which recovered, and that of the Cape, which withered. Between 1902–3 and 1907–8, the Cape's revenue fell from £11,700,000 to £6,980,000, and the decline was reflected mainly in diminishing customs revenue and railway receipts, which in turn followed from a marked increase in the proportion of goods conveyed through Lourenço Marques. Ironically, the Cape's deficit was accompanied by an increase in revenue from direct taxation, Jameson having given the Colony its first income tax, while the railway deficit was met by an increase in rates.*

To overcome the pull of vested interests so much in conflict with each other presented an immense challenge to the members of the new parties in the four colonies. The Cape Bondsmen, as might be expected, remained fiercely protectionist in their outlook. In 1904 and 1905, congress demanded that the railway preference given to Lourenço Marques should be withdrawn, that the Transvaal should restore pre-war customs preferences for Cape liquor over imported products, and that each colony in the customs union should be given fiscal freedom where its own products were concerned, in order to protect them from external competition.* Bond farmers reluctantly admitted that this last point threatened to lead to an increase in the price of foodstuffs, but went on to describe their own acute distress:

'We are all agreed [said Theron in his 1906 presidential address]— though people would have us believe that we have reached the trough of the depression, or that we have turned the corner—that our Colony is in a more depressed state than ever before. In some places they are still experiencing the burden of an unprecedented drought nearly five years old. Waters are drying up. Locusts live and swarm in almost every stage in some of the best parts of the veld. In a word, the experience of the farming community as producers and load-carriers is harder than one can imagine. All sorts of plans are being devised to keep their heads above water [!], but believe me it is hard going. If a general calling in of outstanding debts were to take place, then we should see the sort of things happen in the Colony that have never been seen before.'*

The burden on the farmer was undoubtedly severe, and stemmed from natural as well as fiscal causes, and although the rise in insolvency statistics suggested that the towns were worse hit,[1] the figures for the rural areas, where a not very significant increase was reflected, may well not indicate the extent of the relapse into poor-whiteism— a category for which it is in any case difficult to find firm criteria.

In Parliament it was generally the South African Party representatives who took the lead in asking for change, though they did not encounter much opposition from the government benches. F. S. Malan moved the 1904 congress resolution denouncing the *modus vivendi* in Parliament, and secured its adoption.* In 1905, Sauer moved for a revision of the customs tariff, describing it as 'very much worse . . . [for] this colony than the tariff which existed under President Kruger'.*

---

[1] Total voluntary insolvencies in the Colony in each of the years 1901 to 1908 were as follows: 141, 117, 224, 621, 527, 576, 602 and 730. In each year approximately one-quarter of these occurred in the Cape Peninsula.

Dissatisfaction in the Cape, though, did not necessarily mean satisfaction in the Transvaal, where the Het Volk ministry, on gaining power in 1907, yielded to the pressure of farmers and towns-men and declared its intention to withdraw from the customs union with effect from July 1908.* Het Volk itself, however, was badly divided over the question of protection. Some members, like the Rustenburg farmer who complained that he could not compete with Natal citrus growers on the Standerton market, or A. D. W. Wolmarans, who thought that the Cape and Natal were pushing too many goods into the Transvaal, were in favour of high protective tariffs. But others would reply that it was unwise to tamper with tariffs because of the dependence of western Transvaal maize farmers on Cape Colonial markets; and it was these whose influence prevailed at the 1907 congress, when a motion supporting withdrawal from the customs union was removed from the agenda.* At the 1908 congress, the feeling of the meeting was still—but now less surely—behind Botha's strong appeal for free trade. 'The programme of the protectionists', Botha was reported to have said, 'was a departure from Het Volk principles. They should not allow their organization to be pulled to pieces by these people.' But his desire to remove preferences on South African as opposed to external produce clashed with the views of the Cape farmers. Fundamentally it was the interests of the Transvaal that Het Volk sought to protect, and its representatives attended the Pretoria customs conference in May 1908 with the instruction to 'ensure to the inhabitants of this country the legitimate benefits to which they are entitled on the inland markets by reason of their geographical position'.*

Although the new parties excluded from their programmes most things that might offend the non-Afrikaner, there were certain questions of a general kind which affected the Afrikaners more intimately than they did other South Africans, and in which these parties therefore took a special interest. There was the problem of the poor-whites, which had been a major concern of the Dutch churches before the war, and which had increased in intensity in the post-war period for a multiplicity of reasons—among them the ravages of the war itself, the post-war depression and the drought, the immigra-tion from abroad, and the work shortage. The Transvaal Indigency Commission stated in 1908 that, though the war had not been the main cause of poor-whiteism, it had impoverished the farmers to such an extent that they could no longer support on their land the squatters who had made their living there before. Its report also referred to 'some 10,000 souls' left in the concentration camps at the end of the war, who had 'little education and no training which could fit them for the struggle for employment in the ordinary competitive conditions of industrial life', people whom it had proved impossible to accommodate in the Burgher Land Settlements, with the result that 'the greater number gradually drifted into the towns to swell the poor-white population which lived upon the outskirts'.*

Het Volk and the Orangia Unie both included the rehabilitation of the poor-white in their programmes of principles, urging that steps be taken to stop and turn back the flow of white men to the towns—about the possibility of which the Cape select committee on poor-whiteism in 1906 and the Transvaal Indigency Commission were rather less sanguine than they, save through the medium of carefully supervised rural settlements like the Kakamas labour colony, which had been established by the N.G. Kerk before the war.* Both parties accepted that ignorance was a major cause of poor-whiteism, and therefore urged that schooling should be placed within the reach of all white children, with the provision of far better facilities for industrial training than existed at the time, for it was accepted that hope for a high proportion of the poor-whites depended on their learning the simple skills which would make their absorption in mining, the railways or the lower echelons of the public service possible. So intractable did the problem seem, and so strong the need to safeguard the white man's moral and technical supremacy, that hardly a ripple of opposition came when the Jameson Government introduced its School Board Bill in 1905, letting in the principle of colour discrimination in public primary education in the Cape Colony—a principle for which, it should perhaps be added, precedents existed in the pre-war records of both the South African and the Progressive parties.* People began to look on the labour market as a potential scene of racial conflict. Theron warned the Bond congress in 1906 that 'not only will the rising generation have to compete against those coming in from outside in their struggle for a position, but it will also find that our coloured compatriot is going to be a formidable opponent in the struggle'.* Anxious white men began to note how assiduously the children of Coloured parents seemed to be going to school, and to dwell on the very low percentage of white children actually at school in some rural areas.* Nor could it be forgotten that the poor-whites were potential voters—Afrikaners for the most part, with a presumed disposition to favour parliamentary candidates of their own ethnic group, if those candidates took notice of them. The political side of the poor-white question can be illustrated by such developments as the Bond's decision to set up a branch in the Kakamas labour colony, or the advice of A. B. du Toit to Hofmeyr (in connexion with the 1908 Assembly election) that South African Party candidates in the George and Humansdorp constituencies should make special efforts to woo the poor-whites there,* or Het Volk's runaway victory in the Vrededorp contest of February 1907, Vrededorp being one of the poorest districts in Johannesburg.

There was agreement among the parties over the poor-whites, but the same cannot be said with confidence with regard to the non-whites, for here the old distinction between the Cape Bond on the one hand and its Republican branches on the other reappeared with the emergence of Het Volk and its O.R.C. and Natal counterparts. The Cape Bond continued theoretically to extend the right of membership to 'all people born in or permanently settled in South Africa', whereas the other three organizations explicitly reserved membership for white people.* Although the Cape Bondsmen never followed out the logic of their constitution by admitting non-white people to membership, they professed an attitude to their participation in politics which differed in emphasis from that of their northern neighbours. Their leaders enunciated this difference with such deliberation at times that it would be insufficient to dismiss their remarks as mere expediency. Thus when F. S. Malan stated on 17 January 1908 that 'the South African Party is against drawing a colour line for political purposes', he went on to describe such a policy as not only unwise and unpractical but also unjust.* Merriman, introducing the closer-union resolutions in the House of Assembly on 22 June the same year, described the 'maintenance of the rights of the natives in respect of the franchise in this colony' as a matter on which both sides of the House were 'pledged up to the hilt'.* But were the views of the party leaders shared by the rank and file? If the South African Native Affairs Commission of 1903–5 had included a few Bondsmen among the large number of witnesses whom it examined,*[1] this might well have brought to light a veiled

[1] Hofmeyr and Theron were invited to give evidence but were unable to do so. No other Bond office-bearer seems to have been approached, and the only witness likely to have been a Bondsman was P. R. Rabie of Worcester. Merriman and Sauer gave evidence in support of non-white political rights.

dissatisfaction with the Cape franchise of the sort manifested by G. H. Maasdorp and H. C. van Heerden, the two South African Party representatives of the Cape rural areas at the National Convention.*[1] Unfortunately the evidence which this Commission failed to provide was also not to be found in the record of the closer-union debate in 1908, during which Merriman made the bold statement already quoted, because none of the Bondsmen who spoke committed themselves to supporting the Cape franchise.* Was silence their sanctuary? They could not easily have gone with the Het Volk members who proclaimed in the Transvaal Assembly that one purpose of Union was 'to try to bring the whites of South Africa together, and then they would be in a position to keep the natives in their place', nor with the opposition Constitutionalist in the O.R.C. legislature who thought the duty of the Orangia delegates was to convince their opposite numbers 'of the fact that the people were determined to keep this a white man's country'—even supposing that some of them felt this in their hearts.* The South African Party could not forget its indebtedness to Tengo Jabavu during the elections of 1898 and 1904, nor its dependence on men of liberal outlook like Sauer and Merriman, nor its constant need to keep the African and Coloured voter mellow. A. B. du Toit told Hofmeyr in relation to the 1908 election that he had been 'given to understand by several Coloured people (not of the class that will follow the Malay Doctor),[2] that they are most anxious for the S.A.P. candidates to address them in different places', and he provided a list of the names and addresses of twelve secretaries of Coloured benefit societies.* A mixture of patriarchal aloofness and genuine concern for the welfare of the underdog, together with a sense of the foolishness of alienating potential friends when it might become necessary one day to protect the borders against the 'teeming millions of Darkest Africa', seems to have conditioned Hofmeyr's attitude to Coloured people's rights. His reply to an address of appreciation from the Cape Town Coloured People's Vigilance Committee in March 1909 revealed a conservatism which recoiled from the idea of abandoning the Cape's political compromise in either a more reactionary or a more liberal direction:

[1] Maasdorp and Van Heerden 'said that they feared the Native franchise and if possible they would like to go back'.

[2] i.e. Dr. A. Abdurahman, founder of the African Political Organization (A.P.O.), who energetically opposed the franchise provisions of the draft Act of Union.

'But the very fact that we are so outnumbered renders it necessary to proceed with great care and circumspection in extending our political franchise to races hitherto utter strangers to all constitutional government and to the responsibilities and duties which are inseparable from its privileges.

'I myself and many gentlemen who belong to the same political party as I do have, therefore, deemed it necessary to proceed no further in the present political crisis than to try to safeguard the political rights already bestowed on the coloured people of the Cape.'*

The first report of the National Convention in February 1909 did not recommend the extension of the franchise to non-white people in the northern provinces, and proposed also that they should be debarred from membership of Parliament, but not of the Cape provincial council. It also proposed that the non-white franchise in the Cape province should not be removable except by a two-thirds majority at a joint sitting of the two Houses. Coloured and African reactions to these proposals were widespread and hostile.* The Transvaal and O.R.C. legislatures, on the other hand, maintained an unyielding refusal to consider Union if any further concessions were made in the direction of non-white people.*

When the Cape Town branch of the Bond met to consider the report on 17 February, they decided that the proposals for the protection of non-European political rights in the Cape were inadequate, and recommended by 15 votes to 8 that to remove the non-white electors from the common roll it should be necessary to have a majority of the votes of the Cape parliamentarians, in addition to the proposed safeguards. They also approved, with the chairman's casting vote, of a recommendation that 'a Parliamentary experience of about fifty years has not proved the necessity of the introduction of colour restrictions in respect of the membership of the Parliament of the Cape Colony'.* Congress, meeting in Dordrecht at the beginning of March, adopted the first of these resolutions but not the second. But as the discussion was held *in camera*, and J. G. van der Horst, the Cape delegate, made no mention of it in his report back to the branch, the tenor of the debate cannot be assessed.*

The atmosphere in which the Cape Assembly debated these questions was charged with considerable feeling, and the record of its decisions reads at first like a headlong flight from the principles to which Merriman had said in 1908 that it was 'pledged to the hilt'.

In brief, it would not hear Dr. Abdurahman at the bar. It threw out by 74 votes to 20 a motion by Schreiner to enable non-Europeans to become senators for the Cape, and by 74 to 23 his motion that they might become members of either House. Schreiner's further proposal that the Union Parliament be deprived of competence to exclude members on the ground of race or colour only was defeated by 79 to 16, and when he asked for the entrenchment of the non-white franchise to be conditional not only on the two-thirds majority of the Union Parliament as laid down in the report, but also on a two-thirds majority of the Cape members, this proposal was defeated by 86 votes to 14. Only J. A. Vosloo's motion, for the adoption of the Dordrecht congress resolution requiring a majority of the votes of Cape parliamentarians as a condition for removing non-white voters, came anywhere near to success, and that was defeated by 53 votes to 47.* It was indeed a strange occurrence, that a resolution carried by the congress of the dominant section of the South African Party, which itself had complete control of the House of Assembly, should have been thrown out like this barely a month after its adoption. Analysis of the voting on Vosloo's motion, however, does not reveal a significant swing on the part of any party or interest group, for Progressives and S.A.P. members, and among the S.A.P. members Bondsmen, town and country constituencies, east and west, were more or less evenly divided in their voting. The most probable explanation of what happened is that in the first place the Bond congress vote had been a close one (hence the omission of all details in the report of Van der Horst, himself a supporter of the non-white franchise), and that the Assembly vote on Vosloo's motion was swayed, not by the merits of the issues themselves, on which the members could well have recorded a different decision, but by extraneous considerations forced on their attention, above all the known intransigence of the Transvaal. This would explain why the names of all the Convention delegates, even surprising ones like Beck, Malan, Merriman and Stanford, and even the name of Sauer, appeared among the opponents of the motion. It was not, they might have explained, that they loved the Cape tradition less, but that they loved Union more.

II. THE UNIFICATION OF SOUTH AFRICA

The evidence given in the preceding pages shows that within the circle of the Afrikaner Bond and its associated parties in the other colonies there were arguments both for and against the political unification of South Africa. The success of these parties in the elections of 1907-8 seemed to indicate that if Union were acceptable they could have it very much on their own terms. Furthermore, the preparedness of all three parties to put out feelers towards the white artisan section of the community, which was in some measure an explanation of their electoral successes, seemed also to be a guarantee against the sort of narrow sectionalism which could have wrecked a closer-union movement among white South Africans. But factors which might have prevented unification were the economic rivalry of the individual colonies, which was checked but not overcome at any of the customs conferences before Union, and the danger of deadlock over the sharing of political power, if not between white and non-white, then between colony and colony or between country and town.

The disposition of the Afrikaner leaders to favour unification was a potent factor from the outset, for though members of Milner's kindergarten may have 'taken the initiative' in the matter, closer union was not a notion introduced from outside. So sensitive, in fact, had South Africans become to any attempt to foist a political system on them, that the success or failure of the movement could be said to rest very largely on the extent to which it depended on the initiative of committed South Africans.

'The unification of the British South African Colonies in a Federal Union' was the slogan adopted by the Afrikaner Bond in 1903, as a substitute for the more sweeping objective of a 'united South Africa' which had been its professed aim since 1883. Het Volk declared for a united South Africa in which the interests of the Transvaal would be properly safeguarded, while the Orangia Unie also hoped 'to unite South Africa and bring into being a great Nation'.* In August and September 1906, F. S. Malan contributed a series of articles to *Ons Land* proposing that, once the autonomy of the Transvaal and the Orange River Colony had been restored, British South Africa (including Basutoland and Swaziland—and Rhodesia too if, after clearing its public debt, it wanted to come in) should federate as three separate units—the Cape Colony, Orangia and Natal, and the Transvaal and Rhodesia—on a fairly centralized pattern after the Canadian rather than the Australian or United States model.* The idea of federating any groups other than the existing colonies as separate entities would soon die out, though

Steyn, Smuts and Merriman all toyed with it; but this did not affect the main issue, for as soon as he had declared his purposes Malan began to receive overtures from the English-speaking leaders of the closer-union movement, who had themselves received an initial rebuff from the Het Volk leadership in the Transvaal.* Smuts, Steyn and Merriman were as interested in closer-union as Malan, but deliberately stayed their hands until the control of the Transvaal, O.R.C. and Cape should fall into the hands of the associated parties. Malan, however, went ahead on his own. He secured the tabling of Selborne's federal Memorandum and related correspondence during the 1907 session of the Cape Parliament, and followed this on 23 July with a motion requiring the Cape Government 'during the recess' to 'approach the Governments of the other self-governing British colonies in South Africa to consider the advisability of taking preliminary steps to promote the union of British South Africa' and report back during the following session.* Malan considered that 'union must come from the whole of the people of the country and not from one political party', and as a gesture of agreement with this bi-partisan approach, Jameson, who was still Prime Minister, seconded the motion. It was carried without a division. Smuts feared that the Progressives were using Malan for party political ends and withheld support for the introduction of a similar motion in the Transvaal; but Malan's move did not materially affect developments because the resignation of Jameson in February 1908, following his defeat in the Council elections, gave the associated parties the position of power in all three colonies to which they aspired. When Merriman had formed his South African Party Government in the same month, the time was manifestly ripe for the leaders of the associated parties to put their plans into operation. Moreover, the possibility of an isolationist revival in the Transvaal which was now hinted at, and which had already led Botha's Government to announce its impending withdrawal from the customs union, gave another reason for urgency and pointed to the inter-colonial conference due to be held at Pretoria in May as the right occasion on which to launch formal closer-union proposals.

Smuts and Merriman succeeded without difficulty in getting proposals for the holding of a national convention accepted at the Pretoria conference.* The proposals then became a matter for public debate, and although there were some hostile press reactions at first, the Parliaments in all four colonies expressed their agreement and chose their delegates to meet in convention at Durban in October 1908.* So far as the reactions of the associated parties were concerned, the Het Volk caucus accepted the resolutions on 18 June, though some leaders of the party—notably A. D. W. Wolmarans, who was a member of the head committee—voiced objections on the ground of local self-interest. The Orangia Unie parliamentarians raised no objection to the calling of a convention, though they were apprehensive over the possible submergence of their interests under those of the more powerful colonies. The Cape Bondsmen supported the principle of a convention when their congress met at Robertson on 4 June,* and received the backing of South African Party speakers in Parliament. The members of the Natal Boerekongres supported the plan with some enthusiasm, and were far less apprehensive than the majority of white Natalians.*

In accepting the principle of a convention, the associated parties expected to hold a commanding position in the deliberations. In effect, they got one. From Natal, admittedly, came five delegates of whom none were Boerekongres representatives; but the Unie sent four of the five Orangia delegates, Het Volk five of the eight Transvalers, and the South African Party six of the twelve Cape representatives, of whom four were Bondsmen. This gave them fifteen of the thirty seats which carried voting rights (the Rhodesians being present as observers only), against thirteen held by Progressives, Unionists, Constitutionalists and Natalians together, and two by Cape independents. The ascendancy of the associated parties came, therefore, not from a mathematical preponderance as such, but from the probability that their opponents would not always act together, and from the fact that their own leaders—Smuts and Merriman in particular—were generally better prepared than their political opponents to handle the problems expected to arise. The Bond representatives included Malan, whose influence was considerable; but Hofmeyr declined Merriman's pressing invitation to attend, and Schreiner, who shared Hofmeyr's predilection for a federal rather than a unitary type of constitution, felt obliged to turn the invitation down in order to lead the defence in Dinizulu's trial.*

The Convention sat in Durban from 12 October to 5 November 1908, and then adjourned to Cape Town from 23 November to 3 February, with a break between 18 December and 11 January. At the end of the Cape Town session it produced its first report.*

In substance this favoured a unitary form of government with a bi-cameral legislature, though an element of federalism survived in the proposal for equal representation of the four provinces in the Upper House. The proposed constitution was to be fully flexible, except for safeguards for the equal status of Dutch and English as official languages, and for the existing political rights of non-white voters in the Cape Province, which could be altered only by special amending procedures. The report proposed that the representation of each province in the Lower House should be approximately in proportion to the number of its white male adults, under a system of proportional representation. It contained many other detailed recommendations in its draft constitution; but events would show that the attention of the associated parties was focused on one problem above all others: the question of the future distribution of political power.

The Afrikaner parties in the O.R.C. and the Transvaal reacted favourably to the report. Members of the Orangia Unie were particularly gratified at the success of Steyn and Hertzog in winning the Convention's support for the demand for equal language rights. Only Wolmarans objected in the Het Volk caucus, and Botha and Smuts were able to persuade the electors in the Transvaal country districts to leave any amending that might be necessary to Parliament.* When the Transvaal Parliament began its extraordinary session on 30 March, objections were indeed raised to a few of the Convention's recommendations—notably that in favour of entrenching the Cape non-European franchise—but most members were in a mood for rejoicing and refrained from moving any amendments at all, on the advice of their leaders.* The Parliament of Orangia had a more stormy debate which focused mainly on the topic of the Cape franchise, an amendment being proposed to introduce safeguards against the enfranchisement of non-Europeans in the O.R.C. which only the Speaker's casting vote defeated. Orangia Unie members in the Lower House were concerned to ensure that delimitation commissions after Union would really give the rural areas the advantage of fewer voters than the urban, as the report proposed. The nominated Upper House rejected their proposed amendment, but both Houses adopted the report on the understanding that the substance of the Assembly motion would be communicated to the Convention.*

The Cape Bond, by contrast, raised substantial difficulties. As had so often happened in the past, the Cape Town branch took it upon itself to investigate the report of the Convention on behalf of the party as a whole, and appointed a sub-committee on 11 February, consisting of J. A. C. Graaff (the branch chairman), Hofmeyr, Dr. J. Petersen, J. G. van der Horst and J. J. Michau, to go into the details and report back.* This sub-committee reported on the 16th, and its recommendations were adopted by the branch almost without amendment on the 17th. The report was arranged under fifteen heads,* some of which—such as its demand for a referendum before the adoption of the new constitution, and for a parliamentary inquiry into the likely effects of moving the administrative capital to Pretoria—would soon cease to be talking points of importance. But over and above these, and the proposals already discussed for the protection of non-European political rights, the committee wanted guarantees that the provinces could not be split up without the consent of their inhabitants as expressed through a referendum. It also wanted the extension of the entrenching section of the draft constitution to other parts of the same instrument, but did not specify which parts. Hofmeyr's preference for a federal rather than a unitary constitution, which was manifest from his public statements at the time,* came out incidentally in the first of the committee's observations, which hinted that the Bond was pledged to a federal solution, and then went on to deplore what it considered to be the under-representation of the Cape in the proposed Lower House.[1] Under the same head, they dissented from the principle of equal representation for the provinces in the Senate. In sum, the committee and the branch to which it reported gave evidence of a provincial patriotism at least as strong as that exhibited by the Transvaal. J. G. van der Horst, who would take the Cape Town resolutions to congress at the beginning of March, feared the influence of British imperialists, mining tycoons and Transvaal racists, and expressed these anxieties through his periodical, the *Cape*, with contagious effect.*

His influence and that of Hofmeyr also lay behind the other main category of objections which the Bond raised to the Convention report, which would eventually assume greater importance. These

[1] Thompson has shown that the distribution of seats on a population basis was of greatest benefit to Natal, on a white population basis to the Cape and the O.R.C., and on a white male adult basis to the Transvaal; and that, with some adjustments, the white male adult basis was the one chosen (op. cit., pp. 226–31).

concerned the distribution of power and influence between the associated parties and their opponents, and centred on the proposed electoral system for the Lower House. The principle of proportional representation in multi-member constituencies with each voter having a single transferable vote had first been proposed in the Convention by Smuts, and in section 39 of its draft constitution the Convention made provision for 'electoral divisions, each returning three or four members: provided that in special cases of sparsely populated areas the commission may delimit divisions in which less than three members shall be returned'.* But Van der Horst, indulging in some private mathematics and taking into account the existing advantage enjoyed by rural voters in the Cape, calculated that the introduction of proportional representation might result in the S.A.P.'s exchanging a massive majority, as things then stood, for an actual minority of the Cape Assembly seats.* The question here was not one of provincial autonomy, but of the continued ascendancy of one of the associated parties under a system devised by a leader of one of the others. There was room for considerable speculation as to what the results of an election in the Cape were likely to be under the proposed system, and Smuts and Botha, after first showing consternation at Van der Horst's figures, ended by pronouncing them to be far too pessimistic.* There was an outside chance, however, assuming a delimitation commission hostile to the interests of the South African Party, that Van der Horst's calculation might prove accurate, and fear of this enabled opposition within the party to the Convention proposals to grow. Hofmeyr, focusing his gaze on South Africa as a whole, feared also that the balance of power might be tipped against the associated parties in the event of Southern Rhodesia's electing to join the Union.* Sharing their anxieties were Henry Burton, J. A. C. Graaff and N. F. de Waal, all members of Merriman's Cabinet, and other prominent Bondsmen like J. J. Michau, A. C. A. van Rooy, and Dr. A. L. de Jager.

Van der Horst had been empowered by the Cape Town branch to use his discretion, in consultation with leading members of the party, as to which of his branch's resolutions, if any, he should raise in congress.* But when congress decided on 4 March to go into committee, he put his full case. After a debate behind closed doors, and in the face of strong opposition from Malan, congress then came out with a resolution confirming most of the points submitted by the Cape Town branch and adding some minor ones of its own.* It

upheld the argument that under the proposed constitution the Cape
would be under-represented, and it repeated Cape Town's objection,
as developed by Van der Horst, to the single transferable vote under
proportional representation without a prior investigation by the
Government of its likely political effects. The text of Van der
Horst's report back to his branch shows how much importance was
attached to these two topics, the second of which had also received
prominence in the report of the *Commissie van Toezicht* over the
signatures of Hofmeyr and Michau.*

Yet the actual congress resolution explicitly stated that, though
highly dissatisfied with the mode of representation proposed, the
Bondsmen did not consider themselves free to wreck the closer-
union movement even on grounds such as these. Congress therefore
concluded its resolution as follows:

'The Central *Bestuur* considers the subject of closer union to be
of such overriding importance, that nobody's conscience ought to
be stifled by party influence. For this reason, although the Central
Bestuur earnestly hopes that our Parliament will follow its opinion,
it wishes to explain clearly that it does not desire to prescribe for
members of Parliament in this matter, should they happen to differ
on these points.'

Even Bond members therefore had a free vote, and it was plain
from the reaction of some of the branches—notably Stellenbosch,
Burghersdorp, Dordrecht and Aberdeen—that the Cape Town
resolution did not represent the only view held within the party.*[1]

On the strength of the congress resolution, Bond parliamentarians
might well have used the special session at the end of March merely
to register a preference for an alternative form of representation,
and then have left it to the next session of the Convention to find a
way of meeting their wishes. But when Parliament met, the mood of
some was entirely different. Speakers insisted that the maximum
loading of urban and unloading rural voters' rolls allowed under
the draft constitution (that is, 15 per cent either way from the
provincial quota) should be made obligatory in parliamentary

---

[1] The Stellenbosch branch, after registering support for the draft Union Bill,
resolved as follows: 'This meeting expresses its regret over the resolutions taken
by the Cape Town branch of the Bond, for such cannot serve the interest and
welfare of land and people, but could lead rather to division and estrangement
of the different colonies, which is not only undesirable, but could also be very
disadvantageous for the Cape Colony' [Dutch original].

delimitations. So strong were the feelings expressed that Merriman, after writing to Steyn to tell him of 'a thoroughly organised effort' to destroy the work of the Convention, eventually agreed at a caucus meeting on 5 April to accept amendments to the electoral sections 39 and 40 of the proposed constitution. He explained to Botha that he had been driven to this by 'a knot of people with headquarters in Cape Town who for one reason or another do not like Union'. Hofmeyr was the 'head centre', with Van der Horst an 'able Lieutenant', the group having 'entire control of *Ons Land*', and 'the entire farming community of Dutch and English behind them' in opposition to the principle of one vote one value.*[1] During the committee stage an amendment to the draft Bill was proposed by J. C. Molteno, South African Party member for Jansenville, that the creation of constituencies returning less than three members should be obligatory 'in all cases of sparsely populated areas', such areas to be clearly defined. Despite Merriman's fear, grounded in a warning from Botha that the Transvaal Progressives would not accept any compromise which detracted from the principle of one vote one value, Molteno's amendment was carried. It was a Unionist farmer, Blaine, who then moved that the maximum load on urban and the maximum unload on rural constituencies should be made obligatory on the delimitation commissioners, and the House carried it by a three to one majority. It went on to pass a motion in favour of single-member constituencies for the provincial council.* It would be an exaggeration to call this a stampede; but members of the House, pondering their performance at leisure afterwards, must have realized that what they had taken part in was an agitation led by the representatives of the countryside against the towns, in which even provincial interests had been relegated to second place, and the defence of the 'Cape liberal tradition' to a very poor third.

The agitation was successful, though it nearly destroyed the closer-union movement. It was idle to pretend, as Merriman perforce felt bound to do, that the Cape resolutions amounted to 'elucidation,

[1] Despite the commitment of the editor, F. S. Malan, to the Convention's report, *Ons Land* backed the criticisms of the Hofmeyr–Van der Horst group. Between the publication of the report and the beginning of the parliamentary session Malan was away from Cape Town on departmental business, but showed in a speech at Malmesbury, reported in the issue of 18 March, that he was as keen as Hofmeyr that the Cape should not swallow the report 'with eyes shut and mouth open', but consider it on its merits.

not amendment' of the draft Bill. When the delegates arrived at Bloemfontein in early May for the final stage of the proceedings in South Africa, there was a real danger of complete deadlock between the Transvaal Progressives, who had pressed for one vote one value, and the Cape rural delegates, supported by those of the O.R.C., who insisted on electoral advantages for the country constituencies. After very tense moments on the floor of the Convention, during which the Progressive delegates demanded new securities against the 'bad faith' of the Cape farmers, the deadlock was only resolved by a decision to abandon proportional representation in Lower House elections and create single-member constituencies, and to require the reservation for the King's pleasure of any Bill to amend the sections dealing with the House of Assembly.*

These changes were accepted by the Cape Town branch of the Bond, though it could not resist finding further minor objections to the draft Union Bill;* but Merriman, on Hely Hutchinson's advice and under pressure from Malan, invited Hofmeyr to join the deputation which would take the measure to London, as one of the Cape representatives. This action caused some consternation among the Afrikaner leaders in the Transvaal but proved wise in the event, for although Hofmeyr remained stubborn on procedural points— notably in opposing the idea that any amendments to the Bill should be permitted in the Imperial Parliament—his support for the Bill itself scotched further opposition within his party.*

Neither Hofmeyr nor his supporters in the Bond had in fact ever suggested that the draft constitution should be rejected out of hand; but, as Cape patriots, and lacking that sense of urgency which had led Smuts and Merriman to take time by the forelock lest the chance should never recur, they had sought by their criticisms to improve the measure and protect the Cape. On first hearing of the Cape Town resolutions, Smuts expressed surprise at the way Hofmeyr had 'cut himself practically adrift from the noblest aspirations of the people of South Africa, and apparently on mere paltry grounds'.* But he failed to see that Hofmeyr's real concern was to protect the Afrikaner, so that his position was not basically different from his own. Gideon Krige told an audience in Stellenbosch that when a friend of his had asked Hofmeyr why he had criticized the draft constitution, the reply had been that although he was an old man without personal ambition or interests, he was 'troubled over the future of his people'.* Hofmeyr's letters to Steyn in April and May suggest that it was the Afrikaner people whom he had in mind. But this had been one of the major preoccupations of Boer leadership in the Transvaal as well, with its twin objectives: the fostering of a spirit of union on the one hand, and the protection of their own position against their political opponents on the other. The timing of the political campaign and their handling of the electoral and franchise questions revealed the Transvaal Afrikaners' concern with the problem of power. It was the possibility that the Transvalers might have erred in their calculations which awoke opposition within the Bond; but it was as important for Smuts as it was for Hofmeyr that, if error there was, it must be corrected. If indeed there had been any likelihood of a Progressive victory in the first Union election, it is pertinent to ask whether the Bond or any of the other associated parties would have agreed to closer-union. It was too soon after Milner, too soon after the war, for the Afrikaner political leaders— even Botha—to allow any draught of convention spirit, however heady, to slacken their grip on effective power.

III. THE UNIFICATION OF LEADERSHIP

Jan Hofmeyr died in London on 16 October 1909, shortly after the enactment of the South Africa Act. An unusual intensity of feeling characterized the tributes paid to him, both from within and from outside the Afrikaner Bond. Basil Williams, the historian, wrote of 'a really warmhearted man' and deplored the loss of 'another of the diminishing band of the old Cape liberals', while John Daverin, a South African Party member for Port Elizabeth, told Schreiner: 'I do not remember one instance in which he spoke uncharitably of anyone.'* The Cape Town branch of the Bond recorded their sense of loss in speeches of deep and genuine affection, well exemplified in that of Thomas te Water, who described Hofmeyr's delight at the nickname 'Onze Jan', which had originated, he said, in a toast proposed by Dolf Botha at Graaff-Reinet in 1884. Above all was the branch conscious that Onze Jan had worked with it and through it in the propagation of most of his political decisions.* The party had lost, not a *volksleier*, but a patriarch who had shrunk from theatrical poses, shrunk even from a public political role, for reasons which had as much to do with temperament as with health. His death, following that of Thomas Theron by almost exactly a year, threw new burdens on the surviving leadership of the party at a difficult time. Frederic de Waal may have possessed Hofmeyr's moderation, but he lacked his popularity. F. S. Malan may have had Theron's courage and Theron's ability to identify himself with his people; but in his dealings with Merriman, with whom he differed in temperament and would come to differ over details of policy, he lacked Hofmeyr's immense advantage of years.

Though the two years between May 1908 and May 1910 saw a growing harmony in South African public life as the convention spirit caught the public imagination, for the South African Party this was a period of testing and division, of which disunity over the South African Bill was merely one symptom. At the back of its difficulties lay the severe economic crisis which Merriman's Government had inherited from its predecessor, and the inevitable unpopularity which Merriman himself courted in his determined and ultimately successful bid to bring the Cape into Union in a solvent condition. Malan criticized Merriman's very policy of retrenchment by arguing that, if it was a question of priorities, Union was more important than solvency.* The application of that policy was attacked in June 1908 by white working men who chafed at the immigration of contract labourers—'waitresses, mechanics, tailoresses and shop assistants'—at a time when jobs were short. They saw red at the Prime Minister's bland rejoinder that as white people they really had no complaint because they were 'here in this country as members of an aristocracy'. Six months later, demands by white and coloured unemployed for work on new railway construction projects were turned down by the Government because of the shortage of public money, and the workers' leaders, encouraged by the *Cape Times*, began seriously to discount the value of their electoral alliance with the South African Party.*

Meanwhile agitation against the Scab Act had revived in the north-western Cape because the Government had found it necessary to withdraw some of the financial assistance which helped to make the law bearable. The wine farmers of the western districts also rose up in anger because of Merriman's refusal to remove the excise on spirits which Jameson had reimposed in 1904. At an excited meeting in the Cape Town Drill Hall in April 1908, farmers complained bitterly that they were unable to dispose of their surplus stocks because of excessive retail prices, for which they said the excise was to blame. Merriman was hard put to answer their questions, as were Malan and Frederic de Waal when they faced the crowds outside the hall afterwards. But he refused to reduce the excise when approached by a deputation in June, and it was only at the end of the parliamentary session in December, two months after another approach had been made by Malan, that he reluctantly agreed to cut the duty by half.*

De Waal, who had borne with Malan the strain of the excise agitation, was under additional pressure in that, as Colonial Secretary, he was having to contend with a growing discontent over the Government's educational policy. Congress at Robertson in June 1908 expressed strong opposition to the 1905 legislation, urging a return to the system which had existed before the introduction of school boards, and demanding an adjustment of the local educational rate so that the burden fell on other people as well as landowners. It wanted more rights for Dutch-speakers, state subsidies for 'free' (that is private denominational) schools, and a host of other changes; but the most important of these demands was the financial one.* By 1909, however, the emphasis had shifted more to the ideological field. Congress in that year received a petition signed by clergy (mainly of the Gereformeerde Kerk) and a few prominent Bondsmen and members of Parliament like A. S. du Plessis and H. J. Raubenheimer, stressing the need for the subsidization of denominational schools. This movement stemmed mainly from the north-eastern Cape, where, in step with the revival of Christian National Education in Orangia and the Transvaal, a Gereformeerde gymnasium had been set up at Steynsburg in 1904 'in the interest of parents who desired to educate their children according to their own convictions and baptismal promises'. Though the Cape movement was limited in its territorial extent, congress decided 'by a great majority' to support the petition, 'taking into account the Protestant, religious character of our people'. *Ons Land* described this as a 'resolution of great significance', noting that it was indeed unjust to expect parents who educated their children in private church schools to have to pay the public rate as well, but also wondering whether it was wise under South African conditions to put children of different cultural backgrounds in separate classrooms.*

There was a real danger that public friction over such a combination of bread-and-butter and ideological questions, occurring at a moment of strain within the leadership, might open up a rift between the South African Party and the Afrikaner Bond. Nor was this all. In the early months of 1910, particularly, few members of the Cape or the other Colonial Parliaments could feel sure of winning seats in the Union legislature. A seat on a provincial council was no adequate substitute, carrying less prestige and fewer emoluments. Friction was therefore likely to arise directly from the transition to the new political system. In fact, it was made to focus on two questions: coalition and the premiership.

The first political problem to be dealt with under Union was posed by the Progressive leaders, notably Jameson, Fitzpatrick and Farrar, when they urged that the first Union government should be a ministry of all the talents. As Innes put it to Merriman, 'it would be a good thing for South Africa if our Ship of State could be launched in the same spirit in which its keel was laid down, and by the same hands that built it', because it was 'the work not of one party or of one race, but of both'.* Jameson had pressed Botha to agree to coalition when the two men were in Britain in September 1909, and Botha, though he claimed to have consistently resisted Jameson's arguments, did 'candidly confess that he was able to make out a very strong case'.* Jameson does not seem to have been deceived by Botha, who, as Fitzpatrick noted, had given him no promise in this regard, and he told his brother in February 1910 that when it came to the point Botha would probably 'go with his own people'. He talked, not of immediate success, but of 'getting Botha ultimately to work with our own party even if we can't do it with the first Unionist Government'.* For him, as for Fitzpatrick, whose *The Union: a Plea for a fresh Start* appeared in March 1910, coalition was a long shot but worth working for. The opponents of coalition marshalled a variety of arguments. Onze Jan had feared that it would bring 'quarrelling and division', Steyn and Merriman that it would destroy effective opposition and play into the hands of the magnates.* 'If Botha had formed the Cabinet on "Best Man Lines"', wrote B. K. Long, 'there would have been immediate certainty, throughout Dutch South Africa, that he was no more than a tool of Britain'.* In other words, for the associated parties to work too closely with the Progressives was to risk internal division, for by no means all their supporters could take such a step. There was also the problem of patronage, to which perhaps not enough attention has been drawn. This was put succinctly by the editor of the *Volksstem* when he told Malan: 'We shall have difficulty enough among ourselves as it is, giving our own politicians a place commensurate with their services' without bringing in the Progressives.*

These arguments were conclusive for the associated parties. They held power, and it seemed that coalition could only create disadvantages for them. Botha, Merriman and Fischer decided firmly against 'best man government' when they met in Cape Town at the end of January 1910. But the exclusion of the Progressives from the race for office could not of itself remove all difficulties, not least because coalition had itself become entangled with the question of the premiership. In the absence of Steyn, who could have formed a government without friction but was advised to stand down for health reasons, the only two serious candidates in the field were Botha and Merriman. In Botha's favour were his record in war and peace, his post-war magnanimity and moderation, his natural bonhomie (which contrasted with Merriman's too sharp tongue) and his ability to impress people in Britain during his visits in 1907 and 1909—the last an important consideration, for Engelenburg was right to observe that the choice of the first Union premier depended a little on opinion in England.* In Merriman's favour was a parliamentary experience that went back to 1869, his high standing among Cape Afrikaners, including Bondsmen (who were certainly not alienated by his non-membership of their organization), his budgetary achievements since 1908 (which compared very favourably with Transvaal practice, as reflected in the recent voting of unusually large parliamentary allowances to members),* and an intellectual refinement which contrasted markedly with Botha's almost complete lack of erudition.

It may well be, as B. K. Long suggested, that Merriman realized his personal chance of becoming the first Union premier was small; but he was human enough to take to heart the manoeuvres of Botha and of some of his Cape colleagues to make them even smaller. Botha's carefully negative handling of the coalition question had led the Transvaal magnates and their English friends to back him for premier on the supposition that he and Jameson might ultimately coalesce. Merriman tried to represent this as a bid by Hoggenheimer to return to power by the back door, but whatever the justification his argument awoke little public response.*[1] He angered Botha by

[1] Merriman cautioned Smuts on 15 Feb.: 'As regards the Progressives do not be too effusive. It is quite clear the situation is not unlike 1895. The actors are the same—Jameson—The Press, skilfully engineered by clever fellows from abroad—The Magnates—and above all the object is the same, to secure the dominance of the money power in South Africa, per fas aut nefas. The cry then was "women and children", now it is the "race question", but we are forewarned this time and I pray God the attempt may fail.' This was a rather too frantic

challenging him during February and March 1910 to come into the open on the coalition question. Several leading Bondsmen, notably Malan, D. Graaff, N. F. de Waal and Van der Horst, worked to promote Botha's candidature, in collaboration with Botha himself and his colleagues in the Transvaal. Steyn, who had approached Botha, knew that he would refuse to serve under Merriman, and thought that Smuts would follow suit. Graaff told Malan in January that the Het Volk leaders were 'most anxious not to give our old friend offence, and would like to be as reasonable with him as possible, but there is one thing they will not do, and that is give him the position he covets'.* In February, Botha asked Graaff to persuade Malan and Fischer to 'take a more definite stand with regard to the premiership'.* A substantial correspondence in the Merriman Papers for May and June 1910 suggests a conspiracy by these men against the Cape leader, alleging not only that they tried to deprive Merriman of the premiership, but that they threatened to keep him out of the Victoria West seat in the Union Parliament unless he was prepared to serve in a Cabinet under Botha.* If this was true (and Merriman believed the story*), it must be said in Malan's defence that he tried not to turn it into a personal issue—a temptation which Van der Horst could not avoid—and that at least by 23 June he had given up the idea of turning Merriman out of his seat.*

Merriman's chances of obtaining the premiership, at best remote, were destroyed in the final resort by the attitude of the South African Party press. Malan's *Ons Land* naturally followed a neutral line. In April 1910 Botha and Smuts acquired a controlling interest in the *South African News*. It is a fair assumption that this was prompted by Botha's political ambition, though the letters dealing with this transaction addressed to them by F. J. Centlivres, the managing director, leave a little room for doubt as to whether this was primarily a clever bid to neutralize Merriman's influence, or a simple act of party loyalty to keep the paper out of the hands of possible rivals at a time when it was in financial difficulty.*1 The editor,

commentary on Smuts's observation in his letter of 10 February that 'the Progressives have behaved well over Union and have to some extent rehabilitated themselves'.

1 Centlivres, writing in confidence, was protecting the paper from 'the enemy', once vaguely defined as 'a cash purchaser then residing in Johannesburg, whose name was never disclosed to me', and he sought to keep it in the hands of 'the party' (sometimes capitalized), which is nowhere clearly identifiable with the anti-Merriman section. His public policy over the premiership was one of

Philipson-Stow, was himself a supporter of Merriman, and was quick to jump on public statements which attempted to prejudge the premiership question in Botha's favour, but he complained that his hands were tied, and resigned at the end of May.* Van der Horst's *Cape* was likewise run by supporters of Merriman, namely A. D. Donovan and the cartoonist, D. C. Boonzaier, but they were restrained from advocating Merriman's claims even though the Transvaal papers and the *Cape Times* were openly supporting Botha. When Lord Gladstone passed over Merriman and invited Botha to form a government on 21 May, Donovan and Boonzaier made an open attack on Malan and Graaff, who threatened legal action unless their personal allegations were withdrawn.[1] Rather than withdraw them, Donovan resigned. Boonzaier followed when a cartoon which he had drawn to honour Merriman was published with an amended caption which ridiculed him; and the two of them, with Merriman's agreement and some outside financial backing, launched another weekly, the *New Nation*, in July. This paper affected to be non-partisan in its advocacy of the sort of policies, above all financial stringency, which a Merriman government could assuredly best provide.*[2]

There was purpose in this manoeuvre with the first Union election in prospect and the Botha Government enjoying mere caretaker status; but the rift in the South African Party lute was healed in due course, when it became apparent that Merriman was not only too strong in Victoria West to be easily ousted, but also willing to act the 'humble musket-bearer' on Botha's back benches. When the news of Botha's appointment became known, *Ons Land* reported disappointment in the Bond branches at Aliwal North, Carnarvon and Dordrecht, and satisfaction at Montagu and Robertson. *Het Oosten* regretted that the premiership had not been given to the senior colony. *Onze Courant's* editorial carried the innuendo that Botha's

neutrality, and his quarrel with Philipson-Stow rested on the argument that Stow was taking Merriman's side. This was common cause between them, but Stow objected that the *S.A. News* had no right to let the Cape's case for having the premiership go by default.

[1] I have not been able to locate a copy of the *Cape* of 27 May 1910, but according to Mrs. P. Lewsen and Dr. R. F. Currey the item to which Graaff and Malan took exception was a cartoon in which Merriman was depicted in the act of discovering De Waal and themselves cheating at cards.

[2] The *New Nation* began to appear weekly from 29 July, but in September Donovan and Boonzaier merged it with the Cape *Observer*, which they took over.

appointment was a triumph for the 'English party' because the 'magnates' had pushed his claim with too much fervour for comfort. *De Stem* of Burghersdorp, on the other hand, was unreservedly satisfied. Merriman received many letters from individual Bondsmen regretting that he had not been appointed; but for the most part the public reaction of the party was one of interested silence.* Bondsmen waited to see what course events took, and then gave the stamp of their approval to a *fait accompli*, thus avoiding discord in their ranks.

IV. THE UNIFICATION OF PARTIES

The leaders of all parties were alive to the long-term need of bringing their organizations into line with the new conditions of political union. Thus the various colonial Labour parties joined forces in January 1910, and the Unionists and Progressives merged under the former name in May.* As early as December 1909, Botha had raised the question of the amalgamation of the government parties in letters to Merriman and Malan, telling them that he thought the time had come to organize a 'South African party . . . with a new name and a programme as liberal and on as wide a basis as possible', through the amalgamation of the 'South African, Bond, Unie and Het Volk Parties' and an appeal to the 'moderate men amongst our present opponents' to join it. Such a combination, he wrote, would give the moderate section power 'for a very long period'. The name he proposed in a draft manifesto enclosed in each letter was *De Zuid Afrikaanse Unie*.*

Both the Cape leaders replied cautiously. Malan was apprehensive of hasty amalgamation and reminded him that the Bond was constitutionally linked with the South African Party, and that it would be necessary to consider all aspects of the question before placing any proposals before the Bond congress, which was due to meet in March.* Merriman wrote at length, dissociating himself from the idea of a coalition which Botha had rather cryptically mentioned, warning against the dangers of corruption when governments became too secure in office, and suggesting to Botha that the South African Party already met his essential requirement of a political party under whose umbrella Het Volk and the Unie could conveniently link up with the Bond. He then let Botha know with unmistakable clarity that he did not regard the Bond (and by implication Het Volk as well?) as a political party in the proper sense of the term, but as an 'agricultural association' which worked

20

in harmony with his own parliamentary party. The ploy was as obvious as Botha's avoidance of the name 'South African Party' in his own proposal.* A few days later Merriman suggested to Malan, that Botha aimed at 'a "caucus" and not a "party",' and continued that 'to suppose that the Bond is to efface itself seems to me beyond the mark'.* Merriman had the advantage over Botha in that he already headed the kind of organization that Botha was anxious to create on the national level, and he would not let that advantage go lightly. Botha must yield to him.

After holding discussions in the Transvaal with Graaff, Smuts and Sauer over party amalgamation and other questions, Botha visited the Cape during the last week in January. There he met the Bond leaders, Fischer and Merriman; and before he left Cape Town the local branch of the Bond had already met and carried a resolution for congress to consider closer union between the associated parties, in the hope of obtaining a decision at the following session of the Central *Bestuur*.* That Botha was satisfied with progress appeared from a letter from Smuts to Merriman, in which Smuts also suggested the adoption of 'some such name as "S.A. Party" ' all over South Africa as an antidote to possible provincialist sectionalism.*

But soon after Botha's return to the Transvaal Merriman spoke at Worcester and publicly deplored Botha's failure to make an open rebuttal of the idea of coalition. Botha was privately angry that Merriman should have brought the subject into the open but took Malan's advice not to be drawn into controversy over it.* Instead, he devoted his attention to the improvement of his original manifesto, made overtures to the Transvaal Nationalists, and toured his Colony to ask the Het Volk committees to support a project which he planned to launch at the party congress on 23 March. This was for the transformation of Het Volk into a 'South African National Party' like Merriman's. His plan met with complete success, and in due course the Het Volk congress agreed after discussion in committee to a change of name and programme.*

A week later the Bond congress empowered its executive, together with the members of the *Commissie van Toezicht* and their alternates, to arrange a conference with delegates of friendly bodies 'to consider co-operation, closer contact or closer union' (*samenwerking, toenadering of nauwere vereniging*) and report back — if necessary to a special meeting of the congress.* The Orangia Unie agreed in principle at its congress in April to a merger with the other parties on a very broad basis,* while the Natal Boerekongres, which had resolved at Vryheid on 21 January to purge its constitution of 'everything that might be a stumbling block in the way of our joining hands and co-operating for the welfare of our native land', changed its name in May to the Natal *Volksvereniging* (People's Union) as a gesture of broadmindedness.* It too was reconstituting itself on 'South African Party' lines, though the Natal English press found the posture strange.

At the beginning of June Louis Botha, now Prime Minister of the Union, whose Cabinet included members of Het Volk, the Orangia Unie, the Afrikaner Bond and the South African Party, put out in his own name the manifesto which he had first sent to Merriman and Malan at the end of December, now altered appreciably as a result of criticisms offered by Malan, De Waal and others.* This manifesto provided a blueprint for the eventual amalgamation of the associated parties. But, appearing as it did a week after Jameson's Unionist manifesto of 25 May, it had obvious importance for the general election which was due to be held on 15 September, and which, owing largely to the influence of Malan, the associated parties decided to fight with their existing machinery as separate political bodies. The manifesto contained a draft programme of principles, which served as a common platform for all the Nationalists, as the associated parties were now commonly called.

The first of Botha's points sought to protect local interests, the second those of cultural minorities, and the third lifted native affairs 'above party politics' and proposed 'the fair and sympathetic treatment of the Coloured races'—a point on which Malan had already lectured Botha and Smuts.* Subsequent clauses approved of European immigration (while vigorously disapproving of Asian), stressed the need to look after the interests of labour (especially white labour), and showed concern for the establishment of a good defence system within the Empire, an efficient and well-treated civil service, the expansion of communications, of industry and of commerce, the attraction of capital for mineral exploitation and the development of agriculture in all its aspects. The document thus offered something general to all major ethnic and interest groups save the Asian, but was lacking in specific undertakings. Neither Merriman nor Malan had thought much of it in its original form, and when Boonzaier saw the published version he entertained the readers of the *Cape* to a cartoon depicting the Union's first Prime

Minister as a middle-aged nurse feeding the infant South Africa from a bottle labelled 'Platitudes'.* Furthermore, the Unionist programme, which had already appeared and therefore could not have been designed to obscure the differences between the parties in order to promote the idea of best man government, contained every substantial point in Botha's in a rather more concrete form.*

The election was therefore fought, not over the differences between the policies of the two main contenders, but over a question which was really an internal matter for the Nationalists: the position, the aims and the influence of General J. B. M. Hertzog, whom Botha would gladly have excluded from his Cabinet had it been possible to do so without alienating the sympathies of the Orange Free State. Hertzog's advocacy of strict equality of treatment for the Dutch and English languages in education, which he had begun to implement in the Free State and now wished on South Africa as a whole, aroused a great deal of antagonism among the English-speaking electorate. Botha blamed it for his own defeat by Sir Percy Fitzpatrick in the Pretoria East contest, though this was in fact Fitzpatrick's home ground. But the Nationalists won the election by a comfortable margin in spite of the Hertzog hazard, gaining 67 seats against 39 won by the Unionists, 10 by independents and 4 by Labour—an outright majority, though Botha had hoped for one much larger.*

The election over, the associated party leaders returned to the task of party amalgamation, most of the spadework being done by Malan and Smuts. Malan called for copies of the statutes and programmes of the other organizations and drafted a constitution, which was ready by January 1911. Smuts prepared another draft, and both were discussed at a conference of parliamentary representatives of the associated parties in the parliament buildings on 31 March and 1 April.* Malan took the Bond constitution as his model, while Smuts took that of Het Volk. The conference used Malan's Draft as a basis for discussion and incorporated a few of Smuts's points in a revised text which was then submitted to the parties for consideration, along with a set of draft regulations for the nomination of candidates for the House of Assembly, and the manifesto of General Botha which was proposed as a draft programme of principles. These were to be discussed at a later conference.* The Orangia Unie expressed satisfaction at its congress in June, and empowered its Central *Bestuur* to arrange the party's representation at this conference. The Cape Town Bondsmen appointed a committee which went into the documents with customary thoroughness, compared notes with another committee set up by party members in Steynsburg, and eventually arrived at Botha's conference in November with a long list of proposed amendments.*

Meanwhile Botha and Malan spent the middle months of 1911 in England attending the Imperial conference, which meant that they were conveniently placed for co-ordinating their plans for party amalgamation. Botha's aims appear from a letter he wrote to H. E. S. Fremantle, member for Uitenhage, on 3 July. He wanted invitations to his congress sent to all associated party members of the Assembly, to influential senators, to all district *besturen* of the associated parties, to the Liberal Association, and to a large number of unattached but prominent people in each electoral division, with special attention to those divisions in which the Nationalists were weak and where there were many floating voters. Fremantle was asked to draw up a list for the Cape.*

To perform this task, Fremantle made a tour of the Cape constituencies, and the report which he made on his return told as much about his party's political intentions as about the attitudes which he found.* The situation, he wrote, was 'wavering but hopeful'. Botha was popular, but the Unionist leaders, apart from Jameson, were not. Hertzog had made a favourable impression on people who had met him in the flesh, but he was suspect among English-speakers and had undoubtedly slowed down the drift towards the Nationalists. 'There is a tendency among farmers to join us,' Fremantle continued. 'In the Midlands this is especially marked. There is also a tendency on the part of artisans to sympathise with us. On the other hand there is still a certain social prejudice on the other side, being English counting as a title to gentility and superiority not otherwise apparent, and this makes it difficult to get very strong platforms. This feeling is breaking down, but our strength on the English side, at any rate in the towns, must for a long time lie in the people rather than the smart set.' He found that the English Colonials were bigoted on language matters, but that the Unionists had not been able to win support among the artisans for their immigration policy. If there was apathy in some Dutch districts, he found that sections of the English community were critical of bad leadership and might well be expected to join the Nationalists. His conclusion therefore was that 'the existence of the Unionist party is in peril and . . . if the plain facts are known the Hertzog bogey will disappear, the flood-gates be opened allowing the stream to flow freely our way, and the Unionist leaders be left with no support but what they can get from their personal connections and the withering plant of spontaneous Jingoism and racial snobbery. But we have no papers and we do not hold meetings enough; and at present it is hardly too much to say that in this province the existence of the opposition is due to our inaction.' Given 'constant and active energy' over the next few years however, Fremantle thought it would be possible to 'annihilate the other side or leave the leaders without followers'.

This was the kind of advice which Botha wanted to receive, because he saw the routing of the Unionist opposition as a condition for the growth of an enduring spirit of conciliation among the electors. There had to be a landslide towards the Nationalists, a massive influx of at least unattached individuals into the one party which, in his view, possessed the true South African spirit, so that the amalgamated South African Party would be a far larger, far more representative body than the sum of the associated parties' members. This conception begged some big questions. It involved a sweeping dismissal of the Unionist claim to a South African patriotism. Its assumption that the Hertzog 'bogey' could be expected to disappear was rash even at the date on which Fremantle wrote, for Hertzog was already protesting his discomfort in his new Cabinet surroundings.* But Botha claimed to stand midway between Hertzog and his Unionist critics, which in his opinion and that of most white South Africans represented the centre of the political stage.

When the fusion congress met in the Ramblers' Hall, Bloemfontein, on 21 and 22 November, there were white representatives from all four provinces on the platform, nearly all of whom were members of the associated parties, though the invited audience contained many who were not.* Botha, who was elected to the chair, opened with an exhortation to 'sweep South Africa clean of racialism' and looked forward to 'the amalgamation of the two white races in order that along that line there may be formed a South African nation'. He moved the establishment of a new South African Party. After a large committee representing all provinces had been chosen to look into the draft constitutional documents and the proposed amendments to them, Botha's motion was adopted with acclaim. The congress eventually agreed to leave the finalizing of the constitution to a continuation committee, for report to the first congress of the new party, and accepted the draft put forward by the parliamentary representatives in April as a provisional instrument for purposes of branch formation. A provisional head committee was then elected and the congress closed.

Malan had meanwhile arranged for the 1911 Bond congress to meet in Cape Town on 7 December instead of during the first half of the year, so that action could be taken to implement the Bloemfontein decisions. When congress met he presented a joint report in the name of the *Moderatuur* and the *Commissie van Toezicht*, which explained the Bloemfontein decisions. He then moved the dissolution of the Afrikaner Bond. After a long discussion his motion was adopted by the delegates with applause, and the minutes are silent as to the name of the lone member who cast a contrary vote.*

PART THREE:

THE AFRIKANER BOND IN RETROSPECT

14

The Afrikaner Bond as a Political Party

WHEN Sir Bartle Frere dismissed the first Cape Prime Minister, Sir John Molteno, from office in 1878, even though he had commanded a safe majority in the Assembly during the previous session, the public outcry which followed was not sufficient to prevent the formation of a new government by J. G. Sprigg, who found he could count on the continued support of the House. Sir James Rose Innes rightly considered, the propriety of the Governor's action quite apart, that this change of ministry 'could not have happened without a general election, had party lines been definite, and party discipline strict'. But a change was at hand. When Hofmeyr entered the House in 1879, 'the formation of, at any rate, one real parliamentary party began'.*

The fact that Milner refrained from doing to Schreiner in 1899 what Frere had done to Molteno in 1878 was due, on the Governor's own admission, to the existence of political forces which had simply not been there twenty years earlier.* The formation of the Z.A. Boeren Beschermings Vereeniging had led to the appearance in Parliament of an organized pressure group with a watching brief over a particular set of interests. This group was the nucleus of the parliamentary party that Innes had in mind. But the expression 'parliamentary party' is misleading when applied to its heir and successor, the Afrikaner Bond, for it suggests a political party with the rudiments of cohesion within the House itself, and invites attention to the manoeuvres of politicians there, rather than to the connexion between those politicians and the electorate. To grasp the meaning of the Afrikaner Bond as a political organization, one must take account both of its activities in Parliament and of its articulation in the constituencies.

The Cape Parliament was modelled on the British at a time when the British party system was long established but still relatively immature. There was little demand in Great Britain for the elaboration of party machinery, involving the working out of party constitutions and the development of the party caucus, until the appearance in the second half of the nineteenth century of a mass electorate. The Whig or Tory of tradition had been prepared to accept discipline at a price, but preferred to stand before his electors as a man of independent judgement rather than as the obedient party cipher who was willing to 'leave his brains outside', and he regretted the transition from the age of independents to the age of party machines. At the Cape, too, the tradition of independence proved extremely tenacious. Against a background of Boer indifference, the parliamentary class of English- and Dutch-speaking townsmen had so far enjoyed a security of tenure which made political independence seem as desirable in practice as it was in theory to the individualists of the Victorian era. Nor, at the moment when the Afrikaner political movements began to appear on the scene, had the complexity of government business or the size of the electorate yet created the conditions which necessitated the introduction of full-scale party government.

At the start of his political career Hofmeyr shared the dislike of his contemporaries for a rigid party system, disagreeing with the suggestion of John Paterson, a member for Port Elizabeth, that the Colony needed an arrangement on British lines, even if the names 'Conservative' and 'Liberal' were to give place to 'those of "*Pas op*" and "Press on"'. He wrote that, in reality, 'our parties group themselves only under the exigency of a big question', and he was content with a fluid system of this sort even after Shepstone had moved into the Transvaal.* Furthermore, although his efforts led to the establishment of something like a party system in Parliament, he persistently refused to apply the first convention of such a system inside the House. On every occasion that he was invited, as leader of the largest following in Parliament, to form a government, he turned the invitation down, to the indignation of many who considered that the man who had effective power ought to take on the responsibility. The explanation offered below of Hofmeyr's policy has two main aspects, one mechanical, the other tactical, and when both are considered together the policy itself falls easily into place.

The mechanical explanation rests on the simple fact that the Afrikaner Bond was not as strong in Parliament or in the constituencies as some of Hofmeyr's critics apparently imagined it to be. Its net, though spread widely through the Colony, was of coarser mesh than L. S. Amery imagined when he wrote that the Bond 'by slow degrees absorbed almost the whole of the Dutch inhabitants of the colony'.* Bond membership climbed fairly steadily, with some acceleration during the period of Rhodes's premiership, from 2,002 in 1887 to 11,487 in 1899, and rose gradually thereafter, with little annual variation, to 12,576 in 1911. But the Orangia Unie claimed a membership of 12,586 in 1907, after it had been in existence barely a year, and Abraham Fischer, explaining this figure at the second party congress, maintained that although it was based on incomplete records, 'he could safely say that there were 5,000 more members than officially noted'.* The Cape Bond's claim to a membership of 12,000 in 1911 looks equally unimpressive next to the claim of the Nationalist Party to a membership of 120,000 in the Cape Province in 1953.* Politicians' methods of reaching the electorate improved markedly between 1911 and 1953; but neither this fact, nor the increase in the population (which did not even double itself in the period), nor the Nationalist Party's admission of women to membership, which the Bond disallowed, adequately explains the disproportion. The Bond's failure to grow numerically seems to have been due very largely to the fact that it expended much more of its energy on the registration of voters than it did on the recruitment of new members. The annual subscription of 5s., which from 1909 could be reduced in individual cases, was not prohibitive; and there is evidence of a desire to step up membership from 1905 onwards;* but in spite of this, Bond membership in the Colony as a whole never rose much above one-tenth of the total number of voters on the roll. The steady growth of the voters' roll, on the other hand, owed much to the existence of the Bond and the work of its press and agents. The relative growth of party membership and the Cape electorate can be seen from the following table:*

TABLE I

BOND MEMBERS AND REGISTERED VOTERS IN THE CAPE COLONY

Year	1887	1893	1898	1903	1907	1909
Bond members	2,002	9,237	10,675	11,469	11,948	12,452
Registered voters	88,999	90,679	109,888	135,177	152,121	142,367

A comparison of published data for the years 1897–8 in the two electoral provinces where the Afrikaner Bond was strongest, namely the north-western and midland circles, shows that in no constituency did Bond membership come anywhere near half the number of voters in the rural wards in any district, and that the Bond candidates in the 1898 Assembly elections could usually count on the votes of approximately half of the electorate at best:[1]

TABLE II

THE POLITICAL STRENGTH OF THE AFRIKANER BOND
IN CONSTITUENCIES MOST FAVOURABLE TO IT

	1	2	3	4	
Constituency	Total Voters 1897	Total Rural Voters 1897	Total Bond Members 1897	Votes cast for Bond Candidates in 1898 Assembly Elections (a)	(b)
N.W. Circle					
Worcester	3,752	2,564	514	1,872	1,865
Malmesbury	2,508	2,004	147	1,449	1,349
Piquetberg	1,481	1,322	71	778	646
Namaqualand	1,479	1,059	38	346	320
Clanwilliam	2,209	2,039	438	1,134	1,030
Midland Circle					
Graaff-Reinet	2,283	1,287	454	1,289	1,250
Richmond	2,360	1,342	664	1,067	1,046
Beaufort West	2,727	1,693	607	1,198	1,094
Victoria West	3,013	2,251	728	1,566	1,424

It was only in the north-western, midland and north-eastern circles that the Bondsmen had a reasonable expectation of being able to sweep the board. Here, with the exception of the problem constituency of Namaqualand, they were in control. But in the eastern province, where the British settlers predominated, and the African vote was often though not invariably hostile, in the south-western where rural Afrikaners seem generally to have resisted the Bond's appeal, and in the western, where the Bond had to contend with a good deal of Coloured opposition and had no way of dealing with a largely urban electorate until Merriman devised the Liberal Association, its hold was generally precarious. If the Bond won Bechuanaland, this was often balanced, too, by a failure to hold Griqualand West.

It was not a matter for surprise, therefore, that the Bond never acquired a majority of seats in both Houses, nor enjoyed the

[1] Figures in column 1 are derived from G. 8—'98. Report of the Redistribution of Seats Commission, Appendix D; in column 2, from ibid. Appendix C; in column 3, from the *Notulen*, 1897 congress, pp. 28 ff.; and in column 4 from contemporary press reports.

experience of being in undisputed control of either, until the general election of 1908, by which time it was constitutionally tied up in a parliamentary coalition with South African Party members who were not Bondsmen, from whom it lacked the will if not the power to break away. The parliamentary strength of the Bond and the South African Party—they cannot very easily be disentangled from each other—developed as follows in respect of each House of the legislature:

TABLE III

THE AFRIKANER BOND AND ITS ALLIES IN PARLIAMENT

(A) *House of Assembly*

Year of election	1879	1884	1888	1894[1]	1898	1904	1908
Total seats	72	74	76	76	78	95	107
Seats held by Bondsmen, etc.[2]	±18	±33	±31	±35	**42**	43	**69**
Seats held by Progressives	—	—	—	±14	35	49	33
Seats held by Independents	±54	±41	±45	±27	1	3	5

(B) *Legislative Council*

Year of election	1878	1883	1890	1898	1903	1908
Total seats	21	22	22	23	23	26
Seats held by Bondsmen, etc.[2]	9	**12**	**16**	11	10	**18**
Seats held by Progressives	—	—	—	12	12	8
Seats held by Independents	12	10	6	—	1	—

Holding thus a minority position in the legislature, albeit as the only political party for much of its existence, the Bondsmen were nearly always in the position of having to make terms with sympathizers outside their party.

Let us now turn to the tactical considerations which moved Hofmeyr. The Afrikaner Bond never attempted, as a party, to pit its strength against all comers, partly because the combined voting power of non-Bondsmen would have been too strong for it, but more especially because its leaders felt the need for the talents of certain sympathetic outsiders. A good illustration of this is Hofmeyr's admission at the time of the 1894 general election that if Schreiner's

[1] The figures given by the *Commissie van Toezicht* (see p. 152 above) for the 1894 Assembly election appear to underrate the extent of Bond successes. The distinction between Progressive and Independent, as an index of support or of opposition to the Bond at that time, is largely meaningless.

[2] The term 'Bondsmen' etc. is here taken to include candidates of the *boeren vereenigingen* (1878–9) and members of the South African Party (1898 onwards). Figures take into account the results of by-elections following successful election petitions. Occasions when the Afrikaner Bond acquired a majority of seats in either House are shown in bold type.

candidature were not secured the Bond had nobody among its candidates capable of handling the law department. Onze Jan was acutely aware of the Bond's shortage of professional and commercial men, as well as of members of Parliament who could hold their own in debate. He also appreciated the sensitivity of the English colonial to any manifestation of Afrikaner nationalism, and for all these reasons judged it best to let power appear to reside in other hands, thankfully grasping what he could of the substance, which he could only have held under these conditions.

His method, used time and again with success, was to lend the support of his parliamentary following to whichever candidate for the premiership was prepared to comply with the Bond's legislative requirements of the moment, and to withdraw that support either when their adopted leader ceased to fit in with their needs, or when a rival politician offered better terms. Thus it was that South Africa's Parnell backed Scanlen in order to secure the recognition of the Dutch language, but rejected him two years later on account of his frontier policy; and he supported the Upington and Sprigg ministries in the mid-eighties because their customs, railway and frontier policies were acceptable, only to move over to Rhodes when he offered partnership in the North. In this way Hofmeyr was able to maintain his party in a position of power for most of the time between the fall of Sprigg's first government in 1881 and the outbreak of the South African war. It was able to use this power to win victory after victory for the Dutch language, to maintain the protective tariffs which the farmer desired, to win the battle of the brandy excise, to safeguard its position against possible swamping either by the African vote or by the towns, and so far to influence the external policy of the Government that the Colony's active participation in the conquest of the Boer Republics became unthinkable.

Hofmeyr's manoeuvres called not only for great judgement on his part, and for a good deal of quiet lobbying whenever a change of ministry was in prospect, but also for a strong sense of discipline and party loyalty on the part of his parliamentary followers. His home in Camp Street became the meeting place of what may loosely be termed a party caucus at least from April 1880, perhaps earlier.[1] His supporters were nicknamed the 'White House Party' because of this, though in due course they would commonly meet in the *Ons Land* office. The only caucus records that seem to have survived are

[1] For Bond and S.A.P. caucus meetings, see above pp. 132, 156-7, 218 222, 288.

occasional reports or memoirs of meetings.* These give no indication that meetings were held regularly, and suggest rather an informal *ad hoc* gathering to which non-parliamentarians might be admitted, without office-bearers or strict rules of procedure or disciplinary authority. There are no references to a Bond or a South African Party whip. In the early part of 1892, *Ons Land* ran a series of editorials discussing a current proposal for the setting up of a Bond executive committee (*uitvoerende commissie*) to ensure that steps were taken to secure the passage of congress resolutions into law, and the editor attacked those critics who thought the Bond's representatives did not push congress's demands hard enough in the House. He denied that it was the function of an executive committee to act as a party whip, or to force Bond members to make a declaration of obedience to the 'party line': 'Not one desirable candidate will be found ready to make such a declaration. And if perchance such a cringing aspirant were to offer himself for Parliamentary distinction, he would stand very small chance of being elected.'*

That strict discipline was not enforced on Bond members in the House is borne out by the evidence of the parliamentary votes and proceedings. Among the Boeren Vereeniging men in the sixth Colonial Parliament (1879–83), discipline was lax. Hofmeyr's colleague from Stellenbosch, P. A. Myburgh, voted against the majority of his Vereeniging fellows as often as he voted with them. It is possible to find a few occasions when all the representatives of the Vereeniging voted together in an important division;* but normally one or two of them voted against their colleagues. In the Upper House the persistent opposition of W. A. J. de Smidt to the ideas of most of his party colleagues was mainly responsible for the fact that on no major political issue over which the Council divided during the five sessions did all the Vereeniging's supporters vote in the same way. Nor did its majority in the Council always agree with its representatives in the Assembly. When Merriman moved a vote of no confidence in Sprigg's Government in the Assembly on 23 July 1880, all the Vereeniging members save Myburgh supported it; but all their colleagues in the Upper House save one voted in favour of a contrary motion by Alfred Ebden on the same day. Merriman's motion was that 'the Ministry no longer possessed the confidence of the House'; Ebden's, that 'this Council without entering into the merits of the railway question, desires to record its confidence generally in the Ministry, and to express the opinion that their removal from office at the present juncture would be uncalled for and fraught with danger to the best interests of the Colony'.

Yet there were signs during the life of the same Parliament that the tradition of proud independence was coming under pressure. The Sprigg Government, during its death agonies in April 1881, survived Scanlen's motion of censure by the narrow margin of thirty-seven votes to thirty-four. The Vereeniging men were reasonably solid in their support for the motion, but some of their fellow-Afrikaners were not, and the *Zuid Afrikaan* berated them for putting local interests before ethnic loyalty.* The *Patriot*, with greater audacity, suggested that petitions should be sent to the 'Settlers' Ministry', urging it to resign, by Myburgh of Stellenbosch, Sichel of Albert, Van Zyl of Richmond, De Wet of Somerset East and Watermeyer of Hanover.* Myburgh had already been hauled over the coals at a meeting in Stellenbosch on 1 March for not having supported the 'no confidence' motion of the previous session, and for having allegedly aided in the subjugation of the Transvaal by selling horses and donkeys to the Imperial authorities; Sichel was soon to face the music at the hands of his Albert constituents; Van Zyl received a vote of censure from the Petrusvillers on 20 May; and Watermeyer was a butt for the attacks of the *Zuid Afrikaan* periodically through the year. The last three were not returned to Parliament in the 1884 election. Pressure of this kind, sustained by newspaper attacks, was bound to lead to greater emphasis on party loyalty inside Parliament, and provided an external substitute for the internal machinery which was lacking.

No Bond member of Parliament was ever formally expelled from the party for voting against party policy in the House. The disciplinary authority of the *Commissie van Toezicht* stopped short at the doors of the chamber, and when the David de Waal test case occurred in November 1898, the absence of a disciplinary whip, combined with considerations of party tactics, prevented punitive action being taken against him, even though De Waal's relationship with the Bond leadership was strained to breaking point. He was bombarded with telegrams urging him to resign, which were sent by his constituents but perhaps inspired by Hofmeyr himself;* but he ignored these and continued to cast his vote against the Bondsmen during the remainder of the session with complete impunity. Nevertheless the growing control of the *Commissie van Toezicht* over the nomination of parliamentary candidates largely dispensed with the need for a disciplinary caucus. The fate of S. J. du Toit was an effective object-lesson to all would-be deviationists, and the solidarity of the Bond vote in the House of Assembly during the sessions of 1898 and 1899 was impressive, in divisions ranging in importance from Schreiner's 'no confidence' motion of October 1898 to Sir Henry Juta's proposal a year later for the payment of weekly benefits to sick railway employees: all were party questions, and the free vote was now the exception, not the rule.*

Reference to the pressure of the electorate on individual members raises the question of where power in the Bond really resided. In theory, as S. J. du Toit expressed it, the Bond was governed not from the roof but from the foundations. Bond policy was indeed determined in the first instance by the majority decision of the representatives of the district *besturen*, meeting in congress. This democratic decentralization of power was particularly strong in the early years of the Bond, and although it tended to diminish as the years went by, it was at all stages possible for the rank and file Bondsmen to band together and compel the leadership to listen to their views. The spirit which had led the Cradock congress to deny a deliberative vote to the parliamentarians who were present manifested itself again in the great scab agitation of 1895. The same spirit was present in the decision of the 1891 congress to ensure that parliamentary candidates were democratically elected, by altering the procedure of the circle and nomination meetings so that individual districts and wards, instead of being represented by two delegates with discretionary powers of voting, would be represented by one delegate, with a block vote equal to the number of Bondsmen who had sent him, and with instructions to use that vote in support of the candidates chosen by his branch. His vote could be invalidated by the *Commissie van Toezicht* if it could be shown that he had not done so.*

But if the Bond was decentralized and democratic in much of its working, in some important respects it was the reverse. The explanation of this paradox is partly institutional; but the peculiar arrangement of Bond government at the higher levels, of which a discussion follows, was probably designed mainly to meet the situation in which the parliamentary party found itself. The bare facts of the case are that, although decisions were made democratically at all levels up to and including that of congress, no formal machinery existed for the making of political decisions binding on

21

the party when congress was not in session. It was taken for granted that all Bond committees would have office-bearers. A new congress was elected every two years in terms of the constitution.* According to the *Reglement van Orde*, it had to have a chairman, vice-chairman, secretary and treasurer;* but no official Bond document carried a definition of their functions, and it was nowhere suggested in any of the instruments that these office-bearers should regard themselves as an executive committee when congress was not in session. They were indeed responsible, as individuals, for the continued running of the Bond. They occasionally issued circulars dealing with current issues on which guidance was considered necessary—for example, the instruction in 1899 as to how Bondsmen should behave in the event of war. The demands on the Bond leadership created by the South African war did in fact endow the leaders with a modicum of corporate existence, reflected in the term *Moderatuur*, which emerged during the war and survived in post-war parlance as a collective term to describe them.* But they were usually too far distant from each other to meet regularly in committee, and were certainly not required to do so. Het Volk and the Natal Boerekongres had head committees of seven members elected by their respective congresses; the Central *Bestuur* of the Orangia Unie, which was in effect an executive committee, had thirteen members; and in all three the chairman of the executive was *ex officio* chairman of congress.* The executive committees of these other parties also possessed wide disciplinary powers analagous to those of the *Commissie van Toezicht*, though less fully defined.*

But in the case of the Afrikaner Bond the *Commissie van Toezicht* did not fulfil the role of a full-fledged executive, for three main reasons: firstly, its functions were not all-embracing, but limited to matters concerning elections—it had no power, that is, to make policy decisions; secondly, as already noted, it had no power over the parliamentary party beyond such as may have come from the accidental fact that Jan Hofmeyr dominated both; thirdly, owing to the dominant personality and leadership of Hofmeyr, and to the steady growth in the *Commissie's* authority over the years, especially in 1898, it became too strong to be regarded in the proper sense as a committee of congress. It was able to take liberties with the constitution under which it operated, notably during the general elections of 1894 and 1898, on the assumption that it would be able to secure retrospective validation of its decisions. To this extent, though within a limited field, it was a rival authority to congress. It was the agency through which Hofmeyr was able to build up his personal control over the party outside Parliament. It is clear from the *Commissie's* annotations (*aanteekeningen*) on the general run of electoral complaints that it was nearly always Hofmeyr who made the important decisions. The angry letters reached him first, as chairman. He would send his observations on each case to his colleagues through the post, and they in turn would add their own comments, which nearly always endorsed Onze Jan's judgement, and return the document to him for filing. Hofmeyr was willing to forgo the treasurership of the provincial (later Central) *Bestuur* and his seat in Parliament, but except for a brief spell during his absence in Europe during the war, he did not relinquish the chairmanship of the *Commissie van Toezicht* until separated from it by death.*

The chief limitation on the power of congress arose from the fact that it had no direct means of controlling the parliamentary party. An attempt was made to establish such control at the congress of 1888, with the setting up of a *Commissie tot uitvoering van Bonds-besluiten* (Committee for the execution of Bond resolutions), consisting of six members of Parliament drawn from both Houses.* But the Bond members of Parliament themselves objected to such a body, which seemed to reflect on their own party loyalty and competence. In 1892, therefore, congress accepted the proposal that the chairman should informally assign to two Bond members of Parliament the task of reporting back to congress on the progress made over the implementation of earlier congress resolutions.* Such reports were thereafter regularly made, but until the South African war they were incorporated in the annual statement of either the chairman or the secretary.* A resolution of 1900, however, resulted in the appointment of two Bond parliamentarians with the task of presenting annual written reports, which thereafter became regular procedure.*

The establishment of a standing executive committee of congress might conceivably have bridged the gap between congress and the parliamentary caucus, though this would probably have involved an increase in the capitation levy on its branches in order to cover its members' travelling expenses. (The only Bond official to receive an honorarium was the secretary-treasurer, who received first £25 and later £50 a year.) The practical alternative adopted, which fitted in with Hofmeyr's desire to keep as much control as possible in his own hands, was to establish an unofficial head office in the capital, and to allow the parliamentary party, or the Cape Town branch when Parliament was not in session, to take the lead whenever necessity required. It was the Cape Town branch, for example, which approached Sprigg on the matter of a customs convention in January 1887, which set in motion the spate of protests against the policy of the Imperial Government in July 1899, and which inspired the revolt against 'one vote one value' in the National Convention. This informal arrangement was dictated by the parliamentary position of the Afrikaner Bond, which would have been untenable had the caucus been rigidly subordinated to congress or to a committee of congress. Because the Bond had no outright parliamentary majority, Hofmeyr was obliged to make what terms he could with political leaders outside the party, and for this he required freedom of movement. Had the Bond acquired an absolute parliamentary majority at any time, then the importance of congress would have been immediately enhanced, and the way laid open for a struggle for power within it; but as things were, the requirements of the Bond inside Parliament reacted on the form of its organization outside, by strengthening that tendency towards 'government from the roof' to which the foundation fathers had taken exception.

This tendency increased as time went on. The parliamentary party, which normally did its best to secure the implementation of congress resolutions so far as this could be done without jeopardizing its parliamentary position, was led by Hofmeyr until 1895. When Hofmeyr left Parliament in that year, the leadership of the Bond inside the House, so far as it was exercised by anybody, now passed in practice to Schreiner, and then to Merriman, both non-Bondsmen, though before the end of 1900 Theron, De Waal and F. S. Malan had acquired considerable parliamentary stature. Yet in a real sense Hofmeyr continued to lead from outside the House. This was very evident during the post-Raid crisis, and again in the months preceding the war, and even—though from a distance of 6,000 miles his touch was less certain—during the suspension crisis. Onze Jan's ascendancy may be illustrated from a letter written to him by Theron on 22 June 1899, from his home in Britstown. Theron explained that he had followed the crisis in Ons Land and the South African News, and 'admired' the manner in which Hofmeyr and the Government were conducting affairs. He awaited instructions from Hofmeyr as to when Bond meetings should be called and what resolutions ought to be carried. He who thus waited for orders was not only member for Richmond but also the chairman of the Bond provincial *bestuur*; but he could hardly have played a prominent part in the negotiations from his farm in the Karoo.

The link between the Afrikaner Bond and the South African Party, which dated from the time of Schreiner's ministry, had a decisive influence on the form of the party as well as on its outlook. It stood to reason that once this link had become an organic one, after the Somerset East congress of 1903, and the Bond organization outside Parliament had become constitutionally shackled to a parliamentary group of non-Bondsmen, the Bond was thereby precluded from pursuing political objectives from which only its own members were likely to benefit. It rephrased its long-term political objective to accommodate its parliamentary allies and to take post-war circumstances into account.* Even though it had the power in 1908, after its landslide electoral victory of that year, to form a Bond ministry, it was so tied to the South African Party—by inclination no less than by formal agreement—that no suggestion was made that it should do so. The South African Party, which provided three ministers, including the Premier, in Merriman's Cabinet of seven (the rest being Bondsmen), could claim to have a substantial non-Bond following in the Parliaments of 1903 and 1908;* but it had no formal existence outside the legislature despite the fact that all pro-Government candidates in the Lower House election in the latter year were classified in both the *South African News* and *Ons Land* as 'S.A.P.', the Bondsmen included. As a general rule, 'S.A.P.' candidates in this election were nominated according to the normal Bond procedure, at nomination meetings from which non-Bondsmen were excluded. Merriman, for example, who was not a Bondsman, was selected as a South African Party candidate for Victoria West at a meeting attended only by representatives of Bond branches in the constituency.* Occasionally local initiative would attempt to devise new procedures so as to give the South African Party some concrete existence in the localities. From Oudtshoorn, for example, a report reached *Ons Land* that 'the South African Party has now resolved to support Messrs. J. H. Schoeman, A. Fourie and Advocate Roché Pohl'; and Stellenbosch actually had a 'South African Party nomination meeting', conducted on lines which bore no resemblance at all to the recognized Bond procedures.* At Beaufort West the liaison between the Bond and

the South African Party broke down over the choice of a candidate.[1]
If Bond nomination procedures had worked normally in 1903,
it is doubtful whether such irregularities—for such they were—
would have been tolerated in 1908. The formal association between
Bond and S.A.P. was not intended to alter their relationship but to
establish it on a clearer footing; but by leaving some room for
ambiguity it did the reverse, while the grip of the *Commissie van
Toezicht* relaxed visibly when the tide of public opinion began to
flow in the South African Party's direction. The 1908 election
produced a crop of independent South African Party candidates,
some of whom had not even been mentioned at Bond nomination
meetings, who not only ran against official Bond nominees but in
some cases beat them, and were still classified after the election was
over as supporters of the South African Party Government.[2]

A recent authority on party organization has drawn a broad
distinction between parties which operate from the branch upwards
and those which operate from the caucus downwards. He has noted
'the general coincidence in practice of the caucus system with weak
articulation, of the branch system with strong articulation', observing
as a characteristic of highly articulated parties a 'multiplying [of]
co-ordinating bodies . . . creating, instead of a weakly organized
embryonic authority, a veritable machinery of government, including
a separation of powers: legislative power devolving upon the
"Congress" . . . executive power residing in an Executive Committee
. . . juridical power being entrusted to committees of "Arbitration",
or "Control", or settlement of "Disputes" '.* In the case of the
Afrikaner Bond, we have seen how the principle of strong articulation
applied with respect to the legislative authority of congress, which

[1] Thirty-five petitioners approached F. S. Malan on 19 Dec. 1907 protesting
that 'the S.A. Party (including several members belonging to the Bond) some
time back requisitioned Mr. Julius Robert Jackson of Nelspoort . . . to allow
himself to be nominated as a S.A. Party candidate for the Legislative Assembly.
Upon Mr. Jackson accepting the requisition, a circular letter, signed by influential members of the S.A.P., was sent to the various branches of the Bond.' But
the chairman of the Bond district *bestuur*, according to the petitioners, had sent
a circular to the branches 'intimating that Mr. Jackson cannot under any circumstances be nominated as it would be contrary to the constitution of the Bond',
with the result that at the nomination meetings Jackson got 'practically no
support', many not even knowing that he was a candidate (Hofmeyr Papers).

[2] W. Cloete (Aliwal North), and S. P. H. de Villiers, D. Retief and F. J.
Joubert (Paarl), all succeeded against official Bond candidates but remained
members of the S.A. Party caucus.

was designed ultimately to reflect the views of the Bondsmen in the wards; but also how—and here is to be seen the influence of the caucus principle—the executive authority, in which must be included the power to determine the tactics of the party in the political arena, was essentially informal, and devolved on the parliamentary leadership, whose constitutional relationship with the party outside Parliament was entirely undefined. The fact that the parliamentary leader also supervised party discipline had the effect of further emphasizing this tendency, to the point at which a dissatisfied member of the Bond, with pardonable exaggeration, could imagine that he saw 'a Bond dictatorship . . . established at the *Ons Land* office'. Du Toit, of course, wrote thus in pique; but the party's experience in connexion with the western province election of 1898 exposed the anomalies in an organization in which power was polarized without the relationship between the two extremes of power, the branch and the party leadership, being governed by clear written rules. In the last resort, however, the autonomy of the branch could be destroyed by the *Commissie van Toezicht*'s interpreting the sense of the party as a whole, and congress would endorse this kind of action taken on such grounds. In the last resort, too, congress could bring the parliamentary party to heel, as it did in 1895 over scab; but it normally chose not to interfere.

15

The Afrikaner Bond and Nationalism

THE structural features of the Afrikaner Bond discussed in the preceding pages throw light on its nature as a political party, but do not in themselves illustrate the purposes for which it was created or the ends for which it was used. These, however, are the most fundamental questions which can be asked about it; but since they draw the historian into the field of human motives, the answers offered must be tentative. In one sense or another, however, it can be said that the Afrikaner Bond was the vehicle of a nationalist movement. Yet to categorize it thus is to group it with a multitude of such movements which have filled the pages of historical works in modern times, and to impart no real distinctiveness to it.

In discussing nationalist movements, it is necessary above all to distinguish between those which support, and those which are ranged against, the authority of the state. The nationalism of revolutionary France, which is usually regarded as the prototype of the dynamic nationalist movements of modern times,* was *étatiste* in conception and aim, designed to buttress the state by providing the French people with an alternative focus of political loyalty to the monarchy which they had rejected. The nationalisms of central Europe which developed after the Napoleonic era, on the other hand, whether in their German, Italian, Polish or Austro-Hungarian forms, were usually ranged against the constituted authorities, because their objectives included the breaking up and redrawing of existing political frontiers so that national groups could become political nations in their own right. The importance of this distinction lies chiefly in the fact that, depending on whether or not they have achieved political consolidation and can therefore afford to be *étatiste*, nationalist movements have tended to breathe rather different kinds of fire. In the case of revolutionary France, the nationalist spirit was outward facing, assertive against external powers and disruptive of international order; but within the French frontiers it was reconciled to the existing framework of law and behaved, so to speak, 'normally'. In central Europe, on the other hand, the nationalist leader tended to develop an antagonism towards existing political authority and sought, by building up the group consciousness of his fellow nationals, to prepare them for political self-realization. The nationalism of a politically subject people of European origin, whether it has arisen out of frustration, or humiliation, or whatever cause, has normally been built upon the revival of a broken or derelict cultural heritage, with the emphasis laid in varying degrees on those factors which tend most to differentiate the subject people from their political overlords.[1] There is a danger, of course, in pressing the distinction between these two forms of nationalism too far, for nationalism, whether in the 'French' or 'German' sense as used above, has always depended for its vitality on the union of cultural and political pressures. It was the political act of state-making or state-breaking which gave rise to the revival of group traditions in the minds of central European nationalists, just as a conviction of his nation's cultural superiority helped to produce the French assimilationist or the British jingo. But the quality of the nationalism affects the mood of the nationalist, and mood is perhaps the most important underlying factor.

This book has hardly been concerned at all with nationalism of an *étatiste* kind, but rather with movements which have aimed at internal political change. Most South African nationalists in our period, it is safe to say, wanted to see a greater degree of unification, under more centralized government, of politically separated people. Their general aim, that is, was to consolidate rather than to disrupt, on the analogy of the nationalist movements in Germany or Italy rather than of those within Austria-Hungary. Beyond this, however, the South African nationalist could have desired, basically, one of two things, but not both of them together at the same time. On the one hand, he might have wanted the creation of a single South African state, unitary or federal, on the lines of one or other

---

[1] Mid-twentieth century colonial nationalism, by contrast, has generally been concerned to demonstrate not the superiority of its own indigenous institutions but the competence of its people to work the admittedly superior institutions of the colonial power.

of the schemes envisaged between the time of Sir George Grey and the formation of the South African Union, in which the main stress lay on the machinery to be devised to consolidate and harmonize the different political, economic, regional and cultural interests of the people. Alternatively, he might have intended the creation of a single state, the main purpose of which would be to give expression to the cultural, economic or other needs of the national group to which he belonged, perhaps at the expense of the interests of other groups, in which case the state would be conceived, not as an arbiter for the reconciliation of divergent interests, but as an instrument of power for the better protection of one.

To determine the position of the Afrikaner Bond in relation to these two lines of thought is not easy, because at one time or another different groups within it committed themselves to each of them. The Bond had arisen in the first instance in response to a deeply felt cultural need. Had it continued in existence with the sole object of satisfying that need, it would probably have anticipated by fifty years the 'purified' nationalism of the mid-twentieth century, with which it had certain roots in common. But the outstanding fact about the Afrikaner nationalism of the Cape in the period before 1912 is that the spirit of narrow exclusivism failed to crowd out the broader spirit of tolerance. There were two occasions in particular when it might have done so. The first was in the years between the British annexation of Basutoland in 1868 and of Bechuanaland in 1885, the second between the Jameson Raid and the South African war.

Between 1868 and 1885 many of the normal manifestations of a vigorous cultural nationalism were apparent—the awakening among the Afrikaner people of an awareness of the danger of cultural conquest, and of a sense of the epic quality of their own history, which helped to build up a strong feeling of group unity around the twin pivots of language and religion, fired in due course by the Transvaal's military success against the supposedly superior might of the Imperial conqueror. This combination of favourable circumstances produced a language movement, a national *History*, a national newspaper and a national political party, together with projects for the development of a distinctive national religion with its own system of education, and an economic policy rooted in the idea of group self-sufficiency. But for a multitude of reasons S. J. du Toit's movement failed to carry the Afrikaner people. He alienated the rank and file, as well as most of the leadership, by his unusually austere Calvinism. He was no match in politics either for Jan Hofmeyr or for Paul Kruger, who both had their reasons for rejecting his aims and ideas. Moreover, Du Toit's early concept of Afrikaner *volkseenheid* made no progress in the face of commercial rivalries between the South African states in the late eighties and early nineties, especially after Rhodes had tossed in his apple of discord by inviting help from all quarters in the opening of the North. Finally, though drawn up to fight a battle, the nationalists found when they came to the point that it was a battle hardly worthy of the name. In the Transvaal, it is true, the decision of the Imperial Government to annex lands to the west and north tended to keep anti-British feeling simmering; but there had been no new attempt to take away the independence which the Transvalers had won in their war of liberation. The Free Staters, who might have kept alive a similar resentment at the earlier British interference in their border lands, were satisfied by the eighties to be rid of Basutoland, which the Cape had since proved unable to control, and of the Diamond Fields, for this spared them an uitlander problem. In the Cape, the use of the Dutch language, the focal point of the Afrikaner's campaign for real equality, was extended as asked for without much parliamentary opposition, even if some resistance was still met outside the parliamentary field. If nationalism, in the words of a modern expert,* is 'essentially an anti-feeling [which] feeds and fattens on hatred and anger against other national groups, and especially against the foreign rulers of a subject country', then in the South Africa of the late eighties and early nineties it had to subsist on a spare diet.

The Jameson Raid, however, gave rise to a new cry for Afrikaner *volkseenheid*. The call this time was for more reflective soul-searching, as well as for solidarity in the face of immediate danger, and its fruits were seen in the defeat of those, like S. J. du Toit, who equivocated between support for Rhodes and loyalty to the Afrikaner cause; in the decision of Kruger's Government to eliminate so far as possible the Hollander influence in the Transvaal State; in fresh appeals to the Afrikaner not to allow himself to become tainted with alien mammon, and to return to his Bible. This new drive for *volkseenheid* was further stimulated from outside by the revival of the uitlander movement and the growth of the jingo South African League in the Milner period, coupled with increased Imperial pressure in local South African affairs. Yet, as had happened after Majuba, the Afrikaner national movement failed to gain real momentum. The Transvalers counted upon the unreserved support of the Cape Bond during the crisis of 1899, but they realized by August in that year that they would not be able to rely on it, even though the Free Staters were prepared to fall in behind them. Apart from their difficulties inherent in their situation as citizens of a British colony, the Cape Bond leaders were in any case too critical of the way in which the Transvaal Government had handled their side of the negotiations to come in whole-heartedly on their side. So, as the first phase of the pan-Afrikaner movement had disintegrated for lack of an enemy to fight, the second fell apart because the inner bonds were not yet strong enough to withstand an unusual degree of external pressure.

When war broke out in 1899 the Afrikaner people went through three years of hell. In their suffering and their anger, their attention was forced towards larger questions than those of mere group interest: questions touching the elementary freedoms of movement and self-expression and the use and abuse of arbitrary power; questions, in the last resort, of life and death, in a situation in which law and order often seemed to be contradictory terms. They had drawn up a petition of right, tried a grand remonstrance, and learned the need for self-control in the face of hostile and provocative officials. Pride in the signal successes of their guerrilla leaders had helped to sustain their morale; but the conditions of peace in 1902 were not those under which assertive nationalism could flourish, for the war and the surrender drove deep wedges between Afrikaner and Afrikaner which only time and sympathetic leadership could heal. With the conclusion of peace, therefore, the Afrikaner leaders stored away their desire for a restoration of republican independence, and this was hardly heard of again until the First World War. A campaign for a limited restoration of rights conducted in a mood of conciliation was the only realistic course open to them. The logic behind such a campaign rested partly on necessity, partly on the desirability of reducing tension for its own sake, and partly on the reasonable expectation that if the right kind of atmosphere were created the British Parliament would respond in the right way and remove authoritarian controls.

Conciliation worked, and soon brought in the right atmosphere for the reassertion of the Afrikaner's traditional cultural claims. It was significant that the desire for Christian National Education, which before the war had barely received support outside the Transvaal, should have won a favourable vote at a Bond congress in 1908 when the conciliatory mood was at its height. The original spirit of S. J. du Toit's nationalism was never extinguished altogether, and survived above all in the spheres of religion and language.

Most Bondsmen professed adherence to the Reformed religion, and acted on their profession. This gave their society a distinctive flavour, and a wide range of common standards in public and private life, which even the differences of outlook between the Dutch Reformed Churches did not substantially affect, save on a few important occasions. At the institutional level, first of all, we may note the importation into Bond procedure of various practices common to church meetings, such as the calling for letters of credence (*geloofsbrieven*) from delegates to conferences, and more especially the almost universal practice at all levels of beginning and ending meetings with prayer. Bondsmen were on the whole very conscious of their church membership. Local Bond leaders were often members of their local *kerkraden*. Many clergy were members of the Bond, some of them participating actively in politics both inside and outside Parliament. From their point of view the national revival had a spiritual as well as a secular side. As they had taken the lead in the Dutch language movement, so they expected the politicians to supplement the influence of the pulpit; and many must have derived satisfaction from the amount of attention paid by Bond congresses to topics falling within the range of Sunday observance. The Sunday sermon became a regular feature of the annual congress proceedings, and it was thought proper, at any rate on special occasions such as these, to extol the nationalist virtues from the pulpit.[1]

Equally important as a unifying force was the central position given in Bond propaganda to language questions, both before and after the South African war. Which language was ultimately to secure official adoption was not determined in our period; but so great was the enthusiasm for linguistic emancipation, and so great

[1] See for example the sermon of Ds. D. H. Celliers, addressed to the delegates to the Burghersdorp congress in 1896. He spoke on Mordecai the Jew, 'seeking the best for his people', and commended him for retaining his Jewish identity in alien surroundings as 'the true Patriot, the upright Bondsman', an example for all to follow. The full text was published in the report reprinted from *De Paarl*.

the value of the *Taal* as an emblem under which Afrikaners of varying origins could unite, that language may be taken as the central symbol of the nationalist movement in these years. It proved a successful rallying point at times when other types of appeal—for a republic under its own flag, for economic independence, for Christian National Education—all failed to win general support. The struggle for language rights took place both inside and outside the parliamentary field, and although parliamentary opposition was slight, the campaign required untiring effort on the part of its sponsors in order to maintain the necessary degree of public enthusiasm, which helped to keep the nationalist spirit alive. If Dutch was to achieve equal status with English in practice, it had to be spoken and written, and its use had to be made a matter of pride. The Taalbond took on this task, with its own range of incentives, and it received the warm and material support of Bond congresses throughout the period between its inception and Union. To the efforts of the Taalbond would be added in the post-war period those of the Afrikaanse Taalvereniging and the Afrikaanse Taalgenootskap, and eventually those of the Akademie from 1909.

But once allowance has been made for the enduring influence of cultural factors such as these on the outlook of the Afrikaner, it remains true that the Bond, under Hofmeyr's guidance, did much to resist the tendency towards Afrikaner exclusiveness which was implicit in Du Toit's earlier approach. Its choice of the designation *Afrikaner* Bond has often been taken to imply the opposite, and the Bond slogan, '*Afrika voor de Afrikaners*', has been used as evidence of the narrow racialism of the movement. To the twentieth-century English reader, for whom the term *Afrikaner* has come to signify a white Afrikaans-speaking South African, this argument must have some force. Even to the nineteenth-century reader, *Afrikaner* and its semi-anglicized form *Africander* carried a cultural nuance not present in the geographical though not yet politically meaningful term *South African*. Some English-speaking people, like J. T. Molteno, described themselves as Afrikaners. Others, like Sir James Rose Innes, did not. Yet others, like F. J. Dormer, added the prefix *Anglo-*, which corresponded with the expression *Hollandsche Afrikaanders* normally used by Jan Hofmeyr to describe people of his own language group. All that can safely be said, therefore, is that the word *Afrikaner* and its variants could be used more naturally in the late nineteenth century to describe any white South African than is the case in the mid-twentieth, but that even at that time it did not reassure the English-speaker who was not prepared to be convinced.[1]

The Bondsmen, nevertheless, tried in all their official policy statements to reassure English waverers. Even S. J. du Toit's draft constitution of July 1879 had proposed to admit to membership 'anybody who has chosen Africa as his fatherland, and aims at Africa's welfare, no matter what his national origin is, or to what ecclesiastical or citizen group he otherwise belongs'.[2] The formula adopted at the Richmond congress in 1883, which remained the accepted Bond doctrine throughout our period, stated: 'The Bond knows no nationality of any kind save that of the Afrikaners, and considers as belonging to it everybody, of whatever origin, who aims at the welfare of South Africa.'[3] Hofmeyr stated explicitly on a later occasion that he included in the term *Afrikaner* 'everyone who, having settled in this country, wants to stay here to help to promote our common interests, and associate with the inhabitants as members of one family. That is surely wide enough; it is neither narrow nor exclusive.'* So long as political advantage was to be gained by disarming English-speaking critics or attracting English votes, it would of course have been bad tactics to adopt a narrow definition, and for this reason some caution should be observed in accepting these policy statements at their full face value. But Hofmeyr certainly meant what he said, provided one limits the scope of his definition to white people, and his great personal influence on the Bond makes it reasonably certain that a very high proportion of its members thought like him. Such people, it seems, wanted to build a state in which all white South Africans would feel equal and at home.

Did they still feel the same after the Anglo-Boer war? There was no manifest popular desire among Afrikaners after the war to drive

[1] Compare Fremantle's early 20th century view (pp. 18–19) with Marquard (p. 57), who writes that 'until the first decade of this century' the word *Afrikaner* meant a white South African whose mother tongue was Afrikaans', and that the word has since been narrowed by Afrikaner nationalists to refer to themselves, non-nationalists tending more and more to prefer the epithet *Suid-Afrikaner*.

[2] 'Elkeen wat Afrika tot syn vaderland gekies het, en Afrika's welvaart bedoel, onverskillig wat syn nasionale afkoms is, of tot watter kerkelike of burgerlike party hy origens behoor.'

[3] 'De Bond kent geen nationaliteit hoegenaamd dan alleen die der Afrikaners, en beschouwt als daartoe behoorend een ieder, van welke afkomst ook, die de welvaart van Zuid-Afrika beoogt.'

the English-speakers out, and the whole emphasis of the Boer conciliation policy rested on the assumption that they would remain. It was, in this sense, conspicuously humane. But no Afrikaner political leader between 1905 and 1912 could risk supporting proposals which offered the prospect of effective political power to their opponents. In their negotiations with Campbell-Bannerman and the West Ridgeway Committee in 1906, Smuts and the Het Volk leaders showed more concern over the ultimate distribution of power than over the need for securing a constitution which would give an even reflection of public opinion. The argument over urban and rural constituencies at the Bloemfontein session of the National Convention, during which the Free Staters and Cape Bondsmen refused to accept the principle of 'one vote one value', was treated by them as of greater importance than the argument over provincial quotas and the means whereby these were determined. Hofmeyr showed in his letters to Steyn at that time that he was extremely worried lest the eventual incorporation of Rhodesia in the Union might tip the balance against the associated parties, and saw this as a long-term danger against which it was necessary to make immediate provision. The adamant refusal of the associated-party leaders on the eve of Union to have anything to do with a coalition govern-ment is only in part explicable by patronage difficulties, and must be linked with the conviction of those leaders that the road to proper conciliation lay through the 'annihilation' of the Unionist opposition, both at the polls and as a political party. The only acceptable organization for bringing the white groups together, they said by implication, was one over which they exercised control.

This conviction, for such it assuredly was, stemmed from various roots. Humanly speaking, it would have been asking a lot of a community which had recently paid in suffering for its lack of power to suggest that it should relax its grip on the power which it had now acquired. They would first have needed to be convinced that the pursuits of the Rand capitalists and the outside groups which backed them were not hostile to the long-term interests of the Afrikaner population, and this at a time when the memory of Chinese labour was very fresh, and landless Afrikaners who were beginning to move into the cities were getting their first view of capitalists not merely as aliens but as members of a social class ranged against themselves. From another point of view, genuine South Africanism still meant for most Afrikaners the possession of roots in the South African soil and in no other, and the Unionists were thought to fail by that test. Whether it was possible to possess South African roots which differed substantially from those of the Afrikaner and still pass as acceptable to him was not a subject to which the cultural experts had yet given much thought; but the impression prevails that Afrikaner nationalists at the time of Union did not insist on a high degree of conformity with themselves. The objections to Merriman as a prime minister of the Union did not include the argument that he was deficient in South African patriotism, while the support which he received from Bondsmen in spite of the unpopularity of his economic policy shows that to a very high degree he was accepted by Afrikaners, not as one of themselves but as an outsider in whom they could place complete trust. Hertzog, who stressed the utilitarian reasons for membership of the British Empire and rejected the emotional, was a strict egalitarian in his cultural demands. S. J. du Toit's original brand of Afrikaner exclusiveness would have been out of tune with the times. But the Afrikaner was coming to claim the right, by virtue of his stronger identity with and longer experience of South African conditions, to set the tone of public policy.

The nationalism of the Afrikaner Bond, and of the associated parties after the war, was something wider than the nationalism of an oppressed and exclusive cultural group, and it was narrower than a simple Cape Colonial or South African patriotism. Common sense told the Cape Bondsmen before the war that a narrow cultural nationalism would lead them into a cul-de-sac, for, unlike their Afrikaner kinsmen in the Orange Free State and Transvaal, they did not have political control of the state, nor the apparent prospect of having it except in alliance with others. They were therefore ready to welcome the support of white non-Afrikaners who looked sympathetically upon their cultural aspirations and were prepared to go part of the way along the road. This disposition of the Afrikaner Bond before the war was in general true, not only of itself, but of Het Volk, the Orangia Unie and the Natal Boerekongres afterwards.

On the other hand, these organizations neither had nor, with the exception of the Bond, saw the need to ask for the political support of non-white people, and even the Bond limited membership to whites in practice. From the strictly political angle, this decision had been difficult for the Afrikaner Bond to make. Coloured and African voters did not constitute more than a small fraction of the

Cape electorate; but they did hold the balance in a few constituencies. The Bondsmen nevertheless chose to forgo the political advantages which the accommodation of such people would have brought in its train (though they went to considerable trouble to avoid policy statements which were overtly offensive to them), and were able to get away with it because, when it came to the point, their Progressive opponents declined to make use of the opportunity which the squeamishness of the Bondsmen gave them. If the South African League had risen to the occasion in 1896 and created, out of a multi-racial electorate, a multi-racial political party, instead of contenting itself with ill grace with a poorly developed system of non-white branches, the Bond would not have been able to afford the luxury of racial isolation. Whether it would have been politically possible for the League to act thus is at best a debatable question; but it is safe to argue in reverse that the Cape liberal tradition could only have acquired substantial content, sufficient for it to withstand the buffeting which it received at the National Convention and after-wards, if it had been taken up and consolidated within the framework of the Cape political parties.

Here, then, is the real measure of Bond nationalism. The Bonds-men were able, on the whole, to keep their exclusive group feelings within bounds, save in reaction against the more extravagant manifestations of British imperialism. But together with, and to some extent in advance of, their political opponents, they did much to foster the more insidious racialism of the white colonial. The associated parties amalgamated with each other before they had achieved a proper meeting of minds on questions of race. Northern parties, committed in principle to the doctrine of racial inequality, made common cause with a Cape party which accepted racial equality in a limited political sense. It stood to reason that, unless one side or the other surrendered, they could have no general policy after amalgamation on what became the central question of South African public life. Nor, in view of the necessity of presenting a united front to the electorate, were they very well placed to raise the matter in public at all. Taking their lead from Botha, therefore, whose original proposals were an amalgam of contradictory senti-ments until they were rendered meaningless by Malan, they nailed the only possible flag to their mast and proclaimed as a principle 'the placing of the native question above party politics, and the honour-able and sympathetic treatment of the coloured races in a broad and liberal spirit'. This formula encouraged warm feelings rather than cool thoughts, and helped to establish the convention whereby the development of a purposeful policy over racial questions was kept out of public life altogether. But when minds abdicated the task, traditional sentiments took over, and through the medium of their increasingly efficient and increasingly impersonal organizations the associated parties became instruments for the passing on of the social and political assumptions of the age of the Great Trek into the society and politics of the Union of South Africa.

Notes

CHAPTER 1

society. Scholtz, J. du P., pp. 175–6.

time. Cape Argus, 9 Nov. 1882.

proceedings. Hofmeyr, p. 235. The *Grahamstown Journal* showed on 18 and 19 Sept. 1882 that the number of exotic magistrates was in fact smaller than commonly supposed. Of the 72 who then held office, it claimed, 49 were Cape born, of whom 'about thirty are of Dutch extraction'. But there was undoubtedly a cultural incompatibility even between some Afrikaner magistrates, who had absorbed English influences in their training, and the Boers of the districts which they served.

Dutch. See A. 13—1880: minutes of evidence, pp. 6, 32.

enterprise. See, for example, Varley and Matthew, pp. 190–1, 210; Wepener, pp. 25–7.

bodies. e.g. Graaff-Reinet, Mossel Bay, Burghersdorp and Queenstown. See Immelman, *passim.*

O'Brien. Burghersdorp Gazette, 8 Mar. 1878.

1883. Worcester Advertiser, 1 Mar. 1883.

Vereeniging. Beaufort Courier, 17 Jan. 1882.

new. Zuid Afrikaan, 8 Mar. 1883.

1865. By Act 4 of 1865.

task. Cf. Du Toit, S. J. (2), p. 140: 'Die Distriksrade is omtrent so's die Heem-rade eers was. Een van die voordele hiervan was dat die Boere leer om meer belang te stel in publieke sake' ['The Divisional Councils are like the Heemraden used to be. One of their advantages was that the Boers learned to take more interest in public affairs'.]

result. Scholtz, J. du P., pp. 116–18. English had been made the language of Parliament by section 89 of the Constitution Ordinance of 1853.

carpet-baggers. The Paarl paper, *Die Afrikaanse Patriot,* caught the atmosphere of Boer indifference on 31 Jan. 1879, when it complained that parliamentary candidature was reserved for a few English merchants, Jews and their associates, while the Boer population sat still, nominated no candidates of their own, and either stayed at home on polling day or were obliged to vote for one of these 'self-appointed glory-seekers' (*self-opgeworpe erebejagers*). For a totally different view of the effects of carpet-bagging, see Dormer, pp. 80–1.

stocked. Cape Argus, 25 Sept. 1882.

CHAPTER 2

numbers. On the ecclesiastical conflict, see especially the works by S. P. Engelbrecht, T. N. Hanekom, G. B. A. Gerdener and D. P. Faure, listed in the bibliography.

1870's. See especially Scholtz, J. du P., p. 164; Van Jaarsveld, pp. 93, 112–13.

it. De Waal, J. H. H. (1), pp. 58–60. Cf. Hofmeyr, pp. 138–9.

ministry. Hofmeyr, p. 124.

Blake. Hofmeyr, p. 84. See also Van Jaarsveld, p. 100.

expenditure. e.g. *Zuid Afrikaan,* 1 June 1878, 2 Apr. 1879. 'Alzoo blijft er slechts één middel over om het oor de Rijksregering te bereiken', wrote Hofmeyr on the last of these occasions, 'te weten, in de Transvaal te blijven bij lijdelijk verzet, en in de Kolonie te weigeren te confedereren zoo lang dat verzet voorduurt' ['And so there is only one way left to get at the Imperial Government, namely to stick to passive resistance in the Transvaal, and in the Colony to refuse to confederate for as long as that resistance lasts'].

land-hunger. Zuid Afrikaan, 23 Apr. 1879.

all. Zuid Afrikaan, 26, 29 June 1878.

produce. Patriot, 2 Aug. 1878.

force. Patriot, 15 June 1877. After receiving the printed report of a congress of English-speaking farmers' associations held in Grahamstown, the editor asked why such associations could not be formed in the Western Province, Free State and Transvaal.

time. Hofmeyr set out his ideas at length in editorials in the *Zuid Afrikaan* on 27, 31 July 1878. See also Hofmeyr, pp. 147 ff.

discussion. The account of the formation and establishment of the *Z.A. Boeren Beschermings Vereeniging,* which follows, is based on reports in the *Zuid Afrikaan* and on the printed records of the Vereeniging in the Hofmeyr Papers.

adopted. The text given in Hofmeyr, pp. 643–5, is that of the unamended draft accepted on 12 Aug. 1878, and discussed at the meeting of 31 Oct. On the latter occasion two minor changes were made: (*a*) Article VI was amended to enable more than one local *vereeniging* to exist in any fiscal or electoral division—a concession to Wellington, whose members wished to remain separate from Paarl; and (*b*) Article XIII was altered to increase the membership of the *hoofdbestuur* (head committee) to seventeen.

seats. Article XXIII stated that the Vereeniging would not 'interfere with party politics as such, but . . . pursue [its] objects . . . regardless of any effect such course of conduct may have on the state of Parliamentary parties'. This article, drawn up at a time when no parties existed in the Cape Parliament, seems to have been intended to prevent the Vereeniging from tying itself to any other group in the House, and free it to pursue an independent course—if not as a party in its own right, then at least as a compact and independent pressure group.

PAGE 17

return. Zuid Afrikaan, 13 Nov. 1878.

inactive. A correspondent told the *Zuid Afrikaan*, 10 June 1880, that the Worcester branch 'is in een diepen slaap gevallen'.

PAGE 18

constitution. Volksblad, 23 Nov. 1880.

1882. See Hofmeyr, p. 190.

time. Notulen, Speciale Vergadering der Z.A.B.B. Vereeniging, 10 Mar. 1882 (Hofmeyr Papers).

PAGE 19

Town. Zuid Afrikaan, 5 Oct. 1878.

Bond. This article, by A. S. du Plessis, which appeared in *De Tolk*, 1 Sept. 1882, is also quoted in Du Toit, pp. 150–1.

early. Burghersdorp Gazette, 1 Sept., 6 Oct. 1882. The theory propounded here is that the Albert Vereeniging was formed in 1878 to promote the election of Andries Stockenstrom to the House of Assembly.

PAGE 20

Afrikaan. Burghersdorp Gazette, 4, 11 Oct. 1878; 21 Feb., 7 Mar. 1879. *Zuid Afrikaan*, 9 Oct. 1878.

mercy. Burghersdorp Gazette, 21, 28 June 1878. Hopley, it said, 'preferred the pusillanimous method to sneak away from the ranks of either side and vote neither way when the time came. Such political cowardice our member will find will have its own reward. Happily, the session is the last of this Parliament; we can confidently assert that it will be the last one in which Mr. Hopley will ever find a seat in the House.'

influence. Burghersdorp Gazette, 24 Oct. 1879.

1879. Burghersdorp Gazette, 30 May 1879.

Sichel. Burghersdorp Gazette, 19 Sept. 1879 (my italics).

PAGE 21

Africa. Burghersdorp Gazette, 8 Aug. 1879 (taken over from the *Volksblad*).
importance. Burghersdorp Gazette, 26 Sept. 1879.
peace. Burghersdorp Gazette, 24 Oct., 14 Nov. 1879.

PAGE 22

associations. Zuid Afrikaan, 15 Nov.; *Patriot*, 24 Oct. 1879; Du Toit, p. 33.
spirit. Zuid Afrikaan, 15 Nov. 1879 [Dutch original].

consultation. *Zuid Afrikaan*, 19 Nov. 1879, replying to *Volksblad* of 18 November.

Maraisburg. *Zuid Afrikaan*, 3 Mar. 1880.

elections. *Zuid Afrikaan*, 11 Mar. 1880.

it. *Zuid Afrikaan*, 1, 3 Apr. 1880 [Dutch original].

PAGE 23

crisis. For Van den Heever's expedition, see *Zuid Afrikaan*, 29 Jan., 3, 8, 12, 15, 17 Feb.; *Patriot*, 7, 28 Jan. 1881.

mission. The text of Van den Heever's report on his visit is given in the *Zuid Afrikaan*, 15 Feb. 1881.

desire. *Middelburg Gazette*, 25 Jan. 1881.

PAGE 24

1880. See the manuscript biographical sketch by R. Kilpin in the J. W. Jagger Library, University of Cape Town.

politics. *Cradock Register*, 16 Jan., 25 June 1880.

PAGE 25

name. This is plain from the following reports of meetings: *Zuid Afrikaan*, 26 May; *Patriot*, 27 May 1881 [conversion to the Bond]; *Cradock Register*, 14 Apr., supported in *Zuid Afrikaan*, 27 June, denied by *Patriot*, 30 June, but confirmed beyond question in *Zuid Afrikaan*, 11 Nov. 1882 [return to 'Vereeniging, status].

July. *Northern Post*, 23 July 1881; *Der Boeren Bode*, 8 Apr. 1882.

PAGE 27

party. These points are considered in more detail in ch. 7.

CHAPTER 3

PAGE 29

Paarl. For biographical information on the Du Toit brothers, the fullest source is J. D. du Toit, *Ds. S. J. du Toit in Weg en Werk*. See also Nienaber (2) and Von Wielligh (2).

PAGE 30

schools. For the Paarl split, see Du Toit, pp. 17–18; Oberholster, pp. 21–3.

told. It has been told at greater length by Scholtz and Du Toit in the works referred to. See also De Villiers (2).

Afrikaans. Du Toit, ch. XIV.

worship. Du Toit, pp. 65–70; Von Wielligh (1), pp. 17–21. The rules of the Genootskap were printed in Du Toit, S. J. (3), pp. 51–3.

society. Hofmeyr, p. 75; Du Toit, pp. 78–9; De Villiers (1), p. 98.

PAGE 31

languages. Von Wielligh (1), p. 83.

costs. Du Toit, pp. 65–6, 77–8.

PAGE 32

Toit. For information and commentary on the *Geskiedenis*, see Du Toit, pp. 75–6; Van Jaarsveld, pp. 96–101; Van Niekerk, pp. 18–22.

PAGE 33

action. Patriot, 24 Aug. 1877. ['Soos gewoonlik, meer *gepraat* as gedaan.']

PAGE 34

itself. The following paragraph, taken from an editorial of 1 Dec. 1882, entitled 'Di Volk syn Wil is di Wet van God' ['The Will of the People is the Law of God'], is a particularly good example:

'Di hoogste wet is di wil van di volk. Wat di volk wil moet wet worre. En as 'n volk ni eenstemmig is ni, dan gaat dit by meerderheid van stemme. Di meerderheid maak di wet. . . . Geen regering kan staan teen di volkswil. En so is di wil van di volk di hoogste wet en daar dit tog al te erg sou wees, dat 'n heel nasie sou sê: daar is geen God, en di mens tog ni onder God wil staan, so is dan di wil van di volk di wet van God geworre. . . . '

PAGE 35

afterwards. For example, *Patriot,* 24 Oct. 1879 ['Die Genootskap had . . . sowel 'n politieke as 'n taalkundige doel']; Von Wielligh (2), pp. 52–3.

purpose. Volksblad, 7, 17 June; *Patriot,* 13, 20 June; *Zuid Afrikaan,* 18 June 1879; Du Toit, pp. 142–7.

PAGE 37

House. Zuid Afrikaan, 25 June 1879; Hofmeyr, p. 197; Du Toit, pp. 140–6.

Bond. This document, entitled an *Ontwerp van Bepalings* (draft regulations) was printed in the *Patriot,* 4 July 1879, and reprinted in the *Afrikaanse Almanak ver 1882.*

PAGE 38

follow. Patriot, 12 Dec. 1879.

Netherlands. For S. J. du Toit's theological views, see Du Toit, ch. XVI, and Oberholster, *passim.*

PAGE 39

present. Patriot, 29 Oct. 1880; Oberholster, p. 25.

it. Du Toit, pp. 345–8 [Neo-Calvinism and temperance], 152 [establishment of the Hopetown Bond branch]; *Northern Post,* 12 June; *Burghersdorp Gazette,* 10 Sept. 1880; *Patriot,* 24 Dec. 1880, 21 Jan. 1881 [Ettie Schreiner's mission and subsequent divisions in the Hopetown congregation]. For the persistence of Neo-Calvinist views in the Hopetown Bond branch, see the *Notule Boek,* Tak no. 3, Hopetown, under 25 May, 28 Aug. 1894.

Patriot. *Patriot*, 29 Oct. 1880 [the Elder of Maraisburg].

Bond. Du Toit, pp. 152–4.

PAGE 40

them. *Patriot*, 28 Jan. 1881; Oberholster, p. 27.

branch. *Patriot*, 24 Feb. 1882 [giving as office-bearers of the new Petrusville congregation: Stephanus du Plessis and Andries Izel (elders), and Petrus van der Walt, Kalkpoort, and Corneles Fourie (deacons)]; Du Toit, loc. cit. [mentioning a Stef. du Plessis as a speaker at the Bond meeting of 5 January, and naming as branch committee members A. Yzel, C. Fourie, and Petrus van der Walt, Kalkpoort].

guidance. For the influence of the *Patriot* in the Transvaal, see Du Toit, pp. 224–6; Coetzee, p. 75.

PAGE 41

back. *Patriot*, 22 Feb. 1878.

verset. *Patriot*, 8 Oct. 1880.

PAGE 43

accordingly. *Zuid Afrikaan*, 24 Mar., 9, 14 Apr.; *Patriot*, 1 Apr. 1881. A copy of this constitution exists in the Hofmeyr Collection.

them. *East London Dispatch*, 9 Sept. 1882.

take. Report in the *Zuid Afrikaan*, 21 Oct. 1882.

instead. *Patriot*, 7 Oct.; *Zuid Afrikaan*, 27 Oct. 1881.

PAGE 44

cause. See *Bedford Guardian*, 11 Feb.; *Volksbode*, 24, 31 May; *Bedford Advertiser*, 16 Sept. 1882.

year. See *Opregte Afrikaner* and *Volksbode*, 22 Nov. 1882.

PAGE 45

Patriot. *Zuid Afrikaan*, 10 Mar.; *Patriot*, 11 Mar. 1881.

September. *Patriot*, 29 July, 9 Sept.; *Zuid Afrikaan*, 11 Aug., 17 Sept. 1881.

Bond. *Zuid Afrikaan*, 4 Aug.; *Patriot*, 9 Sept. 1881.

Paarl. *Patriot*, 16 Sept. 1881.

cognizance. *Notulen*, 21 Sept. 1881 (Hofmeyr Papers).

PAGE 46

excise. This emerged very clearly in the debate on the excise at the special meeting of 10 Mar. 1882.

discussed. *Notulen*, 10 Mar. 1882 (Hofmeyr Papers).

Basutoland. *Express*, 20 Jan. 1881.

April. Text in the Hofmeyr Collection. According to Hofmeyr, p. 199, it was drawn up by Borckenhagen in collaboration with Chief Justice F. W. Reitz and Messrs. Voigt and Esselen, two men who had abandoned their medical studies at Edinburgh to tend the Boer wounded in the Transvaal war.

PAGE 47

whole. Express, 12, 19 May 1881.

existence. Friend, 9 June; *Express*, 30 June; *Patriot*, 8 July 1881.

government. Express, 27 Oct. 1881 [text of the Bond address and of Brand's reply]; Fraser, pp. 79–82.

PAGE 48

opinion. Express, 3 Nov. 1881.

charge. Patriot, 4 Nov. 1881, 24 Feb. 1882.

fifty-one. Express, 29 Sept. 1881; *Afrikaanse Almanak ver 1882*, pp. 52–6.

bestuur. Coetzee, p. 215, has noted the absence of any report of the congress at which the Free State provincial *bestuur* was founded, but claims to have discovered that Reitz presided from references which he does not specify.

Brand. See the analysis in Coetzee, pp. 219–21, 239–40.

1881. Mouton, p. 111.

August. Coetzee, p. 222; *Volksstem*, 17 Aug., 2 Nov. 1881.

PAGE 49

gate. Volksstem, 19 Oct., 2 Nov. 1881.

branches. Bond MSS., Library of Parliament, p. 85; *Volksstem*, 24 May 1882; Du Toit, pp. 172–3; Coetzee, p. 225.

Potchefstroom. Bond MSS., Library of Parliament, p. 65; *Volksstem*, 15 Jan. 1884; Coetzee, p. 227.

PAGE 50

Colony. Amphlett, pp. 202–3, shows a steady increase in the Bank's dividend between 1865 and 1881.

depositors. Patriot, 24 Mar. 1882.

bank. Zuid Afrikaan, 12 Oct. 1882.

PAGE 51

paper. Patriot, 29 Apr. 1881, in an editorial outburst against 'the soakers, the robbers and the reds', perhaps the most extreme statement of S. J. du Toit's anti-British position. See also Du Toit, pp. 212–18.

boycott. For Hofmeyr's views on farmer's co-operatives, see *Zuid Afrikaan*, 13, 16 Aug. 1881.

difficulties. Van Winter, i, 54, 91.

it. Text in Du Toit, pp. 185–9. The Programme was issued from the home of D. P. van den Heever at Ventersburg.

principle. Kuyper, pp. 1–6, gives the original *Program* on which S. J. du Toit's was based. The *Patriot* on 3 Mar. 1882 described Kuyper's document as the fruit of years of thought by brilliant men. It had been published on 1 Jan. 1878 by the central committee of the Anti-Revolutionary Party as a platform for the Dutch Lower House elections.

philosophy. S. J. du Toit's commentary was published in pamphlet form as the *Program van Beginselen van de Nationale Partij, Opgesteld, Verklaard en Toegelicht*, being a collection of press articles, the last dated 21 Feb. 1884.

CHAPTER 4

PAGE 54

result. e.g. *Patriot*, 29 July 1881. ['Mar dit word hoog tyd dat die Hoofbestuur van die B.B. Vereniging die voorstel ernstig ter harte neem . . . om te verklaar in welke verhouding hulle tot die Afrikaner Bond staat, en om so molik te verenig.']

August. Patriot, 27 May 1881.

place. Patriot, 10, 17 June 1881.

PAGE 55

purpose. Patriot, 29 July 1881.

vereenigingen. Zuid Afrikaan, 4 Aug. 1881.

within. Hofmeyr, pp. 202–3.

present. Patriot, 17 Mar., *Zuid Afrikaan*, 9 Mar., *Middelburg Getuige*, 11 Mar. 1882; Hofmeyr p. 203.

PAGE 56

purpose. Zuid Afrikaan, 9, 11 Mar. 1882.

PAGE 57

right. Patriot, 17 Mar. 1882.

PAGE 58

principle. Zuid Afrikaan, 3 Aug., 2 Sept. 1882. None of the other branch meetings between May and September expressed themselves clearly on the subject of fusion. Contrast Hofmeyr, p. 203, and Coetzee, p. 114.

event. According to the *Uitenhage Times*, whose editor was present in person, the *Cape Times, Volksblad, Zuid Afrikaan* and the Cradock journals all sent correspondents. The *Patriot* was not represented, but derived its information from the *Volksblad* and *Zuid Afrikaan*, and gave space in the issues of 20, 27 Oct. and 10 Nov. to the account of a dissatisfied member of the congress. A full report, though not a first-hand one, appeared in *De Tolk* on 29 Sept. See also the official *Notulen van het Afrikaansch National Congres gehouden te Cradock* (Hofmeyr Collection).

PAGE 59

kind. See, for example, *De Tolk*, 11 Apr., 23 May 1883 (reports of meetings at Fraserburg and Vlekpoort, Cradock respectively) for reasons why the name 'Afrikaner Bond' could not be given up.

groups. See N. F. de Waal's advice in the *Middelburg Getuige*, 12 Aug. 1882.

strings. Hofmeyr, pp. 203–4.

carried. Volksbode (Bedford), 4 Oct. 1882.

PAGE 60

work. A large majority favoured these proposals. Several of the sources state that 7 votes were cast against the motion, but none indicate whose they were.

Heerden. This was J. A. van Heerden of Murraysburg. There were three other J. van Heerdens present.

latter. Patriot, 15 Sept. 1882.

resolution. Patriot, 3 Nov. 1882.

PAGE 61

instead. Hofmeyr, pp. 201–2.

face. Patriot, 6, 13 Oct. 1882; Du Toit, pp. 165–6.

Cradock. Patriot, 24 Nov. 1882.

Bondsmen. Opregte Afrikaner, 18 Oct., *Zuid Afrikaan*, 24 Oct., *De Tolk*, 27 Oct. 1882.

PAGE 62

Africa. The full text of this long resolution was published in *De Tolk*, 3 Nov., and *Zuid Afrikaan*, 2 Dec. 1882.

without. Hofmeyr, p. 202.

it. Sampson, p. 59.

constitution. Zuid Afrikaan, 28 Oct., 4 Nov. 1882.

resolution. e.g. Queenstown (*Patriot*, 17 Nov. 1882).

haste. e.g. Komgha (*Patriot*, 1 Dec. 1882).

assent. Zuid Afrikaan, 21 Nov. 1882; *De Tolk*, 10 Jan. 1883.

split. Zuid Afrikaan, 16 Nov. 1882.

PAGE 63

bestuur. Coetzee, pp. 118–19, has corrected Hofmeyr (p. 205 on this point).

PAGE 64

consultative. Zuid Afrikaan, 14 Dec. 1882. The *Patriot* supported Hofmeyr's plan on 12 Jan. 1883.

date. De Tolk, 10 Jan. 1883.

public. Zuid Afrikaan, 16 Jan. 1883.

standing. Zuid Afrikaan, 3 Feb. 1883.

purpose. For the Hanover meeting, see *De Tolk*, 21 Feb. 1883.

hoofdbestuur. Zuid Afrikaan, 15 Feb. 1883.

PAGE 65

February. See the *Rapport van de Commissie over de Ineensmelting van den Afrikaander Bond en de Boerenbeschermingsvereeniging* (Hofmeyr Collection).

PAGE 67

outvoted. The attitude of the *Patriot* may be gleaned from editorials and special articles in the following issues: 2 Feb., 9, 16, 23, 30 Mar., 6 and 13 Apr. 1883. For D. F. du Toit's attitude immediately before the Richmond congress, see the report of a Bond meeting at Daljosaphat in the *Patriot*, 18 May 1883.

vereenigingen. The following Bond branches rejected fusion on principle without waiting for the commission report: Prince Albert (*De Tolk*, 10 Jan. 1883), Ceres (*Patriot*, 24 Nov. 1882), Bedford (*Zuid Afrikaan*, 29 May 1883). The report was rejected by some or all Fraserburg branches (*De Tolk*, 11 Apr. 1883),

Vlekpoort, Cradock (ibid.), Daljosaphat (*Patriot*, 18 May 1883), West Uitvlugt, Richmond (*De Tolk*, 23 May 1883), and possibly a few others. Such branches usually wanted the adoption of the Transvaal document. A larger number of branches preferred Du Toit's views on 'Christian' education, or the *Program van Beginsels*, or the colour bar, without rejecting the report as a whole.

Reports of *boeren vereeniging* meetings in the *Zuid Afrikaan* between 3 and 22 May 1883 reveal no major disagreement with the commission report, though Tulbagh and Uniondale preferred 'Christian' education.

bestuur. The *Notulen* of the 1883 Richmond congress, which was classified as the first official Bond congress, were printed together with the *Notulen eener Vergadering van den Afrikaner Bond en de Boerenbeschermingsvereeniging, gehouden te Richmond* (Hofmeyr Collection). See also *Zuid Afrikaan*, 29, 31 May; *De Tolk*, 6 June 1883; Coetzee, pp. 123–33; Hofmeyr, pp. 205–8.

PAGE 69

majority. Eight voted in favour of Du Toit's amendment, according to *De Tolk*; thirty-four Bondsmen and twenty-one Vereeniging men voted against it, according to the *Zuid Afrikaan*.

meeting. *Zuid Afrikaan*, 2 June 1883.

PAGE 70

Naude. Bond MSS., Library of Parliament, p. 65.

Theron. T. P. Theron to Jakob Middel, 22 Feb., 19 Apr. 1884, in Bond MSS., Library of Parliament, pp. 74–5.

CHAPTER 5

PAGE 72

1874. Text in Eybers, p. 64.

towns. Walker (1), p. 63.

majority. See editorial comment in the *Zuid Afrikaan*, 27 Nov., 4 Dec. 1878.

PAGE 73

signatures. Du Toit, pp. 229–30.

introduction. Hofmeyr, p. 167, quoting C. 2374, p. 142.

annexation. Full report in the *Zuid Afrikaan*, 12 Nov. 1879.

Dutch. Worsfold (1), pp. 287, 296.

Gladstone. Text in Hofmeyr, pp. 645–9. This author attributes the initiative to Onze Jan; but contrast Kotze, i, 694, where it is attributed to the *Patriot*.

PAGE 74

commission. Many public meetings took place in the Colony, especially in Jan. 1881, and were fully reported in the *Zuid Afrikaan*.

disaffection. De Kiewiet, p. 266. See also Tylden, chs. VIII–X.

contingency. Walker (3), p. 371.

PAGE 75

pound. C. 2,964, pp. 10 [Sprigg's terms], 12–13 [Robinson's report of 5 Mar. 1881], 20–1 [Robinson to Kimberley, telegram, 29 Apr. 1881, giving details of his award].

railway. Williams, p. 63.

1881. Laurence, p. 59; Hofmeyr, p. 184. Onze Jan had been approached to lead the Opposition, but declined because the 'time was not yet ripe' to form an Afrikaner ministry if he were called upon to do so.

so. Hofmeyr, p. 188.

action. Zuid Afrikaan, 10 May 1881.

PAGE 76

restraint. Patriot, 10, 17, 24 June; *Zuid Afrikaan,* 16, 21 June 1881.

intent. Text in *Graaff-Reinet Advertiser,* 29 Oct. 1881. See also Hofmeyr, p. 191; Laurence, p. 60; Lewsen, i, 94–8 [text of a memorandum in May 1882, for which Merriman was partly responsible, indicating that he drew a distinction between the aims of the Bond and those of Hofmeyr's Vereeniging].

PAGE 77

full. Hofmeyr, pp. 193–4.

PAGE 78

not. This refers to a statement on Basuto policy made against Hofmeyr's advice. See Hofmeyr, p. 189.

level. The brandy excise yielded £58,293 in 1881–2, £43,103 in 1882–3, and £19,469 in 1883–4. The figure rose after amending legislation to £94,686 in 1884–5. The tax was abolished in 1886. For its history see Hofmeyr, pp. 227–8, 263–4, 276, 280–1. It was reimposed after the South African war, and became a controversial issue under the Merriman administration of 1908–10.

PAGE 79

March. Hofmeyr, pp. 223–4.

practice. G. 75–1880, para. 17; De Villiers (1), p. 113; Malherbe, p. 414.

sprang. De Villiers (1), p. 114; Hofmeyr, p. 226.

1884. Eybers, p. 133; De Villiers (1), pp. 115–16; Hofmeyr, p. 266.

1887. De Villiers (1), pp. 118–19.

PAGE 80

explained. For examples of desertions, see *Burghersdorp Gazette,* 25 Feb., *Cradock Register,* 4 Mar., *Zuid Afrikaan,* 24 Mar. 1881. For Bond attitudes, see *Zuid Afrikaan,* 9 Mar. 1882, and *Notulen,* Cradock congress, p. 15.

PAGE 81

Government. Notulen, Speciale Vergadering der Z.A.B.B. Vereeniging, 10 Mar. 1882.

dream. Zuid Afrikaan, 9 Mar. 1882.

disannexation. Notulen, Cradock congress, pp. 20–1: 'that under the existing circumstances the affairs of Basutoland should be left in the hands of the Government; but that it is desirable to repeal the annexation' ['dat onder de bestaande omstandigheden de zaken van Basutoland in de handen van de Regering worden gelaten; doch dat het wenschelijk is de annexatie te herroepen'].

territory. C. 3112, pp. 120–1, 124, 129–30: ministerial minutes of 29 Dec. 1881, 25 Jan., 6, 15 Feb. 1882.

State. C. 3717, p. 34: Robinson to Kimberley, telegram, 28 Mar. 1882.

problem. C. 3717, p. 48: Brand to Robinson, 23 Mar. 1882.

PAGE 82

Africa. Hofmeyr, p. 231 [speech by Onze Jan at Stellenbosch, 16 Jan. 1883]; see also *Zuid Afrikaan*, 28 Dec. 1882.

action. Hofmeyr, p. 235. For illustrations of Brand's clear reluctance to increase his responsibilities towards Basutoland, see C. 3717, p. 117: Scanlen to Merriman, telegram, 13 Mar. 1883; C. 3855, pp. 19–20, quoting Brand to Officer Administering, Cape Colony, 5, 12 July 1883.

failure. Notulen, Richmond congress, item 7: a resolution urging that the Imperial Government be urged to leave Basutoland entirely and unconditionally to the Colonial Government, to deal with as circumstances might warrant.

quickly. C. 3708, pp. 1–3: Ministers' Minute, 30 Apr. 1883.

Basutoland. C. 3708, pp. 14, 35, 37: Merriman to Derby, 29 May; Brand to Derby, 12 May; Derby to Officer Administering, Cape Colony, 14 June 1883.

£20,000. Text in C. 3855, pp. 24–5.

PAGE 83

plan. Votes and Proceedings, House of Assembly, 27 July 1883. The 'rebels' were R. N. Aling, M. Bergh, L. H. Goldschmidt, M. J. Louw and H. Wilman.

1884. Text in Newton, i, 92–4.

Transkei. C. 3708, p. 23: J. X. Merriman, Commissioner to Derby, 11 June 1883, esp. paragraph 15.

Queen. See Eybers, p. 65; Walker (3), pp. 393–4.

PAGE 84

again. A. 3—1892, p. 3.

leaving. Macquarrie, i, 177–9.

farmer. See editorials in the *Zuid Afrikaan*, 4 May, 1 Aug. 1882.

sale. C. 3493, pp. 11 ff.: telegraphic correspondence between Scanlen and General Gordon, June 1882.

it. Notulen, Cradock congress, pp. 17, 25.

Colony. G. 66—1883, pp. 2, 12.

jurisdiction. Votes and Proceedings, House of Assembly, 30 Aug. 1883.

PAGE 85

there. Minutes, 1884 congress, pp. 26–8.

PAGE 86

Convention. Agar-Hamilton, pp. 167–82, gives a full account of the Moysey report.

so. Mouton, p. 90 [the republics as 'toekomstige Transvaalse gebied beskou']; Agar-Hamilton, p. 250 ['Stellaland and Goshen . . . had never been intended to survive, but to be absorbed straightway by their parent'].

PAGE 87

Cape. Agar-Hamilton, ch. XII.

neighbours. Agar-Hamilton, p. 231.

1884. Agar-Hamilton, pp. 272 ff.

suggested. See Agar-Hamilton, pp. 364–5; Hofmeyr p. 257.

PAGE 88

goods. Van der Poel (1), p. 17.

Bechuanaland. Minutes, 1884 congress, pp. 29–30.

war. Agar-Hamilton, pp. 256–8, quoting G. J. van Niekerk to Joubert, 24 Sept. 1883, 3 Mar. 1884; Mouton, p. 90, quoting Joubert to the landdrost of Lichtenburg, June and Aug. 1884.

chairman. De Tolk, 10 Oct., 26 Dec. 1883. See also the issues of 25 Apr., 9 May 1884.

PAGE 90

issues. Hofmeyr, p. 247.

order. See Agar-Hamilton, chs. XIII, XIV, and Campbell, ch. XIV, for sympathetic studies of Mackenzie, who has on the whole been badly treated by historians.

encounter. Agar-Hamilton, ch. XV; Williams, p. 82; Mouton, pp. 91–2.

PAGE 91

humanity. Kotzé, ii, 54–7. Krüger, (1) ii, 71, sees in the reference to 'humanity' an indication of Du Toit's influence on the President, which Kotzé's memoir does not suggest.

Joubert's. On Joubert's recall, see Mouton, pp. 92–8; Walker (1), pp. 182–3; Agar-Hamilton, p. 352; Van der Walt, p. 63; Krüger (1), ii, 70.

flaccid. Text in the Patriot, 17 Oct. 1884. See also Agar-Hamilton, p. 353; Van der Walt, pp. 70–2.

retard. Kotzé, ii, 58–9.

instructions. Leyds, p. 168.

PAGE 92

believed. Du Toit, pp. 240, 256–61.

so. That Du Toit had such enemies is clear from Jorissen, pp. 128–30; Van Winter, i, 45–6; Van der Walt, pp. 27–36, and Krüger (1), ii, 14–17, 76–7. Krüger accepts, in part, the scapegoat analogy.

aller. See Leyds, pp. 500–1, quoting a letter which he had written to H. P. du Preez in November 1884.

PAGE 93

Cape. Sank, pp. 15–23.

Empire. Notulen, Cape Town Bond branch, 28 Oct. 1884.

1885. Agar-Hamilton, pp. 393–401; Leyds, pp. 218–19.

PAGE 94

1886. Notulen, 1885 congress, pp. 5, 16–17.

CHAPTER 6

PAGE 96

bestuur. See the *Verslag van de Eerste Zitting van het Centraal Bestuur* (*Notulen,* 1886 Cape Congress, Bijlage C).

authority. Zuid Afrikaan, 27 Feb. 1886.

protection. Notulen, 1886 congress, p. 12.

scab. The figures in this paragraph are derived from the Cape of Good Hope *Blue Books* and *Statistical Registers.*

1882. See *Blue Book,* 1882, p. 806; *Statistical Register,* 1885, p. 479. Insolvency figures for the worst hit wool, ostrich and wheat districts in 1876–85 were as follows:

		1876	77	78	79	80	81	82	83	84	85
Fraserburg ..	..	1	3	2	9	6	15	31	10	21	12
Oudtshoorn ..	..	8	5	1	8	8	12	34	33	30	67
Malmesbury	..	22	24	16	4	20	27	72	40	33	30

PAGE 97

sown. Cape Argus, 17 Feb. 1882.

scrip. Cape Argus, 14 Jan. 1882.

PAGE 98

account. See, for example, the figures for Beaufort West, Paarl, Richmond and Swellendam, in addition to those quoted above.

Venter. Notulen, 1886 congress, p. 18; 1887 congress, p. 15; Assembly Debates, 1886, pp. 382–3.

producers. For a discussion of the Transvaal monopoly system, see Marais, ch. II.

1884. Minutes, 1884 congress, pp. 42–3.

PAGE 99

tobacco. G. 42–1886, pp. 1–2; State Secretary, Pretoria, to Upington, telegram, 1 Aug. 1885; Brand to Sir H. Robinson, 8 Jan., 6 Mar. 1886. See also Van der Poel (1), p. 22; Walker (1), p. 188; Hofmeyr, pp. 324–5.

Pretoria. Kotzé, ii, 68–71.

basis. Notulen, 1886 Cape congress, Bijlage C.

union. Hofmeyr, pp. 323, 326.

PAGE 100

policy. Printed as G. 42—1886.

rested. See the Ministerial Minutes in G. 42—1886, in which Upington even refused to admit the existence of any customs profit to which the Free State could lay claim.

district. See G. 42A—1886: R. Trower to Resident Commissioner, Maseru, 24 Apr. 1886, protesting against Upington's recent address to his Caledon constituents threatening to impose a duty on grain imported from the Republics. Upington endorsed the arguments of his 'famous Caledon speech' a year later (Assembly Debates, 1887, p. 258).

inconsistent. 'Vindex', pp. 132–44; Michell, i, 218–22. Contrast his advocacy of internal free trade on 20 May, with his advocacy of protection for Colonial wheat farmers on 6 May (with reference to the development of the Vaal-Harts region) and 21 June (when he was addressing farmers in Paarl).

PAGE 101

refusal. Van der Poel (1), pp. 25–6.

PAGE 102

extension. For the involvement of Du Toit and Joubert in the Lewis and Marks project, see Van der Poel (1), p. 30; Van Winter, ii, ch. VII; Van der Walt, pp. 88–92; Lewsen, i, 227–9.

policy. Bond MSS., Library of Parliament, pp. 53–7, 97.

fall. Zuid Afrikaan, 17 July, 23 Oct. 1886.

established. Du Toit, pp. 240–1.

well. Joelson, pp. 32–8.

prospects. Cloete, pp. 26–7.

1888. Te Water to M. Taylor, 12 Apr. 1888, copy (Te Water Papers).

Rhodes. J. W. Sauer to Rhodes, 12 Dec. 1888 (Rhodes Papers); Hofmeyr to Henry Mitchell, Kimberley, and Rhodes, 30 Dec. 1888 to 26 Jan. 1889, copies of telegrams (Hofmeyr Papers).

PAGE 103

union. Notulen, Cape Town Bond branch, 18 Jan. 1887; Hofmeyr, p. 326.

optimism. Printed in *Notulen*, 1887 congress, Bijlage D.

necessary. Notulen, 1887 congress, p. 11.

suit. Coetzee, p. 229, quoting *Volksstem*, 22 Apr. 1887.

April. G. 37—1887. Schermbrucker's telegraphic progress reports during this mission are in the Sprigg Papers. See also De Waal, J. H. H., pp. 116–23.

PAGE 104

Transvaal. Hofmeyr, pp. 330–1.

years. Kruger to A. B. Hofmeyr, 21 Sept. 1887 (Hofmeyr Papers); Mouton, pp. 115–16; Van Winter, i, 221–2.

PAGE 105

recommendations. Notulen, 1888 congress, p. 8.

theirs. Coetzee, pp. 216–17. Opposition to the railway came largely from transport riders, who feared loss of business.

vote. Van Winter, i, 223.

great. A sub-file in the Hofmeyr Papers contains Hofmeyr's correspondence with the Republican leaders. See also Hofmeyr, p. 342.

PAGE 106

Africa. S. J. du Toit to Hofmeyr, 21 Aug. 1888 (Hofmeyr Papers). ['Geloof mij vrij, wij doen zulks niet uit oppositiezucht. Maar eer Paul Kruger's politiek de nek gebroken is zijn al uwe mooie plannen zoo vele zeepbellen. Sprigg's politiek zal die van Kruger ondermijnen; maar de politiek nu onder onze mannen gevolgd maakt Kruger met zijn Hollander-kliek tot Dictator niet slechts over Transvaal, maar over heel Zuid Afrika. Alle pogingen om Z. Afrika's eenheid te bevorderen stuiten hierop af. . . . '] See also Bond MSS., Library of Parliament, p. 100—a still more outspoken criticism of Hofmeyr's policy in Du Toit's hand.

materialize. 'Vindex', pp. 182–9.

respectively. Votes and Proceedings, House of Assembly, 1888, pp. 314 [Hofmeyr Proviso], 353–4, 460–1 [Theron Proviso and its rejection]. Nine Bondsmen voted against the Theron Proviso on the first occasion, and six on the second.

Bloemfontein. Whether Kruger was yet prepared to accept extension of the Colesberg line to the Vaal is doubtful. Contrast Van der Poel (1), p. 38, and Van Winter, i, 225.

step. Esselen to Hofmeyr, 15 Jan. 1889 (Hofmeyr Papers). See also Hofmeyr, pp. 349–51.

PAGE 107

Britain. Williams, pp. 130–5; Van der Poel (1), p. 38.

first. Van der Poel (1), pp. 40–1; Michell, i, 269–70; Headlam, i, ch. 7.

Transvaal. Notulen, 1889 congress, pp. 15, 17.

PAGE 109

constancy. This account of the decline of S. J. du Toit's influence and fortunes is based on Du Toit, pp. 261–6; Van der Walt, pp. 97–103; Van Winter, i, 238–9.

PAGE 110

Steyn. Coetzee, pp. 219–21.

recovered. Coetzee, pp. 228–33.

party. From the congress of 1905 onwards.

CHAPTER 7

co-operation. Notulen, 1885 congress, p. 9.

done. Port Elizabeth Telegraph, 18 Mar. 1886.

month. Notulen, 1886 congress, Bijlagen D, E, F, H [text of correspondence].

April. Zuid Afrikaan, 3 Apr. 1886.

eighties. Convictions for stock thefts (all races) rose from 1,132 in 1880 to 6,016 in 1885, and fell to below 2,000 in 1887–90. Convictions under the master and servant laws, which were enforced by criminal sanctions as in the West Indies after slave emancipation, reached a peak in 1881–2, with figures of 3,885 and 3,508 respectively (all races). 1,406 persons were convicted of pass law offences in 1880; the figure rose to 7,503 in 1883, and fell gradually to 1,576 in 1890. See Cape of Good Hope *Blue Books* and *Statistical Registers*.

1893. The Grahamstown Political Union of 1886 and the Frontier Party of 1888 rose and fell on a basis of regional and economic interests. See Sank, pp. 25–35.

farmers. The 1888 Bond congress resolved (*Notulen*, p. 10) to grant equal language rights in due course ['Dat in vervolg van tijd de Engelsche en Hollandsche talen gelijke rechten zullen worden toegestaan in hare beraadslagingen']; but this decision was revoked in 1889 (*Notulen*, p. 9), and the rule adopted that those who could not speak Dutch should be allowed to speak in English and have their speeches translated. The 1890 congress (*Notulen*, p. 20) decided to have the *Officieële Stukken* translated into English but not into Afrikaans. The farmers' congress does not appear to have made any reciprocal gesture.

element. Bedford Enterprise, 21 Mar. 1888; *Graaff-Reinet Advertiser*, 18 Mar. 1889; G. Lee to Te Water, 15 July 1890 (Te Water Papers).

accused. Report of the Select Committee on District Justice Courts (A. 13–1880).

1882. Acts 10 of 1876 and 40 of 1882.

object. Minutes, 1884 congress, pp. 49–50; *Notulen*, 1886 congress, p. 8; 1887 congress, p. 9; 1888 congress, p. 14; 1889 congress, p. 11; Assembly Debates, 1887, pp. 225, 263, 321.

it. East London Dispatch, 16 June 1883 [report of Farmers' Congress].

councils. For a classic exposition of this view, see *De Tolk*, 4 July 1883 [report of a Bond meeting, Aberdeen]. For other instances of demands for the abolition of local police forces, see *Middelburg Gazette*, 19 Apr. 1881 [memorials from Willem Burgers Rivier and Zuurberg to the Middelburg divisional council]; *Frontier Guardian*, 2 Apr., 22 Oct. 1881, 26 Aug. 1882 [discussion of a demand by the Wodehouse Boeren Vereeniging for the abolition of the local police force, where information is also given that in a period of two years this force had brought about 700 offenders to justice at a cost to the division of about £3,000 a year]. Bond congresses took no firm resolutions respecting police during the 1880's; but see *Notulen*, 1895 congress, pp. 7–10; 1897 congress, pp. 6–10; 1904 congress, p. 18, at all of which the demand was made for placing the police forces under the divisional councils. In 1904 a reduction was demanded.

search. See resolutions on these lines at the Fort Beaufort, Bedford and Graaff-Reinet congresses in *East London Dispatch*, 13, 16 June 1883; *Bedford Enterprise*, 28 Mar. 1888; *Graaff-Reinet Advertiser*, 25 Mar. 1889.

PAGE 115

man. N. F. de Waal in *Middelburg Getuige*, 23 Dec. 1882; St. P. O'S. O'Brien in *Burghersdorp Gazette*, 3 Oct. 1879 [on race and the lash]. For allegations of anti-white prejudice in the magistrates' courts, see *Zuid Afrikaan*, 9 Mar. 1882 [debate on master and servants law at Graaff-Reinet congress of Bondsmen]; *Port Elizabeth Telegraph*, 20 Mar. 1886 [debate on stock thefts at Port Elizabeth Farmers' Congress].

individuals. For full ranges of opinion regarding punishments for stock thefts, including suggestions for the branding, transportation, subjection to the tread-mill, and hanging of culprits, all of which were rejected, see Minutes, 1884 Bond congress, pp. 56–7; *P.E. Telegraph*, 20 Mar. 1886 [farmers' congress].

PAGE 116

property. See Acts 24 of 1857, 17 of 1864, and 22 of 1867—the steps by which the pass system was introduced for Africans, though it had been abolished in respect of Coloured persons in the twenties.

stock. For Bond congress views on pass legislation, see Minutes, 1884 congress, p. 53; *Notulen*, 1885 congress, pp. 14–15; 1886 congress, p. 7 and Bijlage G, in which the support of the farmers' associations is indicated; 1887 congress, p. 9; 1888 congress, p. 17; 1890 congress, p. 20. For the views of the farmers' associations, see congress reports in *E. L. Dispatch*, 16, 23 June 1883; *Bedford Enterprise*, 28 Mar. 1888.

neighbourhood. Minutes, 1884 congress, pp. 51–2.

Governor. Act 37 of 1884.

police. *Notulen*, 1891 congress, p. 39; 1892 congress, p. 19.

stock. Act 33 of 1892.

existed. *Notulen*, 1893 congress, p. 26.

unfavourably. Report of the Select Committee on the Native Location Act (A. 10—1893).

PAGE 117

that. A. 10—1893, Minutes of Evidence, QQ. 311–12.

emphasized. Report of the Select Committee on the Labour Question (C. 2, 2A —1892).

out. *P.E. Telegraph*, 23 Mar. 1886; *Graaff-Reinet Advertiser*, 25 Mar. 1889.

education. See the following resolutions: *Notulen*, Cradock congress, pp. 18–20 ['het Kongres aanbeveelt scholen onder de Naturellen en vooral over de Kei grootelijks te verminderen']; 1885 congress, p. 19 [' . . . dat er te veel gelden aan Inboorlingen scholen besteed worden']; 1887 congress, p. 12 ['De Regeering en Parlement worden gevraagd om . . . op de uitgaven op Naturellen scholen te bezuinigen'].

view. The Report of the Superintendent-General of Education, Dr. Langham Dale, for 1881 (G. 39–1882, pp. 2–5), listed 75 third-class and 13 district boarding schools catering for 3,185 pupils, as against 370 mission and 225 aborigines' schools with a total of 56,781 pupils. Costs per head were 7s. 8d. in the case of mission schools (which were only subsidized), 20s. in the case of aborigine's schools, 30s. in the (unofficially white) public schools, and 112s. 2d. in the case of district boarders. In reply to a complaint by the Bond Cradock congress, Dale stated that £50,000 in a total educational budget of £88,000 had been spent in 1881 on the education of white children (*Zuid Afrikaan*, 9 Nov. 1882).

schools. *E.L. Dispatch*, 20 June 1883.

notice. *Bedford Enterprise*, 28 Mar.; *Imvo Zabantsundu* (*Native Opinion*), 28 Mar. 1888.

interpreter. For the unpopularity of the court interpreter, see Hofmeyr, p. 235; *Notulen*, 1893 congress, p. 34; 1910 congress, p. 46 [recommendations that the employment of non-white people in this capacity be prohibited]; W. F. Juhre to Te Water, 16 Apr. 1898 (Te Water Papers) [a letter from Aberdeen to the then Colonial Secretary, relating that 'an educated Caffir from Lovedale was sent here *ostensibly* as Police Constable, but he really acts as clerk to the Resident Magistrate and is continually employed in registering births and deaths. . . . It is hardly necessary for me to mention what deep-rooted objections the respectable mass of Dutch farmers have to be catechised, as it were, about their private family concerns by a Caffir.' Te Water took steps 'to put an end to the grievance complained of'].

PAGE 118

respect. For a farmers' congress view, see *E. L. Dispatch*, 23 June 1883 [a recommendation 'rather to inculcate industrial habits than to cram the native scholars . . . in the higher class of subjects']. For a Bond view, see *Notulen*, 1893 congress, p. 20 [a congress resolution recommending the limitation of education in mission and aborigines' schools to standard two, a special tax on the hut of every school-going African, and the combination of manual labour with book learning].

action. Minutes, 1884 congress, p. 60; *Notulen*, 1885 congress, pp. 21–2; 1886 congress, p. 8; 1887 congress, p. 17; 1888 congress, p. 14; 1894 congress, p. 29. The farmers' congress dissented from the view of the Native Laws Commission in 1883 that legal recognition should be given to African polygamy. It considered but withdrew a motion condemning *lobola* (*E.L. Dispatch*, 23 June 1883), and endorsed this view in 1889 (*Graaff-Reinet Advertiser*, 25 Mar. 1889).

franchise. *Notulen*, 1887 congress, p. 14; and cf. *Notulen*, 1886 congress, p. 11.

reasons. See the 1886 farmers' congress debate on squatting, when interested motives came to the fore (*P.E. Telegraph*, 23 Mar. 1886), and contrast the tone of debate at Bedford in 1888, when individual tenure was supported because people thought it would weaken the authority of the chief, educate the owners, and enable more Africans to qualify for the vote (*Bedford Enterprise*, 14 Mar. 1888).

PAGE 119

farmers. Hence the refusal of the farmers' congress in the eighties to discuss such questions as the imperial connection or the alteration of the franchise, on the ground that these might arouse political feelings. By the nineties, they were more willing to discuss political issues, the Graaff-Reinet Farmers' Association, for example, inserting the word 'Political' into its title in 1893.

constitutions. Transvaal Bond constitution, art. I ('De Bond vestigt zich onder de blanke bevolking'); Free State Bond constitution (Bloemfontein revision), art. I. The original *Express* constitution had no colour bar.

besturen. Provincial constitution for the Cape Colony, 1883, art. V(*a*).

Tolk. De Tolk, 5 Dec. 1883 (culled from the Humansdorp *Re-Echo*).

women. The *Express* constitution, Art. 27, gave membership rights to women in the Orange Free State; but this privilege was removed by the Bloemfontein Revision.

qualifications. Under the constitution ordinance of 1853, art. 8, the vote had been given to male adults who could show an occupational qualification of £25 or an income qualification of £50 a year (Eybers, p. 48). This was an easy test, but extra qualifications of any kind other than racial would have excluded some whites as well as some blacks.

PAGE 120

appraisal. Zuid Afrikaan, 4, 7 Nov. 1882. Cf. the anecdote recounted in Hofmeyr, p. 309.

kaffirs. Patriot, 13 Dec. 1888.

opposition. P.E. Telegraph, 27 Dec. 1881.

aims. Zuid Afrikaan, 5 Jan. 1882.

PAGE 121

House. Imvo Zabantsundu, 30 Mar. 1887. For examples of attacks on the Bond, see issues of 27 Apr., 23 Sept. 1885, 10 Feb. 1886, 2, 16 May 1889.

Afrikaan. Imvo Zabantsundu, 15 Nov.; *Uitenhage Times*, 6 Dec.; *Zuid Afrikaan*, 4 Dec. 1888. See also the *Patriot's* review of the election results (issues of 13, 20 Dec.): 'Di eerste les is: Di groote mag van di Kafferstem, en di gebruik wat van di stem gemaak word. . . . Ons moet net ons beginsels vas hou, en di moed ni opge, en op die manier bly ons baas in di land. Ons baas of di kaffer baas, dit is di vraagstuk. Laat alle Bondsmanne daaro'er nadenk. Di tyd van speul is virby' ['The first lesson is: The great power of the Kaffir vote, and the use which is made of that vote. . . . We must just stick to our principles, and not lose courage, and in that way we stay boss in the land. Ourselves boss or the Kaffir boss, this is the question. Let all Bondsmen think about that. The time for playing is past'].

activity. See Report of the Select Committee on Queen's Town Registration (A. 19—1888) in which the majority (Innes dissenting) accepted the Bond's case that its opponents had placed large numbers of unqualified Africans on the roll.

The civil commissioner had struck off 133 out of 426 names put before him. See also *Imvo Zabantsundu*, 18 Jan. 1888 [a reference to attempts to eliminate African voters by 'our Dutch neighbours in Herschel, Queenstown, Wodehouse, Tembuland, Victoria East and Fort Beaufort']. See also letters in the Hofmeyr and Te Water Papers from Dr. Arthur Vanes of Uitenhage in 1891-3. Vanes, then a Bondsman, told Te Water on one occasion that 'the native vote has been splendidly pared down'.

electorate. Vanes to Hofmeyr, 23 Feb. 1891 (Hofmeyr Papers), relating how he had authorized his agent 'to secure votes at £7 10s. per cent in Hankey and I fancy we should have 150'; H. J. H. Claassens to Te Water, 14 Mar. 1891 (Te Water Papers), applying for £2 7s. 0d. as electoral expenses because 'eenige kleurlingen moest ik eenige bottels Bier te drinken geven, omdat de heer Auret [opposition agent] . . . te drinken heeft gegeven'.

reached. Notulen, Cradock congress, p. 15; Minutes, 1884 congress, pp. 45-7.

Africans. Sprigg estimated that there were nearly 10,000 whites and nearly 350,000 Africans in the Transkei and Griqualand East in 1887. The 1891 census put the African population of these districts at over 475,000 (see C. G. H. *Statistical Register*, 1892, pp. 26-7).

competence. P.E. Telegraph, 25 Mar. 1886.

PAGE 122

vote. C.G.H. *Government Gazette*, 19, 22 May 1885, pp. 1,050-6, 1,078-9 [two Bills, the first of which provided for the establishment of a Native Council 'in order to give the native population of the Transkeian Territories such voice in the legislation affecting those Territories as circumstances at present require', and the second of which proposed to create two single-member constituencies for the Cape Parliament, and extend the ordinary Cape franchise law to them]; *Notulen*, 1886 congress, p. 11. Both Bills were subsequently withdrawn.

measure. Assembly Debates, 1886, pp. 70-1; Hofmeyr, pp. 283-4.

Bill. Note especially the arguments of Leonard (Oudtshoorn), Warren (King William's Town) and Vintcent (George) in Assembly Debates, 1886, pp. 70, 73, 396. See also ibid., pp. 428-9; Votes and Proceedings, House of Assembly, 1886, pp. 438-9 [passage of the amendment by 31 votes to 28].

Transkei. Act 14 of 1887. The important section was the seventeenth.

advance. Notulen, 1887 congress, p. 13 ['Deze vergadering keurt het nieuwe Wetsontwerp door de Regering te worden ingediend bij de volgende sessie van het Parlement, goed, en verzoekt de leden de Regering daarin te steunen'].

PAGE 123

land. Imvo Zabantsundu, 30 Mar. 1887. See also Jabavu, pp. 29-33.

strong. Dormer to Rhodes, 5 Sept. 1888 (Rhodes Papers).

separated. Sauer to Rhodes, 10 Sept. 1888 (Rhodes Papers).

League. On these ephemeral organizations, see Sank, pp. 29-32.

PAGE 124

mine. Hofmeyr to Rhodes, 3 Oct. 1888 (Rhodes Papers).

right. Notulen, 1889 congress, Bijlage A.

opponents. Arthur Vanes to J. E. McCusker, editor of the *Graaff-Reinetter*, 30 Nov. 1888 (Te Water Papers). A graphic description.

organization. The Graaff-Reinet election is well documented in the Te Water Papers.

so. Notulen, 1889 congress, Bijlage E (Report of the congress constitutional committee).

accepted. Notulen, 1889 congress, p. 19.

PAGE 125

1886. Notulen, 1885 congress, p. 8: *Rapport der Commissie over het Program van Beginselen* (Hofmeyr Collection).

PAGE 126

Toit's. Du Toit's draft, entitled a *Program van Beginselen van de Nationale Partij*, left out most of the politically explosive phrases in his brother's document which offered oblique insults to the English-speaking colonials, such as their exclusion from the biological definition of the *volk* in the first article. He also omitted the phrase '*onder eigen vlag*' in the sixth. The Hofmeyr–Hoffman draft was entitled a *Program van Beginselen van de Afrikaander Nationale Partij*.

draft. Notulen, 1889 congress, Bijlage D.

trusted. A. J. Herholdt of Murraysburg to Te Water, 8 July 1889 (Te Water Papers): 'Unless our party act a little more liberal we will be out of it. We are not so strong here as some people imagine and we are getting more divided daily. Everybody wants his own way and his own railway and what will be the end of it remains to be seen. Hofmeyr does not seem so very delighted with some of the Bond members. He says they are too ignorant and however good a man might be if he lacks education he cannot be a success in parliament. Believe me we have too many of that class here and if we do not send better men the Africaner party will never be able to take the lead and I am sure of it that the first opportunity Sprigg sees to do without us he will show us his back.' R. P. Botha wrote in similar vein on the 18th.

CHAPTER 8

PAGE 127

convincingly. Hofmeyr, pp. 354–7, 382–9. These two passages, which are based on documents in the Hofmeyr Papers, should be considered together.

differ. Hofmeyr, p. 383.

PAGE 128

State. Quoted in Hofmeyr, p. 356. That this was precisely Sir Hercules Robinson's fear is suggested by Robinson, Gallagher and Denny, p. 232.

unfavourably. Hofmeyr to Kruger, 27 June; Kruger to Hofmeyr, 2 July; State Secretary, Pretoria, to Hofmeyr, 19 July 1889, telegrams (Hofmeyr Papers).

North. Notulen, Transvaal Volksraad, 27, 29 July 1889, as published in the *Staatscourant*; Hofmeyr, p. 357.

Town. Rhodes to Hofmeyr, 20 Sept. 1889 (Hofmeyr Papers); Hofmeyr, p. 384. Onze Jan noted the gist of his reply on Rhodes's letter.

PAGE 129

Office. Van der Poel (1), pp. 51–2, quoting G. 49–1890; Hofmeyr, pp. 384–5; Robinson, Gallagher and Denny, pp. 235–6, 248, who appear to date the political alliance between Rhodes and Hofmeyr rather too early.

Republic. On the Swaziland negotiations, see Garson, ch. III; Leyds, pp. 272–310; Hofmeyr, ch. XXIII; Van der Poel (1), pp. 48–51; Marais, pp. 49–52.

PAGE 130

Pont. Hofmeyr, pp. 395–6.

yield. Hofmeyr, p. 403. Contrast the emphasis in Leyds, pp. 296–301; Garson, pp. 321–4; Green, p. 209, where the claims for Onze Jan are less extravagant.

public. Hofmeyr, p. 406; Michell, i, 127; Dormer to Rhodes, 23 July 1890 (Rhodes Papers): 'Hofmeyr . . . so far as I can learn . . . is not ingratiating himself with the Boers, although he is posing as an anti-railway man! Paul's greeting—seriously meant—was significant. "You are a traitor! And you have come up here as a traitor!" This in the presence of a dozen people! It completely flabbergasted the blind man.'

diplomacy. For the purpose of the Joubert mission, see Mouton, pp. 181–3; Garson, pp. 320–1; Van Winter, ii, 102–5. Though Joubert spoke against the Swaziland Convention after it had been signed, in an interview with *The Times*, London, on 15 August, he was reconciled to the abandonment of the North by 1891, on the evidence of his speech quoted in 'Vindex', pp. 256 ff.

part. Hofmeyr, pp. 399–400.

PAGE 131

rested. Lippert to Hofmeyr, 11 July 1890 (Rhodes Papers).

irrevocable. Hofmeyr, pp. 400–1; Garson, p. 326. For the background to British interest in Zambesia, see Robinson, Gallagher and Denny, pp. 222, 225 ff., 411–12.

lines. Sprigg proposed to build lines as follows: Warrenton to Vryburg; Paarl to Worcester via Du Toit's Kloof; Indwe to Molteno; Mossel Bay to Ashton; Mossel Bay—George—Oudtshoorn—Klipplaat—Somerset East—Cookhouse—King William's Town; Graaff-Reinet to Richmond Road; a line linking the eastern and midland systems; and the purchase of the line to Kowie, all at an estimated cost of at least £7,500,000.

West. A. Innes to Te Water, 10 June 1890 (Te Water Papers). The Sprigg Papers contain many memorials in support of the proposals, and it is noteworthy that some came from Bondsmen.

simultaneously. A. J. Herholdt to Te Water, 2 June 1890 (Te Water Papers): Sprigg 'gave me the assurance that the G[raaff] R[einet] extension will be commenced simultaneously with all the rest so that whoever gets into office will be bound to finish the line'.

Rhodes. Jenkins, p. 13, quoting *Cape Times*, 16 July 1890.

Warwick. The phrase was R. W. Murray's. See Hofmeyr, pp. 388–9, for the telegraphic correspondence between Rhodes and Hofmeyr, and Innes, pp. 59–60, for the view that party considerations rather than ill health determined Hofmeyr's refusal of office.

caucus. Innes, p. 80.

asked. Minutes of the caucus meeting, based on a report in the Hofmeyr Papers, are printed in Hofmeyr, p. 388. An eyewitness account, presumably by D. F. du Toit, who attended the meeting though he was not a member of Parliament, appeared in the *Patriot*, 24 July 1890. On 23 July, R. P. Botha gave Te Water the following account (Te Water Papers): 'Om van het tegenwoordige Kabinet een goed denkbeeld to geven, Rhodes, nog voor ingesworen vroeg my, als voorzitter, de Bondsleden by elkaar te roepen. Hy ontmoet ons, en leg zyn program bloot. Wil de Bond hem een kans geven dan ga hy in met toestemming van den Bond anders niet. Zyn regering zal Afrikaans zyn, de Naturelle pollitiek [*sic*] zal zyn eigen zyn; en de Minnester [*sic*] die niet met hem mee gaan moet uit. Hy erken dat geen gouvernement is mogelyk zonder de Bond. Hofmeyr is met hem.'

borders. Michell, i, 279–83.

distributed. Michell, i, 276–7, states that 25,000 were distributed to Colonial applicants; Williams, pp. 141–2, gives 125,000 and 'even more'; McDonald, pp. 116–17, gives 150,000 'applied for'.

recipients. Tielman Hofmeyr, brother of Onze Jan, who recorded the transaction, bought £1,300 Charter stock in November 1890 (evidence in Hofmeyr Papers). D. C. de Waal received 1,000 shares on ten certificates, presumably with a view to distribution, in December 1890 (evidence in Rhodes Papers). Merriman informed his mother on 24 April 1890 that 'shares are being plentifully distributed to members of Parlt., even very obscure ones coming in for a share' (Merriman Papers). This appears to be the earliest contemporary reference to the distribution, though Innes suggests that it had begun before the end of 1889.

denying. Van der Poel (2), p. 4 (note 2), documents the allegation. See, however, *Ons Land*, 4 Aug. 1898 [letter from Hofmeyr enclosing a certificate from his auditors to the effect that his total profits from Chartered shares to that date amounted to £2,465 4s.]; Hofmeyr to Merriman 10, 13 Aug. 1898 (Merriman Papers).

evidence. Hofmeyr to Rhodes, 26 Aug. 1895 (Rhodes Papers). Hofmeyr bought shortly before Kruger closed the Vaal drifts, at a time when De Beers and Charters were soaring. See also Walker (2), p. 65.

him. D. C. de Waal's *With Rhodes in Mashonaland* is a translation of articles recording this expedition which first appeared in the *Z.A. Tijdschrift*.

prospects. R. P. Botha to Te Water, 10 Dec. 1890 (Te Water Papers).

Bondsmen. Quoted in 'Vindex', pp. 264–77.

PAGE 134

sphere. Hofmeyr, ch. XXIV.

occupation. De Waal, D. C., pp. 92–102.

President. De Waal, D. C., p. 109; Michell, i, 313; Williams, p. 155; Krüger (1), ii, 132.

way. Patriot, 2 Apr. 1891. Among the provisional leaders, Adendorff unwisely named A. S. du Plessis of Steynsburg, who indignantly dissociated himself from the trek in the issue of 9 Apr.

PAGE 135

Rhodes. Hofmeyr Papers.

April. See editorial opinion on the Adendorff trek, *Patriot*, 2–16 Apr. 1891.

him. S. J. du Toit to Rhodes, 3 Apr. 1891 (Rhodes Papers). Cf. Rhodes to the Secretary of the Cape Town Bond, quoted in Michell, ii, 20–3.

Adendorff. S. J. du Toit to Rhodes, 14 Apr. 1891 (Rhodes Papers). The Cape Town Bond circular of 22 Apr., *De Afrikaander Bond en de Dreigende Botsing in het Noorden*, and S. J. du Toit's *Open Brief aan mijne Transvaalsche Vrienden, welke den Trek naar Banyailand voorstaan* of 30 Apr., were published by the *Patriot* on 30 Apr. and 7 May respectively.

trekkers. 'Vindex', pp. 277–91; Michell, ii, 24–8.

speech. Innes, pp. 89–90; S. J. du Toit to Rhodes, 8 Aug. 1891 (Rhodes Papers): 'I am continually receiving applications for farms in Mashonaland under the Chartered Co. from different parts of the Colony. . . . Many of them ask, whether your Concession gives you the right to issue *land grants*, or whether your company only holds *mineral rights*. Of course, I put the reply to this question off at present.'

Croesus. Hofmeyr, p. 410; Borckenhagen to Rhodes, 10 Sept. 1891 (Rhodes Papers): a private request for financial assistance for the O.F.S. National Bank, of which Borckenhagen was a director.

PAGE 136

concern. See for example D. F. ['Dokter'] du Toit to Hofmeyr, 5 Aug. 1891 (Hofmeyr Papers). This D. F. du Toit was a cousin of his namesake, like him a foundation member of the Genootskap van Regte Afrikaners, and on the staff of the *Patriot*.

facets. W. P. de Villiers to Te Water, 30 May 1891 (Te Water Papers).

us. S. J. du Toit to Hofmeyr, 19 Oct. 1891 (Hofmeyr Papers) [Dutch in original].

1892. S. J. du Toit to Rhodes, 8 Aug. 1891 (Rhodes Papers).

Hofmeyr. S. J. du Toit to Hofmeyr, 19 Sept. 1891 (Hofmeyr Papers). See also editorial in *Patriot*, 17 Sept. 1891.

bataille. S. J. du Toit to Hofmeyr, 19 Sept. 1891 (Hofmeyr Papers).

policy. Hofmeyr, pp. 418–19. For the farmers' report of their tour, see *Zuid Afrikaan*, 10 Oct. 1891.

object. De Waal, D. C., part ii, ch. XXVI.

PAGE 137

Borckenhagen. Borckenhagen to Hofmeyr (telegram), 3 Nov. 1891 (Hofmeyr Papers).

rights. Patriot, 12 Nov., *Zuid Afrikaan*, 14 Nov. 1891.

arbitration. Hofmeyr to Loch, 26 Nov. 1891 (Hofmeyr Papers).

order. D. F. du Toit and J. van Soelen to editor, *Graaff-Reinetter*, 5 Feb. 1892.

State. Nienaber (2), p. 246.

district. S. J. du Toit to Rhodes, 8 Aug. 1891 (Rhodes Papers).

chair. S. J. du Toit to Hofmeyr, 15 Oct., and Jotham Joubert to S. J. du Toit, 19 Oct. 1891 (Hofmeyr Papers) establish this point in the cases of D. P. van den Heever and Jotham Joubert.

PAGE 138

wilted. Bower to Hofmeyr, 28 Apr. 1892 (Hofmeyr Papers).

Colony. The evidence is in the Rhodes Papers. For reasons of space, only one example is quoted: S. J. du Toit to Rhodes, 16 Jan. 1892 ['I have got fully 150 applications for farms, of which 30 are from Burghersdorp, 47 from Somerset East, 41 from Griqualand East and several other districts including a few from Free State and Transvaal'].

soil. 'Vindex', pp. 256 ff.

congress. S. J. du Toit to Rhodes, 3 Apr. 1891 (Rhodes Papers).

Company. Notulen, 1892 congress, Bijlage H. It seems probable that Marais obtained the help of D. F. du Toit in drawing up his report, in view of S. J. du Toit's comment to Hofmeyr, 27 Oct. 1891 (Hofmeyr Papers): 'Loko is gister avond naar Kimberley: ik denk dat hij met Stiglingh en P. Marais zal probeeren onder dat anti-Rhodes Wesselton gespuis eene resolutie gepasseerd te krijgen.'

PAGE 139

1890. A. 7—1891, especially Appendix K.

for. Ibid., pp. xiii–xviii.

monopoly. Ibid., pp. v–xii. T. P. Theron, J. X. Merriman (Treasurer-General), J. W. Sauer (Colonial Secretary), T. E. Fuller, B. I. Barnato, J. T. Molteno and L. Wiener accepted the majority report.

unimpaired. Notulen, 1892 congress, p. 23, moved by N. F. de Waal and R. P. Botha: '. . . dat ter eerst-komende Parlements-sessie zoodanige maatregelen zullen worden genomen als vereischt door de algemeene belangen der Kolonie' ['That in the next Parliamentary session such measures shall be adopted as are demanded by the general interests of the Colony'].

1894. Notulen, 1893 congress, p. 34; 1894 congress, p. 12.

PAGE 140

point. Arndt, pp. 414–17. The project, which came to nothing, grew out of the reluctance of existing banks to grant extensive credit facilities in a period of depression.

schools. On the Taalbond, see De Villiers (1), pp. 120 ff.; Hofmeyr, ch. XXV; and the contemporary issues of the *Z.A. Tijdschrift*, which became its organ.

Peninsula. Williams, p. 195; Innes, pp. 89–90.

history. Total Bond membership doubled from 4,428 in Mar. 1890 to 9,748 in in Mar. 1894, but had declined to 8,511 by Mar. 1896.

PAGE 141

poll. The *Commissie van Toezicht* files for this and subsequent elections are in the Hofmeyr Papers. The Te Water Papers contain some correspondence, relating mainly to the midland circle election.

1885. Nieuwe Middelburger, 1 May; *Middelburg Getuige,* 4 July 1885.

difficulties. The reasons are obscure; but see C. P. Hoogenhout to Hofmeyr, 4 Aug. 1891 (Hofmeyr Papers). Hoogenhout described the firm as 'op zyn laatste beenen' and suggested a few ways in which it might be rescued. Hofmeyr noted on the letter: 'R[eplied] 7.8.91. Friends ready to help if confidentially consulted.'

English. Editorials on 2, 30 Apr., 5 May, 18 July and 27 Aug. 1891 give a good indication of how far Van Oordt was prepared to back the Rhodes–Bond alliance. His rather long-winded defence of his editorial policy in the issue of 14 Jan. 1892 throws some light on his rift with Hofmeyr.

PAGE 142

Principles. Notulen, 1892 congress, p. 25 [Dutch in original].

years. Ons Land first appeared on 14 Jan. 1892. The *Zuid Afrikaan* amalgamated with it on 13 Jan. 1894. See Molteno (1), p. 38; Hofmeyr, p. 441; De Waal, J. H. H. (1), pp. 192–3.

sense. On the negotiations leading to the establishment of *Onze Courant,* see correspondence in the Te Water Papers.

organs. Hofmeyr to Te Water, 27 Aug. 1891 (Te Water Papers).

opinion. S. J. du Toit to Hofmeyr, 19 Sept. 1891 (Hofmeyr Papers) [Dutch in original].

funds. S. J. du Toit to Rhodes, 3 April 1891 (Rhodes Papers). See S. J. du Toit to Hofmeyr, 19 Sept. 1891 (Hofmeyr Papers,) for a much fuller exposition of the same theme.

money. De Swardt, p. 61, quoting the *Patriot* of 30 Apr. 1891.

PAGE 143

necessary. Hofmeyr to Te Water, 27 Aug., 11 Sept., 1 Oct. 1891 (Te Water Papers).

revealed. R. P. Botha to Te Water, 21 Feb. 1891 (Te Water Papers), indicates that Hofmeyr contributed substantially out of his own pocket to Bond election expenses, and it is possible that the munificence was his.

railway. Van der Poel (1), pp. 54–61; Van Winter, ii, ch. XX; Marais, pp. 33–8.

PAGE 144

Republic. Williams, p. 197.

Vaal. Notulen, 1893 congress, p. 23 [Dutch Original].

worse. Notulen, 1894 congress, pp. 9–13.

1890. Williams, pp. 193–4.

stocks. Hofmeyr, pp. 369–70; Williams, p. 194.

PAGE 145

involved. Notulen, 1891 congress, p. 34; Jenkins, pp. 54–8.

PAGE 146

concession. Marais, p. 24.

affair. Innes, p. 94.

contract. A. 4—1893; Hofmeyr, pp. 443–7; Jenkins, ch. III; Lewsen, ii, ch. III; Innes, pp. 96–7; Michell, ii, 72–5.

Rhodes. Bond congresses agitated for the reinstatement of Bamberger in 1889, 1890 and 1892–4. The dropping of Sivewright from the Cabinet evoked no public reaction from congress, but did lead to a dispute between the *Commissie van Toezicht*, which supported his candidature for the Griqualand East seat in the 1893–4 elections, and the Griqualand East Bondsmen, who opposed it. See p. 150.

Merriman. Rhodes to Sprigg, 27 Sept., 4 Oct. 1892; J. G. Sprigg, 'Short record of negotiations concerning proposal by Mr. Rhodes that I should join his Ministry' (MS., 1893) (Sprigg Papers).

open. See, for example, A. J. Herholdt to Te Water, 21 June 1892 (Te Water Papers): 'I don't think the ministry as safe as some people fancy, in fact I am quite convinced that before many days a change must come, for there is such internal decension [*sic*] with them that it is simply impossible for them to live together. If it were not for the franchise question which we must get through this session Merriman Innes and Sauer would have had to clear out already but Hofmeyr seems to be very anxious to avoid a split before that important measure is settled. Don't be at all surprised if you hear of a burst up. The Bamberger case is another point and I am quite convinced that this is the rock on which the Ministry will be landed.'

him. Laurence, pp. 149–50; Walker (1), p. 227; Innes, p. 99.

PAGE 147

him. Walker (1), pp. 222–38; Williams, pp. 187, 215–18; Hofmeyr, p. 445.

certificate. Notulen, 1891 congress, p. 38.

Parliament. Hofmeyr, p. 431.

carried. See Hofmeyr to Canon A. T. Wirgman, copy, 12 Aug. 1891 (Hofmeyr Papers): 'I consider the result of the debate on my franchise motion highly satisfactory. The Sauer amendment I arranged myself to prevent complications as regards the position of Innes—who, however, would have voted for the motion (this is confidential).'

test. Eybers, pp. 73–4.

PAGE 148

test. Notulen, 1892 congress, p. 11: the previous year's resolution confirmed 'met bijvoeging van het beginsel van beschaving' ['with addition of the civilization principle'].

had. The congresses of 1889, 1890, 1891, 1893, 1894, 1897, and 1898 all considered redistribution. It was felt that some rural constituencies were too large ('ten einde recht te doen aan groote districten, die lijden onder gedeeltelijke vertegenwoordiging' [1893]) and that fiscal and parliamentary divisions ought to coincide [1894]. But when their opponents urged redistribution in favour of greatly increased urban populations, the Bond attitude on the subject became defensive.

House. Assembly debates, 1893, p. 282; Sank, pp. 61–2; Innes, p. 100. Hofmeyr, pp. 451–2, does some special pleading. See also *Notulen*, 1893 congress, p. 22.

vote. According to Fuller, p. 180, they styled themselves the Progressive Committee.

power. Fuller, pp. 164–5.

emerge. Sampson to Te Water, 9 May 1893 (Te Water Papers) [erroneously dated 9 Apr.]. Sampson was an English-speaking white-supremacist lawyer from the Eastern Province, who had not liked 'to see the clay and the iron attempting to combine' and was glad about the expulsion of the musketeers.

strong. E. Y. Brabant to Sivewright, copy, 24 Dec. 1893 (Hofmeyr Papers).

Government. Sank, p. 65, quoting *E.P. Herald*, 22 Sept. 1893.

PAGE 149

November. Sank, pp. 65–70. A notebook of press cuttings in the Hofmeyr Papers, in which these programmes were annotated by Onze Jan, has also been used.

lawyers. Cf. Hofmeyr to Te Water, 19 Dec. 1892 (Te Water Papers), discussing the parliamentary candidature of Victor Sampson: 'We *do* require a barrister in Parliament, who is 1stly heart and soul with us. 2ndly of such standing as to be fit for the Attorney-Generalship. 3rdly not so selfish, as to turn against us should he *not* get that office *through our influence*.'

PAGE 150

achievement. Some account of this election is given in Hofmeyr, pp. 452–7. The *Commissie van Toezicht* records are in the Hofmeyr Papers.

correspondence. This involved unseating the sitting member, W. H. Janse van Rensburg.

Cabinet. Walker (2), pp. 55–8.

PAGE 151

home. Rhodes 927 votes, Schreiner 885, Stiglingh 781.

PAGE 152

struggle. Hofmeyr, p. 473.

step. Both letters were dated 22 May (Hofmeyr Papers). See also Hofmeyr, pp. 473–4.

PAGE 153

Bond. *Notulen*, 1890 congress, p. 28.

report. A. 3–1892.

1893. Innes, p. 104.

settlers. Notulen, 1886 congress, p. 12.

effect. A. 3—1892, p. 4.

PAGE 154

sale. Notulen, 1893 congress, p. 32 ['Indien persoonlijk grondbezit wordt toegestaan aan naturellen, in reserves, locaties of elders, zulks behoort te geschieden zonder het recht van verkoop te beperken'].

motion. Sampson to Hofmeyr, 3 Nov. 1893 (Hofmeyr Papers). Whether Hofmeyr, as his biographer avers, really did 'recognize the necessity of keeping the native reserves free from European intruders' (p. 471) may be doubted in the light of Innes's remarks at pp. 104–5. The present writer has not seen the memorandum submitted by Hofmeyr to Rhodes to which Innes refers. Sampson's *Reminiscences* throw no light on Hofmeyr's attitude.

vote. Sampson to Hofmeyr, 15 June 1891 (Hofmeyr Papers).

over-population. Sampson to Te Water, 6 Mar. 1893 (Te Water Papers).

you. Sampson to Hofmeyr, 22 May 1893 (Hofmeyr Papers).

labour. Sampson to Hofmeyr, 18 July 1893 (Hofmeyr Papers).

both. Enacted as Act 25 of 1894.

PAGE 155

1893. Figures from the C.G.H. *Statistical Registers.* After 1893 there was a sharp decline in prosecutions.

PAGE 156

ignorance. G. 1—1894, p. 28. For the type of ignorance with which the Commission had to deal, see ibid., p. 583, QQ. 13,373–81 [evidence of J. B. Nigrini, a Bondsman from Fraserburg]. See Jenkins, pp. 58–74, for a detailed account of Rhodes's legislation.

councils. Notulen, 1888 congress, p. 13; 1889 congress, p. 12; 1890 congress, p. 22; 1891 congress, p. 34; 1892 congress, p. 16.

it. Notulen, 1894 congress, p. 26; 1895 congress, pp. 7–10, from which the account of the negotiations in Parliament is drawn.

twain. Proceedings of the Victoria West conference were reported fully in the *Victoria West Messenger* [*Nieuwsbode*] 21, 28 Dec. 1894. The conference had been called by a committee established at De Aar in November under Van den Heever's chairmanship. See also Jenkins, p. 70.

PAGE 157

congress. S. J. du Toit to Hofmeyr, 19 Feb. 1895 (Hofmeyr Papers).

inspectors S. J. du Toit to Te Water, 28 Feb. 1895 (Te Water Papers).

report. G. 1—1894, p. 31.

basis. For evidence of friction between farmers and inspectors, see *Notulen,* 1895 congress, p. 17; C. A. du Toit to Te Water, 11 July, and J. F. du Toit to Te Water, 8 June, 18 July 1894 (Te Water Papers).

minority. Notulen, 1895 congress, p. 17. This was, in substance, the same as the resolution adopted by majority vote at the Victoria West meeting.

redressed. Notulen, 1895 congress, p. 20.

branches. An example of a split in a Bond branch occurring after the 1895 congress is given in the *Notule Boek* of Tak No. 3, Hope Town (Cape Archives) under the date 26 Apr. 1895.

suggests. Hofmeyr, pp. 472–3.

PAGE 158

necessary. Assembly Debates, 1895, p. 471.

front. Innes, p. 114.

suspended. W. P. de Villiers to Rhodes, 30 Sept., 2 Dec. 1895 (Rhodes Papers).

subject. Sampson, p. 87.

affair. Molteno (1), p. 39.

PAGE 159

public. These are in the Hofmeyr Papers.

resignation. De Waal, J. H. H., pp. 201–3; Hofmeyr, p. 474 n.

loss. Innes, p. 113.

PAGE 160

role. Van der Poel (2), p. 20.

protest. Innes, pp. 110–11; Lewsen, ii, 171–2; Laurence, pp. 150–1; Michell, ii, 130–1 [suggesting that Robinson returned 'against his better judgement']. The Bond congress welcomed Robinson's impending return (*Notulen*, 1895 congress, pp. 14–15), though Robinson was clearly mistrustful of the Bond and had long been so.

1895. Van der Poel (1), pp. 76–82.

PAGE 161

traffic. Notulen, 1895 congress, p. 18; Van der Poel (1), p. 83; Van Winter, ii, 213.

power. Michell, ii, 93–6; Warhurst, pp. 116–27; Robinson, Gallagher and Denny, pp. 217–21, 415–18; but see also ibid., pp. 428, 431, 440, 445–9.

dividends. Walker (3), p. 442; Michell, ii, 118–26.

June. Walker (3), pp. 446–7.

PAGE 162

get. The Vryburgh election folder in the *Commissie van Toezicht* archives (Hofmeyr Papers) has correspondence dating from 13 June 1895, three days after the debate on Rhodes's motion in the Assembly. The nomination meeting took place on 13 November, and the annexation was proclaimed on the 16th.

necessary. Walker (2), pp. 65–7; Van Winter, ii, 218–19; Van der Poel (2) pp. 39–41.

Transvaal. Hofmeyr, p. 485.

Cabinet. Walker (2), pp. 70–4. Faure was Rhodes's Colonial Secretary.

PAGE 163

Kruger. Hofmeyr to Kruger, copy of telegram, 31 Dec. 1895 (Hofmeyr Papers): 'Ik hoop uwe burgers zullen sich kwyten als helden tegen Jamesons filibusters' ['I hope your burghers will quit themselves like heroes against Jameson's filibusters'].

State. Robinson to Chamberlain, 31 Dec. 1895, quoted in Kotzé, ii, 250.

President. Hofmeyr to Kruger, copy of telegram, 31 Dec. 1895 (Hofmeyr, Papers).

ministers. Onze Jan's memorandum, in the Hofmeyr Papers, is printed in part in Hofmeyr, p. 499.

order. Hofmeyr to Kruger, copy of telegram, 31 Dec. 1895 (Hofmeyr Papers).

PAGE 164

January. Van der Poel (2), p. 119; Kotzé, ii, 254. Contrast Hofmeyr, p. 492.

yet. Hofmeyr to Robinson, copy of telegram, n.d. (Hofmeyr Papers).

idea. S. J. du Toit to Hofmeyr, 1, 6 Jan. 1896 (Hofmeyr Papers).

generous. Hofmeyr to Kruger, copy of telegram, 2 Jan. 1896 (Hofmeyr Papers): '. . . Overwinnaars kunnen grootmoedig zyn.'

publish. The correspondence is quoted in Hofmeyr, pp. 494–5.

discussion. The memorandum is in the Hofmeyr Papers, and very briefly summarized in Hofmeyr, p. 500. See also De Waal, J. H. H., pp. 225–6; Van de Poel (2), pp. 155–6.

CHAPTER 9

PAGE 166

offer. Walker (1), pp. 267–8; Hofmeyr, p. 508; Innes, p. 127.

latter. Sprigg to Hofmeyr, 8 Jan. 1896 (Hofmeyr Papers).

note. The text, in the Hofmeyr Papers, is quoted in part in Hofmeyr, pp. 508–9, but not those parts which indicate Te Water's annoyance at Onze Jan's attitude.

Republics. Walker (2), p. 75.

Agriculture. Sprigg to Te Water, 10, 11 Jan.; Te Water to Sprigg, 10 Jan. 1896, telegrams (Te Water Papers).

PAGE 167

Company. Sir J. G. Kotzé to Hofmeyr, 27, 29 Jan. 1896 (Hofmeyr Papers).

Europe. Cloete, pp. 126–7.

ourselves. S. J. du Toit to Hofmeyr, 1 Jan. 1896 (Hofmeyr Papers).

Republic. Van Winter, ii, 253–4, 264–72; Kotzé, ii, 235–7.

Kruger. Kotzé to Hofmeyr, 14 Feb. 1896 (Hofmeyr Papers).

PAGE 168

these. De Waal, J. H. H., pp. 225–33.

meeting. T. Louw to Rhodes, 15 Jan. 1896 (Rhodes Papers).

Transvaal. Robinson to Hofmeyr, 8, 11 Feb. 1896, and the 'Memorandum on proposed Local Autonomy for Rand District' (MS., Hofmeyr's hand, 11 Feb. 1896); Robinson to Hofmeyr, 11 May 1896, and Hofmeyr's memorandum of 18 May entitled 'Suggestions in connection with proposed Transvaal reforms' (Hofmeyr Papers).

manner. S. J. du Toit to Hofmeyr, 6 Jan. 1896 (Hofmeyr Papers).

guilty. S. J. du Toit to Hofmeyr, 13 Jan. 1896 Hofmeyr Papers): 'Ik ben met u overtuigd dat hij schuldig is.' See also Hofmeyr, N. J., p. 393 [a motion by S. J. du Toit at a meeting in Paarl in early January, in which the Raid is condemned but reference also made to 'redelijke grieven der Uitlanders'].

PAGE 169

did. Walker (2), pp. 79–80; *Notulen,* 1896 congress, pp. 12–13.

PAGE 170

July. A. 6−1896.

charge. Du Toit, pp. 335–6; Hofmeyr, p. 514 [where the evidence may be slightly stretched]; Walker (2), p. 84; Molteno (1), p. 132. De Waal, J. H. H., p. 231, states categorically that financial help was given by Dr. Rutherfoord Harris in connexion with the purchase of premises in Cape Town (from which *Het Dagblad* was published only from May 1897).

Raid. Het Dagblad, 9 Dec. 1896, 7 Jan. 1897.

congress. Notulen. 1897 congress, p. 14; *Het Dagblad,* 13 Mar. 1897.

PAGE 171

else. Notulen, 1897 congress, pp. 23–4 [Dutch original].

unrepresentative. Notulen, 1897 congress, pp. 27, 34.

Raid. For accounts of the League, see Sank, chs. V, VI; Bitensky, especially chs. III, VII; Marais, pp. 161–70.

PAGE 172

one. Innes, pp. 143–4.

party. Het Dagblad, 28 Oct. 1897, 5 Mar. 1898.

PAGE 173

Church. On this movement, see Du Toit, pp. 369–73; Oberholster, pp. 225–46.

seat. Paarl district *bestuur* to *Commissie van Toezicht,* 17 Jan. 1898 (Hofmeyr Papers).

candidature. Sank, ch. VIII, where Faure's candidature is discussed from the League and S.A.P.A. points of view.

Rhodes. See his manifesto in the *Cape Times,* 22 Jan. 1898.

besturen. Het Dagblad, 6, 17 Nov. 1897, gives Du Toit's opposition to this decision, which was made after much correspondence between the members of the *Commissie van Toezicht.*

Colony. D. C. de Waal to Rhodes, 30 Dec. 1897 (Rhodes Papers).

PAGE 174

Faure. Hoffman to Hofmeyr, 3 Nov. 1897 (Hofmeyr Papers); *Het Dagblad*, 22 Dec. 1897.

candidate. Notulen, Cape Town Bond Branch, 23 Dec. 1897. T. Hofmeyr asked for, and received, permission 'alle zoodanige stappen te nemen als hij best zou achten in het belang van ons kandidaat' ['to take all such steps as he might think best in the interest of our candidate']; *Ons Land*, 25 Dec. 1897; *De Kolonist* [supplement to *Het Dagblad*], 15 Jan. 1898.

view. Paarl district *bestuur* to *Commissie van Toezicht*, 17 Jan., and comments thereon by Hofmeyr, 24 Jan., N. F. de Waal, 28 Jan., and S. J. du Toit, 1 Feb. 1898. See also report by T. P. Theron dated 4 Feb. 1898 (Hofmeyr Papers).

positions. Notulen, 1898 congress, p. 12. On the first ballot, the following were the votes for the first five places: J. H. Hofmeyr 76, J. M. Hoffman 49, N. F. de Waal 29, T. P. Theron 22, S. J. du Toit 18—an indication of the poor support Du Toit had in congress.

report. Notulen, 1898 congress, pp. 33, 39, giving the majority and S. J. du Toit's minority reports. The latter is discussed in Du Toit, pp. 182–4.

organization. 'die nadelig is voor of vijandig tegen de organisatie.'

PAGE 175

refusal. Notulen, 1898 congress, pp. 33–4.

endorsed. Theron to N. F. de Waal, 11 Apr. 1898, and annotation by Hofmeyr [Dutch originals] (Hofmeyr Papers).

election. Het Dagblad, 2 Apr. 1898.

principle. Het Dagblad, 26 Apr. 1898, gives the text of the Colonial Union's constitution as adopted at its inaugural meeting.

creation. Het Dagblad, 26 Apr. 1898.

PAGE 176

attain. Het Dagblad, 30 Sept. 1898.

Ishmael. P. J. Nienaber, in a book entitled *S. J. du Toit, die Eensame Ismael.*

idealism. Coetzee, pp. 189–91.

PAGE 177

epidemic. Notulen, 1897 congress, p. 33. So strong was congress's indignation that a proclamation ordering the slaughter of healthy beasts in infected herds had to be withdrawn.

Bond. Headlam, i, 65–7, quoting correspondence between Milner and Sprigg; *Notulen*, 1897 congress, p. 20; 1898 congress, p. 28.

efforts. Notulen, 1897 congress, p. 30 [motion by F. S. Malan].

cable. Notulen, 1898 congress, pp. 27, 40.

Milner. Headlam, i, 249–51.

PAGE 178

camp. Robinson, Gallagher and Denny reveal a substantial fear in the Colonial Office even before the Jameson Raid lest the alliance between Rhodes and the

Bond might disintegrate, and show (pp. 230–1) that this was largely owing to Sir Hercules Robinson's apprehensive advice. For London assumptions of Bond adherence to Kruger after the Raid, see ibid., pp. 433 [where the Cape Dutch are said to have joined with Afrikaner nationalists of the interior 'in defence of republicanism'], 438–46 [Chamberlain's fears, as inspired by Milner]. The authors tend to take these assumptions too much for granted, for they hardly represented the actual state of affairs in the Bond.

endorse. Hofmeyr, chs. XVII, XXVII; but see *Notulen*, Cape Town Bond branch, 9 Apr. 1885, where appreciation of his efforts is recorded.

PAGE 179

defence. Thus S. J. du Toit, in the commentary on his very anti-imperialist Programme of Principles, had written in 1883: 'De te vormen Vereenigde Staten van Zuid Afrika zullen staan onder Britsch Protectoraat, waaronder begrepen is onzer zijds dat wij onze havens openstellen voor de Britsche zeemacht, en in elken haven eene militaire bezetting der Rijksregeering toelaten, waarvoor Engeland op zich neemt ons tegen aanvallen van buitenlandsche, overzeesche mogendheden te beschermen; dat zoodanige bezettingen echter in geenerlei opzicht den vrijen handel mogen belemmeren, anders dan in tijden van oorlog.' ['The United States of South Africa to be formed shall stand under British Protection, whereby is meant on our side that we keep our harbours open for the British navy, and allow the Imperial Government to have a military base at each port, in return for which England undertakes to protect us against external overseas enemies; but that such bases may in no sense interfere with the freedom of trade, except in times of war.']

Governor. Notulen, 1898 congress, p. 31.

ousted. Quoted in Headlam, i, 61.

Republic. Headlam, i, 87, 476–9. The letters were dated 25 Aug. 1897 and 7 Aug. 1899.

PAGE 180

town. C. H. O. Marais to Te Water, 13 Feb. 1898 (Te Water Papers).

past. Onze Courant, 7 Mar. 1898 ['en om aan bloedverwanten in Zuid Afrika die regten te verzekeren die door Hare Majesteit onze Geëerbiedigde Koningin hun goedgunstelijk werden toegezegd in het verledene'].

re-election. Notulen, 1898 congress, pp. 23, 29.

PAGE 181

Republic. Headlam, i, 242–7, where much of Milner's speech is quoted.

criticism. Onze Courant, 10 Mar. 1898 [Dutch original].

life. Michell, ii, 221; Walker (2), p. 105.

harm. For the effect of the Raid on the political loyalties of the Merriman–Innes–Sauer group, see esp. correspondence published in Lewsen, ii, 210 [Merriman to Innes, 2 Feb.], 214–16 [Merriman to Bryce, 29 Mar.], 218–21 [Merriman to Innes, 2, 20 Apr., Innes to Merriman, 15 Apr. 1896].

areas. Walker (2), pp. 98–9.

PAGE 182

Opposition. Walker (2), pp. 106–10.

constituencies. Notulen, 1897 congress, p. 38; 1898 congress, p. 41.

desirable. G. 8—1898: Report of the Redistribution of Seats Commission.

supporters. W. P. de Villiers to Te Water, 6 June 1898 (Te Water Papers); *Notulen,* Cape Town Bond branch, 20 May 1898.

realized. Headlam, i, 253–4, quoting Milner to Chamberlain, 18 May 1898.

PAGE 183

Sprigg. Walker (2), pp. 109–11.

campaign. J. C. Smuts to Hofmeyr, 31 Jan. 1897 (Hofmeyr Papers); Hancock, pp. 67 note 2, 566; Scoble and Abercrombie, pp. 236–7.

fund. Michell, ii, 217–18; Scoble and Abercrombie, pp. 236–40; Marais, p. 225; Headlam, i, 264 note 3.

admitted. Het Dagblad, 3 Dec. 1897, quoting a speech made by Kruger at Standerton.

outside. Michell, ii, 198, 222; 'Vindex', p. 573; Williams, p. 294; Walker (2), p. 113.

PAGE 184

blankets. Marais, p. 225; Walker (1), p. 326. *Ons Land* of 15 Feb. 1898 contains a report of the refutation by Hofmeyr in a speech at Paarl of the rumour that W. J. Leyds had transferred £25,000 to the Afrikaner Bond in the Colony through Carl Borckenhagen. For other such refutations, see a letter from Hofmeyr in *Ons Land,* 23 July 1898; Hofmeyr, p. 527; Molteno (1), pp. 142–3; *Notulen,* 1899 congress, p. 20.

constituency. E. Marshall to Hofmeyr, 17 Aug. 1898 (Hofmeyr Papers): 'Our party kept together but the whole coloured vote turned against us at the last minute, in fact some promised at the door to vote for our candidate and went in and voted solid for S[ivewright]. They had their instructions from Faure. . . . ' Cf. A. F. Weich, Namaqualand, to Hofmeyr, 12 Sept. 1898 (loc. cit.): 'I'm distressed that our coloured people have been bought by Rhodes's money against Afrikaner party'; *Ons Land,* 5 Jan. 1899: 'De overgroote meerderheid onzer kleurling-kiezers bij de jongste electie "progressief" bleek.'

luck. Headlam, i, 275–7, quoting Milner to Chamberlain, 20 Sept. 1898: 'The result may be said to be due entirely to luck, as one of the doubtful seats fell to the Bond by a majority of 2 [Aliwal North], another by a majority of 10 [Somerset East] and a third by a majority of 20 [Oudtshoorn, presumably; but Gert Olivier, Juta's vanquisher, was a Rhodes man]. . . . On the other hand, no seat won by a Ministerialist has been won by less than 135.' Milner calculated, reasonably, that the Progressives had polled 6,500 more votes than the Bondsmen.

Zambesi. Ons Land, 7 Apr. 1898.

PAGE 185

struggle. Imvo Neliso Lomzi [the current title of Jabavu's paper], 31 Mar. 1898.

Rhodes. Jabavu to Hofmeyr, 2 July 1898 (Hofmeyr Papers): ' . . . You may have noticed that I have been roundly abused in Jingo-Quarters for supporting Mr. Sauer, Mr. Merriman, Mr. Solomon, Mr. Hay and others, who are said to have contaminated themselves by voting with the Bond on the no confidence question. I don't mind this as these gentlemen are old friends of mine and of our people; and I know they have sided with your people because they feel they have been wronged. Now I would strongly impress on you & your people not to see them penalised for their stand; and you could do so much for the cause by co-operating with our people in constituencies where there are Dutch, English and Native voters, neither of which sections can command a majority.'

neutrality. Hofmeyr to M. J. du Plessis, M.L.A., 4 July; A. J. Botha, secretary, Queenstown district *bestuur*, to Hofmeyr, 16 July; J. H. de Lange, chairman, Queenstown district *bestuur*, to Hofmeyr, 19 July 1898 (Hofmeyr Papers). Both Progressives succeeded.

stand. D. Janse van Rensburg to Hofmeyr, 30 June; Jabavu to Hofmeyr, telegram, 13 July 1898 (Hofmeyr Papers).

PAGE 186

Transvaal. S. C. Cronwright-Schreiner to Hofmeyr, 14 July 1898 (Hofmeyr Papers).

kind. See, for example, Jourdan, pp. 57–61; Michell, ii, 228–34; Williams, pp. 294–5. To help his campaign, Rhodes established a new Bantu-language newspaper, *Izwi Labantu*, edited by A. K. Soga.

Progressives. Molteno (1), p. 160. See the Oudtshoorn election folder in the Hofmeyr Papers.

votes. Headlam, i, 276, quoting Milner to Chamberlain, 20 Sept. 1898.

PAGE 187

him. De Waal, J. H. H., pp. 247–51.

railway. Theron to Hofmeyr, 28 July; P. J. du Toit to Hofmeyr, 6 Aug. 1898 (Hofmeyr Papers).

seat. Molteno (1), pp. 50–4; Nienaber (2), p. 219. Le Roex's 474 votes compared badly with the 1,566 and 1,424 polled by the Bond candidates.

men. See especially J. A. van Niekerk to Hofmeyr, 17 June; C. J. Kieser to Hofmeyr, 27 June, 1 July with enclosures, 4 July 1898 (Hofmeyr Papers).

surprising. Notulen, 1899 congress, p. 20 ['niet alleen bemoedigend, maar uiterst verrassend'].

PAGE 188

proposed. Headlam, i, 273–7; Marais, pp. 226–7.

Bond. De Waal, J. H. H., p. 253.

CHAPTER 10

PAGE 189

portfolio. Onze Courant, 20 Oct.; *Ons Land,* 15 Oct. 1898. Te Water wished to avoid being dubbed a career politician.

himself. For comments on the composition of Schreiner's Cabinet, see Headlam, i, 280–4; Walker (2), pp. 117–20; De Waal, J. H. H., p. 255; Laurence, p. 166; and for the early use of the name 'South African Party', Walker (2), p. 113.

PAGE 190

Waal. According to Walker (2), pp. 117–18, Hofmeyr urged De Waal's inclusion instead of Richard Solomon. But J. H. H. de Waal states that although his father was earmarked for Agriculture, Onze Jan discouraged the appointment because he was not learned enough for a Cabinet post.

succumb. Walker (2), p. 120; Michell, ii, 242–3.

him. De Waal, J. H. H., pp. 255–61. They began to urge the Piketberg electors to press for his resignation.

PAGE 191

follow. Headlam, i, 280–4, quoting Milner to Chamberlain 19 Oct. 1898.

checked. Butler, pp. 392, 405.

acquaintance. Butler, p. 396.

policeman. Marais, pp. 237–43; Headlam, i, ch. XI; Breytenbach, i, 239–47; documentation in C. 9345, especially pp. 126–32.

PAGE 192

timed. Merriman to Steyn 1 Jan.; Lippert to Merriman 10, 11 Jan. 1899 (Merriman Papers).

compromise. Marais, pp. 247–58; Fitzpatrick, pp. 175–9; Hancock, pp. 86–8.

Rand. Marais, p. 245.

grievances. Marais, pp. 257–8; text in Amery, i, 225–32.

Commissioner. Merriman to Schreiner, telegram, 4 Mar.; Milner to Merriman 13 Mar.; Fischer to Merriman 20 Mar.; Merriman to Fischer, Schreiner and Binns, telegrams, 23 Mar.; Smuts to Merriman 29 Mar.; Fischer to Merriman 6 Apr.; Reitz to Merriman 7 Apr. 1899 (Merriman Papers); Headlam, i, 362–5.

PAGE 193

affairs. Marais, pp. 185–6; Headlam, i, 304–6, quoting Milner to Hely-Hutchinson 23 Feb. 1899; Walker (2), pp. 134–5.

presidents. Walker (1), pp. 332–4; (2), pp. 134, 138, 141.

behalf. Hofmeyr, pp. 533–4 [text of Sivewright's telegram]; Marais, p. 273.

caution. Headlam, i, 375–6; Van der Merwe, i, 162 ff. [Steyn]; Hofmeyr, p. 534; Walker (2), pp. 142–3 [Reitz]; Hancock, p. 91; Walker (2), pp. 143–4; Smuts to Hofmeyr 10 May 1899 (Hofmeyr Papers) [Smuts]. Hofmeyr, p. 535, gives Onze Jan's replies.

PAGE 194

Bloemfontein. Headlam, i, 374–5; Kieser, pp. 137–8; C. 9345, pp. 239–43.

enemy. Headlam, i, 378, quoting Milner to Conyngham Greene, 12 May 1899.

advantageous. Walker (2), pp. 146–8; Marais, pp. 277–8; Headlam, i, 391–2;

Garvin and Amery, iii, 403. See Merriman to Fischer, 17 May 1899 (Merriman Papers), for an attempt by Merriman to have Hofmeyr invited to Bloemfontein.

value. Hofmeyr to Steyn, telegram, 8 or 9 May 1899 (Hofmeyr Papers); Marais, p. 279, quoting Hofmeyr to Sivewright 8 May 1899.

insist. C. 9404, pp. 14–59 [minutes of the Bloemfontein conference]. Marais pp. 280–4.

unreasonable. S.A. News, 8, 9 June; *Het Oosten*, 8 June; *Onze Courant*, 8, 12 June; *Ons Land* 8, 10 June 1899.

PAGE 195

attitude. Walker (2), pp. 154–6.

side. Notes by Hofmeyr on a letter from Olive Schreiner, 3 June 1899 (Hofmeyr Papers).

standing. Te Water to Steyn, copy of telegram, 9 June 1899 (Hofmeyr Papers).

stand. Fischer to Hofmeyr, 8 June; Fischer to Te Water, copy of telegram, 10 June; Smuts to Hofmeyr, telegram, 10 June 1899 (Hofmeyr Papers); Hancock, p. 97.

PAGE 196

consultations. Te Water to Fischer, copy of telegram, 13 June 1899 (Hofmeyr Papers).

held. Fischer to Hofmeyr, telegram, 13 June 1899 (Hofmeyr Papers).

British. Headlam, i, 349–53 [text of the 'helot' dispatch, which is also given, with one paragraph omitted, in C. 9345, pp. 209–12]. For Chamberlain's dispatch of 10 May, see C. 9345, pp. 226–31; Headlam, i, 356–8.

flag. S.A. News, 5 July; *Ons Land*, 6 July; *Onze Courant*, 10 July 1899.

accusations. For evidence in support of Milner, see Worsfold (2), pp. 119–21; Walker (2), p. 164 [reference to a letter in the *Stellalander* which is given in English translation in C. 9345, p. 182]. Conclusions in this paragraph were reached without reference to Scholtz, G. D., ii, 217–18, where a similar analysis is given.

PAGE 197

demonstrations. e.g. by *Het Oosten*, 29 June 1899.

July. S.A. News, Onze Courant, 13 July; *Het Oosten*, 20 July 1899; Hobson, pp. 99–110.

Heever. Notes by Hofmeyr on a letter from Edgar Walton, 19 May 1899 (Hofmeyr Papers).

PAGE 198

party. Smuts to Hofmeyr, 13 June 1899 (Hofmeyr Papers); Hancock, pp. 97–8 [Dutch original].

Bloemfontein. For the proposals which Fischer took to Pretoria, see Hofmeyr, pp. 539–40. Walker (2), pp. 157–8, Kieser, p. 158, and Marais, pp. 290–1, all refer to discussions between Milner and Fischer. Kieser suggests that Milner was satisfied with the proposals, Marais that he thought they were a 'considerable advance' on Kruger's Bloemfontein offer.

Volksraad. C. 9415, p. 13; Headlam, i, 447–8, quoting Milner to Chamberlain, telegram, 30 June 1899; Marais, p. 291.

conciliator. Garvin and Amery, iii, 415–16; Marais, p. 292.

PAGE 199

Government. Hofmeyr and Herholdt to Schreiner, telegram, 3 July 1899 (Hofmeyr Papers): 'In our conference Sunday night with Grobler [and] Smuts we drew attention to many shortcomings in concept and handed them written memo containing following recommendations. Firstly oath not to be obligatory without full franchise. Secondly residential qualification for future arrivals not to be longer than seven years in any case. Thirdly more liberal provision for giving full franchise without delay on passing of proposed law to old residents who arrived after promulgation [of] law of 25 Aug. 90. Fourthly four additional Volksraad members to mining districts and these not to be neutralised by other new members. Fifthly reforms dynamite. Sixthly reference to another and fuller memo in wh[ich] we enter more in detail on sliding scale, registration, and bribery laws, acting in understanding with other party, etc.' A copy of the 'fuller memo' referred to is in the Hofmeyr Papers.

districts. Hofmeyr, pp. 542–3; Walker (2), p. 164; Marais, p. 296.

them. According to Greene, quoted in Headlam, i, 453, Onze Jan appealed to the serpentine wisdom of the members. According to Hofmeyr's biographer, he frightened them into agreement with a piece of spine-chilling oratory (Hofmeyr pp. 543–4).

1890-5. C. 9415, p. 44; Headlam, i, 459–60, quoting Milner to Chamberlain, telegram, 13 July 1899.

Milner. C. 9415, p. 13; Headlam, i, 447–8, quoting Milner to Chamberlain, telegram, 29 June 1899, in which Milner pointedly observed that in the Transvaal's response to Fischer's proposals 'there was no question whatever of agreeing to the minimum demands made at Bloemfontein by me'. For Milner's original attitude to Fischer's mission, however, see the references in note to '*Bloemfontein*' on p. 198, above.

peace. Schreiner to Herholdt, three telegrams, 6 July (Hofmeyr Papers); Herholdt and Hofmeyr to Schreiner, two telegrams, 6 July 1899 (Schreiner Papers); Walker (2), pp. 165–7.

unity. Smuts to Hofmeyr, 9 July 1899 (Hofmeyr Papers).

return. Notulen, Cape Town Bond branch, 12 July; *S.A. News*, 13 July 1899.

PAGE 200

secured. e.g. *Onze Courant*, 13 July; *Het Oosten*, 20 July 1899.

followed. See *Onze Courant*, 24 July, 5 Aug.; *Ons Land*, 25 July 1899.

invalidated. C. 9415, p. 43; Headlam, i, 456, 465–6, quoting Chamberlain to Milner, telegram, 11 July, and Milner to Chamberlain, telegram, 17 July 1899.

field. C. 9415, p. 45: Milner to Chamberlain, telegram, 13 July, quoting State Secretary, S.A. Republic to Greene of same date; Headlam, i, 457, quoting

Greene to Milner, 12 July 1899 [account of conversation with State Attorney, S.A. Republic].

consultation. e.g. Te Water to Smuts, copies of telegrams, 11, 13 July 1899 (Hofmeyr Papers).

Steyn. Fischer to Hofmeyr, telegram, 13 July 1899 (Hofmeyr Papers).

measure. All are in the Hofmeyr Papers [Dutch originals]. Kieser argues, p. 176, that the Cape friends would not have succeeded in their efforts but for the influence of Steyn on Kruger; but their ability to influence Smuts was a factor of major importance.

franchise. Marais, pp. 297–8.

provisions. Marais, pp. 302–3; Headlam, i, 468, quoting Chamberlain to Milner, telegram, 18 July; C. 9518, pp. 7–14, quoting Chamberlain to Milner, 27 July 1899, and telegraphic summary of same date.

war. Te Water to Fischer, 31 July; Hofmeyr to Fischer, 3 Aug. 1899, telegrams (Hofmeyr Papers); Walker (2), pp. 171–2.

servants. Contained in Te Water to Fischer, telegram, 11 Aug. 1899 (Hofmeyr Papers).

us. Fischer to Hofmeyr, 11 Aug.; Te Water to Fischer, 12 Aug. 1899, telegrams (Hofmeyr Papers).

today. Steyn to Hofmeyr, telegram, 14 Aug. 1899 (Hofmeyr Papers).

immediately. For the resultant Smuts–Greene negotiations, see Marais, pp. 308–12; C. 9530, p. 24: Smuts to Greene, two letters, 25 Aug. 1899. For Greene's account of the negotiations, see C. 9521, pp. 44–5: Milner to Chamberlain, two telegrams, 15 Aug. 1899.

suzerainty. The meaning of 'suzerainty' and 'paramountcy', in the name of which Britain claimed the right of exclusive supervision over at least the external relations of the S.A. Republic, is discussed by Marais at pp. 195–200.

clear. Reitz to Hofmeyr, 28 Aug. 1899 (Hofmeyr Papers) [Dutch original].

Rhodes. Smuts to Hofmeyr, 22 Aug. 1899 [signature deleted] (Hofmeyr Papers).

paramountcy. Marais, pp. 310–12; Headlam, i, 493 [referring to Chamberlain's speech on 26 Aug. 1899 in Birmingham], 516 [quoting Milner to Chamberlain, 16 Aug.], 525 [quoting Milner to Chamberlain, telegram, 4 Sept. 1899].

terms. Marais, loc. cit.; C. 9521, pp. 44, 47. Smuts had 'assumed' that H.M. Government, in return for the concessions he offered, would reciprocate in the manner he proposed. Reitz stated that such reciprocation was 'expressly conditional' on the Republic's offer.

kill. Hancock, p. 103.

State. See Walker (2), ch. IX.

Government. Nor was Milner fully informed of their activities, according to Headlam, i, 499–500, quoting Milner to Chamberlain, 30 Aug. 1899. It is noteworthy that Milner ceased to confide in Hofmeyr after his return from Pretoria in mid-July, perhaps because of Greene's information that he had used subterfuge when addressing the Volksraad secret session. See Headlam, i, 453; Herholdt to Steyn, copy of telegram, 15 Sept. 1899 (Hofmeyr Papers).

PAGE 205

Books. Hofmeyr to Smuts, 30 Aug. 1899, quoted at length in Hofmeyr, p. 550.

Town. C. 9521, pp. 52–4; reported in Milner to Chamberlain, telegram, 5 Sept. 1899.

Pretoria. Te Water to Fischer, copy of telegram in Hofmeyr's hand, 6 Sept. 1899 (Hofmeyr Papers).

it. C. 9521, pp. 64–5: Chamberlain to Milner, telegram, 8 Sept. 1899.

rights. Herholdt to Fischer, copy of telegram, 13 Sept. 1899 (Hofmeyr Papers); Hofmeyr, p. 551.

demand. Fischer to Hofmeyr, 13 Sept.; Steyn to Hofmeyr, 14 Sept. 1899, telegrams (Hofmeyr Papers); Hofmeyr, p. 552.

effect. Herholdt to Steyn, copy of telegram in Hofmeyr's hand, 14 Sept. 1899 (Hofmeyr Papers).

PAGE 206

point. Contained in Fischer to Hofmeyr, telegram, 16 Sept. 1899 (Hofmeyr Papers); Hofmeyr, p. 553.

it. Hofmeyr to Fischer, copy of telegram, 18 Sept. 1899 (Hofmeyr Papers); Hofmeyr, p. 554.

date. Ons Land, 21 Sept. 1899.

reply. C. 9530, pp. 15, 18: reported in Milner to Chamberlain, Chamberlain to Milner, telegrams, 21, 25 Sept. 1899.

draft. Walker (2), p. 192.

policy. C. 9530, pp. 39–40, 45. For the background of the Bond petition see Molteno (1), pp. 169, 173–93.

PAGE 207

Queen. Made by the S.A. Vigilance Committee in a pamphlet entitled *The Transvaal, Past and Present, and its Future* (Cape Town, 1900).

arbitrament. Dormer, p. 30.

borders. Coetzee, p. 141, quoting the *Express*, 27 Dec. 1887.

adversaries. Amery, i, 266–7.

PAGE 208

take. See especially Walker (2), pp. 140–1, quoting Schreiner to Smuts, copy, 1 May 1899 (Schreiner Papers; Hofmeyr, p. 550, quoting Hofmeyr to Smuts, copy, 30 Aug. 1899 (Hofmeyr Papers).

PAGE 209

trapped. Fischer to Hofmeyr, telegram, 12 Sept. 1899 (Hofmeyr Papers).

CHAPTER 11

resignation. Walker (2), p. 197; Cloete, p. 149.

Republics. Keith, i, 314; ii, 871–2; Walker (2), pp. 186–7; Headlam, i, 503 [on the neutrality question]; Walker (2), p. 195; Cd. 43, p. 135: enclosures in Milner to Chamberlain, 17 Oct. 1899 [on Steyn's attitude].

persuasion. Keith, i, 122; Headlam, i, 461.

defence. Cd. 43, pp. 11, 33, 37: Milner to Chamberlain, 30 Aug., 6 Sept., with enclosures; Chamberlain to Milner, 7 Oct. 1899.

Kerk. Schreiner to Resident Magistrates and Field Cornets, 9 Oct.; to Ds. J. H. Hofmeyr, 10 Oct. 1899 (Schreiner Papers); Breytenbach, ii, 15; Walker (2), pp. 198–200; Strydom, pp. 101–2.

November. De Afrikaander Partij en de Oorlog, pp. 23–4 [an instruction dated 6 October, signed by T. P. Theron, D. J. A. van Zyl and N. F. de Waal, as chairman, vice-chairman and secretary-treasurer respectively of the provincial *bestuur*].

Taung. Cd. 420, pp. 26–73: Milner to Chamberlain, 14 Aug. 1900, enclosing magistrates' reports on the rebellion.

district. For the Barkly East rebellion, see affidavits by G. F. Wilhelm, A. R. A. Wilhelm, Meshek Maqubela, Aaron Goldberg and others; Resident Magistrate, Barkly East, to Lex, Cape Town, 19 Oct., telegram; D. A. Campbell, 'Report on State of Affairs before and at Occupation of Barkly East by F[ree] S[tate] Commando' (MS., 15 Dec. 1899) (in A. G. 2014); J. P. Smit, Dordrecht, to Merriman, telegram, 8 Nov. 1899 (Merriman Papers). From the evidence of these documents it is legitimate to infer that the rebellion was premeditated to some extent. The O.F.S. appointed as landdrost the G. G. Munnik who had once been colonial magistrate there.

charges. For Van Pletzen's attitude, contrast Merriman to Van Pletzen and others, telegram, 21 Oct. 1899, and Van Pletzen's telegraphic reply (Merriman Papers), and the evidence quoted against Van Pletzen in A. G. 2013–15.

encouragement. For Sauer's mission, see Cd. 43, pp. 220–3; Sauer to Schreiner, telegram, 27 Nov. 1899 (Schreiner Papers); also Cd. 261, pp. 47–8; Cd. 420, pp. 107–8. In view of the handling of this incident in Headlam, ii, 16–17, and of the tendency of contemporaries to belittle Sauer's efforts—see the speech by Col. Schermbrucker in Assembly Debates, 1900, pp. 37–9—it is perhaps necessary to stress Sauer's obvious integrity on this occasion.

Republics. Cd. 903, p. 119: Hely-Hutchinson [Milner's successor as Governor of the Cape Colony] to Chamberlain, 22 Oct. 1901. Figures given here tally with the unpublished returns referred to, in C.O. 48/555, and with the *Notulen,* 1899 congress, pp. 43–4, 53, 74.

legislature. Schreiner to Sauer, draft telegram, 1 Dec. 1899 (Schreiner Papers) Assembly Debates 1902, pp. 176–7 [Joubert]. Cd. 264, p. 2: Milner to

Chamberlain, 16 Jan. 1900, quoting General Grobler to O.F.S. Government, 16 Nov. 1899; and telegraphic correspondence between the Colonial Law Department and the Resident Magistrate, Naauwpoort, 11, 12 Dec. 1899 (Schreiner Papers) [Van der Walt]. J. H. O'Connell, Resident Magistrate, Gordonia to Schreiner, typed copy, 22 Mar. 1900 (Schreiner Papers) [Schröder].

firearms. Cd. 420, pp. 34–73 [replies of magistrates to the question 'What restraints (if any) were imposed upon those who refused to identify themselves with the invaders?']; ibid., pp. 79–81: Milner to Chamberlain, 5 Sept. 1900. Contrast Cd. 264, p. 9: A. S. du Plessis to Schreiner, 2 Apr. 1900.

accuracy. Strydom, pp. 87–8 [Afrikaans original]; Amery, iii, 78–9, 85–7.

Republics. This committee concerned itself purely with relief work. Its letter book and minutes are in the Hofmeyr Papers.

PAGE 213

performance. Assembly Debates, 1900, pp. 48–50 [Theron], 97–109 [Schreiner], 219–21 [Hoffman]; 1902, p. 107 [Theron]; P. Dreyer, Kenhardt, to Schreiner, 1 June 1900 (Schreiner Papers).

over. De Afrikaander Partij en de Oorlog, p. 24. The public reason given for postponement was the futility of meeting before the opposing parties were prepared to talk peace. But see Theron to Hofmeyr, telegram, 25 Oct., N. F. de Waal to Hofmeyr, telegram, 26 Oct. 1899 (Hofmeyr Papers). The latter wrote: 'Your wire received. Theron suggests postponing congress indefinitely. I am strongly same opinion believing that proclamation does away with danger of volks agitation.' Hofmeyr noted assent. The proclamation referred to was presumably that printed in Cd. 43, p. 101, in which Milner on 25 October threatened to bring charges of high treason against Colonials taken in rebellion.

met. Circular dated 17 November, printed in Onze Courant, 27 Nov. 1899.

be. Cd. 261, pp. 182–4: Milner to Chamberlain, 6 June 1900; Notulen, 1900 congress, pp. 6–7, See Cd. 261, pp. 28–9, for arguments against postponement put forward by Ons Land.

men. Walker (2), p. 209; Mackarness to Merriman, 6 Dec. 1899 (Merriman Papers).

20th. Enclosure, 'The Conciliation Committee of South Africa', in W. Hay to Schreiner, 20 Mar. 1900 (Schreiner Papers).

district. Cd. 43, pp. 222–3: report from the S.A. News enclosed in Milner to Chamberlain, 29 Nov. 1899; Headlam, ii, 17.

May. Cd. 261, p. 127: Kruger to Steyn, 20 Jan., enclosed in Milner to Chamberlain, 25 Apr. 1900; Cd. 624, pp. 41–2; Milner to Schreiner, 12 Sept. 1900 (Schreiner Papers). Between 19 March, when it reported an address by Hargrove entitled 'Some talks with Presidents Kruger and Steyn in January 1900', and 20 June when it reported his impending departure for England, the S.A. News followed him through Cape Town, Stellenbosch, Paarl, Wellington, Worcester, Ceres, Montagu, Robertson, George, Humansdorp and Graaff-Reinet.

PAGE 214

origin. Notulen, 1900 congress, p. 24 ['Dit Bestuur, alhoewel met die oproeping en het werk der Volksvergadering als zoodanig niets te doen gehad hebbende, daar het spontaan uit het volk ontstaan is zonder ons toedoen . . . ']. See also the comment by N. F. de Waal in Assembly Debates, 1902, p. 108.

roles. See reports of meetings in Cd. 261, pp. 58–9, 92–4, 148, in all of which Bondsmen played leading roles. At Stellenbosch, where there was no Bond branch, there was an active conciliation committee.

policy. Cd. 261, p. 126: Milner to Chamberlain, 25 Apr. 1900.

gathering. Estimates of attendance varied between 1,200 [Civil Commissioner, Graaff-Reinet, to Secretary, Law Department, copy of telegram, 1 June 1900 (Schreiner Papers)] and 2,500 counted at the gates (*S.A. News*, 5 June 1900). It was a far larger gathering than a normal Bond congress. See also *Ons Land*, 5 June 1900; Strydom, pp. 126–30.

widely. Cd. 261, pp. 184–90 [the *Cape Times* report, from the issue of 1 June 1900].

PAGE 215

Republics. Cd. 261, pp. 53–5, 69–73, 77–83, 94, 139.

independence. Cd. 261, pp. 126–32: Milner to Chamberlain, 25 Apr. 1900, with enclosures.

soil. The original Merriman–Hargrove correspondence is in the Merriman Papers.

recommendation. Cd. 261, p. 150: enclosures in Milner to Chamberlain, 16 May 1900.

PAGE 216

aloof. Hofmeyr, pp. 557–9; Solomon to Schreiner, 22 Mar. 1900 (Schreiner Papers); Walker (2), pp. 209–10.

March. Snyman, pp. 21–4; Cd. 264, pp. 11–12. Chamberlain's dispatch was quoted in Milner's minute of 14 April 1900.

Republics. Headlam, ii, 106–7, quoting Milner to Chamberlain, 26 Mar. 1900.

Ministry. Headlam, ii, 56–8.

justice. Headlam, ii, 106–7 [Milner]; Solomon to Schreiner, 28 Mar. 1900 (Schreiner Papers) [Solomon]. That Chamberlain agreed appears from Cd. 264, pp. 11–12.

PAGE 217

Afrikaner. Te Water to Schreiner, 2 Apr. 1900 (Schreiner Papers).

well. Cd. 264, p. 13: Ministers' minute, 27 Apr. 1900.

itself. Headlam, ii, 106–7.

Indemnity. Solomon to Schreiner, 22 Mar. 1900 (Schreiner Papers).

him. Merriman to Schreiner, 31 Mar. 1900 (Schreiner Papers).

situation. Cd. 264, pp. 14–32; Molteno (1), p. 201.

PAGE 218

will. Cd. 264, pp. 7–8: Chamberlain to Milner, telegram, 4 May 1900.

policy. Cd. 264, pp. 37–40: minute by R. Solomon, 17 May 1900.

term. Cd. 264, pp. 33–4: Chamberlain to Milner, telegram, 10 June 1900.

Colony. Cd. 264, pp. 40–3: Minutes by Merriman, 20 May, and Te Water, 19 May; Hofmeyr, p. 559, quoting Hofmeyr to Schreiner, 22 May 1900; Walker (2), p. 228.

fullest. *S.A. News*, 18 June 1900 [speech by N. F. de Waal]; De Waal, J. H. H., pp. 274–5, quoting D. C. de Waal to an undisclosed addressee, 25 June 1900. The latter account was written by a supporter of Schreiner, stressing the Premier's fear that if the Government proposals were not adopted the rebels might suffer the full effects of the 1892 treason law. Merriman's diary of 8, 9 June 1900 also contains a brief report.

PAGE 220

June. D. C. de Waal recorded that 8 members supported Schreiner, and more than 30 opposed him. Molteno (1), pp. 201–2, gives the opposition 39 and Schreiner 'four or five'. Michell, ii, 283, states that 'only two of his colleagues and ten other supporters stood by him'. Walker (2), p. 233, records the defeat of the Premier by 29 votes to 8. It was at all events a decisive defeat. For Schreiner's explanation of his actions to the Bond, see his letter to N. F. de Waal, 13 June 1900, in the *Notulen*, 1900 congress, pp. 21–2.

impossible. Schreiner Papers.

informer. Solomon to Merriman, 30 Mar. 1900 (Merriman Papers).

colleagues. Ministers' minute on civil servants on active service, 19–24 Apr. 1900 (Schreiner Papers).

demand. Walker (2), pp. 231–2; Merriman's diary 20, 23 Mar., 12 Apr., 11, 18, 23, 28 May, 7, 9 June 1900.

manner. e.g. Merriman's diary 9 Apr., 22, 26 May, 13 June 1900.

PAGE 221

Times. For illustration of the restrictions on the distribution of newspapers, see Strydom, pp. 208–9, and n. 96 below.

members. *Notulen*, 1900 congress, p. 26.

Malan. *Notulen*, 1900 congress, p. 25. The members of the commission were: T. P. Theron, D. J. A. van Zyl, N. F. de Waal (all of the executive), J. H. Schoeman (Middelburg) and F. S. Malan. For the text of the resolution, see *Notulen*, pp. 24–5, and for Malan's speech, *De Afrikaander Partij en de Oorlog*, pp. 15–22.

PAGE 222

Spirit. *De Afrikaander Partij en de Oorlog*, pp. 4–7.

party. Merriman's diary, 9 June 1900.

Schreiner. *Notulen*, 1900 congress, pp. 22–3; *S.A. News*, 18 June 1900.

him. Headlam, ii, 114–15, quoting Milner to Chamberlain, 4 July 1900.

contrary. Te Water to Schreiner, 22, 23 July; Theron to Schreiner, 24 July (misdated Aug.) 1900, and Schreiner's notes thereon (Schreiner Papers).

PAGE 223

released. L. Abrahamson to Rhodes, 9 July 1900 (Rhodes Papers).

June. Assembly Debates, 1900, pp. 186–7.

law. Assembly Debates, 1900, pp. 9–15.

PAGE 224

repealed. Assembly Debates, 1900, pp. 48–50.

it. Innes, p. 188; Snyman, p. 28. Text in Cd. 420, pp. 110–18.

PAGE 225

capacities. Cd. 261, p. 187 [Cartwright]; *De Afrikaander Partij en de Oorlog*, p. 19 [Malan].

PAGE 226

property. Assembly Debates, 1900 pp. 199–201, 249–50.

seats. Herholdt to Schreiner, 26 Nov., 14 Dec.; C. Searle to Schreiner, 25 Nov., 1 Dec. 1900 (Schreiner Papers). For the private referendum, see Walker (2), pp. 239–41.

PAGE 227

time. *S.A. News*, 10 Oct.; Assembly Debates, 1900, pp. 429–30 [Merriman], 48–50 [Theron], 166–70 [Smartt], 219–21 [Hoffman].

Jingoism. *S.A. News*, 20 Oct., 8 Dec. 1900 [report by Ds. P. J. G. de Vos].

me. *S.A. News*, 19 Oct. 1900.

Republics. *S.A. News*, 12 Nov. 1900.

policy. See, for example, the article from the *Worcester Advertiser* quoted in Cd. 547, p. 13, dated 23 November, and the article indicting General French in *Ons Land* of 24 November 1900. These articles formed the main evidence against the Bond editors, J. E. de Jong and F. S. Malan, when they were tried in April 1901.

population. Headlam, ii, 170–2, quoting Milner to Chamberlain, 14 Nov., 5 Dec. 1900.

PAGE 228

result. Merriman to N. F. de Waal, 23 Nov. 1900 (Merriman Papers).

gathering. Assembly Debates, 1902, p. 108.

unwisdom. N. F. de Waal, T. P. Theron, 'Observations on Mr. Merriman's letter of 23rd November' (Merriman Papers).

involved. Full report in the *S.A. News*, 8 Dec. 1900.

PAGE 229

reversed. Cd. 547, pp. 21–3: Milner to Chamberlain, 12 Dec. 1900, enclosing the *Cape Times* report of the interview from its issue of the same date.

policy. Cd. 547, p. 29: Chamberlain to Milner, 18 Jan. 1901.

discipline. Merriman to N. F. de Waal, 23 Nov. 1900 (Merriman Papers).

England. See Walker (1), p. 384; Laurence, pp. 186–7. The confusion apparently arose from De Waal's agreement that Beaufort West would make a suitable venue. The Cape Town meeting is reported in *Ons Land,* 8 Jan. 1901. See also Agnes to Julia Merriman, 8 Jan. 1901 (Merriman Papers), where it is suggested that Merriman had difficulty in winning acceptance for his moderate proposals.

PAGE 230

Volksraad. Hofmeyr to Merriman, 17 Feb. 1901 (Merriman Papers), quoted also in Hofmeyr to Jan de Waal, 20 Feb. 1901 (Hofmeyr Papers); Hofmeyr p. 563. 'Of course your request will not be granted', Hofmeyr told Merriman on 18 March.

settlement. S.A. News, 17 Apr. 1901 [text of the petition, of which an original printed copy exists in the Merriman Papers].

Chamberlain. Laurence, pp. 188–95.

is. Hofmeyr to Jan de Waal, 20 Feb. 1901 (Hofmeyr Papers).

PAGE 231

prisoners. The trials were not reported in the Cape law reports; but see the *S.A. News,* 19, 20 Apr.; *Ons Land Advertentieblad,* 20, 23 Apr. 1901; Gardiner and Lansdown, pp. 1005, 1010–11; Cloete, pp. 152–7.

PAGE 232

file. H. Currey to Merriman, 27 Jan. 1901 (Merriman Papers).

assistance. Cd. 903, pp. 2–3: P. D. de Wet, [D. J. H.] van Niekerk and C. L. Botha to Milner, 19 Feb. 1901. P. D. de Wet was a brother of General C. R. de Wet. See also the *Verslag van de Zending der Vredes Gezanten uit de Oranje Rivier Kolonie,* containing the Peace Committee's correspondence.

on. Beck to Merriman, 27 Feb. 1901 (Merriman Papers).

us. Cd. 903, pp. 5–6: De Wet, van Niekerk and Botha to Milner, 25 Feb. 1901.

authorities. Cd. 903, p. 6: Theron to P. D. de Wet, 20 Feb. 1901.

PAGE 233

mind. Assembly Debates, 1902, pp. 109–12 [Crewe], 289–95 [Smartt].

them. Assembly Debates, 1902, pp. 349–52, 370–3.

out. Assembly Debates, 1902, pp. 104–9 [N. F. de Waal]; *Ons Land,* 4 Sept. 1902. I am indebted to Mr. Noel Garson for confirmation of this peace move from Kitchener's side. See Kitchener to Brodrick, secret, 19 July 1901 (Kitchener Papers). This letter suggests that Kitchener and French had taken some action.

borders. Cd. 1364.

surprising. Afrikaander Bond en Boeren Vereeniging: Naamlijst van Leden, 1893. For evidence that participants in the second rebellion were often very young, see a minute in A. G. 2062, printed in A. 6–1902, where it is shown that of 3,413 rebels who laid down their arms after 31 May 1902, 1,087 were under 21.

PAGE 234

parliamentarians. Assembly Debates, 1902, pp. 104–9.

witnesses. A. 21—1902. Report of the Select Committee on the Afrikander Bond, 29 Oct. 1902. Its members were: H. T. Tamplin [chairman], V. Sampson, D. Harris, J. Lawrence, J. X. Merriman, J. W. Sauer, and J. C. Molteno.

guilty. A. 21—1902, Appendix D: J. J. Graham to the Clerk of the House of Assembly, 25 Oct. 1902; ibid., Appendix A [texts of press statements to which the Bond leaders took exception].

1902. An amendment by F. Oats to broaden the scope of the inquiry was defeated on division by 35 votes to 24 (Assembly Debates, 1902, pp. 382–3).

PAGE 235

Rensburg. Assembly Debates, 1902, pp. 289–95. Bracketed comments and information are by the author.

him. A.G. 2073(*b*): H. G. Watson to J. J. Graham, 4 Dec. 1902; Graham to Watson, 21 Jan. 1903 (Cape Archives). The names were supplied.

CHAPTER 12

PAGE 237

intervals. Headlam, ii, 37–8, 56–8, 59–61, 106–7, 114–15, 115–17, 182–4, quoting Milner to Selborne, 30 Nov. 1899; to Chamberlain, 17 Jan., 21 Feb. 26 Mar., to Sir E. Hamilton, 24 June, to Chamberlain, 4 July 1900, 17 Jan. 1901.

plan. Headlam, ii, 123–5, quoting Chamberlain to Milner, 10 Sept. 1900. See also Garvin and Amery, iv, ch. LXXX *passim*.

out. *Graaff-Reinet Advertiser*, 10 May 1901.

demand. Cd. 903, pp. 50–4.

Times. e.g. *Diamond Fields Advertiser*, 2, 8, 10, 17 May; *Graaff-Reinet Advertiser*, 1 May 1901.

PAGE 238

matter. D. Graaff to Hofmeyr, 14 May 1901 (Hofmeyr Papers). How many of the Bond leaders seriously considered an approach to Rhodes is obscure. Headlam, ii, 406, probably exaggerates their efforts.

worthless. Hofmeyr to Graaff, 12 June 1901 (Hofmeyr Papers), extensively quoted in Hofmeyr, pp. 565–7.

PAGE 239

movement. *S.A. News*, 16 May 1901.

here. Headlam, ii, 406; S. J. du Toit to Rhodes, 4 Feb. 1902 (Rhodes Papers).

substitute. Cd. 1162. Petition for the Temporary Suspension of the Cape Constitution and Reply of His Majesty's Government. The best apologias for suspension are in Amery, vi, 62–71, and Sampson, pp. 101–3.

press. Milner to Hely-Hutchinson, 19 May, in *Cape Times*, 30 May 1902. For his subsequent dispute with Chamberlain, see Garvin and Amery, iv, 105–12.

reasoning. For further evidence, see Walker (1), pp. 394–403; Assembly Debates, 1902, pp. 5–6 [Berry], 273 [Sprigg]; Molteno (1), pp. 230–44; Garvin and Amery, iv, 113–17. There is no mention of the suspension issue in the official report of the 1902 Colonial Conference (Cd. 1299), and the information that the Colonial Premiers made an issue of it on the conference floor seems to derive only from Molteno's memoirs, on which Walker apparently depended.

PAGE 240

advice. Garvin and Amery, iv, 125–30, quoting Milner to Chamberlain, 6 Sept. 1902.

Colony. Garvin and Amery, iv, 122, quoting Chamberlain to Hely-Hutchinson, 26 Aug., Hely-Hutchinson to Chamberlain, 28 Aug. 1902 (telegrams).

problems. The development of Onze Jan's attitude to suspension can be seen in the following correspondence: D. Graaff to Hofmeyr, 16 June (with Hofmeyr's reply in note form), 8 July; Hofmeyr to Graaff, 11 July, to [C. du P.?] Chiappini, 15, 22 July 1902 (Hofmeyr Papers). The last is quoted in part in Hofmeyr, pp. 576–7.

PAGE 241

one. Assembly Debates, 1902, pp. 24–35, 47–59, 70–86 [second reading debate, General Indemnity Bill, which went through all stages without a division].

1904. Assembly Debates, 1902, p. 184 [text of Merriman's motion]. The motion was ultimately adopted without a division.

month. The fullest published accounts of Chamberlain's South African visit are in Amery, vi, 77–98, and in Garvin and Amery, iv, 343–85.

electors. Headlam, ii, 442, quoting Milner to Lady E. Cecil, 15 Feb.; Garvin and Amery, iv, 362, quoting *Cape Times*, 13 Feb. 1903.

PAGE 242

course. Ons Land, 24 Feb. 1903.

PAGE 243

added. Garvin and Amery, iv, 365–8, where use is made of Chamberlain's Business Diary. The S.A.P. leaders had first approached Chamberlain on 8 Jan. See Hofmeyr to Merriman, 23 Dec. 1902, and correspondence between F.S. Malan and H. W. Just, Chamberlain's private secretary, 8–22 Jan. 1903 (Merriman Papers).

afternoon. For Chamberlain's visit to Cape Town, see Garvin and Amery, iv, 369–81; Amery, vi, 94–5; Hofmeyr, pp. 583–5; *Ons Land*, 19, 24, 26 Feb. 1903.

departure. The Hofmeyr–Chamberlain correspondence of Feb.–June 1903 is given at length in Hofmeyr, pp. 585–8, and partly in Garvin and Amery, iv, 378–9. Originals are in the Hofmeyr Papers.

Dutchmen. Hofmeyr to Chamberlain, 20 May 1903 (Hofmeyr Papers) [Passage omitted in Hofmeyr, p. 587].

PAGE 244

all. Hofmeyr to D. P. Graaff, 12 June 1901 (Hofmeyr Papers).

Houses. Hofmeyr, pp. 580–1. The details are obscure.

amendment. *Notulen*, Cape Town Bond branch, 4, 9 Dec. 1902, 13 Jan. 1903; *Ons Land*, 2 Dec. 1902, 28 Apr., 7 May 1903; *Notulen*, 1903 congress, p. 23.

PAGE 245

Crown. 'Zij bedoelt, onder de leiding der Voorzienigheid: de ontwikkeling van een gevoel van nationale eenheid in Britsch Zuid Afrika en de vereeniging der Britsch Zuid Afrikaansche Koloniën in een Federale Unie, met inachtneming van de onderlinge belangen dier koloniën en van het oppergezag der Britsche Kroon.'

zelfstandigheid. The Canadian and Australian analogies seem to have been first expressed by Hofmeyr, before he returned to South Africa in October 1902. See W. T. Stead to Merriman, 4 Oct. 1902 (Merriman Papers).

PAGE 246

congress. *Ons Land*, 7 May 1903.

Land. *Ons Land*, 18 Nov. 1902 [an editorial review of the session].

grievances. Sprigg to Merriman, 25 Aug. 1902 (Merriman Papers). ['In moving the second reading of the Indemnity Bill this afternoon the Attorney-General will state that Ministers will so soon as the Bill is passed advise the appointment of a Commission to enquire into the administration of Martial Law']; Assembly Debates, 1902, p. 26 [the Attorney-General's promise].

cases. Cd. 1364.

trial. For the kind of victimization which the South African Party had in mind, see the affidavit of P. W. Michau, chairman of the Cradock district *bestuur* of the Afrikaner Bond, dated 26 Aug. 1902 (Merriman Papers). Snyman has argued that, all things considered, the record of the military courts was far less reprehensible than it is usually held in Afrikaner circles to have been; but it would be difficult to argue that they administered a satisfactory form of justice. For a contemporary criticism of their performance, see C. W. Slaughter to Merriman, 5 Sept. 1902 (Merriman Papers).

answer. Merriman to Sprigg, copy, 10 Jan.; Sprigg to Merriman, 14 Jan. 1903 (Merriman Papers).

matter. *Ons Land*, 7 Mar. 1903.

claims. Assembly Debates, 1903, p. 656.

PAGE 247

one. Assembly Debates, 1903, pp. 664–5.

advantage. Molteno (2), pp. 74–83.

ranks. Colvin, ii, 210–25; Sampson, p. 105. The Sprigg Papers throw no light on the Premier's intentions.

stand. Assembly Debates, 1903, pp. 667–77. See also F. Mackarness to Merriman, 30 Jan. 1903 (Merriman Papers).

party. Colvin, ii, 218, 235; Molteno (2), p. 92.

PAGE 248

quo. Cuthbert, p. 3, quoting *S.A. News*, 8 Jan. 1904 [Jameson's election manifesto].

electorate. The voters in Cape Town had increased from 9,483 in 1899 to 17,131 in 1903.

independent. L. Wiener to Hofmeyr, n.d. [Sept. 1903?] (Hofmeyr Papers); *S.A. News,* 30 Oct. 1903.

Six. S.A. News, 24 Oct., 7 Nov. 1903. This paper ran a regular weekly column of labour notes from September 1902 until July 1906.

accept. Jabavu to Merriman, 18 Feb. 1904 (Merriman Papers).

Merriman's. H. Neville to Merriman, 24 Feb. 1904. Cf. J. P. Smit to Merriman, 12 Sept. 1903 (Merriman Papers).

800. The registered voters for Wodehouse had decreased from 2,592 in 1897 to 2,001 in 1903. According to the records of the commission established under Act 6 of 1900 in A.G. 3650–2 (Cape Archives) voters from Barkly East and Dordrecht who were found guilty and therefore disfranchised between April and June 1901 numbered 851. These were offenders under the first rebellion only, and the figure does not include those disfranchised by other procedures. According to a memorandum prepared by A. B. du Toit to assist the South African Party in the Legislative Council elections of 1908 (Hofmeyr Papers, n.d.), 1,638 Wodehouse voters were re-enfranchised between 1904 and 1908 — a figure which would include a fair number of young men not yet on the voters' roll in 1904.

persuasion. Colvin, ii, 231, quoting Jameson to his brother, 25 Jan. 1904 ['From now till 10th I am going to do nothing but native constituencies. Practically following round on Tengo Jabavu's track']; Merriman to his wife, 10, 18, 21 Jan. 1904 (Merriman Papers).

way. Smuts to Merriman, 30 May 1904 (Merriman Papers).

rehabilitated. Cd. 1551, pp. 1–4.

themselves. The divisions within Afrikanerdom are well described by Kirstein.

particular. See, as an illustration of the type of arguments used by Transvaal Afrikaners against Chinese immigration, the speech of Louis Botha at Heidelberg on 2 July 1903 (*Volksstem,* 4 July 1903).

did. Cronwright-Schreiner to Merriman, 5 Apr. 1904 (Merriman Papers).

Williams. Quoted in Headlam, ii, 242–4. See also Milner to General Pretyman, 20 June 1900, ibid., pp. 133–4.

limits. Cd. 1551, p. 138 [Transvaal]; Ordinances of the Orange River Colony, 1903, pp. 163–7 [O.R.C.].

battlefield. e.g. Assembly Debates, 1910, col. 297 [Hertzog]; Pienaar, p. 222.

service. See A. 24—1906: Report of the Select Committee on the Dutch Language, p. vi.

PAGE 253

declined. 'Knop', p. 10, quoting the Boer leaders' reply as printed in *Land en Volk*, 20 Feb. 1903. Pyrah, p. 140, seems to place the wrong interpretation on Botha's action.

won. See the report of the *Commissie van Toezicht, Notulen,* 1905 congress, pp. 14–16.

PAGE 254

antagonism. Compare Hancock, pp. 192–3; Engelenburg, p. 116; Amery, vi, 94.
strains. Printed leaflet issued by Van de Sandt de Villiers, based on reports in the *Cape Times* and the *S.A. News*, together with notes and related correspondence (Malan Papers). See also Cloete, pp. 172–84.

PAGE 255

assembly. *Volksstem,* 4 July 1903 [a full report].

PAGE 256

action. *Star,* 12, 15 Feb. 1904, quoting Botha to Lawley, 10 Feb., with enclosure, and Lawley to Botha, 15 Feb. 1904.
spirits. Munnik, pp. 234–9; Headlam, ii, 517 [an unreliable passage which may however be accurate in its broad conclusions].
longer. Ernest Sheppard to Merriman, 28 Mar. 1904 (Merriman Papers); *Star,* 30 Mar. 1904.
Volk. Spoelstra, pp. 324–5, quoting the *Volksstem,* 25, 28 May, and the *Transvaal Leader,* 26 May 1904; 'Knop', pp. 18–37; Newton, i, 275–81 [report of the Pretoria congress].

PAGE 257

none. *Rand Daily Mail,* 29 Jan. 1904; *Star,* 29 Jan., 2 Feb. 1904 [refutation of the charge by N.D.F. leaders J. W. Quinn, Howard Pim and R. Stickland].
money. E. Sheppard to Merriman, 15 Feb. 1904 [referring to a protest against the importation of Chinese 'which I, together with a representative committee of Boers drew up', but which was never circulated because the Boer leaders themselves took the matter up]; Merriman to Sheppard, copy, 26 Feb. 1904 (Merriman Papers) [Merriman's proposals].
Transvaal. *Owl,* Cape Town, 3 June 1904 [enlarged programme]; cf. Merriman to T. Palmer, copy, 29 Apr. 1904 (Merriman Papers).
them. *Ons Land,* 4 June 1904.
camp. *Owl,* 10 June 1904. For the later history of the relations between the Bond and the Liberal Association, see *Notulen,* Cape Town Bond Branch, 11 Aug. 1904 [decision to consult with the Liberal Association over the choice of a candidate for the Legislative Council]; 20 Oct. 1906 [decision to entrust the registration of voters to a special committee 'in consultation with the Liberal Association']; 11 Feb. 1908 [this body is now described as a 'joint committee of Bondsmen and members of the Liberal Association']. Botha made provision for the Liberal Association to be represented at the Bloemfontein congress in

November 1911 at which the associated Afrikaner parties agreed to amalgamate. See Botha to H. E. S. Fremantle, 3 July 1911 (Fremantle Papers).

power. Easton to Merriman, from Bristol, 22 Dec. 1905 (Merriman Papers).

PAGE 258

Boer. Smuts to Merriman, 30 May 1904 (Merriman Papers); Merriman to Smuts, 4 June 1904 (Smuts Papers); Hancock, p. 203.

reappeared. The document sent by Merriman is identifiable from Merriman's letter in the Smuts Papers. For Smuts's draft programme, see Smuts to Merriman, 11 July 1906 and enclosure (nos. 184, 241/1906, Merriman Papers).

interests. Spoelstra, pp. 379–81, quoting the *Volksstem*, 5 Dec. 1906 [the Het Volk programme]. See also Smuts to Merriman, 28 Nov. 1906 (Merriman Papers).

PAGE 259

succeed. Smuts to Merriman, 11 July 1906 (Merriman Papers), quoted in Thompson, pp. 131–2. Hancock, pp. 226–7, quotes Merriman's letter to which this was the reply.

apart. Engelenburg, pp. 131–2.

contained. Spoelstra, pp. 369–70. Beyers was later elected Speaker of the Transvaal Lower House.

funds. Report in the *Transvaal Leader*, 2 Dec. 1904.

1905. *Friend*, 20 July 1905, quoting B. T. Blackwood, acting Colonial Secretary O.R.C., to Hertzog, 18 July 1905.

PAGE 260

home. *Friend*, 4 May 1906.

necessary. Van den Heever, pp. 211–12.

speakers. Jansen, *passim*; De Villiers (2), pp. 660–4.

PAGE 261

Transvaal. J. C. Smuts, 'Memo. of Points in Reference to the Transvaal Constitution', Feb. 1906 (no. 240/1906, Merriman Papers); Thompson, p. 25; Hancock, pp. 207–17. On the West Ridgeway Committee see Amery, vi, 186–9, and Le May, pp. 197–208.

policy. *Bloemfontein Post*, 13 Nov. 1907.

prices. *Bloemfontein Post*, 30 Oct. 1907.

PAGE 262

wobble. Smuts to Merriman, 23 Dec. 1906 (Merriman Papers).

PAGE 263

Afrikanerdom. Molteno (2), pp. 89, 110.

administration. *S.A. News*, 5 Feb. 1908 [text of Jameson's published statement].

PAGE 264

1903. A printed memorandum in the Hofmeyr Papers gives the *bestuur* and the *statuten* of the Taalbond as at its meeting in Stellenbosch on 14 March 1903.

cause. Hofmeyr, p. 591. J. H. H. de Waal's *My Herinnerings van ons Taalstryd* gives his own account of developments.

PAGE 265

Afrikaans. For the texts of Hofmeyr's speech, 'Is 't ons Ernst?', and of Preller's reply, 'Laat 't ons toch Ernst wezen', see the *Hertzog-Annale*, Oct. 1952, pp. 14–50. See also Hofmeyr, pp. 598–600; Pienaar, pp. 244–67.

1905. Pienaar, pp. 269–70 [text of its *statute*]; Dekker, pp. 39–40.

Town. Pienaar, pp. 270–86 [including text of its *statute*].

Taalvereniging. Notulen, 1907 congress, p. 38; 1908 congress, p. 36; 1909 congress, p. 29; 1910 congress, p. 26; 1911 congress, p. 43.

volksklasse. Pienaar, pp. 307–10; *Hertzog-Annale*, Oct. 1952, pp. 72–80 (Dutch original).

PAGE 266

Art. Pienaar, pp. 314–18; Dekker, p. 42.

service. Cd. 3250: Transvaal constitution, 1906, ss. xxxiv, xliv; Cd. 3527: O.R.C. constitution, 1907, s. xxxvi, printed also in Newton, ii, 191; 'Knop', p. 57, quoting resolution of the Het Volk congress, 1908. .

stand. Notulen, 1903 congress, p. 29; 1905 congress, p. 27.

debate. Assembly Debates, 1905, p. 67 [text of Malan's motion and introductory speech].

commission. Assembly Debates, 1905, pp. 195, 199.

appointment. Notulen, 1906 congress, p. 31; A. 24—1906; Assembly Debates, 1907, p. 69; A. 2—1907 [acceptance by the Government].

PAGE 267

Department. Malherbe, pp. 378–9; Fraser, pp. 328–9; Van den Heever, p. 226.

control. Headlam, ii, 513–15, quoting Milner to Lyttleton, 13 June 1904; *Volksstem*, 4 July 1903 [Botha's Heidelberg speech].

language. Malherbe, p. 330.

Smuts. Malherbe, p. 334; Hancock, p. 239.

priority. 'Knop', pp. 42–3; Spoelstra, p. 373.

PAGE 268

education. Van den Heever, pp. 228 ff.; Trollip, chs. III, IV.

underhandedly. Beck to Merriman, 7 July 1904; Maeder to Merriman, 2 June 1905 (Merriman Papers).

PAGE 269

enforced. Assembly Debates, 1905, pp. 25–9 [Malan], 42–5 [Beck]. Merriman at p. 58 claimed to be against compulsion on principle.

people. Notulen, 1908 congress, p. 34; 1909 congress, pp. 32–4.

CHAPTER 13

itself. Transvaal Leader, 6 Feb. 1905 [report of a meeting to establish Het Volk's Johannesburg branches].

Colony. De Waal, N. F., p. 5.

respect. Notulen, 1906 congress, p. 29; 1907 congress, pp. 20-1 [appointment and report of a committee to investigate effective means of liaison].

Afrikanerdom. The Natal Boerekongres apparently had no programme of principles, while the programme of the Afrikaner Bond, dating for the most part from before the war, hardly reflected the new emphases. The three documents compared are located as follows: the Liberal Association programme in the *Owl*, 3 June 1904; the Het Volk programme in Spoelstra, pp. 379-81; and the programme of the Orangia Unie in the *Notulen*, 1910 Orangia Unie congress, pp. 37-9 (Malan Papers).

revenue. Thompson, p. 491.

produce. Van der Poel (1), pp. 118-23; A. 1, 2—1903.

vivendi. Van der Poel (1), p. 109; Newton, i, 176-81.

rates. C.G.H., *Statistical Register*, 1908, p. 49. The yield from income tax rose to over £444,000 in 1907-8.

competition. Notulen, 1904 congress, p. 16; 1905 congress, p. 24.

before. Notulen, 1906 congress, p. 7 [Dutch original].

adoption. Assembly Debates, 1904, pp. 145, 260 ff., 375 ff.

Kruger. Assembly Debates, 1905, pp. 491-3.

1908. Van der Poel (1), p. 138; Thompson, p. 59.

agenda. 'Knop', p. 55.

position. 'Knop', p. 57 [Dutch in original]; *Transvaal Leader*, 9 Apr. 1908. Thompson, pp. 80-1, emphasizes the isolationist revival in the Transvaal in 1908.

outskirts. T.G. 13—1908, p. 12.

war. Het Volk programme, art. viii; Orangia Unie programme, art. vii; A. 10—1906, pp. x-xi; T.G. 13—1908, p. 167.

parties. C.G.H., *Government Gazette*, 1896, pp. 1187-91 [T. P. Theron's School Boards Bill, esp. section 24], pp. 1298-1300 [J. W. Sauer's School Attendance Boards Bill, sections 13, 15, 16]; 1898, pp. 1684-9 [T. W. Smartt's School Attendance Boards Bill, section 35]; 1899, pp. 1420-3 [W. P. Schreiner's School Attendance Boards Bill, section 2, where 'child' is defined as a 'child of European birth or extraction']. I am indebted to Mr. Edgar Maurice for information on this point.

struggle. Notulen, 1906 congress, p. 5 [Dutch original].

areas. e.g. Assembly Debates, 1896, pp. 397–402 [J. W. Sauer, who claimed that 79% of the white children in the Carnarvon district, 72% in Barkly East and 52% in Prieska were not at school]; 1905, pp. 18–25 [C.P. Crewe, who in introducing the School Board Bill concluded that 'one-third of the (white) children who ought to be receiving education in this country were not in any school whatever'].

PAGE 277

there. Notulen, 1905 congress, p. 33 [Kakamas]; A. B. du Toit to Hofmeyr, n.d. [1908] (Hofmeyr Papers).

people. Afrikaner Bond constitution (1910), art. II; Het Volk *statuten*, art. 22 [all white people over 16]; Orangia Unie *statuten*, art. 2(*a*) [all white people over 18]; Natal Boerekongres *statuten*, art. 2 [all white inhabitants of Natal of European origin over 18].

unjust. U.G. 54–1937, p. 224.

hilt. Assembly Debates, 1908 (second session), p. 41.

examined. Report of the South African Native Affairs Commission, 1903–5, i, Annexure 6, pp. 13–18. See also Thompson, p. 114.

PAGE 278

Convention. See Malan, pp. 55–7.

franchise. Assembly Debates, 1908 (second session), pp. 45–7 [F. S. Malan, A. S. du Plessis and T. P. Theron].

hearts. Transvaal Assembly Debates, 1908, cols. 107–8 [J. A. Joubert]; O.R.C. Assembly Debates, 1908, cols. 654–61 [W. Ehrlich].

societies. A. B. du Toit to Hofmeyr, n.d. [1908] (Hofmeyr Papers).

PAGE 279

Cape. Hofmeyr, p. 629. Onze Jan's reply was dated 22 March.

hostile. Thompson, pp. 325–7.

people. Thompson, pp. 327–36.

Colony. Notulen, Cape Town Bond Branch, 17 Feb. 1909.

assessed. Notulen, 1909 congress, p. 37.

PAGE 280

47. Thompson, pp. 336–44.

PAGE 281

Nation. Afrikaner Bond programme of principles (1909), art. 2; Het Volk programme, art. 2; Orangia Unie programme, art. I.

model. Ons Land, 30 Aug., 1, 4, 6, 8, 11 Sept. 1906, reprinted in Malan, pp. 252–69.

PAGE 282

Transvaal. Thompson, pp. 69–74.

session. Assembly Debates, 1907, p. 227; Thompson, pp. 75–7; Cd. 3564 [the Selborne Memorandum].

conference. Thompson, pp. 90–4.

PAGE 283

1908. Thompson, pp. 139–48.

June. Notulen, 1908 congress, p. 30.

Natalians. Jansen, p. 16; Thompson, p. 147, quoting correspondence between Botha and M. Myburgh, May 1908.

trial. Hofmeyr, pp. 616–17; Walker (2), pp. 290–1.

report. Hofmeyr, G. R., pp. 312–45.

PAGE 284

Parliament. Thompson, pp. 313–15.

leaders. Thompson, pp. 327–31.

Convention. Thompson, pp. 331–6.

PAGE 285

back. Notulen, Cape Town Bond branch, 11 Feb. 1909.

heads. Hofmeyr, pp. 625–7, gives in translation the full resolution as carried, with minor amendments, by the branch.

time. e.g. Hofmeyr, pp. 618–19.

effect. Thompson, p. 315.

PAGE 286

returned. Hofmeyr, G. R., pp. 58, 319–20; Thompson, pp. 237–9.

seats. Thompson, pp. 320–2; *Ons Land,* 25, 27 Feb. 1909 [two letters making the same points in detail, signed 'Denker', who on Thompson's identification must have been Van der Horst].

pessimistic. Thompson, p. 322; Botha to Merriman, 19 Mar. 1909 (Merriman Papers).

Union. Thompson, pp. 366, 387, quoting Hofmeyr to Steyn, 21 Apr., 14 May 1909.

congress. Notulen, Cape Town Bond branch, 17 Feb. 1909.

own. Notulen, 1909 congress, pp. 36–8; Van der Horst to Hofmeyr, telegram, 7 Mar. 1909 (Hofmeyr Papers) [with references to 'Malan's strenuous opposition' and the loyal support of De Waal, Michau and Van Rooy].

PAGE 287

Michau. Notulen, Cape Town Bond branch, 16 Mar. 1909; *Notulen,* 1909 congress, pp. 23–5.

party. Ons Land, 23, 27 Feb., 27 Mar. 1909 [reports of branch meetings].

PAGE 288

value. Quoted by Thompson, pp. 339–40.

council. Thompson, pp. 342–4; Assembly Debates, 1909, pp. 111–17 [Molteno's amendment], 117–21 [Blaine's amendment], 125–7 [Tod's amendment].

PAGE 289

Assembly. Thompson, pp. 366–74.

Bill. Notulen, Cape Town Bond branch, 18 May 1909: motion by J. G. van der Horst and C. P. Schultz.

party. Malan told the 1910 congress that he had persuaded Merriman to invite Hofmeyr. See also Hely-Hutchinson to Merriman, 18 May, and telegraphic correspondence between Merriman and Botha, 22–9 May (Merriman Papers), and Merriman to Hofmeyr, 27–31 May 1909 (Hofmeyr Papers); Cloete, pp. 218–19.

grounds. Smuts to Merriman, 19 Feb. 1909 (Merriman Papers). Botha, in letters to Merriman dated 19 February and 9 March (loc. cit.), did not take Hofmeyr's opposition seriously.

people. Ons Land, 23 Mar. 1909. For further evidence of Onze Jan's reaction to the first report of the National Convention, see *Ons Land*, 11 Feb. 1909 [his initial impressions] and Hofmeyr, p. 628 [his address to the Cape Town branch on 16 March].

PAGE 290

anyone. Williams to Merriman, 21 Oct. (Merriman Papers); Daverin to Schreiner, 16 Dec. 1909 (Schreiner Papers).

decisions. Notulen, Cape Town Bond branch, 28 Oct. 1909.

PAGE 291

solvency. Cloete, pp. 204–5.

Party. S.A. News, 5 June, 15 Dec.; *Cape Times*, 15 June 1908.

PAGE 292

half. Malan to Merriman, 25 Sept. 1909 (Merriman Papers).

one. Notulen, 1908 congress, p. 34; N. F. de Waal to Merriman, 16 July, 4 Aug. 1909 (Merriman Papers).

classrooms. Notulen, 1909 congress, pp. 32–4; *Ons Land*, 13 Mar. 1909.

PAGE 293

both. Innes to Merriman, 24 Feb. 1910 (Merriman Papers).

case. Engelenburg, pp. 190–3.

Government. Colvin, ii, 291–2, quoting Jameson to his brother, 9 Feb. 1910; Wallis, pp. 154–5.

magnates. Hofmeyr, p. 636; Van der Merwe, ii, 239–40, quoting Steyn to Hyslop of Natal, *c.* Feb. 1910; Merriman to Steyn, 12 Feb., to Goldwin Smith, 5 Mar. 1910 (Merriman Papers).

Britain. Long, p. 143.

Progressives. F. V. Engelenburg to Malan, 6 Jan. 1910 (Malan Papers).

PAGE 294

England. Engelenburg, p. 198.

members. Thompson, p. 453. For Merriman's views on this, see Merriman to Steyn (copy), 22 May 1910 (Merriman Papers).

response. See Smuts to Merriman, 10 Feb., Merriman to Smuts, 15 Feb., to Goldwin Smith, 5 Mar. 1910 (Merriman Papers).

PAGE 295

covets. Graaff to Malan, 17 Jan. 1910 (Malan Papers).

premiership. Botha to D. P. Graaff, 9 Feb. 1910 (Malan Papers) [Dutch original].

Botha. J. D. de Ville to Merriman, 30 May, 13 June; J. A. Graaff to Merriman, 3, 17 June; P. Rabie to Merriman, 5 June; P. G. Kuhn to Merriman, 5 June; A. G. Visser to Merriman, 8 June; J. H. Claassens to Merriman, 11 June 1910 (Merriman Papers).

story. Merriman to Steyn, 22 May; to P. Rabie, 31 May; to J. A. Graaff, 5 June 1910 (copies) (Merriman Papers).

seat. Malan to Botha, 25 Mar.; to Ds. G. S. Malan, 23 June 1910 (copy) (Malan Papers). Contrast the letter by J. G. van der Horst in the *S.A. News*, 11 June 1910, which aroused a considerable outcry among Merriman's supporters.

difficulty. F. J. Centlivres to Smuts, 18 Feb., 18, 21 Mar., 24 Apr. 1910 (Smuts Papers); Thompson, pp. 453–4.

PAGE 296

May. e.g. the editorial on 13 April attacking a letter to the London *Times* in which Botha's claim to the premiership had been strongly put. See also Philipson-Stow to the Board of Directors, *S.A. News*, 31 May 1910 (copy) (Merriman Papers).

provide. Boonzaier to Merriman, 20 May, 17 June; A. D. Donovan to Merriman, 4, 7 June, 4, 11, 17 July; Merriman to Donovan (copy) 6 June 1910 (Merriman Papers); *Cape*, 20, 27 May, 3, 10, 17 June 1910.

PAGE 297

silence. Ons Land, 24, 26 May; *Het Oosten, Onze Courant, De Stem*, 26 May 1910. Leading Bondsmen who commiserated with Merriman were P. G. Kuhn, member for Prieska, H. J. Raubenheimer, member for George, Dr. J. H. M. Beck, member for Worcester, and P. W. Michau, legislative councillor for the north-eastern circle (Merriman Papers).

May. Thompson, pp. 460–1.

Unie. Botha to Merriman, 29 Dec. 1909 (Merriman Papers); to Malan, 29 Dec. 1909 (Malan Papers). The Malan Papers contain a fragment of Botha's original manifesto.

March. Malan to Botha, 4 Jan. 1910 (Smuts Papers).

PAGE 298

proposal. Merriman to Botha, 5 Jan. 1910 (copy bearing the erroneous date '1909') (Merriman Papers).

mark. Merriman to Malan, 19 Jan. 1910 (Malan Papers).

bestuur. Notulen, Cape Town Bond branch, 25 Jan. 1910.

sectionalism. Smuts to Merriman, 10 Feb. 1910 (Merriman Papers); see also Thompson, p. 441, basing his account on Merriman's diary of 27 and 29 January.

it. Malan to Botha, 7 Feb. 1910 (copy) (Malan Papers).

programme. Botha to Graaff, 9 Feb.; to Malan, 18, 29 Mar. 1910 (Malan Papers).

congress. Notulen, 1910 congress, p. 44.

basis. Verrichtingen van het Vijfde Jaarlijksche Congres der Orangia Unie, 19, 20 Apr. 1910, pp. 19–20.

broadmindedness. Jansen, pp. 16–25.

others. Dutch text in the *Konstitutie van de Zuid Afrikaanse Nationale Partij* (Cape Town, n.d. [1910]. pp. 15–17. Translation is given in Krüger (2), pp. 48–50. For the proposed amendments see Malan to Botha, 7, 22 Feb.; Graaff to Botha, 21 Mar.; Botha to Malan, 4, 18 Mar. 1910 (Malan Papers).

Smuts. Malan to Botha, 27 Feb. (copy) (Malan Papers); to Smuts, 28 Feb. 1910 (Smuts Papers).

Platitudes. Cape, 3 June 1910.

form. Krüger (2), pp. 45–7; Thompson, pp. 462–5.

larger. For a discussion of the 1910 election, see Thompson, pp. 460–79.

April. Notulen van een Konferentie uit de leden van de Hoofdbesturen van de Afrikaander Bond . . . ; De Unie . . . , de Volksvereniging en de Zuid-Afrikaanse Nationale Party . . . te Kaapstad op . . . 31 Maart en 1 April 1911, printed in Jansen, pp. 49–51. Malan's documents relating to party amalgamation are in his papers in the Cape Archives. They include two drafts bearing the title *'Konstitutie van de Zuid-Afrikaanse Nationale Partij'*. One is in galleys with numerous amendments in Malan's hand recording the changes made at the parliamentary conference. The other document with the same heading is in typescript and can be attributed to Smuts. Botha stated at the parliamentary conference that Malan and Smuts had been entrusted with the task of preparing a draft for discussion.

conference. Unsigned circular annotated by Malan, dated Cape Town, 5 Apr. 1911; typed circular over the name of Louis Botha, dated Cape Town, 27 Apr. 1911 (Malan Papers).

amendments. Verrichtingen van de Zesde Jaarlyks Kongres der Orangia Unie (Bloemfontein 1911), p. 30; *Notulen*, Cape Town Bond branch, 24 Aug., 21, 25, 29 Sept. 1911.

Cape. Botha to Fremantle, 3 July 1911 (Fremantle Papers). See also Malan to Fremantle, 16 June; Smuts to Fremantle, 10 Aug.; Burton to Fremantle, 15 Aug. 1911 (loc. cit.).

found. Report by H. E. S. Fremantle dated 26 Oct. 1911 (Fremantle Papers).

surroundings. See Hertzog to Steyn, 13 May 1911, quoted in Van den Heever, pp. 289–90.

not. Notulen van het Nationale Kongres gehouden in de Ramblers' Zaal te Bloemfontein op . . . 21 en 22 November 1911 (Pretoria, 1912).

PAGE 303

vote. Notulen, 1911 congress, pp. 2, 28–33.

CHAPTER 14

PAGE 305

began. Innes, p. 36.

earlier. For Milner's reasons, see Headlam, i, 503–21 *passim.*

PAGE 306

Transvaal. Zuid Afrikaan, 14 Apr. 1877.

PAGE 307

colony. Amery, i, 83.

noted. Bloemfontein Post, 5 July 1907 [report of Orangia Unie congress].

1953. Carter, p. 221.

onwards. Bond constitution (1907, 1909), art. VIII [subscription]; *Notulen*, 1905 congress, p. 29; 1907 congress, p. 29 [membership drive].

table. Sources: Bond congress *Notulen*; C.G.H., *Statistical Register*, 1897, pp. 31–3; *Government Gazette*, 1904, p. 695; 1907 (July–Dec.), pp. 1602–15; 1909 (July–Dec.), pp. 803–16.

PAGE 311

meetings. See also Hofmeyr, p. 170; *Notulen*, 1900 congress, p. 15 [account by T. P. Theron of the caucus meetings in 1884 to discuss the possibility of allying with Upington].

elected. Ons Land, 27 Feb., 12, 17 Mar., 9 Apr. 1892.

division. e.g. on 4 Aug. 1879 [for the repeal of the Griqualand West Annexation Act] and on 27 Apr. 1881 [for Scanlen's motion of censure on Sprigg's Basuto and Transkeian policies].

PAGE 312

loyalty. Zuid Afrikaan, 30 Apr. 1881.

Hanover. Patriot, 6 May 1881.

himself. Tielman [Hofmeyr?] to Rev. Mostert, Porterville, draft telegram, 3 Nov. 1898 (Hofmeyr Papers).

PAGE 313

rule. Votes and Proceedings, House of Assembly, 11 Oct. 1898, 3 Oct. 1899.

so. Cape Bond constitution (1898), arts. XI, XII.

PAGE 314

constitution. Cape Bond constitution (1903), art. VI.

treasurer. *Reglement van Orde*, art. 5. The offices of secretary and treasurer were combined from 1888.

them. The earliest official use of the term *Moderatuur* in relation to the Bond executive seems to occur in the circular put out by T. P. Theron and N. F. de Waal on 30 Oct. 1899, in *De Afrikaander Partij en de Oorlog*, p. 23.

congress. Het Volk *Statuten*, arts. 2, 3; Boerekongres *Statuten*, art. 15; Orangia Unie *Statuten*, art. 7.

defined. Het Volk *Statuten*, arts. 14, 20; Orangia Unie *Statuten*, art. 10, and *Notulen*, 1910 congress, pp. 33–6 [special rules regarding the nomination of parliamentary candidates]; Boerekongres *Statuten*, art. 23.

PAGE 315

death. The continuity of Hofmeyr's tenure of the chairmanship of the *Commissie van Toezicht* is usually assumed; but see his letter to Tielman of 4 Sept. 1902, announcing his resignation before leaving for Europe ['als lid der Com. v. Toezicht op Electies bedankte ik reeds voor mijn vertrek. Maar gij kunt de bedanking herhalen'] (Hofmeyr Papers); *Notulen*, 1900 congress, pp. 28–30 [a resolution which implies that Hofmeyr had submitted his resignation]. He signed the *Commissie's* Report to the 1903 congress however (*Notulen*, pp. 17–18).

Houses. *Notulen*, 1888 congress, p. 18; *Patriot*, 19 Mar. 1891.

resolutions. *Notulen*, 1891 congress, pp. 35–7; 1892 congress, pp. 11, 13.

secretary. e.g. *Notulen*, 1893 congress, pp. 5–8; 1894 congress, pp. 9–13; 1899 congress, pp. 8–10.

procedure. *Notulen*, 1900 congress, pp. 26–7.

PAGE 317

account. Programme of Principles (1903), art. 2, discussed at p. 245.

1908. About one-third of the S.A. Party members of Parliament were not Bondsmen during the post-war period. See De Waal, N. F., p. 12; Fremantle, pp. xvii–xviii.

constituency. Ons Land, 20 Feb. 1908.

procedures. Ons Land, 25 Feb. [Oudtshoorn], 13 Feb. 1908 [Stellenbosch].

PAGE 318

Disputes. Duverger, p. 47.

CHAPTER 15

PAGE 320

times. See Carleton J. H. Hayes, 'Nationalism', in the *Encyclopedia of the Social Sciences*; H. Kohn, *The Idea of Nationalism* (New York, 1946), p. 3; A. Cobban, *National Self-Determination* (Chicago, 1944), pp. 4–5.

PAGE 323

expert. Jawaharlal Nehru, *Towards Freedom* (New York, 1942), p. 74.

PAGE 327

exclusive. Hofmeyr, p. 524.

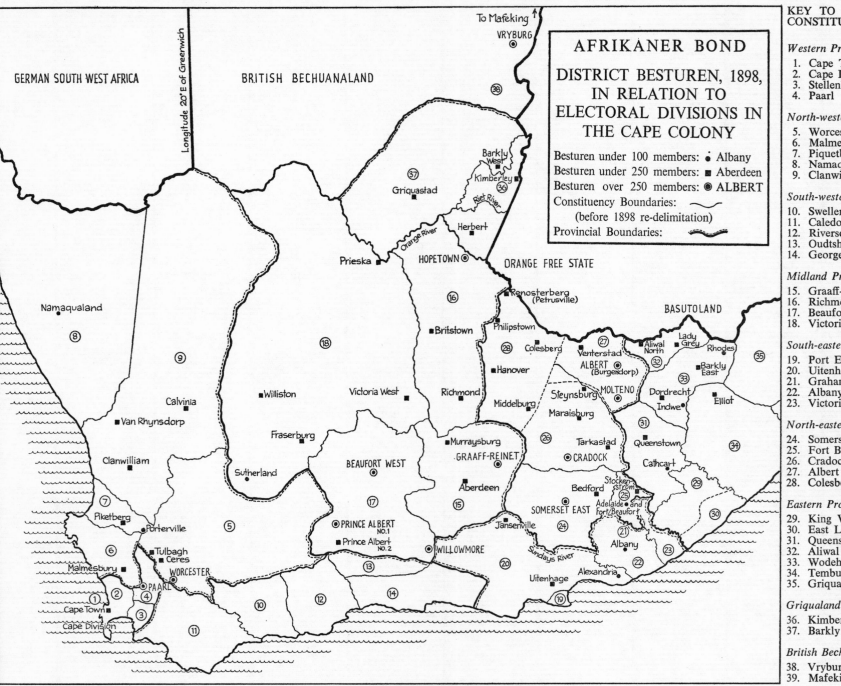

KEY TO CONSTITUENCIES

Western Province

1. Cape Town
2. Cape Division
3. Stellenbosch
4. Paarl

North-western Province

5. Worcester
6. Malmesbury
7. Piquetberg
8. Namaqualand
9. Clanwilliam

South-western Province

10. Swellendam
11. Caledon
12. Riversdale
13. Oudtshoorn
14. George

Midland Province

15. Graaff-Reinet
16. Richmond
17. Beaufort West
18. Victoria West

South-eastern Province

19. Port Elizabeth
20. Uitenhage
21. Grahamstown
22. Albany
23. Victoria East

North-eastern Province

24. Somerset East
25. Fort Beaufort
26. Cradock
27. Albert
28. Colesberg

Eastern Province

29. King William's Town
30. East London
31. Queenstown
32. Aliwal North
33. Wodehouse
34. Tembuland
35. Griqualand East

Griqualand West

36. Kimberley
37. Barkly West

British Bechuanaland

38. Vryburg
39. Mafeking (off map)

AFRIKANER BOND

DISTRICT BESTUREN, 1898, IN RELATION TO ELECTORAL DIVISIONS IN THE CAPE COLONY

Besturen under 100 members: • Albany
Besturen under 250 members: ■ Aberdeen
Besturen over 250 members: ◉ ALBERT
Constituency Boundaries: ⌒⌒
   (before 1898 re-delimitation)
Provincial Boundaries: ⌇⌇

GERMAN SOUTH WEST AFRICA

BRITISH BECHUANALAND

ORANGE FREE STATE

BASUTOLAND

MAP 2

Appendix

OFFICE BEARERS OF THE AFRIKANER BOND IN THE CAPE COLONY

Chairman

1883–6	J. J. Janse van Rensburg (Cradock)
1886–92	R. P. Botha (Graaff-Reinet)
1892–8	P. J. du Toit (Richmond)
1898–1908	*T. P. Theron (Britstown)
1909–11	H. C. van Heerden (Tarkastad)

Vice-chairman

1883–4	D. F. du Toit (Paarl)
1884–6	G. F. Joubert (Graaff-Reinet)
1886–92	P. J. du Toit
1892–8	*J. P. du Plessis (Cradock)
1898–1905	D. J. A. van Zyl (Clanwilliam)
1905–11	P. J. du Toit

Secretary

1883–8	T. P. Theron

Treasurer

1883–8	J. H. Hofmeyr (Cape Town)

Secretary-Treasurer

1888–98	T. P. Theron
1898–1908	N. F. de Waal (Middelburg)
1908–11	J. J. Michau (Barkly West)

Assistant Secretary

1890–8	N. F. de Waal
1898–1903	J. J. Michau
1903–5	P. W. Michau (Cradock)
1905–8	J. J. Michau
1908–11	J. A. Vosloo (Somerset East)

Commissie van Toezicht op Elekties

1889–92	J. H. Hofmeyr (chairman), R. P. Botha, N. F. de Waal
1892–8	J. H. Hofmeyr (chairman), N. F. de Waal, S. J. du Toit
1898–1905	J. H. Hofmeyr (chairman), *J. M. Hoffman, T. P. Theron
1905–9	J. H. Hofmeyr (chairman), *T. P. Theron, F. S. Malan
1909–10	*J. H. Hofmeyr (chairman), F. S. Malan, H. C. van Heerden
1910–11	F. S. Malan (chairman), H. C. van Heerden, N. F. de Waal.

* died in office.

Bibliography

I. A NOTE ON THE CITATION OF PRINTED OFFICIAL SOURCES

The following letters used in notes designate British and South African parliamentary papers:

A.   Papers ordered to be printed by the House of Assembly of the Cape of Good Hope.

C.   (followed by a serial number and a date—e.g. C.2—1892): Papers ordered to be printed by the Legislative Council of the Cape of Good Hope.

C.,Cd. (followed by a serial number but no date): Papers ordered to be printed by the Parliament of Great Britain (e.g. C.2964, Cd.420).

G.   Papers ordered to be printed by the Government of the Cape of Good Hope.

T.G.   Papers ordered to be printed by the Government of the Transvaal.

U.G.   Papers ordered to be printed by the Government of the Union of South Africa.

II. MANUSCRIPT SOURCES

The *J. H. Hofmeyr Papers* in the South African Public Library, Cape Town, constitute the largest manuscript collection relating to the Afrikaner Bond. Vols. 1 to 9, as catalogued by J. M. du Bois and J. H. Davies in 1942, contain the archives of the *Commissie van Toezicht* from its inception in 1889.

A bound volume of *Afrikaner Bond Manuscripts* in the Library of Parliament, Cape Town, contains a small collection of documents relating to the Afrikaner Bond in the Transvaal between 1881 and 1886. These are the records kept by Ds. S. J. du Toit as secretary of the Transvaal provincial *bestuur*, and contain the *Notulen* for the congresses of May, 1882, January 1884 and February 1885.

The *Te Water Papers* in the Cape Archives, folios 56–60, contain the political correspondence of Dr. T. N. G. te Water, one of the few Bondsmen to hold cabinet rank in the period before the South African war. These papers throw much light on the inner history of the Bond, especially in the Cape Midlands, and are particularly valuable for the general election of 1888, an event not covered in the archives of the *Commissie van Toezicht*.

The *W. P. Schreiner Papers* in the South African Public Library throw a great deal of light on developments inside the South African Party during the years 1898–1900.

The *John X. Merriman Papers*, also housed in the South African Public Library, have been most useful for the period 1896–1911. Examined in conjunction with the *F. S. Malan Papers* and the *H. E. S. Fremantle Papers*, both in the Cape Archives, and the *Smuts Archive*, at present housed in the J. W. Jagger Library of the University of Cape Town, they give a solid documentary foundation for the history of the Afrikaner Bond in the decade before Union and party amalgamation.

The collection of *Rhodes Papers* in the library of Rhodes House, Oxford, has also proved useful: much of the correspondence between Rhodes and members of the Bond has not been directly used by Rhodes's biographers.

The *J. G. Sprigg Papers*, now housed in the Cory Library of Rhodes University, Grahamstown, have yielded a few documents of importance, but are a depleted collection.

A few minute books of the Afrikaner Bond branches have survived in public collections, namely: (*a*) *Notulen Boek van de Afrikaner* [*-ander, -aander*] *Bond, Kaapstad*, 3 vols., 26 Apr. 1883 to 18 Jan. 1912, in the South African Public Library; (*b*) *Notulen, Tak No. 3, Hope Town*, 8 Feb. 1888 to 26 Jan. 1912, in the Cape Archives; and (*c*) *Notulen, Oost Uitvlugt Tak van de Afrikaner Bond* (Richmond district), 25 Apr. 1882 to 11 Feb. 1914, in the Cape Archives.

III. PRINTED RECORDS OF THE AFRIKANER ORGANIZATIONS MENTIONED IN THE TEXT. [For details of published works referred to, see Section V below.]

1. THE GENOOTSKAP VAN REGTE AFRIKANERS
   Its rules are given in Du Toit, S. J. (3), pp. 51–3.

2. THE Z.A. BOEREN BESCHERMINGS VEREENIGING
   (*a*) Draft Rules and Regulations (*Bepalingen en Regulatien*) are given in Hofmeyr, pp. 643–5 (originals in the Dutch edition, pp. 706–8). (On 31 Oct. 1878, art. VI was amended to enable more than one branch to exist in any fiscal or electoral division, and art. XIII to enlarge the *hoofdbestuur* to seventeen members.)
   (*b*) A bound booklet in the Hofmeyr Papers contains the *Notulen* of the annual meetings of 1879, 1881 and 1882, as well as the special meeting of March 1882. For the annual meetings of 1880 and 1883 I have used press reports.

3. THE ALBERT BOEREN VEREENIGING
   The Nineteen Points of 26 May 1879 (*Burghersdorp Gazette*, 30 May 1879); the *Regels van het Boerenbeschermings Comité, Albert* (*Burghersdorp Gazette*, 28 Nov. 1879); the *Regels van de 'Boerenbeschermings-Vereeniging' van Albert veerenigd met den Afrikaner Bond* (document in the Hofmeyr Collection).

4. THE AFRIKANER BOND
   (*a*) S. J. du Toit's *Ontwerp van Bepalings* (*Patriot*, 4 July 1879).
   (*b*) The Constitution of the Afrikaner Bond in the Orange Free State (*Express*, 7 Apr. 1881 [the original constitution]); amendments of Dec. 1882 (printed text in the Hofmeyr Collection).
   (*c*) The Constitution of the Afrikaner Bond in the Transvaal (*Patriot*, 9 June 1882); revision of 1885 (Bond MSS., Library of Parliament, p. 5).
   (*d*) The Central Constitution of the Afrikaner Bond: the *Algemeene Constitutie* adopted at Richmond, May 1883 (Hofmeyr, pp. 649–50 [English edition], 712–13 [Dutch edition]); the Constitution adopted at the 1886 meeting of the Central *Bestuur* (*Verslag van de Eerste Zitting van het Centraal Bestuur*, and from 1890 to 1898 in the various editions of the *Officieële Stukken*). Amalgamated with the Cape constitution in 1903.
   (*e*) The Constitution of the Afrikaner Bond in the Cape Colony: the provincial constitution adopted at Richmond, May 1883 (Hofmeyr, pp. 650–2 [English edition], 714–16 [Dutch edition]). A consolidated

edition of the Cape Bond constitution, indicating its growth from 1883 to 1899, is given in my thesis, *The Afrikaner Bond*, 1880–1900, pp. 478–84 (S.A. Public Library).

(*f*) The Amalgamated Central and Cape Colonial Bond constitution (annual congress *Notulen*, 1903–11, where the current constitution is printed in the *Officieële Stukken*).

(*g*) The *Program van Beginselen* of the Afrikaner Bond: S. J. du Toit's original *Program* (document in the Hofmeyr collection [original spelling]; Du Toit, pp. 185–9 [revised spelling]); amendments by D. F. du Toit (*Notulen*, 1886 congress, Bylage A) [see also *Het Program van Beginselen van de Nationale Partij, opgesteld, verklaard en toegelicht door Ds. S. J. du Toit* (Paarl, n.d. [1884]) (Hofmeyr Collection)]. The *Program* adopted at Middelburg, March 1889 (text in the *Rapport der Commissie over het 'Program van Beginselen'*, Hofmeyr Collection, and in the various editions of the *Officieële Stukken*, 1890–8); as amended in 1903 (*Officieële Stukken*, 1903–11).

(*h*) Congress *Notulen*. Official *Notulen* of all congresses save those of 1884, 1885, 1908, 1910 and 1911 are bound in three volumes in the Hofmeyr Collection, S.A. Public Library. These include the *Notulen* of the Cradock congress of September 1882, which did not rank officially as a Bond congress. The *Notulen* of all other congresses save that of 1884 can be consulted in the Library of Parliament, whose holdings are otherwise less complete. Minutes of the 1884 congress, reprinted from the *Zuid Afrikaan*, and of the 1896 congress, reprinted from *De Paarl*, have also been consulted. Press reports are an indispensable adjunct to the official *Notulen*, which do not record debates.

(*i*) Miscellaneous documents (in the Hofmeyr Collection, unless otherwise stated):

Rapport van de Commissie over de Ineensmelting van den Afrikaander Bond en Boeren Beschermings Vereenigingen (1883).

Verslag van de Eerste Zitting van het Centraal Bestuur te Bloemfontein, 17, 18 Feb. 1886. (See also *Notulen*, 1886 Cape congress, Bylage C.)

Een Kort Overzigt van de Geschiedenis van den Afrikaander Bond, zijn Ontstaan, Voortgang en Doel (Paarl, 1890). An address given by T. P. Theron at the 1887 congress. (Dutch and English versions in the bound pamphlet collection, S.A. Public Library.)

Officieële Stukken van den Afrikaander Bond en Boerenvereeniging (editions of 1890, 1892, 1895, 1896, 1898, 1903 and annually thereafter). These include the texts of the *Program van Beginselen*, the general and Cape constitutions, and the *Reglement van Orde* (Standing Rules) of the Bond.

Afrikaander Bond en Boeren Vereeniging: Naamlijst van Leden, 1893. The only complete membership list printed. (Also in the Library of Parliament.)

De Afrikaander Bond en het Dreigende Botsing in het Noorden (Cape Town 1891). On the Adendorff Trek (S.A. Public Library).

De Afrikaander Partij en de Oorlog (Cape Town, 1900). Documents printed by order of the 1900 congress. (In private possession.)

5. THE COLONIAL UNION
Its constitution is printed in *Het Dagblad*, 26 Apr. 1898.

6. THE SOUTH AFRICAN LIBERAL ASSOCIATION
Its principles are given in the *Owl*, 3 June 1904.

7. HET VOLK
Printed editions of the *Statuten*, 1905 (private possession) and 1907 (F. S. Malan Papers), have been consulted. See also 'Knop'.

8. THE ORANGIA UNIE
The *Verrichtingen* of the 1910 and 1911 congresses are in the F. S. Malan Papers. The former contains the text of the *Statuten* (*Aanhangsel A*) and the *Beginselen* (*Aanhangsel C*) of the Unie.

9. THE NATAL BOEREKONGRES/VOLKSVERENIGING
Jansen summarizes the history of the organization and gives the *Statuten van Het Kongres* as Bylaag F. (Library of Parliament.)

10. DOCUMENTS RELATING TO THE AMALGAMATION OF PARTIES, 1910–11
Het Manifest van Generaal Botha, June 1910. Texts in Dutch (Jansen, Bylaag C), Afrikaans ('Knop', pp. 69–70) and English (Krüger [2], pp. 48–50).

Notulen van een Konferentie bestaande uit de leden van de Hoofdbestuuren van de Afrikaander Bond en Boeren Vereeniging in de Provincie Kaap de Goede Hoop; De Unie, in de Oranje Vry Staat; de Volksvereeniging van Natal en de Zuid-Afrikaanse Nationale Party in Transvaal, Cape Town, 31 Mar., 1 Apr. 1911 (in Jansen, Bylaag A).

Notulen van het Nationale Kongres gehouden in de Ramblers' Zaal te Bloemfontein, 21, 22 Nov. 1911 (F. S. Malan Papers).

Konstitusie van de Zuid-Afrikaanse Nationale Party. The draft constitution, incorporating *Statuten betreffende de Benoeming van Kandidaten voor de Volksraad*, accepted at the conference of party leaders on 31 Mar., 1 Apr. 1911, and provisionally adopted at the inaugural meeting of the South African Party in Bloemfontein, 22 Nov. 1911. (Jansen, Bylaag B.)

IV. NEWSPAPERS

Of the newspapers mentioned in the text, the following had a special significance for the Afrikaner Bond:

Afrikaanse Patriot, Di[e] (Paarl, 1876–1904). Original organ of the Genootskap van Regte Afrikaners. Edited by Ds. S. J. du Toit (1876–82, 1891–1904) and by D. F. du Toit (1882–91). Usually opposed to the *Zuid Afrikaan* before 1883, it developed a moderate policy, sometimes antagonistic to the Transvaal Government in the late 1880's, supported the Hofmeyr–Rhodes alliance in the 1890's, but lost its status as a Bond organ in 1897 on account of its continued support of Rhodes.

Albert Gazette verband met de Bondsman, De (Burghersdorp, 1894–9). Successor to the *Burghersdorp Gazette*. Edited by F. S. Collett.

Burghersdorp Gazette, The (1860–93). The best source on the Albert Boeren Vereeniging. An independent paper edited by St. P. O'S. O'Brien, who joined the Bond in the 1890's.

Dagblad, Het (Paarl and Cape Town, 1896–8). Organ of the Colonial Union and vehicle for the views of Rhodes's Afrikaner supporters after 1896. Refused recognition as a Bond organ by the 1897 congress.

Express, De (Bloemfontein, 1875–99). The official organ of the Afrikaner Bond in the Orange Free State. Initially edited by C. Borckenhagen, a German immigrant.

Friend, The (1896–). At first hostile to Afrikaner political movements, it became an organ of the Orangia Unie after the South African war.

Graaff-Reinetter, De (1885–1902). Especially important for the years 1890–1, when the paper opposed the Hofmeyr–Rhodes alliance and supported the Adendorff trekkers. Edited by J. E. McCusker.

Land en Volk (1888–1907). Supporter of the Afrikaner revival in the Transvaal after the South African war. Edited by Eugène Marais.

Middelburg Getuige, De (1882–5). Began as the *Middelburg Gazette*, owned and edited by J. N. Heathcote, but taken over for three years and renamed by N. F. de Waal. Superseded by *De Nieuwe Middelburger* (1885–1902), also edited by N. F. de Waal, who then drove the *Getuige* out of business.

Ons Land (Cape Town, 1892–1930). Founded in opposition to the *Zuid Afrikaan*, in response to a general feeling in the Bond that Dr. Van Oordt's editorial policy was not sufficiently accommodating to the English-speaking section. It forced the *Zuid Afrikaan* to amalgamate with it in 1894. F. S. Malan became editor in 1895.

Onze Courant (Graaff-Reinet, 1891–). Founded to offset the influence of the *Graaff-Reinetter*, and edited by C. H. O. Marais. A full correspondence on the origin of this paper is in the Te Water Papers. Now named *Ons Koerant*.

Oosten, Het (Somerset East, 1892–1917). The leading Bond organ in the Eastern Province. Edited by J. A. Vosloo.

Opregte Afrikaner, De (Bedford, 1882–3). Of special importance for its obstructive tactics over fusion between the Bond and the *boeren vereenigingen*. Edited by N. P. van der Meulen, a radical Bondsman.

Paarl, De (1883–98). Bond organ in the Western Province, published by the owners of the *Patriot*.

South African News, The (Cape Town, 1899–1914). Founded to 'put the ministerial policy to English-speaking readers who were beyond the reach of Malan's *Ons Land*' (Walker). Edited before the S.A. war by A. Cartwright, afterwards by R. Philipson-Stow.

Tolk, De (Paarl, 1882–5). Organ of the Afrikaner Bond, containing no news other than reports of branch meetings. Edited by D. F. du Toit. Issued as a supplement to the *Patriot*.

Volksstem, De (Pretoria, 1873–). Became, under the editorship of J. F. Celliers, the official organ of the Bond in the Transvaal, and fulfilled a similar function for Het Volk after the South African war, when the editorship was taken over by Gustav Preller.

Weekblad voor Phillipstown, Het (1892–3). A Bond organ, edited by J. E. van Minnen.

Zuid Afrikaan, De (Cape Town, 1830–94). Edited by J. H. Hofmeyr (Onze Jan) (1871–83), subsequently by Dr. J. W. G. van Oordt. Having itself merged with Hofmeyr's *Volksvriend* in 1871, it was united with *Ons Land* in 1894.

V. PUBLISHED WORKS QUOTED IN THE TEXT

Agar-Hamilton, J. A. I., *The Road to the North* (London, 1937).

Amery, L. S. (ed.), *The Times History of the War in South Africa* (7 vols., London, 1900–9).

Amphlett, G. T., *History of the Standard Bank of South Africa Limited, 1862–1913* (Glasgow, 1914).

Arndt, E. H. D., *Banking and Currency Development in South Africa, 1652–1927* (Cape Town, 1928).

Breytenbach, J. H., *Die Tweede Vryheidsoorlog* (2 vols., Cape Town, 1948–9).

Butler, General Sir W. H., *Autobiography* (London, 1911).

Campbell, W. B., *The South African Frontier, 1865–1885. A Study in Expansion* (Archives Year Book for South African History, 1959, vol. I).

Carter, G. M., *The Politics of Inequality. South Africa Since 1948* (2nd ed., London, 1959).

Cloete, B., *Die Lewe van Senator F. S. Malan* (Johannesburg, 1946).

Cobban, A., *National Self-Determination* (Chicago, 1944).

Coetzee, J. A., *Politieke Groepering in die Wording van die Afrikanernasie* (Johannesburg, 1941).

Colvin, I. D., *Life of L. S. Jameson* (2 vols., London, 1922).

De Kiewiet, C. W., *The Imperial Factor in South Africa* (Cambridge, 1937).

Dekker, G., *Afrikaanse Literatuurgeskiedenis* (5th ed., Cape Town, 1960).

De Villiers (1) A. J. D., *Die Hollandse Taalbeweging in Suid-Afrika* (Annale van die Universiteit van Stellenbosch, Cape Town, 1936).

De Villiers (2) A. J. D., 'Die Afrikaanse Kultuurstryd', in Van der Walt A. J. H., Wiid J. A. and Geyer A. L., *Geskiedenis van Suid-Afrika* (2nd ed., 2 vols., Cape Town, 1955), ii. 634 ff.

De Waal, D. C., *With Rhodes in Mashonaland* (Cape Town, 1896).

De Waal, J. H. H., *Die Lewe van D. C. de Waal* (Cape Town, 1928).

De Waal, N. F., *The Afrikaner Bond: its history and aims* (Cape Town, 1906).

Dormer, F. J., *Vengeance as a Policy in Afrikanderland* (London, 1901).

Du Toit, J. D., *S. J. du Toit in Weg en Werk* (Paarl, 1917).

Du Toit, S. J. (1), *De Christelijke School in hare Verhouding tot Kerk en Staat* (Paarl, 1876).

Du Toit, S. J. (2), *Die Geskiedenis van ons Land in die Taal van ons Volk* (1st ed., Cape Town, 1877; 2nd ed., with revised spelling in title, Cape Town, 1895).

Du Toit, S. J. (3), *Die Geskiedenis van die Afrikaanse Taalbeweging* (Paarl, 1880).

Duverger, M., *Political Parties: their Organization, and Activity in the Modern State* (trans. B. and R. North, London, 1954).

Edwards, I. E., *Towards Emancipation* (Cardiff, 1942).

Engelbrecht (1), S. P., *Geskiedenis van die Hervormde Kerk van Afrika* (3rd ed., Pretoria, 1953).

Engelbrecht (2), S. P., *T. F. Burgers: a Biography* (Pretoria, 1946).

Engelenburg, F. V., *General Louis Botha* (Pretoria, 1929).

Eybers, G. W., *Select Constitutional Documents illustrating South African History* (London, 1918).

Faure, D. P., *My Life and Times* (Cape Town, 1907).

Fitzpatrick, Sir J. P., *South African Memories* (London, 1932).

Fraser, Sir J. G., *Episodes in my Life* (Cape Town, 1922).

Fremantle, H. E. S., *The New Nation* (London, 1909).

Fuller, Sir T. E., *The Rt. Hon. C. J. Rhodes* (London, 1910).

Gardiner [F. G.] and Lansdown [C. W. H.], *South African Criminal Law and Procedure* (6th ed., Cape Town, 1957).

Garson, N. G., *The Swaziland Question and a Road to the Sea, 1887–1895* (Archives Year Book for South African History, 1957, vol. II).

Garvin [J. L.] and Amery [J.], *Life of Joseph Chamberlain* (4 vols., London 1934–51).

Gerdener, G. B. A., 'Die Kultuurhistoriese Bydrae van die Ned. Geref. Kerk in Suid-Afrika', in Van den Heever, C. M., and Pienaar P. de V. (eds.), *Die Kultuurgeskiedenis van die Afrikaner* (3 vols., Cape Town, 1945–50).

Green, J. E. S., *Rhodes goes North* (London, 1936).

Hancock, Sir W. K., *Smuts: the Sanguine Years* (Cambridge, 1962).

Hanekom, T. N., *Die Liberale Rigting in Suid-Afrika: 'n Kerkhistoriese Studie* (Stellenbosch, 1951).

Headlam, C., *The Milner Papers* (2 vols., London, 1931–3).

Hobson, J. A., *The War in South Africa* (London, 1900).

Hofmeyr, G. R. (ed.), *Minutes of Proceedings of the South African National Convention* (Cape Town, 1911).

Hofmeyr, J. H., in collaboration with Reitz, F. W., *The Life of Jan Hendrik Hofmeyr (Onze Jan)* (Cape Town, 1913). All references are to the English edition unless otherwise stated.

Hofmeyr, N. J., *Die Afrikaner-Boer en die Jameson-Inval* (Cape Town, 1896).

Immelman, R. F. M., *Men of Good Hope* (Cape Town, 1955).

Innes, Sir J. Rose, *Autobiography* (ed. B. A. Tindall, Cape Town, 1949).

Jabavu, D. D. T., *Life of J. Tengo Jabavu* (Lovedale, 1922).

Jansen, E. G., *Die Natalse Boerekongres, 1906–1911* (Pietermaritzburg, n.d.).

Joelson, A. (ed.), *The Memoirs of Kohler of the K.W.V.* (London, 1946).

Jooste, J. P., *Geskiedenis van die Gereformeerde Kerk van Suid-Afrika, 1859–1959* (Potchefstroom, 1959).

Jorissen, E. J. P., *Transvaalsche Herinneringen* (Amsterdam, 1897).

Jourdan, P. J., *Cecil Rhodes: his Private Life* (London, 1911).

Keith, Sir A. B., *Responsible Government in the Dominions* (2nd ed., 2 vols., Oxford, 1928).

Kieser, A., *President Steyn in die Krisisjare* (Cape Town, 1939).

'Knop', *Agt Jaar s'n Politiek: Skoon Geskiedenis van die Suidafr. Nasionale Partij, 1902–1910* (Pretoria, 1910). The author is identified in the Library of Parliament catalogue as Gustav Preller.

Kohn, H., *The Idea of Nationalism* (New York, 1946).

Kotzé, Sir J. G., *Biographical Memoirs and Reminiscences* (2 vols., the second ed. by B. A. Tindall, Cape Town, n.d.).

Krüger (1), D. W., *Paul Kruger* (2 vols., Johannesburg, 1961–3).

Krüger (2), D. W., *South African Parties and Policies, 1910–1960* (1960).

Kuyper, A., *Ons Program* (Amsterdam, 1880).

Laurence, Sir P. M., *Life of J. X. Merriman* (London, 1930).

Leipoldt, C. L., 'Cultural Developments', in the *Cambridge History of the British Empire*, vol. VIII (1st ed., Cambridge, 1936).

Le May, G. H. L., *British Supremacy in South Africa, 1899–1907* (Oxford, 1965).

Lewsen, P., *Selections from the Correspondence of J. X. Merriman* (vols. I and II, Van Riebeeck Society, Cape Town, 1960–3).

Leyds, W. J., *The Transvaal Surrounded* (London, 1919).

Long, B. K., *Drummond Chaplin. His Life and Times in Africa* (London, 1941).

McDonald, J. G., *Rhodes: a Life* (London, 1927).

MacQuarrie, J. W. (ed.), *The Reminiscences of Sir Walter Stanford* (2 vols., Van Riebeeck Society, Cape Town, 1958–62).

Malan, F. S., *Die Konvensie-Dagboek van Sy Edelagbare François Stephanus Malan* (ed. J. F. Preller, Van Riebeeck Society, Cape Town, 1951).

Malherbe, E. G., *A History of Education in South Africa, 1652–1922* (Cape Town, 1925).

Marais, J. S., *The Fall of Kruger's Republic* (Oxford, 1961).

Marquard, L., *The Peoples and Policies of South Africa* (2nd ed., Cape Town, 1960).

Michell, Sir L., *Life of C. J. Rhodes* (2 vols., London, 1910).

Molteno (1), Sir J. T., *The Dominion of Afrikanerdom* (London 1923).

Molteno (2), Sir J. T., *Further South African Recollections* (London, 1926).

Mouton, J. A., *Generaal P. J. Joubert in die Transvaalse Geskiedenis* (Archives Year Book for South African History, 1957, vol. I).

Munnik, G. G., *Memoirs* (Cape Town, n.d.).

Nehru, Jawaharlal, *Towards Freedom* (New York, 1942).

Newton, A. P. (ed.), *Select Documents relating to the Unification of South Africa* (2 vols., London, 1924).

Nienaber (1), G. S. and P. J., *Die Geskiedenis van die Afrikaanse Beweging* (Pretoria, 1941).

Nienaber (2), P. J., *Afrikaanse Biografiese Woordeboek* (Johannesburg, 1947).

Nienaber (3), P. J., *Ds. S. J. du Toit, die Eensame Ismael: 'n Beskouing oor sy Letterkundige Werk* (Pretoria, 1940).

Oberholster, J. A. S., *Die Gereformeerde Kerke onder die Kruis in Suid-Afrika* (Cape Town, 1956).

Pienaar, E. C., *Die Triomf van Afrikaans* (Cape Town, 1946).

Pyrah, G. B., *Imperial Policy and South Africa, 1902–10* (Oxford, 1955).

Robinson [R.] Gallagher [J.] and Denny [A.], *Africa and Victorians* (London, 1961).

Sampson, V., *My Reminiscences* (London, 1926).

Scholtz, G. D., *Die Oorsake van die Tweede Vryheidsoorlog* (2 vols., Pretoria, 1947).

Scholtz, J. du P., *Die Afrikaner en sy Taal, 1806–1875* (Cape Town, 1939).

Schreiner, Olive, *Trooper Peter Halket of Mashonaland* (London, 1897).

Scoble [J.] and Abercrombie [H.R.], *The Rise and Fall of Krugerism* (London, 1900).

Slater, J., *The Birth of the Bond* (London, 1900).

Snyman, J. H., *Rebelle-Verhoor in Kaapland gedurende die Tweede Vryheidsoorlog, met spesiale verwysing na die Militêre Howe, 1899–1902* (Archives Year Book for South African History, 1962).

Spoelstra, B., *Die Bewindsaanvaarding van die Botha-Regering oor Transvaal as selfregerende Britse Kolonie in 1907* (Archives Year Book for South African History, 1953, vol. II).

Strydom, C. J. S., *Kaapland in die Tweede Vryheidsoorlog* (Cape Town, 1937).

Thomas, C. H., *The Origin of the Anglo-Boer War Revealed* (London, n.d.).

Thompson, L. M., *The Unification of South Africa, 1902–1910* (Oxford, 1960).

Tylden, G., *The Rise of the Basuto* (Cape Town, 1950).

Van den Heever, C. M., *Generaal J. B. M. Hertzog* (Johannesburg, 1943).

Van der Merwe, N. J., *Marthinus Theunis Steyn: 'n Lewensbeskrywing* (2 vols., Cape Town, 1921).

Van der Poel (1), J., *Railway and Customs Policies in South Africa 1885–1910* (London, 1933).

Van der Poel (2), J., *The Jameson Raid* (Cape Town, 1951).

Van Jaarsveld, F. A., *Die Afrikaner en sy Geskiedenis* (Cape Town, 1959).

Van Niekerk, L., *De Eerste Afrikaanse Taalbeweging* (Amsterdam, 1916).

Van Winter, P. J., *Onder Krugers Hollanders* (2 vols., Amsterdam, 1937).

Varley, D. H., *Union List of South African Newspapers* (Cape Town, 1950).

Varley [D.H.] and Matthew [H.M.], (eds.), *The Cape Journals of Archdeacon N. J. Merriman, 1848–1855* (Van Riebeeck Society, Cape Town, 1957).

'Vindex', *Cecil Rhodes: His Political Life and Speeches, 1881–1900* (London, 1900).

Von Wielligh (1), G. R., *Baanbrekerswerk, of die Letterkundige, Kulturele en Politieke Betekenis van die Genootskap van Regte Afrikaners* (Pretoria, 1925).

Von Wielligh (2), G. R., 'Persoonlike Herinneringe van die Patriotmanne', in Afrikaanse Studentebond (eds.) *Gedenkboek ter Eere van die Genootskap van Regte Afrikaners* (Potchefstroom, 1926), pp. 59–62.

Walker (1) E. A. *Lord de Villiers and his Times, 1842–1914* (London, 1925).

Walker (2), E. A., *W. P. Schreiner: a South African* (Oxford, 1937).

Walker (3), E. A., *A History of Southern Africa* (London, 1957).

Wallis, J. P. R., *Fitz, The Story of Sir Percy Fitzpatrick* (London, 1955).

Warhurst, P. R., *Anglo-Portuguese Relations in South-Central Africa, 1890–1900* (London, 1962).

Wepener, B. J., *Een Model Afrikaander, of het Leven van T. P. Theron* (Potchefstroom, 1910).

Williams, A. F. B., *Cecil Rhodes* (2nd ed., London, 1938).

Worsfold (1), W. B., *Life of Sir Bartle Frere* (London, 1923).

Worsfold (2), W. B., *Lord Milner's Work in South Africa* (London, 1906).

Wrench, Sir J. E., *Alfred, Lord Milner: the Man of no Illusions* (London, 1958).

VI. UNPUBLISHED WORKS QUOTED IN THE TEXT OR CONSULTED

Bitensky, M. F. [Dr. M. Katzen], *The South African League: British Imperialist Organization in South Africa, 1896–1899*. M.A. thesis, University of the Witwatersrand, 1950.

De Swardt, A. H., *Rhodes en die Afrikaner Bond*. M.A. thesis, University of Stellenbosch, 1941.

Cuthbert, P., *The Administration of Dr. Jameson as Prime Minister of the Cape Colony, 1904–1908*. M.A. thesis, University of Cape Town, 1950.

Du Plessis, J. H. O., *Die Ontstaan van Politieke Partye in die Kaapkolonie tot 1885*. M.A. thesis, Potchefstroom University College, 1939.

Jenkins, S. J., *The Administration of C. J. Rhodes as Prime Minister of the Cape Colony, 1890-6.* M.A. thesis, University of Cape Town, 1951.

Kilpin, R., *Sir Nicolaas Frederic de Waal.* Manuscript article in the J. W. Jagger Library, University of Cape Town.

Kirstein, J., *Some Foundations of Afrikaner Nationalism.* Research essay, University of Cape Town, 1956.

Kleynhans, W. A., *Politieke Stroming en Verantwoordelike Bestuur in Transvaal, 1905-1909.* M.A. thesis, University of Pretoria, 1952.

Malan, C. C., *The Origin and Establishment of the Afrikander Bond until 1883.* B. Ed. thesis, University of Cape Town, 1927.

Sank, Y. P., *The Origin and Development of the Cape Progressive Party, 1884-98.* M.A. thesis, University of Cape Town, 1955.

Smit, G. J., *Die Afrikaner Bond in sy Wording in die Kaapkolonie.* M.A. thesis, University of Stellenbosch, 1931.

Trollip, A. E. G., *The First Phase of Hertzogism.* M.A. thesis, University of the Witwatersrand, 1947.

Van der Walt, C., *S. J. du Toit in die Diens van die S.A. Republiek.* M.A. thesis, University of Pretoria, 1945.

Index

A

Abdurahman, Dr. A., 249, 278, 280
Aberdeen, C.P., 42, 55, 136, 233, 287
Abrahamson, Louis, 222.
Adamson, Dr. J. E., 267.
Adendorff Trek, 134–8, 160
'Adullamites', 222, 226
Advertentieblad, De, 231
African people, relationship with Afrikaner Bond, 115–23, 184–6, 249–50, 329–31
African Political (later People's) Organization, 249, 278.
Afrikaans language, 30, 176, 264, 322.
Afrikaanse Patriot, Die, 12, 15, 20–1; 31–9 (foundation and character); 40–2 (supports Transvaal); 48–53 (propagates Afrikaner exclusiveness); 54, 58 second note, 61, 73; 76 (attacks Hofmeyr); 102 (criticizes Kruger); 135 (opposes Adendorff); 141–2 (rescued by Rhodes); 170, 196–7, 312, 322; 33, 135 (editorship of).
Afrikaanse Taalgenootskap, 265–6, 326
Afrikaanse Taalvereniging, 265–6, 326
'Afrikaner', 1, 28, 35–6, 52, 128, 326–8 (definitions);
Afrikaner Bond
  Foundation of: ch. III *passim*; Cape Colony; 34–40, 42–6; O.F.S., 46–8; Transvaal, 48–9
  Constitutional Structure of (see also *Commissie van Toezicht*): Cape Colony, 59–60, 64–8, 174–5, 244–6, ch. XIV *passim*; O.F.S., 46 and fourth note, 47–8, 62, 66; Transvaal, 49, 66, 68.
    Central bestuur, 36, 47, 56–7, 61, 63, 65, 67, 69–70, 95–6, 99, 103, 110; 245 (equated with Cape Provincial Bestuur, 1903), 287, 298
    Provincial besturen (Congresses), 47, 95, 313–19; Cape Colony: Richmond (1883) 64–70, 82, 84, 96, 119, 125, 327; Graaff-Reinet (1884) 70, 83, 85, 88, 116, 121, 125–6; Beaufort West (1885) 94, 111, 125, (1910)– ; Grahamstown (1886) 94, 96, 99–100, 111, 121–2, 125, 153; Uitenhage (1887) 122, 126; Paarl (1888) 126, 156, 315, (1900) 218, 220–2, 225; Middelburg (1889) 103, 107, 124–6, (1907)– ; Somerset East (1890) 131, (1903) 244, 317; Kimberley (1891) 133–5, 138, 313; Stellenbosch (1892) 134, 139–42, (1904) 273–4; Queenstown (1893) 116, 139, 144; Cape Town (1894) 144, (1911) 303; Port Elizabeth (1895) 157–60; Burghersdorp (1896) 162, 168–9; Malmesbury (1897) 170–3; Worcester (1898) 174–5, 179–80; Victoria West (1899) 211–12; Ceres (1906) 276; Robertson (1908) 283, 292; Dordrecht (1909) 279–80, 285–7. O.F.S.: (1882) 48. Transvaal: Pretoria (1884) 49; Potchefstroom (1887) 104, 109
    District *besturen*, 42, 47, 173–5.
    Ward *besturen*, 119 (control of membership).
    Membership: 307 (subscription), 306–8 (strength in constituencies); 140 and fourth note, 244, 307–8, 329 (numerical details); 119 and fifth note, 307 (non-admission of women); 37, 67 second note, 68, 119, 277, 329–31 (colour bar).
    Cape Town branch, role of, 62, 93, 102–4, 173–4, 195, 199, 244, 249, 279, 285, 289–90, 298, 300–1, 316.
    Commissie van Toezicht op Elekties, 124–6, 140, 141 and first note, 150–2, 159, 173–5, 183–4, 187, 244, 287, 298, 303, 309, 312–15, 318.
    Executive authority in, 210, 303,

Afrikaner Bond (*cont*.)
313–17 (*Moderatuur*); 311 (*Commissie tot Uitvoering van Bondsbesluiten*); 314–17 (office-bearers).
Parliamentary aspects: strength in Parliament, 308–9, 316; relations with S.A. Party, 243–51, 270, 292, 297, 309, 317–19; caucus, 132 and fourth note, 156–7, 218, 222, 288, 310–13; relations between parliamentary and extra-parliamentary elements, 158–9, 169, 305; representation in Cabinet, 71, 75–7, 166–7, 189, 263, 317; shortage of professional men among M.P.s, 149–51, 309–10; registration of voters, 38, 121 and third note, 122, 307; redistribution of seats, 148 and second note, 182, 310; franchise, 118–23, 147–8, 184–6, 278, 310; 148, 248 ('plumping').
Objectives: 35–6 (S. J. du Toit's original plan).
Defence of farming interests, 36, 96–8, 100, 144–5; 155–9 (scab); 83–6, 116–18, 133–8, 152–5 (occupation of land)
Defence of commercial interests, 36, 99, 100, 107, 109, 131, 144, 273–4, 310 (customs and railway questions)
Defence of cultural interests, 112 and third note (language) (see also under Afrikaans, Dutch language, Du Toit S. J., Hofmeyr J. H.); 117 and fourth to eighth notes, 118, 268–9, 276–7, 292 (education).
Programme of Principles (*Program van Beginsels*), 29, 37, 50–3, 56, 60, 66–7 (S. J. du Toit's proposals); 125, 126 and first note, 142 (adopted programme); 244–6 (revised, 1903).
Pan-South African aims: 36, 47, 53, 57, 63, 66, 70, ch. VI *passim*, 108–10, 125, 271, 324; 201–4, 207, 323 (idea of *volkseenheid*); 245, 248, 280–1, 285 (attitude to federation); 280–90 (attitude to unification of South Africa); 271 (pan-South Africanism regretted); 110–12 (becomes a Cape political party).
Attitudes on external questions: Basutoland, 78, 80–3 (Orange River as Colonial frontier); Transkei, 83–5; Bechuanaland, 85–94, 107, 126–7, 161–2; 177 (Langeberg rising); Charterland, 134–8 (Adendorff Trek); 132–3 (Chartered shares); diplomatic ineffectiveness before 1886, 94; Jameson Raid, 159–65; 1899 crisis to outbreak of Anglo-Boer War, 196–7, 199–202, 206–9; Anglo-Boer War, ch. XI *passim*; 213–14 (Conciliation Movement); 214, 220 (attitudes to Republican independence)
'Loyalty' or 'disloyalty' of, 52, 93; 177–81 (Milner at Graaff-Reinet); 196–7, 200, 206–7, 211–14, 233, 241, 244; 177, 242–3, 299 (attitude to Imperial defence); 69, 84, 91, 180, 191, 217, 225, 239, 245 (the Crown); 234–6 (select committee on the Bond).
Dissolution of, 107–10 (collapse in O.F.S. and Transvaal); 302–3 (amalgamation with associated parties).
Relations with other organizations and groups
Genootskap van Regte Afrikaners, 28
Dutch Reformed Churches, 58, 325 (use of prayer, congress sermons, Sunday observance)
Boeren Vereenigingen, 23, 25, 43–6, c. IV *passim*, South African Party, 243–51, 270, 292, 297, 309, 317–19
Colonial Union, 175
South African Liberal Associa-

Afrikaner Bond (*cont*.)
tion, 257 (and see under Liberals)
*Het Volk, Orangia Unie, Natal
Boerekongres*, 257, 271; 297–303
(amalgamation as S.A. National
Party)
The press (for particular newspapers, see index under 'Press' and
Section IV of the bibliography),
141–3, 170–1
Cape Ministries, 71–5, 305, 310–
12 (Sprigg 1878–81); 75–89 (Scanlen 1881–4); 89–94, chs. VI, VII
passim (Upington and Sprigg
1884–90); 139–45, 155, 159
(Rhodes 1890–6); 166, 176–83
(Sprigg, 1898–1900); 241, 246–7
(Sprigg 1900–04); 253, 262–3,
266, 276 (Jameson 1904–8); 263,
289, 291, 294 (Merriman 1908–10).
African people, 115–23, 184–6,
249–50, 329–31.
Coloured people, 115, 120, 184
and second note, 276–9, 308, 329–
31
Urban Labour, 248–9, 272, 299
Capitalists, 181, 252, 254–5, 272,
294, 328.
Afrikaner nationalism, ch. III *passim*,
66–9, 125, 167–8, ch. XV *passim*.
(See also Republicanism)
Agar-Hamilton, J. A. I., 87–8.
Agriculture, Ministry of, 145, 157
Ahmed Effendi, 148
Akademie voor Taal, Letteren en Kunst,
266, 326
Albany, district of, 42, 116
Albert, district of, 19, 23–4, 51, 55, 116,
211, 237 (see also Burghersdorp,
Steynsburg, Ventersburg).
Albert *Boerenvereeniging*, 13, 19–23
(foundation); 37, 43, 54, 197
Alexandria, district of, 18
Aling, R. N.; 83 first note.
Aliwal North, district of, 24, 55, 148,
185, 211, 244, 250, 296; 25, 43
(*Boerenvereeniging*); convention of,
82

Alverstone Commission, 233, 246
Amery, J., 242
Amery, L. S., 207, 307
Anglo-Boer War, 1899–1902, ch. XI
passim; 327–8 (effects of, on Boer
opinion)
Anti-Coin Law League, 15, 17
Anti-Convict Agitation, 1849, 15
Anti-Revolutionary or Christian
Historical Party, Netherlands, 51
and fifth note.
Arbitration (see Transvaal).
Associated parties, 258, 271, 299
(defined)
Aurora Gold Mining Company, 102
Aurora Rederijkerskamer, 3

B

Badenhorst, B. J., 39
Bamberger, A. N., 146 and fourth note
Banks and banking, 36, 50, 97, (see
also Imperial Banks, National
Banks, Standard Bank).
Banyailand (see Adendorff Trek)
Barnato, B. I., 139 third note
Barkly East, 84, 211 and second note
Barkly West, 87, 134, 151, 176, 186–7
Basutoland, 10, 322–3 (British annexa-
tion); 23, 84, 152 (disturbances in);
56, 74, 78, 80–3 (Cape policy for);
82–3, 90 (Cape disannexation); 100
(wheat exports)
Beaconsfield, Griqualand West, 139
Beaufort West, 6, 18, 131, 318; 94, 111,
125 (Bond Congress, 1885)
Beck, Dr. J. H. M., 225, 232, 268, 280,
297 first note
Bechuanaland, 85–94, 127–8 (expan-
sion into); 107, 126 (railway); 135,
160–1 (Border Police) (see also
British Bechuanaland)
Bedford, Cape, 43–4, 55, 61–3 (Bond
branch); 67 second note, 69, 149
(see also Farmers' Associations)
Behr, C., 45
Bekker, Gerrit, 55
Bergh, M., 83 first note
Berrangé, Daniel F., 63

Berry, Dr. W. Bisset, 188, 239
Bethesda, 55
Bethulie Bridge, 144
Beyers, Gen. C. F., 256, 259
Bilingualism, 265, 268
'Bittereinders', 251, 253
Blackwood, B. T., 259 fourth note
Blaine, G., 288
Blignauts Pont, 130–1
Bloemfontein, 47, 48, 63, 70, 82, 95, 215; 106, 107 (customs and railway conference, 1889), 272–3 (customs and railway conference, 1903); 193–5, 197–8, 200, 203 (Milner meets Kruger at, 1899); 259 (Boer congress, 1905); 257 fifth note, 302–3 (S.A. National Party Congress, 1911)
Bloemfontein Convention, 1854, 11
Blood River, battle of, 33
Boer Central Peace Committee, 232
Boeren Vereenigingen, 6, 7, ch. II passim, 54–5, 311, 312; 25 (language medium); 19–25 (in eastern Cape); ch. IV passim (amalgamation with Afrikaner Bond); 256 (in Transvaal after 1902). (For individual vereenigingen see under Albert, Aliwal North, Colesberg, Cradock, Maraisburg, Middelburg, Murraysburg, Petrusville, Somerset East, Wodehouse. See also Zuid Afrikaansche Boeren Beschermings Vereeniging, Farmers' Associations.)
Boerewinkels (Co-operatives), 50
Bondsman, De, 197
Boonzaier, D. C., 252, 296, 299–300
Borckenhagen, Carl, 46–8, 135–7, 141, 184 first note
Botha, C. L., 232 second note
Botha, Gen. Louis, 230, 254, 260; 255–6 (speech at Heidelberg); 256–8 (founds Het Volk); 262 (his 1907 cabinet); 275 (and Transvaal isolationism); 284, 286, 290 (and National Convention); 293–4, 297–8, 302 (and idea of coalition); 294–5 (and Union premiership); 297–303 (and party amalgamation); 297 third note, 298–

300, 330–1 (Manifesto of 1910); 300 (defeat in 1910 election); 301 (1911 Imperial Conference)
Botha, J. N. P., 223, 234
Botha, R. P. ('Dolf'), 56, 77, 85, 112, 125, 126 third note, 132 fourth note, 133, 142, 150, 290
Bouwer, J. J., 56
Bower, Sir Graham, 163, 165
Bowler Trek, 130
Boycotts, advocacy of, 50–1, 322
Brabant, Col. (later Gen.) E. Y., 148–9; 223 (Brabant's Horse)
Brand, President J. H., 47–8, 76–7, 82, 86, 99, 104–5, 108, 205
Brandfort, Boer congress at, 259
Brandvlei, Calvinia, 156
Brink, J. S. O., 63
British Bechuanaland, 93–4, 161, 177, 248, 308, 322
British Government (see Colonial Office, Imperial Government)
British Resident (Agent) at Pretoria: 86 (see also Greene, Conyngham)
British South Africa Company, 128–9, 132, 134, 137, 160–1, 164, 181; 165, 167–9 (demands for abrogation of charter) (see also Chartered Shares, Jameson Raid, Rhodes, C. J.)
Britstown, 42, 55, 176, 226
Bryce, James, 230
Bultfontein, 138
Burger, Schalk, 193
Burgers, President T. F., 40
Burgher Land Settlements, 276
Burghers, Cape Colonial (see Militia)
Burghersdorp, 5, 43, 144, 287; 137 (conference, 1892); 197, 208 (public meeting, 1899) (see also Albert, district of)
Burghersdorp Gazette, 19
Burton, Henry, 246, 247, 263, 286
Butler, General Sir William H., 191, 197–8, 204

C

Cachet, Professor J. L., 197, 208
Caledon, Cape, 17, 18, 90, 249

Calvinia, 233
Camdeboo, 55
Camp Street, 310
Campbell, D. A., 211
Campbell, Griqualand W., 151
Campbell-Bannerman, Sir Henry, 261, 328
Canada, Canadians, 179, 217, 245
Cape, The, 285, 296
Cape Argus, The, 73, 77, 97
Cape Colony (Cape of Good Hope), Government of, 86–7, 129; 210, 310 (extent of involvement in Anglo-Boer War); 90, 92, 161 (annexations of territory) (see also Suspension Movement)
Cape Division, 18
Cape Dutch (see Afrikaans, Afrikaner, Dutch language)
Cape Times, The, 58 second note, 163, 181, 214, 221, 237, 291, 296
Cape Town, 7, 15, 73, 148, 176, 242, 248–9; 104 (customs conference, 1888), 161 (1889); 229 (S.A. Party meeting, 1901); 291 (Drill Hall meeting, 1908) (see also Afrikaner Bond, Cape Town branch)
Capitalists and Capitalism, attitudes towards, 181 (Merriman), 252 (Afrikaners), 254–5 (F. S. Malan), 272, 328; 192 (capitalist negotiations, 1899)
Carnarvon, Cape, 62, 141, 158, 296
Carnarvon, Lord, 41
'Carpet-bagging', 7–8, 38
Cartwright, Albert, 213, 225, 231–2
Cathcart, Cape, 43
Celliers, Ds. D. H., 325
Celliers, J. F., 48
Centlivres, F. J., 295–6
Central Bestuur (see Afrikaner Bond)
Ceres, 61, 67 second note, 229, 276
Chamberlain, Joseph, 161, 227, 256; 162 (Drifts crisis); 164 (and Jameson Raid); 168 (on self-government for Rand); 192–6, 198, 200–6, 209 (crisis of 1899); 216–18, 225 (and Cape rebels); 229–30

(rejects Cape peace proposals); 236, 241–3, 254 (visit to South Africa); 237–41 (opposes suspension of Cape constitution)
Chartered Company (see British South Africa Company)
Chartered shares, disposal of by Rhodes, 126, 132 and sixth and seventh notes, 133 and first and second notes
Charterland (see Rhodesia)
Chinese labour, 251, 255–6, 262, 299, 328
Christian National Education (C.N.E., C.N.O.), 30, 31, 37, 67 and second note, 68, 292, 322, 325–6 (in Cape Colony); 266–9, 292 (in Transvaal and O.R.C. after 1902); 31, 37 (S. J. du Toit's De Christelijke School)
Civil liberty, loss of during Anglo-Boer War, 221, 324
Claassens, J. H., 295 third note
Claassens, H. J. H., 121 fourth note, 229
Cloete, W., 318
Cobden, Richard, 15
Colesberg, 23, 25, 39, 42–3, 55, 105, 107, 170, 211, 237; 25 (Boeren Vereeniging)
Colonial Conferences, 178 (1887); 151, 178 (1894); 177 (1897); 239 (1902) (see also Imperial Conferences)
Colonial Office, London, 73, 82, 161, 178, 202, 209, 256 (see also Downing Street, Secretary of State for the Colonies)
Colonial Union (Koloniale Unie), 175–6, 186–7
Coloured people, relationship with Afrikaner Bond, 115, 120, 184 and second note, 276–9, 308, 329–31
Commando system, 80
Commissie van Toezicht op Elekties (see Afrikaner Bond)
Concentration camps, 251
Concession policy (see Transvaal)
'Conciliation', 236, 243, 253–63, 302, 324, 328

Conciliation Movement, 213–14, 276
Confederation (see Federation)
Constitutionalist Party, O.R.C., 260–1, 278, 283
Co-operatives (*Boerewinkels*), 50
Corporal punishment, 114–15
Courts (see Justice, administration of)
Cradock, 7, 23, 43, 124, 174, 233; 7, 24, 43, 55 (*Boeren Vereeniging*); 56–61, 64, 81, 83–4, 121, 125, 313 (congress, 1882); 273–4 (Bond congress, 1905)
Cradock Register, 24
Crewe, C. P., 223
Cronwright-Schreiner, S. C., 186, 228, 252
Currey, H. L., 263
Customs Union, 96, 98–9, 103, 107–8, 127, 130, 272–5

D

Dagblad, Het, 172–6
Daljosaphat, 29, 45, 67 second note
Daverin, John, 290
Dawkins, Sir Clinton, 179
De Aar, 137, 156 fourth note
De Beers, 133–4, 138, 151, 159, 160
De Jager, Dr. A. L., 286
De Jong, J. E., 227 fifth note, 231
Delagoa Bay, 99, 101, 104, 106, 107, 127, 143, 160–1, 273
De Lange, J. H., 185 third note
De la Rey, General J. H., 256
Derby, Lord, 82, 86–7, 90
De Smidt, W. A. J., 311
De Ville, J. D., 295 third note
De Villiers, B. J. van de Sandt, 11
De Villiers, J., 262
De Villiers, Sir J. H. (later Lord), 79, 132 146, 166, 193, 239
De Villiers, J. I., 228
De Villiers, S. P. H., 318
De Villiers, Ds. W. P., 21, 76, 79, 136, 158, 172, 182
De Vos, Ds. P. J. G., 167, 227 second note
De Waal, Daniel, 55

De Waal, David Christiaan, 103, 132 seventh note, 133, 135, 138, 142, 144, 159, 165, 168, 173, 187–8, 190 and first note, 218–19, 222, 264; 187–8, 190, 312 (his defiance of Bond leadership)
De Waal, J. H. H., 264
De Waal, Nicolaas Frederic, 24, 141 (early career); 125, 174–5, (on *Commissie van Toezicht*); 157; 213 second note, 218–19, 221 third note, 222, 228, 232, 233, and third note (and Anglo-Boer War); 234 (and select committee on Afrikaner Bond); 242–3 (and Chamberlain's visit); 271 (address to Liberal Association); 263, 290–1 (in Merriman's Cabinet); 286, 295, 296, 299 (and unification of South Africa); 316
De Waal, Pieter, 151–2
De Wet, General C. R., 228, 231, 262
De Wet, J. A., 312
De Wet, P. D., 232 second note
De Wet, P. J., 185, 222, 227, 234
De Winton, Sir Francis, 129–30
Diamond Fields, British annexation of, 10, 205, 323
Diamond Fields Advertiser, 237, 239
Diamond industry, 1, 138–9; 139, 272 (tax on diamonds)
Dinizulu, 283
Disarmament under Peace Preservation Act, 73, 74, 81 (Basuto); 221, 248 (Boers)
Disfranchisement (see Franchise, Cape Colony)
District Six, 249
Divisional Councils, 6–7
District *besturen* (see Afrikaner Bond)
Donovan, A. D., 296
'Doppers' (see *Gereformeerde Kerk*)
Dordrecht, Cape, 6, 24, 84, 211, 213, 287, 296
Dormer, F. J., 4, 8, 62, 123, 178, 207, 326
Dort, Synod of, 38
Douglass, Arthur, 111, 148, 182, 249

Downing Street, 93, 254
Drifts crisis, 133, 160–2
Du Plessis, A. S., 19 second note, 134 fourth note, 182, 223, 234, 292
Du Plessis, J. P., 174
Du Plessis, M. J., 185 third note
Du Plessis, Stephanus: 40 second note
Du Preez, H. P., 15, 17, 56
Durham, Lord, 225
Dutch East India Company, 32
Dutch language, use of in public life, 3, 4, 7 and second note, 36, 46, 56, 71, 75–80, 113, 120 (campaign in Cape before 1900); 243, 248, 255, 266–9, 292 (campaign in Cape and ex-Republics after 1900); 140, 264, 326 (Taalbond); 30–1, 236, 264–6 (rivalry of Dutch and Afrikaans); 252 (Treaty of Vereeniging); 284 (equality with English in S.A. Act) (see also Education, Christian National Education)
Dutch Reformed Churches, 28, 29, 38–40, 255, 266, 325 (and Afrikaner political movements) (see also *Nederduits Gereformeerde Kerk*, *Gereformeerde Kerk*, *Kruiskerk* movement, Christian National Education, Neo-Calvinism)
Du Toit, A. B., 263, 277, 278
Du Toit, D. F. (D. F.'s son), 136 first note
Du Toit, Daniel François (D. P.'s son), 29 (early career); 31, 33 (edits *Patriot* as 'Oom Lokomotief'); 57, 60, 66, 67, 69 (and amalgamation of Bond and Vereenigingen); 69 (vice-chairman, Cape Provincial *bestuur*); 96 (on Central *Bestuur*); 102 (joins mining syndicate); 125–6 (on Bond Programme of Principles Commission); 132 fourth note (attends caucus); 134–8 (opposes Rhodes's northern policy, backs Adendorff, retires to O.F.S.)
Du Toit, P. J., 39, 115, 116; 177 (Peace motion); 212, 232

Du Toit, Ds. Stephanus Jacobus:
Early career to 1882, 29; 22, 26, 37, 44–6, 52, 54 (relations with Hofmeyr and *boeren vereenigingen*); 23, 40–2 (and Transvaal crisis 1877–81); 28–34 (and *Genootskap van Regte Afrikaners*); 32–4, 50–1, 322–3 (character of his early nationalism); 20, 35–9, 327 (proposes an Afrikaner Bond, 1879)
Transvaal period, 1882–90, 30–3 (appointed Superintendent-General of Education in Transvaal as sponsor of Christian National Education); 49 (founds Afrikaner Bond in Transvaal); 70 (mission to Europe, 1883–4); 91–2, 162 (involvement in Bechuanaland crisis); 102 (criticizes Kruger's concession policy); 101–6 (criticizes Kruger's railway policy); 106, 167 (criticizes Hollander influence); 101–2, 109 (business interests, failure, return to Cape)
Second Cape period, and alliance with Rhodes, from 1890, 135; 138 (defends De Beers); 136 (opposes Adendorff Trek); 141–3 (revives Bond press); 157 (supports Rhodes's Scab Act); 164, 168, 170 (associates with Rhodes after Jameson Raid); 168–76 (breach with the Bond); 170–4 (establishes Colonial Union and *Het Dagblad*); 151, 162, 176, 187 (unsuccessful parliamentary candidatures); 239 (urges suspension of Cape constitution)
Relationship with Afrikaner Bond, 20, 35–9, 327 (proposal to establish); 39, 173–4, 313 (views on Bond constitution); 50–3, (proposed Programme of Principles; 49 (founds Bond in Transvaal); 67 (message to Richmond congress); 70, 96 (chairman of Central *Bestuur*); 141–3 (and Bond press); 150, 174 (membership of and expulsion from *Commissie van Toezicht*); 168–76 (breach with Bond)

Du Toit (cont.)
Press activities, 33–4, 135 (*Patriot*);
141–3 (views on a press union and
approach to Rhodes); 170 (*Dagblad*)
Relations with Dutch Reformed
Churches, 28; 38–9, 51 (Neo-
Calvinism and debt to Kuyper); 173
(Kruiskerk movement); 322–3
Character of his Nationalism,
32–3 (*Geskiedenis van ons Land*); 50,
140 (proposals for a national bank);
51 and first note (boycott doctrine);
171–2 (moderation in late 1890's)
His personality, 109, 176, 322–3
Du Toitspan, 138
Dynamite monopoly (see Transvaal)

E

East London, 93, 249; 114 and fourth
note (Farmers' Congress, 1883)
East London Dispatch, 43
Eastern Province Herald, 237
Easton, Herbert, 257
Ebden, Alfred, 311
Economic depression, 95–8 (early
1880's); 143–4 (gold crisis, 1890–1);
274, 291 (1903–9)
Edgar incident, 191
Education in Cape Colony, 31–2
(*Genootskap van Regte Afrikaners*);
57 ('voluntary principle'); 79 (Dutch
permitted in secondary schools); 79
(Commission, 1880), 140 (Commission, 1891); 117–18 (farmers' opposition to education for black
children); 268–9, 276 and second
and fourth notes, 292 (white politicians and growth of educational
discrimination)
Education in Transvaal and O.R.C.
after 1902, 266–9; 167, 252, 255, 267
(Transvaal); 267–8, 300 (O.R.C.)
(see also Christian National Education)
Elections, Cape Colony, House of
Assembly, 17–19, 71–2 (1879); 71,
85, 89 (1884); 120–2, 124, 127 (1888);
125, 139, 147–52, 154, 185 (1894);

120, 175–6, 183–8, 278, 308 (1898);
241, 247–50, 278 (1904); 261, 263
(1908); 72, 190, 244 (by-elections)
Elections, Cape Colony, Legislative
Council, 17–19, 71–2 (1878); 71, 89
(1883); 140 (1891); 173–5, 180
(1898); 247–9 (1903); 261–3 (1908)
Elections, O.F.S. Volksraad, 261–2
(1908)
Elections, O.R.C., legislature, 261–2
(1907)
Elections, Transvaal presidential, 109
(1888); 180 (1898)
Elections, Transvaal, legislature, 261–2
(1907)
Elections, Union of South Africa, 296,
299–300 (1910)
Emigrant Tembuland, 83, 152
English language, 2, 3 (official in Cape
Colony); 252 (official in Transvaal
and O.R.C.); 4 (use in courts)
Engelenburg, F. V., 293 and sixth note,
294
Esselen, Ewald, 106, 256
Excise on spirits, Cape Colony, 13–16,
18, 26, 46, 71, 78 second note, 149,
291–2, 310
Express, The, 46, 136, 141, 207

F

Farm-buildings, Anglo-Boer War, 227
Farmers' Associations (Dutch-
speaking) (see *Boeren Vereenigingen*)
Farmers' Associations (English-
speaking), 15 and second note, 26–8,
43–4, ch. VII *passim* (origin and
relationship with Dutch-speaking
bodies); 25, 112 (language medium)
Congresses: East London (1883),
114 and fourth note; Port Elizabeth
(1886), 111, 121; Bedford (1888),
114 sixth note; Graaff-Reinet
(1889), 114 sixth note
Political attitudes: 114–15 (justice
and police), 116–17 (pass laws and
squatting), 117–18 (African education and land tenure), 156 (scab);
118, 119 and first note (non-party

Farmers' Associations (*cont.*)
political character of); 149 (opposition to redistribution of parliamentary seats); 26–7, 95, 111–13 (possible emergence of an Anglo-Dutch farmers' party)

Farrar, Sir George, 293

Faure, J. A., 173–5

Faure, Sir Pieter H., 162, 166, 182, 237

Fauresmith, 48

Federation of South Africa, 10, 11, 12 fourth note, 73 (British efforts to achieve); 52, 245, 248, 261, 280–1, 285 (Afrikaner attitudes on); 161, 169 (Rhodes); 283–5 (National Convention and). (See also Unification of South Africa)

Field-cornets, 6, 114

Fincham, A. W., 184

Fingo, 116; 83 (Fingoland)

Fischer, Abraham, 192, 195, 196, 198 and second note, 199, 200, 202, 203, 205, 207 (and crisis of 1899); 262 (Premier of O.R.C.), 294–5, 298

Fitzpatrick, Sir J. Percy, 192, 293, 300

Flags, issues affected by, 66, 68, 90, 91, 96, 111, 112, 126 first note, 196, 212, 255

Fort Beaufort, 148, 185; 114 sixth note (Farmers' Congress, 1883)

Fourie, A., 317

Fourie, C., 40 second note

Fourteen Streams, 93

Fox, C. J., 243

Franchise, Cape Colony, 118–23 (discussion of, and 1887 amendment); 21 (changes considered by Albert *Boeren Vereeniging*), 56 (at Graaff-Reinet congress, 1882); 147–8 (Franchise and Ballot Act, 1892); 154–5 (Glen Grey Act and); 216–20, 225–6, 236, 241, 243, 247–50 (disfranchisement of Cape Colonial rebels and political effects); 263 (re-enfranchisement of rebels)

Franchise, Transvaal, 193–203 (uitlander franchise, 1899); 202–8 (joint inquiry proposals)

Franchise, Union of South Africa, 284

Fraser, Sir J. G., 260, 261

Fraserburg, 67 second note, 69, 96 fourth note, 187

'Freebooters', 86

Fremantle, H. E. S., 257 fifth note, 301–2, 327

French, General Sir John, 227 fifth note, 231, 233

Frere, Sir H. Bartle, 12, 20, 72–4, 210, 305

Frontier Guardian, The, 24

Frontier Party, 112 second note, 123

Frontier Wars, 11, 14, 84, 152 (in 1870's)

Frost, J., 148, 153, 157, 237

Fuller, Sir Thomas E., 139 third note, 148, 182

Gaika-Gcaleka war, 14, 74

Garrett, Edmund, 163

Genootskap van Regte Afrikaners, Die, 28–34, 50, 265

George, Cape, 18, 223, 277

Gereformeerde Kerk, 261, 292 (see also Dutch Reformed Churches)

Gereformeerde Kerke onder die Kruis (*Kruiskerk* movement), 173, 176, 187

Germans, Germany, 92, 192

Geskiedenis van ons Land in die Taal van ons Volk, Die, 31–3, 37, 52, 322

Gladstone, Lord, Governor-General, 296

Gladstone, W. E., 41, 73, 243

Glen Grey, 152–5 (Act, 1894); 153 (Commission, 1892)

Goede Hoop, De, 264

Gold-mining, 95, 98, 102, 143

Goldschmidt, L. H., 83 first note

Goldwin Smith, 293 fourth note, 294 third note

Gordon, General Charles, 84 fourth note

Gordonia, 211, 234

Goshen, Republic of, 85, 88, 90–3

Graaff, David P. de V., 238, 262, 263, 295, 296, 298

Graaff, J. A. C., 285, 286, 295 third note

Graaff-Reinet, 19, 23, 24, 55, 56, 62; 76–7 (Bond address to Merriman); 102, 124, 131, 150; 179–81 (Bond address to Milner); 237, 242; 54–7, 61, 81, 125 (congress at, 1882); 70, 83, 85, 88, 98, 116, 121, 125, 126 (Bond congress at, 1884); 114 sixth note (Farmers' congress at, 1889); 213, 214 and fourth note, 225, 227 (conciliation movement congress, 1900); 19, 119 first note (Farmers' Association)
Graaff-Reinet Advertiser, The, 181, 237
Graaff-Reinetter, De, 136, 141–2
Grabe, J. G., 96
Graham, J. J., 234 third and sixth notes
Graham, T. L., 246
Grahamstown, 7, 111, 249; 94, 96, 99, 100, 111, 121–2, 125, 153 (Bond congress at, 1886); 111–12 (conference of Bond and Farmers' Associations at, 1886)
Grahamstown Political Union, 112 second note
Great Trek, 1, 11, 32, 331
Greene, Conyngham, 192, 194, 203, 204
Grey College, Bloemfontein, 47
Grey, Sir Edward, 179
Grey, Sir George, 322
Griqualand West, 75, 138, 212, 248, 308
Griquatown (Hay), 234
Grobler, Piet, 199
Groote Kerk, Cape Town, 3

H

Haarhoff, D. J., 184, 186
Hague Convention, 1899, 200, 221
Hamelfontein, 62
Hamilton, Francis, 24
Hammond, John Hays, 161
Hanbury-Williams, Major, 252
Hankey, 121 fourth note
Hanover, Cape, 61, 62, 64 and fifth note, 65
Hargrove, E. T., 213–15

Harris, D., 234 second note
Harrismith, 48, 107
Hay (Griquatown), 234
Hazenjagt, 45
Headlam, Cecil, 178
Heathcote, J. N., 24, 141
Heidelberg, Cape, 17, 18
Heidelberg, Transvaal, 48, 49, 255–6
Heidelberg Catechism, 38
Heilbron, 48
'Helots', 196–218
Hely-Hutchinson, Sir Walter, 211 fifth note, 212, 237, 240, 289
'Hensoppers', 233, 251, 260
Herholdt, A. J., 126 third note, 146 sixth note, 189, 198–9, 223, 226
Herholdt, M. J., 55, 56
Hertzog, General J. B. M., 226, 254, 259, 260, 262, 329; 267–8 (education policy); 284 (at National Convention); 300 (and 1910 Union election); 300–2 (and Botha's Cabinet)
Het Volk, 256–8 (established); 258, 264, 271, 329 (principles); 261 (wins 1907 Transvaal election); 275, 281–4 (attitude to South African unification); 270, 276 (concern for poor whites and urban artisans); 295 (and Union premiership); 298, 301 (and party amalgamation); 298 (changes name); 314 (head committee)
Heyns, J. J., 234
Hicks Beach, Sir Michael, 73
High Commissionership in South Africa, 74, 83, 86, 90, 101, 130, 137, 159, 160, 163, 172, 192, 193, 194, 203, 225 (see also Frere, Robinson, Loch, Milner, Selborne)
Hobson, J. A., 178
Hoffman, Dr. J. M., 60, 125, 170, 173, 174, 212, 227, 245
Hofmeyr, Ds. A. J. L., 164
Hofmeyr, Jan Hendrik ('Onze Jan'): Personal characteristics, 11, 12 (childhood and education); 10, 11, 142–3 (editor of Volksvriend, Zuid Afrikaan, and view on the press);

Hofmeyr, Jan Hendrik (*cont.*)
26, 290 ('Mole', 'Onze Jan'); 90, 158, 164, 222 (health); 102, 133, 159, 183 (investments); 290, 306 (death and appraisals)
Relationship with farmers' movements, 13, 14, 78 (opposition to excise on spirits); 13–18 (establishes *Boeren Beschermings Vereeniging*), 45–6 (proposes its reform); 26–7 (uses a farmers' movement to push cultural demands); 22, 64 (attitude to eastern *vereenigingen*); 111 (attitude to English-speaking farmers' associations); 144–5 (backs Rhodes's agricultural policy).
Relationship with Afrikaner nationalist movements, (*a*) *Genootskap van Regte Afrikaners*, 30–1; (*b*) Afrikaner Bond, 36 (resists S. J. du Toit's original proposals); 44–6, 61, 76 (competes with Du Toit for support); 56, 59, 60 (at Graaff-Reinet and Cradock congresses, 1882); 55, 62 (joins Afrikaner Bond); 63, 64, 67, 69 (at Richmond congresses, 1882–3); 69, 315 (Treasurer, Cape provincial *bestuur* and member of Central *Bestuur*); 124–5, 151–2, 174, 314–15 (chairman of *Commissie van Toezicht*, q.v.); 125–6 (on Bond Programme of Principles commission); 142–3 (on Bond press); 175, 244–5 (and Bond constitutional changes, 1898, 1903); 26–7, 289–90 (concern to preserve Afrikaner's cultural identity)
Attitude to language questions, 12, 30–1 (prefers Hollands to Afrikaans); 76, 79 (urges Dutch in Parliament and public service); 264–5 (*Taalbond*, q.v., and second language movement; *Is 't ons Ernst?*)
Parliamentary activities, 72, 151–2, 158–9 (represents Stellenbosch and resigns, 1879–95); 18, 71, 75–6, 77 (enters and leaves Scanlen's Cabinet); 89–90, 123–4, 131, 132 and

second note, 149, 166, 306 (his refusals to form a government); 71, 310 (as 'king-maker'); 305–11 (his tactics considered)
His constitutional and political ideas, 12, 26, 59, 326 (opposes racialism); 52–3 (respect for British parliamentary system); 122, 147–8 (views on franchise); 125–6 (and Bond principles); 175, 244–5 (and Bond constitution); 238–41 (and suspension of Cape constitution); 283, 285–6, 288–90, 328 (non-participation in and views on National Convention; prefers federal to unitary constitution, opposes proportional representation; delegate to London); 293 (opposes coalition after Union)
His attitude to external questions, 12, 73 (opposes confederation before restoration of Transvaal independence, 1880); 56 (is proposed for Transvaal presidency); 73, 76, 78, 80–3 (on Basutoland); 84 (on white settlement in Transkei); 87–8, 92 (on Bechuanaland); 99, 101, 105, 106, 127–9 (on customs union and railway extension); 129–31, 160 (and Swaziland negotiations); 132 (refuses seat on B.S.A. Company Board); 135–7 (and Adendorff Trek); 163–5, 316 (and Jameson Raid); 177–9 (and protection of Imperial navy); 168, 193–208 (views on Transvaal Government and participation in diplomacy of 1899); 198–9 and first note (mission to Pretoria); 216 (and Hargrove mission); 222 (retirement to Europe, 1900); 229–30 (resists Merriman's 'grand remonstrance')
His attitude over racial questions, 115 (abstains over Strop Bill); 120 and first note, 148, 278–9 (relations with coloured people); 184–6 (courts African vote in 1898 election, with support of Jabavu); 154–5 (Glen

Hofmeyr, Jan Hendrik (*cont.*)
Grey); 277 (did not testify before
S.A. Native Affairs Commission)
His relationship with individuals,
12 (Sir Bartle Frere); 24 (N. F. de
Waal); 44–6, 52–4, 76, 135–7, 142,
157, 164, 168–9, 173–5 (S. J. du
Toit); 64 (T. P. Theron); 77, 229–30,
283, 289 (J. X. Merriman); 127–8,
133, 136, 163–5 (C. J. Rhodes); 160
(Sir H. Loch); 166 (J. G. Sprigg);
243 (J. Chamberlain); 150–1, 181,
218, 220 (W. P. Schreiner)
Hofmeyr, Professor N. J., 29
Hofmeyr, Tielman J. R., 132 seventh
note, 174 and second note
'Hoggenheimer', 252, 294
Hollanders in Transvaal, 102, 106,
167–8, 323
Hoogenhout, C. P., 30, 141 third note
Hopetown, 39, 42, 136; 51 (Hopetown
bank)
Hopley, F. H., 20 and second note, 21
Huguenots, 32, 33
Hull, H. C., 261, 262
Humansdorp, 18, 277
Hyslop, T., 293 fourth note

I

Immigration, 1, 5, 299, 301 (see also
Chinese labour)
Imperial Banks, 50 (see also Standard
Bank)
Imperial Conference, 1911, 301 (see
also Colonial Conferences)
Imperial Government, 73–4 (Confederation policy); 83, 85, 86, 89, 90
(and Basutoland, Transkei, Bechuanaland); 129–31 (Swaziland); 138
(Adendorff Trek); 161 (release of
Bechuanaland Border Police); 162
(and Drifts crisis); 163–5 (and
Jameson Raid); ch. X *passim*
(relations with Transvaal before
Anglo-Boer War); 10, 189, 192,
203–4, 208, 209, 220 (paramountcy
doctrine); 203, 208 (suzerainty
doctrine)

Imperial League, 93, 112
Imperial Navy, 52, 178–9
Imperial Secretary, Cape Town, 131
Imperial troops, allegations against,
221, 226–7, 231
Imvo Zabantsundu (alternatively *Imvo
Neliso Lomzi*), 121 and first note,
185
Indemnity legislation, 219, 220, 223,
224, 240
Innes, Sir James Rose, 132, 135, 145,
149, 154–5, 158–60, 171–3, 177, 182–
3, 185, 188, 223–5, 293, 305, 326
Insolvencies, 97–8, 274
Inter-Colonial Council, 253
Irvine, 84
'Isolationists', 253, 282
Izel (see Yzel, A.)
Izwi Labantu, 186 second note

J

Jabavu, John Tengo, 117, 120, 123; 185
and second note; (accepts Hofmeyr
as ally) 249, 278
Jacobsdal, 48
Jackson, J. R., 318
Jameson, Dr. L. S., 135, 160, 223, 237
249, 301; 252 (leads Progressives);
253, 262–3, 266, 273, 276 (Ministry,
1904–8); 282 (and F. S. Malan's
federal motion); 293, 294 (and
coalition proposals); 299 (and 1910
election)
Jameson Raid, 133, 158–65, 221, 322,
323; 169–70 (Cape select committee);
170–1 (commission of inquiry)
Johannesburg, 128, 145–6, 160, 162,
191, 203; 273 (railway conference
at)
Joint inquiry (see Franchise, Transvaal)
Jorissen, Dr. E. J. P., 41, 73
Joubert, F. J., 318
Joubert, Jotham, 20, 21, 55, 84, 137,
197, 212, 222, 234
Joubert, J. S., 136
Joubert, General P. J., 41, 73 (agitates
for Transvaal independence); 48, 70
(and founding of Bond in Transvaal);

Joubert, General P. J. (cont.)
88–92 (and Bechuanaland); 96 (on
Central Bestuur); 102, 104, 109
(opposition to Kruger); 130, 138
Justice, administration of; 114 (in
country districts); 8 (Boers and jury
service); 8, 117 and eighth note
('Kaffir' interpreters)
Juta, Sir Henry, 186, 239, 313

K

Kakamas Labour Colony, 276–7
Keate Award, 85
Kemp, General J. C. G., 256
Kenhardt, 211, 213
Kimberley, 102, 132, 137, 139, 165;
99, 101–3, 105, 128–9 (railway
extension)
'Kindergarten', Milner's, 253, 281
King William's Town, 120, 121, 131,
148, 185
Kitchener, Lord, 212, 216, 231; 227
(farm-burnings); 230 (Middelburg
negotiations)
Klein Drakenstein, 69
Klerksdorp, 128
Klipplaat, 131
Kohler, C. W. H., 102
Kokstad, 84
Kolbe, Rev. Dr. F. C., 228, 229
Koloniale Unie (see Colonial Union)
Kolonist, De, 174 second note, 176
Komatie, 49
Kommissie van Toezicht (see Afrikaner
Bond: Commissie van Toezicht)
Koopmans de Wet, Marie, 227
Kosi Bay, 129, 130
Kotzé, Sir J. G., 26, 91, 99, 167–8
Krige, Gideon, 152, 289
Krige, W. A., 151–2
Kritzinger, Commandant P. H., 226
Kroonstad, 48
Kruger, President S. J. P., 40, 41, 73
(and Transvaal independence); 86,
91–3 (Stellaland and Goshen); 99,
101, 104–7, 127, 128 (and railway
extension); 130 (Blignauts Pont
meeting); 134–5 (opposes Adendorff

Trek); 160, 162 Drifts crisis); 180
(re-election 1898); 191; 193–5 (meets
Milner at Bloemfontein); 198, 199,
205–6 (crisis of 1899); 213–15
(Hargrove); 274, 322–3
Krugersdorp, 256, 257
Kruiskerk movement, 173, 176, 187
Kuhn, P. G., 295 third note, 297 first
note
Kuyper, Dr. Abraham, 29, 38, 51–2

L

Labour parties, 262, 297
Labour tax, 155
Ladybrand, 48, 136
Laing, J., 160, 162
Land, 149, 153–4 (ownership by
Africans); 84–5, 98, 133, 135 and
sixth note, 177 (demand for by
white men)
Land en Volk, 264
Langeberg rebellion, 177, 181, 186
Langlaagte Estate Mines, 102
Language (see Afrikaans, Dutch,
English)
Lawley, Sir Arthur, 256 first note, 267
Lawrence, J., 234 second note
Leribe, 81
Le Roex, A. S., 68, 187
Letsie, 81
Lewis and Marks, 102 (see also Kim-
berley railway)
Leyds, Dr. W. J., 184 first note
Liberalism, 32, 52 (theological); 37,
52–3, 113, 122, 190, 288, 330
(political)
Liberals, 132, 145–8, 152–5, 160, 185,
278; 254, 257, 260 (Liberal Party in
Great Britain); 254–5, 257 and fifth
note, 258, 270, 271, 301, 308 (S.A.
Liberal Association)
Lichtenburg, 88 third note
Lippert, E. A., 130–1, 137–8 (land con-
cession); 192 (dynamite concession)
Lobengula, 131, 134
Lobola system, 118
Loch, Sir Henry, 130, 131, 133, 159–60
Logan, J. D., 146, 150, 158 (contract of)

London Convention, 1884, 90–2, 129, 162, 200
Long, B. K., 293, 294
Lötter, C. J., 234
Lourenço Marques (see Delagoa Bay)
Louw, M. J., 83 first note
Louw, Thomas A. J., 100, 164, 168, 171
Lydenburg, 49
Lyttleton Constitution, 258, 260

M

Maasdorp, G. H., 278
Mackarness, Frederick, 213
Mackay, J., 121
Mackenzie, Rev. John, 87, 90 and second note
Maeder, Ds. G. A., 268
Mafeking, 129, 144
Majuba, battle of, 74, 95, 323
Makwassie, 49
Malan, Daniel, 102
Malan, Dr. Daniel François 265
Malan, D. J., 134, 136
Malan, François Stephanus, 102; 167 (edits *Ons Land*); 168–9 (at Burghersdorp Bond congress); 200 (and 1899 crisis); 221, 227 fifth note, 228 (leads Bond resistance to Imperial Government's war policy); 231, 234 (trial and conviction for seditious libel); 243 (meets J. Chamberlain); 254–5, 260 (addresses Liberal Association); 263, 291–2 (in Merriman's Cabinet); 281 (federal proposals of 1906), 283, 286, 288, 289 (influence at National Convention); 277, 280 (opposes political colour bar); 293 opposes coalition, 1910); 295, 296 (promotes Botha for premier); 297–303 (views on party amalgamation); 299, 330 (views on Botha's Manifesto); 244–6 (views on Bond constitution); 245 (elected to Central *Bestuur*); 265–6 (prefers Dutch to Afrikaans, backs equality of Dutch and English); 274 (and tariff policy); 301, 316
Malan, Ds. G. S., 295 fifth note

Malmesbury, 17, 18, 23, 96 fourth note, 233, 288; 170–1, 173 (Bond congress, 1897)
Mankoroane, 86, 92
Mansvelt, Dr. N., 167
Marais, C. H. O., 142, 172, 179–81
Marais, Eugène, 264
Marais, J. S., 15, 68, 69, 75, 79, 151
Marais, P. J., 138, 151
Maraisburg, 55; 22, 24, 43 (*Boeren Vereeniging*)
Maritz, J. C., 234
Marks, Sammy, 99 (see also Lewis and Marks)
Marquard, Leopold, 327
Martial Law, 219, 223, 246
Mashonaland, 130, 133
Massouw, David, 86
Master and Servant Laws, 1, 56, 112, 114, 115 first note, 125–6, 145
Matabele Rebellion, 170
Matabele War, 155, 161
Matabeleland, 105
Matatiele, 154
McCusker, J. E., 124 third note, 141
Merriman, John Xavier, 48, 54, 76–8 (early hostility towards Bond); 82, 189–90, 220, 291, 294 (Colonial Treasurer in Scanlen's, Schreiner's and his own Ministries); 132 seventh note, 139 third note, 143, 145, 146, 153, 154 (and Rhodes Ministries); 263, 282, 317 (forms Ministry in Cape); 185, 249–50, 295–6 (fights Wodehouse and Victoria West seats); 181, 234 (association with Bond); 191 (crisis of 1898–9); 169, 294–5 (his anti-capitalism); 211, 215, 217–19, 223, 225, 227–30 (opposition to Imperial policy during Anglo-Boer War); 234 second note (and select committee on the Bond); 241 (and suspension movement); 257–8 (founds Liberal Association); 277–80, 282, 283, 288, 289 (role at National Convention); 293–8 (attitude to coalition and Union premiership); 297–303 (attitude to party

Merriman, John Xavier (*cont.*) amalgamation); 291, 294 (personal relations)

Michau, J. J., 285, 286

Michau, P. W., 297 first note

Middel, Jacob, 49

Middelberg, G., 160

Middelburg, Cape, 23, 24, 43, 51, 242; 23, 43 (*Boeren Vereeniging*); 103, 107, 124–6 (Bond congress, 1889)

Middelburg Gazette, The, 23

Middelburg Getuige, De, 24, 141

Middelburg negotiations (Transvaal), 230

Middelburg Road (Rosmead), 131, 144

Midlothian campaign (Gladstone's), 41, 73

Migrant labour, 154–5

Militia, Cape Colonial, 74, 80 and note, 84

Mills, Sir Charles, 146

Milner, Lord, 172 (arrival); 177, 188 (and Sprigg Ministry); 179–81 (Graaff-Reinet Speech); 190–1, 216, 222, 305 (and Schreiner Ministry); 192–5, 200–9 (Bloemfontein conference and 1899 crisis); 210, 213–15 (and Conciliation Movement); 216, 227, 229 (and Cape rebels); 216, 237–41 (and suspension of Cape constitution); 236, 251–3, 266–7 (anglicization of ex-Republics); 260, 273 (*modus vivendi* with Portugal)

Missionary societies, 33, 86

Modus vivendi with Portugal, 273, 274

Molopo River, 88

Molteno, Cape, 131

Molteno, Sir John C, 20, 305

Molteno, J. C., 234 second note, 288

Molteno, Sir James Tennant, 139 third note, 158, 239, 263, 326

Monopolies (see Transvaal, Concession Policy)

Montsioa, 86, 91, 92, 93

Morgan, Rev. George, 30

Mosenthal, 5

Moshete, 86

Mossel Bay, 157

Mostert, Ds., of Porterville, 312 third note

Muir, Dr. Thomas, 268

Muller, General C. H., 256

Municipal Boards, 6

Munnik, G. G., 211 second note, 256

Myburgh, M., 283 third note

Myburgh, P. A., 78, 311, 312

'My Dutch' (see Rhodes)

N

Namaqualand, 92, 308

Natal, 99, 101, 104, 107, 108 (and customs union); 160–1 (railway); 283 (unification of South Africa)

Natal Afrikaner, De, 260

Natal Boerekongres, 260 (formerly *Boerenvereeniging*); 283, 299 (changes name to *Volksvereeniging*); 314 (head committee); 329

National Association (see 'Nationalists')

National Banks, 50, 140 (demand for, in Cape); 50 (in O.F.S)

National Convention, 270, 279, 282 (proposed at Pretoria railway conference); 283 (representation at); 330; 283–4 (Durban and Cape Town sessions); 289, 328 (Bloemfontein sessions)

National Democratic Federation, 256

National Gold Mining Company, 102

National Scouts, 251, 253

Nationalists, 258, 262, 298 (= National Association); 299–302 (= Associated Parties, q.v.)

Nationalism, ch. XV *passim*

Native Affairs, Cape portfolio of, 148, 271–2

Native Council, proposal for, 122

Native policy, 101, 126, 149; 299, 330–1 (Botha's Manifesto)

Naude, P. J., 70

Nederduits Gereformeerde Kerk, 10 (heresy trials of 1864); 38–9 (opposes S. J. du Toit); 39–40, 47, 325 (relationship to Afrikaner Bond); 79 (and Dutch language); 210, 233

Nederduits Gereformeerde Kerk (*cont.*)
(role during Anglo-Boer War); 276
(and poor whites)
Neethling, M. L., 173–4
Nehru, Jawaharlal, 323
Nellmapius, A. H., 98
Neo-Calvinism, 38, 50, 125, 176, 322
Netherlands South Africa Railway
Company, 101–2, 160, 167, 213
Neville, H. M., 249
New Nation, The, 296
Newspapers (see Press, and under
individual names)
Newton, A. P., 178
Nieuwe Middelburger, De, 141, 232
Nigrini, J. B., 156
'North', The, 106, 127, 131, 132, 133,
139, 159 (see also Rhodesia, Zam-
besia)
Northern Post, The, 24
Noorder Paarl, 29, 173

O

Oats, F., 234 fourth note
O'Brien, J. V., 24
O'Brien, St. P. O'S., 5, 19, 20, 21,
24
Observer, The, Cape Town, 296
Olivier, Gert C., 184 third note; 186
Olivier, Commandant, 213
Onder Zeekoerivier, 42
Ons Land, 141–2, 149, 167, 174, 197,
220, 221, 227 fifth note, 231–2, 246,
265, 281, 288, 292, 295, 296, 310,
311, 316, 317, 319
Ons Weekblad, 232
Onze Courant, 141–3, 189, 196–7, 232,
296
'Oom Lokomotief', 31, 33, 40, 60
Opregte Afrikaner, De, 44, 61
Orange Free State, 10, 81, 323 (Diamond fields and Basutoland); 46–8,
107–9 (Afrikaner Bond in); 99, 101,
104, 107, 108 (and customs union);
ch. VI *passim*, 128 (railway policy);
100 (wheat exports); 107, 209
(treaties with Transvaal); 205, 209
(1899 crisis)

Orange River Colony (Orangia) 236;
260–1 (self-government in)
Orangia Unie, 258, 259 (foundation);
260, 264, 271, 329 (principles); 261
(wins 1908 election); 262 (forms
Government); 276 (and poor whites);
281, 283, 284 (and unification of
South Africa); 298–300 (and party
amalgamation); 307 (membership
larger than Bond's); 314 (central
bestuur of)
'Organization of the People' (see Het
Volk)
Orpen, Francis, 75
Orpen, J. M., 121
Ostrich-farming, 96
Ottawa Colonial Conference, 1894,
151
Oudtshoorn, 18, 44–5, 58, 96 fourth
note
Owl, The, 257 third note

P

Paardekraal, 61
Paarl, 11, 15–18, 23, ch. III *passim*,
41, 63, 73, 77, 102, 135, 136, 151,
173–6, 233, 239; 126, 156, 315 (Bond
congress, 1888), 218, 220–2, 225
(ditto, 1900); 227 (women's con-
gress, 1900); 265 (language congress,
1907)
Paarl, De, 142, 170, 325
Paarl Gymnasium, 29
Paarl-Pretoria Company, 102
Pakeman, A. G., 258
Palmer, T., 257 third note
Pannevis, Arnoldus, 29
Paramountcy, British (see Imperial
Government)
Pass laws, Cape, 116 and first and
second notes
Paterson, John, 306
Patriot (see *Afrikaanse Patriot, Die*)
Patronage, problem of at time of
Union, 293, 328
Peace Preservation Act (see Disarma-
ment)
Pearston, 55, 136

Petersen, Dr. A. H., 249, 262
Petersen, Dr. J., 285
Petrusville, 39, 40, 42, 51; 25 (*Boeren Vereeniging*)
Philip, Dr. John, 33
Philippolis, 48
Philipson-Stow, R., 296
Philipstown, 42, 55, 133
Philipstownsche Weekblad, De, 142
Phylloxera, 89, 144
Pietersburg, 134
Pietermaritzburg, 273 (railway conference, 1906)
Piketberg, 186–7
Pim, Howard, 257 first note
Pioneer Column, 130
Pohl, Adv. Roché, 317
Police system, 114 and fifth note (Cape Colony) (see also 'Zarps', S.A. Constabulary)
Political Labour League, 249
Polygamy, 118
Pondo, Pondoland, 84, 155
Poor Whites, Poor Whiteism, 98, 119, 149, 154, 274–7
Port Elizabeth, 7, 241; 157–60 (Bond congress, 1895); 111, 121 (Farmers' congress, 1886)
Port Elizabeth Telegraph, The, 120
Port St. Johns, 90
Portugal, Government of, 107, 161, 192
Potchefstroom, 48, 49, 128; 104, 109 (Transvaal Bond congress, 1887)
Prayer, at Bond meetings, 58, 325
Preller, Gustav, 264–5
Press, 5, 302 (generally English-owned); 141–3 (Bond press in Rhodes era); 191, 194, 196–7, 200 (and 1899 crisis); 220, 227 and fifth note, 231–2 (Cape press during Anglo-Boer War) (see also under individual newspapers)
Pretoria, 48, 49, 85, 91, 128, 130, 160, 162, 221, 226; 282 (customs conference, 1908)
Pretoria Convention, 1881, 86–7, 203
Prieska, 176, 211, 212, 234

Prince Albert, Cape, 17, 18, 45, 67 second note, 69
Programme of Principles (see under Afrikaner Bond, Het Volk, Orangia Unie)
Progressive Party, Cape Colony:
First Progressive Party, *c.* 1894, 112, 148–9, 152
Second Progressive Party, 1898–1908, 173–81 (win 1898 Council elections); 183–7 (fight and lose 1898 Assembly elections); 191 (Milner on); 237–41 (and suspension of Cape constitution); 247–51 (win 1903–4 elections with aid of disfranchisement of rebels); 252 (oppose Chinese immigration); 254–5 (criticized by F. S. Malan); 280 (and Cape franchise); 182–3, 190, 238–9, 240, 248, 253, 262 (and redistribution of seats); 283, 293 (and unification of South Africa); 263 (renamed Unionists); 297 (merge with other Progressive parties); 330 (and colour bar)
Progressive Party, Transvaal, 260; 283, 288, 289, 293 (and unification of South Africa) (see also Constitutionalist Party, O.R.C., Unionist Party)
Proportional representation, proposed at National Convention, 284, 286
Protective custody (see Concentration Camps)
Provincial *besturen* (see Afrikaner Bond)
'Purified' Nationalism, 322
Purcell, Isaac, 249
Pyrah, G. B., 253 first note

Q

Queen, The, 52, 69, 84, 91, 177–8, 180, 191, 206, 217, 225, 239, 245
Queenstown, 43, 84, 121 third note, 148, 185; 116, 139, 144 (Bond congress, 1893)
Queenstown Political Association, 149
Quinn, J. W., 257 first note

R

Rabie, P. R., 277, 295 third note

Ramsbottom, A. E. W., 262

Rand (see Witwatersrand)

Rand Daily Mail, 256

Railways, extension of, 98, 103, 127, 131, 139, 143–4

Raubenheimer, H. J., 223, 224, 292, 297 first note

Rebellion in Cape Colony, 1899–1902, 210–11, 226, 227, 230; 216–20, 223–6, 235, 240, 243, 248, 251 (treatment of rebels) (see also Franchise, Cape Colony)

Rebellion of 1914, 254

Redistribution of Parliamentary Seats, 148 and second note, 182, 310 (Bond interest in); 149, 182–3, 190, 238–9, 240, 248, 253, 262 (Progressives and)

Reinecke, Dr., 229

Reitz, F. W., 47, 48, 67, 68–70, 106–8, 127, 129, 193, 204, 213

Republicanism, 52, 196–7, 226, 242, 253–4, 324

Resident Magistrates and Civil Commissioners, 4 and first note, 6

'Responsibles' (see Transvaal Responsible Government Association)

Retief, Piet, 1 (Manifesto)

Retief, D., 318

Rhodes, Cecil John, 75, 151 (Member for Barkly West); 87, 90, 93 (and occupation of Bechuanaland); 100 and fourth note, 108, 143–4, 160–1 (railway and customs questions); 102, 126, 127–8, 131–4, 159, 307, 310, 323 (partnership with Hofmeyr and Bond); 123, 131–2 (premier of Cape); 133–4, 143–5 (relations with Cape farmers); 134–8 (Adendorff Trek); 141–3 (support for Bond newspapers); 145–7 (attitude to parliamentary system and formation of second ministry); 147–8 (and franchise); 152 (and 1894 election); 152–5 (and Glen Grey Act); 155–9 (and Scab Act); 160 (and Sir H. Loch); 159–65 (Drifts crisis and

Jameson Raid); 164, 165, 168, 171, 172, 186–8 ('My Dutch'); 166 (resignation as premier); 168–71 (rejected by Bond); 170 (supports *Dagblad*); 170, 173, 181, 190, 223 (his political come-back); 237–41 (supports suspension of Cape constitution)

Rhodesia, 186, 281, 286, 328 (see also 'North', Zambesia)

Richmond, Cape, 6, 43, 62, 124, 176, 187, 212; 61, 62, 63, 64 (congress at, Nov. 1882); 64–70, 82, 84, 96, 119, 125, 327 (Bond congress, May 1883)

Ridgeway Committee, 258, 261, 328

Rietfontein (Hanover), 42, 62, 137

Rietvallei, 88

Rimington's Scouts, 226

Rinderpest, 176–7

Ripon, Lord, 161

Rissik, J., 262

Riversdale, 17, 18

Robertson, Cape, 18, 296; 283, 292 (Bond congress, 1908)

Robinson, Sir Hercules, 74–5, 90, 92–3, 99 (Governor and High Commissioner); 159–60, 163, 164, 168 (second term)

Rooigrond, 86, 91

Rosmead Junction, 131

Rosmead, Lord (see Robinson, Sir Hercules)

Rustenburg, 48, 49

S

Sampson, Victor, 62, 148 and sixth note, 149 second note, 154, 158, 234 second note, 237

Sand River Convention, 11

Sauer, J. W., 123, 131, 139 third note, 146, 147, 153, 160, 181, 184, 185, 189, 193, 211, 213, 215, 220, 229, 230, 234 second note, 250, 263, 274, 277, 280, 297

Scab disease and legislation, 96, 145, 149, 152, 155–9, 261, 291, 313

Scanlen, Sir Thomas C., 71, 75–89, 100, 310, 312

Scheepers, Commandant Gideon, 226

Schermbrucker, Colonel Frederick, 103–4, 211 fourth note

Schoeman, J. H., 221 third note, 234, 317

School Board Bill, 1905 (Cape), 268, 276

Schreiner, Ettie, 39

Schreiner, Olive, 181, 186, 227

Schreiner, William Philip, 150–1, 309–10 (candidate for Parliament); 162–3, 169 (and Jameson Raid); 181–2 (associates with Bond); 166, 183, 188, 313 (opposition to Sprigg); 177, 188–91, ch. X passim, 210–20 (as premier of Cape); 199, 204, 206, 208, 214, 305 (and 1899 crisis); ch. XI passim, 212–15, 218–19 (and problems of Anglo-Boer war); 220 (independence of Republics); 220 (resignation as premier); 226 (resignation as M.P.); 249 (defeat in 1904 election); 280 (defends Cape franchise); 283 (declines invitation to National Convention)

Schröder, Ds. C. W. H., 212, 222, 234

Schultz, C. P., 289 second note

Scoble and Abercrombie, 178

Scottish clergy and schoolmasters at Cape, 2, 8

Scouts' Kerk, 251

Sauer, W. J., 211

Searle, Charles, 223, 226

Secretary of State for the Colonies (see Carnarvon, Hicks Beach, Derby, Ripon, Chamberlain, Lyttleton)

Selborne, Lord, 260, 267; 282 (Selborne Memorandum)

Seven Circles Act, 72 and first note

Sheppard, E., 256 third note, 257 and second note

Shepstone, Sir Theophilus, 10, 12

Sichel, G., 5, 19, 20, 21, 312

Sigcau affair, 1895, 155

Simonstown, 177

Sivewright, Sir James, 128, 129, 131, 143, 145–6, 150, 160, 182, 184 and second note, 193

Slagters Nek, 32

Slater, Josiah, 178

Smartt, Sir Thomas W., 133, 150, 227' 233–5, 240, 241, 249

Smeer, F. de V., 234–5

Smithfield, 47, 48

Smuts, General Jan Christian, 193, 195, 198, 199, 201, 203, 204 (and crisis of 1899); 251, 254, 256–62, 328 (and restoration of Transvaal self-government); 267 (Education Act); 282–4, 286, 289–90 (proposals over unification of South Africa); 295 (Union premiership question); 298, 300 (party amalgamation)

Smuts–Greene negotiations, 1899, 203–7

Sneeuwberg, 55

Soga, A. K., 186 second note

Solomon, E. P., 262

Solomon, Sir Richard, 153, 185, 189–90; 215–26 (Attorney-General in Schreiner's Cabinet)

Somerset East, 55, 233; 25 (Boeren Vereeniging); 227 (women's congress, 1900); 244, 317 (Bond congress, 1903)

Somerset West, 129

South African Association, 171

South African Constabulary, 255

South African League, 171, 177, 186, 191, 201, 323, 330

South African Native Affairs Commissions, 277–8

South African News, The, 196, 213, 228, 231–2, 295, 316, 317

South African Party, 189 (name for supporters of Schreiner's Government); 218, 222, 288, 310–13, 318 (caucus); 223, 226, 229 (and Anglo-Boer War); 236, 240, 242–3, 247–50 (suspension, Chamberlain's visit, elections of 1903–4); 262–3 (1908 election); 274 (and tariff reform); 278, 280 (and franchise); 280–90 (and unification of South Africa), 243–51, 292, 296, 309, 317–19 (relationship to Afrikaner Bond); 297–303 (amalgamation with other associated parties)

South African National Party, 302–3 (established, 1911)

South African Political Association, 171, 173

South African Republic (see Transvaal)

South African Vigilance Committee, 215, 237, 239

South African Liberal Association (see Liberals

Sprigg, Sir J. Gordon, 131, 15 (excise policy, 1878); 41, 73 (and confederation); 71–5, 305, 310–12 (Ministry of 1878–81); 76, 103–6, 129, 131, 144, 247 (and railways extension); 99, 105, 177 (and tariff policy); 122–3 (franchise reform); 131 (Ministry of 1887–90); 146–7 (and Rhodes's second Ministry); 157 (and Scab); 166, 172, 176–83, 191 (Ministry of 1896–8); 222, 226, 241, 246–9 (Ministry of 1900–04); 237–41 (against suspension of Cape constitution); 247 (leaves Progressive Party); 93, 204, 206, 243

Springfontein, 144

Squatters, squatting, 84–5, 116–17, 129, 145, 153

Standard Bank, 34, 50, 160, 184

Standerton, 49

Stanford, Colonel W. E. M., 280

Stellaland, 85, 86, 90–2

Stellalander, De, 196 fifth note

Stellenbosch, 15, 16, 17, 18, 58, 151–2, 158–9, 186, 264–5, 287, 317; 134, 139, 141–2 (Bond congress, 1892), 273–4 (ditto, 1904)

Stellenbosch District Bank, 51

Stellenbosch Seminary, 29

Stem, De, 297

Sterkstroom, 62

Steyn, President Marthinus Theunis, 110, 191–2, 193–4, 195, 201, 203, 205, 213, 215, 282, 284, 288, 289, 293, 294, 295

Steynsburg, 43, 55, 292, 301

Stickland, H., 257 first note

Stock thefts, 112 and first note, 115 first and second notes, 116

Stockenstrom, Andries, 20, 21

'Strop Bill', 115, 145, 149, 184

Strydenburg, 187

Strydom, C. J. Scheepers, 212

Sunday observance, 125; 145 (trains)

Suspension of Cape constitution, movement for, 236–41, 242–3, 246, 316

Sutherland, 51

Suzerainty (see Imperial Government)

Swaziland, 129–31

Swellendam, 17, 18

T

Taalbond, 140, 264, 326

Tamplin, H. T., 234

Tariff and Excise League, 123

Taung, 211

Taxation, 98 (see also Excise on Spirits; Diamond Industry)

Tembu, 152; 83, 84–5, 90, 122, 148 (Tembuland); 84 (Tembuland Commission)

Tennant, Sir David, 152

Tennant, F. R., 5, 21

Te Water, Dr. Thomas N. G., 150 (M.P. for Graaff-Reinet); 166, 172, 176, 179–80, 182 (in Sprigg's third Cabinet); 216–20 (in Schreiner's Cabinet); 195, 201, 202 (and 1899 crisis); 216–17 (and treatment of rebels); 234 (in danger of arrest); 102, 112, 131, 133, 142, 154, 157, 290

Theron, Thomas Philippus, 56, 60, 64 (and amalgamation of Bond and vereenigingen); 68, 69 (secretary, Cape provincial bestuur); 70, 96, 103 (on Central Bestuur); 100, 106 (and railway and customs); 111–12 (and English Farmers' congress); 132, 139 third note (and Rhodes); 174–5 (and Commissie van Toezicht); 182 (on redistribution commission); 274, 316–17 (chairman of

Theron, Thomas Philippus (*cont.*)
provincial *bestuur*); 276 (fears black competition); 212, 213 and second note, 221 and third note, 222, 223, 226, 228, 232-3 (and Anglo-Boer War); 243 (and Chamberlain); 290 (death)
The Times, London, 165
Thomas, C. H., 178
Toerien, J. P., 134
Tokai jail, 243
Tolk, De, 19, 58 second note, 59, 68, 69; 119 (on colour bar); 141
Tot Nut van 't Algemeen, 3, 12
Transkei, 83-5, 90 (political control of); 85, 122 and first note, 147 (enfranchisement of); 121 and sixth note (incorporation in Cape Colony; 181 (Transkeian Territories Act)
Transvaal, 10, 28, 40-2, 74 (War of Independence, 1880-1); 37 *Volks-Comité*); 87 (delegation to London, 1883); 85, 86, 127 (frontier question); 99, 101, 107-8 (and customs union); 107, 209 (treaties with O.F.S.); ch. VI *passim*, 143-4, 160, 161 (railway policy); 159-65 (Jameson Raid); 183-4 (secret service); 98, 102, 192-5 (concession policy); 91-2, 128, 199, 201 (Executive Council); ch. X *passim* (crisis of 1890's); 195, 196, 198, 200, 203, 208, 214 (arbitration of disputes); 10, 189, 192, 203-4, 208-9, 220 (paramountcy and suzerainty questions); 252-4, 260-1 (constitutional development after 1902)
Transvaal Indigency Commission, 275-6
Transvaal Responsible Government Association, 258, 267
Treason, Law of, 209, 213 second note, 217, 219, 223, 226, 235, 238, 241
Trooper Peter Halket of Mashonaland, 186
Tsomo, 154
Tudhope, J., 131
Tulbagh, 17, 18, 67 second note

U

Uitenhage, 121, 124, 150, 301; 122, 126 (Bond congress, 1887)
Uitenhage Times, The, 58, 121
Uitlander questions, 160, 191, 192, 201, 203, 207, 323; 191-6 (Uitlander Petitions)
Umzimvubu River, 90
Unification of South Africa, 68, 89, 96, 134, 149, 280-90, 321 (see also Federation)
Uniondale, 18, 67 second note
Unionist Party, 283, 293, 297, 299, 301-2, 328-9 (see also Progressive Party)
Upington, Cape, 234
Upington, Sir Thomas, 83, 89-94, 99, 100 and third note, 121, 122, 139, 146, 170, 310
Utrecht (Holland), 49
Utrecht (Natal), 260

V

Van den Heever, D. P. ('Oom Daantje'), 20-3, 25-6, 43, 54-5, 56, 59, 60, 67, 68, 97; 156-7 (Scab Conference, Victoria West); 172, 197
Van der Horst, J. G., 279-80; 285, 295 and fifth note, 296
Van der Lingen, Ds. G. W. A., 29, 31
Van der Merwe, F. J., 212
Van der Merwe, Paul J., 63
Van der Meulen, N. P., 44, 61-3
Van der Rijst, H. M., 234
Van der Spuy, C. J. M., 6
Van der Spuy, Herman, 44
Van der Walt, I. J., 182, 212, 222, 234
Van der Walt, P. J., 40 second note
Vanes, Dr. Arthur, 121 third and fourth notes, 124 third note, 150
Van Eyk, 174
Van Heerden, Hercules C., 278
Van Heerden, J. A., 60 and second note
Van Niekerk, D. J. H., 232 second note
Van Niekerk, G. J., 88 third note
Van Oordt, Dr. J. W. G., 141-2
Van Pittius, N. C. Gey, 88, 93

430 INDEX

Van Pletzen, C., 211 and third note
Van Prinsterer, Groen, 38
Van Rensburg, J. J. Janse, 7, 23, 55, 56, 58, 67, 69, 83, 84
Van Rensburg, N. A. J., 235
Van Rensburg, W. H. J., 150 second note
Van Rooy, A. C. A., 286
Van Soelen, Johannes, 136, 137
Van Zyl, D. J. A., 157, 221 third note, 232
Van Zyl, J. J. W., 312
Venter, M. M., 98, 133, 171
Ventersburg, 20, 55
Vereeniging, Treaty of, 241, 251, 252, 263
Vermaak, J. A., 19
Victoria East, 148
Victoria West, 141, 187, 295, 296; 156 and fourth note (Scab conference, 1894); 211-2 (Bond congress, 1899)
Viljoen, Dirk, 229
Vinkelfontein, 20
Visser, A. G., 295 third note
Visser, C. J., 96
Vlekpoort, Cradock, 67 second note
Volksblad, Het, 11, 13, 15, 22, 26, 33, 58 second note, 73
Volksraad, O.F.S., 105, 106, 197
Volksraad, Transvaal, 48, 91, 128, 135, 198, 199, 203
Volksstem, De, 40, 48, 264, 293
Volksvriend, De, 10, 60
'Voluntary principle' in education, 57
'Volunteers' (see Freebooters)
Vorster, Barend, 134
Vosloo, J. A., 142, 231, 280
Vryburg, 86, 90, 129, 161-2, 184, 186, 211, 226, 244
Vryheid, 260

W

Wakkerstroom, 49
War Office, 198
Warren, General Charles, 92-4, 95
Warren, W. J., 121
Warrenton, 157
Watermeyer, P. J. A., 312

Wellington, Cape, 15, 16 first note, 17, 18
Wessels, C. H., 262
Wessels, D. H. W., 223, 226
'White House Party', 310
Widows and Orphans Fund, 206, 212 and fourth note
Wienand, F. F., 223
Wiener, L., 139 third note
Wijnbouwers Vereeniging, 14, 15
Williams, Basil, 290
Williston, 187
Willowmore, 18, 233
Wilman, H., 83 first note
Winburg 48
Witwatersrand, 95, 98, 161, 162, 192, 272
Wodehouse, Cape, 133, 148, 150, 185, 211-12, 249-50; 25, 114 fifth note (Boeren Vereeniging)
Wolmarans, A. D. W., 256, 275, 283, 284
Wolseley, General Sir Garnet, 191
Women, 119, 307 (not eligible for Bond membership); 227 (protest at farm-burnings); 260 (monument to, Bloemfontein)
Wool, export of, 96, 158
Worcester, Cape, 5, 6, 15, 17, 18, 58, 298; 174-5, 179-80 (Bond congress, 1898); 228 (protest meeting, 1900)
Worcester Advertiser, The, 231
Working Men's Union, 249
Worsfold, W. B., 178
Wrench, Sir J. E., 178

X

Xanthium spinosum (burr-weed), 96, 153

Y

Yzel, Andries, 40 second note

Z

Zambesia, 127, 135, 161; 135-6 (Colonial farmers' deputation); 137 (applications for farms in) (see also Adendorff Trek, North, Rhodesia)

'Zarps', 191

Zietsman, L. S., 150

Zoutpansberg, 49; 256 (*Boeren Vereeniging*)

Zuid Afrikaan, De, 10 (amalgamates with *Volksvriend*); 11, 13 (opposes *Volksblad*); 14 (and *Wijnbouwers Vereeniging*); 20; 33, 35, 41, 44, 50, 56–7, 60 (relations with *Patriot*); 77 (Hofmeyr resigns from Cabinet); 101–2 (favours Transvaal's railway policy); 120–1 (discusses African voters' loyalties); 30 (language question); 35 (on foundation of Bond); 96 (criticizes Central *Bestuur*); 141–2 (breaks with Bond, amalgamates with *Ons Land*); 312 (disciplines M.P.s)

Zuid Afrikaansche Boeren Beschermings Vereeniging, 13–18 (established by Hofmeyr); 16, 18, 305 (aims); 16, 65 (constitution); 16–18 (formation of branches); 45–6 (Hofmeyr's attempts to reform); ch. IV *passim* (amalgamation with Bond); 44–6, 61, 76 (friction with S. J. du Toit and Bond); 67–9 (represented at Richmond congress, 1883); 69 (dissolves itself); 71–2 (and 1878–9 elections) (see also *Boeren Vereenigingen*, Farmers' Associations)

Zuid Afrikaansche Handelsmaatschappij, 51

Zuid Afrikaansche Tijdschrift, De, 30, 37

Zuider Paarl, 183

Zuid Winterveld, 62

Zwartruggens Farmers' Association, 112